Claude McKay

Claude McKay

The Making of a Black Bolshevik

Winston James

Columbia University Press / *New York*

Columbia University Press
Publishers Since 1893
New York   Chichester, West Sussex
cup.columbia.edu

Library of Congress Cataloging-in-Publication Data
Names: James, Winston, author.
Title: Claude McKay : the making of a Black Bolshevik / Winston James.
Description: New York : Columbia University Press, [2022] |
    Includes bibliographical references and index.
Identifiers: LCCN 2021044661 | ISBN 9780231135924 (hardback) |
    ISBN 9780231135931 (trade paperback) | ISBN 9780231509770 (ebook)
Subjects: LCSH: McKay, Claude, 1890–1948. | McKay, Claude, 1890–1948—Political
    and social views. | African American authors—Biography. | Authors,
    Jamaican—20th century—Biography. | Jamaican Americans—Intellectual life. |
    Socialism—United States—History—20th century. |
    Black nationalism—United States—History—20th century.
Classification: LCC PS3525.A24785 Z743 2022 |
    DDC 811/.52 [B]—dc23/eng/20211216
LC record available at https://lccn.loc.gov/2021044661

Cover image: Private Collection Prismatic Pictures / Bridgeman Images
Cover design: Lisa Hamm

In loving memory
of
Mary Turner, Hayes Turner, and William Brown
and
the heralds of a new day yet to be born
John Coltrane
and
Nina Simone

Every Negro who lays claim to leadership should make a study of Bolshevism and explain its meaning to the colored masses. It is the greatest and most scientific idea afloat in the world today. . . . Bolshevism . . . has made Russia safe for the Jew. It has liberated the Slav peasant from priest and bureaucrat who can no longer egg him on to murder Jews to bolster up their rotten institutions. It might make these United States safe for the Negro.

—Claude McKay, 1919

In the East the clouds glow crimson with the new dawn that is
    breaking,
And its golden glow fills the western skies.
O my brothers and my sisters, wake! arise!
. . . . Lift your heavy-lidded eyes, Ethiopia! awake!
. . . . Wake from sleeping; to the East turn, turn your eyes!

—Claude McKay, from "Exhortation," 1920

I have spent a lot of my life in association with Marxists of a variety of colours. But I have never in my life met a Marxist baby. Never. Never. Nor have I ever met a Christian baby. When a man tells me he is a Marxist, that is of great interest, but there is a matter that fascinates me more. I want to know how he got there.

—George Lamming, November 1982

Contents

Abbreviations

"ANPP"	Claude McKay, "A Negro Poet and His Poems," *Pearson's Magazine*, September 1918
B	Claude McKay, *Banjo: A Story Without a Plot* (New York: Harper, 1929)
BB	Claude McKay, *Banana Bottom* (New York: Harper, 1933)
CB	Claude McKay, *Constab Ballads* (London: Watts, 1912)
CKOF	C. K. Ogden Fonds, William Ready Divisions of Archives and Research Collections, Mills Memorial Library, McMaster University, Hamilton, ON
CMI	Claude McKay Manuscripts, Lilly Library, Indiana University, Bloomington
CMPS	Claude McKay Papers, Schomburg Center for Research in Black Culture, New York Public Library
CMPY	Claude McKay Papers, James Weldon Johnson Collection of Negro Literature and Art, American Literature Collection, Beinecke Rare Book and Manuscript Library, Yale University, New Haven, CT
G	Claude McKay, *Gingertown* (New York: Harper, 1932)
H	Claude McKay, *Harlem: Negro Metropolis* (New York: Dutton, 1940)
HBJ	*Handbook of Jamaica* (Kingston: Government Printing Office, annual)
HG	Claude McKay, *Harlem Glory: A Fragment of Aframerican Life* (Chicago: Kerr, 1990)
HH	Claude McKay, *Home to Harlem* (New York: Harper, 1928)

"HH"   Claude McKay, "Review of *Home to Harlem*, in "Significant Books
          Reviewed by Their Own Authors," *McClure's* 60, no. 6 (June 1928)
HS   Claude McKay, *Harlem Shadows* (New York: Harcourt, Brace, 1922)
JESP   Joel E. Spingarn Papers, Rare Books and Manuscript Collection,
          New York Public Library
JRRCP   J. R. Ralph Casimir Papers, Schomburg Center for Research in
          Black Culture, New York Public Library
LW   Claude McKay, *A Long Way from Home* (New York: Lee Furman,
          1937)
MGH   Claude McKay, *My Green Hills of Jamaica* (Kingston: Heinemann,
          1979)
"MGH"   Claude McKay, "My Green Hills of Jamaica," MS, Schomburg
          Center for Research in Black Culture, New York Public Library
MGP   Robert A. Hill, ed., *The Marcus Garvey and Universal Negro
          Improvement Association Papers*, 13 vols. (Berkeley and Durham:
          University and California Press and Duke University Press, 1983—)
NA   Claude McKay, *Negroes in America* (1923; Port Washington, NY:
          Kennikat, 1979)
NCC   Nancy Cunard Collection, Harry Ransom Humanities Research
          Center, University of Texas at Austin
SJ   Claude McKay, *Songs of Jamaica* (Kingston: Gardner, 1912)
SNH   Claude McKay, *Spring in New Hampshire and Other Poems*
          (London: Grant Richards, 1920)
SP   Claude McKay, *Selected Poems of Claude McKay* (New York:
          Bookman, 1953)
TNA   The National Archives, Kew, Richmond, Surrey, UK
WAB   William Aspenwall Bradley Archive, Harry Ransom Humanities
          Research Center, University of Texas at Austin
WD   *The Workers' Dreadnought*
WSBP   William Stanley Braithwaite Papers, Houghton Library, Harvard
          University, Cambridge, MA

Acknowledgments

One of the distinct pleasures of finishing a book such as this is the opportunity it affords to publicly thank those who've helped along the way. I have accumulated many debts which cannot be repaid but ought to be publicly acknowledged.

I am grateful for the courteous assistance that I received from librarians and archivists especially in the United States, Britain, and Jamaica. I wish to thank those at the Schomburg Center for Research in Black Culture, New York Public Library; the Beinecke Rare Book and Manuscript Library, Yale University; the British Library, especially its newspaper division when at Colindale; Columbia University libraries, especially the Interlibrary Loan Office; the Harry Ransom Humanities Research Center, University of Texas at Austin; the Lilly Library, Manuscripts Department, Indiana University, Bloomington; the International Institute of Social History, Amsterdam; the Labour History Archives and Study Centre, People's History Museum, Manchester, UK; the William Ready Divisions of Archives and Research Collections, Mills Memorial Library, McMaster University, Hamilton, Ontario; the Moorland-Spingarn Research Center, Howard University; the Houghton Library, Harvard University; the National Archive (previously the Public Record Office), Kew, Surrey; the National Archives, Washington, DC; the Library of Congress, Washington, DC; the Rare Books and Manuscript Collection, New York Public Library, New York City; the Albert H. Small Collections Library, University of Virginia; the West India Reference Library, University of the West Indies, Mona, Jamaica; the National Library of Jamaica. Richard Smith efficiently and successfully chased down some of the items I was not able to ken myself in London. Cecil Gutzmore provided similar help in Kingston. I thank them both.

This project formally started life many moons ago during my studies at the London School of Economics and Political Science, University of London. I wish to thank Martin Bulmer, Percy Cohen, and Alan Swingewood for their help in its initial formulation and development. Professors Stuart Hall (Open University) and Eric Mottram (King's College, London) served as external examiners of my dissertation. I drew strength from their enthusiasm for the project and benefited from their helpful suggestions. Mottram died soon after our meeting, but Stuart (who died in 2014), for all the years I knew him (stretching back to the 1980s), was invariably generous with his time, thought, and encouragement. George Lamming kindly took the time to read an early draft of the book and provided valuable comments. I'm indebted to Ken Weller, who was enormously generous with his time and knowledge of the radicals around the Pankhurst group, including Reuben Gilmore. I'm also grateful to Robert Hill for his support and encouragement over the years and particularly for sharing access to some rare issues of the *Negro World*, including one containing McKay's "letter" from London.

I was moved by the kindness and hospitality of McKay's relatives in Clarendon, when I, a stranger, first arrived unannounced in their midst many summers ago. I am especially grateful to Mr. Hartley McKay (one of McKay's nephews, who took me under his wings, guided operations and directed me to other family members), Miss Claudette McKay, and Mrs. Icelyn McKay Binger. I also owe a debt of gratitude to Rev. Luke N. Shaw, the pastor of Mount Zion Baptist church at the time for granting me an interview and sharing documents about the history of his church with me. In London, McKay's niece (and U. Theo McKay's daughter), Mrs. Eloise McKay Edwards, was most generous with her time, memory, and documents. Carl Cowl, McKay's friend and last literary agent, was a great source of information and encouragement. He was equally generous with his time and knowledge. He never tired of talking about McKay and his milieu, and spoke of the man and his time not only with knowledge but great insight, too. He opened up to me McKay's world and struggles (especially the latter part of McKay's life) with a unique and unparalleled immediacy. An active Marxist and outspoken Trotskyist right up to his death at the age of 93, Cowl had great sympathy for the political McKay that I have been trying to recover. After I moved from London to New York in 1991, it was easier to call him up or pop down to his Brooklyn apartment to talk McKay and share archival findings with him. Even though we had our disagreements, I shall always treasure his friendship and generosity.

Over the years a number of institutions have provided fellowship support that enabled me to do the research and writing for the book. Becoming the Arturo Schomburg Fellow at the City University of New York (supported by the Rockefeller Foundation) was among the most important of these. I came to the United States on the basis of that fellowship. The others were a fellowship at the Frederick Douglass Institute (supported by the Ford Foundation)—awarded to last a year, but used only for a semester—at the University of Rochester; a Scholar-in-Residence fellowship, Schomburg Center for Research in Black Culture, New York Public Library (supported by the National Endowment for the Humanities); the Josephus Daniels Fellowship, National Humanities Center, Research Triangle Park, North Carolina (supported by the National Endowment for the Humanities, and the Ford Foundation). These were all vital to making the book possible.

Portions of part one draw upon an earlier and much briefer introduction to McKay's Jamaican years and his early creole poetry, contextualized and anthologized in *A Fierce Hatred of Injustice: Claude McKay's Jamaica and His Poetry of Rebellion* (London: Verso, 2000). But the history and sociopolitical analysis of McKay's Jamaica, his island experience, and the poetry he produced have all been radically revised and expanded here in light of more and deeper research. Segments of chapter 7 were published previously as "Claude McKay's Bolshevisation in London," in *The Red and the Black: The Russian Revolution and the Black Atlantic*, ed. David Featherstone and Christian Høgsbjerg (Manchester University Press, 2021). I am grateful for the opportunity to revise and expand that analysis.

For more than a decade, my colleagues in the History department of the University of California, Irvine have provided a supportive and congenial environment, one conducive to the production of this and other publications. I especially appreciate the support of Heidi Tinsman, Steven Topik, Vinayak Chaturvedi, Robert Moeller, David Igler, Jeffrey Wasserstrom, Mark LeVine, Sarah Farmer, Susan Morrissey, and Ian Coller.

Peter Dimock, Columbia University Press's senior executive editor at the time, commissioned this work. I shall always be grateful for his unwavering support, advice, and enthusiasm for the project. Bill Schwarz, a friend for almost four decades and a staunch supporter, has read various segments of this work over the years and always provided valuable insights. He has been one of my fiercest critics and most loyal cheerleaders. Similarly,

Clive Harris—a brother, comrade, and collaborator since our undergraduate days—one of the finest scholars I know, read the full manuscript and provided helpful comments. Peter Hulme, whose work I've long admired, but whom I met only four years ago, was kind enough to conduct a close reading of the entire manuscript which I found highly valuable. Philip Leventhal, my editor at Columbia University Press, has not only steered the manuscript through the (prolonged) publication process but also provided close and helpful readings along the way.

Both my immediate and extended family have, as always, provided unstinting support. I can never thank them enough.

Claude McKay

Prologue

If I were a Negro I couldn't be anything but a revolutionist!

—Max Eastman to McKay, 1919

Where scarlet pennants blaze like tongues of fire,
There—where high passion swells—is my heart's desire.

—Claude McKay, "Travail," 1920

"**E**very Negro who lays claim to leadership should make a study of Bolshevism and explain its meaning to the colored masses." Thus declared Claude McKay in the pages of the *Negro World*, organ of the Black nationalist Universal Negro Improvement Association (UNIA), founded and led by Marcus Garvey. In his exchange with the paper's literary editor, William Ferris, he went further. Bolshevism, McKay insisted, "is the greatest and most scientific idea afloat in the world to-day"; it can not only aid the working class as a whole to "better its material and spiritual life" but also assist the liberation of oppressed Black people. Bolshevism "has made Russia safe for the Jew. It has liberated the Slav peasant from priest and bureaucrat who can [no] longer egg him on to murder Jews to bolster up their rotten institutions. It might," he believed, "make these United States safe for the Negro."[1] Less than two years later, in July 1921, he asserted that the Russian Revolution was "the greatest event in the history of humanity;

much greater than the French Revolution, which is held up as a wonderful achievement to Negro children and students in white and black schools." He did so in a public condemnation of another editor, that of the *Crisis*, accusing W. E. B. Du Bois of "sneering" at the Russian Revolution.[2]

These were not the empty pronouncements of an armchair socialist intellectual removed from the practical engagement of radical politics. In 1919, an increasingly radicalized McKay joined the Industrial Workers of the World (IWW), the revolutionary and most racially inclusive political group in the United States at the time. Later that year, he sailed for London and quickly joined forces with Sylvia Pankhurst, Britain's most ardent supporter of Bolshevism and the Russian Revolution. McKay not only worked with her on the *Workers' Dreadnought*, which he helped to edit, but also became a member of the Workers' Socialist Federation (WSF), the organization she founded and led. Membership, let alone active participation, in both the IWW and the WSF carried a great risk of persecution from established authority on both sides of the Atlantic, especially given the paranoia and "Red Scare" surrounding Bolshevism.

* * *

McKay's stature as one of the most important and pioneering Black writers of the twentieth century is both secure and imposing. *Songs of Jamaica* and *Constab Ballads*, his anthologies of poems written in his native Jamaican creole language and published in 1912, are, along with *Gingertown* (1932) and his chef d'oeuvre, *Banana Bottom* (1933), acknowledged by literary critics and cultural historians alike as founding texts in Caribbean literature.[3] His Harlem Renaissance contemporaries and peers repeatedly recognized and acknowledged his pioneering role in that movement, corroborated and reaffirmed by historians and literary scholars. Since at least 1963—when Lilyan Kesteloot's seminal work, *Les ecrivains noirs de langue française: Naissance d'une littérature*, first appeared—the fact of McKay's profound influence on Black writers in the Francophone world (both Caribbean and African) had been established and subsequently reinforced by others.[4]

But despite the growing and welcome body of literature on McKay, an important aspect of his work has been so inadequately addressed by scholars that it constitutes a large lacuna: McKay's political trajectory and political philosophy, in the widest sense of the latter term—his worldview.

"I have never been a political writer; I never claimed to be one," McKay declared in 1946, two years before his death.[5] But the most cursory reading of his work belies the disclaimer: his poetry and novels—not to mention his more explicitly political, journalistic, and sociological texts—are all replete with political imperatives, some more explicit than others. Sympathetic as well as hostile commentators noticed and registered the political nature of his work dating from before he left Jamaica in 1912, and especially after his defiant outburst in the form of a sonnet, "If We Must Die," was published during the height of the 1919 racist mob attacks known as the Red Summer. Included among these commentators was no less a figure than the attorney general of the United States, A. Mitchell Palmer, and the American intelligence services. In "Exhibit No. 10: Radicalism and Sedition Among the Negroes as Reflected in Their Publications," which forms an integral part of his notorious 1919 report, Palmer explicitly mentioned McKay and his poem more than any other person or piece of writing in his compendium of "seditious" literature among African Americans.[6] Indeed, from this date to his death three decades later, McKay was to receive the unwelcome and unblinking attention of intelligence services, not only those of the United States but also—during his period in Europe and North Africa—those of the United Kingdom, France, and Germany. Yet no one has undertaken a systematic analysis of this aspect of McKay's oeuvre, his political evolution, despite the fact that McKay's political thought constitutes one of the most valuable and enduring components of his legacy.

The uncommonly sophisticated character of his political thinking as well as the rich and textured quality of his writings—fiction and nonfiction— are in large measure explicable by the fact that McKay was the most traveled member of his generation of Black intellectuals, spending more years abroad than any of his peers. After seven years in the United States (1912– 1919), he spent fourteen years in Europe and North Africa between 1919 and 1934. All told, after leaving Jamaica for the United States in 1912, McKay spent no less than a third of the remainder of his life outside the United States. In addition to Jamaica and the United States, he traveled to and lived in at least nine different countries, developing varying levels of competence in several languages. And he made the most of his strangely unremitting itinerancy. A keen observer, he was forever analyzing his experience in letters, essays, novels, poems, a travelogue, and a memoir. He emerges as one of the most perceptive, sensitive, and uninhibited analysts of the Black condition, especially that of the African diaspora in the United States and Europe, in the turbulent times in which he lived, a witness without peer. McKay's lack of inhibition was both a strength and a weakness. His determination, for instance, to draw his fictional characters realistically did not endear him to either W. E. B. Du Bois or Marcus Garvey. The two men, who bitterly disagreed with each other, were united in their strong condemnation of McKay's first novel, *Home to Harlem* (1928).[7]

Moreover, a key part of his life's work—largely in spite of himself—was an unrelenting meditation on what it meant to be Black in a white man's world, a world dominated by Europe and its far-flung diaspora. In McKay's work we have one of the most intellectually rewarding, sustained, and engaging dialogues between the seemingly incompatible and competing ideologies of Black liberation—Black nationalism and socialism. The product of his diligent search for political strategies in the fight against the oppression and exploitation of Black people around the world, the tension between these two projects—both of which, in varying combination, simultaneously commanded his sympathy—characterized his work to the end of his life. His exceptional analytical skill is widely acknowledged, and the relevance and resonance of his political thought to the old and new challenges that Black people face are undeniable and undenied. Writing at the height of the Black Power movement, the distinguished African American sociologist and activist St. Clair Drake, in a fine introduction to the 1970 edition of *A Long Way from Home*, drew attention to this aspect of McKay's ideas for a later generation. Similarly, Addison Gayle, a leading figure in the Black Arts Movement, the cultural arm of the Black Power movement, averred two years later that McKay's poetry "serves as a living inspiration for those who refuse to bow down at the feet of alien gods."[8]

Yet in the critical literature, the scattered remarks on McKay's politics—many of which are to be found in highly influential texts—betray, in varying degrees, hasty and ill-informed judgments or conclusions reached from perverse readings of his life and writings. This is partly because McKay was the most controversial figure of the Harlem Renaissance, reviled and loved in equal measure but for different and incommensurate reasons. To the younger Harlem writers, especially Langston Hughes, Zora Neale Hurston, Gwendolyn Bennett, Dorothy West, and even the young and cantankerous curmudgeon Wallace Thurman, McKay was a hero worthy of emulation and celebration. "It was Claude McKay's example that started me on this track," acknowledged Hughes. The almost-impossible-to-please Thurman—he was hard on others and even harder on himself—in a remarkably perceptive essay, expressed his admiration for McKay's radical ardor. "He is such an intense person that one can often hear the furnace-like fire within him roaring in his poems," Thurman observed. Furthermore, McKay possessed "more emotional depth and spiritual fire than any of his forerunners or contemporaries" and seemed to have "considerably more mental depth too." McKay, the "glorious revolutionary," Thurman wrote approvingly in 1928, "is the only Negro poet who ever wrote revolutionary or protest poetry." To James Weldon Johnson, McKay was "one of the principal forces in bringing about the Negro literary awakening."[9]

But to detractors such as George Schuyler, McKay was a "black fascist." To others, he was the opposite—"essentially a 'white-folks nigger'" was Arthur P. Davis's verdict. Schuyler and Davis cannot both be right, not to mention Thurman.[10] Addressing the Congress on the Dialectics of Liberation in London in 1967, Stokely Carmichael (Kwame Ture), a leading advocate of the Black Power movement, claimed McKay for the cause. "If We Must Die," he told the audience, is "our poem today in the US." Addison Gayle hailed McKay as the "warrior-poet of his people."[11] Yet in the same year Carmichael gave his speech, Harold Cruse, in his influential book *The Crisis of the Negro Intellectual*, denounced McKay as a "stand-offish" West Indian, "not the type to be embroiled in any action involving the American Negro problem in the United States."[12] But as Langston Hughes noticed years ago, "some folks are STILL mad at Claude, even though he is daid [sic] and gone!"[13] One of the challenges of this undertaking is to make sense of these incommensurate and incompatible assessments of McKay.

Remarkably, despite McKay's centrality to the development of Caribbean literature, the Harlem Renaissance, and the *négritude* movement, Wayne Cooper's *Claude McKay: Rebel Sojourner in the Harlem Renaissance* is the only full-length biography of the man.[14] Although Cooper succeeds in providing a portrait of McKay that helps to clear up many misconceptions, his book is not without flaws. His archival range was rather limited, and errors of fact as well as judgment disfigure Cooper's biography. Some of its shortcomings are both understandable and forgivable. His book was published in 1987, and since then a cornucopia of archival material has opened up, most notably in the former Soviet Union, especially the archives of the Communist International (Comintern). The Freedom of Information Act in the United States has similarly made accessible material that was previously unavailable to scholars. But despite its shortcomings, Cooper's is a pioneering work. I, as well as others following in his footsteps, have benefited from the path he opened up. But the new archival evidence as well as the new interpretation it summons radically alter previous portraits of McKay.

We are now, for instance, in a position to understand more fully McKay's complex and ambivalent relationship to Garveyism and the public debates he had with Garveyites. Indeed, the meaning, reach, and complexity of Garvey's project can now be better understood, especially after the publication of the stupendous multivolume papers edited by Robert A. Hill and his colleagues.[15] Similarly, McKay's membership of and important work with the African Blood Brotherhood can now, thanks to new archival material, be more fully revealed and analyzed. And McKay's controversial political interventions after his return to the United States in 1934 can be better understood. In short, it is possible to paint a more comprehensive political portrait of McKay than hitherto.

I have analyzed McKay and his work in order to paint such a portrait of this important but in many ways misunderstood and maligned figure. I have examined the political trajectory of the young McKay, covering the crowded first thirty-two years of his life, from 1889 to 1921. Accordingly, the book traces McKay's politics from his Jamaican childhood and youth through his migration to the United States in 1912 and his sojourn in Britain from 1919 right up to his return to New York in 1921.

McKay entered the United States as a twenty-three-year-old Jamaican with Fabian socialist sympathies—gradualist, nonviolent, social democratic, reformist—headed to Tuskegee Institute, founded and run in Alabama by the conservative African American educator Booker T. Washington. Seven years later—by the time he left the United States for London in the fall of 1919—McKay, as he put it, "became Bolshevik" and a publicly committed Black radical.[16] Before leaving for London, he had already made his revolutionary sympathies clear, but during his time living, working, and moving in London's radical circles—which he later called "the nest of extreme radicalism"—McKay grew even more radical, joining Pankhurst's far-left Workers' Socialist Federation (WSF) and working full-time on the *Workers' Dreadnought*.[17] Resolutely anti-imperialist and antiracist, the WSF was Britain's most radical socialist organization, recognizing and fearlessly defending the Bolshevik Revolution before all others. It was the first British organization to join the Moscow-based Communist International (Comintern)—the "Central Committee of the world revolution," Trotsky called it—founded by the Bolsheviks in March 1919. Filled with "plenty of radical knowledge," McKay returned to New York from London in January 1921. Having clearly committed himself to Bolshevism, both ideologically and in practice, McKay embarked upon a new phase of his life in New York. And the moment of his return is where this present volume closes.

* * *

In the reconstruction of his political journey, *Claude McKay: The Making of a Black Bolshevik* draws upon McKay's poetry, short stories, and novels, but primarily upon his nonfiction texts—his substantial and scattered work of journalism, his sociological studies (*Negroes in America* [1923] and *Harlem: Negro Metropolis* [1940]), along with his autobiographical travelogue (*A Long Way from Home* [1937]) and memoir of his Jamaican years (*My Green Hills of Jamaica* [1947; 1979]). To aid the reconstruction and analysis, I have additionally called into service McKay's unpublished no less than his published work, including his enormously rich and substantial body of correspondence. It seems self-evident that without a critical examination of the entire corpus of McKay's work, along with other relevant material, such a portrait—although covering here only a part of his life—cannot be adequately drawn. Accordingly, I have used not only McKay's own writings but also all the known—and in some cases hitherto unknown—archival resources, including those of his friends, acquaintances, and adversaries, such as the illuminating American and British intelligence reports on the author. Thus, even when much of the archival material is not explicitly deployed in this volume, knowledge of it informs the overall analysis and adds authority to the argument.

In carrying out this project, my most important methodological ambition has been to remain constantly alive to the necessity of locating McKay and his ideas in time as well as space. Without this to guide me, the meaning of McKay's political behavior and ideas would have been easily lost or misconstrued. It should go without saying—but it still needs to be said, especially in the light of certain pronouncements on McKay—that "the political character of a body of thought can only be established by a responsible study of its *texts* and *context*."[18] I am interested, however, not only in McKay's texts and context but also his political *behavior*—his actions. To this extent, I will inevitably make reference to his biography for more than merely contextual purposes. Nevertheless, the objective of this effort is not a conventional "political biography"—partly because I find it difficult to conceive of a *non*political biography. Biographies are primarily works of description and disclosure. What I have attempted is, first and foremost, a work of interpretation, analysis, and explanation.[19] Consequently, contexts and processes—social, economic, political, cultural, and so on—are crucial facets of the project. There are few models for what I have attempted.[20] The book does not fit into a prefabricated genre, nor does it need to. What a book does and what it is should be considerations of greater import than how one categorizes it.

In sum, my ambition is this: a critical deciphering, retracing, and reconstruction of the political journey traveled by McKay, an exploration of his political thought and political behavior in time and space. Since, as George Lamming reminds us, radicals are not born but made—"I have never in my life met a Marxist baby"—the question arises: How had this baby of the Black Jamaican peasantry grown up to embrace Bolshevism and revolutionary socialism in such a passionate, courageous, and public manner by the beginning of 1921?[21] How does one explain his simultaneous attraction to Black nationalism and to revolutionary socialism? His origins, trajectory, and destination constitute an unlikely combination. How, then, does one explain his political evolution? What does it tell us more generally about the Black experience and the world and times in which McKay lived? By extension, how does one account for the deep radicalization of the kind black intellectuals such as McKay underwent during the first two decades of the twentieth century? Previously unaddressed, these are the fundamental questions that the book raises and brings into sustained focus and attention. The answers elicited are complex, intriguing, surprising, and instructive.

* * *

Claude McKay: The Making of a Black Bolshevik begins by locating McKay in fin de siècle colonial Jamaica. "Properly to understand the work of Claude McKay, it is essential to know about his Jamaican origins," Mervyn Morris, the distinguished Jamaican literary scholar and poet, observed.[22] I agree, but I would break this down further and make the recommendation even more explicit: Without an understanding of Jamaica *and* his Jamaican origins, it is impossible to understand the man and the trajectory he followed in subsequent years. The book is organized chronologically but also thematically.

Part 1 is concerned with McKay's Jamaican years. Chapter 1 is devoted to locating McKay, his family, and his class—the Black peasantry into which he was born—within the social structure and political economy of the island. Particular attention is paid to the highly unusual, if not unique, social position occupied by the McKays. They were very dark skinned—"black," by Jamaican standards, as opposed to "brown" or "colored"—yet were relatively and increasingly prosperous and financially independent by the time McKay left the island. The chapter delves into this set of circumstances and its ramifications for McKay and his family. Also included in this chapter is a more micro analysis of the McKay family dynamics and how Claude fitted into them. Apart from McKay's relationship with his parents, the chapter highlights his relationship with two profoundly influential figures during his childhood and early adulthood: his older brother, Uriah Theodore McKay (known to all as U. Theo), a distinguished schoolmaster and political activist; and Walter Jekyll, an English aristocrat, folklorist, and eccentric man of letters who had settled in Jamaica in the 1890s. Chapter 2 provides an overview of the Jamaica into which McKay was born in 1889 and in which he lived until his departure from the island in 1912, never to return. It focuses in particular upon the plight of the Jamaican workers and peasants, urban and rural, which profoundly affected McKay. In order to understand the roots of their underlying condition, the chapter addresses the colonial structure that shaped the island and its political economy and culture, including its articulation of race and color. Chapters 3 and 4 attend to McKay's experience as a member of the police force, with its traumatic and radicalizing impact on the sensitive young Jamaican and the poetry he wrote. These chapters focus in particular on what McKay's poetry reveals about his thinking, feelings, changing social consciousness—including his growing racial consciousness—and dissenting politics, prefiguring many of the political and intellectual tendencies manifested during his years abroad.

Part 2, comprising chapters 5 and 6, examines McKay's early American years, the traumatic nature of his experience, and its impact upon his increasing radicalization. In the United States, McKay quickly abandoned his allegiance to reformist British Fabianism and by 1919 became, as he said, "Bolshevik," adopting the radical ideology articulated by Russian revolutionaries (especially Vladimir Lenin and Leon Trotsky) that had culminated in the overthrow of the czar and the conquest of power in Russia in 1917. These chapters, especially chapter 5, document McKay's horrified reaction to the virulent racism he encountered in the United States—the everyday humiliation and oppression of Americans who happened to be of African descent and especially the barbaric practice of lynching, which was commonplace, banal, and routinized, lacking sustained opposition if not receiving general acquiescence from the white population, north and south. The widespread and senseless slaughter of the Great War—"this great catastrophe," he called it—was both shocking and unfathomable to McKay, undermining his confidence in "Western Civilization" and all that he was taught to "respect and reverence."[23] In this context, the Bolshevik Revolution restored his "golden hope."[24] The Red Summer of 1919, when anti-Black mob violence broke out in more than thirty major U.S. cities, including Washington, DC, and Chicago, slaughtering, terrorizing, torturing, and wounding thousands of African Americans, further radicalized McKay. It was during that summer that he penned his most famous poem, "If We Must Die," a bold, rallying cry for Black resistance. Chapter 5 focuses on McKay's time as a student at both Booker T. Washington's Tuskegee Institute and Kansas State College and his move to New York. Chapter 6 analyzes the events of 1919, McKay's response to them, and his public advocacy, for the first time, of Bolshevism. It ends with his departure for England in the fall of that year.

Part 3 (chapters 7 and 8) follows McKay to London and explores the radicalizing impact of his British sojourn. Chapter 7 documents his involvement with the radical left in London and especially his relationship with Sylvia Pankhurst and the group she founded, the Workers' Socialist Federation. It examines the racially hostile Britain that he entered, the different milieus in which he operated, and their impact on him. Chapter 8 discusses the publication of his first book of verses since leaving Jamaica (*Spring in New Hampshire and Other Poems* [1920]) and its British reception. It examines McKay's troubled relationship with C. K. Ogden, the distinguished linguist and editor of *Cambridge Magazine* who oversaw the publication of the book, as well as the crisis of the British left, McKay's caustic observations and reflections on Britain, and his decision to return to New York, arriving there in January 1921.

The book is thus chronologically bracketed by McKay's birth in 1889 and his return to New York at the beginning of 1921. The objective of *Claude McKay: The Making of a Black Bolshevik* is a radical reevaluation of the man as well as his work and times. The ambition is to draw a detailed, comprehensive, and more accurate political portrait of this most remarkable thinker, political activist, and courageous child of the African diaspora, who endured and articulated, like no other, the long and powerful storms of Black despair and struggle punctuated by days of sunshine and hope.

Part I

Jamaican Beginnings: The Formation
of a Black Fabian, 1889–1912

Map of Jamaica, Clarendon Parish highlighted

Land over 650 feet

Parish boundary

20 miles

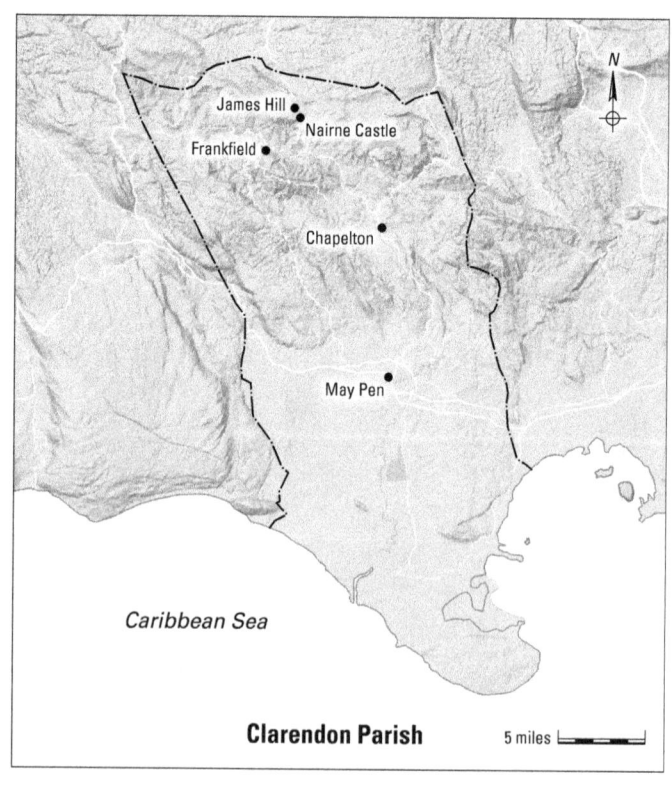

Clarendon Parish

5 miles

1

A Son of the Soil

Jamaica's Claude McKay

De mango tree in yellow bloom,
De pretty akee seed,
De mammee where de John-to-whits come
To have their daily feed,

Show you de place where I was born,
Of which I am so proud,
'Mongst de banana-field an' corn
On a lone mountain-road.

—Claude McKay, "My Mountain Home," 1912

The Place and World of the McKays

Festus Claudius McKay was born on September 15, 1889, in the parish of
Clarendon.[1] Claude was the youngest of the eleven children of Thomas and
Hannah Ann Elizabeth McKay (née Edwards), eight of whom lived to maturity (seven boys and one girl).[2] McKay's grandparents—at least the paternal ones—were enslaved Africans. According to *My Green Hills of Jamaica*,
his account of his childhood and youth, McKay's paternal grandfather was
a member of the Asante nation (from today's Republic of Ghana), and his
mother's side of the family traces its roots to the island of Madagascar, off the
East African coast.[3]

Heroic legend is associated with his mother's family. First made public by Max Eastman, McKay's closest friend, the story is that McKay learned as a boy of his mother's ancestors in Madagascar, their life of freedom before their violent abduction, their transportation to the New World, and their enslavement in Jamaica. On their arrival in Jamaica, the family resolved not to be broken up and sold separately. Each member would kill him- or herself if this demand was not met. According to Eastman, this decision, "solemnly announced in the [slave] market by the oldest white-haired Negro among them, had such an effect upon prospective buyers that it was impossible to sell them as individuals, and so they were all taken away together to those hills at Clarendon which their descendants still cultivate." Eastman infers from the story that "with the blood of these rebels in his veins, and their memory to stir it, we cannot wonder that Claude McKay's earliest boyish songs in Jamaican dialect were full of heresy and the militant love of freedom."[4]

McKay's father, an illiterate man who had earlier been a road mender, was, upon his marriage to Hannah Ann, given a small plot of land by his father-in-law, Thomas Edwards.[5] According to his son, Thomas McKay "did not believe in renting land; so he had worked grimly hard, buying a piece of land wherever it was for sale until he owned over one hundred acres in and around the village."[6] Mr. McKay was one of the few winners in the growing economic differentiation of the peasantry in late-nineteenth-century Jamaica.[7]

In the 1930s, an ex-governor and keen student of the island, Lord Olivier, calculated that fifty acres "form a prosperous property for an industrious and capable man, enabling him to keep a car and give some time to public duties."[8] The distinguished scholar Ken Post suggested that somewhere between twenty and seventy-one acres was "the watershed between rich peasants and small capitalist farmers" no longer working manually themselves and managing their holdings strictly as a profit-making venture.[9] Though Post's is an unsatisfyingly wide "watershed," which diminishes its analytical value, clearly a man with more than one hundred fertile acres and significant wealth in other forms was well beyond both his and Olivier's threshold of prosperity. Although all the evidence suggests that Thomas worked on the land well into his old age—he died at ninety-four—he was also tied into the market and wage system. In other words, he fulfilled any reasonable criteria for qualifying as a capitalist farmer. Given his economic circumstances, Thomas did not exaggerate when he gave as his occupation the grand and loaded title "planter"—as opposed to "small farmer," "farmer," or "peasant"—when he registered Claude's birth.

The economic position achieved by Thomas McKay and his family was not unique, but it was extraordinarily rare in fin de siècle Jamaica. The McKays were not only Black, they were very dark skinned, what may be described as "black" Black Jamaicans, in a society characterized by an almost invariable overlapping of class and color. One could almost read a person's social class from the color of his or her skin: white and lighter-skinned people occupied the higher class positions, and the dark-skinned majority inhabited the rungs below. And the darker they were, the lower the position they occupied. Wealth, power, and professional jobs went with whiteness and lightness; poverty, powerlessness, and menial, poor-paying jobs were associated with darker-skinned people. The McKays violated this pattern.[10] Though Black and illiterate, Thomas climbed up the steep and slippery socioeconomic pole to achieve exceptional wealth. Moreover, on this economic base, he ensured the education of his eight dark-skinned children, which propelled them into the professions and on to the upper echelons of the socioeconomic ladder, endowing the family with an extraordinary level of independence. The situation of the majority of Black Jamaicans was very different. This was especially true at the time of Claude's birth in 1889, a time when the island was in the throes of rapid social and economic change adversely affecting the mass of the people. Exceptionally sensitive to these transformations, McKay was shaped politically by them, forming the subject matter of much of his early writings.

Thomas McKay's wealth provided the material underpinnings of his and his family's self-confidence and poise. One writer claimed, a little misleadingly (as we shall see), that Mr. McKay's eldest son, Uriah Theodore (generally known as U. Theo), had himself become "independent enough, financially," to leave teaching in 1910, before he was forty.[11] Beyond question, however, is the fact that the very dark-skinned McKays were a rare Jamaican family: they were Black, yet unlike the vast majority of dark-skinned Jamaicans, they were not economically beholden to *buckra*, the white plantocracy. It was this capitalist status that provided the economic security and the psychic resource of confidence that, in turn, facilitated and nourished the development of Claude McKay's independent thought and action that moved, somewhat ironically, in a decidedly *anti*capitalist direction over the years.

Thomas McKay was, in another important respect, a member of a rare species of men in turn-of-the-century Jamaica: a Black person prosperous enough to qualify to vote under a tightly restricted franchise. So prohibitive were the financial qualifications to vote that only 1.5 percent of Jamaicans were registered voters in 1884—9,176 out of a population of 600,000. In 1901, when the population stood at 756,000, there were only 16,256 registered voters—hardly an improvement.[12] The franchise skewed in favor of the wealthy—merchants, landowners, and attorneys, the vast majority of European and Levantine origin—and worked against the Africans who comprised the overwhelming majority of the population. Among non-Europeans, the "coloreds" (those of "mixed" descent; the "brown"), being economically better-off than the Africans, constituted a proportion of the voters greater than their demographic weight on the island. Not surprisingly, the proportion of Black voters was substantially below the proportion of the population that was Black. In contrast, white voters vastly overrepresented the 2 percent of the population they comprised in 1886, even though many qualified whites did not bother to register. Of those who did register, few bothered to vote—probably calculating, not incorrectly, that their vital interests were well taken care of without the charade and inconvenience of going to the polls.[13] Similarly, the coloreds, who made up less than a fifth of the population, accounted for more than a third of all registered voters.[14]

As if the veto power of the British governor and the cabal of oligarchs around him were not enough, Black Jamaicans were disenfranchised even further after 1893 as literacy tests and hard times knocked them off the voter registration rolls. From a peak of more than 42,000 in 1893–94, the number of registered voters declined to some 16,000 in 1901, and to less than 9,000 four years later. In 1911, just a year before McKay left for the United States, the number of voters had increased but still amounted to just over 3 percent of the population—27,000 out of 831,000. The proportion was even smaller in Clarendon.[15]

Black working-class women were completely disenfranchised during McKay's time on the island. It was not until 1919 that Jamaican women were allowed to vote. And the "enfranchisement" legislation (Law 22) was never meant to benefit working-class women. Brigadier General E. A. Moulton Barrett, the custos of St. Ann and a nominated member of the Legislative Council, captured the general sentiment of that body when he inveighed against the bill, introduced by the colored elected member for Kingston, H. A. L. Simpson. Jamaica, he declared, would be the "laughing stock of the world" if some of the women who pay "ten shilling taxes were allowed to vote. They were absolutely unfit to exercise any franchise altogether," he insisted. Moulton Barrett urged the council to impose "a very high franchise" if women were to be granted the vote at all. He then made the class/racial basis of his opposition plain: "No one who knew Jamaica and knew the majority of the peasants in Jamaica would disagree with him." The governor, Sir Leslie Probyn—whose wife had chaired a large meeting organized by upper-class white women agitating for the vote—essentially agreed with Moulton Barrett. Probyn suggested that the vote should be given to women only if the qualifications were "really safe" and if after its implementation the government had the capacity to make such qualifications "more rigid" if needed.[16] And so it was. When the franchise was conceded to women in May 1919, they had to be twenty-five years old, as Probyn had proposed, in order to vote (one member of the Legislative Council had proposed thirty); for men, the age was twenty-one. Similarly, the female franchise was tied to property qualifications more punitive than those for men. Whereas one of the qualifications for men to vote was the payment of taxes or rates on real property amounting to no less than ten shillings per year, women were required to pay taxes or rates on real property amounting to no less than two pounds—four times the sum required of men.[17] Women were also banned from running for public office, local or national. Whereas men registered before 1893 did not need to be literate to vote, all women did. Thus, while the vast majority of Black Jamaican men were denied the vote, an even greater proportion of Black women suffered disenfranchisement, and for a more prolonged period. This was indeed the object of many of those who agitated for women's suffrage, including the white women who made their voices heard: to keep the women's vote white, just like that of male voters.[18]

It was within these tight constraints, what McKay euphemistically called "the English political system prevailing at the time," that Thomas McKay survived as "one of the few peasants who possessed enough worldly goods to establish himself as a voter."[19] Moreover, as his son pointed out, Thomas "never yielded to any of the political trickeries of the political machine at voting time when he might have earned a few pounds because of his influence over the rest of the peasants."[20] His disinclination to succumb to the planter-politicians' blandishments was not only due to his pride and dignity; it was also an outgrowth of his economic independence. Universal adult suffrage did not come until 1944, and then only after the workers and peasants, men as well as women, revolted, frightening their overlords into making political concessions.[21] Thomas McKay, then, was one of a tiny minority within a tiny minority.

Black, economically superior, educated (with the sole exception of Thomas himself), respected, the McKays had little patience with the colorism of mulatto society or the racism of the whites. They nevertheless were very conscious of the fact that they were less than a generation removed from the struggling working class. This knowledge was a source of pride as well as inspiration for the McKays. Young Claude grew up in a family undergoing the transition from one class to the next, and the tracings—especially ideological and cultural ones—of the old class lingered and nourished the family. This transitional character of the McKay family forms part of the explanation for the radicalism of both U. Theo and his younger brother.[22] It is never possible to read, as if on a grid, one's political behavior and ideology from one's class position. Forces other than social class shape, transform, and refract political ideology and political behavior. And when an individual or family is in a state of social mobility, either upward or downward, it is even more difficult to precisely gauge the role of class position in determining politics. In the case of the McKays, their political ideology and action were further influenced, if not determined, not only by their "race," but by their color, too. If Thomas McKay's success as a farmer elevated the family's economic status, their dark skin still denied the McKays full acceptance in middle-class Jamaican society with its color snobbery. The family, always aware of this, deeply resented the colorism surrounding them. U. Theo and Claude were not the only members to give expression to their resentment of this kind of discrimination.

Rachel McKay, in writing to her brother Claude about the career prospects in Jamaica for his daughter, Hope, noted: "You know in Jamaica the colour question is so strong that there [are] scores and scores of girls that have been to these high schools, and can get nothing to do, but sit at home under their parents' support, after spending so much on them. Others have to go to College and be trained as teachers so as to get something to do."[23] Rachel was herself reasonably fortunate: she was a postmistress near her village. Very few, if any, other dark-skinned Black women held such an esteemed position in Jamaica at the time. The power and prestige of the McKay family certainly helped Rachel to enter this mulatto occupational preserve. McKay's brother Tommy—christened Thomas Edison McKay—contradicted himself when he wrote in 1929: "It is quite true that the black population have less chance in getting decent jobs than the mulattoes do, but it goes by ability and capacity." And in the very next sentence he informed McKay that Hope, being relatively light-skinned—her mother, McKay's ex-wife, was a "mulatto"—"will get a decent job at any time." A few years later, Tommy, a trained clergyman of the Anglican Church, was less equivocal about the color question in Jamaica. In a series of rather desperate letters written in 1936—spawned by the exceptional hardship of the

Depression—he sought Claude's help in getting to the United States. He had had enough of Jamaica. "There is too much red-tape here and the church is more oppressive and colour prejudiced than even the Civil Departments," he told McKay. "Jamaica," he wrote in another letter, "is all white and brown [mulatto]; there is no scope for one, and too much favouritism."[24] So much for getting by on "ability and capacity."

One therefore needs to be cautious with McKay's remark that "in our village, I grew up on equal terms with white, mulatto and black children of a certain class because my father was a big peasant [and] 'belonged.' "[25] The statement is probably true, but the reader should not extend the applicability of the remark outside of McKay's village and immediate community, which served as a cocoon. Well-known, established, prosperous, and respected in James Hill and the surrounding areas, outside of their village the McKays were at best dark-skinned, middle-class Jamaicans with the abridged and grudging respect accorded Black Jamaicans, even middle-class ones.

Sometimes even grudging respect was denied. In a 1932 letter, McKay recalled that when he achieved local fame as a poet, at one home to which he was invited, "the light-colored servants didn't want to wait on [him]." Addressed to Nancy Cunard, the eccentric and rebellious British heiress, who was planning a trip to Jamaica accompanied by her African American lover, the letter advised her on the etiquette of color on the island. "I think, if your friend is dark, you might have some difficulty seeing the mulatto smart set in their homes with him. . . . But," McKay added, "the social and material prestige of your name may cow them."[26] Rosalie, who Langston Hughes met in Paris during one of his stays there in the 1920s, was evidently a member of Jamaica's "mulatto smart set." While Hughes and his friend raved about the recently published *Spring in New Hampshire*, McKay's 1920 collection, Rosalie—Hughes never disclosed her last name—described by Hughes as a "light-skinned Jamaican" with a "violent prejudice toward dark Negroes," said that "she did not like Claude McKay because he was too black." "Color had nothing to do with the quality of one's writing," Hughes retorted. "But Rosalie said it had to do with the quality of one's affections, and that was that."[27]

Tommy's aside about the "oppressive and colour prejudiced" civil departments, by which he meant the colonial civil service, is not at all surprising, nor was it hyperbolic. To Black Jamaica, especially its emerging Black intelligentsia, the colonial civil service was the prime site of race and color prejudice on the island. In 1911, the colonial government in

Jamaica discontinued competitive examination for positions in the civil service. This effectively blocked Black people, especially the dark-skinned bright children of the peasantry, from entering the service. Competitive examinations had been introduced in 1885, but in response to opposition from the privileged few, including some within the civil service itself, the colonial authorities made changes in 1894, allowing exemptions from the examinations. In 1905, open competition returned, only to be disbanded again six years later.[28] Thus, an important avenue for upward social mobility for educated Black people was blocked overnight. The measure contributed to the outward flow of Black talent from the island. Indeed, in McKay's novel, *Banana Bottom*, set in turn-of-the-century Jamaica, one character, a bright and ambitious young son of the peasantry, left for the United States explicitly because of this change in policy. As the narrator explains: "The competitive examinations for the local Civil Service upon which he had fixed his hopes had been abandoned for a system of selection. The selection was made by the special recommendation of people in respectable and responsible positions. And the result of this new order was to limit the minor Civil Service posts to the light-coloured middle classes and bar aspirants from the black peasantry."[29] J. A. Rogers, who emigrated from the island to the United States in 1906, condemned the policy (light-skinned though he was) from his new base in Harlem. The Reverend E. Ethelred Brown, one of the few dark-skinned Jamaicans to have worked within the service, denounced it and continued to denounce it long after leaving the island for Harlem. Marcus Garvey, in his very first article, vented his rage against the policy. Writing two years after the authorities ended competitive exams, Garvey observed that "when the Government twenty or thirty years ago, threw open the doors of the Civil Service to competitive examination, the Negro youths swept the board, and captured every available office, leaving their white competitors far behind. This system went on for a few years, but," he noted, "as the white youths were found to be intellectually inferior to the black, the whites persuaded the Government to abolish the competitive system, and fill vacancies by nomination, and by this means kept out the black youths."[30] The year before Garvey's article appeared, C. A. Wilson, one of island's leading Black intellectuals, declared: "If you are white and with ever so little ability every avenue of service and promotion is thrown open to you. If you are black you are always running up against barred gates."[31] Though he did not to mention it by name, the Jamaican civil service was the primary target of Wilson's criticism.

Small wonder, then, that the colonial civil service in the British Caribbean, but especially in Jamaica, from the late nineteenth century right down to independence in the 1960s, had been a key focus of nationalist agitation and colonial discontent.[32] It was in the recruitment process to the civil service and the treatment of colored and Black people who made it into the service that racism was most transparent and explicit within the structure of colonial rule in the islands. It is not surprising, then, that Jamaica's first openly nationalist organization, the National Club, was begun by a disgruntled colored civil servant with bitter grievances over his treatment in the service. Marcus Garvey and W. A. Domingo served their political apprenticeships under Sandy Cox, the man who founded the club.[33]

Hannah and Her Husband: A Portrait

Thomas and Hannah McKay, their dark skin notwithstanding, were members of what was then called the "respectable peasantry."[34] McKay tells us that Thomas "was a very just man," and that he was "something of a village leader, as they have in Africa." Instead of going to court, people would often ask Thomas to adjudicate and settle their differences; his rulings were generally obeyed. Mr. McKay was very strict about the law and "hated" dishonesty and trickery.[35] A deeply religious man who eschewed and condemned tobacco and alcohol, Thomas McKay served as a senior deacon in the local Baptist church—a position of great prestige among the villagers.

The story of Thomas's rise to prominence in James Hill, where the McKays lived, is an intriguing one. The son of formerly enslaved Jamaicans, he was born around 1840—a mere two years after the formal end of slavery on the island—in the village of Staceyville, some twelve miles east of James Hill. Industrious, enterprising, and ambitious, he worked at various laboring jobs in upper Clarendon. One of his friends who lived in James Hill wanted him to meet a woman who he thought would make a good wife for Thomas. Instead, Thomas met and fell in love with the beautiful Hannah Ann Elizabeth Edwards, the twenty-one-year-old daughter of well-to-do Thomas Edwards, a senior deacon in Mount Zion Baptist Church. Thomas, no doubt in his Sunday best, "tramped," McKay tells us, to Hannah Ann's village every Sunday to court her. He was about eight years older than she, but Hannah Ann's father approved of the match, and the couple were married in 1870. Thomas Edwards gave the newlyweds a piece of land, and from there Thomas McKay built a small cottage, worked extremely hard, and embarked upon a seemingly continuous process of accumulating more land.[36]

Unlike Thomas McKay, Hannah Ann could read and write. She learned her letters, according to her son, from Mother Woolsey, the light-skinned, quadroon matriarch of the Woolsey clan, a rather unpleasant local colored family in the throes of decline. Mother Woolsey prided herself on having taught Hannah Ann and claimed that Hannah Ann was much better at learning her letters "than all the other members of the Negro families around."[37] Hannah Ann's proficiency was such that when her firstborn, U. Theo, arrived in 1872, she taught him to read and write herself. She apparently did the same for all her other children before they went to school. U. Theo never went to school until he was eleven.[38] Hannah Ann, however, seemed to have done little for U. Theo's arithmetic, which, when he went to school, was discovered to be "not very brilliant." But she excelled at teaching him reading and writing.[39] By the time he started formal schooling, U. Theo was, said the *Jamaica Times*, "dux in reading in his class." The *Times* writer averred that U. Theo's "success in life is largely due to the love of reading which [his mother] inculcated into him."[40]

McKay recalled that, although his mother was a relatively young woman in her forties, all the villagers called her "Mother Mac." That was, he said, "a great mark of love because only certain native women are honoured with this distinctive title of 'Mother.'" Mrs. McKay, like her husband, was a leader in the church, where, among other things, she directed the women's prayer meetings. McKay remembered that the women often visited his home to discuss church business with her.[41]

McKay loved and admired his mother deeply. She reciprocated his love. "I was the baby of the family and the favourite of my mother," he openly confessed.[42] Indeed, there is evidence, from McKay's own writings, that his mother rather indulged, perhaps even "spoiled," him as a boy.[43] But a certain sadness overshadowed the relationship. As McKay wrote in his autobiography some thirty-four years after leaving Jamaica, and almost forty years after Hannah Ann's death: "One thing I do remember sharply is that my mother was ill and it was generally said that she became ill right after I was born."[44] He never said so explicitly, but McKay felt personally responsible for his mother's deteriorated health and early death, a burden he never relinquished. In *Banana Bottom*, McKay's novel of Jamaican peasant life, the mother died at the heroine's birth. "The village folk said that she had killed her mother. That was the way the black peasants referred to a child that survived when the mother had died giving birth to it."[45]

The guilt was compounded. Carl Cowl, McKay's friend and last literary agent, said that McKay felt guilty because he was not at his mother's bedside when she died. Young Claude left his mother for a short time to go to the field, and she died before he returned. Cowl believed that McKay never fully forgave himself for his absence. Even though he talked to Cowl about the incident on several occasions, it was always with self-recriminating anguish that McKay remembered the circumstances of his mother's death.[46] His sonnet "My Mother" tells the story of Hannah Ann's last moments:

> Reg wished me to go with him to the field;
> I paused because I did not want to go,
> But in her quiet way she made me yield
> Reluctantly,—for she was breathing low.
> Her hand she slowly lifted from her lap
> And, smiling sadly in the old sweet way,
> She pointed to the nail where hung my cap;
> Her eyes said: I shall last another day.
> But scarcely had we reached the distant place
> When o'er the hills we heard a faint bell ringing,
> A boy came running up with frightened face,
> We knew the fatal news that he was bringing:
> I heard him listlessly and made no moan,
> Although the only one I loved was gone.[47]

Hannah Ann's son devoted some of his finest poems to her memory. When he went to the United States, the first poems he published—including one of his most accomplished and celebrated, "The Harlem Dancer"—were under the nom de plume of Eli Edwards—a masculinization of his mother's maiden name, Elizabeth Edwards.[48] "I always thought my mother was very beautiful," he said. "She was round faced and brown skinned with two plaits of curls, one on each side of her head." He described her as

> a wonderful person and all the peasants around liked her. She was especially nice to the young girls who had produced babies out of wedlock. She used to give them food and clean rags. These girls were likely to be snubbed by the older married women who were in the church and considered themselves very respectable. Although my mother was a deaconess in the church, she treated those girls just as she would anybody else. Perhaps the quality most

prominent in my mother was her goodness. She loved people and believed in being kind to everybody.[49]

Mrs. McKay, her son tells us, "didn't care very much about what people did and why and how they did it. She only wanted to help them if they were in trouble. She wanted to help those who were outcast, poor and miserable."[50] The reverence with which McKay remembered her was shared by other members of the family. His brother Tommy, a good Anglican, remarked to him twenty years after his mother's death: "I hope you have not forgotten God and you are following dear mother's footsteps."[51] McKay's letter responding to his brother has not survived. It would, however, not have been inaccurate for him to tell the Reverend Thomas that he had long forgotten God, but that he always attempted, however imperfectly, to follow in his mother's footsteps.

The songs of praise to Mrs. McKay were not sung only by her favorite son and the other members of her large Clarendon clan. Everyone who knew her was deeply impressed by Hannah Ann's exceptionally fine, almost saintly, qualities. The anonymous writer of her obituary, who had known her "very, very intimately for over 30 years," said that he had never known her to have a quarrel with anyone. He corroborates McKay's testimony to Hannah Ann's generosity: "Her bounty was small but her charity was large and her neighbours, especially those not circumstanced as she, know full well the depth of her kindness. Her life was full and the large attendance at her funeral . . . is a tribute to her worth and work."[52]

McKay's relationship with his father could hardly have been more different from that with his mother. Indeed, in his autobiography, he quite often contrasted his parents—invariably to his father's disadvantage. To the warm, generous, and loving mother he counterposed the cold, remote, and austere father with his authoritarian tendencies. His mother, McKay wrote, was "quite different" from his father, "who believed in justice, a kind of Anglo-Saxon justice"; "very stern and upright." All the children preferred their mother,

who was so much more elastic and understanding. She was a virtuous woman too. My father, however was a Presbyterian Calvinist. A real black Scotchman. We boys wondered how his education could have made him that way. He was so entirely different from all our coloured neighbours with their cockish-liquor drinking and rowdy singing . . . So top-lofty, one might say. Yet everybody liked and respected him.[53]

Mrs. McKay always took the children's side in dealings with her husband.[54] Thomas, like most Jamaican parents, then as now, was not averse to meting out corporal punishment to his children. McKay managed to get himself exempted in a spectacular fashion, showing great courage—not for the last time—facing a figure of authority. A rambunctious teenager, Claude thought that at the age of fourteen he had outgrown being beaten by his father. McKay was, he confessed, "very impertinent"—forced-ripe, the Jamaicans would call it—and one day went too far. "You cannot whip me, sir," he told his father. "I am a man." Provoked, Thomas promptly tied him to a post and dropped his trousers. The boy had to be taught a lesson. In proper Jamaican fashion, Thomas went to get a strap. But when Claude saw him coming, he started to "curse and used every swear word that a small boy could think of." Shocked, Thomas changed his mind: "I can't whip the boy. Why! he's gone crazy!" His father left the tied-up boy and went off to the fields. By Jamaican standards, Claude's was a very lucky reprieve. Pleased with his defiance, McKay proudly reported that it was "the last time he ever tied me up or laid a hand on me."[55]

Despite McKay's unhappy relationship with his father, he did respect Thomas even if he did not love, or perhaps even like, the man. McKay's depiction of the relationship in *My Green Hills of Jamaica* is probably more negative than it was in reality. In the correspondence with members of his family, especially with U. Theo and Rachel, McKay consistently inquired about his father. He repeatedly requested a photograph of Thomas from both U. Theo and Rachel, and he got many promises from them to send the picture. "I will try to send you [father's] picture," U. Theo told him in April 1929. But in August of the same year, U. Theo wrote: "I saw father about three days after I got your letter and in conversation with him he said that he has not heard anything about money for photograph." "You will soon get father's photo," his sister Rachel reassured him in December 1929. "Thanks for the photographs," he wrote in August 1932 to Nancy Cunard, who was on a visit to Jamaica. "Sorry you did not get one of Father. Been asking my brother for one for three years."

The old man probably had stronger feelings for the son than the son had for him, and a more tender heart than his rebellious son gave him credit for. In a letter sent to McKay in August 1927, Rachel wrote: "Our heart pines and yearns after you; especially your aged father who believes that the Lord has heard his prayers in allowing him to hear from you before he dies." U. Theo had also told McKay that his father would love to see him before he dies. Although McKay never returned to see his father, when the old man died in 1933 he still willed to his absent son the family home and "the lands around it," even though Rachel was allowed to live there till her death.[56]

If there is doubt about McKay's love for Thomas, there is none about his admiration and respect for the old man. Consistent and explicit on this point, McKay admired his father's industry and enterprise. He was proud of the old man's remarkable accomplishments and principled positions. And he acknowledged that Thomas did his best—if only in his own peculiar way—for his eight dark-skinned children in a society riddled with colorism, if not downright racism. In an autobiographical sketch published in 1918, McKay described his father as a "firm believer in education" and acknowledged that Thomas had "tried to give all his eight children the best he could."[57] Thomas never allowed his sons to carry loads on their heads "like other peasant boys."[58] Ambitious for his children, on more than one occasion he made it clear to his seven sons that he was not educating his "boys" for any of "these village girls no matter how pretty they might be." "I never did run around with girls," he told them, "and I've never known another woman besides your mother. And God helping me, never will." (He kept his word, even though he survived his wife by almost twenty-four years.) But his sons, "the boys," had different ideas up there in the Clarendon hills: "all of us," McKay reported, "went after the village girls."[59]

McKay related with admiration and pride his father's bold stand against a hypocritical Scottish missionary, the pastor of their church, Mount Zion. The Baptists, as McKay explained, were very strict in their prohibition against drinking, smoking, dancing, and other "sins." Rumor had it that the Scotsman was a heavy smoker. Thomas McKay, who was head deacon, said that the man should not be accused unless there was proof of transgression. McKay's father was surprised when one day he visited the minister in his library and found the place full of smoke. The pastor had managed to put out his pipe, but the smoke and scent gave him away. Thomas was shocked and disappointed. "It is true then what people say about your smoking?" The missionary, condemned for the gap between his preachings and the cloud of smoke around him, attempted a clumsy lie. "Without batting an eye," he told Thomas that he was not smoking. "How can you say you are not smoking when we are enveloped in the fog of hell?" Thomas asked. He offered not to bring charges against the pastor but insisted that the Scotsman give up the ministry and leave Mount Zion.[60]

When the pastor refused, Thomas resigned as deacon and stayed away from church. The villagers rallied round him and also boycotted the church. According to McKay, Mount Zion "went down to the devil. And the mountain country became a hell for that missionary. Even the children jeered at him along the roads when he went riding by."[61] The villagers held meetings with the church hierarchy to resolve the crisis. The missionary, an arrogant man, stoutly refused to heed the congregation's demand. In fact, he added fuel to the fire. He abused his status of titular head of the Mount Zion church school by firing the local teacher, replacing him with his own wife. That to the villagers, McKay remembered, was a "terrible offence because the teacher was a good man. There was nothing against him." Children and parents revolted. Parents sent their children to other schools, even though the other schools were several miles away. To make matters worse, the pastor began doing "things that no other minister had ever done," including embezzling missionary funds for his own use.[62]

Another large members' meeting was convened with all the other Baptist ministers from the surrounding areas in attendance. The white ones especially urged the minister to leave: "he was bringing a bad name upon all the white clergy." The missionary's wife, who by this time had already sent their two sons off to Canada, decided to leave her husband and take the two remaining children with her. Having got on well with the villagers, his wife found herself in an invidious and uncomfortable position. With the pressure piled upon him to the rafters and his wife now threatening to leave him, taking the children with her, the minister finally threw in the towel. The whole affair had lasted no less than five years.[63] On the morning they were leaving, the missionary's wife went over to the McKays and she and Hannah Ann "mingled their tears." "My mother," McKay wrote, "was always very kind and hated to see anyone suffer." But when the missionary went over to his father to shake hands and say good-bye, things went less smoothly. "I will not shake your hands because they are dirty," Thomas told him. "A dirty white hand is the same to me as a dirty colored hand. *No sir*, I will not shake your hand." Another minister was appointed, this time a colored man who had been educated at the Calabar Institution, a prestigious college in Kingston. Thomas went back to the church and was made deacon again.[64] The victorious congregation returned to the pews, and the children returned to Mount Zion's school.

For McKay, these events symbolized his father's resolve and strength of character and also demonstrated the power of collective action on the part of ordinary people. The struggle for Mount Zion, which took place during his boyhood, made a profound impression on him. It is no accident that this anecdote is told twice, a decade apart, in writing.[65] Later, McKay supported the boycott of the Canadian-owned trams in Kingston after a particularly unpopular fare increase in February 1912. His poem on the subject, "Passive Resistance," published in April 1912, anticipated the militant defiance of "If We Must Die" and other poems of protest written in the United States.[66] The example of the Mount Zion battle also echoed in McKay's firm and public support of the Black boycott of racist retailers in Harlem during the Depression. The white store owners in the "Negro Metropolis" explicitly refused to employ Black people in any except the most menial jobs. "Don't Buy Where You Can't Work" became the rallying cry. Of all Harlem's Black intellectuals, McKay provided the most vigorous and passionate defense of the boycotters. He paid a heavy price. He was criticized by those on the left (the Communist Party) as well as those on the right, Black and white. George Schuyler, an African American journalist, among others, accused McKay of being a "black fascist." But McKay, like Thomas and the congregation and children of Mount Zion, remained steadfast.[67]

McKay offered other vignettes of his father and of the complex relationship between himself and Thomas. He vividly recalled the unprecedented and surprisingly open expression of tenderness from his father when Thomas discovered that young Claude, who had recently moved to Kingston to study, had escaped the terrible earthquake that hit the city in 1907. In the aftermath of the devastation, McKay picked his way through the rubble and managed to get a dray headed for Clarendon. The dray reached Clarendon in the blackness of the rural night. Unexpectedly, he met his father near May Pen, the parish's capital. Anxious about his son, "the baby of the family," Thomas had made his way to the small town, calling out to the different drays to see if Claude was on any of them. Finally, he spotted the one carrying his son. McKay remembered the drayman stopping. As his son got off, Thomas hugged and kissed him. "It gave me the strangest feeling," McKay remembered, "my father's beard against my face—because I had never before been kissed by him. He was always a very stern man; but now he must have felt that I'd escaped from something terribly tragic as he held me in his arms."[68]

Although Thomas frowned upon some of the customs of the peasants—especially the boisterous tea meetings—this puritanical and rigidly Christian man, so much a child of the European missionaries, managed never to forget and remained proud of his African roots. "Sometimes when he became angry with us boys for any foolish practice he would say to us: 'Your grandfather (meaning his father) was a slave and knew how cruel the white man could be. You boys don't know anything about life.'" Thomas, McKay tells us, was a "wonderful teller of African stories."[69] Hannah Ann, too, was a highly accomplished teller of Anancy stories, the African-derived Jamaican folktales.[70] McKay recounted that his father told them of West African customs. One of the tales left a particularly sharp imprint on Claude's childhood memory: "I vividly remember his telling us that when Ashanti mothers gave birth to albino babies they were regarded as types who were mixed up with magic and thus caused bad luck, so they were exposed to die."[71]

Thomas McKay, however, vigorously rejected the African-derived, magico-religious practice known locally as obeah. McKay, more likely than not, exaggerates the extent of the practice of obeah among the peasantry when he writes: "My father's family and the Constable[s] our cousins, were the only two in our village which did not practice the magic of obeah."[72] McKay heartily approved of the rationalist premise upon which his father rejected the purported magical powers of the obeahman. Thomas used to say that "one could be hurt only by being poisoned, or through some other physical contact with an enemy."[73]

McKay also wrote in awe about his father's stoicism and puritanical behavior. The son linked these qualities to Thomas's amazingly robust constitution—even though he was "as lean as a greyhound"—and astonishing longevity:

> I remember that my father besides his mules and horses had two milch cows and my mother and we kids, between us, had a flock of Shaggy goats; but father did not drink cow's milk or goat's milk. He preferred the milk that came from the dried nut of the coco-palm tree. The coconut was grated, the milk strained from it, and put into coffee. It gives the coffee an entirely different taste from that of either goat's or cow's milk, or cream. It is delicious indeed, if you acquire the taste. My father would drink about a pint of coffee with coconut milk and go to work all day and return only in the evening for dinner.
>
> People used to say that he would ruin his health; but my father knew what he was doing. I remember, too, he would never touch a drop of anything that came out of a bottle, even plain soda pop. At Christmas time, my brother used to bring home or if he did not come, would send two bottles of Moet and Chandon. Mother and the older boys used to drink it with the orange wine and Port wine with which we celebrated Christmas. Father never touched it and he lived until he was 98. Mother died at 53. None of us boys are like our father; all of us do all the things that he wouldn't do, without any regrets[.] Only my sister lived up to his standards of austerity.[74]

U. Theo McKay: Big Brother and Mentor

Although McKay powerfully recalled his parents' presence in his life, the most influential figure in his formation, including his intellectual formation, was his eldest brother, U. Theo. Born on March 23, 1872, U. Theo was more than seventeen years McKay's senior. He graduated from the most prestigious teacher-training institution in Jamaica—and arguably the most highly regarded of such institutions in the British Caribbean at the time—Mico College, in Kingston, where he excelled. According to *Who's Who in Jamaica*, he passed "first in Honours" and, the entry intriguingly added, "also in other subjects." U. Theo studied at Mico between 1891 and 1896, and received broad academic training in the natural sciences, mathematics, music, and the humanities. Claude particularly recalled that he had a "very sound grounding" in Latin and French. It is probably true that for the time and place, as one writer suggested, it was the best education available.[75]

U. Theo became one of the island's most distinguished schoolmasters. Somewhat of a Renaissance man, he loved cricket (which he also played) and good literature (which he read widely). A music lover, he played the piano and was renowned as a choirmaster and impresario. McKay vividly recalled his organizing a choir in Clarendon that performed Handel's *Messiah* to national acclaim. He kept abreast of current affairs, subscribing to a large number of foreign journals and newspapers. He moved with confidence and ease between the classes. He loved a good conversation and in *Who's Who* listed "Political and Economic discussions" among his recreations.[76] Unlike his little brother, who was always shy and never enjoyed speaking in public, not even to recite his own poems, U. Theo was an accomplished orator. Indeed, a distinguished contemporary claimed that he was "one of the ablest speakers in Jamaica" and was accurately described as "one of the smartest of the elementary teachers of the island."[77]

When Claude was seven, his parents entrusted his upbringing and education to their firstborn and distinguished eldest son. At that time, U. Theo and his wife lived in Mount Carey, a small town about ten miles southwest of Montego Bay, and, at the time, about a day's journey from the McKay family seat in Nairne Castle, Clarendon.[78] He served as headmaster of the local school. It is not clear why Thomas and Hannah, along with U. Theo, came to this arrangement about Claude's upbringing, but such practices were commonplace in Jamaica at the time.[79] McKay attended his brother's school and, by his own account, relished it—albeit not necessarily for the best of reasons:

There was one thing that gave me a great deal of physical and mental joy. That was the fact that I was my brother's brother and because of this received so many little privileges. I was made a member of all the important school clubs even though I was not of age. In the school I was put into much higher classes than the kids of my own age. Very often I had to depend on other classmates to work out my problems for me. They were all willing to do it. Then I soon discovered that except for figuring I had a good brain. I was good in geography and history, reading and writing and the natural sciences.[80]

It was at his brother's school, as well as at U. Theo's home, that Claude developed and cultivated an appetite for books. His love of literature and music was nourished by U. Theo, and by the age of ten, McKay started to write poetry.

Unlike his parents, U. Theo was a committed freethinker. In a 1929 letter to Claude, who was then living in Europe, he confessed: "I believe in independence, especially intellectual independence. . . . I still stand a free man, where revealed religion is concerned. Try as I may, I cannot but regard the teachings of priest and prophet as anything but superstition."[81] Like his father before him, U. Theo was disdainful of the practice of and belief in obeah. He, however, went further than Thomas: he spoke out against it. Twenty years after leaving the island, McKay recalled that when he was "a kid" growing up with him, U. Theo used to "lecture against [obeah] and try to convince his friends among the well-off peasants that obeah was a fake. But," concluded McKay, "I am sure he had no success."[82]

The boy voraciously devoured his big brother's library—Arnold, Draper, Spencer, Hegel, Spinoza, Haeckel, Schopenhauer, Kant, and Berkeley, among others.

When my brother saw me reading those books he was very happy. He loosened up and started to tell me about the lives of the great freethinkers of the times such as Thomas Huxley, Bradlaugh the great Parliamentarian, Mrs. Annie Besant and Mr. John M. Robertson also a Parliamentarian. Now I read the freethinking books with greater interest and saw and thought of life solely from the free thought angle.[83]

U. Theo, pleased with his little brother's interest in progressive ideas, encouraged the young man along this path. "By the time I was ten," McKay recalled, "my brother was pushing free-thinking books my way."

I devoured Huxley and Lecky, Haeckel and Gibbon and others. Gibbon I especially loved as an historian. My sister-in-law was very religious. When she saw me reading Haeckel's *The Riddle of the Universe*, she said it was a bad book, and tried to stop me. My Brother said: "Let the boy read anything he likes."[84]

Writing in an American magazine in 1918, McKay fondly remembered the years with his brother as "a great formative period in my life—a time of perfect freedom to play, read and think as I liked."[85] Thus, by the time Claude, his big brother, and his sister-in-law returned to live in Nairne Castle, when Claude was about fourteen, the young McKay had become a committed freethinker in a sea of believers; not only that, he began proselytizing: "Soon I began talking to the younger set . . . boys of my age, some older and some younger. Many of them believed as I believed. We went to my brother for enlightenment and instruction. Soon there was a young crop of agnostics way up there in the hills of Jamaica."[86]

McKay's education continued in Clarendon for the next couple of years. Although he was no longer formally taught by U. Theo, the brothers actively maintained their intellectual relationship. U. Theo's interest in music continued and flourished with his organization of a distinguished local choir. McKay proudly participated in its activities.[87]

Not long after his return from Mount Carey, events in Nairne Castle severely tested McKay's intellectual resolve and courage. A wave of religious revivalism, emanating from as far away as Wales, hit the Clarendon hills and other parts of Jamaica in 1906. Claude and U. Theo stood firm while the local villagers fell like tenpins to the spiritual allurements of a small, fiery Welshman "who had a personal friendly way of appealing to people, talking to them and singing." Unlike previous revivals that lasted a few days, this was the first McKay encountered that lasted "for weeks and months." Mount Zion was set alight: "life was one long excitable thrill from seven o'clock in the morning until long after midnight." By the time the little Welshman had reached Nairne Castle, he had accumulated a fervent body of followers. "Strong, husky men who had not been in church for years would suddenly break down babbling like babies and be taken to the penitent form to kneel and pray and to confess and rejoice in a new life." With lively singing interspersed with the missionary beckoning to the onlookers—"Come to Jesus. He wants you. He waits for you. Come to Jesus now"—the tally of the converted increased rapidly. Even the vibrant young lovers of the Clarendon hills would confess their sins, seek forgiveness, and surrender to the Lord. McKay's father was "right in it," as were his mother, sister and all his brothers, except of course U. Theo.

The villagers gossiped that McKay had been "trained in ungodliness" and this was why he resisted the Welshman's message. An uncharacteristic chill pierced the air of the little village. "All the people" were angry with U. Theo. "They prayed for him in the church . . . prayed for God to convert him. But in their prayers there was," McKay remembered, "a menacing tone as if they would like to lynch him." When they met him in the street, they would not speak to him. They felt that he was "the child of Satan while they were the holy children of God." Confident of his militant rationalism, U. Theo took it all in stride. He harbored no hard feelings against these "simple country people who laboured under the illusion that they had seen God personally and were talking to Him day and night." The villagers concluded that U. Theo's education was "something more of a compact with the devil than real education."[88]

With time, Nairne Castle settled down, back to its usual, benign rusticity. The bad feelings quickly evaporated into the Clarendon sky like the morning mist covering the hills, and McKay, mischievously, had the last laugh:

> After the first wave of excitement was over in the beginning weeks of the revival, it was discovered that scores of our young girls were *enceinte*. On this occasion, however, the young men who had committed the acts admitted to them. So there were many marriages. . . . revival marriages we called them, because in many cases there was nothing of the usual merry making and high feasting. The missionary just got a cheap ring and married the offenders.[89]

It was after the revival that McKay set to work, cultivating his "young crop of agnostics." For a time, he had to endure the anguish of isolation and hostility directed at him and his brother for swimming against the tide and holding fast to his convictions. This was not the last time he would find himself in such a predicament, but the first time he became acquainted with the price of following the lonesome road.

U. Theo McKay was not an isolated, ivory-tower freethinker, but a member of a group of organic and deeply engaged Black intellectuals who came into prominence during the 1880s and 1890s.[90] As a well-read, nationalist, and race-proud teacher, he would have read Dr. Love's *Jamaica Advocate*.

Between 1894 and 1905, Dr. J. Robert Love, founder and editor of the *Jamaica Advocate*, provided the key oppositional Black voice in Jamaica.

Born in Nassau, Bahamas, in 1835, Love studied (theology and then medicine) and worked in the United States and Haiti before migrating to Jamaica in 1890.[91] Taking advantage of the extension of the franchise in 1895, Love was elected to the Kingston City Council in 1898 and to the Legislative Council in 1906. Soon after his arrival in Jamaica, Love dedicated himself to speaking out against the wrongs committed against the masses of Jamaican people. Love, who was a Pan-Africanist thinker and activist from his period in the United States, preached "race consciousness" and race pride. He lectured and wrote in his newspaper about Toussaint Louverture and the majesty and grandeur of the Haitian Revolution at a time when the maligning of Haiti by racist ideologues as well as the colonial authorities in the Caribbean was especially intense.[92] Love's lectures on Toussaint Louverture were especially remarked upon and celebrated even in some unlikely quarters. Indeed, his talks on Louverture were said be "so brilliant that people travelled from all parts of the Island to hear him in Kingston and Spanish Town." Remarkably, the custos of St. Catherine, the Honorable Thomas Lloyd Harvey, who chaired a certain occasion, was said to be "so carried away by Love's oratory that he showered praises on him."[93] Love appreciated the pivotal role of Toussaint Louverture and the Haitian Revolution in the Black struggle for liberation; he appreciated their symbolic significance, and he also knew how important they were to Black nationalist ideology. Such considerations motivated his translation and publication of that historic document, Haiti's Declaration of Independence, in the Atlanta-based African American journal, *Voice of the Negro*, in 1905.[94]

Love lectured on the eighteenth-century African American poet Phillis Wheatley and celebrated her achievements in the *Advocate*. He made it his duty to keep his readers informed about the wider Black world, breaching the walls of parochialism while forging Pan-African consciousness and solidarity. He exercised a formative influence upon the young Marcus Garvey; he apparently gave Garvey, who became an outstanding orator, elocution lessons. Love struggled to expand and protect the rights of Black women— if only in the problematic terms in which nationalists the world over often articulated the position and role of women: look after the women for the benefit of the men, and therefore the benefit of the nation—in this case, the Black nation, the "Negro race."

> We have concentrated on the elevation of our men—clergymen, lawyers, etc.—but not on our daughters. The race must rise by families not by individuals. Men are still despised in spite of their achievements. The race rises

as its women rise. They are the true standard of its elevation. We are trying to produce cultured men without asking ourselves where they are to find cultured wives. We forget that cultured families constitute a cultured race and that a cultured race is an equal race. The elevation of women to equality with [their] white counterparts is the Condition *Sine Qua Non* of the elevation of the Negro race.[95]

Despite its now obvious limitations, for the time and place, Love's position was a marked improvement upon what had existed. And the championing of certain progressive measures, such as the education of women, could be separated from the somewhat questionable motives behind them. "Every pound spent to educate the black boy tends to elevate a class only, but," declared the *Advocate*,

every pound spent to educate a black girl, tends to elevate the whole race. Fathers and mothers, bear these facts in mind, and send as many of your black daughters to England as you can. Some tell you that your girls can be just as well educated here. Ask them, why then do they send theirs to England.[96]

Love fiercely defended the rights of poor Black people. In addition to struggling to protect their right to migrate, he advocated for land reform; he agitated for the more accessible distribution of Crown lands; he fought against regressive land taxes and, like Ethelred Brown after him, against the practice and rationale of the heavily subsidized importation of indentured labor.[97] Love subscribed to the ideas of the American social reformer Henry George, especially his advocacy of the abolition of private landownership, and carried extensive excerpts of his writings in the *Advocate*.[98] Though an Anglican, Love was not afraid to express his admiration for Robert Ingersoll, the American atheist and orator.[99]

Love enjoyed a close association with the Jamaica Union of Teachers and had himself claimed more than a little credit for the union's formation in 1894.[100] One commentator went so far as to claim that the *Jamaica Advocate* "became the official publication of the Jamaica Union of Teachers."[101] In fact, the official publication of the JUT was the *Jamaica Teacher*, but after its demise in December 1898, the *Advocate* covered the activities of the union more extensively than previously.[102] In his capacity as teacher, then, U. Theo McKay would have encountered the work of Dr. Love.

U. Theo also participated in the People's Convention, organized by Robert Love. The convention first met in August 1898 for the purpose of "celebrating in a sympathetic and useful manner the sixtieth anniversary of the abolition of slavery."[103] In a 1909 article aptly titled "August 1 in Its True Setting," U. Theo made a passionate plea for the continued celebration of Emancipation Day. Observing that the abolition of slavery liberated not only the slave but also the slaveholder from a barbaric and backward system of economic and social organization, he wrote:

> We the black and white ought to hasten to drink deep of the wine of joy and be intoxicated with pleasure at this August season; and if there is any time when the emotional part of our nature . . . should be encouraged to a prodigal use, it is at this season when we should not be satisfied to leave the First day of August as a dry, historical fact but should by pageantry and varied other ways of celebrating, make it a living day in our existence, a day that obtrudes itself on us without our having to go to the pages of history to search for it. If we—the black and the white residents in Jamaica—had a healthy conception of the essentials of communal life and a just appreciation of the event which the First of August 1838 recorded for all Time, we would not allow the valuable asset of the commemoration of this day to depreciate with the years. Let us hope that soon we shall see the event in its true perspective. Perhaps the centenary of Freedom will give the desired impetus. Let us hope.[104]

One of the contributors to Love's newspaper was a remarkable Jamaican scholar and one of the most distinguished members of that generation of post-emancipation Black intellectuals in the Caribbean, Dr. Theophilus Scholes. Of humble origins, the dark-skinned Scholes studied medicine in Edinburgh and Brussels and served as a Baptist missionary in Central and West Africa. But his most important and enduring contribution has been his scholarly and robust rebuff of racist theories and his attacks upon European, and especially British, imperialism during his time. Imanuel Geiss, in his pathbreaking work, *The Pan-African Movement*, correctly noted that "Theophilus E. Samuel Scholes deserves to be better known, since he was an active spokesman for Pan-Africanism during the first half of the twentieth century."[105] Regrettably, Dr. Scholes remains largely unknown and unremarked. We may not know the finer details of his biography, but we do have the eloquent testimony of his intellectual efforts. His magnum opus, *Glimpses of the Ages: or the "Superior" and "Inferior" Races, so-called, Discussed in the Light of Science and History*, published in London in two volumes (1905 and 1908), is a work of remarkable scholarship, unforgettable wit, and analytical power. In its discussion of the ancient world, especially

Egypt and Greece, it anticipated the work of the Senegalese scholar Cheikh Anta Diop by half a century and that of Martin Bernal's *Black Athena* by more than three generations.[106]

Love and Scholes were outstanding but not alone. As Patrick Bryan has shown in his pathbreaking study, there was a sizable and interconnected group of intellectuals in fin de siècle Jamaica debating and writing about issues of land reform, the degradation of the peasantry, the exploitation of Black workers, the relation between Africa and the diaspora, and the ideology of racism.[107] There also emerged among this group of Black intellectuals—who were by and large just two generations removed from slavery—what Karl Mannheim would call a "style of thought," a broad set of ideas, positions, and intellectual preoccupations held in common.[108] Key components of this style of thought were hostility toward the plantation system, advocacy of land reform, extension of education to the masses of the people, the need for state education, an attack on doctrines of racial superiority, a growing allegiance to an emergent Jamaican identity if not complete independence from Britain, and more questionably, promotion of the Christian faith and its extension to Africa along with "Western civilization."

In key respects, U. Theo McKay's worldview coincided with that of his peers. But in a number of important areas, U. Theo diverged from his contemporaries. He could not in good conscience promote the Christian faith, and his militant rationalism set him apart. He went so far as to view the abolition of slavery, for instance, as the outgrowth of rationalism and of "the expulsive power of that humanitarian spirit which is a product of Social Evolution." Elsewhere in the same article he wrote, "Slavery was so pre-eminently a curse to the world's civilization, and so inimical to all that is best in human progress, that as soon as men saw it in all its hideousness, they as it were lost their judicial calm in their desire to strangle such a monster." The rationalism and optimism of the Victorian era was not confined to the metropole.[109]

His rationalist commitments set U. Theo conspicuously apart from his Jamaican contemporaries. I know of no Black freethinker in Jamaica at the time apart from U. Theo and his little brother. Love was an Anglican priest; even Scholes—the most radical and extravagantly gifted of the contemporary writers—had been formed by Christianity and served as a missionary in Africa. The hegemonic position of Christianity as an ideology among intellectuals at the time is hardly surprising: these men were almost without exception the product of denominational schools; the ideology of Christianity came along with the "three Rs." Indeed, some have argued persuasively that another "R"—religion—was the most important of the lot in the formation of British Caribbean educational doctrine and practice.[110]

U. Theo stood apart from his peers in another important way. Unlike most, he was a socialist. To be sure, he was not a revolutionary socialist,[111] but he was to the left of the Fabians, for whom he nonetheless had great admiration. (Jamaica's governor, Sydney Olivier, and Annie Besant were two of the Fabian socialists he admired the most.) U. Theo was regarded by his contemporaries, including the Jamaican press, to be one of the most radical of his generation—and they were right. He, for instance, advocated a progressive income tax—at a time when incomes were not taxed at all. Taxes were levied, but indirectly and in an obscenely regressive manner, as discussed in the next chapter. Thus, U. Theo gave qualified support to the Income Tax Bill that was under discussion in 1919 because, as he put it, "it may eventually touch the pockets of the rich men."[112]

He differed from the majority of his contemporaries in yet another respect: like Dr. Love, he supported equal rights for women. During the heated debate that raged in the Jamaican legislature and press between 1918 and 1919 over a bill proposing the enfranchisement of women, U. Theo was one of only a handful of Black men who spoke out in favor of the measure. In fact, of the men supporting the bill, his position was the most unequivocal and outspoken. "Woman has proven herself as capable as man in the management of affairs, and it is only hide-bound conservatism for which the twentieth century has no use that would oppose the measure," insisted U. Theo. Furthermore, "No less a savant than John Stuart Mill advocated the enfranchisement of women years ago, and the justice of her claim has grown with the years."[113]

In marked contrast to U. Theo, the two most prominent Black men in the Legislative Council, D. T. Wint and the Clarendon representative, J. A. G. Smith, opposed the bill.[114]

Like his father, U. Theo was Black, proud, and independent. "I have never wanted anything from the white man save recognition," he wrote Claude. "I mean by that a fair field and no favours."[115] He was outspoken against injustice, writing in the *Jamaica Times*, "one part of our people cannot be kept down and the other part progress." Capital, he declared, is "useless without labour and a down trodden and discontented peasantry does not augur well for the progress of a country."[116] U. Theo's admiration of the working class and his loyalty to his humble roots were a matter of public record. In 1912, for instance, he wrote to the press about the exploitation of laborers in

Clarendon building roads and extending the railway line. "In every work or great enterprise dealing with human progress," he observed, "the horny-handed son of toil is an indispensable unit." The engineer's work and the architect's work are incomplete without the intervention of manual labor. Mental and manual labor, he argued, are "inter-dependent, the one is as essential as the other." U. Theo wrote about the common laborer with undisguised sympathy and a lyricism that had never before been associated with this humiliated and maligned class of exiled Africa in Jamaica. "We see the son of labour, the horny-handed son of labour, jacketless, begrimmed [*sic*] with dirt and saturated with honest sweat," U. Theo took the time to notice and record. "Sometimes he is coarse in his expressions and his argument is punctuated by oaths and fiats and sticks and stones," conceded U. Theo. But

> as you watch the shovel making the dirt fly, the pick levelling the rock, the "borer" drilling with persistency a hole in the rock, the barrow going backward and forward the whole day through while the rays of the sun beat down on him mercilessly, a wave of admiration for such a one passes over you. A man like this should get the reward of his labour. . . . And oftentimes he is in some way or another cheated out of what is his by right.[117]

From these general observations, U. Theo addressed the specific problems of the laborers in Clarendon. "The work on the New Roads and on [the new railway line] in Clarendon furnishes many cases in which he [the laborer] has not been rewarded for his toil. Surely," he concluded, "it won't be long before the horny handed sons of toil are given ample protection for every day the world is awakening more and more to their great importance."[118]

For U. Theo to have adopted such a passionate stance on behalf of labor was remarkable, especially since his changing economic position militated against it. After years of teaching, for unexplained reasons, U. Theo gave up the profession, moved back to Clarendon, and leased a very large estate of "some hundreds of acres" near Nairne Castle. The estate was officially known as Palmyra, but the local peasants had a less romantic name for it. They called it Boghole, "because periodically there were floods and the best portions of the estate would be under water."[119] Palmyra was the property of an absentee landowner, "a [L]ord Penhryn who lived in England and never visited the island of Jamaica." His agent in Jamaica collected his money and forwarded it to him. "There are," McKay added, "many such properties in the West Indies which are owned by famous English families, some of them belonging to members of the royal family."[120]

Within two years of U. Theo's leasing the estate, a major flood over-whelmed Palmyra. In *My Green Hills of Jamaica*, McKay described it in the following terms:

> The waters gushed out of the vast sink holes, spreading over the land, cov-ering the sugar canes and peas and yam hills. The flood lasted for days. The main road which led over to the neighbouring parish of St. Ann was under water for a quarter of a mile.
>
> Because this road was flooded, many of the peasants coming from villages far and near to go to the Cave Valley market in St. Ann, could cross only by the help of boats, which were always available for the dire event.
>
> From the neighbouring villages the young people came to Boghole during the moonlight evenings and on Sunday, just as they went to a picnic. They paid the boatman to take them all over the flooded areas, while they ate sandwiches and fruit, chattered and sang. I remember one song they sang:

> The boat is filled with sail and oar . . .
> . . . .
> Then row, row, row . . .
> Over the beautiful waves we go
> Then row, row, row
> So merrily, merrily, oh . . .[121]

McKay wrote another and rather different narrative of these events, which he suppressed. This "untold" rendition of the story, left abandoned in a notebook he kept, bring out more realistically some of the underlying class contradictions in his village. One consequence of the flooding of Bog-hole was that these subterranean discontents broke to the surface, gushing up for all to see like the water bursting out of the sinkholes on U. Theo's estate. McKay's notebook reveals that every day his brother rode from his house, about a mile away, to Palmyra and "mixed with his tenants, talking to them about the crops, advising them how to cultivate it [*sic*] better." But with the inundation of Boghole, the easy camaraderie between U. Theo and his tenants turned into something else:

> The best crops of the peasants were ruined, including sugar cane, bananas & yams. From the neighbouring villages the young people came to Boghole

as if they were on a picnic. They paid the boatman to take them all over the flooded estate. And they sang their songs. . . .

While they were so happy they seemed totally unaware of the personal tragedy. The flood set my brother back a great deal for the peasants could not pay him. And that year he could not pay the full bill to Lord Penhryn's agent. When he tried to get as much from the peasants as he could they murmured & said he was a hard man to deal with.

There were even more far-reaching repercussions:

My brother also quarrelled with my father because of his wrangling [with] the peasants. He reminded my brother that he had given him an education to live among the peasants & teach them. How after all the years he had spent supporting him in college, he had given that up to become a third rate tenant of a white man in England.[122]

My brother did not like all this especially because it was so true. Because of this quarrel my brother stopped coming to the house. But my sister-in-law always came to see my mother.[123]

McKay evidently found the ramifications of Boghole's flooding especially unpleasant and difficult to deal with, and in the end he downplayed them. This veritable censoring of the story of the flood, I believe, was reflective of his love and deep loyalty to his eldest brother. Apart from his mother and his sister Rachel, U. Theo was the only person with whom McKay had close relations whom he never criticized. Always mercilessly frank—even about his closest friends and acquaintances—McKay never refrained from exposing the weaknesses of others. His memoir, *A Long Way from Home*, is seen by many as a catalogue of indiscretions. Warranted or not, the criticism most often leveled at McKay by his detractors was that of disloyalty, often coupled with the charge of ingratitude.[124] Max Eastman, his closest friend, and even Walter Jekyll, a mentor and benefactor, were at one point or another reproached in print by McKay. U. Theo, however, never was. And in the twilight of his life—indeed, less than a year before he died—as he recollected his Jamaican childhood, McKay was not going to break the pattern of a lifetime and risk embarrassing his big brother. The "untold" story also gives us insights into the personalities of U. Theo and his father as well as the class conflict at work in Nairne Castle, which McKay suppressed in the final version of *My Green Hills*.

The story reveals that, despite his writing to the press in support of the Jamaican peasants and workers, because of his class location U. Theo himself could, no doubt reluctantly, be "a hard man," as the peasants charged. The crisis brought on by the flood exposed, in a mercilessly naked manner, the fundamental difference in interests between U. Theo's social class and that of the small tenant farmers. It was Algernon Sidney's allegory with a vengeance: Lord Penhryn wanted money from his agent; the agent wanted the money from U. Theo; U. Theo wanted the money from the peasants, hit though they were by catastrophe. U. Theo's tenants were expected to ultimately bear the burden of the disaster that Mother Nature wrought on Boghole.

The incident also shows U. Theo as a strong-willed and independent-minded person. Here was a man who had studied to be a teacher—a highly prestigious occupation to this day in Jamaica—who achieved success only to give it all up for agriculture. It was a radical departure from the expected pattern. The peasantry educated their children to escape the soil—even as landholding farmers—and enter the professions. Having acquired a profession, one does not return to the soil, not even in retirement. A poor teacher was more highly regarded in the eyes of fellow Jamaicans than a successful, even relatively wealthy, farmer. As far as Thomas McKay was concerned, U. Theo had broken an unwritten rule, a taboo, letting down the old man by taking a step back and down.[125] Thomas McKay may even have felt betrayed by U. Theo. Worst of all, his eldest son, in whom he had invested so much, had become "the third-rate tenant of a *white* man in England." The crisis of the flood brought into the open Mr. McKay's disappointment with what must have been viewed by his neighbors as eccentric behavior on the part of his son. Indeed, in the same notebook, McKay wrote that his new schoolmaster in Clarendon, a man who had studied at the same college as U. Theo, "thought my brother was quixotic to give up school-teaching to become a small time landlord." If this was disconcerting to U. Theo, he did not show it. McKay noted that U. Theo did not think much of the fellow and regarded him as his intellectual inferior: "My brother disliked the teacher because he thought him a shallow man who did not appreciate books—free-thought books, great novels, & poetry. He was only a competent teacher. Whenever I met my brother he would tease me about my new teacher."[126] U. Theo had once again demonstrated to his young brother that he had the courage to swim against the tide—the guts to violate what he regarded as anachronistic, if stubbornly enduring and powerful, conventions.

In a relatively short time, U. Theo became a very successful farmer. He would later also become an agent of the notorious United Fruit Company, buying bananas from the peasants on its behalf. This would have undoubtedly deepened the tensions between himself and the poor peasants, especially in times of crisis such as the Great Depression of the 1930s.[127] These agents were extremely unpopular with the peasants—and for good reasons.[128]

In 1919, U. Theo was once again in the limelight, making pronouncements on the needs of returning ex-servicemen. He publicly forewarned of the dissatisfaction that the veterans would express about prevailing conditions on the island.[129] In the same year, U. Theo was at the center of a cause célèbre because of his firm stand against government interference in the activities of the Jamaica Agricultural Society (JAS), a farmers' educational and pressure group. In the tumult after the First World War, colonial officials were anxious to silent oppositional voices, and the JAS was one institution in which the peasants could organize and speak their mind, despite the involvement of some large farmers. But the expression of discontent within the JAS against the state became so intense that the government attempted to proscribe political discussions at branch meetings. Pressed by the colonial authorities, the Board of Management of the JAS—comprising some of the large landowners—issued a circular in November 1918 to the individual branches telling them, in the words of U. Theo, "the subjects they have right to discuss at their branch meetings." U. Theo was indignant. "I sincerely hope," he wrote to the *Gleaner*,

> that every branch society in the island will say to the Board of Management "Hands Off." . . . The branch societies are popular organisations; they are not under government rule; they are free and independent, and the Board of Management has no power on earth to dictate to them. These societies are used as clubs, as meeting places where the members discuss all sorts of subjects acceptable to them, and at these meetings they are learning citizenship, learning to take an intelligent interest in their own affairs, learning to think for themselves; finding out those who are seeking their own interest.[130]

As far as U. Theo was concerned, the branches of the JAS were unparalleled in their "splendid educative work among the mass of the people . . . and it would be a sorry day when any reactionary is allowed to scotch progress in this direction." He concluded his letter, somewhat melodramatically, with fighting words:

The time has come when we are thinking for ourselves and can see through
the veil of self interest, and the most they can do is to use their power and
influence in crushing those who dare to speak, but as a man can die but once,
there seems to be nothing to fear in this.[131]

Within half a year, his youngest brother and protégé would be uttering similar words to an embattled Black America. To be sure, the situation in 1919 was
far graver for Black people in the United States than it was for the peasantry
in Jamaica. It is nevertheless striking that "If We Must Die" has a similar coda
to that of U. Theo's letter.[132] Neither Claude nor his big brother was afraid of
death in such situations: you can die only once, said U. Theo; why should one
be especially bothered about an open grave in dire circumstances such as
the Red Summer, his younger brother asked. Both declared that if the fear of
death is conquered, then there is no reason to refrain from fighting when one
has to. In U. Theo, then, McKay had an exemplary fighter, whom he observed
and sought to emulate from his boyhood days.

During the 1920s, U. Theo continued to be outspoken, becoming
increasingly nationalistic in his outlook. In 1922, on a platform of the
Jamaica People's Association, U. Theo, considered a radical by the ruling
class, went beyond the aims of that organization by explicitly calling for
self-government for Jamaica. "The man from over the seas could not know
much about Jamaica. Jamaicans wanted their own sons to manage their
affairs. The day must come when this would be so," U. Theo told the conference.[133] His nationalist call came sixteen years before the formation of
the People's National Party—generally viewed as Jamaica's first "nationalist"
organization—and a whole generation before the winning of a semblance
of self-government in 1944. Not surprisingly, his remarks generated considerable public debate, not to mention censure from the colonial elite.[134]

U. Theo was on the platform at a Universal Negro Improvement Association (UNIA) meeting that Garvey chaired and spoke at on New Year's
Day, 1928. Garvey had arrived in the island on December 10, 1927, after his
prison release and deportation from the United States. The colonial intelligence report does not indicate if U. Theo spoke, but given that he was on
the platform and was not chairing the proceedings, it is likely that he did.[135]
The meeting took place at the Ward Theatre in Kingston. U. Theo lived in
Frankfield, rural Clarendon, and therefore would most likely have had to
make some special effort to participate in the event.

By August 1929, however, U. Theo had radically altered his position
toward Garvey and the UNIA, as is clear from a letter he wrote to McKay:

Garvey is having a big convention here during the month of August. He appeared in court as witness in a case which one Marks has against the U. N. I. A., and I must say from the evidence he gave he cut a very sorry figure. He was the little, sniffling, dodging-the-issue, mean-hearted, little[-]minded fellow and his bigness was eclipsed by his semi-truths. I think he has gone down immensely. I am not a Garveyite and never will be but I must confess to a secret desire that the man may eventually show himself to be *somebody*. I do not think he can rise to the occasion. He publishes a paper here[,] the "Blackman"[,] which is just a dirty rag. When I see the chance he has of doing something and making a name and uplifting those who believe in him[,] I can assure you that I feel that the man is his own enemy.[136]

There is more pity than censure in these words.

Elected vice-chair of the Parochial Board of Clarendon in 1923, U. Theo carried on his civic activities during the 1930s. Through his work with the Frankfield Citizen's Association and the Clarendon Old Boys Association, he was credited with helping to develop a sense of nationalism within the parish. Thus, in 1932, as far as the *Gleaner*—the island's leading newspaper—was concerned, there was one district in the island with "national spirit." That district was "Frankfield and its immediate neighbourhood, in Upper Clarendon." And the "gospeller in the promotion of a national feeling" among the people in the area was U. Theo McKay, who became known as the "Mayor of Frankfield."[137]

Jekyll and Claude

Four of McKay's brothers were teachers, and one became a pastor. At the age of sixteen, McKay was undecided about a career. Though unclear about what he would like to do, he was categorical about what he did *not* want to do for a living: he had no intention of becoming either a teacher or a preacher. He would not follow in his brothers' footsteps. Farming, the occupation of his father and later U. Theo, held no attraction for him either. And even though he took and passed the examination to enter teacher-training college, he never followed it up.[138] He passed an entrance examination and received a scholarship to be trained as a craftsman at the government trade school due to open in Kingston. McKay did go to Kingston, but before term began, the earthquake of 1907 shattered and mangled the city, forcing him to return home to Clarendon. With the brand-new trade school turned to rubble, McKay was obliged to pursue an apprenticeship outside of Kingston. His family eventually found him a trade master in the "lovely little town" of Brown's Town, in the neighboring parish of St. Ann. McKay learned little:

> My master was a light mulatto, kind of crabbed, yet kindly in a way. He was a jack-of-all-trades—a wheelwright, a carriage builder and an excellent cabinet maker. . . . I stayed with this master about two years without learning anything of consequence. He was one of those men who wanted to guard his trade secrets and was not eager to teach me anything.[139]

But there were compensations. McKay saw the lavish interiors of the houses of the "whites and near-whites" as he went about collecting his master's money from the big landowners for work done. The experience deepened his appreciation of inequalities in Jamaica. McKay also enjoyed reading his poems to his boss's poetry-loving young son. Most significantly, during his two years working with Old Brenga, as he called his master,[140] McKay met Walter Jekyll.

When his mother became fatally ill, McKay abandoned his apprenticeship and went back home to help nurse her. Because he was learning nothing from Old Brenga and because of the special bond between him and his mother, he gave up trade without objection from the rest of the family.[141] After her long struggle with "cardiac trouble"—including several very close brushes with death—Hannah McKay succumbed four days before Christmas in 1909. "The only one I loved was gone," he declared in his poem "My Mother";[142] in another, written on the tenth anniversary of her death, he lamented: " 'Tis ten years since you died, mother, / Just ten dark years of pain."[143]

McKay left Nairne Castle for Kingston almost immediately after his mother's death, as if nothing was left in Clarendon to keep him there. Not even "de loved, de hallowed spot / Where my dear mother rest," of which he wrote in an early poem, could detain him.[144] He had no specific plans in going to Kingston apart from getting closer to Walter Jekyll, with whom he had corresponded about his poetry from the time they met at Old Brenga's place in St. Ann. The relationship between McKay and Jekyll was born out of a flippant remark of Brenga's. Knowing Jekyll was a man of letters, he introduced McKay to him one day joking, "Here I have an apprentice who writes poetry." To Brenga's amazement, Jekyll expressed genuine interest in seeing McKay's poems and agreed for them to be sent to him as McKay had none with him.[145]

Walter Jekyll, who settled in Jamaica in 1895, was born into an upper-class family in Surrey in 1849. A Cambridge graduate, he excelled in music, literature, languages, and philosophy. After university he was ordained by the Church of England and served for a number of years, including a stint as a chaplain in Malta. But in the great contest between religion and science that rocked late Victorian Britain, Jekyll opted for science and renounced Christianity. He had been a friend of Robert Louis Stevenson, and Stevenson's famous character was probably named after him.[146] At the time McKay met him, Jekyll had recently published the first authoritative documentation of Jamaican folk songs and stories, *Jamaican Song and Story*, published in London by the Folklore Society in 1907.[147]

By all accounts, Jekyll lived a simple life in Jamaica; he spent his time collecting stories and songs from among the peasantry, reading and writing books, and translating others, most notably Schopenhauer, into English—he apparently knew six European languages. He deepened McKay's knowledge of German philosophy and poetry: "Schopenhauer, Kant, Nietzsche, and Hegel. Besides these he had translated some poems from Goethe, Schiller and Heine. . . . Mr. Jekyll always read the German, deep and sonorous before he translated it into English for me." He also improved McKay's French. They read and discussed Berkeley, Hume, and Spencer, among others.[148]

It has been suggested that Jekyll was gay and that, even though they may not have developed a physical relationship, a "homoerotic component most likely underlay" McKay's relationship with him.[149] This may well have been true, but the quality of the purported evidence—even allowing for the obvious difficulty of acquiring this type of information—is far from satisfactory, let alone conclusive. Jekyll may have been gay, but, as of now, such a statement remains only conjectural, at best probabilistic. We do know that in subsequent years, after his departure from the island, McKay had heterosexual as well as homosexual relations. But this in itself tells us nothing of his relationship with Jekyll in Jamaica. A bachelor, Walter Jekyll was an ascetic man—a fact abundantly testified to by McKay and others—rather asexual, with Buddhist inclinations and sympathies.[150]

McKay provides a revealing snapshot of Jekyll's politico-philosophical perspective:

> Mr. Jekyll hated the British Empire but he used to say, "What is there to take its place, Claude? The Germans are still too young and arrogant; they will never do."

He was disillusioned with British liberalism, yet he did not believe in socialism or any of the radical parties of the day. He always said to me that the British upper class would know how to handle radicals and that Lloyd George who was the famous liberal radical then, would finish up as a lord. He was a great follower of Leo Tolstoy, and a pessimist. Mr. Jekyll was also something of a Buddhist and did not think that the world could be reformed. He used to say that the politicians would fool the people all the time, until the end of time. He was a member of the English upper class and knew that class thoroughly.[151]

Jekyll's best friend at the time was the private secretary of King Edward VII; his eldest brother, according to McKay, was a high-ranking colonial official in India. Other members of his family were in politics or engaged in banking in the City of London. Gertrude Jekyll, one of Britain's leading landscape gardeners and a prolific and distinguished writer on gardening, was Jekyll's older sister. According to his brother Herbert, Jekyll suffered terribly from asthma and spent several winters in Jamaica in the 1890s, avoiding the damp British weather. Jekyll loved Jamaica and decided to settle there after his mother died in 1895. The island had another attraction for Jekyll: it provided him with the scope to live the quiet, unencumbered life he sought. Herbert Jekyll reported that his brother found the restraints of British society "irksome" and that he "preferred to live his own life and follow his own pursuits unmolested."[152] McKay tells us that Jekyll turned his back on English society for Jamaica and decided "to live like a peasant except for his books."[153] Live like a peasant? What McKay, for once, was too polite to say was that Jekyll could afford it—no real Jamaican peasant had the financial wherewithal to follow Jekyll's "peasant" lifestyle. If they did, they would no longer have been peasants. As McKay knew full well, Jamaican peasants worked grimly hard, and for very little, if any, reward. Jekyll was in the very privileged position of not having to work, and did not. "I am not sure that he [Jekyll] is anything more than a loafer," Sydney Olivier told his wife after an early encounter with Jekyll.[154] Jekyll had a substantial private and unearned income to finance his "peasant" life in Jamaica.[155] McKay, for understandable reasons and laudable motives, was overly indulgent in his portrait of the eccentric aristocrat. Some fourteen years earlier, when McKay depicted Jekyll as Squire Gensir in *Banana Bottom*, he was perhaps more accurate in his portrait when he declared in a telling sentence: "The peasants were his hobby."[156]

McKay also registered Jekyll's class snobbery. "In spite of his gentleness and otherworldliness, he possessed a curious kind of class pride. In fact he was strangely proud of his class." McKay recalled an example of this, which tells more about Jekyll than just his "class pride." One weekend, Sydney Olivier, then governor of Jamaica, visited Jekyll while McKay was there. Toward the end of the evening, in the course of the after-dinner conversation, Olivier requested to stay overnight. "Evidently," McKay narrates, "he relished the simplicity of Mr. Jekyll's surroundings and wanted to stay for a night instead of returning to King's House (the Governor's residence) or perhaps staying in some hotel in the Blue Mountains with its large retinue of servants." But Mr. Jekyll refused and said to him "quite sharply": "There's no place for you to stay." Olivier nodded toward McKay and said: "But he stays here." Jekyll replied: "But he is my special friend." After Olivier left, Jekyll "raved." McKay had never seen him in such a temper. "That's English middle class bad manners," said Jekyll. "No person of my class would ever say that to me. We just cannot stand them because they never know when to say the right thing." Taken aback by all this, McKay said to him: "But Mr. Jekyll, how can you tolerate me? I am merely the son of a peasant." "Oh", Jekyll replied, "English gentlemen have always liked their peasants, it's the ambitious middle class that we cannot tolerate."[157]

As McKay noted, Jekyll at first regarded him as an exotic novelty, a member of a somewhat peculiar, talking-horse-like species: "a Negro who was writing poetry."[158] George Bernard Shaw, a childhood literary hero of McKay's, had a similar reaction—albeit one that was blunter and more insensitive—when McKay, with uncharacteristic, even hadj-like, reverence, visited him at his home in London in 1919. "It must be tragic for a sensitive Negro to be a poet. Why didn't you choose pugilism instead of poetry for a profession?" Shaw demanded. "You might have developed into a successful boxer with training." Poetry had "picked me as a medium instead of my picking poetry as a profession," McKay told him.[159]

Jekyll's interest in McKay as merely "a literate phenomenon among the illiterate peasantry" was to alter. McKay noticed that, in time, there was a subtle change "from a general to an individual interest." Jekyll also became "keen" on McKay's intellectual development and on his verse as "real" poetry.[160]

McKay distinctly remembered Jekyll's reaction to the first batch of poems he showed him. While Jekyll was reading the poems, he suddenly broke into laughter. Claude became angry because he thought the Englishman was laughing at him. All the poems were written in "straight English" except a short one "about an ass that was laden for the market—laden with native vegetables—who had suddenly sat down in the middle of the road and wouldn't get up. Its owner was talking to it in the Jamaican dialect, telling it to get up." That was the poem, Claude discovered, that Jekyll was laughing about. Jekyll told Claude that he did not like his poems in straight English. He thought them repetitious. "But this," said Jekyll, holding up the donkey poem, "this is the real thing. The Jamaican dialect has never been put into literary form except in my Annancy stories. Now is your chance as a native boy [to] put the Jamaica dialect into literary language. I am sure that your poems will sell."[161]

McKay's reaction was as interesting as it was understandable: "I was not very enthusiastic about this statement, because to us who were getting an education in the English schools the Jamaican dialect was considered a vulgar tongue. It was the language of the peasants. All cultivated people spoke English, straight English."[162]

McKay's response could hardly have been otherwise. The ethos of colonial education was to inculcate into the colonized—the conquered—the superiority of the metropole and its culture. As Frantz Fanon eloquently demonstrated in *Black Skin, White Masks*, language constituted one crucial and strategic site of struggle.[163] The acquisition of and facility with the language of the imperial power were signs, as well as prerequisites, of social elevation. The French and Portuguese were perhaps the most explicit of the colonial powers on this question with their systems of "assimilation," providing special privileges to natives who mastered the European tongue. In reality, of course, this was and is nothing less than a calculated policy of cultural genocide: systematic deracination, in both senses of the term—uprooting and whitening, Europeanizing and thus destroying: "Wherever colonialism is a fact the indigenous culture begins to rot."[164] For the aspiring colonial, the culture of the so-called mother country, becomes what Mervyn Alleyne aptly terms the "target culture."[165] According to the ethos of colonial education, there was no beauty, no nobility, no history, no culture—in short, nothing of any worth (barring the natural resources and markets for manufactures)—in what was local or native, including the people and their culture.

The task of the colonial educator, then, in the far-flung hinterland of empire—insofar as there was any education to speak of at all—was the eradication of local cultural forms: to elevate the hapless colonized—"Ham's children," "the Natives," "the Wogs"—from their pathological condition; to lead, coax, cajole, and coerce them—the more insidious, inconspicuous, surreptitious, and covert the better—out of the long night of their heathen darkness into the clear light of day of Western civilization. Colonial education inculcated Black inferiority, as force alone could never do. Commander Bodilly, an Englishman stationed in Jamaica as a resident magistrate, spelled this out as recently as the early 1930s in an interview in Britain. British rule in the colonies, he declared, depends upon a "carefully nurtured sense of inferiority" in the governed.[166]

Colonial domination—direct as well as indirect—is never unmediated, devoid of local collaboration. This is the key to its longevity: it imbues in the colonized over the generations the lie of its indispensability, its perennial necessity—"But what is there to take its place, Claude?"—its "natural," reified permanence, thus attempting to make the colonized complicit in their own oppression.[167]

The psychic wounds of colonialism are far more unyielding than its formal political structures. Even elements of the so-called colonized masses, especially those in or near urban centers—the breeding ground of colonial culture—are affected. And there develops the unconscious formal collusion in the suppressing of local forms.

Louise Bennett, for decades the leading poet writing in the Jamaican language, had what was, given the colonial cultural legacy and milieu, a predictable experience at one of her early performances in the 1940s. A voice from the audience rang out the rhetorical question: "A dat yuh modder sen yuh a school fa?"[168] Even the most casual and moderately observant visitor to Jamaica, or indeed to anywhere else in the Caribbean, will know that the attitude implied in this pathetic cry of the first half of the century is still all too prevalent.

Aimé Césaire, the great poet of *négritude*, born some twenty-three years after McKay and brought up in a poor household in rural Martinique, was, like many colonials, not allowed to speak Creole, the common language of the people, at home: his paternal grandmother and his father read to the boy in the language of the metropole, the texts of the metropole—the French classics. Because of his family's strenuous effort in this endeavor, Césaire, as one authority noted, "repressed Creole in favor of French quite completely and at a very early age. He was consequently even less able than other writers of his generation to envisage Creole as a vehicle for Martinican cultural expression. Creole was never a real choice for him precisely because of the dynamics of culture and power to which he was introduced as a young child."[169]

It was not until Césaire became a student at the Lycée Schoelcher in Fort-de-France, the island's capital, that he received encouragement by an extraordinary teacher, Eugène Revert (1895–1957), a native of Normandy, to see beauty in the rich flora and fauna—which were to so lavishly and effectively inhabit and decorate his poetry—that surrounded him in great abundance. For the first time, there was positive affirmation of something Martinican. And this came from a Frenchman. Such are the ironies of colonialism.[170]

McKay—who had a direct influence on Césaire in the 1930s—was similarly encouraged to see beauty in his island home. Although it is unlikely that McKay needed this education, Jekyll's love and enthusiasm for the Jamaican landscape, flora and fauna clearly made a lasting impression on him. McKay noted that they went for long walks over the hills. "Heaps of wildflowers spilled themselves along the roadside and Mr. Jekyll," McKay said, "gave me lessons in higher botany, telling me the Latin names for all the flowers." Writing forty years after, McKay admitted that he had "quite forgotten" the Latin names; but, "it was nice," he said, "listening to these high-sounding Latin names for our hibiscus and painted ladies, trailing feefees, bluebells, water lilies of all kinds, bell flowers, four o'clock, crotons and the rest."[171]

When one bears in mind the colonial milieu in which McKay grew up and lived, what is remarkable is not that he wrote all but one of the poems he showed to Jekyll in straight English, but that he wrote any at all in the language of the common people. Even more remarkable was that McKay had the added audacity to show the poem to a white man, a white aristocratic stranger no less, albeit one interested in Jamaican folklore. The poem burst out of McKay in a moment of truth when he heard a man, a peasant on his way to market, coaxing his harassed and overburdened donkey:

> Ko how de jackass
>   Lay do'n in de road;
> An' him ondly car'
>   Little bit o' load.
>
> Kue, jackass, git up!
>   'Tan' up 'pon you' foot!
> Dis ya load no load,
>
> You's a lazy brut'.[172]

One can understand the impulse behind the poem and the language that it took. But what inspired the author to show it to Jekyll, in the very first batch of poems he ever allowed Jekyll to read, is more difficult to fathom.

Louise Bennett also started her apprenticeship as a poet writing in straight English. And she also had her Saul-on-the-road-to-Damascus moment by the sheer power of the arresting eloquence and humor of the Jamaican folk language. Mervyn Morris tells the story:

> One day she [Louise] set out, a young teenager all dressed up, for a matinee film show in Cross Roads [Kingston]. On the electric tramcars which were then the basis of public transportation in Kingston, people travelling with baskets were required to sit at the back, and they were sometimes resentful of other people who, when the tram was full, tried to join them there. As Louise was boarding the tram she heard a country woman say: "Pread out yuhself, one dress-oman a come." That vivid remark made a great impression on her, and on returning home she wrote her first dialect poem, "On A Tramcar," which began:

> Pread out yuhself deh Liza, one
> Dress-oman dah look like seh
> She see de li space side-a we
> And waan foce harself een deh.

As Morris noted, this was young Louise's beginning.[173]

That incident occurred in the 1930s. McKay had written his first creole language poem in 1909, ten years before Louise Bennett was born.[174] Bennett, in fact, had the exemplary work of McKay to go by, and McKay's creole language poetry directly influenced her own artistic development.[175] Revert had encouraged the young Césaire to see beauty in his native Martinique; Jekyll did the same for McKay's Jamaica. This, I think—more than the discussions of European philosophy and literature, music and folklore—was Jekyll's signal contribution to the intellectual growth of the young colonial: the reassurance that there was genuine beauty in the Jamaican language and, by extension, in the culture of the ordinary Jamaican people, and especially the peasantry, that one can celebrate without fear or favor outside of the narrow, though warm and protective, confines of Clarendon. McKay learned quickly to see the beauty that Jekyll had identified in his "dialect" poems and happily shared his own discovery of this beauty in the Jamaican language with others. His poetic outpourings were published on a regular basis in the Jamaica press. After writing each poem, McKay sent it to Jekyll:

He wrote back to say that each one was more beautiful than the last. Beauty! A short while before I never thought that any beauty could be found in the Jamaican dialect. Now this Englishman had discovered beauty and I too could see where my poems were beautiful. Also my comrades and sometimes the peasants going to market, to whom I would read some of them, liked them. They used to exclaim, "Why they're just like that, they're so natural." Then I felt that I was fully rewarded for my efforts.[176]

McKay was especially gratified by the response of the ordinary people, the subject of his poetry. Twenty years after leaving Jamaica, thousands of miles away in Morocco, he clung to the vivid and warm memory of the response of higglers (market women) to his poems: "I remember when my first poems came out, the market women stopped me by the roadside and asked me to read to them. Those were the happiest readings I ever gave—I dislike audiences."[177]

U. Theo McKay and Walter Jekyll: A Balance Sheet of Influences

Apart from my earlier effort,[178] discussions of McKay's intellectual and political development invariably diminish U. Theo's role while exaggerating that of Walter Jekyll.[179] It is therefore worthwhile to pause, take stock, and reflect upon the relative impact of U. Theo McKay and Walter Jekyll, beyond what has already been established—in short, to critically gauge their influence upon Claude.

The impression is often given that after McKay left Clarendon for Kingston (probably in January 1910) there was little or no contact between him and his big brother and that he, as it were, passed over to another mentor, Walter Jekyll. But the surviving correspondence between McKay and his brother attests to the fact that contact was maintained between them, and that U. Theo knew Jekyll.[180] That the brothers kept in touch after McKay's emigration is also clear. Although U. Theo, at least on one occasion, chided his brother to make a greater effort to write more frequently, the link remained intimate and unbroken. The exchange of ideas between them was maintained, and U. Theo continued to have influence over his brother. It appears, for instance, that the very idea of writing a novel about Jamaica came from U. Theo.

In a letter dated March 1, 1929, McKay was informed of Walter Jekyll's death. U. Theo suggested, "It would be a good thing if you could write a short tribute of him and send it to me and I would see it published in the Jamaica press. I do think he has been really good to you," U. Theo added, "and it would be fitting for you to do so if time will allow." In ending his letter, U. Theo remarked, "I must now close wishing you still greater success than you have already achieved and I hope that one of your books will deal with Jamaica life, altho there may not be much money in it as your audience may be restricted."[181] McKay's next book and best novel, *Banana Bottom*, was indeed set in rural Jamaica. It was dedicated to Walter Jekyll. (Alas, U. Theo's forebodings were realized: *Banana Bottom*, published in New York at the height of the Depression, was a commercial flop.) It is known that U. Theo received a copy of the book, but we may never know what he thought of it, as the correspondence beyond 1933 has apparently not survived.[182] What is known, however, is that U. Theo contributed to the construction of the novel by providing McKay with background information. "I am glad," wrote U. Theo, "that the materials I sent you proved of some use to you and the compiling of your last volume [*Banana Bottom*] and I hope that you shall earn enough from literary efforts to put you beyond the pale of want and that before long you will pay us a visit when we will give you the welcome which you have so richly earned."[183]

Political differences undoubtedly existed between the brothers. They differed in the 1920s over their estimation of the influential Jamaican journalist, Herbert de Lisser.[184] While U. Theo, perhaps mellowing with age, claimed that "it is not in our blood to be revolutionists,"[185] the younger McKay, as we have seen, was politically and spiritually nourished by the memory of his ancestors' defiant stance on the auction block. And while McKay became increasingly critical of British imperialism, the older brother had different thoughts on the subject:

> You have travelled widely and have gained experience which I have had no chance of getting, so your judgment must be worth infinitely more than mine, but at present, I do hold that the British Commonwealth of Nations with all its most glaring faults is the best national organization in existence.[186]

Although there is no reason to doubt McKay's claim that Walter Jekyll's education was "acres broader" than U. Theo's,[187] it should never be forgotten that McKay's formative years were spent under the personal and educational guidance of his brother. Until McKay left Clarendon at the age of nineteen, U. Theo was effectively the only teacher he had had. Old Brenga, under whom he spent two years as an apprentice, hardly made an impact. McKay first met Jekyll when he was eighteen and did not see him on a regular basis until about 1910, when McKay was twenty years old. This more frequent contact in Kingston was interrupted when McKay went to Spanish Town and joined the constabulary force. After joining the force, he spent at least six months in Spanish Town before he was transferred to Half Way Tree in Kingston. After having spent ten months in his village in Clarendon, in July 1912 he was on the boat to Charleston, South Carolina. In short, the level of contact and the intensity of interaction between McKay and Walter Jekyll do not compare to those between McKay and his brother, who was a second father to Claude—and with greater influence than the biological one. Indeed, U. Theo was, in many ways, more of a father to Claude than Thomas ever was. This is not to say that Thomas was a neglectful father; it was just a matter of circumstances. McKay himself wrote that he had "scarcely known" his father and mother when he left to live with U. Theo. He was, after all, only seven years old. And while living in Mount Carey, he "had been entirely cut off from [his] associations" with his parents. He never visited them, nor did they visit him. (The roads were terrible.) Additionally, he noted, "I had never written my father, mother or any of my brothers. When my brother [U. Theo] received letters from home he would sometimes say that my father or my mother had said 'hello' to me." Returning to Nairne Castle after more than seven years—more than half his life—of living with U. Theo, McKay said he had "found a new world" to the one he had left behind as a small boy. "Now," he wrote, "I had to become acquainted with my own family."[188] It is significant that he said acquainted, not reacquainted.

There is no doubt that Jekyll influenced McKay; the problem is the weight given to that influence. The misunderstanding and inflation of Jekyll's role stems partly from McKay's own portrait of the man in *A Long Way from Home*. It is notable, however, that it was only after Jekyll's death in 1929 that McKay began to extol his importance in his intellectual formation. McKay, as we saw, was encouraged by U. Theo to recognize Jekyll's contribution. Far away in Tangiers, McKay did not attend Jekyll's funeral. For unknown reasons, he apparently did not write a tribute to Jekyll for the Jamaican press, as his brother had suggested. (If he did, it was certainly not published; there is no evidence among his papers that he wrote it.) McKay may very well have overcompensated for these shortcomings after 1929.

An audit of the value McKay placed on his brother's contribution to his intellectual formation puts U. Theo in an unrivaled position. In an interview published in the *Gleaner* in October 1911, for instance, McKay—described as reticent, diffident, modest to a degree, monosyllabic—was nevertheless forthcoming and clear in his remarks about U. Theo's role in his education. Asked to clarify if the famous U. Theo McKay was his brother, "Yes," said McKay, "and all I know I learnt from him." Jekyll is thanked for his "kindness" in helping to bring out *Songs of Jamaica*, but there is no other mention of Jekyll in the interview.[189] In *Pearson's Magazine* in 1918 and in *Negroes in America* (1923), U. Theo and Jekyll are both acknowledged, but precedence is given to U. Theo.[190] And as late as 1927 he wrote an autobiographical sketch that hardly mentions Jekyll:

> When I was of school age I was sent to my brother who was a schoolmaster in a small town in the North-Western part of the island. He educated me. He was a free-thinker and I became one, too, so soon as I could think about life and religion. . . . My brother had a nice library with books of all sorts and I read . . . free-thought writers[,] Shakespeare and the great English novelists and poets . . . before I was fourteen.

Jekyll, is accorded one sentence: "An English gentleman who was collecting Jamaica folklore became interested in my dialect verses and helped me to publish my first book: *Songs of Jamaica*, in 1911."[191]

Banana Bottom, published in 1933, was dedicated to Jekyll. Squire Gensir, an important character in the novel, was based on Jekyll, as McKay himself pointed out in a prefatory note to the novel. McKay's was a warm and generous portrait of Jekyll, but it was by no means uncritical. The other post-1929 mention of Jekyll and U. Theo occurred in *A Long Way from Home*, published in 1937, followed by a little essay published in 1945.[192] McKay's final written remarks were made in *My Green Hills of Jamaica*, which was finished less than a year before he died.

My Green Hills of Jamaica carries charming and richly textured portraits, brimming with love, warmth, generosity, and humor, of both U. Theo and Walter Jekyll. But he attributes to U. Theo the primary role in his education. Jekyll contributed to McKay's intellectual growth, but he was a secondary resource in McKay's formation. McKay summed it up: it was "U. Theo who had trained me."[193] There is every reason to believe that were McKay alive today he would heartily disapprove of the belittling of his brother in the discussions of his own intellectual and political formation.[194]

McKay's race pride, class and peasant consciousness, combative tone, outrage at injustice, and the self-confidence exuded by his early Jamaican poetry cannot be adequately explained without due recognition of the profound influence—through both teaching and example—of his big brother. With the sun going down on his life, and reflecting upon his childhood years spent with U. Theo, McKay wrote, "There was one thing that gave me a great deal of physical and mental joy. That was the fact that I was my brother's brother."[195] *My Green Hills of Jamaica* testifies to the fact that the joy and pride he felt in being his brother's brother lasted to the very end of his life.

McKay Became a Red-Seam: Joining the Constabulary

After the money he took with him from Clarendon to Kingston ran out, the twenty-year-old McKay worked in a match factory, "but the hours were long and there was no fun in it." He met a new friend who had been kept a long time by the "most beautiful" prostitute in Kingston. Like McKay, his new friend was "fed up . . . and wanted to get away from it all." According to McKay, impulsively, they both decided to go to Spanish Town and join the Jamaica Constabulary, the police force.[196] The real story, though still unclear, appears to be more complicated and more painful. In his 1911 conversation with the *Gleaner*, McKay was "very reticent as to why he joined the Force," reported W. A. Stephenson, his interviewer. "It is said," Stephenson wrote, "that the underlying cause is a pitiable love story. I hear he has poured out poem after poem on this subject, but he would not discuss the matter." "I cannot touch the public with my heart," McKay told Stephenson, "it would be of no interest to them."[197] Clearly, there was something in what Stephenson had heard, probably from Jekyll, who had apparently set up the interview. But the heartache that drove him to the police force, unrevealed by McKay himself, remains unidentified. (It is not evident in his poems.) Why McKay thought he could gain solace in the constabulary is also a mystery. His description of having joined the force on an impulse seems plausible enough, even if the catalyst remains unknown.

McKay reports in his memoir that when he and his friend got to Spanish Town, the recruiting officer told them they were a little too short to join the constabulary. But the officials liked them and allowed them to join.[198] The real reason the officials allowed them to join is probably less flattering: the constabulary was understaffed and encountering serious difficulty in filling its vacancies. Indeed, in 1910 and 1911 (the years McKay served in the constabulary), the force failed to reach its targeted size.[199]

Nothing in the archives or the press reveals what U. Theo and the rest of McKay's family made of his joining the force. From McKay's own evidence, they were not consulted before he joined, as it was a decision made on the spur of the moment after he had left his job at the match factory. The McKays were probably faced with a fait accompli, but it is doubtful that Claude's decision would have been met with their immediate approval. In his memoir, Herbert Thomas, a white Jamaican who served as an officer in the constabulary for almost half a century until the early 1920s, reported that men from the more respectable families who joined the police force were looked down upon by their relatives.[200] The McKays, on account of their love and respect for Claude, probably acted more charitably toward Constable McKay. But it is unlikely that this came easily. Apart from everything else, the job would have been well below the status of one that the family expected him to pursue. A temporary job in a match factory was one thing, a career as a policeman quite another. One of U. Theo's nieces remembered that when she was a little girl, he asked her what she wanted to be when she grew up. She told him she wanted to become a nurse. U. Theo told her in no uncertain terms that "No McKay is ever going to wash sores." She became a teacher.[201]

The roots of the Jamaica police force go back to 1716, when a bill was passed for the "more easy serving of constables." Though there were changes to this act in the eighteenth and nineteenth centuries, the modern police force came into being in the aftermath of the Morant Bay Rebellion of 1865. It was out of the panic that the event generated among the island's ruling class that the British authorities created the Jamaica Constabulary Force in 1867. According to one authority, the rebellion "exposed the need for an improved Police Force; it showed the entire absence of cooperation between parishes, the drawbacks of allowing men to serve in their native parishes and the absence of effective control of the police."[202] Modeled on the Royal Irish Constabulary (the notorious RIC), centrally organized, and more professionally trained and structured, the new force established a systematic and formidable presence islandwide.[203] This body of men was buttressed by an auxiliary force of district and special constables, who were generally called upon during emergencies. The early Jamaican constable is often likened to the British bobby. But unlike the British bobby (and like its true counterpart, the RIC), the constabulary's men dealt directly with the dirty business of colonial rule and were armed with more than truncheons.

In 1867, each man was issued an Enfield muzzleloader, known as the Brown Bess, and a long narrow bayonet. In 1884, the old Brown Bess musket was replaced by the Martini Henry carbine, and training in the use of firearms was improved. Along with the Martini Henry was issued a "pioneer sword," two feet seven and a half inches long. These, in turn, were replaced in 1900 by .303 Martini-Enfield Artillery carbines with short bayonets.[204] It is not clear to what extent these men patrolled the streets and byways of Jamaica armed. In the nineteenth century, they apparently did so.[205] It appears, however, that by the time McKay joined the force in 1910, the men generally carried out beat duty without firearms—they carried truncheons—though they had ready access to firearms in times of crisis.

The Irish connection with the constabulary was strengthened in 1895 when thirty men from the RIC were recruited to serve as sergeant-majors and sergeants in Jamaica. The measure was undertaken in an effort to "increase the efficiency of the Force" after the police were worsted the previous year by rioting men belonging to the West India Regiment.[206] After 1895 and up to McKay's time in the force, the subofficer class (sergeant-majors, sergeants, and corporals) comprised disproportionately men of Irish descent. But a substantial number of "mulattoes" served as subofficers. British and white-led, the Jamaica Constabulary had the same color structure as the remainder of the colonial state apparatus on the island. The authorities systematically blocked Black and colored men from rising above the subofficer ranks. Smug and self-confident, they provided no explanation for the proscription—at least not publicly. Though racism was at the root of the matter, the cheap justification, transmitted indirectly, was that Black policemen would not obey nonwhite officers, be they colored or Black.

A retired inspector, Herbert Thomas, a racist and generally obnoxious little man, took it upon himself to explicitly articulate the authorities' position, raising the latter, for the first time, above the status of mere rumor. Despite his many weaknesses, Thomas had the audacity to speak frankly. He also possessed sufficient self-awareness and foresight to declare: "I expect to be called a hide-bound old fossil."[207]

In the course of writing his 1927 memoir, *The Story of a West Indian Policeman or 47 Years in the Jamaica Constabulary*, a remarkable historical document, Thomas, who was born in Jamaica but spent most of his childhood and youth in Yorkshire, decided to address head-on the long-standing but growing discontent about the blockage of nonwhites from commission status within the constabulary. Thus, Thomas embarked upon what he calls his "little heart-to-heart talk with the sergeant-majors and sergeants, to whom I intend to address direct—using the second person—the fatherly advice which I have given verbally to more than one of my own trusted men who have felt—and quite rightly—that I was the very best friend for them to consult." He then moves, in earnest, onto the "vexed question of promoting the native sub-officers to commissions." For Thomas, the very idea that nonwhite Jamaicans should be able to become officers is based on "the utterly fallacious theory that all men are born equal," which, he says, "as any fool can see, they are not." He counsels the men to reconcile themselves to the status quo. After all, "Society is constituted in a certain fashion to-day, and not one of you will ever live long enough to see any marked change in it; no matter what the far distant future may have in store."

In any case, Thomas explains, you would be silly to want promotion: you would have to "cut yourselves loose from those persons who are now your associates, and you would find yourselves boycotted by the upper classes of society." You would find yourself completely out of place, "hovering," says Thomas, "from a social point of view, between heaven and earth, like Mahomet's coffin." For those who remained unpersuaded, Thomas spells out the implication of his argument: "Do you think the Custos and Resident Magistrate would invite you to tea? And if by any chance they did so, how would you feel in their drawing-rooms? A fish out of water would be in Paradise in comparison."

But the men should not despair, there is consolation: "you are fit to take your places alongside of the non-commissioned officers of any police force in the world." Thomas advises the men to "be content with that, and not to aspire to a false position, which you would find to contain for you nothing but unhappiness, if not downright misery." He did not finish there; that was just the argument against promotion from the "social angle." He now moves on to the "official point of view." But Thomas pauses; he glimpses the specter of Marcus Garvey. "I am, of course," he writes in parentheses, as if sotto voce, "taking it for granted that there are none among you who have been contaminated by the teachings of the U. N. I. A. [Universal Negro Improvement Association]." Having re-assured himself, he takes courage and proceeds:

The men like their officers to be white—or "pass as such". . . . And you like it also, if you will be honest with yourselves; and you know perfectly well that if you were promoted to commissions there would be endless trouble about the saluting—not to mention anything else—especially those whose complexions are of darker hue.

Thomas rounds off his case for the continuation of racism in the Jamaica constabulary by warning his men-children: "do not allow noisy demagogues or blatant politicians to undermine your loyalty with specious arguments." He concludes his lecture:

> Having attained as high and respected a position as you are fitted by Nature, education and training to fill, be content to continue serving your country in that position with the loyalty and efficiency which have raised you to it, instead of aspiring to become square men in round holes.[208]

It is an extraordinary performance. The length at which Thomas expounded his discourse is an index of the extent to which the racist, colonial foundations were being undermined in the 1920s. It is no accident that he openly worried about the influence—contamination, he would call it—of Black nationalism and anticolonial sentiment expressed in the form of Garveyism. Only a decade before, the white ruling class and its organic intellectuals, such as Thomas, felt no need even to answer the objections to their racist policies in the career structure of the constabulary. Thomas's own case, made only in 1927, was the most explicit one ever put forward in defense of the status quo, but its sandy foundation was evident to all those with a modicum of intelligence and honesty. In the same chapter in which Thomas tries to persuade his readers that nothing can be done about the promotion of Black men to commission status because "the men like their officers to be white," he boasts that although from 1899 constables were permitted to smoke while on patrol, he told the men under his command that he did not approve of it—and they refrained from smoking on duty.[209] Even if one concedes that there probably were recruits to the Jamaica Constabulary who would attempt to be insubordinate to a Black officer simply because of his color, why should that constitute an argument against having Black officers? Many recruits hated getting up early in the morning, but they had to because of their obligations as recruits. Similarly, as U. Theo McKay pointed out in a letter to the press on the matter as early as 1910, if the objection really exists, it could easily be overcome: "If the men promoted have not sufficient force of character to command the men over whom they are placed revert them to their former position and if the men in the ranks are insubordinate they should be punished and made to obey."[210] Inspector Thomas never tolerated insubordination among his men; he even got them to obey orders that did not officially exist.

It was not until the mid-1940s that the first Black Jamaicans were appointed officers[211]—decades later than U. Theo would have liked, but decades earlier than Inspector Thomas expected and feared. But be they Black or white, given their repressive function, the Black population, especially the poor, generally detested the police. And, as we will see, the clash between force and populace not infrequently erupted into riotous violence.

From the outset, McKay hated life in the police force. But although he "despised" the institution and his period in it, the police force provided him with invaluable knowledge and insight into Jamaican society and class structure. McKay's first collection of poetry, *Songs of Jamaica*, was published in January 1912. Nine months later, it was joined by a second, *Constab Ballads*. Both volumes received local and international acclaim. The books not only tell of McKay's experience in the police force but also reveal his political awakening. Indeed, these texts are the most valuable resources and the most reliable documents available for an understanding of McKay's early social and political perspective. A critical engagement with these collections, along with other poems published in the Jamaica press, will enable us to come to terms with the politics of the young Jamaican and to plot from its very point of origin the remarkable trajectory of McKay's political thought and activities. But a proper understanding and appreciation of McKay's early poetry and political thinking necessitate an understanding of key dimensions of the Jamaican society in which he grew up.

2

Holding the Negro in Subjection

Claude McKay's Jamaica

You hab all t'ings fe mek life bles',
But buccra 'poil de whole
Wid gove'mint an all de res',
Fe worry naygur soul.

—Claude McKay, "My Native Land, My Home," 1912

The Power of Home: Jamaica and McKay's Imagination

In July 1912, Claude McKay, just a couple months shy of his twenty-third birthday, left his island home to study in the United States. As it turned out, despite his initial intention to return after his studies, McKay was never to see Jamaica again. In fact, instead of returning, he ranged even farther afield from native ground. "Gripped by the lust to wander and wonder," as he later disclosed,[1] McKay spent more than a year in Britain between 1919 and 1921; spent eight months in Lenin's Russia between 1922 and 1923; and between 1923 and 1934 lived in Berlin, in various parts of France (mainly Marseilles), in Spain (mainly Barcelona), and for several years in Morocco (Tangiers) before returning to New York. Although McKay left Jamaica, Jamaica never left him, despite his decades of wandering, his wide experience, and his traveling half a world away. Exiles inevitably carry memories of home with them, especially in the early years of separation, but in McKay's case, all the evidence suggests that his formation on the island and his memory of Jamaica held him in an uncommonly powerful grip. He could never forget Jamaica, and he never wanted to. Fighting against what Edward Said called the exile's "crippling sorrow of estrangement," McKay "embalmed" his Jamaican days and carried them with him.[2] In his darkest moments abroad, he took refuge in this memory, this nostalgia, writing some of his most accomplished and moving poems. Indeed, the struggle to remember, to deepen and nourish his memory of Jamaica against the corrosive power of time and distance, often became the subject of his poetic reverie. "Flame-Heart" captures well this struggle and sense of loss:

> So much I have forgotten in ten years,
> So much in ten brief years! I have forgot
> What time the purple apples come to juice,
> And what month brings the shy forget-me-not.
> I have forgot the special, startling season
> Of the pimento's flowering and fruiting;
> What time of year the ground doves brown the fields
> And fill the noonday with their curious fluting.
> I have forgotten much, but still remember
> The poinsettia's red, blood-red, in warm December.[3]

But although the detailed, seasonal, quotidian rhythms of flora and fauna at times escaped him in exile, he remembered much of greater significance than the "poinsettia's red, blood-red, in warm December." Moreover, his Jamaican upbringing and experience shaped him in profound ways. His perception of and preoccupation with injustice and inequality, his attitude toward women, and his position on color and class hierarchies largely issued from his time on the island. Although his attitudes adjusted and developed over time, they were clearly evident before he left Jamaica. Similarly, his freethinking and socialist views emerged before he emigrated, albeit in less radical forms than they would subsequently take. In addition to his autobiographical writings and much of his poetry, McKay's best works of fiction, notably *Banana Bottom* and *Gingertown*, explicitly evoke the world of his Jamaican childhood and youth. Mervyn Morris, the Jamaican poet and critic, is therefore right in noting that McKay's "most characteristic concerns and attitudes were planted early in Jamaica" and that to appreciate his work, it is "essential to know about his Jamaican origins."[4]

To know McKay's Jamaican origins, we need to know more than the immediate family and the Clarendon hills depicted in the previous chapter. A wider, more panoramic, lens is now called for, one capable of capturing the larger Jamaican scene and environment in which he lived and which so profoundly influenced and conditioned his political outlook and intellectual formation. In particular, we need to know about the political economy of his island-colony in order to understand McKay's early preoccupation with the condition of the poor that he documents and analyses so extensively and so well in his early Jamaican poems. We need to understand the formation and struggles of the Jamaican peasants—the class into which he was born—that so powerfully commanded his attention and drew his sympathy. We need to understand the dynamics of the rapid and baneful urbanization that overwhelmed the island in the late nineteenth and early twentieth centuries, forming the backdrop of so much of his early protest poems emerging out of his Spanish Town and Kingston experience. We cannot understand McKay without an appreciation of the articulation of race and color on the island that broke his heart and drew his wrath. We need to understand the cultural and intellectual milieu of his Jamaica.

Thus, I map out the wider socioeconomic context in Jamaica between his birth in 1889 and his departure in 1912. A knowledge of this period of Jamaican history cannot be taken for granted, not even among those who possess a good grasp of the general history of the island, as this period of Jamaican history is underexplored and inadequately understood. The period of slavery has been extensively covered and the post-emancipation period up to 1865 only slightly less so. The decades extending from the labor uprisings of 1938 to the end of the 1970s also have a rich body of literature. However, the same cannot be said for the period stretching from the Morant Bay Rebellion (1865) to the 1930s, which remains, as Alistair Hennessy observed three decades ago, the "least studied" and understood of all.[5] There is a growing body of sound analyses of different aspects of this period, but the coverage is fragmentary, scattered, and partial;[6] no one has so far synthesized the available material. It is therefore hardly surprising that one of the major weaknesses of the existing literature on McKay is an inadequate grasp and appreciation of his Jamaican context. The primary objective of this chapter, then, is to build upon the extant scholarship and draw the broad contours of McKay's Jamaica.

The Lay of the Land

By the time McKay was born, Jamaica had undergone four centuries of European, mainly British, colonial domination. This experience constitutes the most important force in the island's historical formation. As in the rest of the

Caribbean, the period of colonialism was accompanied for almost its entire duration by chattel slavery. The enslavement of Africans by Europeans and its institutionalization over the centuries, in turn, created the especially sharp salience of race and color—socially, politically, and economically.

Colonialism configured the economy of the island for the benefit of the metropole to the severe detriment of the overwhelming majority of the Jamaican people. Jamaica, like the rest of the Caribbean islands, was annexed, its indigenous people subjugated and decimated. The conquerors then colonized the island with European settlers and further populated it through the forced migration of enslaved Africans.

Unlike in Africa, Asia, and much of continental (especially South) America, where the indigenous population formed the large base of the colonial edifice, in the Caribbean the native population was not only conquered but also largely, if not completely, destroyed. Upon the bones of the vanquished, the conquerors created a new society fashioned according to European colonial desires. To the colonialists, the Caribbean became a site of plunder and the unrestrained fabrication of wealth. In more ways than one, then, the Caribbean has been a construction of Europe—albeit a persistently contested and unsteady one.

John Stuart Mill's observation that Britain and its Caribbean possessions had a relationship of town and country has the merit of drawing attention to the close economic relationship between the center and the periphery—what some would later call the relationship of metropolis and satellite.[7] But this formulation also oversimplifies the relationship, for the Caribbean colonies were never simply the country to Britain's town. As colonies, they became integral to Britain, but they were also *foreign*, overseas—here, as part of the Empire, but always over there, in "the West Indies." As a part of Empire, they were defined as British and thus central, but by the same token, as colonies, they were by definition marginal, paradigmatically Other—a fundamental and inherent tension of the imperial idea.[8] Despite the ideological smokescreen, the truth is that, not only politically but also economically, the colony was subordinate and subordinated to the imperial heartland—the colony *belonged* to the "mother country."[9]

McKay was born into an especially tumultuous world. By 1889, the conquest of Africa was well under way. At the Berlin Conference of 1884–1885, the European powers had decided how to distribute the spoils of their handiwork of coordinated and premeditated plunder. For more than half a millennium confined to the coast, imperial Europe now busied itself with penetrating Africa's vast hinterland, joining its conquests from the Atlantic to the Indian Ocean; contemporaries dubbed the exercise the "Scramble for Africa."

Africa, however, was not the only victim of the times. In Asia and Latin America, an increasingly vigorous penetration of capital, characteristically accompanied by the displacement of peasants from the land, was in progress. Increasing poverty and widening economic inequality attended the process. By the beginning of the twentieth century, the Philippines, Guam, Cuba, and Puerto Rico had fallen under the overt tutelage of the United States. Emerging as by far the most powerful industrial nation in the world, the United States had transformed the Caribbean Sea into a de facto American lake.[10]

From Sugar to Banana: Economic Crisis, Transition, and Consequences

In part aggravated by this new U.S. presence, the archipelago was riven by complex and uneven changes. Two distinct economic tendencies emerged within the Caribbean, both connected to the sugar industry. On the one hand, sugar continued its long boom in the Spanish-speaking Caribbean, especially Cuba, successfully standing up to increasing competition on the world market from beet sugar producers as well as old rivals such as Brazil. On the other, in marked contrast to these economies, the sugar industry in the older British colonies such as Barbados, St. Kitts, and Jamaica entered a period of sharp decline. The British planter class spoke in increasingly apocalyptic terms about the state of the industry. It was indeed a period of catastrophic decline and painful reorganization in the British Caribbean as a whole; however, the main victims were not the planters and merchants but the workers they exploited.

The British-colonized islands, from a preeminent position in the 1820s producing more than half the total output of Caribbean sugar, by the first decade of the twentieth century contributed only a tenth of the region's output. Cuba's output corresponded inversely to that of its Caribbean neighbors. From producing less than a fifth of the Caribbean total in the 1820s, Cuba was by the first decade of the twentieth century the unrivaled leader in the production of Caribbean sugar, accounting for three-fourths of the region's total output.[11]

Severe hardship for Jamaican workers accompanied the decline in production. Indeed, the two decades between 1889 and 1912—the years between McKay's birth and emigration—were among the most trying since the end of slavery in 1838. The fate of this overwhelmingly Black population had been tied to the sugar industry, which the British colonizers had made the raison d'être of the island since its capture from Spain in 1655. And sugar had now collapsed. Outcompeted by Cuban and Brazilian cane sugar, supplanted by subsidized beet sugar in Europe, and mercilessly exposed to international market forces by Britain's removal of preferential tariffs, King Sugar by 1889 had been dethroned in Jamaica. Despite the massive growth in world consumption of sucrose, Jamaica's exports fell by two-thirds between 1838 and 1890, and by 1900 the price of sugar was less than a quarter of what it had been sixty years earlier.[12] Only with the First World War's devastation of Europe's beet fields did an upturn occur, but the respite that favorable prices brought lasted little longer than the war itself. The fall in the number of sugar estates on the island was even more precipitous. From 670 in 1836, the number dwindled to 74 by 1910.[13] Despite amalgamation and consolidation of estates during the nineteenth century, the area under sugar cultivation shrank drastically. Within the space of only a generation—between 1869 and 1900—the already diminished area under sugar cultivation had almost halved.[14]

Sugar's decline affected some areas of the island far more than others. King Sugar had been dethroned but was by no means dead. Severely wounded and enfeebled, he strategically retreated to the western plains of Jamaica while still maintaining a foothold in the flatlands of southern Clarendon, not far from McKay's birthplace. Under the whip of international competition, made more painful by Britain's free-trade policy, members of the island's ruling class embarked upon ruthless capitalist reorganization and rationalization.[15] Consequently, although the number of sugar estates declined substantially, the average size of the surviving ones increased by almost 60 percent between 1880 and 1910.[16] The average yield per acre had also increased by a quarter between 1846 and 1896, and with the amalgamation of the estates, the average output per sugar factory doubled between 1880 and 1910.[17] One consequence of this dialectic of decline and rationalization was fewer jobs in the industry. Thus, between 1891 and 1911 employment in the sugar industry fell by 41 percent, with male employment falling by a third.[18] This had repercussions well beyond the immediate well-being of those who lost jobs. As the laborers and their supporters testified time and time again before the members of West India Royal Commission sent out in 1897 to investigate the crisis, the sugar workers' immediate families and dependents were not the only ones affected: small farmers found it difficult to sell their produce, small shopkeepers around the estates went out of business, the incidence of "praedial larceny" (theft of crops) born of desperation, increased, children were more malnourished than before, and the death rate increased, including infant mortality.[19]

During the last two decades of the nineteenth century, however, a new agricultural sector emerged into prominence almost overnight, eclipsing sugar with astonishing rapidity: the banana trade. Introduced into Jamaica in the sixteenth century, the banana was a humble but valued fruit cultivated primarily by enslaved people on their provision grounds and by their descendants, the Black peasantry, in the post-emancipation era. The Gros Michel, introduced from Martinique in the nineteenth century, quickly emerged as the most successful variety. To flourish, the banana needs fertile soil with vegetable mold along with good rainfall and drainage. It therefore thrived in the "black soils" of Portland, St. Mary, St. Thomas, and St. Catherine—areas with the heaviest rainfall, the eastern parishes of Jamaica.[20] Up to the late 1870s, banana remained essentially a peasant crop. According to Lord Olivier, banana cultivation was "despised as a backwoods 'nigger business,' which any old-time sugar planter would have disdained to handle, or, if tempted by undeniable prospects of profit, would have thought an apology was required."[21] Thus in 1879, in the entire island, only one large estate was under banana cultivation.[22] Large-scale banana cultivation began the following year when Jamaican merchants and professionals, "whom their neighbours regarded as cranks," moved into the "nigger business" on a grand scale.[23] Fourteen of St. Thomas's eighteen sugar estates had changed over to banana cultivation by 1899.[24] In 1875, St. Mary had up to thirty large sugar estates. By 1897, only two remained; the rest had become banana plantations.[25] In short, "bananas meant money," as a member of the Jamaican ruling class told an English visitor in 1903.[26] In the fertile upcountry of Clarendon, Thomas McKay and many of his peasant neighbors became deeply involved in banana cultivation. In subsequent years, U. Theo McKay, as we have seen, would leave his profession as schoolmaster and become a banana grower and agent.

The revolution in banana cultivation and marketing was initiated by an American, Lorenzo Dow Baker, who, unburdened by the historical snobbery of sugar cultivation, had proven in 1871 the feasibility and profitability of large-scale banana shipment to the United States. By the 1880s, acutely aware of the profits to be scooped up in Boston and New York, Baker was busy purchasing and leasing thousands of acres in eastern Jamaica for the growing and export of bananas. Others followed in Baker's footsteps, but the Bostonian and his corporate creation, the Boston Fruit Company (BFC), which later (in 1899) developed into the notorious United Fruit Company, were not to be denied. Hidden beneath his beatific New England smile and Puritan veneer (no drinking, smoking, or swearing) was a ruthless capitalist.[27] Baker, who was said to have a "twinkle in his eye,"[28] punished and vanquished not only his capitalist rivals: the peasants of eastern Jamaica suffered a historic defeat at his hands. Baker had friends in high places and was aided and abetted by the colonial state, especially the policies of British Colonial Secretary Joseph Chamberlain, which encouraged large landholdings in the British Caribbean.[29] Small wonder that Baker was effusive in his praise of the economic and political setup in Jamaica. "Investments in this country are safe," he declared. "Values are normal; titles are as good and as well protected as any in the world. Our Governors have been the best that Britain can give her colonies. By them we enjoy guaranteed safety and success." Neither he nor his companies knew "anything but kindness from this Government."[30]

Banana cultivation grew exponentially. From two thousand stems of banana in 1869, Jamaica was producing 8.25 million stems by 1900,[31] making the island the world's premier producer of bananas for more than two generations, from 1876 to 1929, when it fell behind Honduras.[32] In 1870, sugar accounted for 44.5 percent of the island's export earnings and banana a negligible 0.06 percent. By 1900, banana had become the island's most important agricultural export earner, bringing in more than three times the amount earned by sugar.[33] In that year, the export earnings of banana were almost twice the combined earnings of sugar and rum. Ten years later, banana made up more than half of Jamaica's export earnings, while sugar and rum together brought in only one-seventh.[34] By 1911, banana employed 77 percent more people than the sugar industry did.[35]

However, the consequences of the expansion of banana cultivation under the hegemony and virtual monopoly of Baker were not all happy ones. With initially high prices, Baker lured the peasantry of St. Mary, Portland, and St. Thomas into agreements to exclusively supply his company with bananas. Having captured the market, he then controlled the price.[36] Baker instructed his agents to bargain hard with peasant producers. And by insisting that the producers bring their fruit to the ports, he not only avoided the cost of transportation but also adroitly obviated the risk and cost of damage—such as the all-too-common bruising—of the bananas en route; the peasant suppliers would bear these burdens. Acutely aware of the powerful position that he had successfully maneuvered himself into, Baker told his son, "You need not make any extra exertion for bananas. Tell the people if they wish to sell their fruit they must bring it down." He briefed his agents to accept only top-quality bananas and to reject all fruit deemed below his prescribed standards. "Never mind what people say," Baker told his son, "throw it back on their barrels, let them suffer for it if they will not mind you."[37] This became easier and easier for Baker's company to do. Not only did the strategy generate fierce competition among the peasant suppliers, but by the 1890s Baker had become not just a buyer of bananas but also the fruit's foremost cultivator on the island. Able to supply its own ships, the Boston Fruit Company thus became less dependent on peasant producers. As Charles King and a group of landless peasants (they rented their plots) from Port Antonio told the Royal Commission in 1897: "We are ruined by banana cultivation. How can we sell to Boston Fruit Company when they have all of their own?" They informed the commissioners that they "subsist by hard toil. We are cultivators of the soil, but we are oppressed. . . . We are not independent freeholders." They appealed for land of their own at a reasonable price and a fair market for the fruits of their labor: "We want proper market for our produce. We do not want, when our produce comes in, and the rich man's comes in, he puts aside ours, and only when his is out he calls for ours at prices that cannot pay."[38] Many corroborated Mr. King's and his fellow petitioners' complaints against Baker's company. A Black Jamaican minister, Rev. H. F. Humphreys, resident of St. Thomas in the east, testified that the people in his district got "a very small price" for their bananas. In fact, he insisted, "they are not paid for them comparatively speaking." He calculated that a bunch of bananas that would fetch eight to nine shillings (96 to 108 pence) in the United States was at times sold for as little as six pence locally to Baker's company—around 5 percent of the price in Boston. Moreover, "there are times that bananas cannot be sold at all."

> I have known the people sometimes bring down heaps of bananas, and have seen them lying at the cross roads, and the man who comes from the Boston Fruit Company to buy just buys a few wagon loads and he is gone, and the other heaps are left there, and these poor people who have been working all day bringing down their bananas, to their great sorrow and grief have to leave them or sell them to anyone for 1½ [pence] a bunch. We should be very glad if we could have competition in the purchase of our produce. That is what is required, and the people would work more and would be benefited.[39]

"Are bananas profitable?" asked the commission chair, Sir Henry Norman, of a Black Jamaican witness. "They are if you can sell them," came the reply. The witness, Thomas Smickle, a former schoolteacher and chair of the St. Thomas parochial board, though a man with 150 acres of his own, sympathized with the poor farmers. He understood and recognized their plight under the Boston Fruit Company's hegemony. As he explained:

> The Boston Fruit Co. are about the only persons who purchase fruit [bananas] in the neighbourhood. They themselves own large properties and plantations of bananas, and as a matter of fact at some times of the year they reject all fruit but their own. As a matter of fact the Americans do own a very large portion of Jamaica. It is only when they wish extra fruit for their vessels that they purchase from outsiders. There are many times when they reject the small settlers['] fruit, because they have enough of their own. Their policy seems to be to extend their own cultivations as much as they can. On the whole the small settlers can get no profit by the cultivation of bananas at all.

He, too, saw the small farmers returning home "with these bananas" after they had traveled miles with them and found no purchaser.[40]

The commissioners, apparently persuaded and moved by the plight of the small farmers, recommended that the British government exert greater effort to expand the trade to North America and to Britain itself.[41] Thus in 1901, Sir Alfred Jones, then managing director of Elders, Dempster, and Company, established the Imperial Direct Line of steamers and a fruit and shipping company, Elders & Fyffes, expressly aimed at shipping bananas from the Caribbean to the United Kingdom. With a successful record of importing bananas from the Canary Islands to Britain, Sir Alfred had been encouraged by the British government to enter the Jamaican banana trade and was provided with a subsidy of £20,000 per year for ten years to do so. The agreement with the government stipulated that a minimum of 20,000 bunches of bananas were to be shipped every fortnight from Jamaica to England. However, a greater quantity of bananas was needed for the Imperial Direct Line to make a profit, so Sir Alfred's aim was to secure more than 20,000 bunches of good-quality bananas each fortnight. Elders & Fyffes sent out energetic and capable young Englishmen to secure supplies for the Imperial Direct Line. But they were inexperienced in things Jamaican and underestimated the "active rivalry of the United Fruit Company," which according to Olivier, "strained every nerve" to divert supplies from the British ships. The UFC offered more money to some and intimidated others from supplying the Imperial Direct Line. Sir Alfred soon realized that he had to come to terms with UFC if his ships were ever to be supplied. United Fruit agreed to supply his 20,000 bunches per fortnight, but when he sought more in order to reduce his losses, the UFC "held him to ransom."[42] When Elders & Fyffes increased its share capital, the United Fruit Company pounced and purchased almost 50 percent of the company's shares. And when the 1903 hurricane destroyed Jamaica's banana fields, Sir Alfred's company was at the complete mercy of the United Fruit Company, which agreed to supply the Imperial Direct Line from its plantations in Central America. The United Fruit Company quickly acquired enough shares in the company to gain control over Elders & Fyffes, which in turn enabled it to demand higher freight rates from Elders, Dempster for Jamaican shipment to Britain. With its control of supplies in Jamaica, markets, and shipping lines to both the United States and Britain, United Fruit chose to export its fruit to Britain from Central America rather than Jamaica. A decade after Sir Alfred's attempt, Jamaica's banana exports to Britain were less than a tenth of the amount that went to the United States—£101,000 versus £1,200,000.[43] The British attempt to open up a new market for Jamaican banana had failed, as had the effort to break the monopoly of the United Fruit Company. Indeed, the situation had worsened: not only had United Fruit maintained its monopoly in the lucrative United States banana market, it had extended its tentacles, through control of Elders & Fyffes, to exercise hegemony over the British market also.

Sir Sydney Olivier, who served as secretary to the 1897 Royal Commission and as governor of Jamaica (1907–1912), exposed and denounced both the Boston Fruit Company and its successor, the United Fruit Company, in his 1936 book, *Jamaica: The Blessed Island*. In one of his longest, most engaging and spirited chapters (aptly titled "Banana War"), Olivier, who described United Fruit as "the American octopus," castigated the company's dictatorial strategies, revealed its dirty tricks and monopolistic practices, and disparaged its "system of mixed solicitation and terrorism."[44] Strong words indeed for a Fabian and former governor—but they tell us more about the outrageous practices of United Fruit than about the ex-governor's supposed radicalism.

Powerful though it was, Olivier's philippic failed to point out that while United Fruit's solicitation was directed at the large plantation owners, the terrorism was unleashed against the little people, the peasants of Jamaica. The fundamental objectives were the same: bending the producers to the will of the company. This system of solicitation and terrorism had been introduced by Baker from the inception of the island's banana trade and successfully applied by him and his companies and agents over the years. Even when, in 1889, he was forced to provide inducements to producers in order to foil the entry into the market of the ill-fated Atlas Steamship Company, he established differential rewards. As he told his son, Loren, who purchased bananas for the BFC, "put on about ten shillings more to the small people and about 10 percent more to the plantation than what you pay the small people." When Atlas wearied of the competition and dropped the price paid to the banana producers, Baker followed suit, but instructed his son not to lower the price just yet for "property fruit,"[45] by which he meant fruit from the large plantations. Thus, the small grower was hit hardest and first when the price of fruit fell. After Baker became more entrenched and able to supply his ships largely from his own purchased or leased plantations, both large and small producers suffered. But it was not the big man's fruit that he told his son to throw back on the barrel, nor was he referring to the big men when he told his son to "let them suffer for it" if they refused to succumb to his demands. After the quick dispatch of Sir Alfred Jones in 1903, the UFC monopoly lacked any serious challenge until the Jamaica Banana Producers Association was formed in the late 1920s—the very moment when Jamaica's preeminence as the world's largest producer of bananas was eclipsed by Honduras, United Fruit's premier "banana republic."

But the problems generated by the Boston and United Fruit companies extended beyond those outlined. Both companies, through their voracious and rapid acquisition of land, significantly contributed to raising the price of land beyond the reach of the peasantry. Indeed, some peasants were reduced to becoming tenants on Baker's estates.[46] Many Black Jamaicans even lacked the opportunity for employment on the banana plantations because these estates recruited Indian indentured laborers. Indeed, the 2,745 indentured laborers brought into the island between 1899 and 1906 were headed to banana plantations; United Fruit was the largest recruiter of indentured laborers at the beginning of the twentieth century.[47] The rapid expansion of banana cultivation and the extensive irrigation it demanded also meant that malaria—a disease carried by mosquitoes that breed in stagnant water—became more prevalent, indeed became a "typical disease of banana workers," in the eastern parishes as a direct result of large-scale cultivation of the fruit.[48]

Land and the People

In marked contrast to the McKays, the Jamaican peasantry fared increasingly badly in the late nineteenth century. In his pioneering study of land transactions in Jamaica from 1866 to 1900, Veront Satchell shows in laudable detail the powerful mechanisms used by the ruling class to squeeze the peasantry during this period. Despite the removal of so-called "squatters," the late 1860s marked the expansion and consolidation of peasant holdings.[49] To a significant degree, this occurred because of official attempts to pacify, on their own terms, the rural population in the aftermath of the Morant Bay Rebellion of 1865. But from the 1870s, things became increasingly difficult for peasants and agricultural workers. Smallholders (those in possession of five acres or less) were sold Crown land (public land under the control of the state) at five times the price paid by large landowners (those with acquisitions over five hundred acres.)[50] From the 1870s to the 1890s, the colonial government embarked on a policy of selling land in large tracts, which the peasantry could not afford. The price of small units were thus artificially inflated.[51] Only a quarter of the lots sold in the 1870s were under fifty acres; by the 1880s, the proportion had dropped to less than one-seventh.[52] To make matters worse, the land acquired by peasants was far less fertile, more hilly, and less accessible than that acquired by the merchants and planters. Furthermore, the massive expansion of Crown land, secured largely through the eviction of smallholders, inflicted one of the most devastating blows upon the peasantry. By retaking control of more than 240,000 acres between 1867 and 1912, the colonial authorities not only made those removed landless but also artificially shrunk the supply of land, thus increasing its price. This vigorous consolidation was concentrated at the very end of the century, with 128,000 acres reverting to the government during the eight years between 1894 and 1901.[53] Given these policies and trends, it is little wonder that by the mid-1890s, eighty-one individuals had become the owners of no less than 97 percent of the rural land offered by the government for sale.[54]

A similar dynamic of expansion and consolidation of large plantations at the expense of smallholders occurred in private land transactions over the same period.[55] The evidence suggests, however, that in one key respect the situation was even worse. More "squatters" were evicted from private than government land. Despite the label pinned on them, many of these people had in fact purchased the land they were evicted from but had not been given deeds by those they had handed their money over to. The only crime they had committed was being the hapless victims of heartless swindlers.[56] Thus, it is not surprising that by the end of the nineteenth century the peasantry were acquiring considerably less land than they had been in the 1860s. They were boxed in by corporate capital on one side and a resurgent plantocracy on the other. With the exception of parts of the Windward Islands, this was characteristic of the British Caribbean at the turn of the century. One historian aptly describes the period as one of "saturation," when the peasantry in the British territories failed to expand their holdings and experienced contraction in a number of instances, including in Jamaica.[57]

With the boom in the banana trade, it became increasingly difficult for smallholders to acquire land in the banana parishes. Thus, the 1890s were marked by rapid consolidation of land holdings in the eastern parishes. By 1900, four landholders, including Baker, came to acquire more than 65,000 acres of land in the principal banana parishes during the late nineteenth century.[58] In addition, the colonial government had offered 76,800 acres (79 per cent of which was in Portland and St. Thomas) to an American syndicate, the West India Improvement Company (WIIC), for extending the island's railway by 120 miles.[59] Under the law enacted in 1889, the company was offered one square mile of Crown land for every mile of track laid. Apparently the deal was not sweet enough for the company; the government handed over the land free of all charges and taxes, including quit rents, for ten years. By 1897, more than 70,000 acres had been given to the company, but according to the surveyor general, the land remained idle and undeveloped by the WIIC, which had mortgaged all of it.[60]

Thus, although the McKays did not live in one of the premier banana parishes, Thomas McKay's extensive acquisition of land during this period of contraction of the Black peasantry was quite exceptional. Indeed, according to the account given by his son, Thomas McKay was an indirect beneficiary of the misfortunes of the poorer elements of the peasantry. "He was always," his son revealed, "ready to snap up a piece of land that was for sale through the death of its owner or its being encumbered by taxes."[61] Between 1869 and 1900, the colonial regime ejected and repossessed from "peasant squatters" some six thousand acres of land in the parish of Clarendon alone. In fact, Clarendon had by far the largest area of land repossessed in this way, accounting for more than a third of the colony's total, even though the parish covered only about a tenth of the island. During the same period, Clarendon, one of Jamaica's fourteen parishes and home to less than 10 percent of the its population, had the largest number of "peasant squatters" ejected—just under 29 percent of the island's total.[62] Clarendon thus emerged as the most favorable area in Jamaica for one in Thomas McKay's financial position and with his ambition for acquiring land; bargains were to be had if one got to the encumbered peasants a step ahead of the bailiff. Given his enterprise, ambition, and resources, along with the processes unfolding in the Clarendon countryside, it is not surprising that by the time McKay left Jamaica in 1912, his father had established himself as a prosperous, progressive commercial farmer with at least one hundred acres of fertile land. By this time also, Thomas McKay possessed his own little sugar mill, one of the coveted Chattanooga mills, so called because they were built in the Tennessee town of the same name. In addition, he had his own boiler and sugar house in which he manufactured sugar, and he had earlier acquired his own dray and mules for transporting his produce to far-off markets.[63] From being an illiterate and humble road mender at the time of his marriage in 1870, Thomas McKay, through his exertions and primitive accumulation in the Clarendon countryside, had transformed himself by 1912 into a prosperous capitalist farmer. Thus, although McKay to the end of his days described himself as a son of the Jamaican peasantry, by the time he left the island, his family's economic position exceeded such a definition.[64] If the McKays were a breed apart from the Clarendon peasants who surrounded them, their economic position was even more remote from that of the Jamaican proletariat, the workers. Thomas had come out of that world but, by the time Claude was born, had long escaped its harsh confines.

In 1838—the year in which slavery finally came to an end with the close of the apprenticeship system—an agricultural worker could expect to earn between seven and fourteen pence for a day's labor. In 1890, the figure was between nine and twenty-one pence; in 1910, it ranged from six to eighteen pence.[65] Thus, even nominal—let alone real—agricultural wages had declined or remained stagnant over three generations. This did not stop employers from cheating workers of their already meager wages, a recurring complaint made to the 1897 Royal Commission. Thomas Smickle, for example, testified to knowing men who walked ten to twelve miles to work, only to be cheated by their employers. "I have known cases," he said, "where men were promised 1 [shilling] a day and have worked for five or six days and then have only got 1 [shilling] or 3 [shillings] and 6 [pence]." In order to buttress his point, he had with him, he told the commission, "a batch of evidence which will substantiate this statement." There is, he continued, "a large number of persons who are not paid what they have been promised and what they have worked and earned." The people complain that "they do not get what they work for, and they are not satisfied." Asked by the chair of the commission if the people complain before a magistrate, Smickle responded, "No, not before a magistrate. You know small people are afraid to take their superiors to court for more reasons than one."[66] What Smickle could have said but did not, even though the implications of his words were heavy, is that frequently the very magistrates who passed judgment on the people were culprits themselves, many being some of the largest landowners on the island. There was nowhere to turn for justice. "We can assure you, gentlemen," a group of Portland petitioners wrote to the commission, "that justice is really wanting at our pay-table in this island. The paymasters here are judges and jury at the pay-table, and do just what they think." The root cause of the abuse, the petitioners thought, was that "competition is so great and work can be done for such nominal sums."[67] The chattel slaves of Jamaica had become wage slaves, with hardly any wages at all.

In fact, in certain important respects conditions were worse in the post-slavery period than they were during the years of bondage. A good example of this is medical care. Forced by the Slave Acts to provide medical care for their slaves, plantation owners employed doctors at the rate of six shillings per annum for each slave. As a result, many doctors were said to be "extremely prosperous" during the early part of the nineteenth century. No doubt attracted by the lucrative venture, two hundred doctors practiced in Jamaica in 1830—a doctor for every 1,855 people. But within a generation of emancipation, only fifty doctors were practicing on the island. The former slaves, poverty-stricken and no longer the charge of their erstwhile masters, had none of what neoclassical economists would call "effective demand" for the luxury of a doctor's care. Thus, from a ratio of one doctor to fewer than two thousand people in the days of slavery, in 1860, after more than a generation of "freedom," there was one doctor for every nine thousand people; as late as 1921, the ratio was still only one to more than six thousand inhabitants.[68] "In no other country, probably, does there exist such a paucity of qualified medical practitioners," one missionary complained.[69] Doctors, as early as the 1840s, were concentrated in Kingston and commanded fees of up to five pounds six shillings and eight pence (£5. 6s. 8d) per visit—more than a hundred times the average daily wage. Faced with a population too poor to be patients, some doctors returned to Britain, others took up residence in the United States or Canada, and a significant number remained in the island but received the bulk of their income from other lines of work. Some ran drugstores; others left the profession altogether to pursue careers as planters.[70] Small wonder, given the conditions under which ordinary people existed—including the abysmally low wages— that their health deteriorated. Infant mortality increased by more than 21 percent between the mid-1880s and 1910. It is true that the figure for the first decade of the twentieth century was inflated because of the Kingston earthquake of 1907, but the average for the five-year period 1911–1915 was still high (179.2 per 1,000 live births). In 1910, 70 percent of the population suffered from hookworm.[71]

While Jamaica's population increased by 43 percent between 1881 and 1911, that of Kingston increased by more than half, exemplifying the marked drift from the Jamaican countryside to the towns. Indeed, while the island's population increased by more than 10 percent between 1881 and 1891, the three main banana parishes experienced an increase of less than half the national average.[72] Significantly, the population of St. Thomas actually fell by more than 5 percent between 1881 and 1891, reflecting, at least in part, the dispossession, hardship, and displacement caused by banana magnates such as Baker and the United Fruit Company. Indeed, the district engineer of the Public Works Department, D. Santfleben—a man well acquainted with conditions in the banana parishes, having lived and worked in St. Mary, Portland, and St. Thomas for twelve years—corroborated the evidence of movement from the eastern parishes and its underlying causes. "Many of the people are going to other districts," he informed the 1897 Royal Commission, because of the increase in the price and rent of land in these parishes, the large proprietors having "taken land from them" and "forced the people to go further back" from the banana estates and the seaports.[73]

In keeping with the general trend of the time, the proportion of the island's labor force employed in agriculture declined. From an estimated 68 percent in 1871, it fell to just over 58 percent by 1911. At the same time, those employed in "domestic service" increased from 10 to 15 percent of the labor force.[74] These developments reflected the disruptive effect of agrarian capitalism in the late nineteenth century. While powerful enough to uproot and displace the peasants, the capitalist upheaval in the countryside lacked the dynamism to absorb and transform them into fully fledged agrarian proletarians. In the absence of a rapidly expanding manufacturing sector to use their labor power, many of the displaced peasants and rural workers reappeared, especially in the towns, as domestic servants, petty traders, prostitutes, and, of course, the chronically unemployed—that category of the labor force that Marx aptly described as the "lazarus-layer" of the working class.[75] Fewer than one in five female workers in Kingston and St. Andrew (Jamaica's largest urban center) was a domestic servant in 1891; by 1911, it was one in four, and by 1921, nearly one in three.[76] "The large increase in female domestic servants was no evidence of a high standard of living enjoyed by a small section of the community," one economist observed. "On the contrary," she maintained,

> it was the response of a much wider community to the needs of surplus rural population. By the end of the century the custom had grown up to provide shelter, food and training to "school-girls" in return for service. This cheap labour supply enabled far lower income groups to enjoy personal services than is usually found in more fully developed societies.[77]

But considerably less reciprocity inhered in such arrangements than Gisela Eisner suggested. Abuse and exploitation more typically defined the lot of domestic servants. Employers took advantage of the economic vulnerability of domestics, a subject about which McKay (living in Kingston at the time) had much to say. Even relatively humble persons indulged in conspicuous consumption at the expense of their servants. "It will be apparent," one contemporary observed in 1913, "that if out of a population of less than nine hundred thousand, most of whom serve themselves, the number of domestics is forty thousand, almost everybody who has the slightest pretensions to be considered anybody employs a servant. In fact," he added, "you are not respectable if you have not a servant. That at least is one law of Jamaica life."[78]

As with the growth in the number of domestic servants, a greater number of petty traders did not mean a general upturn in the island's prosperity. On the contrary, as people became more desperate, many turned to petty trading, especially in the urban areas. Black working-class women figured prominently in this practice; as with their sisters in domestic service, the number of female petty traders—known locally as "higglers"—increased dramatically during the period. Indeed, between 1891 and 1911, the number of women engaged in this form of economic activity more than doubled.[79] As they became more visible than ever in Kingston, McKay noticed and wrote some of his finest poems about them.

The Law of Inverse Ability: Taxing the Poor and Coddling the Rich

Despite the revolt of the Jamaican peasants and workers at Morant Bay in 1865,[80] one of whose main causes was the blatantly unfair and regressive taxation system, such a system remained essentially unchanged during McKay's time in Jamaica. In an attempt to manage the chronic fiscal difficulties that accompanied the demise of the sugar industry, the government deployed a battery of measures to extract tribute from the people. The rich objected to income tax, so there was none. In the absence of direct taxes, the authorities resorted to customs and excise, which accounted for between 70 and 80 percent of government revenue. Jamaica's customs duty was the highest in the British Caribbean.[81] Inherently regressive (exacted without regard to income levels), such taxes in Jamaica became doubly so, falling not only disproportionately but almost exclusively on the items consumed by ordinary Jamaicans—salted cod (known locally as salt-fish), corned beef, flour, cloth, clothing, etc. This led Thomas Macdermot (better known as Tom Redcam), editor of the *Jamaica Times*, to observe that "every being who wears clothes and eats food is a taxpayer owing to our heavy import duties."[82] But the items consumed by the upper class were hardly touched by the taxation system. Contemporaries noted that the white upper class bought their clothes in London or New York when they made their trips abroad. The planter and merchant classes were relieved of export duties as early as 1891. Furthermore, all plantation machinery, implements, fertilizers, and manure entered the island duty free. No such leniency was extended to the poor. Their donkeys and mules were taxed; their carts were taxed (by the wheel); even matches were taxed.[83] Ordinary Jamaicans also had to carry the burden of parochial taxes. The tax on housing was so designed that "the heaviest burden [fell] on the poorest class."[84] Its deleterious effects upon the material condition of the people were well known but illustrated most powerfully by the Reverend Henry Clarke in his testimony to the 1897 Royal Commission. The smallest huts were taxed, he told the commission. "People who have not a single thing in the world, not a bit of furniture or a bed to lie on are taxed in this way. During the last three months I have had people come to me bringing these surcharge papers. They cannot raise the money if it were to save their lives; they have not it and yet they are taxed." The whole exercise was akin to getting blood out of a stone, he told the commission.[85]

After a coldly sober review of the taxation regime at the time, the ever so polite Gisela Eisner succinctly concluded: "If the criterion of a just system of taxation is ability to pay then the Jamaican system could not be called just."[86] This is, of course, an appalling understatement: by almost any measure, the taxation regime was *profoundly unjust*. And the people felt and perceived it that way, as they, time and again, informed Sir Henry Norman and the other commissioners in 1897.

The tax on holdings was one of those they objected to most strongly and repeatedly. This tax egregiously favored large landholders over smallholders and renters of land. Law 11 of 1891 required the holder, whether owner or renter, to pay two shillings of tax each year on any holding up to five acres. In marked contrast, it demanded only two pounds thirteen shillings and four pence of a landlord ("landgod," the people sometimes called such individuals) with 1,500 acres.[87] It was this set of arrangements that led the Jamaican scholar and medical doctor Theophilus Scholes to speak of a law of "inverse ability" operating in Jamaica: "those who have more property shall pay less taxes, and those who have less property shall pay more taxes."[88] Behind the island's taxation regime, Scholes detected a principle that he calls "Class Government." The ruling-class notion is that the "Ethiopian" can live on very little. "They don't require as much as white people." And the state will not intervene to relieve the burden on the Ethiopian.[89]

In practical terms the holding tax meant that a man renting an acre of land would be required to pay two shillings (24 pence) per acre and the landgod with 1,500 acres would pay just over a quarter of a penny (0.26 penny) per acre. Thus, a poor man renting a scrap of land would pay taxes at a rate ninety times that of the rich man with a massive estate. Moreover, the "small man" (another apt Jamaicanism) renting an acre here, a quarter of an acre there and elsewhere was required to pay two shillings on each piece of land. Consequently, a peasant owning or renting half an acre around his hut and two acres farther afield, which frequently occurred, would be required to pay four shillings per year in holding taxes. Thus, the residents of Birnam Wood, a village in Portland, asked the Norman commission to "re-adjust" the holding tax "so that each small settler may have only one holding tax to pay, and not at present a tax on every patch of ground he cultivates."[90]

The unfairness of the tax is further underlined by the provisions for estates over 1,500 acres. The holding tax on an estate of more than 1,500 acres was capped at three pounds. This meant that a landgod with a plantation of ten thousand acres or more would be required to pay only three pounds per year. Theoretically, then, the small man owning fragmented holdings amounting to five acres could very well end up paying the same amount of taxes as the "big man" with an estate of ten thousand acres.[91]

Furthermore, the tax structure encouraged, rather than punished, the underutilization of land. The property tax law, which was separate from the law on holdings, stipulated: "Upon every acre or fraction of an acre of land in cane, coffee, ginger, arrowroot, corn, groundnuts, cotton, tobacco, cocoa, vegetables, bananas, cocoanuts or ground provisions," a yearly tax of 3 pence would be levied; upon every acre or fraction of an acre in Guinea grass, 1.5 pence; in common pasture, or in pimento, or in common pasture and pimento, 0.75 penny; in ruinate (that is completely unused) or wood, 0.25 penny.[92] Not only was this law obviously regressive, it punished the owner or renter who cultivated the land, while the person who left his or her land idle paid virtually nothing. Once again, the peasants, who cultivated their land far more intensively than the large landowner, were the victims of the system. The property tax, furthermore, encouraged land speculation and eschewed the taxation of wealth in land. Given the provisions of the law, it is small wonder that in 1896 some 65 percent of the land in private hands was officially designated as idle (in ruinate and wood)—1,269,000 of 1,960,000 acres. Furthermore, of the 694,000 acres said to be "under cultivation," more than 511,000 (or 74 percent) was described as "grazing lands,"[93] which every Jamaican recognized as little more than a synonym for idle land. Indeed, not only was there undercultivation on the part of large landlords, as Olivier found, sometimes the owners (especially absentee owners) of large estates had so much land and were so nonchalant about its use that they were not even aware of the full extent of their holdings, the real acreage being "conjectural."[94]

The pattern was that at any given time only a tiny proportion of the land on the large estates would be under cultivation. This was especially so on the large sugar estates in the late nineteenth and early twentieth centuries.[95] In 1896, Frome, a sugar estate of 1,058 acres in Westmoreland, had less than 22 percent (229 acres) of its land under cane cultivation, with the rest in "grass, woodland and ruinate." The Fort William estate in the same parish had even less in cultivation (350 of 2,680 acres), a mere 13 percent; Roaring River grew no sugar at all but held onto its 948 acres, unused. In St. Elizabeth, another cane-growing parish, the famous Appleton estate cultivated less than 1 percent of its land—56 of its 5,740 acres. On the Denbigh estate in Clarendon, 150 of 7,503 acres were cultivated; the rest, or 98 percent, was idle. Only 5.3 percent of the Worthy Park estate in St. Catherine was cultivated—425 acres in sugar with 7,543 acres left idle. Rarely was less than 75 percent of the sugar estates' land left in "grass, woodland and ruinate." By the time McKay left the island in 1912, the portion under sugar had increased, but only slightly.[96] The official statistics do not give a breakdown of the idle land on the banana estates, but we know that there was always more land in grass, common pasture, and pimento than there ever was under banana cultivation or any other crop in St. Thomas, Portland, and St. Mary. In short, extensive tracts of land were aggregated in the banana parishes by large landowners, such as the Boston Fruit Company and John Pringle, but a significant percentage of it was always idle.[97]

The agrarian relations in Jamaica thus appear paradoxical. On the one hand, great tracts of land remained underutilized or unused altogether; on the other, there was "land-famine" among the peasants and agro-prole-tarians.[98] The sugar estates periodically rotated the area of land cultivated, leaving some land fallow to facilitate rejuvenation. But even after allowing for this primitive mode of agriculture, developed during slavery, the size of tracts left idle was exorbitant. The property tax regime clearly contrib-uted to this situation: it provided no sanction against leaving the land idle and no incentive to sell or even rent. It cost virtually nothing to leave the land uncultivated, and it increased in value without any exertion on the part of the landlord, especially in the banana parishes where land prices rose most steeply.

A Burning Shame: Land Famine and the Great Refusal

But there was another, more pervasive and sinister motive behind the large landgods' holding out against selling or renting to peasants. The reluctance or outright refusal to sell, rent, or lease land to Black peasants and workers was part of the larger strategy articulated even before emancipation—to separate the former slaves and their descendants from the soil. This inhibited and prevented Black economic independence while fostering dependence upon the large estates for survival.[99] What the ruling class sought was the mass pro-letarianization of the Black population by blocking its access to the means of production, especially land. Without land, without independent means, one was left at the mercy of employers. Wages and conditions of work could be determined unilaterally by capital, especially the large landgods. A man with adequate and fertile land could hardly be forced to work for starvation wages under slavelike conditions.

Thus, groups of prospective cultivators, noticing the "extensive tracts of land, which are allowed to remain in a wild unworked state in the parish of St. Andrew," decided to approach the owner, Louis Verley. Verley, who was, among other things, the "Bread King" of Jamaica in the late 1890s, owned the Mona estate. The only sugar plantation in the parish in 1897, Mona cov-ered an area of 1,072 acres but had only 195 acres under cultivation; the rest languished in "grass, woodland and ruinate," as the *Handbook of Jamaica* recorded.[100] To the local land-hungry people, this was a shame. According to one of the would-be cultivators, the estate's soil was "deep and fertile, and if properly cultivated, would produce any quantity of various kinds of eatables." Desirous of "suitable allotments for cultivation under conditions suitable to both sides," the people "ventured to approach" Verley on several occasions. They were "repelled with the sharp reply: 'No. I'll neither sell, rent, nor give one foot to any body. I prefer it to remain, covered all over with woods.'" A member of the aggrieved party who reported Verley's rebuff noted:

> I do not write under the impression that a man is obliged to do with his goods as others would like; but feel that it is a burning shame to allow good intending citizens of the earth to perish for lack of bread and water; while, contrary to the laws of God and man, arable lands are allowed to remain in a wild state. This disposition of large land owners in general, together with the unthoughtful Government in reference to the poor, has been one of the most potent factors in congealing the atmosphere of depression which to-day, is revolving around Jamaica on every side.[101]

As the writer of the letter suggests, this was the general attitude of the large landowners and especially those in the sugar parishes, such as Westmoreland, St. Elizabeth, and Trelawny. There, as another correspondent to the *Jamaica Advocate* asserts, "it is a notorious fact" that the large landowners—"sugar kings," he calls them—in order to "positively coerce the peasantry to work for starvation wages," neither "sell, rent, nor lease a foot of [land]" to them.[102] Remarkably, even the official report of the 1897 Royal Commission recognized this state of affairs, using almost identical language to that of the correspondent to the *Jamaica Advocate*:

> The settlement of the labourer on the land has not, as a rule, been viewed with favour in the past by the persons interested in sugar estates. What suited them best was a large supply of labourers, entirely dependent on being able to find work on the estates, and consequently, subject to their control and willing to work at low rates of wages.[103]

Some of the viciousness on the part of the planter class stemmed from long-standing and deep-seated resentment harbored against the very emancipation of the former slaves and what the plantocracy regarded as the ruin it brought upon them.[104]

The practice of withholding the land continued well into the twentieth century, and not only in Jamaica.[105] Hon. Rev. A. A. Barclay and Mr. William Cradwick of the Jamaica League, a Black reform group, gave a telling example of its operation as they reported the frustration of a returned Jamaican migrant. The man had been born into severe poverty but after years of hard work in Cuba, returned home in 1920 with "some hundreds of pounds saved." He tried to buy land but had "the greatest difficulty" in finding some to buy. Unable to afford a large property, he managed to buy ten acres in St. Mary. He wanted more to buy but encountered such reluctance to sell from local planters that in the end he resorted to buying eighty acres of badly situated Crown land.[106]

The difficulty of the returnee was aggravated by the fact that the planter class especially resented those Black Jamaicans who returned from Panama and Cuba with newfound wealth. (McKay in his novel *Banana Bottom* provides some acute observations on the subject.) Symbols of independence for those who remained behind, these returnees encountered great obstacles to purchasing land. Traveling in the Caribbean soon after the First World War, Harry Franck, a white American who was hardly sympathetic to the plight of Black Jamaicans, reported that one of the sponsors of these returnees (presumably a white Jamaican) expressed dismay at the reluctance of the plantocracy to sell them land. "Negroes who come back from Panama and Cuba with in some cases hundreds of pounds are seldom able to buy property," he told Franck.[107] When the large landowners did condescend to rent (and less often sell) to Black Jamaicans, they almost invariably offered up the most infertile, stony, remote, and mountainous parts of their estates—at exorbitant rates.[108]

Writing in 1888, the Reverend S. J. Washington, one of the island's leading post-emancipation Black intellectuals, identified the "want of more and better roads" as one of the main hindrances to development of the island.

> Much of the best lands for tillage has not been, and cannot yet be, placed under regular cultivation, on account either of the entire absence of roads, or of the dangerous condition of such as lead to these facilities. Much and profitable business, too, in boards, shingles, and lumber of all kinds, has been prevented in several of the parishes from the absolute want of roads, or from the uninviting condition of the existing nominal ones.[109]

This lack meant surplus food and timber in some areas and not enough in others, and that the island imported items that could have been acquired locally if only the transportation infrastructure were in place. "More and better roads," concluded Washington, "are an urgent need, and must prove an effable blessing to the Island."[110] More than a generation later, the plea remained unanswered: the landgods vigorously resisted the opening up of roads and rail transportation for rural folk to prevent and inhibit peasant agriculture and to secure a cheap and dependent workforce.[111] In Clarendon, they bitterly opposed the extension of the railway from May Pen to Chapelton, where it would be in reach of peasant cultivators. But through the energetic efforts of U. Theo McKay and the peasants in Upper Clarendon, the line was finally built and opened in 1913, and by 1925 it had been extended to Frankfield, further into Clarendon's northern hinterland.[112] Shamelessly, in an effort to have his cake and eat it too, one of those who strenuously objected to the extension (H. Q. Levy, the ex–agricultural instructor of St. Ann and Upper Trelawny) decided to move to Upper Clarendon and settle as a banana grower—once the line to Chapelton had been opened.[113] He now wanted to benefit from the improved transportation facilities he had previously opposed.

As if conditions were not bad enough for Jamaica's peasants and workers, the planter class conspired to undermine the already low wages of the poor by bringing to the island tens of thousands of Indian and Chinese indentured laborers.[114] To compound the injury, the very taxes extracted unfairly from the Jamaican masses would be used to help defray the cost of importing cheap Indian labor.[115]

The whole strategy of the ruling class, one articulated and followed even before emancipation, was to use as many devices as possible to inhibit the independent economic development of the Black population. The ruling class hoped that through taxation, restrictions on emigration, the importing of indentured laborers, and the raising of land prices beyond the reach of the Black population, it could secure for itself a pliable and cheap labor force for the plantations. As an American traveler to the island noted, the whites "strive to keep their estates intact and hold the negro in economic subjection."[116] They did not succeed fully, but they caused untold suffering and sorrow to the Jamaican people, especially its Black working class.

Shafts of Light

Four powerful shafts of light relieved some of the darkness over the land. First, there was the grim determination on the part of the peasants and workers to survive, despite the severity of the hardship. This resilience manifested itself in myriad ways: through the persistent attempts to make a living out of a recalcitrant soil; through the diversification of crops; through sheer hard work; through migration to the cities; through petty trading and domestic work; and most of all, through the solidarity of poor Black people in the countryside and in the towns supporting one another in struggle. The people overtly resisted, too, punctuating the years with sporadic revolts in the countryside as well as in the towns, including in Montego Bay in 1902 and in Kingston a decade later.[117]

On April 5 and 6, 1902, rioting broke out in Montego Bay, the capital of the northwestern parish of St. James. Contemporaries regarded it as the most serious incident since the Morant Bay uprising of 1865. The combined anger of the poor townspeople against police brutality and the landless and overtaxed of the surrounding countryside culminated in attacks on the police and the besieging of the town's police station. Serious injuries were inflicted on the police, including its white officers and the inspector general, by groups numbering thousands on both nights. The city was relieved only after reinforcements were sent from Kingston and elsewhere, including soldiers of the West India Regiment and a Royal Navy ship. Two people, unconnected to the rioting, died of gunshot wounds from indiscriminate firing by police officers. Scores more were injured, including some who were bayoneted, and hundreds were arrested. Damage and loss of property ran into tens of thousands of pounds.[118]

It is remarkable but unsurprising that a dynamite cartridge with a charred fuse was found at the Montego Bay Court House in the office that dealt with property valuation for tax purposes. Apparently dropped through the window during the second night of protests, it speaks volumes: grievances against a new increase in taxation and aggressive tax collection had reached a boiling point. Bailiffs and their underlings (so-called runners) were especially unpopular in the countryside. Theirs was the ugly face of an iniquitous tax system. Not obliged to give receipts—indeed, not even allowed to give official receipts, as St. James's acting collector of taxes told the inquiry into the riot[119]—they frequently abused their powers by charging more than once. When the peasants could not pay, bailiffs and runners used powers of confiscation to seize their tools, animals, and whatever else of value they could lay their hands on. The inquiry heard of men who had their crosscut saw and axes seized; another man complained of not being able to work his ground because his tools had been confiscated; yet another had his ginger and yam plants uprooted and taken away. Edmund Stewart, the overseer of an estate, told of a case in which "a woman had gone into Town to pay taxes on a donkey [and] while she was gone the bailiff came and levied on the donkey and seized it."[120] Seldom do we hear the voice of the people in these documents, and when we do, the tone is generally beseeching—anguished rather than angry. But rather like the anonymous and pseudonymous letters that threatened colonial officialdom during and after the Morant Bay Rebellion, a letter signed "The inhabitants of Noble St. James" was sent to "the Honourable Collector General." Objecting to the new taxes, these inhabitants "positively refuse to pay one cent more than what we paid last year." It would therefore save the government "a great amount of trouble" if it would withdraw the tax increases. If the law was not rescinded, the letter writer promised to "make a complete change of the scene" in Jamaica. The bailiffs would have to "look out for themselves," the officers of the tax department would have to do the same, and "if they dont nobody is going to do it for them." The letter continued:

As for the Constabulary Department they will be blown millions of miles from the face of the earth[.] The Government building also will bow down in subjection Under our feet. So according to the old saying it[']s better to stop quarrel before fight come. I the writer of this letter is undoubtedly a true loyal subject to my country, but if we are to be made slaves to taxes we will have to fight for our freedom and put loyalty aside. We therefore trust honourable Sir that you will submit this correspondence to the Governor and that he will immediately withdraw this Valuation Tax (and allow us to pay the same amount of the Taxe[s] which we had last year) before further trouble because as a matter of fact we do not want to raise a riot unnecessarily, but if we are pushed to do it we will not be responsible for the consequences. Trusting great notice will be taken of this correspondence (or prepare for further trouble)[.]

The letter was signed "Your Obedient Servant, / The inhabitants of Noble St. James" and dated March 27, 1902,[121] just over a week before the uprising and the discovery of the stick of unexploded dynamite.

The second shaft of light was that the typical worker and peasant, despite the hardship, were anxious and determined that their children acquire an education. This education, basic though it was, did not come cheaply. In 1867, the government agreed to subsidize the denominational schools, which provided elementary education. But the state also insisted that, to be eligible for state support, these schools should charge fees. The fees ranged from 1.5 pence to six pence per week—a considerable sum given the miserly wages. In 1871–72, the fees collected amounted to almost £6,000; the government grant was less than £10,000. Parents suffered the fees unrelieved until 1892, when they were finally abolished. After 1892 the poor would still pay, but this time indirectly, through additional taxation. In spite of all the obstacles, the literacy rate increased dramatically, doubling between 1861 and 1911, when it reached more than 62 percent. The number of those able to read as well as write increased almost fourfold to almost 50 percent.[122] The proportion of children between the ages of five and fourteen enrolled in schools increased from 37 percent in 1861 to a peak of 61 percent in 1891, falling back with the hard times of the fin de siècle to 58 per cent in 1911. The actual number attending school tripled over the two generations up to 1911.[123] Given the impediments, these were mammoth accomplishments. The herculean effort of the little people perplexed their overlords; the poorer classes, noted one governor, were "curiously tenacious & sensitive" on the question of education.[124]

The Jamaican people, then, over the course of these two generations became substantially more educated and arguably less vulnerable to manipulation. This enabled the voices of the children of slaves, and of those children's children, to become more audible and distinct. Thus, in May 1895, about a thousand wharf laborers went on strike in Kingston, and one of them took time out to publicize their grievances. In a letter to the *Daily Gleaner*, the island's most influential newspaper, he wrote: "I ask you to occupy a space in your paper concerning the striking of the labourers. We the labouring classes do strike for higher wages . . . we asked for more wages so that we may be able to sustain ourselves and families in a respectable manner. We have to support our families, pay rent, and tax and water rates." More wages, he argued, "will enable us to spend more, and the merchants will receive more"; they won't have to "trouble" the government "often for coffins, and hole for the burial of the dead; we will be able to bury them ourselves. . . . The Alms House won't be having so much paupers on the list." Pointing to the higher wages enjoyed by his counterparts in Trinidad, he wondered why Jamaican workers had "been suffering" for such "a long time under the tyranny of small wages." We mean, he declared, "to be determined for good wages, in our Island." Everybody would inherit the benefit. Higher wages would not only lift the standard of living for working people but also help to restore and enhance their battered dignity: "There are more stealing going on now than if we were getting good wages, if we got good pay, there is no need for us to steal; but on account of the wages is so small, we have to steal, we are going to prison and disgrace ourselves."[125]

Like U. Theo, discussed in the previous chapter, some of the descendants of the enslaved Africans in Jamaica—the "children of the emancipated,"

as one Black organization described them—had acquired higher education and entered into the professions. These were teachers, lawyers, doctors, dentists, clergymen. The growth in the number of those employed
in the professions in the late nineteenth and early twentieth centuries was
remarkable. For while the population of the island grew by 43 percent
between 1881 and 1911, those in the professions almost doubled in number.
Over the same period, the number of professional public servants grew by
more than 50 percent, teachers by 74 percent, doctors and dentists by more
than 104 percent, and lawyers by more than 205 percent.[126] It is difficult to
determine precisely what proportion of these professionals were Black and
colored, but all the contemporary evidence suggests that the growth in the
number of professionals was due largely to the emergence and expansion of
a Black (as opposed to "brown") middle class.[127]

A significant segment of this cohort would form a contingent of organic
intellectuals of the Black masses, giving voice to their suffering and strivings. The emergence of these intellectuals constituted the third significant
positive development of the time.[128] Among them was Ethelred Brown, who
was to become an ordained Unitarian minister and a radical political activist in Harlem in the 1920s. In a pioneering and impressively documented
essay, "Labor Conditions in Jamaica Prior to 1917," he wrote:

> After seventy-eight years in this fair island . . . there are still hundreds and
> hundreds of men and women who live like savages in unfloored huts, hud-
> dled together like beasts of the field, without regard to health or comfort.
> And they live thus, not because they are worthless or because they are wholly
> without ambition or desire to live otherwise, but because they must thus
> continue as economic slaves receiving still the miserable pittance of a wage
> of eighteen pence or 36 cents a day that was paid to their forefathers at the
> dawn of emancipation.[129]

Brown was by no means alone in articulating such views. The others included,
as we have seen, McKay's eldest brother and mentor, U. Theo McKay, as well
as the young Claude himself, as we shall see.

The fourth shaft of light was provided by emigration, especially emigration to Panama and later Cuba. The opportunity to participate in the
construction of the Panama Railroad and the Panama Canal appeared to
Jamaican and other Caribbean workers like acts of divine intervention.
Hemmed in on the islands—underpaid and underfed, overworked, overtaxed, exploited, and often unemployed—they were suddenly, like a clap of

thunder out of a clear blue sky, being pursued by foreigners vying for their labor in the Isthmus of Panama and willing to pay far in excess of what they could ever earn in Jamaica. The stream from Jamaica began in the 1850s during the building of the Panama Railroad,[130] but the first major wave of migration occurred in the 1880s, when the French made their bid to construct the canal. Although the Compagnie Universelle went bankrupt without completing the canal, it provided work and relatively good wages for ten years (1880–1889), when tens of thousands of working people and their families fought hunger in Jamaica. Some 78,000 Jamaicans migrated to the isthmus between 1881 and 1890. The American-controlled Isthmian Canal Commission (ICC) succeeded where the French had failed, and under its auspices the Panama Canal was built between 1904 and 1914. The activity on the canal was like a magnet to Jamaican workers. Between 1891 and 1915, almost one hundred thousand left the island for Panama, about 12 percent of the island's population in 1911.[131]

The mighty flow of Black Jamaica to Central America is easily explained. Jamaicans knew about the construction of the canal. Transportation was readily available. Panama, unlike Jamaica, had tens of thousands of better-paying jobs available. As early as the 1850s, unskilled Jamaican workers on the Panama Railroad earned more than double the prevailing wages for unskilled labor on the island. In the 1880s and during the ICC period on the canal, the differential between wages in Jamaica and wages in Panama widened even further.[132] Jamaica had work; it was just that the employers, including many who could afford it, did not believe in paying workers a living wage—and, as we have seen, many believed in paying no wages at all. This explains the simultaneous mass migration to the isthmus and the importing of tens of thousands of indentured laborers from the Indian subcontinent. As Eric Williams noted, "for every East Indian added to the British West Indian labour force before World War I, three West Indians were subtracted."[133]

During their control of the construction of the canal, the ICC instituted a complex hierarchy of skill and payment overlaid with American Jim Crow racism.[134] The Jamaican migrant workers also complained of profiteering by merchants and shopkeepers. But at the end of the day, real wages were still much higher than those in Jamaica. That tens of thousands still clamored to go to Panama despite knowing about the brutal racism of the ICC, the diseased environment, and the high death rate tells us far more about the conditions in Jamaica than about those on the isthmus. Between 1905 and 1907, the death rate of Black workers in Panama was more than twice that in Jamaica.[135] To appreciate the full significance of the human devastation that these figures indicate, one needs to bear in mind that those who went to Panama were in the prime of youth, strong men (and they were overwhelmingly men) between the ages of twenty and thirty-five,[136] capable of doing hard work. Their employers, the ICC, would accept nothing less—they weeded out and mercilessly rejected all applicants who failed to measure up to their strict criteria of physical suitability for the heavy work on the canal. In marked contrast, the Jamaican death rate figure was for the population as a whole, including the elderly, paupers, those in workhouses, the infirm, and vulnerable infants, who died in large numbers. This was the population against which the cream of Afro-Caribbean labor fared badly. Yellow fever, malaria, tuberculosis, pneumonia, and ghastly injuries and deaths through accidents devastated the Black workforce in Panama.[137] And yet between January and March 1906, for instance, a span of merely three months, more than five thousand Jamaicans left the island for the isthmus. Jamaicans could have said the same of Panama that a British Caribbean migrant said of the Dominican Republic in 1899:

> Her Majesty's black and colored subjects in the West Indies . . . have to choose between death from starvation in their native islands and suffering ill-treatment in St. Domingo, where many have sought employment under the circumstances that their native islands are merely Islands of Death.[138]

But the Jamaican planter class was not going to be easily undermined by the lure of Panama. If it was impracticable to stop altogether the emigration of the workers, the ruling class was determined to make such migration difficult. From 1893, when the Emigrant Labourers' Protection Law was brought into being, the colonial state placed more and more obstacles in the way of would-be emigrants. The law of 1893 gave the governor the authority to declare any country he thought appropriate "a proclaimed place." A "proclaimed place" was one for which Jamaicans required a permit to emigrate. No permit, no emigration—at least no legal emigration. Naturally, Panama, other popular destinations such as Cuba and Costa Rica, became proclaimed places. The crucial clause of the law required the prospective emigrant to produce two persons with property worth ten pounds who agreed to repay any money that the government of Jamaica, British consular officials, or any other authorities in the proclaimed place spent to assist him or her.[139]

As the laborers desperately sought escape from the island, the authorities at the behest of the plantocracy made the laws against emigration increasingly draconian—in 1895, 1902, and 1904.[140] Even a member of Kingston's notoriously hard-hearted merchant class, A. N. Henriques, spoke out against the measures. Dr. J. Robert Love of the *Jamaica Advocate* was, as usual, on the job in no time. In an editorial written before the bill became law, he described it as "a damnable cut-throat law." It was. in his view, "an infernal piece of legislation . . . calculated to crush to earth the class upon which so much of the prosperity of the country depended."[141] Sir Alexander Swettenham, the governor of the island, told the U.S. secretary of war William Howard Taft and ICC officials, at a meeting in 1904, that local employers were "very jealous of emigration of able-bodied laborers," which probably explained his puzzlingly steadfast refusal to loosen the emigration laws despite official U.S. pleadings, concessions, and a commitment to cover the cost of any needed repatriation.[142] Jamaican workers and the poor would therefore be punished for their attempts to escape the island and its "tyranny of small wages."

Despite the obstacles placed in the Jamaican workers' path, traffic between the island and the isthmus was heavy and brisk, with approximately 170,000 people departing and 120,000 returning between 1882 and 1915. In 1912, the year McKay left for the United States, there began a new wave of migration to Cuba to partake in the "dance of the millions"—that island's spectacular boom in sugar production and profits in the early twentieth century. The authorities imposed even more punitive departure taxes, but the migration continued unabated.[143] There were many places that Jamaicans desired to be in preference to their native land in the late nineteenth and early twentieth centuries, and they were determined to leave. To many, it was a matter of life and death.

Jamaican Chiaroscuro: The Pride of Amended Blood

Our sketch of McKay's Jamaica would be incomplete without a few brush-strokes highlighting the place of "race" and color within the island's historical and social landscape. In fact, it is impossible to fully understand McKay's attitude to race and color without also understanding their prominent presence and role within Jamaican history and society.

In Jamaica, and the Americas more generally, the image of Africa and Africans was continuously and systematically maligned.[144] In the eyes of the slave owners, humanity was not only conceived to be congenitally hierar-chical—with the European in the superordinate position—but the African barely reached the lowest rung of the human species.

In the Caribbean, a complex hierarchy of human shades evolved in direct correspondence with this worldview. This in turn led one distin-guished scholar of the region to describe Caribbean societies as "multi-layered pigmentocracies."[145] Those who approximated most closely to the European type—in skin color, hair texture, facial characteristics, and so on—were accorded high status. Those who least resembled Europeans were relegated to the bottom of the social ladder. Thus the "coloureds" (those of "mixed" descent)—offspring of the union of Europeans (almost invariably men) and Africans (almost invariably women)[146]—were regarded as con-genitally superior to "pure Africans" (so-called "Negroes") and, moreover, were treated as such.[147]

Jamaican coloreds during the slavery era were frequently manumitted and, moreover, bequeathed substantial property and wealth by their slave-owning fathers. This transmission of economic resources into non-Euro-pean hands alarmed sections of the ruling class, who regarded the practice as dangerous. Thus, as early as 1761, after an inquiry by the Jamaican House of Assembly discovered that property already bequeathed to "freedmen"—people born into slavery but later manumitted, the vast majority of whom were "coloured"[148]—was valued at between £200,000 and £300,000, leg-islation was promptly enacted making it unlawful for whites to leave real or personal property worth more than £1,200 to any colored or Black per-son.[149] The law, however, like similar attempts elsewhere in the Americas, did not—nor was it meant to—undermine the relative material privilege of the coloreds over the Africans in the Caribbean pigmentocracy. The intention was to protect white privilege and superordination. Indeed, even when they were kept as slaves, the coloreds received preferential treat-ment and occupied "superior" positions in the slave hierarchy. They were granted greater opportunity to learn skills, which enabled them to become artisans—"the flower of the slave population," as one planter dubbed them—and many worked as house or domestic slaves, positions much sought after by slaves, male as well as female, in preference to the more arduous work and harsher regimen of the fields.[150] The color preference manifested itself early in the development of the slave system on the island. Even before the colored population became sizable, many of the enslaved Africans who were put to work as house slaves in Jamaica were the ostensi-bly lightskinned "Madagass" slaves—so called because they were imported from the island of Madagascar.[151] The pigmentocracy, then, operated not only at the level of ideology but also as a material force tightly joining color with class position and privilege, neatly overlapping, overlaying, and imbricating the two. As such, it generated and upheld the forced coincidence of color and class on the island that has endured to the present.

Profoundly race and color conscious, the ruling classes in Jamaican slave society generated a plethora of social types based on "race" and skin color. They designated and hierarchically structured these types in a conscious and thoroughly organized manner. In Jamaica and the other British colonies, for instance, the following categories obtained:[152]

Negro:	child of negro and negro
Sambo:	child of mulatto and negro
Mulatto:	child of white man and negress
Quadroon:	child of mulatto woman and white man
Mustee:	child of quadroon (or pure Amerindian) and white man
Mustiphini:	child of mustee and white man
Quintroon:	child of mustiphini and white man
Octoroon:	child of quintroon and white man

In the British Caribbean (with the sole exception of Barbados), one was designated legally white after the category of mustee and became automatically free.[153] Thus the expunging of "African blood"—"impure" blood—over a series of generations led to freedom. The Spanish were perhaps the most explicit about the process; they spoke of *limpieza de sangre*, the cleansing of the blood, underlining of the concatenation of blackness with servitude and whiteness with freedom.

But regardless of their location on the color ladder, nonwhites were never entirely free of the scorn and contempt of the white overlords. A white patroness of a ball in the Eastern Caribbean "strongly criticized" a British captain for having danced with a "costie," a person onesixteenth Black. She then provided the ignorant guest with a list of the various castes between mulattoes and costies, making clear to the transgressing newcomer that it simply would not do for an English officer to dance with a costie. This incident occurred two decades after the formal abolition of slavery in the British Caribbean.[154]

It was difficult to become "white" and humiliating to have been "un-white"—including being "colored" (even costie), not just "black." The coloreds were segregated, demeaned, and humiliated by the Europeans even after death: they had separate burial grounds from the whites, and church bells rang longer for the white deceased than the colored.[155] Despite all this, the coloreds had few qualms in pouring scorn upon their darker compatriots, including those legally free like themselves. According to planter-historian Edward Long, the coloreds

> despise the Blacks, and aspire to mend their complexion still more by inter-mixture with the Whites. The children of White and Quateron are called English, and consider themselves as free from all taint of the Negroe race. To call them by a degree inferior to what they really are, would be the highest affront. This pride of amended blood is universal, and becomes the more confirmed, if they have received any smattering of education; for then they look down with the more supercilious contempt upon those who have had none.[156]

Ostracized and scorned by the whites, the coloreds in turn ostracized and scorned those of dark complexion. They held spectacular balls from which the dark-skinned, but not whites, were excluded. They expressed their social insecurity by ruthlessly oppressing the enslaved in their possession, earning notoriety, even among the white plantocracy, for exceptional cruelty against slaves.[157] A common Jamaican saying among the African slaves reflected this state of affairs: "If me fe have massa or misses, give me a Buckra one—no give me mulatto, dem no use neega well."[158] According to Mrs. Carmichael, an upper-class British settler who lived in Jamaica and Trinidad, "To be sold to a colored owner is considered by a Negro to be an extreme misfortune."[159] After examining the dynamics among whites, mulattoes, and Africans in prerevo-lutionary Haiti, C. L. R. James declared in resigned exasperation: "It all reads like a cross between a nightmare and a bad joke."[160] His remarks apply with equal poignancy to the situation in Jamaica.

Understandably, the enslaved Africans and their descendants in Jamaica imbibed many of the values attributed to different human "types." Even though Jamaica was renowned for its relatively high retention of African cultural forms in the Americas, eighteenthcentury accounts testify to the contempt with which newly arrived Africans were often met by their "cre-ole" (locally born) counterparts. Some creole slaves referred derogatorily to Africans as "saltwater negroes" and "Guiney birds." "The one class," observed one contemporary commentator, "forced into slavery, humbled and degraded had lost everything and found no solace but the miserable one of retrospection. The other, born in slavery, never had freedom to lose;

yet did the Creole proudly assume a superiority over the African."[161] It was not always like this, but contempt was the general attitude of the creoles toward the Africans.[162]

Emancipation did little to change the color-class complex. Three centuries of African chattel slavery and pigmentocracy made colorism seem as entrenched and as deceptively natural as Jamaica's green hills. Banana uprooted vast plains of cane, cane that seemed as permanent as the hills, but what was there to uproot colorism? Given this history, it would have been miraculous if a subconscious element of selfdoubt, if not selfcontempt, had not afflicted the dark-skinned section of the population in slavery's aftermath. As Marx put it, "The tradition of the dead generations weighs like a nightmare on the minds of the living."[163]

McKay was not alone in complaining about these psychic and political wounds of European colonialism. "Colour is an asset too highly esteemed in Jamaica," observed a distinguished Black Jamaican, Rev. C. A. Wilson, in 1912.

> Clear skin and straight hair are amongst the best recommendations. Whilst Jamaica is not under the regime of the blind, wicked, unreasonable race prejudice of America, it is subjected to an irritating and silly caste system, which too often sees virtue in everything that has a touch of whiteness. Incorrect values are wantonly placed on men. To a nauseating extent does the idea prevail, that whatever pertains to the white man is good, that what is connected with the black man is evil, or of little consequence.[164]

"Black men here are never truly honoured," his compatriot, Marcus Garvey, told an African American visitor to the island four years later.[165] In contrast, "the mulatto has prestige, no matter how he happened to come by his light skin," as the sharp-eyed Zora Neale Hurston observed during her 1936 visit to the island. Hurston, an African American novelist and Columbia-trained anthropologist, noticed that "the system of honoring or esteeming [the mulatto's] approach to the Caucasian state is so elaborate that first, second, third and fourth degrees of illegitimacy are honored in order of their nearness to the source of whiteness." It reminded her of the French ambassador's boast in George and Ira Gershwin's 1931 musical, *Of Thee I Sing*: "She is the illegitimate daughter of the illegitimate son of the illegitimate nephew of the great Napoleon." By substituting the word Englishman for Napoleon, suggested Hurston, one captures the Jamaican malady.[166] In keeping with this outlook, Hurston also noted the erasure of blackness practiced by light-skinned Jamaicans. The Black mother is "literally and figuratively kept out of sight as far as possible, but no one is allowed to forget the white father, however questionable the circumstances of birth."

> You hear about "My father this and my father that, and my father who was English, you know," until you get the impression that he or she *had* no mother. Black skin is so utterly condemned that the black mother is not going to be mentioned nor exhibited. You get the impression that these virile English-men do not require women to reproduce. They just come out to Jamaica, scratch out a nest and lay eggs that hatch out into "pink" Jamaicans.[167]

Hence her description of Jamaica as the "rooster's nest," the land where "the rooster lays an egg."[168] Shocking though it was for Hurston, the phenomenon was familiar and unremarkable to Black Jamaicans. Indeed, some fifty years before Hurston's observations and a year before McKay was born, another Black Jamaican, J. H. Reid, noted drily: "A coloured man generally has no relatives on the mother's side."[169]

Writing a few years after Hurston, Eric Williams observed that among the Caribbean middle classes, "prospective brides look for lightskinned men. They pray for 'light' children, who might marry white. Expectant mothers abstain from coffee and chocolate. As the saying goes in Martinique, one who has reached the dining room should not go back to the kitchen."[170] But endeavors at lightening and whitening, such looking, praying, and abstaining, were by no means confined to Black women, as Williams unfairly implied; Black men were equally assiduous in their efforts to achieve such ends. Rev. Wilson noted: "A full-blooded Negro is sometimes silly enough to think he has made quite a step in advance when he turns up his nose at a well-trained, cultured girl of his own colour, and consorts with an incapable fair or white girl."[171] Garvey went so far as to claim that the "educated black gentleman" seeking a wife "generally marries a white woman."[172] The contagion of colorism was not only endemic but also agile enough to scale the walls of gender; indeed, the primary carriers of this disease were not the women, but the men, who possessed greater power than women in the choice of a spouse. The terrible truth is that the general societal line of march was toward white-ness. Long's two-centuries-old observation applied to McKay's Jamaica: No mulatto ever wished to "relapse into the Negro."[173] Here is a Jamai-can speaking to an American visitor some seven years after McKay's emigration:

The nigger always gets cocky when he is given either authority or encourage-ment. If I invite a negro to my house, the next thing I know he is proposing to my daughter and I have to kick him out, for in Jamaica the colored girl forever loses caste by marrying a black man. I would rather die than marry a negro woman.

The remarkable thing about the speaker was that, although he sounded like an unreconstructed white southern racist, he was in fact a "colored"—an "octoroon"—man, and proudly identified himself as such.[174] He confirmed Hurston's observation: "To avoid the consequences of posterity the mulattoes give the blacks a first class letting alone. There is a frantic stampede white-ward to escape from Jamaica's black mass."[175]

The internalization of the pigmentocracy did not, however, occur to the same depth and range among all Jamaicans. Those most affected by what Jamaican sociologist Fernando Henriques termed the "white bias" in Caribbean society were the urban colored and Black middle classes.[176] But they were not the only participants in the "frantic stampede white-ward." The colored and Black petit bourgeoisie were the most enthusiastic and energetic in the stampede, but the working class and even segments of the peasantry also took part.

* * *

This, then, was McKay's Jamaica: a society undergoing far-reaching, rapid, and bewildering economic and social changes; one characterized by deepen-ing class inequality; but also one in which the peculiar salience of color and its imbrication with class had stubbornly persisted in the postslavery period. A society in a protracted crisis, the simultaneous collapse of its sugar econ-omy and the continued monopolization of the land by the white ruling class had catastrophic repercussions on the mass of its inhabitants—unemploy-ment, poverty, destitution, sickness, and hunger. The peasants' hopes raised by the export market for banana and the rapid expansion of the cultivation of the fruit in the 1880s and 1890s quickly proved illusory and short-lived; the predatory capitalist activity—the type of fin de siècle practice that Lenin would later describe as "imperialism"—of Lorenzo Dow Baker's Boston Fruit Company and United Fruit Company saw to that.

The governing colonial caste, wedded as it was to the interest of the moribund plantocracy, proffered no solution to the crisis of the economy and the society. Instead, it tried to overcome the fiscal crisis by squeezing surplus out of the already impoverished Black population, getting blood out of a stone, as Rev. Henry Clarke put it. The plea from the weak for a fairer distribution of the land went unheeded and was later explicitly rebuffed when Joseph Chamberlain, a proud and overt white supremacist, became Britain's colonial secretary. This failure of governance was at the root of the Morant Bay uprising of 1865 and the progressive questioning of colonial authority in the ensuing period, including McKay's time in Jamaica.

This landscape formed the wider backdrop against which McKay gained his voice and emerged as the people's poet. His own deep and increasing awareness of the wider processes unfolding in Jamaica was one of the most remarkable qualities of the young McKay. Extraordinarily alive to the ways these developments impinged upon his own life and that of others, McKay gave sustained expression to his thoughts and feelings in his early poetry.

3

You Caan' Mek We Shet Up

McKay's Jamaican Poetry of Rebellion

A t'ink buccra ha' jawed enuff.

—Claude McKay, "Peasants' Ways o' Thinkin'," 1912

A Breaking Voice and "Peculiar Sensitiveness"

The twenty-two-year-old author of *Constab Ballads* wrote a charming and surprisingly self-disclosing preface to the volume. "Let me confess it at once," McKay began,

> I had not in me the stuff that goes to the making of a good constable; for I am so constituted that imagination outruns discretion, and it is my misfortune to have a most improper sympathy with wrongdoers. I therefore never "made cases," but turning, like Nelson, a blind eye to what was my manifest duty to see, tried to make peace, which seemed to me better.

He, moreover, possessed an "unadaptive" temperament, which meant that it was not in him to "conform cheerfully to uncongenial usages." Added to what he called the "natural impatience of his race"—identified as "we blacks"—was, in his particular case, "a peculiar sensitiveness which made certain forms of discipline irksome, and a fierce hatred of injustice." He never openly rebelled, but the rebellion was in his heart, "fomented by the inevitable rubs of daily life—trifles to most of my comrades, but to me calamities and tragedies."

To relieve his feelings, he wrote poems, and into them, McKay revealed to his readers, he "poured" his heart in its various moods. The book comprises a selection of those poems.[1]

The passage is especially striking in two ways. First, McKay gives the reader a sketch of his basic social outlook and temperament, an enlightening peep into his inner world and its turmoil. He not only tells about the rebellion of his heart but gives a glimpse of the heart itself. Second, when looking back at his life as a whole, one is struck by the uncannily consistent degree to which the self-portrait of 1912 would essentially remain true of the man for the remaining thirty-six years of his life, as if it were a declaration of intent, a credo to live by. McKay's "improper sympathy *with*" (note the preposition: not *for* but *with*) wrongdoers is one of the hallmarks of his work. Prostitutes, "good-hearted bums," vagabonds, and the motley outcasts of polite society inhabit with dignity all his novels and many of his poems, including two of his finest poems, "A Midnight Woman to the Bobby" and "Harlem Shadows," whose chief protagonists are prostitutes. Felice of *Home to Harlem* and Latnah of *Banjo* are also prostitutes; so are two of the leading characters in his novel *Romance in Marseille*. An arresting and unforgettable gallery of "wrongdoers"—living in Jamaica as well as in Harlem—appeared in his 1933 anthology of short stories, *Gingertown*.[2]

McKay's declaration that it is not in him to "conform cheerfully to uncongenial usages" would be echoed, almost verbatim, in his remarks to an ex-Trotskyist friend who had become a Cold Warrior in the 1940s. Although by that time he had partially renounced his Bolshevik—if not his socialist—past, McKay made clear that he would not allow himself to be used by either British or American imperialism.[3]

McKay talked of his "peculiar sensitiveness" and unaffectedly spoke of his "fierce hatred of injustice." These two motifs—the highly developed sensibilities of the poet and the battle against injustice—are among the most powerful in his work and life. He wrote of the rebellion in his heart "fomented" by what he euphemistically described as "the inevitable rubs of daily life." While the latter were "trifles" to most of his comrades in the constabulary, to him they were "calamities and tragedies." This was an expression of what he, groping naively toward self-knowledge, called his peculiar sensitiveness—the capacity to feel with extraordinary intensity and depth. Being exceedingly alive—to feel what others do not, perhaps too much for his own good—and the ability to give expression to those feelings were constants in McKay's life.

McKay's poems in *Constab Ballads* corroborate his preface. But a substantial number of his creole language poems were not explicitly political—or rather, not concerned with explicitly political subjects. McKay was primarily a lyric poet. However, he possessed an unusual range. Writing in the most wistful and delicate manner about childhood, nature, and rural life, he could, in the next breath, summon up a fiery ball of words, blazing with rage. Few poets had the ability to express with equal facility such different and contrasting moods—sorrow and happiness, rage and ecstasy. This rare ability, to give expression to a wide range of feelings, was noticed before he left Jamaica[4] and soon after his arrival in the United States in 1912. James Weldon Johnson, one of McKay's most discerning admirers, put it best. "Reading McKay's poetry of protest and rebellion, it is difficult," says Johnson,

> to imagine him dreaming of his native Jamaica and singing as he does in "Flame Heart" or creating poetic beauty in the absolute as he does in "The Harlem Dancer," "Spring in New Hampshire," and many another of his poems. Of the major Negro poets he, above all, is the poet of passion. That passion found in his poems of rebellion, transmuted, is felt in his love lyrics.[5]

Songs of Jamaica and *Constab Ballads* have been described as a diptych,[6] but this is somewhat misleading. The first volume contains fifty poems (plus an appendix of six poems put to music), the second twenty-eight. If these two volumes, published a few months apart in 1912, constitute a diptych, it must have been a rather lopsided one. This point is important because it is often said that *Constab Ballads* is the more militant, as it has fewer pastoral poems than the earlier volume. However, this is a rather superficial appraisal of the two volumes: *Constab Ballads* is not *Songs of Jamaica*'s counterpoint. *Songs of Jamaica* is far more varied in its preoccupation and tone than *Constab Ballads* because it contained many poems written before McKay joined the constabulary, alongside some written after he had entered the force.[7] This does not mean that the first volume is less "radical" and oppositional than the second. Instead, what is most noticeable in comparing the volumes is the remarkable level of continuity in their political outlook and narrative voice of protest.

Songs of Jamaica and *Constab Ballads* not only represent McKay's entry onto the literary stage, but they constitute—very much like the breaking voice of an adolescent boy—the young Jamaican's stammering but eloquent, maturing political voice. In these eighty-eight poems (including the ten others published in the press), McKay's lifelong concerns with race, color, class, justice and injustice, oppression, and revolt are given expression for the first time. We also see in these early poems McKay's feminist sympathies—which abided with him for the rest of his life—first publicly expressed. Indeed, two of his most accomplished poems in the volumes, "A Midnight Woman to the Bobby" (in *Songs of Jamaica*) and "The Apple-Woman's Complaint" (in *Constab Ballads*), are often read as documents of state oppression and class difference, ignoring the fact that they also constitute powerful works of protest against the oppression of women qua women. It is in these 1912 collections that the origins of McKay's most memorable fictional female characters—Latnah (of *Banjo*), Crazy Mary and Sue Turner (both of *Gingertown*), and Bita Plant (of *Banana Bottom*)—are to be found.

It is, however, undeniably the case that McKay directed his most spirited and eloquent protests against class (and thereby racial oppression) and racial oppression (and thereby class exploitation)—and the imbrication of the two in the Jamaica in which he lived. Our interest is not in the poems as such but in what they reveal about McKay's political thought and feelings: McKay threw in his lot with the Jamaican victims of oppression and exploitation—in particular, the peasantry and the urban poor of Spanish Town and Kingston, where he served as a policeman. True to his preface, the poems display, more than anything else, his "fierce hatred of injustice."

Shot through with moral outrage, the poems betray the distinctly oppositional views harbored by their author. They communicate McKay's social protest, his rebellion of the heart. But McKay's worldview contained discernible contradictions at that point in his life, tensions reflective of the social forces that penetrated his world and impinged upon his intellectual formation. McKay left no doubt in his reader's mind as to what he was *against*, the objects of his social protest. But as to what he was *for*, McKay was less helpful, primarily because he himself was uncertain. Perhaps it is to expect too much of McKay, or any artist, to present a clear alternative to the object of his social criticism. Some, even on the left, have argued that the proffering of alternatives is not and should not be any of the artist's business.[8]

On the face of it, McKay juxtaposes the rural and the urban, with the rural generally depicted positively and the urban environment as an alien, somewhat forbidding, almost diabolical world. But closer inspection reveals that McKay's views of country life were not entirely positive, nor was he entirely dismissive of urban life. At a more prescriptively ideological level, one finds more than a hint of Fabianism in his work from this time— gradual social reform within the existing capitalist framework. *Songs of Jamaica*, McKay's first book, was dedicated in the most adulatory manner to the island's governor and former secretary of the Fabian Society, Sir Sydney Olivier. Nonetheless, McKay's protest was far more radical, unambiguous, and vivid than any vision he might have had of an alternative to the status quo. He was still searching ideologically.

This observation is further supported by some of the other contradictions in the young Jamaican's thought as expressed in *Songs of Jamaica*. Here was the Schopenhauerian intellectual pessimist with the rebel heart of the optimist; here was one of the island's first nationalists declaring his love for the "mother country," Britain; here was the proud African espousing social Darwinism. Granted, there were distinctive tendencies in the movement of his thought—increasingly anticapitalist, anticolonial, and antiracist—but also these far from trivial contradictions. One of the challenges of this work is to account for them.

Jamaica's problems of social class, color, race, and gender are intertwined and permeate these verses. McKay's poems, however, possess identifiable themes by which they may be profitably ordered and engaged.

The Struggling Peasant

McKay possessed a detailed and intimate knowledge and a sympathetic view of the world of the peasant, a world with which he identified all his life. The turbulence of his Jamaican world is chronicled, reflected, analyzed, and interpreted in his poems.

Songs of Jamaica appropriately opens with a direct and especially forceful poem, "Quashie to Buccra." Quashie and buccra represent opposite ends—bottom and top—of Jamaica's social hierarchy. Quashie—the black country bumpkin, the peasant, the subaltern—occupied the base of the pyramid, while buccra—the white man, the symbol of power, the oppressor—occupied its apex.[9] Quashie is giving buccra a piece of his mind:

> You tas'e petater an' you say it sweet,
> But you no know how hard we wuk fe it;
> You want a basketful fe quattiewut'
> 'Cause you no know how 'tiff de bush fe cut.[10]

The peasant complains that the white man simply devours the fruits of his labor without a thought to the effort put into their cultivation. Moreover, there is the constant haggle over the price, the persistent attempt to get the sweet potato for as little as possible—a "basketful fe quattiewut." The peasant enlightens buccra about the hardship involved in growing the potato—the prickly plants that he has to negotiate and clear with his cutlass, enduring the prolonged, merciless, roasting rays of the sun ("hot like when fire ketch a town") and the predations of the neighbor's pig, borne without complaint "sake o' we naybor tongue." But though he suffers, and *because* he sacrifices so much, he is proud of his work.[11] McKay is revealing the difficult production process, as it were, of the sweet potato as a commodity, a commodity that the rich whites consume with greed and nonchalance from their wide China plates. Thus, Quashie provides buccra (and the reader) with an overview of the life cycle of this commodity, the role of labor power in the process of its creation—the harsh and unsparing regimen of preparing the soil, the cultivation and care of the plant—accompanied by sacrifice and suffering. In so doing, McKay reveals the role and value of labor in the whole enterprise as well as how the peasants are cheated of their hard work through buccra's merciless battering down of the already meager prices for their crop.

The peasant's troubles are also aired in "Hard Times":

> De mo' me wuk, de mo' time hard,
>   I don't know what fe do;
> I ben' me knee an' pray to Gahd,
>   Yet t'ings same as befo'.[12]

His wife is sick, he cannot pay his taxes, and for this he is stalked by the bailiff ("I hear de bailiff's v'ice"). His children went to school without a "bite fe taste," despite the fact that he has worked "like a mule, / While buccra, sittin in de cool, / Hab 'nuff nenyam [food] fe waste." On top of the inequalities, the crops are failing: "De peas won't pop, de corn can't grow." No wonder "Poor people face look sad." Yet there is the flinty perseverance of the peasant: "I won't gib up, I won't say die."[13]

The inequalities seen from the peasant's point of view are also powerfully represented in "Fetchin' Water," where the (white) tourists are being observed gazing and thinking that the rigors of peasant life are somehow exotic. "But I can tell you say, / 'Nuff rock'tone in de sea, yet none / But those 'pon lan' know 'bouten sun."[14] The boy coming up the hill with a gourd full of water is also the target of the tourists' gaze. The boy feels the "weight," the burden of the load, while the tourists "watch him gait." No doubt admiring the boy's "natural" balance, his "natural" rhythm, the tourists are blind to the boy's suffering: "It's so some of de great / High people fabour t'ink it sweet / Fe batter in de boilin' heat."[15]

The hardship of the life of the peasant child is also graphically depicted in "Retribution," where the boys are required to catch the mules and the donkeys before nightfall—not an easy task: "for de whole o' dem [donkeys and mules] can run," and the field is the fiercely guarded kingdom of formidable grass lice:

> Grass-lice dat mek you trimble long time more
>   dan when you meet
> A man dat mean to fight you who you know you
>   cannot beat;
> Dem mek you feel you' blood crawl from you' head
>   do'n to you' feet . . .[16]

There is no tongue-in-cheek humor in "Two-an-Six," one of McKay's finest poems. Here we have pathos, relieved only at the very end by a ray of hope. In no less than fifteen stanzas and 136 lines, McKay describes a day in the life of a peasant, Cous' Sun. It is not an ordinary day, it is "Sateday," a market day. He gets up early: "de light shine from de moon," and "de cocks crow on de hill / An' de stars are shinin' still."[17] He and his wife have six children. He's off to market with his produce and a lot on his mind—how to endure, how to survive, despite the backbreaking work.[18] It is a bad day for sellers of sugar—it is going at "tup and gill" (two and three-quarter pence) per quart. And despite the fact that the tyrannous market for sugar is already ruling in their favor, the buyers still take advantage:

> . . . de people hab de heart
> Wantin' brater top o' i',
> Want de sweatin' higgler fe
> Ram de pan an' pile i' up,
> Yet sell i' fe so-so tup.[19]

In fact, it turns out that sugar was selling for only "two-an-six" (two shillings and six pence) per tin. Dejected, Cous' Sun made his way home without even making the usual stop at the candy store to buy the children sweetmeats; he had nothing to spare. When he reached home,

> . . . de children scamper roun',
> Each one stretchin' out him han',
> Lookin' to de poor sad man.
> Oh, how much he felt de blow,
> As he watched dem face fall low,
> When dem wait an' nuttin' came
> An' drew back deir han's wid shame![20]

His wife kissed and consoled him. She was determined to

> Cut an' carve, an' carve an' cut,
> Mek gill sarbe fe quattiewut';
> We mus' try mek two ends meet
> Neber mind how hard be it.
> *We* won't mind de haul an' pull,
> While dem pickny belly full.[21]

Sun's spirits lifted. He and his wife got down to the business of reckoning the day's takings against their outlay. They discovered that "A'ter all de business fix', / Was a princely two-an-six."[22]

The realism of this poem is corroborated by the anthropological research conducted by Martha Beckwith in Jamaica in the 1920s. She reported the chorus of what the peasants call a "hard time" song that is remarkably similar to McKay's poetry. It is even possible that McKay's poetry influenced the tune:

> Annotto can't sell, the price is unfair,
> Pimento a blossom and drop.
> Hard time, hard time,
> Hard time a carry the day.
> Hard time, hard time,
> For they won't put cramouchin' [grudging] away.[23]

In "Whe' Fe Do?" we have the clearest evidence of the poet's debt to Arthur Schopenhauer. The poem's narrator reviews the troubles and pain of peasant life and finds no way out—it is simply the way of the world, about which nothing can be done. Hence the title and refrain "Whe' Fe Do?" What *can* we do? It is, in this context, a rhetorical question.

We've got to wuk wid might an' main,
To use we han' an use we brain,
To toil an' worry, 'cheme an' 'train
Fe t'ings that bring more loss dan gain;
To stan' de sun an' bear de rain,
An' suck we bellyful o' pain
Widouten cry nor yet complain—
            For dat caan' do.

He vows to struggle on, to

        fight de wul' de best we can,
        E'en though it hard fe understan'
            Whe' we mus' do.

        For da's de way o' dis ya wul';
        It's snap an' bite, an' haul an' pull,
        An' we all get we bellyful "
            But whe' fe do?[24]

"Whe' Fe Do?" is the most pessimistic of McKay's Jamaican poems and indeed, with perhaps one exception,[25] the most despairing of the poet's entire oeuvre.

Arthur Schopenhauer was one of Walter Jekyll's favorite thinkers. *The Wisdom of Schopenhauer as Revealed in Some of His Writings*, a fine tome of Schopenhauer's writings, edited, translated, and introduced by Jekyll from his redoubt in the hills above Kingston, is just one indication of the esteem in which the Englishman held the German philosopher. Although McKay had made an earlier acquaintance with Schopenhauer through U. Theo's library, Jekyll undoubtedly deepened his knowledge and appreciation of Schopenhauer's philosophy. Indeed, in *A Long Way from Home*, McKay recalled that during his early acquaintance with him, Jekyll was translating Schopenhauer and he "read a lot of his translation."[26]

"Life is a task to be worked off," Schopenhauer declared, "in this sense *defunctus* is a fine expression."[27] Human existence was a synonym for "work, worry, toil, and trouble."[28] According to Schopenhauer—who ranks among the most broody and melancholic philosophers—were it not for necessity and the intense pleasure derived from sex, it is doubtful that human beings would want to reproduce themselves as a species because of the inherent suffering that constitutes the task of life: Were procreation "a matter of pure rational deliberation," would not, Schopenhauer asked, "everyone feel so much sympathy for the coming generation that he would prefer to spare it the burden of existence, or at any rate would not like to assume in cold blood the responsibility of imposing on it such a burden?"[29] Human existence is "a uselessly disturbing episode in the blissful repose of nothingness. At all events even the man who has fared tolerably well, becomes more clearly aware, the longer he lives, that life on the whole is *a disappointment, nay a cheat*, in other words, bears the character of a great mystification or even a fraud."[30] In fact, the whole business of living was much worse than disappointing: "The world is just a *hell* and in it human beings are the tortured souls on the one hand, and the devils on the other."[31]

McKay described Jekyll as a pessimist who thought that the world could not be reformed, and Jekyll's worldview coincided with and was strongly influenced by that of his hero, Schopenhauer. But McKay's cheerless philosophy in "Whe' Fe Do?" cannot be entirely attributed to his encounter with Schopenhauerian philosophy through Jekyll's ideology or his own reading of the German philosopher's work. Two other sources of such thought existed. One was the worldview of the peasants themselves: the fatalism in relation to natural disasters such as storms and hurricanes, floods and droughts, which were not infrequent visitors to the island, especially when McKay lived there.[32] This experience, combined with elements of Christian ideology, would have given Jamaican peasants and workers a rather hardened and somewhat pessimistic view of the whole business of life. Second, there were affinity and homology between the conjuncture within which McKay wrote and Schopenhauer's melancholic philosophy. When McKay wrote these poems, the Jamaican people, as we have seen, were experiencing unspeakable hardship, with little prospect of relief. The moment harmonized with a philosophy of despair. For the overwhelming majority of peasants and workers, Jamaica *was* a hellish place—a place very much like Schopenhauer's world, where understandably poor people put their hands on their head, look to the heavens and ask the gods in despair: "Whe' fe do?"

But although Schopenhauerian motifs may be found from time to time in McKay's writings in exile, in general such pessimism was fundamentally at odds with his personality and outlook on life. Over the years, McKay endured sadness, sorrow, and loneliness in the most intense forms, but he never committed himself to a philosophy of melancholy and disillusionment with life and the world. He loved life and reveled in the adventure of living. From time to time he slipped into desperately dark moods of despair—hardly surprising given his sensitive nature and the horrors of the world and times in which he lived, especially as a man of African descent. He privately bemoaned the fact that "the really fine people in this world are so few and *so powerless* that sometimes one is seized with a fit of despair in contemplating life."[33] But McKay also knew how to climb out of these troughs, how to laugh—and laugh heartily. Max Eastman, his close friend, spoke about the "ironical and mischievous" side of the man. In a biographical sketch (as revealing about himself as about McKay), Eastman wrote: "His laughter at the frailties of his friends and enemies, no matter which—that high, half-wailing falsetto laugh of the recklessly delighted Darky—was the center of my joy in him throughout our friendship of more than thirty years."[34] McKay, partly because of his appreciation of the transient and unpredictable nature of life, also had more than a little sympathy for hedonism; *Home to Harlem* and *Banjo* make that clear. For him, joy, not just sorrow, were to be found on this side of the grave. Like Jake, the protagonist of his novel *Home to Harlem*, "sometimes he was disgusted with life, but he was never frightened of it."[35] His characteristic posture was a combination of defiance and struggle, not despair and resignation.

Accordingly, McKay's peasant and proletarian world was not all hardship and struggle. The world of peasants and workers was also one of community, of an ordered pattern of existence (albeit one increasingly disturbed by the expansion of agrarian capitalism), of camaraderie and systems of mutual support, as well as of gossip, quarrel, inequality, and praedial larceny. McKay hardly said a negative word about the Jamaican peasantry. We would have to wait some thirty years before some of the unpleasant aspects of peasant life would be critically interrogated. For the moment, McKay's rural folk would only be censured, half-jokingly, for being "too bad" and for believing in "obeah"—and then it was not specifically the peasantry but Black people in general, "naygur," who were criticized.[36] After McKay joined the police force in 1910 and worked in Spanish Town and Kingston, exposed to the harshness of urban life as an enforcer of the law, not even these mild criticisms would escape his lips. His Clarendon hills would become his rural idyll.

Cleave to the Black: On Black Solidarity

In *My Green Hills of Jamaica*, written in the premature evening of his life (roughly a year before he died), McKay vividly recalled his first visit to

Kingston as a child accompanied by U. Theo's wife. He was struck by the size of the city, "so many times larger than the little village where my brother taught school." His sister-in-law had gone to the city to shop, and they visited its main thoroughfares.[37] He remembered going to the stores on Harbour Street, King Street, and Orange Street. "I gazed with wonder at the stores, thinking they were so large and beautiful. Years later I was just as over-whelmed and bewildered when I first arrived in New York City." It was on one of these visits to Kingston that he had his first ice cream, which he liked, even though it "played havoc" with his front teeth, and "snowball"—shaved ice with plenty of syrup poured onto it.

McKay also remembered that on his first trip to Kingston he vomited on the train when the trees "seemed to be rushing by, as we rode along." They "turned my stomach," he said. His sister-in-law scolded him for vomiting. He could not eat lunch on the train, "but when I got off and we drove through the city I was so excited that I did not care about eating."[38] Thus we have the beginnings of McKay's fascination with cities. Over the years, as he traveled in the United States, Europe, and North Africa, McKay grew to love some cities more than others, but he developed a strange and powerful attraction to urban life in general that abided with him for the rest of his days.

Critics have frequently misread McKay's views of cities and registered what they consider to be his negative posture toward them at the expense of noticing the enormous thrill that he also got from them—especially large cities, such as New York. They miss the nuance and ambivalence toward cities and urban life. "Hatred of the city," reads a typical commentary, "is one of the principal motifs in McKay's Jamaican poems, and the American poems will offer variations on the same theme."[39] McKay's rich and complex response to cities is lost in such a remark. It may be legitimately asked how critics such as Jean Wagner square McKay's supposed "antipathy for the city"[40] with, for example, this passage evoking his feelings and thoughts as his ship approaches New York harbor on McKay's return from Europe in 1921:

Like fixed massed sentinels guarding the approaches to the great metropolis, again the pyramids of New York in their Egyptian majesty dazzled my sight like a miracle of might and took my breath like the banging music of Wag-ner assaulting one's spirit and rushing it skyward with the pride and power of an eagle.

The feeling of the dirty steerage passage across the Atlantic was swept away in the immense wonder of clean, vertical heaven-challenging lines, a glory to the grandeur of space.

Oh, I wished that it were possible to know New York in that way only—as a masterpiece wrought for the illumination of the sight, a splendor lifting aloft and shedding its radiance like a searchlight, making one big and great with feeling. Oh, that I should never draw nearer to descend into its precipitous gorges, where visions are broken and shattered and one becomes one of a million, average, ordinary, insignificant.[41]

Wagner, who was a thorough researcher, must have known better. His notes on McKay[42]—made during the research for his book—included the opening poem to a remarkable anthology that McKay entitled "Cities."

Oh cities are a fever in my blood,
And all their moods find lodgement in my breast,
Whether they sweep me onward like a flood
Or torture me as an unwanted guest,
With wormwood flavoring my scanty foods,
I love all cities, I love their changing moods.
I love all cities, I love their foreign ways,
Their tyranny over the life of man,
Their wakeful nights and never-resting days,
Their mighty movements seeing without plan,
Their pavement stones on which the broken fall,
Their damning wickedness: I love it all.[43]

It should perhaps come as no surprise that this poem is nowhere to be found in Wagner's book—neither in the original French nor in the English edition—nor is it even referred to.[44] The poem certainly would not sit well under the section of Wagner's discussion entitled "Rejection of the City," and clearly it is incongruent with the bald thesis "Hatred of the city is one of the principal motifs in McKay's . . . poems." In reality, McKay's attitude toward cities was always ambivalent, but he loved them more than he hated them.

The foregoing is aimed at bringing into focus the questionable orthodoxy in McKay criticism on the poet's alleged hatred of cities. This erroneous, or at best distorted, view of his response to the urban environment has obfuscated an important dimension of McKay's Jamaican poetry. McKay's poems set in Kingston and Spanish Town while in the constabulary are traditionally read primarily as documents against urban life in general, and that of Kingston in particular. But a more careful reading of these poems reveals that McKay's time in Spanish Town and Kingston cannot be separated from his experience in the police force. On closer inspection, one finds that poems that have been viewed as writings about Kingston are in fact less about Kingston per se than about the experience of a reluctant Black policeman serving in Jamaica in 1910 and 1911. In other words, McKay's Kingston would have been a very different place had he not been in uniform, not seen it on the beat, so to speak. His policeman's badge and duty gave him access to forms of life in the city that he otherwise would not have encountered, and certainly not with the same degree of frequency and depth of familiarity. Indeed, prior to his entering the police force, all of his references to Kingston were favorable ones.

Before the 1907 earthquake, McKay very much enjoyed his stay in Kingston. He had no complaints. "The change from the hills of Clarendon to the city of Kingston was stupendous," he said. His cousin, with whom he lodged for part of his stay in the city, looked after him well and saw to it that he had a good time. "My cousin knew many of the better class girls from the villages who were working in Kingston as clerks and maids. They all came to his apartment and of course I was impressed by their stylish dress and hairdo. We went to concerts in Queen Victoria Park and to the beaches where we swam."[45] Not surprisingly, McKay wanted to remain in Kingston, but the earthquake's destruction of the trade school and its thorough mangling of the city's infrastructure meant that he had to find a tradesman in the countryside for his training. Disappointed that he was not able to stay, McKay was reluctant to leave the city even after the devastation: "I wanted to stay in Kingston for a year because I liked the glamour of the city, and I thought that in the meantime I could find what trade I wanted to take up."[46] McKay summed up this period of his stay in Kingston: "I was very happy."[47]

How do we reconcile these words with the poetry in Songs of Jamaica and Constab Ballads? The reconciliation is relatively straightforward, but only if we step outside of the poems themselves and examine them in their proper context. In marked contrast to the young, aspiring apprentice that he was when he first moved to Kingston in 1907, McKay was in 1910 a policeman, a hated "red seam," as the peasants (alluding to their uniform) derisively dubbed members of the constabulary. And McKay himself, as we shall see, found his job utterly detestable. His poems in Constab Ballads are directed far more against the police than against Kingston as such. These poems were not entitled "urban blues," partly because they were not, but they could easily be described as "constab blues." The poems tell of the hypocrisy of the police force ("Papine Corner," "The Apple-Woman's Complaint");[48] of the class snobbery and abuse of power in the force ("Pay Day," "Flat-Foot

Drill," "The Apple-Woman's Complaint," "A Labourer's Life Give Me");[49] of petty corruption in the force ("A Recruit on the Corpy," "The Bobby to the Sneering Lady");[50] of mindless callousness ("De Dog-Driver's Frien' ").[51] But these poems also tell of the incidental friendship and camaraderie that developed in the force, especially in the early part of his tenure.[52]

The most valuable aspect of these poems in understanding McKay's political evolution is that in them the young poet expresses, even more explicitly than in the earlier poems in *Songs of Jamaica*, his identification with the Black oppressed, including Kingston's Black poor. His unhappy experience in the force pushed him to what we may call, for want of a better expression, an openly Black nationalist position, in which he identified with the Black masses of Jamaica—with those who in Jamaican (as opposed to American) parlance would be described as Black or Negro, as opposed to colored or mixed. These were, literally, the darkest members of the nonwhite population. Such people, as discussed earlier, crowded the lowest rung of the social ladder. Thus, to identify with this group also meant identifying with an economic category or class—Black working people, and more generally the Black poor in the city and the countryside, the peasantry and agro-proletarians or agricultural laborers. One therefore has the conceptual linking, indeed imbrication, of race and class in the thought of the young McKay, reflective of the social structure sketched earlier. This connection with the Black populace is brought out most forcefully in "The Bobby to the Sneering Lady" and in "The Heart of a Constab."

In "The Bobby to the Sneering Lady," the narrator, a policeman, who very well might have been Constable McKay himself, is called to the home of a white or light-skinned upper-middle-class Kingstonian, who wants the police to arrest "her" dark-skinned servant girl (for reasons unspecified in the poem) even though she has already beaten the girl. The policeman tells the woman that although he is an enforcer of the law, he has feelings too. He refuses to arrest the girl: "Our soul's jes' like fe you, / If our work does make us rough; / Me won't 'res' you servant-gal / When you've beaten her enough."[53]

The woman wrongly accuses the Bobby of being the girl's friend and threatens to report him for refusing to arrest her. The policeman acknowledges that his inspector is "flinty hard" and that he would lose a "few days' pay" or be locked in a cell were she to lodge a complaint against him. Nevertheless, such "pains and losses" are nothing new to him; he has been fined heavily in the past for petty violations of the police code of conduct. His superiors are keen and zealous in the imposition of fines, as such fines are used to build up the reward fund—out of which rewards are ostensibly given to constables for meritorious work.[54] But the policeman sticks to his guns; he will not be disloyal to his "own" poor Black people: "Ef our lot, then, is so hard, / I mus' ever bear in mind / Dat to fe me own black 'kin / I mus' not be too unkind."[55]

In "The Heart of a Constab," the narrator sorrowfully and regretfully reflects upon the heavy personal price he has paid for joining the police force. He feels the pain of his rejection by those whom he regards as his people; he hates that he has effectively betrayed them by taking a job "Where I mus' be hard on me own kith an' kin, / And even to frien' mus' prove foe." He had entered the force with honest intentions, to carry out "pure honest toil"; the experience proved otherwise: "But no, de life surely is bendin' me do'n, / Is bendin' me do'n to de death." He is trapped in a deep and lonely vortex of despair. Most agonizing of all is his own people's rejection of him: " 'Tis grievous to think dat, while toilin' on here, / My people won't love me again, / My people, my people, me owna black skin, / De wretched t'ought gives me such pain." Desperate to be one with his people again, he resolves to do the right thing, to follow his conscience and leave the force—"though flow'rs here should line my path"—to save himself: "For 'tis hatred without an' 'tis hatred within, / An' how can I live 'douten [without] heart? / Then oh for de country, de love o' me soul, / From which I shall nevermore part!"[56]

"I . . . joined the Jamaican Constabulary . . . despised it and left," McKay wrote years later.[57] His 1932 anthology of short stories, *Gingertown*, contains an incongruous, hybrid, and remarkable text called "When I Pounded the Pavement." Not strictly fiction, not straight autobiography either, written in a direct first-person singular, it stands in sharp contrast to the other eleven stories in the volume. The story is based on his experience in the force and is substantially autobiographical. It tells of a sensitive Black policeman trying to withstand the pressure to "make cases"—arrest, charge, prosecute, win conviction—however unjustly they may be made. The protagonist yearns to leave the force without making a case: "Nothing could please me more and my peasant friends and relatives who abhorred my profession."[58] The peasants' attitude to the police is described and explained:

> As a son of peasants, I also had in my blood the peasant's instinctive hostility for police people. In spite of night marauders who rifled their fields and stole chickens and goats, the peasants liked the police less than the thieves. When the thieves were caught, it was invariably the peasants who did themselves and brought them to justice. The "red seams"—so the peasants called the

uniformed police—always distinguished themselves in other ways that were hateful to the peasants. They always butted in on family feuds and quarrels and made arrests when such troubles might have been easily settled by our old heads. And on popular marketing days, mostly Saturdays, when the peasants crowded the towns with their stuff, drinking rum and making merry with the rough obscene vocabulary of the fields, the uniformed police would pounce on them for disorderly conduct and thus take most of the money they made out of their pockets.[59]

One of the narrator's friends and fellow policemen was also put under pressure for not having made a case. He quickly made one in order to get his superiors off his back:

My friend had made his case by the easiest opportunity that came to him. While he was on his beat he was accosted by a street girl that we both used to visit in common. She teased him a little for doing patrol duty, and he arrested her for "obstructing a constable on his duty." The girl had thought it was all a joke. But when the court fined her ten shillings with twenty-one days imprisonment, her smiling turned to a terrible howling.[60]

This was more than the narrator could bear: "The last thread of feeling attaching me to the place had snapped and all my desire now was to get out and away from it."[61]

In "When I Pounded the Pavement," McKay deftly illustrates the manner in which the Black police were used to stifle Black advancement. Mr. Klinger, a white official working in the colonial bureaucracy in Kingston, used the Black police constable to arrest the lover of his female domestic servant. At Klinger's insistence, the policeman arrived at his home early and unobtrusively. The policeman hid and waited until the "intruder" was in the maid's shed at the back of the house. The lover, a Black man, duly apprehended while in bed with the servant girl, was arrested on grounds of illegally trespassing. It turned out that this man was a candidate for the Legislative Chamber. "I learned later that his opponent, a European, was a friend of Mr. Klinger's; some said he was even a relative." The narrator continued:

I had to arrest him. He dressed himself and I took him to the lock-up. The next day his father bailed him out. And he was front-page news, photograph and all. When the case was tried he received a maximum sentence. Six months in prison and twenty-one strokes of the tamarind switch. Convicted as a common criminal, his political career was broken. But I think that what broke him most of all was the switch. Policemen holding him down on a block and taking down his pants and whipping him for sleeping with a girl.

It was my first and last case. Before I could make another I managed to obtain my discharge from the constabulary.[62]

Experiences such as this in the police force, however fictionalized, honed McKay's Black nationalist consciousness and sensibilities.

The realism of McKay's portrait of the callousness of the force and its oppression of poor Black people, at the instigation of colonial officials, is amply buttressed by contemporary reports in the Jamaican press. The following, for example, was carried without comment by the *Gleaner* in 1913: "Charged with trading on the Lord's Day—selling curios to tourists on Sunday last, David Roberts was in the Police Court yesterday fined 5 [shillings] or 7 days [in jail]. He was prosecuted by Sergt.-Major Black who asked that he be made an example of."[63] The fine of five shillings amounted to more than a week's wage for a highly skilled worker at the time. Roberts probably had to spend seven days in jail, and the jails were notorious for their inhumane conditions.

The authorities were determined to see to it that tourists to the island were not inconvenienced in any way. Thus, Thomas Campbell was arrested in Kingston for begging from tourists. Without money for a lawyer and without the authorities providing legal counsel, he represented himself in court. He explained that he was from the country, a recent arrival in the city, and did not know it was illegal to beg. "You are a perfect pest to the unfortunate people [the tourists]," Justice Burke told Campbell and sentenced him to six strokes of the tamarind switch. In the same session of the police court, Burke fined Jacob Jones ten shillings and six pence or fourteen days in jail for using indecent language in the presence of tourists.[64]

Then there was the case of John Hylton:

Piloted by a "limb of the law," John Hylton, a blind old man, found his way into the Police Court dock yesterday forenoon, to answer a charge of soliciting alms.

Hylton, who is well known in Kingston, has for a good many years been deprived of his sight, and thus depends on charity for daily sustenance. Not long ago, in his wanderings around the city seeking alms, Hylton used to be guided by a faithful member of the canine tribe which, with a string attached to its neck and held by its blind master, would lead him safely out of danger.

The dog has died and now Hylton depends on his stick and the kind assistance of more fortunate folks.

On Saturday last, Hylton was in King Street, where he hailed each passer with his usual cry: "Pity the blind." Constable McEwan was nearby and he was called upon by one of his superior officers to take the man in charge. The crowd which gathered was a sympathetic one and there were cries of "Shame!" but the law had to be carried out.

The magistrate was just as kind-hearted as the officer who ordered the arrest and the policeman who made it. When the case was brought up, a Mr. Lake spoke up on behalf of Mr. Hylton. He had known Hylton for a number of years and he thought it "pretty hard to expect a man who had lost his sight and had no means of getting support to do anything beside seeking alms." Lake thought that "if His Honour admonished and discharged the defendant, he would be sufficiently punished." But the magistrate said that he would remand Hylton in custody for "a few days," and so Mr. Hylton was sent to jail.[65] Far from being aberrations, the cases of David Roberts, Thomas Campbell, and John Hylton are merely a few of many similar experiences endured by the poor at the hands of the Jamaica Constabulary and the colonial judicial system.

McKay's anguished days in the police force haunted him and lingered in his memory. Some twenty years after leaving the constabulary, he confessed to a friend that "being a cop, even though it was for a short time, was one of the few things that I ever did that I profoundly regretted."[66] Small wonder, then, that in subsequent years McKay was, whether consciously or unconsciously, uncharacteristically less than frank when it came to disclosing how long he had served as a policeman. The rather self-servingly vague "1910–11," mentioned in 1918 in his first autobiographical sketch after immigrating to the United States, which could mean anything from a month to two years, was the nearest he got to an accurate answer. In 1923, the Russian translator of *Negroes in America*, who received his information from McKay himself, wrote that the poet had worked for the police as a "clerk" "for a whole year." (Did he not work in any other capacity for an additional period? Did McKay shorten his time and minimize his role in the force out of added embarrassment before the Bolsheviks, hardly the best friends of the colonial police force?) By 1927, he had shaved down his tenure in the force to ten months, which perhaps led James Weldon Johnson to write in 1931 that McKay served "almost a year" in the Jamaica Constabulary. A decade later, in his autobiography, McKay claimed that he served a year. But that was in a context in which he was at pains to show that, because of his experience as a cop, he knew how to "nose out a secret agent whether he is red or white." Finally, in his last statement on the subject, which appeared in *My Green Hills*, McKay was once again vague, but the suggestion of ten months reappears.[67]

So what are we to believe? Instead of the ten months he suggested, McKay in fact spent almost twice as long as a constab—seventeen months, to be precise.[68] Unable to erase or disown completely his policeman's past, McKay had been sufficiently revolutionized by the experience that he became acutely ashamed of and embarrassed by it. Finding it impossible to deny, McKay, probably more subconsciously than consciously, sought to shorten the episode of his life as a colonial cop.

In a similar effort, by, as he put it, "frankly writing" the story of "When I Pounded the Pavement," McKay boldly claimed: "I have expiated." But he was far too sensitive a person to effect such an easy expiation. He was, however, able to recognize that although he "loathed" it, "the experience was interesting." Being a policeman provided him with the opportunity of "studying the type of mind that exists solely to make trouble for others because it fattened on that. And also," he continued, "it serve[d] me well to estimate and understand the same type among different peoples."[69]

A final note: There is a striking incongruity between the note of dedication in *Constab Ballads* and the content of the book itself. The note reads: "To / Lieut. Col. A. E. Kershaw, / Inspector-General of Constabulary, / and to / Inspector W. E. Clark, / Under Whom the Author had / The Honour of Serving, / This Volume is / Respectfully and Gratefully Dedicated." It appears, at least from McKay's own explanation given in private correspondence, that the dedication was the combined result of manipulation on the part of Jekyll, the sponsor of the volume, calculated Realpolitik, and genuine regard. "I never could stand this book [*Constab Ballads*]," McKay wrote,

> because for one thing it was dedicated to the Inspector General whom we all (constabs) disliked. But the Englishman [Jekyll] who sponsored the publication thought it was "good taste" to give the Inspector General the dedication especially as he was trying to get my discharge from the service. I wanted the dedication to go solely to Inspector Clark whom we all liked.[70]

McKay and his colleagues did have a genuine fondness for Clark. The new recruits suffered more directly at the hands of the lower-ranking officers, especially the drill sergeants, a number of whom were apparently confused and cruel light-skinned men who had nothing but contempt for the dark-skinned beat policemen—described by a visitor to the island as "virtually all jet black"—who came mainly from the countryside.[71] The poem "Flat-Foot Drill" depicts the verbal abuse that the raw recruits suffered at the hands of these colored underlings of empire. It presents the barked admonishments and insults of the Black recruits by a drill instructor. To the instructor, the recruits are hopelessly stupid and clumsy.

The attack upon the "class" background of the country recruits becomes even more brutal and dense:

> "Right tu'n, you damn' bungo brut'!
> Do it *so*, you mountain man;
> Car' behin' de bluff lef' foot,
> Seems i' frighten fe de boot!
> Why you won't keep do'n you' han'?"

The ferocity of the insults cannot be fully appreciated without a proper understanding of some of the vocabulary used. *Bungo* is translated in McKay's glossary to *Constab Ballads* as "black African," but this does not fully impart the deeper meaning of the term. In Jamaican creole it is synonymous with nincompoop: very black, ugly, stupid, a country bumpkin.[72] Today it still carries a negative connotation in Jamaica, even though the Rastafarians, following the practitioners of the African-derived Kumina religion, have tried to invert and subvert its racist implications. (They are happy to dub themselves *Bongoman*.) The drill instructor thus added charge to the already potent insult by describing the recruit as a "damned bungo brute." To call the recruit "mountain man" is to further enforce, if not repeat, bungo brute. When the instructor shouts "Car[ry] behin[d] de bluff lef[t] foot, / Seems i[t's] frighten fe de boot!" he is insulting the size of the of the recruits' feet and their unfamiliarity with wearing shoes and boots. *Bluff* means big or clumsily large, and when the instructor surmises that the foot is frightened of the boot, he is suggesting that the recruit is used to going barefoot and is flummoxed by having to move with something on his feet.

The instructor will brook no explanation or complaint, let alone protest from the recruits. "Shet you' mout'!" he yelled, "A wan' no chat!" He suggests that it is only because they are now, for the first time, eating decent food provided by the police force ("nyamin' Depot fat") and having a bed to sleep in instead of bare mats ("so-so mat") that they have even the strength, let alone the pluck, to talk back. But he will soon put them back in their proper place and teach them not to talk back to their betters, such as himself. "A mean fe pull you' tongue," he promises them. "Wonder when unno wi' fit / Fe move up in-a fus' squad, / Use carbine an' bayonet!" he thinks aloud. But he resolves to make these bungo men into constables despite their grievous failings—even if he has to drive them insane: "Wait dough,—unno wi' larn yet,— / Me wi' drill you ti' you mad."[73]

McKay responds to the drill instructor in "A Labourer's Life Give Me." He extolls the virtues of rural life, letting the instructor know that he was "never ashamed o' de soil." He expresses his regret at having joined the force and wishes to return to the land. The instructor, he suggests, knows little of the peasant's life.[74]

Ellen Tarry, an African American writer who became a close friend of McKay's during the last decade of his life, also thought that McKay's experience in the constabulary had enduring effects upon him. She reports that one of McKay's Jamaican friends in New York, who had known him back in Kingston, told her that when the poet was in the police force, his immediate superior, "a stern, uncompromising, sometimes unreasonable task-master, was a mulatto." Tarry believes that the "indignities—real and imaginary—which Claude suffered at this man's hands left their mark."[75]

In sharp contrast to the drill instructor of "Flat-Foot Drill," Inspector Clark was regarded as tough but fair, and McKay had written two poems in his praise.[76] McKay fired a parting shot at the drill sergeants as he left the police force. He concluded his preface to *Constab Ballads*, a book that was published after he had sailed for the United States, with the following words: "As constituted by the authorities the Force is admirable, and it only remains for the men themselves, and especially the sub-officers, to make it what it should be, a harmonious band of brothers."[77]

It is doubtful that McKay believed that the constabulary was admirable as constituted. As with the dedication, this sentiment might have been Jekyll's rather than McKay's. It might also have been a calculated way of currying favor with the top brass in order to gain his discharge. Nevertheless, McKay did not refrain from having a final dig at the subofficers of the force. Unfortunately, McKay never explicitly gave his reasons for not liking Kershaw, but, significantly, he never wrote a poem in praise of the head of the force.

Jamaican Nationalism and Its Limits

As intimated earlier, McKay's position in relation to Jamaican nationalism was complex compared to his almost instinctive and visceral expression of solidarity with the Black poor and oppressed. The young poet articulated his

Jamaican nationalism most explicitly in "My Native Land, My Home," published in *Songs of Jamaica.*

> Dere is no land dat can compare
>   Wid you where'er I roam;
> In all de wul' none like you fair,
>   My native land, my home.
>
> Jamaica is de nigger's place,
>   No mind whe' some declare;
> Although dem call we "no-land race,"
>   I know we home is here.[78]

In an additional six stanzas, McKay elaborated upon his love and devotion to
Jamaica, including a willingness to die for his beloved *patrie.*[79]

Jamaica is seen as an island naturally endowed with all that its Black
inhabitants could ever need: "Your fertile soil grow all o' ti'ngs / To full
de naygur's wants." However, this near-paradise is despoiled by buccra,
the white ruling class—who, the poet implies, are not really a part of the
nation—who oppress its Black inhabitants.[80] Despite this, his love remains
undiminished: such "little chupidness" [stupidness] will not nullify his
devotion. But the love is not entirely unconditional: "De time when I'll tu'n
'gains' you is / When you can't give me grub."[81] There is a deliberately menacing tone in this, the final, couplet. The ruling class were being warned that
they should not take the "patriotism" of the Black population for granted—
there is a limit to how far they could go. Indeed, in a poem published in the
Gleaner in January 1912, McKay suggested that the limit had been reached.
In "Peasants' Ways O' Thinkin'," he endorses the Black migration to the
Isthmus, as conditions on the island had become unbearable for the majority of its inhabitants. The poem informs the reader that the peasants have
no illusions about conditions in Panama and Costa Rica, but they have
no choice but to go if the opportunity arises. Contrary to buccra's advice
against emigration, "dis is wha' we got to say: / We hea' a callin' from Colon,
/ We hea' a callin' from Limon, / Let's quit de t'ankless toil an' fret / Fe where
a better pay we'll get." Even though the "law is bad" for them in Panama, the
work and wages there keep hunger at bay—"beat de ban's."[82]

In any case, McKay's enthusiastic embrace of Jamaica in "My Native
Land, My Home," a veritable claiming of the island for the Black "race,"
was a very rare posture in Jamaica at the time. It certainly was hardly typical of the peasantry or the Black working class. This is because the Black

masses have always been suspicious of those with ambitions of national autonomy. The posture goes back to the days of slavery, when the local white ruling class (with its not insignificant mulatto underlings) exercised autonomy at the expense of the enslaved. The island's oligarchy of slaveholders resisted the abolition of the slave trade and fought tooth and nail against the abolition of slavery itself, which the British Parliament had approved.[83]

The abolition of both the slave trade and slavery itself were thus carried out over the heads of the local ruling class. To the slaves—thanks to the propaganda and misinformation of missionaries and others—the ending of slavery, the long night of unspeakable suffering, had been brought about by the British Crown over the objections of the wicked local planters. Thus, the idea that "Victoria the Good"—the Good Queen Victoria, "Missis Queen"—had freed the slaves took hold of the heads of the ex-slaves throughout the British Caribbean to a greater or lesser degree. Writing in 1921, McKay remembered that as a boy growing up in Jamaica, Queen Victoria was to him "what Lincoln is to the little American Negro child."[84] He vividly recalled that during the Diamond Jubilee celebrations in 1897—Claude was not quite seven at the time—his teacher and parents told him that "Victoria had freed the slaves. She had mounted the throne of England with the words, 'I will be good,' on her lips. The Bible was her light. From her great love for her colored subjects she had freed them from slavery."[85] It was such imperial indoctrination that helped to cultivate the remarkable love and devotion on the part of the Caribbean working people for Victoria.[86] As one historian put it, the queen "stood as a protective symbol and the source of their liberation from slavery."[87] Just as Afro-America's love for Abraham Lincoln was never shared with any other president of the United States (with the recent exception of Barack Obama), so it was that this love for Victoria was never extended to any other British monarch before or since her reign. Herbert Thomas, who served as an inspector in the constabulary for almost a half-century after joining in 1877, reported in his memoir that among the older generation "the name of Queen Victoria was always uttered with love and reverence." News of Victoria's death was received like that of a personal calamity, the effect as visceral as a punch to the gut. Thomas distinctly remembered "the old cook of a friend with whom I was staying at the time of the Queen's death coming into the room where I was sitting, folding her hands over her abdomen—which is the attitude prescribed by etiquette—bobbing me a curtsey and saying:

"Please, Inspector, is it true I hear 'missis' Queen dead?" On my answering in the affirmative, she bobbed a second curtsey, then cast both her hands and eyes heavenward, which is the gesture of despair, and heaving a deep sigh, turned and left the room without another word. They all used to think that it was Queen Victoria herself who brought about the emancipation of the slaves.[88]

McKay also recalled that when Victoria died there were "strange rumours" among the Jamaican peasantry. "They said that the women's hair would be sheared off and taxation increased for the Queen's son, Edward VII was a spendthrift who would be demanding more and more money."[89] Like Thomas, McKay also remembered that "all the peasants in the village believed that it was the good Queen Victoria who had liberated them from slavery."[90]

Thus, right up to the middle of the twentieth century, the masses of Black people in the British Caribbean believed that the imperial Crown, not the local ruling class, had their interests at heart. (They were right in thinking that the local ruling class meant them no good, but they were wrong in believing that the Crown would look out for them. The 1865 rebels of Morant Bay, who made a desperate appeal to the Good Queen, learnt this lesson in the most painful way of all.) Given this ideological formation, nationalist pronouncements, not to mention more serious agitation of the nationalist variety, against British rule was relatively rare. Demands for reforms? Yes. Demands for national autonomy and independence? Not until well into the twentieth century. This pervasive ideological posture is summed up in the remark made by Alexander Bustamante, the premier labor leader of early-twentieth-century Jamaica: "Self-Government means brown man rule."[91] The coloreds, not African Jamaicans, Bustamante was saying, would take control. Left to the tender mercies of these forces, Black Jamaicans would have no recourse to imperial "protection." The nature of the relationship between the imperial center and the local ruling class vis-à-vis the Black masses holds the key to the enigma of the relatively late (compared to Cuba, Puerto Rico, and the Dominican Republic) development of nationalism in the English-speaking Caribbean.[92]

The sentiments of "My Native Land, My Home," were therefore extraordinary. But they were in tension with those of another early poem, "Old England." In the latter, McKay talks of his longing to visit and "view de homeland England."[93] He mentions the usual tourist sights—St. Paul's Cathedral, Westminster Abbey, and so on—that he would like to see. Interestingly, among these would be Victoria's grave: "de lone spot where in peaceful solitude / Rests de body of our Missis Queen, Victoria de Good."[94] Ironically, there is a subversive—if somewhat confused—intent behind this sentiment, given the history of the island and its relation to the British Crown. In the mythology of the Black peasantry, such a visit would be that of the child of the emancipated visiting the tomb of the "liberator" of her or his ancestors—the equivalent of a Black American child of slaves visiting the Lincoln Memorial in Washington, D.C. Thus, the attachment is not to the British Crown per se, but to the perceived symbolic importance of the British monarchy as a bulwark against the tyranny of the local oligarchy.

The traditional reading of "Old England" as an ode to colonialism and England thus misses the poem's greater symbolic importance because it ignores the concrete, complex, and overdetermined content of the colonial relation.[95] Moreover, the poem defies the traditional simplistic reading in another way. In the very last line, McKay explains that he would be happy and contented after visiting these sights in England to "sail across de ocean back to *my own / native shore.*"[96]

What we have here, then, is divided loyalty. England is his "home-land"—"our home," he calls it in another poem[97]—but so also is Jamaica. In acknowledging England, he does not renounce Jamaica, and in embracing Jamaica, he does not reject England. What is clear, however, is that he felt passionate about Jamaica, his "native land," while his loyalty to England was necessarily more abstract, more from the head than from the heart. Significantly, all that the young colonial desires in "Old England" is to *visit* England, not to take up residence there, not to make it his real home, but simply to visit: "I'll rest glad an' contented in me min' *for / evermore,*" with this simple visit, after which he would return to what he called "my *own* native shore."[98]

Despite this, however, as he wrote in an autobiographical fragment with somewhat bemused hindsight: "Our education was so directed that we really honestly believed that we were little black Britons."[99] Rather than being the expression of an intellect in the ideological grip of colonialism, what we have in "Old England" is the implicit questioning of the ideology of colonialism itself by the articulation of a divided loyalty, instead of a solid, undivided, and univocal commitment to Britain as the mother country. Indeed, Jamaica is given precedence over Britain in the poet's affective bonds. "I've never felt I was legitimately British, which I am not after all," McKay wrote to a friend in the 1930s.[100] Beyond the orchestrated and organized childhood euphoria over Victoria's Diamond Jubilee, the statement is probably true. He no doubt *thought* he was British, but it is unlikely that he *felt* British. And after his encounter with British racism when he lived in London between 1919 and 1921 (discussed in chapters 7 and 8), McKay definitely *knew* he was not British in any meaningful sense.

McKay was not alone in the expression of such ambivalence. No one called for independence, and practically no one called for self-government within the British Empire, a considerably less radical request.[101] When the demands for nationhood were made, U. Theo's voice was one of the earliest and clearest heard, but this was in the 1920s. McKay's friend Thomas Mac-Dermot, who had influenced and encouraged him in his writing of poetry, had occupied a similarly ambivalent position.[102] Indeed, it is undoubtedly the case that MacDermot occupied an even more pro-British position than McKay. Nonetheless, he had identified a political space for pride in a Jamaican cultural identity, a kind of cultural nationalism without the demand for political sovereignty.[103]

Sandy Cox's National Club was formed in March 1909 largely out of its leader's grievance against the governor at the time, Sir Sydney Olivier. Cox, a light-skinned Jamaican civil servant, felt that the local British colonial authorities denied him promotion because he was not white. The National Club called for self-government, but this call was suborned to demands for much more basic reforms. Cox was hounded by his colonial adversaries and by 1911 ended up in Boston as a lawyer. The National Club collapsed quickly thereafter; the objective bases for its survival simply did not exist.[104]

The position taken on the national question by Rev. C. A. Wilson typified that of the Black intelligentsia in Jamaica at the time. Wilson, as earlier discussed, was involved in a number of Black uplift organizations in the early twentieth century, most notably the Jamaica League. Though deeply committed to the advancement of Black Jamaicans, Wilson could not find it in his heart even to mention J. Robert Love and Sandy Cox in *Men with Backbone* (1913) and *Men of Vision* (1929), his praise songs to distinguished Jamaicans. Indeed, in *Men with Backbone*, he chided both Love and Cox, without mentioning them by name, for being "short-sighted" in calling for "Jamaica for Jamaicans."[105] While Wilson thought that "men from abroad should not be given positions that natives are competent to fill," he nevertheless felt that Black Jamaicans should count their blessings rather than agitate for self-government.[106] After all, they were much better off than the sons of Africa living under Spanish and United States rule. "With the Union Jack floating over his head," Wilson proudly declared, "the Negro is a unit in the greatest Empire. He enjoys full liberty, and immunity from the base crimes perpetrated on the Spanish Main. . . . The barbarous and nefarious practice of lynching is unknown in Jamaica."[107]Jamaicans, Wilson wrote, "must not be content to be treated as children," but in the next breath he implicitly subscribed to the imperial notion, which Love and Cox inveighed against, that Black colonials, such as those in Jamaica, were not yet "ready" for self-rule. Jamaicans, Wilson declared, "must seek to grow to political manhood."[108]

Although in general terms McKay and his eldest brother would have shared some of Cox's aspirations, they most certainly would not have agreed with his attacks on Olivier (Cox's main local target and nemesis), whom both U. Theo and the young McKay admired. Olivier had publicly praised McKay's poetry, telling the *Gleaner*: "I have seen a selection of Mr. McKay's poems, and I appreciate the talent they exhibit."[109] And McKay "respectfully dedicated" his first volume of poems to Olivier, "who," he wrote, "by his sympathy with the black race has won the love and admiration of all Jamaicans."[110] Indeed, McKay refrained from publishing one of his poems, "De Gub'nor's Salary," out of his respect for the governor and out of loyalty to Jekyll, who was, as discussed earlier, a close friend of Olivier's. Jekyll and McKay decided to show the poem to Olivier before its publication. "He dissuaded us from publishing it," reported McKay. "He said that the politicians of Jamaica might use it to attack the position of Governor."[111] Claude did make his political compromises, even then. He correctly judged, however, that the most powerful forces attacking Olivier at the time were profoundly reactionary and meant the masses of Jamaicans no good. The opposition from the left led by Cox and the National Club, though troublesome for Olivier, lacked potency. U. Theo admired Olivier's Fabianism and the quality of his mind, and was grateful for his role in extending the railways into upper Clarendon. The extension, carried out in the teeth of opposition from the island's oligarchy and the *Gleaner*, was seen as a measure aimed at helping the peasantry gain better access to markets for their produce.[112]

The McKays' admiration for Olivier was by no means unique. Black Jamaicans were sad to see him leave and grateful for his continued interest in the island from afar. Over the years, many Jamaicans wrote to Olivier and told him so. Among them was Una Marson, the distinguished Jamaican poet and playwright, who spoke of Olivier's "wonderful love of Jamaica" and thanked him for "all you have done and are doing for our Island's welfare." Mrs. Dorothea Simmons, having finished Olivier's 1936 book, *Jamaica: The Blessed Island*,[113] wrote him straightaway: "I kept exclaiming inwardly, 'Bless him for saying that! Oh bless him for that!' you have opened the way for a better understanding of our people and problems."[114]

It is indeed a good book, but the truth is that Sydney Olivier was one of the rare breed of people who grow more radical as they grow older. Some of his early policies while he was involved in the colonial administration of the island, most notably his attempt to restrict the migration of poor Jamaicans to Panama and elsewhere, were plainly reactionary and reprehensible.[115] But his policies became more sympathetic toward the peasants and workers as his governorship (1907–1913) came to an end, and for this the island's oligarchy was always after him. In later years, he was especially appalled by the deteriorating conditions of workers in the British Caribbean, and Jamaica in particular. In retirement and unencumbered by the protocols of colonial officialdom, he became more and more outspoken and anti-imperialist in outlook, especially in the 1930s, and swung back at his enemies in Jamaica in his journalism and his book, *Jamaica*. Indeed, in 1941, during the height of the Second World War, he went so far as to declare, albeit in a letter to his fellow Fabian and close friend Leonard Woolf, that "Hitler and Haw-Haw have told the truth about the British Empire, the Coloured people are still paid at starvation wages and are getting tired of it."[116] Olivier died two years later, age eighty-four.

McKay's "De Gub'nor's Salary," long believed to have been lost to posterity and willingly suppressed by its author during Olivier's administration, did emerge into the light of day.[117] Thanks to the *Gleaner*, in the immediate aftermath of the governor's resignation, the poem appeared.[118] It is unclear whether McKay, who was then at college in Kansas, greenlighted its publication; in his memoir, he seems to have forgotten that it was ever published. The *Gleaner* explained that it had had the poem for "some time in our hands, but there were various reasons why it could not be published earlier. Those no longer exist, and we therefore give the public an opportunity of sharing our own pleasure in a very spirited piece of work." It confirmed that Olivier had seen it in manuscript form and was "much amused." In fact, he "thoroughly enjoyed it," and his only "adverse criticism" was the use of one particular metaphor.[119] The *Gleaner* failed to mention that the governor counseled against its publication and wished the poem suppressed. We now know why Olivier eagerly sought to keep it from an impoverished and restive public.

"De Gub'nor's Salary" is one of McKay's most radical critiques of the Jamaican power structure. As with most of his creole poems, it is articulated through the voice of one of the island's workers or peasants, one of the poor and dispossessed. The discovery that the governor was paid a salary of £5,000 per year (an unimaginable sum for the ordinary worker, let alone the poor) served as the occasion for meditation and complaint. Running to eleven stanzas, the poem outlines the oppressive condition of the Jamaican poor. "A we de feel the burden, Sah," the poem begins. "An' yet dem min' we less; / De best t'ing dat dem do fe we / Is eber to oppress."[120] The narrator then points out that it is people such as himself/herself (the speaker's gender is never revealed)—the workers and peasants—who are holding up the economic edifice, which benefits the rich: "a we min'in' unno,[121] Sah, / We bearin' all the brunt, / An' don't t'ink we no feel i' hard / 'Cause you no hear we grunt." Moreover, because they are poor ("no hab de 'nuff t'ings"), they are disparaged and maligned as nothing: "you all say we is nuttin', Sah." McKay's peasant/worker narrator points out—articulating an argument that has its roots in Marx's labor theory of value (and very similar to the one advanced by U. Theo about the exploited road menders)—that he/she is aware of the working people's true worth and value, proudly declaring: "But a we mek de t'ousan's dough,/ While unno mek the tens" and it was the collective contribution of the working people that the whole society and "Gubberment depen's." The narrator insists on talking about the hardships endured by workers and peasants and won't be silenced:

> You caan' mek we shet up;
> A we deh feel oppression yoke;
> An' drink de bitter cup.
>
> We hab to pay official dem
> An' keep up bridge an' road,
> P'lice, bailiff—persecution lot![122]—
> We bear all o' de load.

On top of all the burden carried by poor Jamaicans comes the governor's fat salary—"de big five t'ousan poun'"—which they, through their taxes, will have to pay. And why all that money—"Dat debil of a big pay"—for just one man, coming from the pockets of the poor?

The narrator would not mind so much if the colony were prosperous, but those days were long gone. Now, the narrator continues, "we t'ink it bery hard / Fe payin' so much cash, / When we so poo' an' naked-'kin / An' gruntin' under lash."[123] Thus, the peasant/worker narrator concludes: "We wantin' many changes, Sah, / An' one o' dem should be / A cuttin' an' a prunin' o' / De gub'nor's salary."

Emergent Feminist Sympathies

"Jane," he continued impressively after a pause, "Kingston is a very big an' wicked city, an' a young girl like you, who de Lord has blessed wid a good figure an' a face, must be careful not to keep bad company. Satan goeth like a roaring lion in Kingston; seeking who he may devour. . . . Don't stay out in the street in the night, go to church whenever you' employer allow you. If sinners entice thee, consent thou not."

—Herbert G. De Lisser, *Jane's Career: A Story of Jamaica*, 1914

As previously discussed, McKay's mother figured prominently in his life and memory. Some of his earliest poems were about her. He even used a version of his mother's name as a nom de plume for his first poems published in the United States. Living in London on the tenth anniversary of her death, Hannah Ann's favorite son penned some of his most moving poems in lonely commemoration of her. But his mother was not the only woman made the subject of his early poems: ordinary Jamaican women were also well represented in their different moods and settings. One of the most remarkable features of the poetry McKay wrote during his youth is the extraordinary degree to which the experience of Black Jamaican women is woven into the overall tapestry of his work. In fact, he wrote a substantial number of his poems in the female voice, and even more had women as their subject. "A Midnight Woman to the Bobby" and "The Apple-Woman's Complaint," two of the most accomplished poems in his entire oeuvre, were written in the female voice. In all his writing, his unforced, unpatronizing, but sympathetic portrayal of women, with their different desires and myriad struggles, is one of the most consistent motifs in McKay's work from beginning to end. This is true of his fiction as well as his nonfiction work, his poetry as well as his prose. Remarkable, too, is the fact that this motif is underexplored in the critical literature on McKay.[124]

McKay's women are primarily of peasant and working-class background. They are young and old, mothers and childless, wives, fellow workers, higglers, and prostitutes. They are depicted in love and out of love. They are seen suffering and defiantly struggling and in deep despair. But most of all, McKay skillfully portrays, with respect and compassion, the precarious and difficult lives these Black women led in an unforgiving time.

We have already encountered Cous Sun, the peasant-higgler, his wife, and their struggle to survive in "Two-An-Six." In "Ribber Come-Do'n," there is fourteen-year-old Milly looking after her six-week-old sibling and three other brothers and sisters marooned by a flooded river. Her mother had gone to a seaport to buy fish (to resell) and her father had been working his provision ground some distance from home when they were both cut off by the flood from their home and children. There was no food at home. It was night and the children were hungry, but the parents still could not get home. Little Milly sought assistance from a neighbor:

> "Ebenin', cousin Anna,
> Me deh beg you couple banna,
> For dem tarra one is berry hungry home;
> We puppa ober May, ma,
> We mumma gone a Bay, ma,
> An' we caan' tell warra time dem gwin' go come."[125]

Cousin Anna, whose name suggests she might very well have been based on McKay's generous mother, gave Milly bits of yam, some cornmeal, "An' a pint o' milk fe de babe." The parents didn't manage to make it home that night, but through the assistance received "de picknanies went to bed / Wid a nuff nuff bellyful."[126]

Not only is "Ribber Come-Do'n" a testimony to the peasant community's structure of mutuality, it is also a good illustration of the hand-to-mouth existence of the rural poor, who had no reserves, absolutely nothing to spare. The parents were not able to return home for only one night—unable to return with quarry for the day, as it were—and the children were literally stranded without food. At the center of the drama of "Ribber Come-Do'n" is a little girl, her struggling parents, and a female neighbor, all portrayed in realistic terms.

In "A Country Girl," the narrator, Fed, meets up in Kingston with Lelia, a girl from his own village. Finding Lelia working as a prostitute, Fed is shocked and disturbed. Asked why she stays in Kingston, Lelia explains, "Country life . . . has no pleasures for me."[127] She wants the excitement of the city and some of the good things in life, such as pretty dresses, as well as the basic needs. And prostitution is the only way she can earn a living: "Dat was the gift dat a gay town could give." Asked whether she has not "swopped out your honour for gold," Lelia tells of her downward spiral. She tried to escape the "horrid . . . lone country life." She suffered in the country, "for sometimes e'en hunger was rife; / An' when I came, Fed, to try my chance here, / I thought there would be no more troubles to bear. / But troubles there were an' in plenty, my lad." She has now become accustomed to life in the city, and is also too ashamed to return home. She is reconciled to her new life, albeit "deep sunk in the shame."[128]

McKay's childhood sweetheart, his first love, Agnes—"a light mulatto with very black hair, buxom of body and with a face that radiated sunshine"—years later "died miserably in one of the brothels in Kingston."[129] This event affected McKay deeply, reverberating in his work for the rest of his life. Almost forty years after Agnes's death, McKay could still vividly remember the passion they shared. Agnes was older than Claude, but that did not prevent his becoming "fascinated" by her. They did not see each other outside of school, but during the recess periods they would "get together in a ring and play 'Drop the Handkerchief.'" They passed notes to each other in class, and Agnes started to write him long letters. Not knowing what to write in response, McKay got his friend the stable boy, who was older than he, to write his letters for him.[130] U. Theo, under whose guardianship he lived at the time, discovered some of the letters, and Claude paid a heavy price for his secret romance with Agnes:

> My brother took the letters to his wife; they both read them and they thought that Agnes and I were wrong in writing such letters. They thought that the letters were very passionate, not the kind that children should be writing each other. My brother whipped me for the first time. He whipped me and said he was astonished that a small boy like me could have such adult thoughts. Agnes was very angry when she heard about the beating and the finding of the letters by my brother.[131]

But McKay reported, "The beating did not change us." And although the other schoolchildren by then knew about them, Agnes and he "hugged our love very closely." "It was my first love. But," as he explained, "before I could even be aware of it Agnes had blossomed into a young woman and I was still just a boy in knee-pants. Then she left the village and I never heard from her again." The next time he heard of Agnes was the news of her "miserable" death in a Kingston brothel.[132] He wrote a long poem to her memory, "Agnes o' de Village Lane," and published it in the *Gleaner* in 1911. It tells the story of their love, how they were parted, how the passion died away, but the memory lingered on, and then after many years, the painful news of "fallen" Agnes's death.[133]

The *Gleaner* reported, within a fortnight of its publication, that "Agnes o' de Village Lane" was the public's "general favourite" of McKay's poems.[134]

While writing *My Green Hills of Jamaica* in Chicago just a couple of years before he died, McKay could not recall any of the poem's words, but he remembered that "friends who read it said it was one of my most touching poems."[135] Agnes's story resonated precisely because it was far from unique. Her downfall was rooted in and symptomatic of the limited and terrible choices that poor people were forced to make in order to survive the hellish conditions that prevailed. Lelia's fall stemmed from that conjuncture, McKay argued.

It appears that Agnes's tragedy and McKay's previous relationship with her lie at the core of his deep and abiding sympathy for prostitutes. *Banana Bottom* is the only one of his six novels that does not have a prostitute as a character; in all of the others, prostitutes figure prominently. They are present in his short stories, and they are perhaps most conspicuous of all in some of his finest poems, including the title poem of his most celebrated anthology, *Harlem Shadows*.[136] Indeed, McKay used the tragedy of the prostitute as a metaphor for the condition of Black people in general.[137]

In "A Midnight Woman to the Bobby," McKay provided a different kind of sex worker, one defiant and resilient, unlike Agnes and Lelia. McKay's admiration for the hardened but refreshing defiance of the prostitute is undisguised. Her attack is a no-holds-barred, scathing, and sustained onslaught on the policeman, the "bobby."[138]

The woman immediately goes on the offensive. She, a prostitute, scorns the policeman and considers his touching her as making her unclean, a defilement: "No palm me up, you dutty brute."[139] She audaciously suggests that he, not she, will "grunt under the law." No country bumpkin, she was born right in the heart of Spanish Town. More worldly wise than he, she suggests that he is out of his depth when he harasses and messes with her: "You t'ink you wise, but we wi see; / You not de fus' one fas' wid me." And she confidently predicts his demise:

> Care how you try, you caan' do mo'
> Dan many dat was hyah befo';
> Yet whe' dey all o' dem te-day?
> De buccra dem no kick dem 'way?[140]

From start to finish, she keeps up a barrage of priceless Jamaican insults. She insults his mouth ("Mash," "like ripe bread-fruit"); his nose ("jam samplatta nose"); his feet ("big an' ugly ole tu'n-foot" with "chigger" looking "like herrin' roe"). All in all, he is a "dutty ugly brute." Not finished with him, she moves on to his background; she "trace(s)" him. In the Jamaican language, "tracing" has the double meaning of cursing a person and digging up dirt in someone's past, which does not necessarily stop with the individual but can extend to that person's lineage and antecedence.[141] Before he joined the police force, he was in a sorry state: he had never worn shoes; he never had enough to eat; he never had any clothes. Hard times—"de pinch o' time"—pushed him to "join buccra Police Force."[142]

But now, because he wears a police uniform, he feels he can throw his weight around: "'Cos you wear Mis'r Koshaw clo'es / You t'ink say you's de only man."[143] The woman is convinced that time is on her side, that she will outlast the policeman, her tormentor: "But wait, me frien', you' day wi come, / I'll see you go same lak a some."[144] She laughs derisively at him when he attempts to arrest her: the judge, she is certain, will not accept his word against hers without the corroboration of a witness. It is the final insult: the judiciary has no respect for the police force, and a policeman's word carries no greater weight than that of a common prostitute. At any rate, this is what the prostitute wants the policeman to believe.

What McKay effectively does here is identify prostitution with policing. Indeed, McKay gives the distinct impression that he believes policing is morally more reprehensible than prostitution. Both "professions" are fruits of desperation, but the policeman's job is more repugnant. In joining the enemy—"buccra Police Force"—the policeman betrays his already oppressed race and beleaguered class; he is a traitor to his race and class. The peasant girl, very much like Lelia, experiencing hard times, moves from the country to the city and becomes a prostitute; but his form of prostitution is to join the constabulary and sell himself to buccra in the person of Mis'r Koshaw—Lieutenant-Colonel Kershaw, the inspector-general of the police—by joining the constabulary. The nocturnal quarrel between police and prostitute is between two Black victims of the same socioeconomic system superintended by buccra, which effectively reduces each to the same status, that of de facto prostitute.

In questioning the police force in this way, McKay invites his readers to question the traditional attitude to both policing and prostitution. Why should one form of prostitution (policing) be regarded as legitimate and socially acceptable while another is proscribed and scorned? Indeed, why should one prostitute be given power to enforce the law over another prostitute? Who should be scorned, and who is really obscene? McKay indicates where he stands by making the policeman mute—we hear the voice of the prostitute only, not a word from the bobby. The police's position is indefensible. And the poet reveals his hand by making the woman look upon the peasant-policeman as unclean, as a defiled abomination. "I have often wondered," McKay revealed many years later, "if it is possible to establish a really intelligent standard to determine obscenity—a standard by which one could actually measure the obscene act and define the obscene thought."[145]

"A Midnight Woman to the Bobby" is a furious, lacerating, and cathartic auto-critique on McKay's part, an early installment in his "expiation." The feeling of honor sold and bought, and of remorse, is as powerfully communicated in this poem as it is in "The Heart of a Constab" and "A Country Girl." The fact that McKay, too, and not only Lelia, had bartered his own "innocent youth" and had "swopped out" his "honour for gold" also helps to explain his bold and extraordinary sympathy for prostitutes. He, after all, had been a prostitute too.

In a peculiar way, although the prostitute in "A Midnight Woman to the Bobby" is depicted as courageous, extraordinarily eloquent, perceptive, strong, and even honorable (she finds despicable any peasant who joins "buccra police force"), we learn far less about her than we do about the police force. She acts as a mirror or, perhaps more accurately, as a bright, penetrating beam of light cum X-ray machine exposing the character and rotten innards of the police force. It is a measure of McKay's contempt for the force that he could have written such a poem—and a measure of the agonized contempt with which he viewed himself at a time when he was still a member of the constabulary.

From the prostitute's attack we move to the higgler's complaint—"The Apple-Woman's Complaint." The reader is led to admire—even to incite and applaud—the prostitute, but to sympathize with the higgler. Colonial Jamaica was such, McKay tells us, that the resilient and worldly-wise prostitute felt more at home in it than the hardworking higgler, or peddler, from the country. The higgler is stunned and appalled that the policeman ("yawnin' on his beat") has stopped her from selling her apples: "Me mus'n' car' me apple-tray." She has no alternative mode of survival, but this does not bother the policeman, who is upon her "like a ravin' bull."[146] She complains about the injustice of her predicament, about the rank hypocrisy of the constabulary, and about the perverse pleasure that the head of the Kingston police gets from the gratuitous persecution of poor, hardworking Black people:

> Black nigger wukin' laka cow
> An' wipin' sweat-drops from him brow,

Dough him is dyin' sake o' need,
P'lice an' dem headman boun' fe feed.

P'lice an' dem headman gamble too,
Dey shuffle card an' bet fe true;
Yet ef me Charlie gamble,—well,
Dem try fe 'queeze him laka hell.

De headman fe de town police
Mind neber know a little peace,
'Cep' when him an' him heartless ban'
Hab sufferin' nigger in dem han'.[147]

She complains and complains, and she has a lot to complain about: "While we go batterin' along / Dem doin' we all sort o' wrong."[148] She feels that the action of the police force is aimed at pushing Black women into prostitution, and prostitutes are persecuted by the police—she cannot win: "Dem wan' fe see we in de street / Dah foller dem all 'pon dem beat; / An' after, 'dout a drop o' shame, / Say we be'n dah solicit dem."[149] But her complaint falls on deaf ears. It is the complaint of the powerless, the heedless voice of one of the little people, the wailing of the condemned. And she *feels* doomed. She desperately bawls for divine intervention. She lifts her head to the heavens and begs Jesus for help because she cannot help herself:

We hab fe barter-out we soul
To lib t'rough dis ungodly wul';—
O massa Jesus! don't you see
How pólice is oppressin' we?

. . . .

Ah massa Jesus! in you' love
Jes' look do'n from you' t'rone above,
An' show me how a poo' weak gal
Can lib good life in dis ya wul'.[150]

"The Apple-Woman's Complaint"—perhaps rivaled only by "Whe' Fe Do?"—is certainly one of the most sorrowful and despairing of McKay's early poems, and indeed of his entire oeuvre.

But McKay's women do not only suffer and struggle. They also laugh, they play, they fall in love (even with policemen), and they fall out of love (most notably with policemen). With the significant exception of the bourgeois woman of "The Bobby to the Sneering Lady" and the fallen Agnes, McKay's women are all a dark shade of black, overwhelmingly poor, and of peasant and working-class background. Thus, one finds in McKay's discussion of women in his early poems an intricate imbrication of oppression based on sex, race, color, and class—"intersectionality," in today's parlance.[151] McKay recognized the impossibility of identifying with precision where one form of oppression ends and another begins. What is most evident in these poems, however, is the young McKay's sincere attempt to represent the lives of Black Jamaican women as he observed them, albeit mediated by his imagination and art. The poems do not lack verisimilitude, dovetailing as they do in a most remarkable way with what we know of Jamaican society at the time. Significantly, some of the most successful of McKay's early poems are written in the female authorial voice. Indeed, the best of his creole language poems is written in the female voice: for faithfulness to the Jamaican language, for rhythm, and for critical social commentary, skillfully and organically embellished with humor, "A Midnight Woman to the Bobby" is unsurpassed. It stands beside the very best creations of Jamaica's most accomplished creole language poet, Louise Bennett.[152]

How do we explain McKay's extraordinary openness to exploring important aspects of Black women's experience in Jamaica at the time? How do we explain his deep compassion and empathy for the women who inhabit so many of his early poems? Indeed, can phenomena such as this be ever adequately explained? There are essentially five considerations that at least help to account for McKay's emergent feminism.

McKay's relationship with his mother is highly significant here—not simply because she was a woman and mother, but because of the *type* of woman and mother she was and the influence she had on her son. He had a close relationship with his mother; he loved her deeply and repeatedly expressed his great respect and admiration of her. Apart from U. Theo, with whom he clearly had a very special bond, of all his other siblings he was closest to Rachel, his only sister, who was only a few years older. As small children they were especially close, with Claude apparently taking a keen interest even in her dolls—an unusual thing for a Jamaican boy at the time.[153] They loved each other, as the extant letters from his sister bear witness. Rachel's letters to Claude are intimate and warm, bubbling over with love and regard for her little brother.[154] Such sisterly love, combined with his worship of Hannah Ann and what she stood for, more likely than not contributed to his regard and general respect for women, especially poor Black women.

McKay observed his mother, "Mother Mac," over the years helping poor and unfortunate women within her community in a selfless and nonjudgmental way at home in Clarendon, and he admired her "goodness." Mrs. McKay, perhaps more than anyone else, helped to develop her son's capacity for compassion, especially compassion for suffering women.

Second, he simply hated to see suffering, injustice, and oppression. As he wrote in one of his earliest American poems, "misery / I have the strength to bear but not to see."[155] In McKay's Jamaica, poor Black women (rural and urban) were the bearers of much misery; insofar as we may measure such a thing, women bore far more than their fair share: Jamaican women held up more than half the sky and were overburdened by the island's sorrows and suffering. Given his exceptional powers of observation, combined with what he euphemistically called his "peculiar sensitiveness" and hatred of misery, it is not at all surprising that these women should figure prominently in McKay's poetry.

Third, an important factor that helps to account for the conspicuousness of women in McKay's poems is the very straightforward one of demography. It was simply hard to miss the fact that women comprised the majority of adult Jamaicans, especially in the cities. From the early part of the nineteenth century right down to our own age, the female has exceeded the male population. Not only were there more women than men during the late nineteenth and the early twentieth centuries, but the female population also grew more rapidly. Thus, from 1881 to 1921, the female proportion of the Black population increased from 51 percent to 53 percent.[156] The island's sex ratio (the number of males per thousand females in the population) declined significantly during the late nineteenth and early twentieth centuries, from 950 in 1881 to 881 in 1921. For the crucial age range of young adults fifteen to twenty-nine, the fall was even more dramatic—from 929 in 1881 to 791 in 1921. Although the lower overall sex ratio for Kingston increased from 704 to 721 over the same period, when these totals are disaggregated into age cohorts and race/color groupings a more meaningful pattern emerges. The sex ratio for those between the ages of fifteen and twenty-nine fell from an already low of 700 to 671 between 1881 and 1921— for every hundred women there were only sixty-seven men in this age group.[157] At the time that McKay was writing his poems in 1911, the sex ratio of the Black population of Kingston was as low as 676. Migration—internal

and external—provides the primary explanation for this demographic dis-
equilibrium in Kingston in particular, and on the island as a whole.

Between 1911 and 1921, 63 percent of the migrants from rural parishes to
Kingston were women. Women also constituted two-thirds of all internal
migrants to the parish of St. Andrew, a de facto extension or suburb of
Kingston.[158] These women were the victims of the dislocation of the agrarian economy and the increasingly skewed economic and political relations
in the countryside. They moved to Kingston and St. Andrew to escape the
growing hardship of the rural hinterland and to seek employment in the
service sector of urban Jamaica, many as domestic servants. In the census
of 1911, a quarter of all women of working age in Kingston and St. Andrew
gave their occupation as domestic servant. Employers showed an overwhelming preference for female, as opposed to male, domestic servants. In
1891, eight out of ten domestic servants in Kingston and St. Andrew were
female, rising to more than nine out of ten by 1911.[159] A significant number
of the women who drifted into Kingston from the countryside ended up as
prostitutes.

Jamaica experienced a net loss of more than 77,000 people through
migration between 1911 and 1921. Almost two-thirds of the emigrants
were men,[160] who left for work on the Panama Canal and the sugar plantations of eastern Cuba. External migration thus exacerbated the male/
female imbalance in Jamaica and nowhere more conspicuously so than in
Kingston—the place (along with Spanish Town) where McKay served as a
constable. This female presence—its sheer magnitude impossible to miss—
was reflected, perhaps not even consciously, in McKay's poetry. Needless to
say, this observation itself does not pretend to account, nor can it account,
for the sympathy with which McKay portrays and discusses women in his
poems. I do believe, however, that these demographic processes, which
impinged upon his finely attuned senses, help to explain the weighty presence of women in McKay's early work.

Fourth, McKay knew personally some of the women who form the subject matter of his poems. In some cases, most notably that of Agnes, these
were people he had loved, admired, and cared for. Others he got to know
during the course of his work as a bobby on the beat. That he should write
about such people with sympathy, understanding, and tenderness should,
therefore, not surprise.

Fifth, as a Fabian socialist, McKay no doubt would have been influenced
by the feminist component within that movement's ideology. Annie Besant,
feminist and prominent member of the Fabian Society, was someone whom

McKay read and explicitly recalled discussing with U. Theo.[161] McKay also read many of the female writers of Victorian Britain. He was especially interested in the life and work of George Eliot, who, apart from being the author of novels such as *Middlemarch*, was a prominent freethinker and translator of Ludwig Feuerbach's pioneering demythologization of Christianity, *Das Wesen des Christentums*. Although Walter Jekyll did not know Eliot personally, he had lived near her. McKay reported that Jekyll, an ardent admirer of Eliot's work, made overtures to get acquainted with her, but Eliot, known for her aloofness, rejected them, "saying she preferred not to make any new friends." The rebuff did not diminish her standing in Jekyll's pantheon of heroes and heroines. He discussed all of this with McKay, who remembered experiencing "a specially piquant human interest" in reading George Eliot.[162] Thus, McKay was exposed to feminist ideas (including those advocated by U. Theo), and what the late Victorians called "the woman question" likely shaped his perception of the condition of women in Jamaica.

McKay's very advanced ideas about women, developed at a relatively tender age, remained with him for the rest of his life. There is much talk in the literature on McKay about his attachments to "father figures," at the expense of examining his relations with women. In fact, some of his closest friends—not lovers, but friends—and comrades were women. These included, in his early years in America, Grace Campbell, Crystal Eastman, and Louise Bryant; in Britain, Sylvia Pankhurst and the other women around the *Workers' Dreadnought* on which he worked and at the International Socialist Club; in Bolshevik Russia, Clara Zetkin; in Germany, France, and North Africa, Josephine Herbst and Nancy Cunard (with whom he later had a fierce quarrel and falling-out). When he returned to the United States in 1934, among his closest friends and confidantes were Grace Campbell, Ellen Tarry, Dorothy West, Gwendolyn Bennett, and Dorothy Day of the *Catholic Worker* movement. McKay's relationship with these women, about which the archives eloquently testify, have been underexplored or completely ignored in McKay scholarship.

On Cruelty

McKay's extraordinary sensitivity and aversion to suffering, oppression, and cruelty were important impulses that led to his growing and deepening radicalization over time. Class, color, gender, and racial oppression in Jamaica started him on his socialist journey and, more than anything else, the gigantic horrors of racism in the United States—especially lynching—deepened his Black nationalism and Bolshevized his erstwhile Fabian socialism.

"Strokes of the Tamarind Switch" provides a good illustration of such a response. An erring young boy is sentenced by the court to be flogged with a tamarind switch. The tamarind switch, made from young branches of the tamarind tree, is pliable but hard, knotty, and strong. A dreaded instrument of punishment dating from slavery, it was designed to inflict fiery and lingering pain; it stings and cuts. McKay witnesses the boy's flogging, executed by his colleagues. But he could not bear to watch. He left.

> I dared not look at him,
> My eyes with tears were dim,
>   My spirit filled with hate
>   Of man's depravity,
>   I hurried through the gate.

He returned angry. As he put it in an intriguing stanza:

> I went but I returned,
> While in my bosom burned
>   The monstrous wrong that we
>   Oft bring upon ourselves,
>   And yet we cannot see.[163]

There is a double meaning in "ourselves." It may be interpreted as McKay referring to, and extrapolating from, the boy in the poem: the boy brought the misfortune upon himself, as people often do. It is also possible that when he speaks of "ourselves," McKay is not referring to the boy at all but to a collectivity, Black people in general, and in particular to the policemen involved in carrying out the punishment. Thus, McKay would be referring to the way Black people cause other Black people to suffer "And yet we cannot see." Given similar pronouncements elsewhere in his poetry, it is probable that the latter interpretation more accurately captures what McKay was trying to impart.

McKay graphically depicts the brutality of the punishment.

> The cutting tamarind switch
>   Had left its bloody mark,

> And on his legs were streaks
>> That looked like boiling bark.

> I spoke to him the while:
>> At first he tried to smile,
>>> But the long pent-up tears
>>>> Came gushing in a flood;
>>>>> He was but of tender years.[164]

The boy with "eyes bloodshot and red" told McKay that his father was dead and explained how he had fallen into bad company with boys "who goaded him to wrong." He "promised to be good." His mother was sending him abroad.

> I wished the lad good-bye,
>> And left him with a sigh:
>>> Again I heard him talk—
>>>> His limbs, he said, were sore,
>> He could not walk.[165]

McKay remarked that when he was small and admittedly "very rude," he too was beaten. He was not beaten as brutally as the boy, but he felt that such punishment was ineffectual: "has it done me good?" Thus, to McKay, not only was the beating of the boy barbaric, it was mindless, depraved, ineffective, and consequently, nothing less than gratuitous cruelty. McKay was so upset by the incident that he felt the need to append a note to the poem.

> This was a lad of fifteen. No doubt he deserved the flogging administered by order of the Court: still, I could not bear to see him—my own flesh—stretched out over the bench, so I went away to the Post Office near by. When I returned, all was over. I saw his naked bleeding form, and through the terrible ordeal—so they told me—he never cried. But when I spoke to him he broke down, told me between his bursts of tears how he had been led astray by bad companions, and that his mother intended sending him over-sea. He could scarcely walk, so I gave him tickets for the tram. He had a trustful face. A few minutes after, my bitterness of spirit at the miserable necessity of such punishment came forth in song, which I leave rugged and unpolished as I wrote it at the moment.[166]

McKay stated that the boy "deserved the flogging," a "miserable necessity." Yet the content, the tone, and the deeply human response to the boy's suffering undermine the claimed legitimacy of his punishment. He is torn: the flogging may be legal, but it is morally wrong.

However, this tension is not present within the poem itself; at least, it is not there in the same way. In the poem, the flogging is not a "miserable necessity"—it is not a necessity at all. But by the same token, McKay's response becomes even more creditable: although he felt that the boy "deserved" the flogging, he nevertheless had the moral courage to recognize and to declare that such punishment is barbaric. Had he not felt that the boy deserved the beating, it would have been more straightforward morally for him to have said that the beating was simply wrong. In other words, McKay is saying that not even wrongdoers should be treated in this way. No human being should be treated in such a barbaric and humiliating manner.[167]

McKay writes that he "could not bear to see . . . my own flesh . . . stretched out over the bench" made ready to be flogged. There is a double meaning, perhaps deliberately articulated, to the phrase "my own flesh." In a most immediate sense, it means a Black person, just as he used the expression "fe me own black 'kin" in "The Bobby to the Sneering Lady," and he talked of "My people, my people, me owna black skin" in "The Heart of a Constab."[168] But "my own flesh" also means, quite simply, another human being.

McKay was similarly moved by the incident that occasioned "Jim at Sixteen" to append an authorial note to that poem too. The poem opens with the complaint of a prisoner: "Corpy, it pinch me so, / De bloomin' ole handcuff; / A dunno warra mek / You put it on so rough."[169]

The note reads:

> On Friday I went to Court on duty for the first time since my enlistment. I happened to escort a prisoner, a stalwart young fellow, and as I was putting on the handcuff, which was rather small, it pinched him badly, making a raw wound. And yet he was so patient, saying he knew that I could not help it. Although it was accidentally done, I felt so sad and ashamed. The above poem grew out of this incident.[170]

McKay's aversion to cruelty is given added emphasis by his repugnance to the ill-treatment of animals. This attitude is brought out most clearly in "De Dog-Driver's Frien,"[171] in which McKay admonishes his colleagues in the force for their cruelty to dogs. There is a certain amount of enlightened self-interest here—the dogs provide companionship for the police on patrol at night, their "night-time frien." But McKay makes a claim for their more generous treatment on moral grounds. Human beings have no greater claim to the earth than animals. The last four lines of this opening stanza serve as the refrain of the poem:

> Treat dem kindly, treat dem kindly,
>   For dey are God's creatures too;
> You have no more claim, dear comrades,
>   On de earth dan what dey do.[172]

In "Killin' Nanny," he tells of two small boys, no more than two years old, watching the capture and slaughter of a goat. It is a gruesome scene. The children watch as the goat is "bawlin' fe mussy" and the butcher "re'ch his sharp knife, / An' 'tab wid all his might." The narrator is intrigued and troubled by the differing responses of the children. One child cries in his "mudder's bosom," with tears "fallin' down hotly"; the other looks on "wide-eyed" and stares with "joy" while "clappin' his han's with glee." Years later, "When dey had forgotten Nanny," the two were seen again as grown men. According to the narrator, "de forehead of de laugher / Was brand' wid de mark of Cain."[173] This is perhaps too harsh and deterministic a judgment: a two-year-old boy is the father of the man. Indeed, the implication is that the laughing boy was somehow born evil. McKay also suggests that exposure to and enjoyment of the slaughter of animals may lead to the slaughter of human beings.

But to my mind the most remarkable thing about "Killin' Nanny" is that it was written at all. Children in the Caribbean, in the urban areas as well as in the countryside, have grown up witnessing the slaughter of animals. Frequently these animals—especially goats, pigs, and chickens—were children's pets, with names and biographies. Little boys and girls nursed them through their ailments and anthropomorphized these animals only to discover that adults looked upon the children's pets as food. To their horror, not only are these animals nonchalantly killed in front of their eyes, but sometimes the children are even asked to catch the poor creatures that are to be turned into dinner. Such incidents are seldom forgotten as easily as McKay suggests in the poem: it is doubtful that the crying boy forgot the stab to Nanny with the sharp knife and the goat "bawlin' fe mussy." How can the adult John forget Peggy, the frail chick, won as a prize at Sunday school, nursed back to health by the proud child, her neck wrung on a bright Sunday afternoon, turning her into the Sunday dinner? Adults talk about such traumatic events of their childhood, some bear a permanent grudge against their parents for the death of their goat or chick, but such matters have never been registered in the literature of the Caribbean. McKay comes the closest to discussing them and, to my knowledge, no one has written about them since. To this extent, then, "Killin' Nanny" is a most remarkable artifact of the Caribbean experience and a tribute to McKay's poetic sensibilities.

In "Snared!," published in the *Jamaica Times* in 1912, McKay once again gives evidence of his poetic capacity to see everyday practices with fresh and questioning eyes—making the commonplace strange, as the Russian formalists would put it. On the face of it, the poem is a banal tale of country life—a boy setting a snare to catch a bird. But the poem goes beyond the adventure story of a boy excited by the thrill of the hunt. "Snared!" is understated, meditative, somber, and calm. Although the poet adopts the position of omniscient narrator, he sides with the doomed bird, a John-to-whit, which he calls Johnnie. The bird is singing, ignorant of its impending death. It is a beautiful morning; the sun is rising over the hillside, it shines bright on the big mammee tree, "An' John-t'whit is eating de red fruit, / As happy as happy can be." The opening stanza serves as a refrain, a refrain of foreboding:

> Though, Johnnie, so sweetly you're singin',
>   Your life is jes' heng on a hinge;
> De next hour your doom will be bringin',
>   For Butty's a-settin' his springe.

The narrator watches Butty, springe under his arm, make his way through the dewy grass and up into the mammee tree, eyeing Johnnie singing, "so gaily / Not thinkin' dat he wi' soon die." Butty sets the snare and climbs down from the tree. The narrator watches Johnnie hop toward his doom, but, as in "Strokes of the Tamarind Switch," the narrator could not bear to witness the dénouement.[174] Once again the Schopenhauerian moral undertones are evident—the wanton cruelty to animals, and the absurdity and cruelty of life itself.

Unlike "Strokes of the Tamarind Switch" and "Snared!", "Cotch Donkey" is written in a light vein, but its underlying message is just as serious. The donkey, overloaded with produce for the market, goes on strike. It sits down in the street refusing to go any farther. Its owner claims that it is lazy. But we learn that not only is the donkey expected to carry more than is reasonable, the poor creature also has a sore back. McKay points out that although the owner may be prosecuted for ill-treating the animal—a policeman inspects the creature's back—that won't stop the donkey's owner from continuing as before:

> Ef dem summons me,
>> Mek me pay few mac,
> Dat caan' mek me 'top
>> Wuk you wid sore back.[175]

Like most poor societies, Jamaica was not and is not renowned for its kindly treatment of animals. Nor, it should be said, was it or is it notorious for the ill-treatment of animals.[176] But McKay's ideas on the treatment of animals were by no means typical of his fellow Jamaicans, especially those from the countryside. Dogs were generally regarded as useful guards and handy scavengers, seldom as pets in the European or Euro-American sense of that term. They typically received scraps of food, leftovers (if any) from the human plate. The poor and the hungry could hardly afford to be generous to animals; indeed, all too often they competed with animals for food. And animals were certainly not seen as having an equal claim to planet Earth.

So where did McKay get this attitude from? It emanated from his extraordinary sensitiveness, and especially his sensitivity to cruelty and suffering. But his aversion to human misery does not fully explain the position that he takes on the place of animals in the scheme of things. "You have no more claim, dear comrades, / On de earth dan what dey do," he tells his fellow dog-drivers. It appears that McKay's already sensitive disposition to such cruelty was given reinforcement and philosophical underpinning, legitimacy, and cohesion by the ideas of Arthur Schopenhauer. There was an elective affinity between McKay and Schopenhauer on this particular subject.[177] From what we know of McKay's reading at the time, it is probable that Schopenhauer was an important influence in this regard, both directly and indirectly through Walter Jekyll.

Schopenhauer regarded animals with a passionate respect that is unsurpassed in modern Western philosophy. We should recognize, Schopenhauer wrote, that "in all essential respects, the animal is absolutely identical with us and that the difference lies merely in the accident, the intellect, not in the substance which is the will. The world," he affirmed, "is not a piece of machinery and animals are not articles manufactured for our use."[178] Schopenhauer objected to the caging of birds and the chaining of dogs.[179] He found vivisection "cruel and shocking." The eating of animal flesh he found "unfortunate" and felt that, insofar as this had to be resorted to, "the death of the animals we eat should be rendered quite painless by the administration of chloroform and of a swift blow on the lethal spot."[180] Schopenhauer went so far as to declare that "The *greatest benefit of railways* is that millions of draught-horses are spared a miserable existence."[181] He was convinced that not only truth but also morality was on his side.

Jekyll probably had some direct impact here, too. For on top of his love of Schopenhauer, Jekyll, McKay reported, was "a great follower of Leo Tolstoy, and a pessimist."[182] He was also "something of a Buddhist."[183] And, according to the Oliviers, who knew him well, Jekyll was also a vegetarian.[184]

McKay's Fabian connections might also have had an impact in this area. Henry Salt, the founder of and driving force behind the Humanitarian League (1891–1919), started his political life as a Fabian. Though it developed a separate identity, the League's membership overlapped significantly with that of the Fabians and the two organizations frequently put out joint publications.[185] The League advocated an end to cruelty to animals, a ban on cruel sports, and an end to vivisection and other forms of animal experimentation; many of its members were leading lights in the Royal Society for the Prevention of Cruelty to Animals (RSPCA). League members advocated for protection of the environment, an end to flogging and the death penalty, and penal reform. Socialists and vegetarians, the League's founders embraced an all-encompassing vision of the Good Society and of the relation between humanity and nature. Their ideology drew freely upon the findings of Darwin, Marx, and Spencer. Salt argued that it was "impossible to maintain in the light of newer knowledge . . . the idea that there is a difference in kind and not in degree only between human and non-human intelligence."[186]

Among the League members were such notable figures as Thomas Hardy, Keir Hardy, George Bernard Shaw, Edward Aveling, Eleanor Marx, Ernest Bell, Alice Lewis, Christabel Pankhurst, Edward Carpenter, and Mahatma Gandhi, who attributed his conversion to vegetarianism to the direct impact of reading Salt's book, *A Plea for Vegetarianism* (1886). Many dismissed Henry Salt and his colleagues as cranks and faddists, but the League's influence was far from negligible. Raphael Samuel described the League as "a Fabian *alter ego*."[187] Through his dual familiarity with both Fabianism and freethought, McKay would have been exposed to the ideas advanced by the Humanitarian League. In the end, however, the degree to which the ideas of others helped to shape McKay's own worldview was dependent upon the extent to which he was already receptive and predisposed to welcome and embrace them.

Religion and Christianity

Although he wrote it after his surprising conversion to Catholicism later in life,[188] *My Green Hills of Jamaica* carries McKay's fond recollections—without the slightest hint of apology or discomfiture—of his rationalist and freethinking childhood. Before his conversion, religion, and especially Protestant Christianity, was for him one of the greatest humbugs on earth, and one of the strongest chains holding back Black humanity, in Africa as well as in the diaspora. His heaviest artillery was aimed not only at the murderous superstition of race and the cruel tyranny of capitalism and imperialism, but also at the "cant" of Christianity. Ray, his roving Haitian intellectual hitman, makes that abundantly clear, especially in the 1929 novel, *Banjo*. "As far as I have been able to think it out," said Ray to a white acquaintance, "the colored races are the special victims of biblical morality—Christian morality. Especially the race to which I belong." He went on to say: "I don't think I loathe anything more than the morality of the Christians. It is false, treacherous, hypocritical."[189] But to what extent do these early poems corroborate the claims in *My Green Hills of Jamaica* of McKay's rationalism before migration? (After all, McKay wrote the memoirs of his childhood not prior to his leaving Jamaica, but in the late 1940s.) Is there any intimation of an incipient or maturing atheism in these early poems—of his being, as he puts it, "a hard little agnostic" from his childhood? McKay's early poetry supports the claim of youthful atheism, with a well-developed worldview confidently articulated by the young poet.

McKay's commitment to the rationalist outlook is most explicitly presented in "Old England," discussed earlier in another context. Included in the itinerary of his imagined tour of England would be a visit to see St. Paul's Cathedral where he would also "hear"—not listen to, but hear— "some of de great / Learnin' comin' from de bishops, preachin' relics of old fait."[190] He is more interested in listening to the powerful organ and feasting his eyes on the architecture of St. Paul's. His preferences are revealed by his animated response to the music and the building; the verbs are more active: "I would ope me mout' wid wonder at de massive organ soun', / An' would 'train me eyes to see de beauty lyin' all aroun'."[191] As far as McKay was concerned, then, the bishops—despite their "great learnin'"—could just as well have been thrown into the Thames. They hold no interest for him; the massive organ with an organ player, plus the architectural splendor of the building, would do very nicely.

He did not stop there. He moved on to make a direct contrast between, on the one hand, what he saw as the failing anachronism of religion and, on the other, the majesty of Reason, which has the future on its side. He would go to the City Temple, "where the old fait' is a wreck," then go where "de men of science meet togeder in deir hall, / To give light unto de real truths, to obey king Reason's call."[192]

In "Cudjoe Fresh from de Lecture," McKay once again explicitly expresses his preference for a rationalist, as opposed to a religious, mode of thought. The *Origin of Species*, not the Book of Genesis, wins his support. Evolutionism, not Creationism, he finds persuasive. "Yes, from monkey we spring: I believe ebery wud," Cudjoe declared. "It long time better dan f'go say we come from mud."[193]

God does not get a particularly good press in these poems either: he consistently fails to answer prayers. He is either deaf, dumb, blind, uncaring, or dead. One poor mother "told of futile prayers / Said on her wearied knees."[194] The peasant of "Hard Times," said "I ben' me knee an' pray to Gahd, / Yet t'ings same as befo'."[195] "O massa Jesus!" the apple-woman cries, "don't you see / How pólice is oppressin' we?"[196]—and nothing happens.

McKay seamlessly weaves his rationalist philosophy into his poetry, making it organic to his art. In "Mother Dear," for instance, the dying woman is being advised to concentrate on Jesus, but instead she embraces and almost worships the enveloping natural world: "de sound of horses neighin', / Baain' goats an' donkeys brayin', / Twitt'rin' birds an' children playin'/ Was all she heard." Although dying she is far more interested in this world—the concrete, sensual world that she herself has helped to fashion—than the Other World.[197]

Interested parties did not fail to notice McKay's militant rationalism. The London-based *Literary Guide*, official organ of the Rationalist Press Association, praised *Songs of Jamaica* and, in its review, went out of its way to claim McKay as one of their very own. The book, it informed its readers, "is by a keen young member of the R. P. A., whose portrait appears on the frontispiece. The volume gives a delightful presentation of the thoughts and feelings of a black man, which," it continued, "in all essential points will be found precisely like our own."[198] Like the *Literary Guide*, the *Christian Commonwealth* was generous in its review of the book. But unlike the *Guide*, with its praise also went a Christian reproach. The review in the *Commonwealth* was written by the Reverend W. Marwick, an English missionary serving in Jamaica, who "never loses an opportunity of doing a good turn to Jamaica and Jamaicans."[199] But the good reverend felt obliged to chide the young Jamaican—albeit in his ever-so-English way—for the sin of Rationalism. "It is to be hoped," Marwick concluded his review, "he [McKay] will be able to correct his rather crude views of the teaching of the City Temple pulpit, and of the value of Rationalism, with increased knowledge and experience of the real relations of Faith and Reason."[200] What McKay thought of this review, we do not know. But knowing something of their character, I can very well imagine him and U. Theo together poring over the passage at the dining table, reading it aloud in a good Jamaican imitation of an upper-class English accent, and having a nice little African giggle as they raised their heads from the page.[201]

Thoughts on Africa and Intimations of *Négritude*

Although there is relatively little reference to Africa in these early poems, the young McKay's ambivalence toward his ancestral home is nevertheless discernible. The narrator in "Cudjoe Fresh from de Lecture" concedes that slavery was terrible for those who experienced it. "But," he continues, "I t'ink it do good, tek we from Africa / An' lan' us in a blessed place as dis a ya."[202] Cudjoe drives his point home, and in the process, gives us an indication of his perception of Africa. It is one inherited from the colonial masters, which he did not transcend. And there is no irony in his words: "Talk 'bouten Africa, we would de deh till now, / Maybe same half-naked . . . / An' tearin' t'rough de bush wid all de monkey dem, / Wile an' uncibilise', an' neber comin' tame."[203]

Yet Cudjoe's exposure to the theory of evolution increases his pride in his blackness, in his race. As far as Cudjoe is concerned, Darwin's theory shows that human beings are fundamentally the same—we all, regardless of color, "spring" from the monkey. The lecturer has convinced Cudjoe that human beings are essentially equal. Cudjoe has undergone an almost religious conversion; he looks upon himself with new eyes: "Him [the lecturer] tell us 'bout we self, an' mek we fresh again." Cudjoe looks upon his blackness with a new pride:

Me look 'pon me black 'kin, an' so me head grow big,

Aldough me heaby han' dem hab fe plug an' dig;

For ebery single man, no car' about dem rank,

Him bring us ebery one an' put 'pon de same plank.[204]

This is the message, this is the news—uncommonly good tidings for Black folks—that Cudjoe is trying to impart when he hails, with the zeal of the newly converted, his cousin to tell of what he has learned.[205] Cudjoe himself recognizes that the rest, including his discourse on Africa, is a diversion. "I lef' quite 'way from wha' we be'n deh talk about,"[206] he admits. Yet it is interesting that commentators invariably notice Cudjoe's digression and ignore the essence of "Cudjoe Fresh from de Lecture": the scientific rejection of racism and the buttressing of Black pride by science.

In "Gordon to the Oppressed Natives," McKay proudly identifies with the sons of Africa in Jamaica, if not with Africa itself, as we have seen:

Wake de lion in your veins,

   De gorilla in your blood;

Show dem dat you ha' some brains,

   Though you may be coarse an' rude.[207]

The imagery is problematic—lion in the veins, gorilla in the blood—echoing notions of the primitive African. True, the words are ostensibly those of Gordon. But Gordon uttered no such words, and he was in Kingston, not in Morant Bay, during the revolt. The choice of words is therefore McKay's and his alone. With time and education, McKay's view of his ancestral homeland would radically alter. In "Africa," one of his finest sonnets, he celebrates her illustrious past: "The sciences were sucklings at thy breast. . . . / New peoples marvel at thy pyramids."[208] But that perspective on Africa came a decade after leaving Jamaica.

If the young McKay had a problem with his depiction of Africa, he had none with his conception of blackness. It is little wonder that his poetry of exile and his novels, especially *Banjo*, had a profound effect upon Aimé Césaire, Léopold Sédar Senghor, and Léon-Gontran Damas, chief founders of the *négritude* movement in Paris during the 1930s. One of the key ideological components of *négritude* is the recognition and affirmation of beauty in blackness. All of the main protagonists in the *négritude* movement pay homage to McKay as a primary source of inspiration. McKay's 1929 novel, *Banjo*, quickly became something of a Bible to these young

Black intellectuals from the Caribbean and West Africa in Paris.[209] But the respect with which McKay wrote about Black people, especially the Jamaican peasantry, the simple beauty and integrity with which they were portrayed in these early poems, made *Songs of Jamaica* and *Constab Ballads* founding texts in the ideology of *négritude* even before this ideological current had a name.

There is in these poems, written and published a generation before the emergence of *négritude*, an explicit articulation of blackness with beauty that is extraordinary. This concatenation of blackness with beauty is remarkable given the times and context in which McKay wrote, when the prevailing ideology denied and militated against such a connection. The very definition of the African, the so-called Negro, was the antonym of beauty. In a most explicit way, McKay went against this colonial orthodoxy, which was not only intrinsic to the colonial project but was also imbibed, accepted, and rearticulated by the colonized, as discussed in Chapter 2. Many ordinary Black people took for granted these negative ideas about themselves. The astonishingly persistent phenomenon of colorism would be inexplicable in the absence of such Black popular complicity.[210] Thus, when McKay linked beauty with blackness, he was going against the grain of a powerful and widely accepted ideological orthodoxy.

McKay embedded this linkage in two of his love poems. In "My Pretty Dan," a woman sings of her love for a Black policeman. Her pretty Dan, her policeman lover, is "de prettiest [bobby] you could set eyes 'pon." Dan has a "pretty cap to match his pretty face." She concludes: "Prettiest of naygur is my dear police, / We'll lub foreber, an' our lub won't cease."[211] The "prettiest of naygur" is nothing less than a revolutionary phrase. Nowhere in Anglophone Caribbean letters, or even folklore, had beauty and naygur been linked in this way before. *Nayga* or *naygur* is seldom used in Jamaica, and never in a positive way. As an expert on the Jamaican language notes, naygur "is used by black people to condemn those of their own color. In the song 'Sammy Dead Oh' there is the line, almost a proverb, 'Nayga kean [can't] bear fe see Nayga flourish,' which Louise Bennett echoes in the poem 'Oonoo Lie!' as, 'Nayga won't meck nayga prospa.' *Naygur* is often tantamount to 'good-for-nothing,' and *neegrish* is 'mean or despicable.'"[212] Instead of "pretty," most Jamaicans would be familiar with hearing the adjective "dutty" (dirty) before the noun "naygur." A "dutty nayga"—an epithet that still has currency—is the lowest of the low, more or less the worst insult to be found in the language. "Pretty naygur," never mind the "prettiest of naygur," is a contradiction in terms. McKay is inviting his fellow Jamaicans to remake the language—to remake it in their own image.

In "Fe Me Sal," McKay once again challenges the orthodoxy. It is the policeman's turn to sing of his love, "de darlin'" of his life, Sal, who he describes as "de prettiest black gal in de wul'; / An' whereber you may go you won't find anedder so, / Wid more tender min' an' better sort o' soul."[213] "De prettiest black gal in de wul'" is almost as heterodox as the description of Dan. The depiction of Sal's mind and soul is also transgressional.

These motifs of *négritude* would be further developed by McKay in his poetry, and especially in his prose, in the harsher, more diabolically racist, and more alienating environments of exile.

The Weapon of Lyric Poetry

McKay's most passionate lyrics of rural Jamaica were written against the backdrop not so much of Kingston as of his experience in the police force. As I argued earlier, it is a mistake to read McKay's poetry as simply or primarily antiurban. His most biting social commentary is not concerned with the urban environment—Kingston or Spanish Town—per se, but with what he depicts as the near-malevolent and destructive powers of the police and, by extension, the colonial state. There was certainly ambivalence in his attitude, but McKay loved Kingston far more than he hated it.

"Papine Corner" is often cited as evidence of McKay's dislike of Kingston. It is nothing of the sort. "Papine Corner" is a tongue-in-cheek description of the goings-on late at night in this lively terminus, where town meets country, on the outskirts of Kingston. The *Gleaner* described Papine as "our local Coney Island . . . the favourite resort of the 'smart set,' especially on Sunday nights."[214] McKay's poem alludes to the hypocrisy of the Jamaican middle class and especially of his fellow police officers: no fewer than four of the nine stanzas are specifically directed at the carryings-on of the police at Papine Corner. But it is evident from the poem itself that McKay found the place exciting and that he got enormous—if somewhat vicarious, almost voyeuristic—pleasure from simply watching the behavior of the motley group of humanity milling around and at play in this part of the city.

> When you want a pleasant drive,
>   Tek Hope Gardens line;
> I can tell you, man alive,

It is jolly fine:
Ef you want to feel de fun,
   You mus' only wait
Until when you're comin' do'n
   An' de tram is late.[215]

As McKay remarked in his memoirs, "I didn't intend the poem ['Papine Corner'] as an attack on the place, because I was very fond of it." But that did not stop some ministers in Kingston, when the poem was published in the *Gleaner*, from using the poem "as a sermon to inveigh against the wickedness of life in our city."[216]

To McKay, the countryside was less an idealized counterpoint to the city than a refuge from the police force and a symbol of freedom. The countryside is home, and home is the countryside. This is illustrated most powerfully by "My Mountain Home," where his childhood in the country is defined as freedom and his time in the police force is one of suffering and unfreedom. The picture of home is pastoral, serene, idealized.[217] This existence ended abruptly when he became an adult and joined the police force and "found myself among / Strange folks in a strange lan." It was a psychically brutalizing form of imprisonment:

My little joys, my wholesome min',
   Dey bullied out o' me,
And made me daily mourn an' pine
   An' wish dat I was free.[218]

McKay is healed and made whole by the countryside. "Sukee River," written after McKay had left the force, expresses this most eloquently. The river provided the needed balm, by dashing against his "broken heart" and cooling his "fevered brow." As he floated, he asked "crystal Sukee River": "Kiss me on my upturned face / Clasp me in your fond embrace."[219]

McKay's intense celebration of the countryside is reactive to the pain of his ordeal in the police force in Kingston—not reactive to Kingston per se. The yearning expressed in "De Days Dat Are Gone," "The Hermit," "Kite Flying," and "Heart Stirrings"[220] can only be explained against the backdrop of the sorrow and alienation experienced in "buccra police force." To this extent, McKay's pastoral and highly subjective outpourings were—to borrow Adorno's apt description of lyric poetry—"socially motivated behind the author's back."[221] The counterpointing of these two worlds—a rural idyll versus the incarcerating world of the constabulary—provides an added dimension to his critique of the police force and all that it represented. Like the Jamaican rebel slaves of old, he abandons the plains—where the ruling class holds sway and the sugar cane grows—and escapes to the relative security of the hills, the traditional refuge of the runaway slave, maroon country.

The most astonishing feature of these early poems is the degree to which McKay's lifelong passions, concerns, hatreds, and loves were conspicuously prefigured in his Jamaican years. To this extent, then, the remarkable thing about McKay's political trajectory in exile is not the ruptures that it manifested but the extraordinary continuity that it had with that of his Jamaican youth.

Birth in the District of Mean   Parish of Clarendon

137

Date and Place of Birth.	Name (if any).	Sex.	Name and Surname and Dwelling-place of Father.	Name and Surname and Maiden Surname of Mother.	Rank or Profession of Father.	Signature, Qualification and Residence of Informant.	When Registered.	Baptismal Name if added after Registration of Birth and Date.
Fifteenth September 1889 Nairne Castle Clarendon	H.Q.	Male	Thomas Francis McKay Nairne Castle Clarendon	Hannah McKay formerly Edwards	Planter	X the mark Thomas Francis McKay Father Nairne Castle Clarendon	Twenty Seventh September 1889	

Signed by the said Thomas F. McKay ___ in presence of   J.M. Mercer

        Registrar of Births and Deaths   Mean   District, Parish of Clarendon

3 Facsimile of McKay's birth certificate

Source: Island Record Office, Jamaica.

4 Thomas McKay, ca. 1920s

Source: Claude McKay Collection, Yale Collection of American Literature, Beinecke Rare Book and Manuscript Library.

7 Walter Jekyll, ca. 1890s.

Source: National Library of Jamaica

8 Banana plantation, St. Thomas, ca. 1890.

Source: Caribbean Photo Archive http://www.caribbeanphotoarchive.com/licensing/

9 Women carrying banana on large plantation, St. Thomas, ca.1890.

Source: Caribbean Photo Archive

10 Women loading banana on a steamer, Kingston, 1905

Source: Caribbean Photo Archive

11 A peasant family and their home, ca. 1900.

Source: Caribbean Photo Archive

12 Children carrying water in May Pen (Clarendon), 1904.

Source: Clarendon, 1904. (Getty Images)

13 Claude McKay in constabulary uniform, 1911.

Source: Frontispiece, *Songs of Jamaica*.

14 Peasant Women to Market, ca. 1905

Source: Cambridge University Library: Royal Commonwealth Society Library

15 Peasant returning from market on his donkey, 1908.

Source: Getty Images

16 Downtown Kingston street scene, 1900.

Source: Caribbean Photo Archive

4

The Man Who Left Jamaica

Claude McKay in 1912

O, you sons of Afric's soil,
    Dyin' in a foreign land,
Crushed beneat' de moil and toil,
    Break, break de oppressors' hand!

—Claude McKay, "George William Gordon to the Oppressed Natives," 1912

That McKay got out of the police force within seventeen months of joining was largely due to Walter Jekyll's quiet but influential intervention. Such an early release was unheard of. "One joins the Constabulary," McKay later wrote, "for five years and there is no hope of getting out before the term is up unless one has very badly misbehaved. Then you are dismissed with a stain upon your character."[1] He was as surprised as anyone by the favorable turn of events. Not until McKay obtained his release did Jekyll tell of the behind-the-scenes effort.[2]

Incredulous at his good fortune, McKay celebrated his discharge from the force with the gusto and joy of a man condemned to death who is suddenly and unexpectedly given his freedom.

Scarce can I believe my eyes,
Yet before me there it lies,
Precious paper granting me
Quick release from misery.

So farewell to Half Way Tree,
And the plains I hate to see!
Soon will I forget my ills
In my loved Clarendon hills.[3]

He kept his word. Released at the end of October 1911, he fled Kingston and was back in Clarendon within days.[4] His father had "plenty of land," so McKay planted peas, corn, and yams, which brought the prodigal son quick returns. "Oh, Jamaica was a happy place for me then," he remembered. "I thought I was walking always with flowers under my feet."[5]

McKay continued his contented "labourer's life" as he awaited the publication of his book of poems. Published in January 1912, *Songs of Jamaica* met with "ready sale" and gained a rapturous reception at home and abroad. "Praise, Praise, Praise!" is how McKay recalled the response to the volume. "The praise of the book in the island press was amazing. It was all praise—not a derogatory word. . . . From different parts of the British Empire it was all the same."[6] He exaggerated, but only a little.

Thomas MacDermot, editor of the *Jamaica Times* who was also a poet, wrote the most extensive and informed review of *Songs of Jamaica*. He was delighted with the book but did not refrain from voicing reservations. Noting that McKay was only twenty-one (in fact twenty-two) and that *Songs* was his "first printed collection," he presciently wrote:

> I say this is a *first* collection, with an emphasis on that first, because we find here such evidence of a rich gift both in poetic conception and in the art of literary expression that assures us that we have a heart and a mind destined, as one of our mountain springs pours forth its streams[,] to yield a great deal more of work as excellent as this, and still more. . . . Here we have a mind and heart stirring with the truly poetic impulses. We venture to say it: here we have a poet.

MacDermot registered, as James Weldon Johnson and others in the United States would later, McKay's versatility as a poet—"the ready sense of humour and of pathos, the spontaneity of feeling, and the facility with which feeling finds varied forms of expression." He averred that some of the poems "might have been more wisely left out." "Quashie to Buccra," in particular, could have done with "a little further touch of lyric ease and flow," but this, MacDermot thought, would come with practice. McKay, he wrote, needed to be on his guard "against colourless lines stealing in to round the verse" and the "didactic tone that creeps in here and there."

But to MacDermot, these were minor blemishes: "taking the collection as a whole, and speaking of the great majority of the poems, we have here outstanding merit." He adjudged it "absolutely correct to say that the publication of this volume is an event of note in Jamaica Literature." He offered a "hearty, sincere welcome to *Songs of Jamaica*. We are proud of the volume." "It does its author credit; it does Jamaica credit, Jamaica who has produced him. We shall," he concluded, "look forward to his future work not only with hope but with confidence."[7] Coming from such a distinguished man of letters, one admired by McKay himself, the review, careful and generous, understandably pleased young Claude.

"Resistance": The Tramcar Riots of 1912

It is just as well that McKay had left the police force at the end of 1911, for early in the new year, Kingston's uneasy peace was shattered by a popular uprising that was unprecedented in the city's history. And in the end, the primary target of the people's fury was the police.

The whole affair started innocently enough. On February 17, 1912, the Canadian-owned West India Electric Company (WIEC) that operated Kingston's tramway services, announced that it would no longer offer seven vouchers for one shilling, but six. This effectively amounted to a more than 16 percent increase in the cost of travel. The residents of Kingston were outraged. Their representatives on the City Council and in the Legislative Council protested to the governor and the company on their behalf. The mayor of Kingston was especially peeved at the governor for allowing the increase without any prior consultation with the people's local representatives. In its reportage and editorials, the *Gleaner* was more critical of Governor Olivier than it was of the WIEC.[8]

The people took matters into their own hands. They refused to buy the one-shilling voucher and instead bought a single voucher at a time for two pence. Moreover, they augmented their opposition to the increase by paying in farthings.[9] The protest soon escalated to more ingenious ways of inconveniencing the company in order to force it to back down. One man started the practice of paying one farthing in the box and then hand the conductor a two-and-six-pence piece to take the remaining seven farthings from. Another dropped a farthing into the fare box and then handed the conductor a shilling piece for him to take the remainder and provide him with change. These and other obstructionist tactics soon went under the name of "passive resistance" with the practitioners being called "passive resisters." The resisters succeeded in slowing down the progress of the conductors to such an extent that many passengers reached their destination without ever having been asked for their fare. Such practices had the desired result of reducing the WIEC's revenue. But the company refused to buckle.

The resisters responded by increasing the pressure: they now asked for vouchers, receipts verifying payment, to which they were entitled but had never previously demanded. They also asked for transfers slips to which they were now entitled. Remarkably, the WIEC had neither the vouchers nor the transfer slips requested by the disgruntled passengers. It also did not have enough farthings to provide change for passengers. Caught off guard, it sent to England to get more farthings to counteract the resisters. But one ingenious group of citizens, a "syndicate," the *Gleaner* called it, attempted to gather up and hoard as many farthings as possible to frustrate the company's countermove.

As the protest escalated, drivers and conductors stopped their trams, refusing to continue the journey so long as some passengers refused to pay without receiving vouchers. This frustrated the remaining passengers, who then demanded a refund because they were not taken to their destinations. Conductors and roadmasters working for the company frequently called the police to break stalemates. But the police, perhaps fearful of being attacked by an enraged citizenry, generally refrained from arresting the resisters. Two members of Kingston's middle class were arrested, however, after Harry McCrea, the deputy inspector of the Constabulary and head of the Kingston police, called up reinforcements, including mounted policemen, when one passenger refused to pay without receiving a voucher. F. A. Judah, a member of a prominent Jewish merchant family, who witnessed the incident, remarked: "Why should a man who has done nothing wrong be arrested?" For this, McCrea asked for Judah's name and address. Judah refused, and he too was arrested. McCrea quickly became the most hated man in Kingston. The *Gleaner* attacked him, the mayor and Kingston's city council called upon the governor to dismiss him, as did H. A. L. Simpson, the city's popular representative in the Legislative Council. Crowds booed and jeered Inspector McCrea whenever he appeared.[10]

Initially, the protest was genteel and good-humored. For a week, Kingston bathed in a carnivalesque atmosphere as the passengers and the people as a whole felt their strength and noticed the company's growing discomfiture. According to the newspapers, the prime movers behind the passive resistance were young men, mainly clerks, who depended upon the trams to get to and from work in the commercial area of the city. The conductors suffered the most, as they were increasingly frustrated in the execution of their work. "For God sake, Sir, caut [sic] you behave yourself?" one exasperated conductor asked a passive resister.[11] But soon they too resigned themselves to the situation, many not even bothering to collect the fares.

The whole affair was like an elaborate game of chess played out on the streets of Kingston between the WIEC (white) and the resisters (black), with daring moves and countermoves. But by the end of the first week of protest, a different game was being played. The management of the WIEC, failing to checkmate the resisters, grew increasingly frustrated and resorted to a less metaphorical form of warfare. Instead of relenting by rescinding the fare increase, it pressured the government to intervene on the company's side, it chided the *Gleaner* for supporting the resisters, it insulted the mayor in a most disrespectful manner, and it called upon the forces of law and order to take action. McCrea was happy to oblige, and when the police beat up a group of working-class protesters on the night of Saturday, February 24, tempers got short. Drawing upon a long tradition of working-class solidarity on the island, the little people of Kingston decided to take a greater hand in the protest and to defend their own. The increasing violence of the police was met with the counterviolence of the Kingston poor. Aggrieved, they sought revenge the following night in the downtown area of Kingston.

The violence escalated on Sunday evening and reached its climax on Monday night. The city leaders' calls for calm went largely unheeded. Three of the company's streetcars were damaged; another was taken possession of and commandeered by the crowd, who drove it down Orange Street, then on to the foot of King Street, where it was then set on fire and partially destroyed. The stoning of the policemen intensified, placing the forces of law and order on the defensive for the first time. Inspector Kershaw had the temerity to drive into one of the hot spots at the corner of Orange and North streets. He reported that his vehicle was "followed by a shower of stones." When he turned the corner, he found two of his subinspectors and small party of policemen "bombarded by a hurricane of bricks and stones from the yards on both sides of the street." His men made repeated charges, but as they could not get to close quarters and as they were nearly all injured, he "ordered a retreat to Barracks which was carried out."[12] Laying siege to the main police station in Kingston on Monday night, the crowd was dispersed only after Inspector Kershaw read the Riot Act and the police opened fire, killing one person and wounding more than thirty others during a series of running battles in the commercial area of the city. A large group of rioters wielding sticks, bricks, and iron pipes caught a group of seven policemen unawares. The seven, recognizing that they would be overwhelmed by the large, angry crowd, took to their heels. The crowd chased after them. "Away with the policemen!" went the cry. "Lick them! Lick them!"[13] shouted the crowd, as it bore down upon the police. "Pursued by the mob like wolves pursuing their prey," the policemen made a narrow escape into Burke's rum shop at the corner of Orange and Beeston streets in the downtown area of the city. A quick-witted (and kindhearted) barmaid bolted the doors behind the fleeing policemen just in time. The crowd laid siege to the bar. "Murder! Murder! Help! Help!" came the desperate bawling from the bar— strange noises from Missa Kershaw's "bullyin'" policemen but music to the ears of Kingston's avenging poor. Governor Olivier, who happened to be passing in his car, saw the commotion and heard the screams. He ordered his driver to stop, got out of the car, and sought to relieve the trapped group of noisy policemen. "You are a brave man," a member of the crowd told the governor, "but we mean to get square with these policemen." The governor remonstrated with the crowd, telling them "how surprised he was at their behaviour and asking what had come over them."[14] But soon he too was the object of attack. He was hit twice by flying bricks, but not seriously hurt, as his aide-de-camp bundled him back into his car and sped off. The policemen managed to escape through the rear of the bar while the crowd was distracted by its exchange with the governor.

Kingston had seen nothing of the kind before. Respectable Jamaica was shocked. "What a week of it! This is a visitation!" some cried.[15] The *Jamaica Times* trawled the history books to find out if there was any parallel for this sort of treatment of a representative of the Crown, the governor, anywhere in the British Empire. It discovered that Lord Elgin (who had served in Jamaica between 1842 and 1845), had been pelted by English-speaking Canadians in Montreal in 1847 for passing an unpopular law while he was governor there.[16]

The newspapers first reported that the governor was hit by accident— that the flying bricks were not meant for Sir Sydney. That he could have been a target of the crowd's fury seemed unthinkable. But the trial of the two men charged with the assault, Cyril McKoy and Joel Mallacci, told a story of deliberate intent to harm Olivier. The men had no legal representation in court, but the evidence against them—even with the requisite skepticism in such circumstances—including that of their own witnesses, was damning. According to the chief witness, Charles Clarke, McKoy was one of the ring-leaders of the group that besieged Burke's rum shop. When the doors were bolted behind the policemen, McKoy went and got a hatchet, which he gave to another man to chop open the saloon window. When Olivier's car came along, two men got out and made their way to the window. Mallacci is said to have called out, "Do you know who that is? It is Olivier. Lick him!" He hurled a brick at Olivier, and McKoy sent another, hitting the governor, and others in the crowd let their bricks fly at the car as it quickly sped away. Clarke, a former schoolmate of Mallacci's, saw all of this and reported it to the authorities. Another witness reported that McKoy had boasted to her that he was the second man to hit the governor. Mallacci called another witness, but the man testified against Mallacci, saying he saw the accused pick up two bricks in Luke Lane that night. Mallacci, according to this wit-ness, cried out: "White give black authority to shoot and I am going to kill two before they kill me." He is said to have boasted afterward of "licking the Governor."[17] McKoy and Mallacci were both found guilty and each sen-tenced to twelve months in prison.

Sir Sydney, no doubt embarrassed that such events should have occurred on his watch, made light of the whole affair in his telegram to his superiors at the Colonial Office in London. He blamed the disorder on "crowds of roughs" and the "dangerous and criminal class" of the city. He explained that on the Monday night "it became necessary" for the police to use fire-arms and fixed bayonets. The governor informed the Colonial Office that a young man was killed, but did not say that the youth killed, Thomas Bar-clay, was an innocent party going about his lawful business when he was shot by the police. Sir Sydney reported that two officers and twenty-five policemen were injured by the mob that night. But he lied when he wrote elliptically of "several persons wounded[,] a number injured principally by weapons of mob"; he knew full well that the crowd targeted the police and left practically everyone else alone. (The single exception was a roadmaster, who the crowd thought was too keen on protecting the WIEC's property.) The crowds attacked the police and property, especially company prop-erty. By Wednesday, February 28, when Olivier dispatched his telegram, Kershaw had called for and received reinforcement from St. Catherine, Clarendon, Portland, and as far away as St. James, at the other end of the island. With this and the display of force on Monday night, the city had returned to an uneasy calm.[18] Olivier tried to allay Whitehall's anxieties: "I have no reason to expect further trouble but every precaution taken.

Damage not serious to property in city except broken window lamps and a little shoplifting." He asked the Colonial Office to tell his wife in London that he was all right.[19]

In many ways, the WIEC fare increase and the violence of the police merely served as catalysts for the expression of the pent-up frustration and smoldering rage of working-class Kingston. The uprising of February 1912 provided the island's authorities and polite society with a glimpse of the subterranean discontent and neglect of Jamaica's working class and poor, especially in Kingston. The riot put paid to any prospects that Olivier may have had of an extension of his term as the colony's governor. Recalled to London in February 1913, he was appointed permanent secretary to the Board of Agriculture and Fisheries, a lowly job compared to that of governor of Jamaica, at a salary of £1,500, less than a third of the £5,000 he had earned as governor.[20] It was difficult not to interpret this move as a major demotion. The plantocracy and the *Gleaner*, its mouthpiece, were happy to see him go. Thomas MacDermot, a firm supporter of Olivier's, bemoaned his departure. The hated Deputy Inspector McCrea died suddenly of a heart attack on the streets of Kingston soon after the riots.

McKay and the "Resisters"

From his tranquil retreat in the hills of Clarendon, McKay followed the turbulent events in Kingston with great interest. Despite his distance from the action, he sought to make his voice heard across the island as he expressed his sympathy for the protesters. He did not condone the rioting, but he fully supported the passive resisters. McKay not only gave vent to his Jamaican nationalism but also articulated the defiance that later came to be associated with "If We Must Die." The poem was called "Passive Resistance."

> There'll be no more riotin',
> Stonin' p'lice an' burnin' car;
> But we mean to gain our rights
> By a strong though bloodless war.
>
> We will show an alien trust
> Dat Jamaicans too can fight
> An' dat while our blood is hot,
> They won't crush us wi' deir might.

The poem continues by promising to "hold 'the boys' in check, / There'll be no more riotin'." It apologizes for the inconvenience caused, but ends boldly:

> Our vict'ry day shall come.
> There are aliens in our midst
> Who would slay us for our right;
> Yet though vipers block the way
> We will rally to the fight.
>
> We'll keep up a bloodless war,
> We will pay the farthings-fare
> An' we send the challenge forth,
> "Only touch us if you dare!"[21]

Significantly, McKay did not condemn the rioting, nor did he apologize for it; his "sorry" was only for "the worry given some." Whereas the *Gleaner* and the *Jamaica Times* along with the governor denounced the rioters as "hooligans," "roughs," "the criminal elements," "the dangerous and criminal class," and other nice things, McKay affectionately referred to them as "the boys"—evidence again of his sympathy with "wrongdoers." He is resolutely on the side of the people and makes himself a member of the collective "we," in whose voice the poem is enunciated. It is noticeable, too, that he made repeated reference to an oppressive alien presence on the island in the form of the West India Electric Company.

McKay also struck the note of revolt in another poem of 1912, published in the press but not included in his collection of poems. First published in a British magazine in April of that year, "George William Gordon to the Oppressed Natives" imaginatively reconstructs the message and sentiments of the celebrated martyr of the Morant Bay Rebellion of 1865.[22] In a desperate bid for justice and relief, the poor peasants and workers of St. Thomas rose up against their oppressors. Beginning on October 11, 1865, the uprising was vanquished within the space of a fortnight with the capture and execution of its leader Paul Bogle (1820–1865), a small farmer and Native Baptist leader, and his supporter George William Gordon (1820–1865), an outspoken colored member of the Jamaica Assembly, representing Bogle's followers. Gordon, a fierce critic of the governor and the ruling class, was not directly involved in the uprising (he was in Kingston), but in the bloodletting authorized by Governor Edward Eyre on behalf of the plantocracy, Gordon was arrested and transported to Morant Bay, tried under martial law, and summarily executed. The figures are imprecise, but estimates vary from the official number of 439 to 3,000 killed. On top of those, hundreds were brutally flogged (women as well as men) and thousands of huts were burnt to the ground.[23]

The poem is of the hortatory kind that is most powerfully exemplified by "If We Must Die." Perhaps more than any other of his Jamaican poems, "Gordon to the Oppressed Natives" provides clear evidence that McKay's poetry of resistance written in exile was anticipated before he left the island. In McKay's rendition, Gordon's address is aimed at the exiled African nation in Jamaica:

> O, you sons of Afric's soil,
>   Dyin' in a foreign land,
> Crushed beneat' de moil and toil,
>   Break, break de oppressors' hand!

The poem runs for another seven stanzas. The downtrodden are urged to rise up and "Show dem dat you ha' some brains, / Though you may be coarse an' rude." Gordon reminds the oppressed that slavery has ended and reminds them of the efforts of the abolitionists—Wilberforce, Sharpe, Buxton, and Clarkson—in their struggle for freedom. But the freedom of the African is still being denied, hence the need to "Trample on de tyranny / Still continued by a few!" He tells them it is lawful to use force—"use our might"—to put an end to "dis great shame" of their continued oppression. He points out that England has already compensated the slaveholders, that the Jamaican peasants and workers are also subjects of the British Crown, and that Englishmen would never tolerate such oppression. "Rise, O people of my kind!" he pleads, "Struggle, struggle to be free!" He ends by urging Black Jamaicans to shake off their oppressors and to seek victory or death:

> Show de tyrants dat you're strong;
> Fight for freedom's rights, you blacks,
>   Ring de slaves' old battle-song!

> Gordon's heart here bleeds for you,
>   He will lead to victory;
> We will conquer every foe,
>   Or togeder gladly die.[24]

In his autobiography, McKay reports that "George William Gordon became one of the legendary heroes of Jamaica that the peasants were always talking about."[25] McKay had, according to the *Gleaner*, written a prize-winning essay in the *Jamaica Tribune* on the Morant Bay Rebellion.[26] "Gordon to the Oppressed Natives" was first published in London in *T. P's Weekly*, a magazine published by T. P. O'Connor, the distinguished Irish Home Rule advocate, MP, and journalist. It had won a prize in an international poetry competition organized by the *Weekly*. The Jamaican newspapers proudly reported the honor bestowed upon a native son and reprinted the poem.[27] According to McKay, when the poem was republished in Jamaica, "it created as much of a stir as 'If We Must Die' created in the United States." He further writes that "Gordon to the Oppressed Natives" was "denounced by the leading ministers of various denominations as inciting to riot; but Mr. Jekyll wrote to the *Daily Gleaner* that it was only a poet's way of expressing his appreciation of a great personality."[28] That there would have been a fuss over the poem is understandable, for "Gordon to the Oppressed Natives" came fresh on the heels of the tramcar riots and McKay was perhaps inspired to write it precisely because of those events. He probably wrote the poem during the riots—around the same time as he wrote "Passive Resistance." The Jamaican ruling class *would* be alarmed.

Peasants' Ways o' Thinkin'

It is clear what McKay was against, but what was he for? What was his vision of the good society? The clearest answer comes from his long poem "Peasants' Ways o' Thinkin." Published in the *Gleaner* in January 1912, the poem lists the complaints of the Jamaican peasants and voices their demands as McKay perceived them. It is petition and manifesto combined. At the heart of the peasants' demands is the need for land:

> Havin' we owna mancha-root,
> Havin' we dandy Sunday suit,
> We'll happy wi' our modest lot
> An' won't grudge buccra wha' dem got.
>
> A piece o' lan' fe raise two goat,
> A little rum fe ease we t'roat,

A little cot fe res' we head—
An' we're contented tell we dead.[29]

These modest and basic demands, congruent with the Fabian socialism that McKay professed at the time, were by no means anticapitalist. However, the "piece o' land" and his own "mancha-root" (banana tree) that the peasant dreams of would hardly fall into his possession like manna from heaven. Given the skewed distribution of land and the intransigence of the oligarchy, land reform would undoubtedly have challenged powerful interests. McKay's peasant-narrator demands land but is silent on what to do if the demand is not met. His father's owning of large tracts of land may have conditioned the son's position on the agrarian question. At the end of the day, McKay seems to be saying, the peasants are willing to reconcile themselves to some inequality between themselves and buccra; there is a stoical and fatalistic coming to terms with this:

We may n't be rich like buccra folk;
For us de white, for dem de yolk,
Das's de way dat the egg divide,
An' we content wi' de outside.

Thus, although signaled and intimated in his early poetry, McKay's anti-capitalist and revolutionary socialist positions were to develop and mature only in exile.

Jamaica Farewell

Walter Jekyll was horrified: "America . . . Claude, do you know how Negroes are treated in America?" Jekyll understood McKay's desire to emigrate but was shocked when Claude told him of the intended destination.[30] It appears that McKay came to the decision at the end of 1911, but the serious planning came several months later.[31]

Placed in its proper historical context, McKay's decision was not that surprising. Black Jamaicans had been emigrating to the United States in rapidly increasing numbers. His mother's doctor (an Edinburgh University–trained Black Barbadian) had left three years earlier. Despite widespread knowledge of the oppression of its Black citizens, the United States was perceived, especially by the island's young and ambitious, as the place to be. McKay remembered that his contemporaries considered Europe, and some went there to be educated, but America was thought of differently. It was seen as "the land of education and opportunity. . . . It was the new land to which all people who had youth and a youthful mind turned."[32]

Two other developments in 1912 influenced and undergirded McKay's decision to go to the United States. The first was the publicity surrounding Booker T. Washington's International Conference on the Negro, held at Tuskegee in April 1912. The conference attracted considerable attention in Jamaica. In the *Jamaica Times*, MacDermot questioned the composition of the Jamaican delegation chosen by the governor and offered nationalist advice as to how the delegates should keep Jamaica's "end up" in the United States. The *Gleaner* carried extensive reports. For McKay, perhaps the most important information that came out of the conference was the long report written by one of the delegates, Margaret Geddes of Kingston's Shortwood Training College, a women's teacher-training college, on her impressions of Tuskegee.

Geddes opened her report by approvingly quoting Paul Laurence Dunbar's celebratory poem on Tuskegee, "pride of the swift growing South, / Oh, Mother Tuskegee, thou shinest today / As a gem in the fairest of lands." Her own remarks coincide with Dunbar's poem: "Tuskegee is big and beautiful. Not only is there the natural beauty of trees and well kept lawns and shrubberies, and flower beds but there is the spiritual beauty of cultivated minds, of a well and disciplined ordered life." Her article, written in the same vein throughout, reads like one long advertisement for Tuskegee: she has nothing but praise for Washington, whom she compares to a king; the students and staff were all exemplary. She reported that there were twenty-three Jamaicans studying there and another seven on the staff. Another article in the *Gleaner* expressed the hope that Washington would make a trip to Jamaica and reported that the British Union, a Tuskegee society made up of British Caribbean students and teachers, had passed a resolution urging the Caribbean delegates to induce their governments to extend an early invitation to Washington to visit the Caribbean.[33] Washington never made it to the Caribbean, but his name and work were widely known. "The fame of Mr. Washington has spread all over the world and I wanted to be in his school," McKay recalled.[34]

Coinciding with the Tuskegee conference was a tour of the island by the distinguished African American actress Henrietta Vinton Davis and one of her colleagues. A few years later, Davis would become one of the leading officials and propagandists of Garvey's Universal Negro Improvement Association. She was the highest-ranking woman in the UNIA, becoming its vice president, and was one of its most respected and effective orators.[35] During her 1912 tour, McKay and Jekyll went together to see her perform at one of Kingston's theaters. She read selections from Shakespeare, for which she was famous in the United States. McKay enjoyed her performance, and Jekyll, a keen musician himself, who had been reluctant to go, was so impressed with her, especially the ring of her voice, that he and McKay went backstage to meet her. Jekyll invited her to visit him at his home at Mavis Bank in the St. Andrew hills.[36]

McKay visited Davis and spoke to her about America. She informed him that she was a good friend of Washington's and that she often visited Tuskegee. There were many West Indian students at Tuskegee, she told him, and she thought that he might like it there, for Washington was "a highly respected man and the students at Tuskegee were well protected."[37] Davis provided the reassuring news McKay had hoped to hear.

Added to the widespread publicity of Tuskegee and the discussion with Davis was the agricultural policy of the colonial government in Jamaica. Beginning in the 1890s, the government sent out agricultural instructors to advise the rural population on how they could improve their cultivation and livestock breeding. Jekyll thought that if McKay received training in agriculture, he could also become an instructor on his return to the island. Such a career, Jekyll believed, would have the added benefit of keeping McKay close to the peasantry and its aspirations and ways of thinking.[38]

But given his many songs of praise to his bucolic Clarendon hills, why did McKay seek to leave them again so soon after his return, even for a relatively short period of study abroad? The evidence suggests that McKay became discontented soon after returning home and that not only did he want to go to the United States, but he also wanted to leave Clarendon and Jamaica. In *My Green Hills of Jamaica*, he tells us that the villagers no longer perceived him in the same way as they had before he left for Kingston: he was no longer simply young Claude from Nairne Castle but a poet, "a little personage." This made him uncomfortable. The villagers knew that he was a poet, and that made him "different," even though he "wanted so much to be like them." He observed that even his closest friends at home were never the same. "I tried to be as simple as simple, but they would never accept me with the same simplicity."[39] McKay went so far as to claim that he was "much happier in Kingston," where he "went with the crowd" and nobody knew him. He also felt more comfortable at Jekyll's place, "where it was not at all embarrassing to be known and accepted as a poet."[40] Given the contemporaneous evidence of his poetry (as opposed to his memoir, written almost forty years later) we can safely discount the notion that he was "much happier in Kingston"! Despite his shyness and the undoubted discomfiture caused by his new celebrity, I am not convinced that this was sufficient to drive him from Clarendon. Surely, had he been determined to stay, he and the villagers could have come to a satisfactory modus vivendi over time.

"Clarendon Hills, Farewell!" gives a deeper and more convincing, if still somewhat mysterious, cause for his discontent. The poem, published in the *Gleaner* just two weeks after McKay sailed for the United States, declares:

> Clarendon hills, my homeland hills, farewell!
> 'Twas in my heart with you for aye to dwell:
> Returning, I had hoped to find repose
> Within your bosom; but the old sad woes
> Drive me from you again, and now meseems
> 'Tis you that cause them, for in those day-dreams
> Wherein I chiefly live I find of late
> My love for you is turning into hate.

McKay does not explain or even name "the old sad woes" of which his poem speaks. His autobiographical writings are mute, too. But surely they could not have been the new embarrassment that came with his status as a poet. Though still unclear, it seems from his second stanza that his discontent might have been caused by the place itself rather than the behavior of the people there:

> "Ah fickle lad!" I hear my reader say,
> "But yesterday you loved and hate to-day:
> Is this a poet's license that you take,
> Faith with your old associates thus to break?"
> To which I make reply: Hills have no heart,
> I wound them not, they will not feel the smart,
> And taking love from them, to make amends,
> I give a double portion to my friends.[41]

"Christmas in de Air" and "Peasants' Ways o' Thinkin'," in which he lists the troubles and hard times of the rural population, suggest that McKay

was particularly disillusioned with the prevailing conditions in the countryside in 1911 and 1912. Both of these poems were written after his return
to Clarendon. The island as a whole was afflicted by an unusually prolonged
drought in 1911 and 1912; in Clarendon in particular, conditions were exacerbated by the fact that work on a government road-building project had
come to an end. Published in December, 1911, "Christmas in de Air" tells
of the sadness that overwhelmed the season of celebration and merriment.

> Dere is Christmas in de air:—
> But de house is cold an' bare,
> . . . .
> Oh! de time is 'tiff wid me!
> Coffee parch up 'pon de tree,
> All de yam-plants tek an' die
> 'Counten o' de awful dry:
> Ah, I wonder how we'll fare,
> Although Christmas in de air.

The peasant, in whose voice the poem is enunciated, relates that his wife is
sick in bed, he has children to feed, yet the baby on his knee "Is as hungry as
can be."

> Wuk is shet do'n 'pon de road,
> An' plantation pay no good,
> Whole day ninepance for a man!
> Wha' dah come to dis a lan'?
> Lard, I trimble when I hear
> Dat dere's Christmas in de air.

Like the peasant of "Peasants' Ways o' Thinkin'," he complains about the price
of food, the heavy taxes on the poor, and the government's callous disregard
of the suffering. The poem ends on a now familiar note:

> O sweet life so sad, so gay,
> Oh why did you come my way,
> All your gaiety to vaunt
> An' yet torture me wid want?
> I'm a-dyin' o' despair
> While dere's Christmas in de air.[42]

As if thinking that the eight stanzas of "Christmas in de Air" had not adequately portrayed people's suffering, McKay a month later published the thirty-one-stanza "Peasants' Ways o' Thinkin'" in the *Gleaner*. It was an appeal for relief that McKay, as the poem itself relates, thought of presenting in prose form (rather like one of U. Theo's missives on behalf of the poor to the press):

> I sort a be'n dah wan' fe try
> To put i' in prose cut an' dry,
> But a'ter all a caan' do worse
> Dan dish i' up in rhymin' verse.

Thinking, that the ruling class ("buccra") have had more than their fair share to say ("jawed enuff"), the persona thought he would intervene on behalf of quashie:

> Aldough we cheerful-like an' glad,
> Life well an' bitter, well an' sad;
> So eben when we 're mute an' dumb,
> We prayin' hard dat change may come.[43]

Given his unease with his new status in Clarendon and his aversion to witnessing suffering, it is understandable that McKay sought to leave Clarendon and its woes. Moreover, he heard the call of the United States, that "great modern land."[44]

But before he paid for his passage to the United States, McKay went to see William Plant, headmaster of the prestigious Titchfield School and one of the island's leading and most celebrated educators. Plant, a man of mixed descent (Black mother, white English father) had been a member of the Jamaican delegation to Tuskegee. McKay talked to Plant about America and Tuskegee. Plant confirmed what Davis had told him. America, Plant said, was "a great, big, wonderfully industrialized country" where McKay could get a very liberal education. He thought that at Tuskegee, McKay would be protected from prejudice because of Washington's prestige. Plant's pretty picture of the United States was, however, tarnished. He told McKay that traveling down from New York to Tuskegee he could not travel by Pullman, but his wife, who was very light-skinned and easily mistaken for white, could; they had made the journey in separate coaches. "My heart sank," said McKay, "to think that one of our great educators was humiliated in such a way." Plant tried to assuage McKay's feelings by telling him that the incident did not bother him that much because he was not going to live in the United States. He thought that it was just "one of the vagaries of American life."[45]

Shortly before leaving the island, McKay organized an important cultural event, almost as a party to give thanks to the villagers of Nairne Castle and the surrounding area. As secretary of the James Hill Literary Society, he was the driving force behind a remarkable evening of recitations and readings from the works of Jamaican writers, and Jamaican writers only. McKay, several members of his family, and a host of others read excerpts from books and stories and recited poems. The event, held on June 5, 1912, was well attended, hugely entertaining, and regarded by all as a great success. Thomas MacDermot, a native of Clarendon himself, who was a participant, was so impressed with the evening that he recorded the program and proceedings for posterity. It was, he said, a unique and historic evening. One author plausibly claimed that Frankfield—largely through the efforts of U. Theo—was the "intellectual capital of black Jamaica." But little James Hill, about ten miles farther north in the Clarendon hills could make a good claim to that accolade.[46]

Two weeks after his "All Jamaica" entertainment, the *Jamaica Times* announced to the public at large that McKay "intends proceeding to the Tuskegee Institution in September to get a course on Agriculture." McKay in fact sailed on July 25, 1912, for the United States. He intended to return after his course of study was over.[47]

Members of his family accompanied him to Kingston, where they said their good-byes. McKay went alone to see Jekyll at his place at Mavis Bank, which Jekyll preferred because he feared that he might break down and cry in public. McKay later had lunch with MacDermot and his wife.

He left Jamaica for, of all places, Alabama—a synonym for racist barbarity, the "Egypt land" of Afro-America—the bottom of America's Deep South. Many people warned him. MacDermot expressed his misgivings in words tinged with foreboding: "Claude, we hate to see you go because you will be changed, terribly changed, by America." But McKay preferred to take his chances. Going to America, he said, was "the greatest event in the history of our hills. . . . Surely there would be opportunity in this land even for a Negro."[48]

MacDermot was deeply moved by the young Jamaican's departure. He shared his thoughts and feelings with his readers. "The last week of July," he told them, "is marked on the tablets of my memory because I bade good-bye then to Claude McKay."

> We parted in Kingston and our surroundings were dust, hot zinc roofs, noise and other city horrors. But I think we felt that we were away in the woods listening to some quietly murmuring brooklet and catching the notes of the John-to-Whit concerning which that very week this paper printed a song by McKay. He is off to a training centre in America, to study Agriculture and he is not likely to be back within three years. My heart smites me at the thought. Change he must in some things, still I feel pretty confident that the inner man of native modesty and simple beauty is going to defy "the world's coarse finger and thumb." He is [of] loveable disposition and after we parted I felt that Jamaica was suddenly a lonely place.[49]

On the eve of departure, McKay confessed to having been "weak-kneed," "maddened by a thousand fears," but was also quietly confident of his prospects in the new land. As he concluded in his farewell poem, "To a Friend":

> The boy you know
> Will come back home a man:
> He means to make you proud of him,
> He'll breast the waves and strongly swim
> And conquer,—for he can.[50]

No doubt, as a child, Claude must have heard the popular Jamaican saying beloved by his elders: "If yuh cyaan hear, yuh ha fe feel."[51] In the end, his American experience proved a painful and traumatic one. He endured new and previously unimagined sorrows; but America also served as his crucible. He squeezed his suffering and frustration into his sonnets, bulging with searing and suffocating pain, which, in his most powerful efforts, erupt like volcanoes shooting red-hot lava of rage way up into the sky, creating a crimson canopy of fire. Was the game worth the candle? That is a question that only McKay himself could answer. However, if his poem "America" is anything to go by, he apparently felt the enterprise was worthwhile:

> Although she feeds me bread of bitterness,
> And sinks into my throat her tiger's tooth,
> Stealing my breath of life, I will confess
> I love this cultured hell that tests my youth![52]

This was written in 1921; McKay died in 1948. He might have felt differently earlier in his American sojourn and changed his mind in the years before he died.

MacDermot's fear and prediction that McKay would be "terribly changed" by America, as will be demonstrated later, was simultaneously confirmed and contradicted by the course of events.

McKay's Jamaican Inventory

A number of features of McKay's life in Jamaica were of cardinal importance in the formation of his personality and worldview by the time he left the island in 1912.

First, McKay was a freethinker, a confident and proud rationalist and member of the Rationalist Press Association in London, a militant and proud child of the European Enlightenment. Prior to his conversion to Catholicism in 1944, less than four years before his death, his atheism was one of the most powerful and enduring threads of continuity in his outlook on life. He spent time and effort attacking religion, especially Christianity of the Protestant variety. Indeed, it is no exaggeration to say that he went out of his way—especially in his novels—to attack religion. Not even the idealized peasants in his late novel, *Banana Bottom*, escaped censure on this score.

Second, accompanying his rationalism was socialism, Fabian socialism to be precise. He went so far as to claim that he had "imbibed" the stuff with his mother's milk. McKay explained this by pointing out that his beloved brother and mentor, U. Theo, was a Fabian socialist. Walter Jekyll was "a Buddhist and something of a Fabian." Even the governor of the island, Olivier, to whom McKay dedicated his first book, was a Fabian and the friend of McKay's hero, George Bernard Shaw, a founding and leading member of the Fabian Society.[53]

Third, one sees clearly from his autobiography and early poetry McKay's strong identification with and love for the Jamaican peasantry, the folk. Significantly, one of the motives behind his going to America in the first place was to study "scientific agriculture" in order to be able to serve and be near his people. His respect for these Black small farmers is illustrated by two examples he gave of their interaction with supposedly British experts.

The British colonial authorities sent agricultural instructors to the islands to spread the wonders and benefits of modern science to the benighted peasants of Jamaica and elsewhere in the Caribbean. All too often, they found themselves humbled by the country folk of the islands. Governor Sir Henry Blake, who established the Jamaica Agricultural Society in 1895 to spread the gospel of the white god of science among the small farmers, was not optimistic about the chances of success. After all, the peasants are Black, and Black people are stupid: "What the ultimate result will be I cannot say. A black population not very intelligent and saturated with suspicion of any attempt to interfere with their crude and wasteful system is not easily influenced."[54]

Before planting, the peasants would clear the land. Two to three weeks later, they burned the shrub, grass, and other debris. Generations of enslaved Jamaicans and their peasant descendants had done things this way—the tried and proven method. But the British agricultural instructors, of course, knew better. They protested against the burning of the debris, saying that it should be plowed under to enrich the soil. "Well," reported McKay, "some of the peasants followed their advice and when they did their planting, the leaves of what they had planted were consumed by worms as soon as they had grown a few inches. Those who insisted on burning this debris found that their planting had developed very healthily." McKay distinctly remembered one of the instructors telling a peasant that the young cocoa plant he had uprooted would not grow. "The peasant insisted that it would and planted it. The next year when the instructor returned, he found a flourishing cocoa tree." The agricultural instructors, McKay concluded, "made their mistakes."[55] So much for "crude and wasteful systems." As Bertolt Brecht rejoiced, "Praise be doubt!" McKay's celebration of the peasantry at times, however, became excessive. "No Jamaican peasant," he declared, "imagines he is inferior to anybody but God."[56]

In another passage in *My Green Hills of Jamaica*, McKay explicitly objected to the way townspeople look upon country folk. Anticipating the surprise and condescension—if not total incredulity—with which most people would react to the idea of a group of committed free-thinking peasant children in turn-of-the-century Jamaica, he went on the offensive:

> People who are born and grow up in large towns and cities have a tendency to imagine that people from small towns and villages are naturally stupid and unintelligent. There is no greater fallacy. Personally I believe that the masses of the cities are woefully less intelligent than people who make up the population of a country town or a village. The country or small town man may not be as slickly dressed but somehow he does use his brains to think. I have

known so many city people from truck driver to professor who just cannot think at all.[57]

He praised the openness, tolerance, and generosity of spirit that he believed characterized the Jamaican peasantry. "Yes, the country people *are* wonderful," he told Nancy Cunard. "They just have *no idea* of the hard and fast moral standards of Europe and America. Any really fine-minded person could live among them in *any way* he pleases."[58] Cunard, who visited the island in 1932 to gather material for her remarkable compendium, *Negro: An Anthology*, like so many visitors before and since, fell under the spell of the Jamaican peasantry and concurred with McKay. Impressed by their energy, curiosity about the wider world, and sense of justice, she particularly noted the subtlety of their minds, which works at such a "slant angle" that "you have the impression no other people in the least like them exist in the world." Cunard viewed them as a "most lovable and interesting people," whom she described as "a lusty, strong and dignified people, without the least trace of any of the surface "inferiority" or exterior hesitancy that has been beaten and pumped into some of the American Negroes by the bestiality of the American whites."[59]

Fourth, and on a somewhat different note, there was the presence of exemplary Black individuals. McKay never suffered from a shortage of these, particularly, as discussed, among his family.

Outside of his immediate family was—as shown in chapter 1—a visible, vocal, and growing body of Black professionals. But other Black people exercised an influence far more subtle and less direct. These individuals, because they figured in memorable incidents and sharply defined situations, helped to create the ambience within which McKay's "unselfconscious black pride"[60] could develop and flourish.

McKay tells us two stories. One is of a Black doctor, the other of a Black preacher. They may almost be described as tales, even parables, of Black superiority. But, in fact, they are not morality tales, separated from a larger narrative; they are unforced and integrated within the wider fabric of the story of his Jamaican childhood and youth. The vividness with which they are recalled some forty years after the events to which they refer makes it clear that these were major, formative moments in the young man's life.

We gather from McKay that the most effective doctor his ailing mother ever had was not white, but Black; indeed, the Black doctor was spectacularly effective, while the white doctor, whom he replaced, failed. McKay wrote that when he was sixteen, his mother became "desperately ill." He remembered coming home from school, finding the house full of people, many of them weeping, for his mother seemed to be paralyzed. "She could not talk, and seemed as if she did not want to talk. They had discovered her in a dead faint in the kitchen and brought her to her room where she was lying like a dead person in the great carved mahogany four-poster bed which had belonged to her father." Instead of the white family doctor, they called in a Black doctor who was relatively new to the area. Described as a "very black man," the new doctor was born in Barbados and educated at Edinburgh University. The people admired him very much, said McKay, "as they do anything foreign that is any good." A close friend of U. Theo's, the doctor prescribed some medicine for Mrs. McKay and ordered that the gable ends be boarded up. McKay remembered that U. Theo and the doctor had "quite a controversy" over the gable ends. "My brother said that we were living in a tropical country and it would be better for the people to live in tents and hammocks than in closed houses." However, Thomas McKay, knowing full well that U. Theo was not trained in medicine, decided to ignore his son. He had plenty of boards so he had the gable ends boarded up as the doctor recommended. Hannah Ann made an astonishing recovery. McKay remembered the old quadroon woman who had delivered most of the McKay children saying to his mother, "You have had a wonderful escape, Anna. That new doctor is surely a wizard."

Four years later, Mrs. McKay was not so lucky when she was once again dangerously ill. The Barbadian doctor, following in the footsteps of many Caribbean professionals, had by then left for the United States. The white family doctor, who was living ten miles away, was called. He did not attend to Mrs. McKay. He sent word saying that there was nothing he could do and that "her battle with life is ended."[61]

The preacher's story is more straightforward but of equal significance. At the time of his mother's death, the minister at Mount Zion was white. However, "one of our brilliant young Negro preachers, a Presbyterian whose name was Barkley, and a member of the legislative council had visited mother when she was ill. She had indicated that she would like to have him preach the funeral sermon. So the Reverend Barkley, who had lived quite a few miles away, came."[62]

The final point that I would like to emphasize is this: McKay was privileged in having been exposed to different facets of Jamaican life. He became remarkably well acquainted with a number of different worlds. He came from the peasantry and knew that world intimately. He had also lived the life of a member of the Jamaican Black middle class, especially when he lived with his brother near Montego Bay. U. Theo's, however, was a first-generation Black middle-class household that remained loyal to and interested in its humble beginnings.[63] A confident young Black man, Claude McKay interacted easily with white people. As he told his friend James Weldon Johnson many years later, in his village he grew up on "equal terms" with white, mulatto, and Black children of a certain class because his father was a big peasant and "belonged."[64] And in his communication with and observation of them, he knew that white people did not possess a monopoly on intelligence or knowledge or beauty. He knew that they were human beings and not gods, and he acted accordingly. Indeed, he had no qualms in registering the glaring shortcomings of some of them. The case of the British agricultural instructors is a vivid example of this. Through living in Kingston as a factory worker, and later serving as a member of the police force in Spanish Town as well as in Kingston, he became acquainted with the plight of the urban working class and the desperation of the Black poor, especially women, of Kingston. He also took advantage of the opportunity to keenly observe for the first time the marketing end of peasant economic activity—"higglering"—in urban Jamaica. McKay also encountered at close range the vicious species of colorism and class snobbery that the "brown" middle class practiced in both Spanish Town and Kingston. Through his membership of the constabulary force, he learned firsthand about the colonial police force and the nakedness of its class rule and corrupt practices. His membership in the force radicalized him, and he learned to detest the institution.

It was also in Jamaica that he served his apprenticeship as a writer. He left to study scientific agriculture but also determined to become a better poet. At the time of his migration, his remarkable range as a writer was already apparent, his ability to express forcefully both thought and a spectrum of disparate feelings and emotions evident.

Perhaps the most remarkable feature of McKay's early years was the extent to which he lived on the borders, intersections, and interstices of many worlds. Though of the peasantry, he was sufficiently separated from it to view with discernment and clear eyes the world of the peasant. He was of the Black middle-class world of Mount Carey, but he never forgot the peasant world from which he was plucked, and though he was of the middle class, his perspective of that world was profoundly informed by his blackness, his very dark skin. McKay joined the police force, but never felt at home within it. On leaving the force, he went back to his village, but never felt at home there either; among other things, his success as a poet had robbed him of the relaxed warmth of village life. As he put it, when he returned home, he was treated like a "little personage."[65] McKay was always a rather shy person; he had always hated the limelight, although he never let that stop him from speaking out—in written form, if not orally. In truth, the restlessness, the wanderlust, the inquietude, so evident during his period of exile, was there from the age of seven when he joined the world of U. Theo at Mount Carey. Once he left the world into which he was born, the world of the Black Jamaican peasantry—a world to which he could not fully return after his seven-year absence at Mount Carey—he never knew peace. This restlessness and deep loneliness—a palpable loneliness—was the fount of his need for creative expression.

Part II

Coming to America: From Fabianism to Bolshevism, 1912–1919

5

"Six Silent Years"

McKay and America, 1912–1918

> But why have you been silent all these six years? . . . For six years you were
> silent in the night, like James Thomson, who wrote *The City of Dreadful*
> *Night.* . . . Perhaps you too have a *City of Dreadful Night* pent up in you as a
> result of your six silent years?
>
> —Frank Harris to Claude McKay, 1918

Horrified

America shocked him. It shocked him with the depth and intensity of its racism. The fact that McKay had entered the United States via what he regarded
as its putrid and stinking southern underbelly did not help. He first set foot
on American soil in Charleston, South Carolina, and traveled on a segregated (Jim Crow) train to Tuskegee, Alabama.[1] It was the first time he had
come face to face with such "manifest, implacable hate of my race," McKay
wrote in 1918 as he reflected upon his six-year experience as a Black Jamaican
man living in different parts of the United States. His feelings were "inde-
scribable." Even in supposedly progressive New York City, McKay recalled
that because of his color he had difficulty finding a decent restaurant on
Sixth Avenue to accommodate him and his white friend Max Eastman for
lunch. They finally had to lunch in "a very dirty place." The experience so disgusted Eastman that he remarked, "If I were a Negro I couldn't be anything
but a revolutionist!"[2]

McKay had heard of American racism but "never dreamed of it being so intensely bitter." He knew prejudice in Jamaica, but it was "the English sort, subtle and dignified, rooted in class distinction—color and race being hardly taken into account." In the United States, he found "strong white men, splendid types, of better physique than any [he] had ever seen, exhibiting the most primitive animal hatred towards their weaker black brothers." The Southland's "daily murders of a nature most hideous and revolting" battered his sensibilities.[3]

No doubt the case of Mary Turner would have been at the forefront of McKay's mind when he wrote that passage in September 1918.[4] Five months earlier, news broke of one of the most gruesome and notorious lynchings in American history. Hayes Turner, Mary's husband, was lynched on May 18, ostensibly for the murder of his employer, an infamously cruel plantation owner named Hampton Smith. In fact, Hayes Turner was not involved in Smith's murder, and on hearing the news of her husband's lynching, the inconsolable Mary protested her husband's innocence and vowed to have those guilty of his murder brought to justice. For her "unwise remarks," the good white citizens of Brooks and Lowndes counties, Georgia, determined: "We'll teach that damn' nigger wench some sense." The mother of two small children, Mary was more than eight months pregnant. But such considerations were irrelevant. The mob tied a rope around her ankles, hung her upside down on a tree, and soaked her with gasoline. Walter White, assistant secretary of the NAACP, after "careful investigation and corroboration" of the events, related what happened next. While Mary "writhed in agony and the mob howled in glee, a match was applied and her clothes burned from her person." A member of the mob boasted to White: "Mister, you ought to've heard the nigger wench howl!" Mary was still alive after her southern *auto-da-fé*, but "a knife, evidently one such as is used in splitting hogs, was taken and the woman's abdomen was cut open, the unborn babe falling from her womb to the ground. The infant, prematurely born, gave two feeble cries and then its head was crushed by a member of the mob with his heel." Hundreds of bullets were then fired into Mary's body, "now mercifully dead, and the work was over."

> Under the tree of death was scooped a shallow hole. The rope about Mary Turner's charred ankles was cut, and swiftly her body tumbled into its grave. Not without a sense of humour or of appropriateness was some member of the mob. An empty whisky-bottle, quart size, was given for headstone. Into its neck was stuck a half-smoked cigar—which saved the delicate nostrils of one member of the mob from the stench of burning human flesh.[5]

McKay noted that the North was not blameless, with its "silent acqui-escence, deep hate half-hidden under a puritan respectability, oft flaming up into an occasional lynching—this ugly raw sore in the body of a great nation." He was at first "horrified"; his spirit "revolted against the ignoble cruelty and blindness of it all." He soon found himself "hating in return," but this feeling, he said, "couldn't last long for to hate is to be miserable."[6]

McKay's exposure to this virulent and pervasive strain of racism height-ened his political consciousness and quickened his radicalization. Not only did his American experience augment his identification as a Black person, but it also schooled him in a greater appreciation of class inequality on a global scale that went beyond the bounds of the Fabian socialism he had adopted in Jamaica. He gained this new consciousness by looking about him with "bigger and clearer eyes," as he put it. And McKay was always looking. He even *looked* as if he was always looking. "His eyebrows arched high up and never came down," observed a close friend.[7] By the time he wrote his autobiographical profile in 1918, McKay had come to realize that, dreadful though their condition was, Black people were not the only vic-tims of oppression: "I saw that this cruelty in different ways was going on all over the world." He also noticed, however, that Black people tended to be the victims of even the other victims. "Whites," he said, "were exploiting and oppressing whites even as they exploited and oppressed the yellows and blacks. And the oppressed, groaning under the lash, evinced the same despicable hate and harshness toward their weaker fellows."[8] McKay had taken the first, tentative steps that would lead him away from his native Fabianism onto the path of revolutionary socialism.

It was not that unusual for a Caribbean migrant such as McKay to develop a more sharply defined racial consciousness as a result of living in the United States. In fact, this was the common experience of his fellow Black migrants.[9] What *does* cry out for explanation is the rapidity with which McKay took his steps toward a profoundly radical ideological posi-tion, manifesting itself in the form of an internationalist revolutionary socialism.

War and Revolution

Two epoch-making, partially overlapping, but contrasting events combined to lay the foundations for this new political consciousness and accelerated radicalization. The first was the outbreak of war in Europe in 1914—the Great War, as contemporaries called it—and the astonishing savagery and carnage by which it was accompanied, defined, and expanded. The impact of this world-enveloping cataclysm profoundly affected McKay, overturning and throwing into bewildering disarray key ideas imparted to and accepted by him through the Victorian and colonial education he received in Jamaica. The unspoken, taken-for-granted belief in the superiority of European civilization, the faith in ineluctable progress in human affairs and in European rationalism that he took so extraordinarily seriously during his childhood and early youth, were all suddenly blown sky high and cut to bits with the booming guns, bombs, and shrapnel on the Sommes. "This great catastrophe," he said of the war, "has come upon the world proving the real hollowness of nationhood, patriotism, racial pride and most of the things which one was taught to respect and reverence."[10]

The war haunted his consciousness for the rest of his life. In his two earliest novels, *Home to Harlem* (1928) and *Banjo* (1929), the impact of the war—its repercussions on human affairs and thought—hovers in the background like a large cloud, casting its shadow over everything below. And in his 1937 memoir, McKay reported that when he visited George Bernard Shaw in London in 1919, he vividly remembered that the old man once mentioned the Great War and "let out a whinny which sounded exactly like a young colt in distress or like an accent from his great drama, *Heartbreak House*. I felt at once," McKay recalled, "that in spite of his elegant composed exterior," the war must have had a "shattering effect" on Shaw. Like other Fabian socialists, Shaw, prior to 1914, probably thought that "a wholesale war of slaughter and carnage between the civilized nations was impossible; that the world was passing gradually from the cutthroat competitive to a co-operative stage. I myself," McKay confessed,

> under the influence of the international idealistic thought of that period, used to think that way. I remember when I was a school boy in Jamaica that the local militia was disbanded by the Governor, Lord Olivier, Shaw's friend and the most brilliant statistician of the Fabian Socialists. The local paper printed his statement that "such training for citizens is not necessary in an age of established peace, and anyway the people of the West Indies could not be concerned in any imaginary war of the future." Seven years later conscription was declared in Jamaica . . . before it became effective in England, and West Indian contingents served in France, Egypt, and Arabia.[11]

The First World War epitomized, for McKay, the "blind brute forces of tigerish tribalism which remain at the core of civilized society." As he told a young white friend, during the war it was "brother against brother and friend against friend. They were all trapped in it and they were all helpless."[12] The very occurrence of the war provided one of the key pieces of evidence that McKay mobilized against H. G. Wells's racist and Eurocentric *Outline of History*. "It is entirely too funny," said McKay wryly, "to think—seven years after the appallingly beastly modern white savagery of 1914–18—of Mr. Wells naïvely wondering whether the Negro is capable of becoming a civilized citizen of a world republic."[13]

During the course of another war, when he was gravely ill and less than four years before his death, the Great War was still on McKay's mind: "I used to have great faith in agnosticism, up until World War I, when the German and British agnostics or rationalists lost all sense of reason, became rabid nationalists and began denouncing one another."[14] McKay knew through direct experience that the madness afflicted some of the most unlikely people. No less a person than his good friend and mentor Walter Jekyll—a man who loved Heine and Schiller and Goethe, adored and played on his piano in the hills of Jamaica Beethoven and Wagner, and worshipped and translated Schopenhauer—wrote to McKay in New York, all the way from his Jamaican rural redoubt, to accuse an innocent man of being "pro-German."[15] As a consequence of the outbreak and prolongation of this shockingly brutal war, McKay lost his intellectual and philosophical moorings. He was living in a turbulent world at a moment when he valued stability and clarity more than ever. McKay, after all, was still in the throes of a painful adjustment to life in a new and hostile society which he entered only two years earlier. With the undermining of his belief in European rationalism and Victorian optimism, McKay sought an alternative and sturdier philosophical and political home.

The second constitutive event at the base of his political radicalization provided him with a concrete alternative: the Bolshevik Revolution of 1917. Like a phoenix rising from the ashes of war and destruction, "Holy" Russia, as he dubbed Soviet Russia in 1920, had returned to McKay—as it had also to so many of his generation—his "golden hope."[16] Indeed, such was the impact of the Russian Revolution upon his worldview that before its second anniversary, McKay was debating the subject hammer-and-tongs with members of the Black nationalist Garvey movement, vigorously promoting the virtues of the October Revolution and its great relevance to the struggles of Black people the world over. McKay was by no means alone in advocating Black liberation through Bolshevism, but he emerged as one of the first Black persons—not only in the United States, but in the world—to do so, and do so vigorously, openly, and boldly.[17]

Thus, McKay's radicalization soon after arriving in the United States cannot be adequately explained without reference to the triple, combined effect of his encounter with American racism, the impact of the First World War upon his worldview, and the promise and the hope he perceived the Bolshevik Revolution to carry for all oppressed humanity. The outbreak of nationwide racist violence in 1919 was to throw into even sharper relief the existence of a new and deeply radicalized McKay.[18]

Listening to Silence

From 1912 to 1918—from when he left Jamaica to when he was featured in *Pearson's*—with the exception of a couple of poems published under a nom de plume in October 1917, McKay was absent from the literary stage and entered a period of relative public silence. Although he made no explicitly political public statement in these six years, it is possible to at least partially retrace his political journey.

Within a couple of months of his arrival at Tuskegee, McKay left for Kansas State College. He did not like Tuskegee, with its "semi-military, machinelike existence."[19] Although he did not say so openly, Tuskegee evidently reminded McKay too much of the Jamaican constabulary from which he had only recently escaped. But it is not entirely clear why he chose Kansas State Agricultural College (later Kansas State University),[20] and he never explained. Max Eastman wrote, however, that McKay "had learned that a free life and a more elective system of education prevailed" there.[21] This is perhaps the nearest we will ever come to an explanation of this move on McKay's part. In a letter to his literary agent, who requested biographical information, McKay pointed him to Eastman: "Max Eastman's preface to my book of poems, *Harlem Shadows*, gives *exact* information about myself."[22]

McKay studied in Manhattan, Kansas, for just under two years: he matriculated on October 30, 1912, and left in the spring of 1914 for New York City. As at Tuskegee, McKay studied agriculture at Kansas, specializing in agronomy according to his college transcript. However, he also took subjects in the humanities, such as English.[23] Indeed, one early biographical note—somewhat corroborating Eastman's remark—spoke of "the opportunity presenting itself of [his] studying 'literary English' at Kansas State

College." Indeed, "Advanced Grammar" was the subject for which he earned the highest mark during his time at KSU, an "E" (excellent).[24] It was at Kansas that McKay's English teacher, a white woman, told him about *The Souls of Black Folk*, W. E. B. Du Bois' remarkable 1903 collection of essays on the Black experience in America. A quarter of a century later, McKay recalled that he found it in the public library in Topeka. The Jamaican, who had lived through the devastating Kingston earthquake of 1907, recalled that the book "shook [him] like an earthquake." Dr. Du Bois, McKay revealed in his memoir, "stands on a pedestal illuminated in my mind," primarily because of the impact of that first reading of *The Souls of Black Folk* in Kansas.[25]

It was also in Kansas that McKay joined "a small group of white students with a socialist bent." According to this account, given by McKay's Russian translator, these students were all "sons of poor people and, while studying at the college, took various odd jobs to support themselves."[26] The claim that McKay was involved with socialist students is plausible. Already a socialist, the lonely McKay in such an environment would, more likely than not, seek the company of sympathetic and like-minded students. It is also plausible and not surprising that such a group existed on the campus of Kansas State College, as the Midwest in general, and the state of Kansas in particular, boasts the United States' strongest radical tradition, stretching back into the nineteenth century. During the American Civil War, some of the most doggedly determined and radical generals in Lincoln's Union Army came from Kansas. The populists in the nineteenth and early twentieth century had strong roots there, and the Industrial Workers of the World (IWW) had some of its strongest and most loyal chapters in and around Kansas. Both James Cannon, the father of American Trotskyism, and Earl Browder, the leader of the American Communist Party in the 1930s, had roots in the Kansas-Missouri area. Cannon was born in Rosedale, near Kansas City, in 1890; Browder was born in Wichita, Kansas, a year later and would, like Cannon, live in Kansas City and become radicalized there. During McKay's student days, Kansas continued to be the fulcrum of much radical activity in the United States. As one writer put it, the region was "Socialism's American heartland."[27] *The Toiler, Socialist Appeal*, and *The Workers' World*, some of the most influential socialist newspapers and formative organs in early-twentieth-century American radicalism, came out of Kansas City.[28] McKay almost certainly read them in his socialist student group.

Despite Kansas's atmosphere of socialism, McKay was largely inactive politically. Outside of the intense study required by his course, McKay spent most of his time observing and learning about America—including Black America. "During my first couple of years in the States as a student," he wrote, "I had a real admiration for the many colored students I came to know and the refined colored society I was introduced into at Tuskegee, Manhattan (Kansas), Kansas City, Wichita, [and] Denver."[29] Of Manhattan itself, however, McKay noted that there were "too few Negroes in the college town for any lively social life."[30] Unlike Tuskegee, whose student body included those from all over the Black world, including more than twenty from Jamaica alone, at Kansas State McKay was one of a mere handful of Black students and the only Jamaican in a student body numbering around three thousand during his time there.[31] McKay said nothing about his living arrangements in Kansas, but he probably obtained lodgings with a local Black family in the small Black community, numbering around three hundred on the south side of Manhattan, or found rooms closer to campus with a "devoutly religious family interested in missionary work."[32] These were the usual accommodation arrangements Black students had to make on predominantly white college campuses at the time. It was unheard of, almost unthinkable, for them to be given lodgings in dorms with white students. Less than a month after McKay's arrival on campus, the *Students' Herald* (the student newspaper) revealed something of the ambience of the place. It carried the advertisement: "Wanted—Negro boy to wait tables."[33]

McKay claimed that for the two years he spent there, he "lived austerely and wrote no poetry."[34] It is unlikely, however, that McKay did not spend some of his time writing in verse—this was an almost involuntary habit with him—refining his art, setting his thoughts and feelings down on paper about life in this new and strange land, especially about life as a Black man in white America. When Frank Harris, *Pearson's* editor, met McKay in 1918, he wondered why McKay had not written anything since leaving Jamaica in 1912. Harris wanted an explanation of his six years of silence. "I said that I had not been really silent at all," McKay wrote in his memoir. "It had been necessary for me to do some practical thing to exist. And it had been a big experience, finding out about America and knowing the commonality of American Negroes. I had continued all along to write at intervals and rewrite to make my writing better, I said."[35] McKay in fact published at least six poems in the Jamaica press between 1913 and 1914, in addition to several he wrote on the eve of departure but published after he sailed.[36] In a letter written in February 1916, he disclosed that he was involved in "making fair copies of the poems I have written for the last four years with the intention of submitting them to some publisher."[37] Clearly, he never stopped writing and in fact had attempted, unsuccessfully, to publish some of his poems in the United States as early as 1915.[38] Furthermore, he claimed that the five poems published in *Pearson's* were written during his "first year's residence in America."[39] Nevertheless, McKay's poetic output declined as a result of his horrified response to the American condition. He implied in one of his early American poems that he had been paralyzed artistically, shocked into silence, by the new environment, of his tongue being "too leaden for song."[40] But he *did* sing, albeit with less frequency and gusto. One striking feature of this moment is an unprecedented religious turn in his poetry. Though beautifully rendered, the sentiment of "The Jamaica Eucharis" is at odds with McKay's atheism and his entire oeuvre up to that point. The flower is described as the "angelic eucharis / That opes its heart to heaven as we / Who do trust God—who feel that his / Will be the triumph day." The flower's beauty, the narrator continues, "brings to me real happiness, / And lays the gaunt ghost of despair, / And says: In God's world nought's amiss."[41]

One can only wonders what the Apple Woman would say to that: "we who do trust God"; "In God's world nought's amiss." Nor was this a singular aberration: the "Almighty" restrained him in "To the White Fiends"; "God sent me pain," he declared in "After the Storm"; "O God! is it worth while?" he asked in "Is It Worth While?"; and he told Braithwaite, "Art is as sublime as He who gave it to man."[42] McKay was likely so shaken by his American experience and felt so powerless and isolated—stalked by "the gaunt ghost of despair"—that he sought the help, solace and guidance of the divine, which he had previously dismissed and ridiculed. He would, however, quickly return to his militant freethinking ways. Hubert Harrison (about whom more later) most probably helped McKay in returning to and reinforcing his rationalist stance.

Manhattan Transfer: Discovering Harlem

In the spring or early summer of 1914, armed with a gift of money (probably from Jekyll), McKay suddenly left college without graduating and headed to New York City.[43] He opened a restaurant in a rough part of Brooklyn with an unnamed friend who had accompanied him from Kansas. The venture quickly failed, and he worked at a variety of menial jobs to survive. But during the war, most of his time was spent as a waiter on the Pennsylvania Railroad. For McKay, the most significant and wonderful thing about going to New York was his discovery of Black Harlem, then a new, vibrant community taking shape in upper Manhattan. It was as if he were a blue-gilled, gasping fish thrown back into the water just in the nick of time after being stranded on dry land. Harlem saved him: "After two years in the blue-sky-law desert of Kansas, it was like entering into a paradise of my own people when at last I fell into the dark warm throbbing bosom of Harlem."[44] After the bleak lone-liness of Manhattan, Kansas, McKay felt that Harlem—New York's "Black Manhattan"—was the closest he would ever get to a home from home. His passionate love affair with Harlem, one that lasted to the end of his life, had begun. "All was unique and novel, yet nothing was strange," he said of his first impression of Harlem.

> It was as if my boyhood's seminude backwoods life, or the jungle if you will, was all dressed up and parading itself in the biggest city in the world. Here were our simple palm-booth tunes delightfully syncopated, our picnic jigs jazzed, the lazy animal movement of the tropics quickened to the beat of New York's double-marching time, the same variegated pigment and matty hair refined by the beauty-shop bleaches and Kink-no-more processes, the same ripe voices uttering a different vernacular, the same deep-moving Afri-can rhythm.[45]

Harlem, like the rest of Afro-America, was undergoing rapid change. Facilitated by the war, the Great Migration—the mass movement of African Americans from the South, mainly to the industrial North and Midwest—was under way. Between 1900 and 1930, the proportion of the African American population living in the South dropped by 12 percent. Over the same period, the Black population in the North increased by 174 percent, from 881,000 to more than 2,409,000, while those in the West increased 298 percent, to 120,347.[46] New York City, and Harlem in particular, received its share of migrants from the South and was the principal destination for those from the Caribbean. The city's Black population increased by more than 50 percent between 1900 and 1910, and by another 66 percent between 1910 and 1920. From 61,000 in 1900, New York City's Black population reached over 152,000 by 1920, which more than doubled to 328,000 by 1930.[47]

These were days of hope in Black America, but they were also days of sorrow. An epidemic of lynching engulfed the southern states. President Wilson, fresh from reintroducing segregation in the nation's capital, had pledged to "make the world safe for democracy," and about two hundred thousand African Americans served abroad in the First World War. W. E.

B. Du Bois, as editor of the *Crisis*, organ of the National Association for the Advancement of Colored People (NAACP), told his fellow African Americans to forget their "special grievances," "close ranks" with white America, and join the struggle against Germany. But while Black soldiers were dying in France to save "democracy," their parents, grandparents, brothers, and sisters left behind in the United States had neither democracy nor safety.[48]

In East St. Louis, roving white mobs killed a still indeterminate number of Black people in an appalling July 1917 pogrom and destroyed thousands of Black homes. Escaping Black children were thrown back into their burning homes while adults were pinned down in the furnace by gunfire. The perpetrators went unpunished. The pogrom of East St. Louis, even by the prevailing racist and barbaric standards of America, was a horrifying event. The NAACP organized a highly publicized silent protest march down New York's Fifth Avenue to draw attention to what Black America called the "Massacre of East St. Louis." Garvey's eloquent and moving speech on East St. Louis won him great support from Black Harlem. St. Croix–born Hubert Harrison, "the father of Harlem radicalism," told Black people to arm themselves and fight back, leading the Justice Department to seek his deportation. In the same year as the pogrom of East St. Louis, thirteen Black soldiers were court-martialed and executed in Texas for retaliating against racist attacks by the white police force of Houston.[49] Events such as these provided the fuel for unprecedented levels of Black agitation in America at the time. And Harlem was the acknowledged home of the new Black radicalism.

Among the Black migrants who arrived in New York around this time were those who would later be renowned for their political agitation and leadership. Marcus Garvey (1887–1940) arrived in New York from Jamaica on a fund-raising and speaking tour the year before East St. Louis. He quickly moved the headquarters of the Universal Negro Improvement Association from Kingston to Harlem, where he settled. A. Philip Randolph (1889–1979), editor of the *Messenger* magazine and future leader of the Brotherhood of Sleeping Car Porters, left his native Florida for New York in 1911. His close friend and coeditor of the *Messenger*, Chandler Owen (1889–1967), arrived from Virginia in 1913. Cyril Briggs (1887–1966), future leader of the African Blood Brotherhood and editor of the *Crusader*, arrived from St. Kitts in 1905. Wilfred A. Domingo (1889–1968), future radical editor and journalist, migrated from Jamaica to Boston in 1910, then moved to New York in 1912. Richard B. Moore (1893–1978), soon to be one of the great orators of the Black left, arrived from Barbados in 1906. And last, but not least, Hubert Henry Harrison (1883–1927), at the age of seventeen, went to New York from St. Croix, the Virgin Islands, in 1900.[50]

Almost overnight and rather like mushrooms in fertile soil, a fine crop of journals and magazines popped up on Harlem's political landscape—the *Voice*, the *Messenger*, the *Negro World*, the *Promoter*, the *Challenge*, the *Crusader*, the *Emancipator*, the *Veteran*. They all gave voice to the new spirit of optimism and combativeness in the struggle for Black rights. In addition to the street corners—sites of Harlem's stepladder orators—indoor venues became available in Harlem, where the dreams, yearnings, needs, demands, and plight of Afro-America gained articulate voice. Garvey's Liberty Hall, the meeting room of the Lafayette Theatre, and Rev. Ethelred Brown's Harlem Community Church were among the primary ones. Hubert Harrison was the distinguished pioneer of Harlem's political oratory and education, but Marcus Garvey quickly superseded him in popular following, if not analysis. Garvey's outstanding oratory and lionhearted Black nationalism won over the Black masses.[51]

On the left, W. A. Domingo, Richard B. Moore, Grace Campbell, A. Philip Randolph, and Chandler Owen gained a respectable, loyal, and growing following at regular meetings at the Harlem Educational Forum, which they organized and held at the Lafayette. The Educational Forum also invited outside speakers. Franz Boas, the distinguished anthropologist, came up from Columbia to debunk racist myths. Elizabeth Gurley Flynn, a leading member of the Socialist Party, also spoke. On occasion, the NAACP men were invited, with James Weldon Johnson being the person in the organization that the young radicals exercised the most patience with. He was not one of the "New Negroes" or "New Crowd Negroes," as the young Black radicals described themselves, but he was one of a handful of "Old Crowd Negroes" that was looked upon with respect and affection. Walter White, the assistant field secretary of the NAACP and Johnson's junior colleague, was also invited. White was an expert on lynching; because of his complexion, he was able to penetrate enemy lines to investigate this ghastly southern pastime on behalf of the NAACP. Very light-skinned, Walter White could have passed for white, but he committed himself to the Black cause for justice and identified himself as a "Negro." Respected for his work, White was invited to the Forum to talk about lynching. At times refugees, fresh escapees from the lynch mobs of the South, would give their harrowing testimony to rapt audiences in Harlem.

Harlem quickly became the home of the best-informed Black community in the world on issues relating to Black people in the United States, in the rest of the Americas, as well as in Europe and Africa. One Black conservative contemporary disapprovingly noted that during the First World War, "Harlem was filled with street preachers and flamboyant orators haranguing the people from morning till night upon Negro rights and wrongs. Radical magazines sprang up suddenly whose utterances were calculated to inflame the minds of the people."[52] The indefatigable special agent "P-138" of the Justice Department could not keep up with the level of political activity in Harlem. He would at times have to run from one meeting to another, unable to catch all that was said at any.[53]

This was the Harlem that, wide-eyed and excited, McKay watched taking shape. It was the political culture of Harlem that helped to shape him and to which McKay, in turn, contributed his own shaping.

Hubert Harrison and His Impact

McKay knew personally the main protagonists involved in the political agitation of the time—Cyril Briggs, Richard B. Moore, Grace Campbell, W. A. Domingo, Marcus Garvey, A. Philip Randolph. But, at least prior to McKay's departure for London in the fall of 1919, Hubert Harrison was perhaps his closest associate among the Harlem intelligentsia. He loved and admired Harrison, with whom he had much in common. Like him, Harrison was very dark in complexion—"very black," as McKay would put it. And like him, Harrison was at peace with his blackness and his African roots, not averse to letting people know how he felt about his blackness. Harrison boasted about his "unmixed" African ancestry. Like McKay, Harrison deeply resented the colorism of the "colored elite" in the Caribbean and the United States.[54]

McKay's and Harrison's intellectual formation were remarkably similar. They both came to free thought and rationalism at an early age and had a somewhat peculiar and early admiration for the sociology of Herbert Spencer. They both became socialist in their early youth and had a deep, sincere, and abiding commitment to women's liberation. Harrison also had a very close relationship with his mother and his older sister. His father died when he was very young, and he was brought up by his mother and sister, whom he joined in New York in 1900. It is claimed that, apart from socialism's intellectual appeal, Harrison became a socialist in large measure because of his abhorrence for the oppression of women.[55]

In other ways, too, McKay and Harrison resembled each other. Joel Rogers, who knew Harrison well, said that most of the enmity against him was "incurred by his devastating candor. . . . He spoke out freely [about] what he thought, and more often than not it was with such annihilating sarcasm and wit that those whom he attacked never forgave him."⁵⁶ The same was true of McKay, who was encouraged in his outspokenness—not that he needed much encouragement—by Hubert Harrison. McKay was, as he himself put it, "suicidally frank."⁵⁷ "I am a fanatic about intellectual independence and frankness even to the point of indiscretion," he told one of his correspondents.⁵⁸

Harrison never abandoned his socialist beliefs but felt it necessary to operate as a radical Black nationalist in a racist United States. He served as an editor of Garvey's *Negro World* and coined the slogan "Race First," adopted by Garvey and the Universal Negro Improvement Association (UNIA). He felt that this was what white people—including his erstwhile comrades of the Socialist Party—practiced, and it therefore made sense for Black people to do the same, if only for defensive purposes. Harrison, McKay said, had come to "the conclusion that out of the purgatory of their own social confusion, Negroes would sooner or later have to develop their own leaders, independent of white control."⁵⁹ McKay adopted a political position in the 1930s that was remarkably similar to that of the later Harrison, but in the early 1920s he evidently preferred Harrison's earlier attempt to simultaneously hold fast the categories of race and class in his social analysis—a potent compound of Black nationalism and socialism.

One of the most distinctive features of Harrison's political thought, compared to that of his Black radical (socialist and Black nationalist) contemporaries and his Black nationalist predecessors of the nineteenth century, was his high opinion of the peoples and cultures of Africa. Much of his time was spent in the study of Africa, and his knowledge on that subject, as well as many others, was described as encyclopedic. This hard-earned knowledge—grounded in the best historical and scientific data available—coupled with his quietly proud identification with the African continuities in his native St. Croix, led Harrison to develop a respect for the African past and African potential that the overwhelming majority of his contemporaries did not have. There is in Harrison's outlook none of the arrogant New World "civilizationism" that one finds, for instance, in Garvey's pronouncements. For Harrison, Africa was primarily a teacher, not a primitive unschooled child in need of "civilization" and instruction. His unrelenting and systematic study of the African past had convinced him of the mendacity of the ideologies of European colonialism and racism. "Let us American Negroes," said Harrison, "go to Africa, live among the natives and

LEARN WHAT THEY HAVE TO TEACH US (for they have much to teach us)"—a complete inversion of New World Black nationalist orthodoxy.[60] He implored Black people to stop reading and believing "the silly slush which ignorant missionaries put into our heads about the alleged degradation of our people in Africa" and recommended instead the "scientific works" of explorers such as Mary Kingsley, for whom he had the greatest admiration.[61] In 1919, he suggested that the Black colleges in America should drop their "silly smatterings of 'little Latin and less Greek' and establish modern courses in Hausa and Arabic, for these are the living languages of millions of our brethren in modern Africa. Courses in Negro history and the culture of West African peoples, at least, should be given in every college that claims to be an institution of learning for Negroes. Surely," Harrison declared, "an institution of learning for Negroes should not fail to be also an institution of Negro learning."[62]

Harrison was the most important force in correcting some of McKay's residual Eurocentric ideas about Africa. The Virgin Islander, who was six years McKay's senior, managed to exorcize the demon of his earlier European colonial education. McKay had clearly made significant progress in this eradication before he left Jamaica, but Harrison helped him to go much further.

McKay and Harrison enjoyed each other's company. McKay admired Harrison's analytical mind and breadth of learning. Harrison lectured on a bewildering variety of subjects, always with "fine intelligence and masses of facts."[63] Harrison, however, was a man not only of learning but also of mischievous fun and sharp wit. He sharply disagreed with Du Bois—especially after his notorious "close ranks" *Crisis* editorial—and the people in control of the NAACP, whose acronym he deciphered as the "National Association for the Advancement of Certain People." In an especially memorable passage in *A Long Way from Home*, McKay related the pleasure that Harrison got from a joke about his late nemesis, Booker T. Washington, fully aware of his friend's having had the temerity to cross swords with the Wizard of Tuskegee—and the consequence of his doing so. "Hubert Harrison," McKay wrote, "had . . . criticized the Negro policy of Booker T. Washington in powerful volcanic English, and subsequently, by some mysterious grapevine chicanery, he had lost his little government job."[64] McKay described Harrison's sense of humor as "ebony hard" and loved to see and hear him laugh. On hearing a funny story about Washington, Harrison "exploded in his large sugary black African way, which sounded like the rustling of dry bamboo leaves agitated by the wind."[65]

Harrison is the most prominently featured Black member of the drama-
tis personae of McKay's memoir, *A Long Way from Home*. And it was Harrison's advice he sought when, in 1919, he was offered the opportunity of a
trip to Europe. Harrison, like a big brother—a new U. Theo—thrashed out
the idea with McKay.[66] McKay claimed that at this point he "knew nobody
among the Negro intellectuals, excepting Hubert Harrison."[67] It is unlikely
that this statement is strictly accurate, though the evidence suggests that his
closest relationship was with Harrison. It was after his return from London,
in January 1921, that McKay became more familiar with the radical intelligentsia of Harlem, especially with those involved in the African Blood
Brotherhood. But right up to his departure for the Soviet Union, in the
autumn of 1922, Hubert Harrison would remain his closest friend in Harlem and arguably, with the exception of Max Eastman, his closest friend in
the United States.

Their intellectual friendship also included frequent socializing. On the
eve of McKay's sailing to England in 1919, at a little send-off dinner at McK-
ay's place, Harrison—who had traveled the world as a cabin boy before
he came to New York—entertained the party with a "little monologue on
going abroad." Harrison assured McKay that the trip would do him good.
He requested articles from McKay for the *Negro World*, which Harrison
helped to edit at the time. After the meal, Harrison accompanied McKay to
Connor's Cabaret, "the most entertaining colored cabaret in Harlem at the
time," for McKay's last fling before sailing to Europe.[68]

When McKay returned from London in 1921, Harrison was quick to
greet him and to congratulate him on his becoming an editor of the *Liberator*, one of the most widely read and prestigious of the socialist magazines.
It was Harrison who suggested a meeting of the leading members of the
Black left—the "black reds," McKay called them—at McKay's downtown
Liberator office in an attempt to push the Garvey movement in a more
"class-conscious" direction.[69]

Harrison tried to impress upon him the need to honor what he considered to be McKay's racial obligations. McKay never liked speaking in public,
and liked even less to recite his poems. But he constantly received demands
and requests to do so at Harlem meetings, especially after the publication of
"If We Must Die" in 1919. He felt that he could never reproduce the sponta-
neous emotion that had created these works in the first place. He resented
standing up on platforms "like an actor to repeat my poems and kindle
them with second-hand emotions." He suggested that poets and novelists
"should let good actors perform for them." But Harrison implored him

to participate in these meetings because McKay, he said, "owed it to [his] race." And so McKay did. Harrison, like the rest of the Black radicals, loved McKay's poetry. He never ceased to promote McKay's work and sing his praises. He loved McKay's "famous poem of New Negro manhood . . . 'If We Must Die.'" To Harrison, McKay's "proud title of distinction consists of two simple words: The Poet," describing McKay as "the greatest living poet of Negro blood in America today."[70]

The night before he sailed for Russia in 1922, McKay met Harrison at a Harlem nightclub. They had a casual drink together. "But," said McKay, "I did not inform him or any of my few familiars that I was sailing for Europe the next day. Sentimental adieux embarrass me."[71] This would be the last time that the two men met. Harrison died suddenly in 1927, and McKay did not return to the United States until 1934.

McKay took one of Harrison's books with him to Soviet Russia, and in his preface to *The Negroes in America*, he explicitly acknowledged that he "obtained valuable statistics . . . from the book *The Negro and the Nation* by Hubert Harrison."[72] But there was more than statistics from Harrison's books in McKay's work.

The literature on McKay abounds with exaggerated claims of the influence on McKay of white "mentors" and white "father figures," but the profound influence of Hubert Harrison, his brother and comrade, is never given its full due. It is as if W. A. Domingo had not said that all the Harlem radicals followed in Harrison's footsteps; it is as if A. Philip Randolph had not described Harrison as the father of Harlem radicalism; it is as if all the major Black newspapers at the time of his death did not sum up and pay handsome tributes to the remarkable contribution of Hubert Henry Harrison; and it is as if McKay himself did not pay his own generous tribute to Harrison in writing. The fact is that a substantial portion of McKay's so-called "silent six years" (1912–1918) was profitably spent in the company of Harrison, who played a crucial part in his political education, the reinforcement of his atheism and deepening radicalization.

But those six years involved more of pertinence to McKay's political formation. In an early passage of *A Long Way from Home*, McKay, reflecting on his growing maturity as a poet, spoke of his first five years in America speeding by "like a rivulet flowing to feed a river. I had accumulated much," he said, "and from the fullness of my heart I poured myself out with passion of love and hate, of sorrow and joy, writing out of myself, waiting for an audience."[73] One of the strongest currents driving his rivulet headlong to the river of greater maturity—not only of his poetry but also arguably of his political outlook—was his close involvement with working-class Afro-America.

McKay as Black Worker

In the years after the collapse of his restaurant venture, McKay worked as a porter, tended furnaces as a "fireman," made a living as a waiter, a barman, a houseman, a butler, a janitor—"anything that came handy," he disclosed in *Pearson's*. As a close friend remarked, McKay earned his living "in every one of the ways the northern Negroes do, from pot-wrestling in a boarding-house kitchen to dining-car service on the New York and Washington express."[74] "I waded through the muck and the scum," he wrote in his 1937 memoir. Three years before he died, he used more euphemistic language: "I went to work at any job a young Negro could find."[75] In exile as in Jamaica, he identified most closely with the Black oppressed, not with the middle class of polite Negro society. In a characteristically trenchant response to his critics—who were virtually all Black—McKay frankly disclosed:

> It was not until I was forced down among the rough body of the great serving class of Negroes that I got to know my Aframerica [*sic*]. I was perhaps then at the most impressionable adult age and the warm contact with my work-mates, boys and girls, their spontaneous ways of acting and living for the moment, the physical and sensuous delights, the loose freedom in contrast to the definite peasant patterns by which I had been raised—all served to feed the riotous sentiments smoldering in me and cut me finally adrift from the fixed moorings my mind had been led to respect, but to which my heart had never held. During the first years among these Negroes my only object in working was to possess the means to live as they did.[76]

McKay developed a deep and abiding loyalty to the Black working class. In his post-Jamaican exile he always considered himself a bona fide member of this class, describing himself as "an ordinary worker, without benefit of a classic education" and as "not only a Negro but also a worker."[77] Whether or not he succeeded, he at least tried—right to the very end of his life—to look at politics not just from the perspective of a Black person in a white man's world, but from the perspective of the Black working class, the Black poor, the Black "masses," in a racist and class-stratified society.

McKay's sustained lack of enthusiasm for calls for "desegregation" is very much related to the position he adopted, taking the perspective of the Black worker. As far as McKay was concerned, ordinary Black folk had more burning priorities and desperate needs than the call for "no segregation." He felt that this demand came primarily from those whom he once described as "nice Negroes."[78] This position earned McKay many enemies, but he held onto it to the end of his life. In one of his last poems, he once again brings the issue of class divisions among Black people into focus on the question of desegregation. "Must fifteen million blacks be gratified," he inquired,

> That one of them can enter as a guest,
> A fine white house—the rest of them denied
> A place of decent sojourn and a rest?
> Oh, Segregation is not the whole sin,
> The Negroes need salvation from within.[79]

His commitment to the Black working class was a significant factor in his drift toward revolutionary socialism. It was his experience as a worker, a *Black* worker, that nourished his abiding commitment to trade unionism and—as we will see—developed in him a deep sympathy for syndicalism. It was its syndicalism together with its principled and remarkably unflinching commitment to racial and sexual equality that attracted McKay to the Industrial Workers of the World. The fact that his good friend Hubert Harrison was a leading member of the IWW when he first met him must have contributed to McKay's enthusiasm for the organization and its leader, William "Big Bill" Hayward. McKay joined the organization in early 1919 when he was working in a factory in New York City.[80] He would articulate his strong support for the IWW in his writings in the early 1920s.

However, McKay was no ordinary worker. He was a book-loving one with writing ambitions—"a peasant and proletarian aspirant to literary writing," he once described himself.[81] His love of books was undiminished by exile, and he spent much of his early period in America reading and trying to make sense of his new environment and much else. The main branch of the New York Public Library, at Forty-Second Street and Fifth Avenue—which he frequently referred to as the "big library"—was one of his favorite haunts. The Harlem branch of the New York Public Library, at 135th Street and Lennox Avenue—which later became the Schomburg Center—also consumed much of his leisure time. McKay knew these libraries so well that he could write from France and give his friend Harold Jackman precise instructions as to where a particular book was located in the "big library" so that Jackman could check a reference for him to use in his novel.[82] He used these libraries to keep up to date with journals and magazines but most of all, it appears, to read African history and radical literature. Hubert Harrison played a role here, too. A renowned lover of good books, Harrison not only would have recommended particular books to McKay but would have helped his friend to find his way around the "big library," which Harrison knew intimately.[83] The New York Public Library system undoubtedly played a crucial role in McKay's education, including his political education, during these early years.

As McKay pointed out to Frank Harris, he was hardly silent between 1912 and 1918. Not only had he been writing all along, but he also succeeded in publishing some of his work. *Seven Arts*, a prestigious avant-garde magazine, published two of McKay's poems in 1917 under the pen name Eli Edwards. But it was in September 1918, when Frank Harris in *Pearson's Magazine* made a two-page splash of his life and work—including a photograph of the poet—that McKay, without the disguise of a nom de plume, stepped onto the American literary stage.

There are at least nineteen poems that we can identify as having been written between 1912 and 1918. These include the two poems that were published in *Seven Arts*, "Invocation" and "Harlem Dancer," and five poems that *Pearson's* carried in September 1918: "To the White Fiends," "The Conqueror," "The Park in Spring," "Is It Worth While?," and "Harlem Shadows." In addition, five unpublished poems were sent in 1916 to William Stanley Braithwaite, the distinguished Black literary critic and editor: "In Memoriam: Booker T. Washington," "When I Have Passed Away," "Remorse," "My Ethiopian Maid," and "My Werther Days." "To the White Fiends" was also included among the batch of poems sent to Braithwaite. The final poem that we can date to that six-year period is "The Lynching," which McKay included among those he submitted for publication to *Pearson's Magazine* in 1918. Frank Harris, *Pearson's* editor, rejected it. It first saw the light of day in Britain in 1920.[84]

McKay wrote more than these nineteen poems between 1912 and 1918.[85] No doubt, some written during this six-year period were later published without indication that they had been composed before 1918; others have simply not survived and are thus lost to posterity. In addition to the six poems sent home to the *Jamaica Times* and the *Gleaner*, the other thirteen identified from the period, however, are helpful in plotting McKay's political trajectory. Like his Jamaican poems for an earlier period, these early

American poems—given the absence of other relevant contemporaneous material—are the most reliable sources we have for mapping McKay's political development during those years.

The Sound of Silence

It is possible to establish a rough chronology of these poems. Six were published in Jamaica between 1913 and 1914. The ones that were sent to Braithwaite were written before 1916, and the ones published in *Seven Arts* were written sometime before October 1917, when that magazine carried them. Likewise, the ones published in *Pearson's* were written before September 1918, when they were published by Frank Harris.

Thus, we know the latest point in time when they could have been written and the earliest, but we cannot be more precise than this as the poems may not have been published—or mentioned in correspondence—in the order in which they were written. "Is It Worth While?," for instance, published in 1918, could very well have been written in 1912 or 1913, as McKay claimed, but we cannot be certain.[86]

Along with "The Jamaica Eucharis," already discussed, McKay also wrote in 1913 "The Liquid Negro Language of the South," a praise song to creole as a language of artistic expression and mischievously "Dedicated, if they so allow, to opponents of dialect poetry."[87] Throughout 1912 and 1913, a spirited debate unfolded in the pages of the Jamaican newspapers. McKay intervened not only with this poem but also with a long letter to the *Gleaner* in defense of dialect poetry. "Poetry written in the Jamaica dialect is, and should be, essentially an interpretation of the life of THE COMMON FOLK; and, consequently, must be realistic poetry. But what can more interpret the life of a people than their own language?" He drew upon the examples of other poets who used local folk language in their art—Robert Burns, William Barnes, Tennyson, and one of his Jamaican supporters, Thomas MacDermot (editor of the *Jamaica Times*, who wrote poetry and prose under the pen name Tom Redcam)—in defense of using Jamaican creole as poetic language. He had no objection to writers' using either creole or "pure English" for their poetry and saw no reason why Jamaicans should be "ashamed of the dialect." But McKay, given his own accomplishments in the language, rather strangely suggested that, though "strong and expressive," one of creole's limitations is that it "cannot express all the emotions of the heart." He concluded with sentiments that anticipated those later expressed by Langston Hughes (which McKay himself would also repeat) in relation to those who would disparage Black popular cultural forms and their representation in poetry and fiction: "With the unadulterated blood of my ancestors coursing through me, I have no cause to be unreasonably prejudiced against or ashamed of a dialect, the charm of which lies in its perfect artlessness."[88]

His other two noteworthy poems sent to Jamaica, "Longing for Thee" and "Home," expressed his deep loneliness and yearning for both his sweetheart and his home. The first is set in the midwestern winter, "where the snow lies on the ground / And grey-brown squirrels do abound / Climbing the naked maple tree, / I'm longing, O my love, for thee." A shorter poem, "Home" declares:

> Rob me of all that childhood gave, O Time,
>   But leave—not leave, for never shalt thou take—
> That love and hope for one dear Southern clime
>   Which life a high and noble purpose make.[89]

In the winter of 1912, perhaps a bit tired of watching squirrels climb the naked maple trees, he returned to his digs and created one of the most sublime comic sketches written in the Jamaican language, "Bestman's Toast at a Rustic Wedding Feast." Written for the yearly Christmas number of the *Jamaica Times*, it reveals McKay's comedic gifts and, even more than his creole poetry, his extraordinary powers of observation and his abiding love—despite the best man's hilarious malapropisms, he charms and entertains—for the ordinary people. It also reveals, once again, the hold that his Jamaican world had on him during the winter—literally and figuratively—of his exile.[90]

"My Werther Days" (which explicitly echoes Goethe) and especially "When I Have Passed Away" are beautiful poems, but they have no direct or explicit political content as such; neither does "Remorse," which is concerned with the breakup of his marriage.[91] "Remorse" is a direct, concise, and hauntingly beautiful poem of sorrow. "My Ethiopian Maid" is once again a poem concerned with his former wife—his love for her and the anguish of being apart from her. This poem, however, also possesses a certain political significance insofar as it reiterates some of the *négritude* motifs that first appeared in his Jamaican poems.

> My love she is sweet, and my love she is brown,
>   Oh brown is my love, and so sweet

Her wealth of black hair, and the cream-colored gown
  Displaying her fairylike feet.

He sings of her face, her voice, her eyes, her heart, her soul. He ends:

I love you, O African maid, from afar
  I worship your heavenly smile;
But ne'er shall I touch you, O beautiful star,
  With hands that can only defile.[92]

Obviously not one of McKay's better efforts, but the evocation of Ethiopia and Africa in this manner was to develop into one of the primary motifs of *négritude* poetry. Césaire, Senghor, Damas are all preempted here. One also wonders about the defiling hands. Was this an expression of a bisexual desire, which McKay perceived as unclean? We know that McKay had gay relationships later in his life. Did he at the time of his brief marriage have such desires and act upon them? One can only speculate.

"To the White Fiends" is classic McKay protest poetry:

Think ye I am not fiend and savage too?
  Think ye I could not arm me with a gun
  And shoot down ten of you for every one
Of my black brothers murdered, burnt by you?
Be not deceived, for every deed ye do
  I could outmatch: am I not Afric's son,
  Black of the black land where black deeds are done?

But, says McKay, the Almighty counsels restraint. The poet has been placed upon the benighted earth to shed light:

Thy sable face I set among the white
  For thee to show thyself of highest worth;
Before the world is swallowed up in Night,
  To point a path to Heaven go forth, go forth.[93]

The invocation of the Almighty—even with a capital "A"—is uncharacteristic, as discussed earlier, but otherwise, this defiant posture would develop into a typical McKay sentiment in subsequent years. "To the White Fiends" is clearly in a direct line of continuity with his Jamaican protest poems. It is noticeable, however, that McKay is restrained. The poem is not written in the let-us-go-down-fighting tone of "If We Must Die." The victory is won over the enemy by the very forbearance of the tormented, not through direct confrontation. Self-restraint, moral superiority, not superior force, wins the day.

There is, finally, among the poems sent to Braithwaite, the most intriguing of McKay's entire poetic works: a warm and generous tribute to Booker T. Washington, "In Memoriam: Booker T. Washington." It ends with the following stanza:

> I vividly recall the noonday hour
>   you walked into the wide and well-filled hall:
>   We rose and sang, at the conductor's call,
> Dunbar's Tuskegee hymn. A splendid tower
> Of strength, as would a gardener on the flower
>   Nursed tenderly, you gazed upon us all
>   Assembled there, a serried, sable wall
> Fast mortared by your subtle tact and power.
>
> O how I loved, adored your furrowed face!
>   And fondly hoped, before your days were done,
> You would look in mine too with paternal grace.
>   But vain are hopes and dreams!—gone: you are gone;
> Death's hand has torn you from your trusting race,
>   And O! we feel so utterly alone.

The poem was written in the immediate aftermath of Washington's death on November 14, 1915, and sent to Braithwaite in the January 11, 1916, letter mentioned earlier. McKay's poem is a human and very personal response to the news of Washington's death. But the poem also reveals that by the beginning of 1916 McKay's radicalism had not developed to the degree that such a tribute would have been impossible for him to make. At the time, fundamental political differences would have made it impossible for a Black radical such as Hubert Harrison, even without the personal entanglement with Washington, to make utterances of this kind in Washington's memory. McKay—who was at the time of Washington's death working as a waiter in Hanover, New Hampshire, and so isolated from the animated responses of Black Harlem to Washington's death—was still not as radicalized as he would become in the space of a couple of years. The poem does not mean, however, that when he wrote it McKay was in agreement with Booker T.

Washington's project or general political outlook. One does not need to agree with someone in order to pay tribute, especially when the person has died: *de mortuus nil nisi bonum*. It should also be noted that apart from feeling "utterly alone" in the aftermath of Washington's passing, every other utterance is describing McKay's experience when he was at Tuskegee as a student. The main subject of the poem is actually McKay's *memory* of Washington during the time that McKay—recently arrived from Jamaica and in shock—was one of Washington's charges. Precisely what McKay thought of Washington after he had left the "serried, sable wall" at Tuskegee, the poem does not say. (In reality, of course, he quickly grew to hate the place—it reminded him of the Jamaica Constabulary—and bolted to Kansas State before the term even began.)

"In Memoriam: Booker T. Washington" delimits and brings into full relief the outer boundaries and contours of McKay's political ideology. The poem serves as a marker of what McKay was *not*. It tells us that McKay was not enough of an iconoclastic Black radical to attack, or at least refrain from honoring, the memory of the Wizard of Tuskegee. However, it does not tell us with any precision what McKay *was* politically. By 1919, for instance, it is unthinkable that McKay could have written this tribute. Indeed, by 1919 McKay had become highly critical of Washington's racial uplift project and would soon write articles that said so in unequivocal terms. Moreover, it is noteworthy that McKay never published this poem. He had more than ample opportunity to put it into print, but never did. He did not even retain a copy among his papers. "In Memoriam: Booker T. Washington," an artistically splendid poem, is known to us only because William Stanley Braithwaite, a conscientious literary critic, kept the copy McKay sent to him in 1916 among his papers deposited at Harvard.

Under the name of Eli Edwards, McKay published "Invocation" and "Harlem Dancer" in 1917. These are not explicitly political poems, but they are important windows on McKay's inner world and are significant expressions of his *négritude* philosophy and aesthetic. In "Invocation," McKay, perhaps for the first time, explores the tensions between his being, by default, of the West—the white man's world—and his desire to reconnect with his African roots. The duality is heightened by McKay's fascination with the modern industrial world, on which he gazes "in awe and wonderment," blocking his connection with the African past. He yearns to be one with the spiritual world of his ancestors and the glorious past of the Ethiopian. He prays for inspiration ("Let fall the light upon my sable face") and begs to be embraced and used as an instrument for his race: "Lift me to thee out of this alien place / So I may be, thine exiled counterpart, / The worthy singer of my world and race."[94]

"The Harlem Dancer," one of McKay's most accomplished sonnets, is yet another of his sensitive portrayals of a Black woman. The poem may also be read as an allegory of the attempt on the part of Black people to maintain their dignity and transcend their humiliating condition, even in the most trying circumstances. The subject of the poem is not just a dancer but also a fine singer, with a voice "like the sound of blended flutes / Blown by black players upon a picnic day." The scene is powerfully evoked. Beautiful but "half-clothed," she sings and dances "gracefully and calm" on the Harlem street for money. She is both applauded and laugh at by the crowd, even the young prostitutes, but to the narrator "she seemed a proudly-swaying palm / Grown lovelier for passing through a storm." Despite the tossed coins, the laughing crowd, and the devouring of her shape "with eager, passionate gaze," she attempts valiantly and successfully to shield her dignity: "looking at her falsely-smiling face, / I knew her self was not in that strange place."[95]

In "Harlem Shadows," first published in *Pearson's* in 1918, McKay observes and reflects upon the young girls operating as sex workers in Harlem:

> I hear the halting footsteps of a lass
>   In Negro Harlem when the night lets fall
> Its veil. I see the shapes of girls who pass
>   To bend and barter at desire's call.
> Ah, little dark girls who in slippered feet
> Go prowling through the night from street to street!

The girls tread the streets until the "silver break of day," even during the snowy winter nights, though only "half-clad." Meditating upon this scene of humiliation and suffering, McKay suggests, through extrapolation, that the condition of the prostitutes serves as a metaphor for the condition of his race as a whole: "Ah, stern harsh world, that in the wretched way / Of poverty, dishonor and disgrace, / Has pushed the timid little feet of clay, / The sacred brown feet of my fallen race!"[96]

"Is It Worth While?" another of the poems published in 1918, is one of McKay's gloomiest. He expresses the anguish felt during his early years in the United States, pushing him to contemplate suicide. He has grown "Sick of life's thankless task," even his tongue is "too leaden for song," and so he asks, "Oh God! is it worth while?" He talks of the racism, the arrogance of

white people, his Black loneliness, and his dissipated dreams. He tells himself that he "must go on," but in the end he remains unsure:

> All alone,
> Through the splashing, lashing torrent,
> Along the eternal mile,
> I must go on
> With this thought ever recurrent:
> Is it worth while?[97]

"The Park in Spring" has been alluded to in an earlier chapter and
need not detain us further, save to say that it testifies to McKay's aversion
to human suffering. Apart from "To the White Fiends," "The Conqueror"
is by far the most explicitly political of the 1918 poems. The "Conqueror"
of the title is never openly identified, but it is nonetheless clear that
McKay is speaking in one breath of modern technology, the white man,
and the Western world, interchangeably. He acknowledges the remarkable technological conquests achieved. The forces of production have
developed to the extent that "Earth, Sea and Air" have all been subdued.
But to McKay, the victory is incomplete, indeed hollow: "He has won
everywhere, / He has under control . . . all things / But his Soul."[98] Once
again, this is an indictment of the West that the poetry of *négritude*, especially that of Césaire and Senghor, would proffer over and over again in
subsequent years.

Finally, there is "The Lynching," written during this period but published
only in 1920. It is a delicately constructed, fragile, somber thing. Du Bois
used the term "sorrow songs" to describe the spirituals.[99] "The Lynching" is
not a spiritual, but it has the same pathos. It is a song of sorrow with hauntingly powerful images of the aftermath of routinized brutality and violence
and the ugliness of racism carried to a new generation.

> Hung pitifully o'er the swinging char.
> Day dawned, and soon the mixed crowds came to view
> The ghastly body swaying in the sun:
> The women thronged to look, but never a one
> Showed sorrow in her eyes of steely blue;
> And little lads, lynchers that were to be,
> Danced round the dreadful thing in fiendish glee.[100]

Frank Harris turned down "The Lynching" in a rather patronizing, schoolmasterly tone. "Now in this sonnet, 'The Lynching,'" he pontificated in his deep lion-roar of a voice, "you have not given of your best. A sonnet like this," he said, "after reading the report of the [East] St. Louis Massacre, which I published in *Pearson's*, sounds like an anti-climax." Harris went on to tell McKay what he should have done: "You should have risen to the heights and stormed heaven like Milton when he wrote 'On the Late Massacre in Piedmont':

> *Avenge, O Lord! thy slaughtered Saints whose bones*
> *Lie scattered on the Alpine mountains cold. . . .*

There you have the sublime human cry of anguish and hate against man's inhumanity to man. Some day," Harris told McKay, "you will rip it out of your guts."[101] Harris was wrong to have rejected "The Lynching," at least on the grounds on which he rejected publication. His impatience with the poem is understandable in the wake of East St. Louis, but sorrow, under the circumstances, is as legitimate an emotion as rage to express poetically. McKay, like many other Black people at the time, felt both sorrow and rage over the incident.

"The Lynching" is ultimately a testimony to McKay's anguished response to an aspect of American life. Interestingly, as in "To the White Fiends," a religious overtone is present in "The Lynching," which, as we saw, was completely absent in his early Jamaican poems. It was as if the species of horror—particularly lynching—specially set aside for Black people in the United States required divine intervention, given the balance of forces between African Americans and their tormentors. To this extent, "The Lynching" is somewhat reminiscent of "The Apple Woman's Complaint": they are both about victims, the important difference being that the apple woman actually complains while the victim of the lynching is mute, isolated, lonely, a swaying, charred body, abandoned even by the gods. The active ones in "The Lynching" are those with steely blue eyes and fiendish glee; they are the demonic ones, the torturers and the torturers to be.

Thus, in the early years of his sojourn in the United States, we can almost see McKay feeling his way and finding his feet and his voice in a strange land. He experienced the shock that most Caribbean migrants of his generation felt. The tyranny of race and racism occupied much of his thought; it is a telling and dreadful testimony to the salience of racism—the almost demonic power of the phenomenon of racism—in American society at the time that this occurred despite McKay's predilections. "As a rule," he wrote Braithwaite in early 1916, "the race problem does not inspire me very much to poetic efforts." Partly pandering to the conservatism of Braithwaite, who had advised him not to reveal his race in his poetry, he declared: "Of the many things I have written very few are of racial themes, but," he went on, "sometimes my emotions are stirred by something above the ordinary, I feel the urge to write and the thought will not down."[102] The problem of course, was that there was always "something above the ordinary" about race in America for a Black person formed in the relatively benign racial environment of Jamaica. The wonder is not that McKay wrote a great deal about it during his early years in America, but that he managed to write about anything apart from racism. His sensitive personality and his provenance in the Caribbean made McKay especially prone to be emotionally "stirred" by the relative starkness and cruelty of racism in America.

Another significant and related feature of these early poems is the testimony that they bear to the swiftness with which McKay identified with African Americans. In describing antiBlack pogroms and lynching in the United States in "To the White Fiends," he speaks of his "brothers" being murdered and burnt. In the same poem he matter-of-factly identifies himself as one of "Afric's sons." In "In Memoriam: Booker T. Washington," McKay is a part of the "we" of Washington's race who feel so "utterly alone" at the leader's passing. In "Harlem Shadows," McKay and the prostitute are one in that he and she both belong to "my fallen race."

Those early years were, indeed, far from silent. McKay busied himself with serving his American apprenticeship, artistically as well as politically. Significantly—as his autobiographical essay in *Pearson's Magazine* indicates—his racial consciousness heightened at the same time that his appreciation of the significance of social class was growing. This is no mean achievement for someone entering such a racially polarized society as America was at the time. The racial and ethnic centrifuge of American society threw individuals into their discrete "racial" and "ethnic" groups. For Claude McKay to have taken social class as seriously as he did in such an environment was to swim very much against the tide. This was the route that other Caribbean radical intellectuals also took. The early Hubert Harrison, Cyril Briggs, Richard B. Moore, Wilfred Domingo, and others all tried, like McKay, to hold fast to the political and conceptual importance not only of race, but also of social class.[103]

6

Fighting Back

Claude McKay and the Crisis of 1919

In the [*Negro World*] of September 20 [1919] there occurred an exchange
of letters between Claude McKay, the author of the much-quoted
poem about the negro with his back against the wall and fighting to
the death, and W. H. Ferris, literary editor of the *Negro World*. McKay
advocates Bolshevism as a means of freedom for the negro.

—A. Mitchell Palmer, attorney general, United States of America, November 1919

In the dark times
Will there also be singing?
Yes, there will also be singing
About the dark times.

—Bertolt Brecht

McKay, along with his poetry, shifted into a higher gear of radicalism
after the First World War. He no longer restrained and smothered
his bursting anger and rage, as he had in "To the White Fiends." He
allowed himself greater freedom of expression. This was because the "white
fiends" went on a rampage of unparalleled breadth and savagery against
Black people in 1919, and McKay had grown increasingly radical during his
time in the United States. The new openness, and the uninhibited rage and
sorrow of his poetry, gained release in a largely involuntary way. McKay
could hardly help his feelings and their expression. There was much for a

Black man to be enraged about, and more than enough to cause him deep despair in America in 1919.

Red Summer, Black Resistance

Nearly four dozen racist mob attacks—from Orono, Maine, in the east to San Francisco in the west; from Chicago in the north to Mulberry, Florida, in the south—with their blood and fire, death and destruction, convulsed urban America.[1] James Weldon Johnson saw the blood and the fire and dubbed the events of 1919 the "Red Summer."[2] In fact, the rampage started before the summer and extended well beyond it, running from April 1919 to January 1920. If ever there was a time for Black people to fight back, this was it. And African Americans did, with great courage, fight back. McKay exhorted them, his Black brothers and sisters, his "kinsmen"—not that they needed much encouragement—to fight back. McKay's rivulets had finally conjoined to form a deep and powerful river.

Coming as it did on the heels of the October Revolution and the First World War, to which it was organically connected, the Red Summer cleared up any lingering doubts McKay may have harbored about crossing the political Rubicon. It had a catalytic effect upon him; more than anything else, it made McKay into a revolutionary. And it was McKay's open and militant response to the momentous events of 1919 that first brought him into the limelight in America. Indeed, it is for his reaction to the Red Summer that he is most widely remembered. We must therefore turn, albeit briefly, to these remarkable events in order to properly gauge McKay's political development, his veritable metamorphosis. His political trajectory for 1919 can be plotted only against the backdrop of the impact of the Red Summer and his response.

Triggered by white racist mobs attacking Black people, the Red Summer occupies an important place in the nation's history. Two of America's most distinguished historians, John Hope Franklin and C. Vann Woodward, judged its position. "The greatest period of inter-racial strife the nation had ever seen," decided Franklin.[3] C. Vann Woodward described the white fury of 1919 as "a reaction of violence that was probably unprecedented."[4] Officially, at least seventy-seven Black people were lynched, including ten soldiers and one woman.[5] But a recent study established that between December 15, 1918, and December 28, 1919, there were at least eighteen documented cases of Black veterans being lynched.[6] One of them, Wilbur

Little, was beaten to death in Blakey, Georgia, for wearing his uniform for "too long."[7] As many as a hundred or more Black cotton farmers and laborers perished in a pogrom—notorious even by the standards of that blood-soaked year—at Elaine, Arkansas. They had the temerity to expect the price they received for their crop from the local white cartel of landowners to reflect the general market for cotton. Cheated for years, they formed a union, the Progressive Farmers and Household Union of America, and began planning a campaign of action. Their enemies viewed such efforts as a challenge and went on the offensive. To make matters worse, these Black farmers had the audacity to return fire after white hoodlums attacked a meeting of their union at a church in Phillips County. One of the white assailants was killed and another, a deputy sheriff, wounded. The authorities disarmed and arrested hundreds of Black people in the county and gave the confiscated arms to whites. The mob gathered reinforcements from "all parts of Arkansas" and from as far afield as Mississippi and Tennessee. There was carnage. Walter White, who visited Arkansas and investigated the massacre for the NAACP, said that those Black people who escaped arrest took refuge in the canebrakes near the town, where they were "hunted down like animals." The final death list states that five whites and twenty-five Black people were killed. But White found the official estimates unconvincing; several white men in Helena, the county seat of Phillips County, told him that "more than one hundred Negroes were killed, and that in their opinion the total death list would never be known." The NAACP later estimated that as many as 250 Black people were slaughtered by the mob with the help of troops called in by the governor of Arkansas.[8]

In Omaha, Nebraska, a white mob, after setting fire to a part of the courthouse, stormed the building, overwhelmed police, and dragged out William Brown, a Black man—to the delight of the baying crowd outside—with a rope forming a noose around his neck. Forty-one-year-old Brown, a packinghouse worker, had been wrongly accused of rape by a nineteen-year-old white girl, Agnes Loebeck. When he was presented to her for identification, even she expressed doubt: "I can't say whether he [Brown] was the man or not." A physical examination showed that Brown was "too twisted by rheumatism to attack anyone," and those who knew Brown and others who saw him in jail corroborated that judgment.[9] He was taken into custody by the police, but the mob demanded to have him. The police refused. The mayor, Edward P. Smith, a sixty-year-old lawyer, urged the crowd to go home and let the law "handle" the case. "If this man is guilty of the crime he is charged with," Mayor Smith is reported to have said to the crowd, "he will be severely punished, but the law must punish him and not a mob. If you take him from this courthouse it will be over my dead body." "If we can't get the nigger, we'll lynch you!" came the reply. "He's no better than a nigger; get the rope!" "Lynch him!" a voice yelled. Smith was dragged from a police emergency car as he tried to leave. "I will give my life if necessary, but I will not surrender the Negro. He may be innocent. I am going to enforce the law at whatever cost," the mayor told the mob. One rioter placed a rope around Smith's neck, and the mob hanged the mayor from an electric light pole. A brave citizen, against some resistance, cut Smith down and bundled him into a car, which took him to a nearby hospital. He arrived at the hospital in "serious" condition, unconscious, battered about the head, with rope burns around his neck.[10] The NAACP telegraphed the injured mayor congratulations on his "courageous attempt to check mob violence."[11]

William Brown was not as lucky as Mayor Smith. He was shot at least twice as he was dragged through the crowd. By the time he was strung to a light pole he was "practically dead." Brown was "never heard to utter a word and he was not given an opportunity to speak before being stretched full length before the gaze of thousands," the *Wichita Protest* reported. But Sheriff Michael Clark claimed that Brown was hysterical and crying out, "I am innocent, I never did it, my God, I never did it."[12] His corpse was burned and lynched, "mutilated beyond recognition of a human being," riddled with "a thousand bullets." "It was the most horrendous sight I'd ever seen," recalled Henry Fonda, who as a fourteen-year-old witnessed the whole grizzly scene from the window of his father's printing office opposite the courthouse. "I could not sleep that night and a lot of other nights after that." What remained of Brown's corpse was then dragged through the streets at the end of a rope pulled by fifty members of the mob. The crowd entertained themselves in a carnival atmosphere with Brown's corpse for hours, well into the small hours of the morning, when its members finally relented and went to bed.[13] White residents, women as well as men, later "laughed" and "bragged" to a *Washington Post* reporter about kicking the burnt torso of Will Brown around the streets of Omaha like a "huge football."[14] Lynched on Monday, September 28, William Brown—what remained of him—was buried on Wednesday, September 30. The authorities buried his remains without a funeral service, without any ceremony, without mourners. An additional two people were killed and more than fifty injured in Omaha.[15]

In Chicago, thirty-eight people—twenty-three Black and fifteen white—were killed and 537 injured in the outburst of violence.[16] Across the nation, thousands of Black people's homes were destroyed by the frenzied mobs, who used not only the gun, the club, and the stone but also the torch in their rampage of terror.

In an illuminating NAACP memorandum submitted to Congress at the beginning of 1920, two significant observations highlight the specificity of 1919. In urging a reluctant Congress to investigate the "riots" and lynchings, the NAACP pointed out that, first, there was an "increase in cruelty and ferocity" of lynchings. The association noted that the number of Black people burned alive at the stake in 1918 was two; four others were burned after death. In 1919, more than five times as many (eleven) were burned alive at the stake, and white mobs burned three others at the stake after they had been killed.[17] In 1918, sixty-three Black people were lynched;[18] in 1919, it was at least seventy-seven, a 22 percent increase. The phenomenal increase in the number of people burned alive at the stake—an increase of no less than 450 percent between 1918 and 1919—evidently far outpaced the increase in total lynchings. This diabolical ratcheting-up of the torturing of Black victims, by burning them alive, was one of the remarkable features of 1919.

The NAACP also registered that local law enforcement officers allowed prisoners to be taken from them without making "bona fide efforts" to protect the prisoners and to hold them for legal trial. The escalation of such incidents between 1918 and 1919 is noteworthy: thirteen in 1918 and thirty-four in 1919,[19] an increase of some 161 percent. As with the number of Black people being burned alive, the pervasiveness of such practices increased faster than total lynchings over the year.

No one was convicted for any of these heinous murders. The NAACP found that there were convictions in two related cases in 1918 and 1919, and neither was for the lynching of a Black man. In Winston-Salem, North Carolina, fifteen men were sentenced to serve from fourteen months to six years for attempting to break into the local jail for the purpose of lynching Russell High, a Black man. In the second case, fines were imposed on twelve men who pleaded guilty to the lynching of Frank Foukal, a white man, at Bay Minette, Alabama. The men pleaded guilty by agreement, and the fines ranged from $100 to $300.[20]

But there was another special quality—and one that ought not to be overlooked—to the conjuncture of 1919. This was, as one writer put it, the "manifest readiness" of Black people to offer "determined resistance" to white racist mobs.[21] This remarkable feature of the year may very well hold the key to explaining the surplus cruelty—the fiendish practices, seemingly straight out of Beelzebub's chamber—enacted by the murdering racist mobs in 1919. At the end of the most prolonged of the riots, that in Chicago, fifteen of the thirty-eight fatalities were white.[22] As one historian, with unwitting redundance, wrote: "The Chicago riot was a two-sided conflict."[23]

A young African American lawyer who witnessed the events emphasized the readiness of Black people to resist in armed combat. He reported that on the second day of the violence, white police officers opened fire "promiscuously" into a crowd at a street corner—Thirty-Fifth and Wabash—on the grounds that a mounted officer had been hit by a brick. (The brick was meant for a passing truck.) Six innocent Black people were killed or injured by the police in the incident. But the police did not go unpunished. One Black man was so incensed by the "cowardly action" of the police that he "walked out into the street with an automatic and shot several of the white officers. He was not hit by any of the bullets from the officer's guns and has not been captured."

"Everything from a knife to a machine gun," the witness said, was used by Black people to defend themselves. And Black Chicagoans made every effort to acquire arms in self-defense. "Quite a bit" of ammunition was procured from as far away as Gary, Indiana, he told the interviewer. Asked whether the delay in the use of federal troops benefited or injured the "Negro cause," he unequivocally responded: "Benefited it." He believed that "the delayed use of troops caused the loss of many innocent lives, colored as well as white." But he added, the delay "afforded an opportunity for the Negroes to impress upon the whites their readiness, willingness, and eagerness to fight the thing through." He was optimistic about the impact of African American resistance on the future position of the Black community.

> The riot will make the future relations between the races decidedly better. It will bring about "a meeting of the minds" to the effect that the colored man must not be kicked about like a dumb brute. Our white friends, seeing the danger that besets the nation, will become more active in our cause, and the other whites will at least have a decent respect for us based on fear.[24]

Black veterans of the First World War—disillusioned and radicalized—played an important role in the struggle against the marauding mobs. The frequent and specifically earmarked targets of white thugs, they had more reasons than most for fighting back.[25] On the South Side—Chicago's largest Black settlement—for instance, African American veterans prepared to deal with attackers. Harry Haywood, a veteran of the war who later became a leading African American member of the Communist Party, was active in the community's defense. He recalled:

> One of the guys from the regiment took us to the apartment of a friend. It had a good position overlooking Fifty-first Street near State. Someone had brought a Browning submachine gun; he'd gotten it sometime before, most likely from the Regimental Armory. We didn't ask where it had come from, or the origin of the 1903 Springfield rifles (Army issue) that appeared. We set to work mounting the submachine gun and set up watch for the invaders. Fortunately for them, they never arrived and we all returned home in the morning.

Haywood pointed out that theirs was not the only group that used its recent army training for defending the Black community. He heard about another group of veterans who set up a similar ambush:

> On several occasions groups of whites had driven a truck at breakneck speed up south State Street, in the heart of the Black ghetto, with six or seven men in the back firing indiscriminately at the people on the sidewalks.
>
> The Black veterans set up their ambush at Thirty-fifth and State, waiting in a car with the engine running. When the whites on the truck came through, they pulled in behind and opened up with a machine gun. The truck crashed into a telephone pole at Thirty-ninth Street; most of the men in the truck had been shot down and the others fled. Among them were several Chicago police officers—"off duty," of course!

Reflecting upon his life some sixty years after the Red Summer, Haywood identified the Chicago "riot" as a "pivotal point" in his life.

> Always I had been hot-tempered and never took any insults lying down. This was even more true after the war. . . . I began to see that I had to fight; I had to commit myself to struggle against whatever it was that made racism possible. Racism, which erupted in the Chicago riot—and the bombings and terrorist attacks which preceded it—must be eliminated.

This outlook, he pointed out, was shared by many young Black people at the time. "The returned veterans and other young militants were all fighting back. And there was a lot to fight against. Racism reached a high tide in the summer of 1919."[26]

Stanley B. Norvell, one of Haywood's fellow Chicago veterans, told a reporter soon after the riot: "Today we have with us a new Negro. A brand new Negro, if you please. . . . You will find that 'Uncle Tom' that charming old figure of the literature contemporary with the war of the rebellion is quite dead now and that his prototypes are almost as extinct as is the great auk, [and] the dodo bird. . . . You will have committed," Norvell added, "an unpardonable faux pas if you should happen to call any eminently respectable old colored lady, 'mammy' or 'auntie.'"[27] He insisted that the African American "must and will have industrial, commercial, civil and political equality." America, Norvel said, has "already given [the African American] these inalienable rights, but she has not always seen to it that he has received them. America," he declared, "must see that the Negro is not deprived of any right that she has given him."[28]

With "brand new Negroes" like Stanley B. Norvel, like Harry Haywood and his brother veterans, like the man with the automatic at Thirty-Fifth and Wabash, Black Chicago defended itself courageously against the white mobs. As one writer observed, except for Black people killed by policemen, "the number of casualties was about equal on both sides."[29] The Black community in Chicago had indeed inflicted sufficient retaliatory damage on the marauders to make such sallies too costly to be lightly embarked upon.

Black Chicagoans, in the heat of the Red Summer, must have been heartened—through the bond of fellowship, strengthened by a history of common oppression and by the centripetal force of a racist America on the rampage—by the exemplary resistance of their brothers and sisters in Washington, DC, which took place only a few days before the violence erupted in Chicago.[30] Black people in Washington demonstrated with conviction that they were prepared and organized enough to resist the white terror of 1919.

Goaded by sensationalist racist reporting—"mob violence propaganda," James Weldon Johnson called it—in the *Washington Post*, hordes of white sailors, soldiers, and marines attacked Black people going about their ordinary business.[31] Along with white policemen and assigned troops, white "civilians" raided the Black community.[32] For the first two days, African Americans were, in Johnson's words, "mobbed, chased, dragged from street cars, beaten and killed within the shadow of the dome of the Capitol, at the very door of the White House." The worst attacks against Black Washingtonians were perpetrated on Sunday night, July 20. Late that night, Carter G. Woodson, a Howard University professor and founder of the Association for the Study of Negro Life and History, was walking home to his rooming house—apparently contemplating the revision of his paper "Relations of Negroes and Indians in Massachusetts"—when suddenly, at the corner of Pennsylvania Avenue and Eighth Street, "there ran by me a Negro yelling for mercy . . . pursued by hundreds of soldiers, sailors, and marines, assisted by men in civilian attire." Woodson was startled because he had read in the papers about the "race riots in the southwest" of Washington, which he avoided, not "think[ing] for a moment that the mob had control of the whole section of the city." Woodson quickly took refuge in the "deep entrance of a store" as shots rang out. Crouching with his back to the mob, Woodson was suddenly joined by two white women, pleading for protection. "I felt like appealing to them to save me." Luckily, their presence hid him from view. After some minutes, which seemed like an eternity, Woodson politely took his leave of the ladies and stealthily resumed his journey home. But he had hardly finished breathing a sigh of relief when, "instead of getting away from the violence," he encountered a second mob and "the most harrowing spectacle" he had ever encountered. The "mob had caught a Negro and deliberately held him as one would a beef for slaughter, and when they had conveniently adjusted him for lynching they shot him. I heard him groaning in his struggle as I hurried away as fast I could without running, expecting every moment to be lynched myself."[33]

It was hunting season: "nigger hunting." "Here's one!" as if pointing to a hapless deer in the forest. " 'Here's one!' some one would yell when the crowd saw a negro, and the chase would begin."[34] "There he goes!" was another trigger to begin the chase—the mob "hooting and shouting"—after its human prey. Women were not spared, nor were the elderly; they just had to be Black.[35] District and federal authorities did virtually nothing to stop the mayhem. When a white man approached three policemen, as a Black man ran by chased by the mob, and asked why someone did not do something to stop the rioting, "That is what we would like to know!" one officer replied.[36] As the New York Age—one of the most conservative Black newspapers at the time—noted, the local and national authorities "to all intents and purposes threw their organized influence against the colored people, the victims of the fury of the mob."[37] The Black population of the nation's capital had to literally save itself. Clearly, no one—not even the constituted authority—was going to stop the mob. From a state of shock, disorganization, and leaderlessness when the rioting started on Saturday night, Black people by Monday rallied and prepared to defend themselves. They defended themselves—in the words of Jeannette Carter, the New York Age's Washington correspondent and eyewitness to these events—with a "grim determination to exact a life for a life. They entered into the strife with more determination than the whites who started it, and," as Carter put it, "they stuck to the job all week like heroes of many battles." The level of organization was remarkable, the audacity breathtaking:

> On Monday the Negroes had three machine guns placed in high-powered automobiles, with hand grenades, and before the riot ended had begun to make bombs. They had plenty of ammunition and guns which were handed around to all colored people who were not able to buy them. The bootleggers who had been making plenty of money went to Baltimore and bought ammunition and guns amounting to more than fifteen thousand dollars['] worth and gave them out to Negroes.[38]

Carter acknowledged the role played by ordinary folk, and indeed by some of the poorest and most disparaged elements of the community, in defense of Black Washington in its moment of need:

> Too much cannot be said in praise of the so-called common people who equipped themselves to meet the emergency. It was splendid. The poolroom hangers-on and men from the alleys and side streets, people from the most ordinary walks of life were the people who really saved the day by striking terror into the hearts of the white mob. They had a regular organization of their own, with a private code. They had a flying automobile squadron that took in every section of the city, including the school of Miss Nannie H. Burroughs, on Lincoln Heights, and places thereabouts, they made several trips to the school, after a report got into circulation that the white mob intended to attack the school.
>
> They made their trip in their high-powered automobiles, every man in the trucks being armed, while the chauffeurs who ran the trucks, steered with one hand and held a gun with the other. They kept one truck with plenty of ammunition, stationed in the neighborhood of Lincoln Heights. The daily newspapers did not report one-half the deaths or casualties.

Mindful of the honors won by Black troops in France during the First World War, it was suggested that a Croix de Guerre "with palm" be given to a seventeen-year-old girl "who is accused of picking off a detective when he went into her bedroom at night without a warrant and when no riot call had come from that house."

The Washington racist rampage that at the beginning had threatened to become another East St. Louis massacre had been transformed into a carnival of the Black oppressed. The confidence of the Black masses was palpable and contagious. "Your correspondent," Carter reported back to New York, "personally visited the scene of the rioting, realizing withal that I was in much danger of getting a stray bullet, but having no fear of being attacked, because I was surrounded by that splendid crowd of brave young men."[39]

James Weldon Johnson, who arrived in Washington from New York in the early evening of July 22, contrasted the anxiety he and others felt as his train approached Washington with the reality on the ground. As the train slowly entered Union Station, the Black porters and waiters, Johnson observed, "plainly showed the strain under which they were doing their work"—

> the strain of suppressed excitement with, perhaps, an added sense of dread of going into something, they knew not what. They moved about quietly, in fact, grimly and entirely without their customary good humor and gaiety. One of the porters who knew who I was questioned the wisdom of my going through with the trip. I may have felt that his question was not absolutely without reason, but I did not admit it. When I left the car he said to me, "Take care of yourself." I assured him that I would spare no effort to do so.[40]

But the Washington Johnson arrived in was very different from that dreaded by the porters and waiters on the train. "When we reached the Northwest Section of the city, I found the whole atmosphere entirely different." Johnson had expected to find the Black community "excited and, perhaps, panicky." But instead: "I found them calm and determined, unterrified and unafraid."

Johnson noted that although "shots had blazed all through the [previous] night" in the neighborhood, he detected "no signs of nervousness" among the Black people. "They had reached the determination," Johnson noticed, "that they would defend and protect themselves and their homes at the cost of their lives, if necessary, and that determination rendered them calm."[41]

Back in New York, Johnson reflected on his journey to the battleground. "I returned disquieted, but not depressed over the Washington riot; it might have been worse," he reported. "It might have been a riot in which the Negroes, unprotected by the law, would not have had the spirit to protect themselves." But the people "saved themselves and saved Washington by their determination not to run, but to fight. . . . If the white mob had gone on unchecked—and it was only the determined effort of black men that checked it—Washington would have been another and worse East St. Louis." Johnson came to the conclusion that as "regrettable" as the events in Washington and Chicago were, "I feel that they mark the turning point in the psychology of the whole nation regarding the Negro problem."[42]

Jeannette Carter's came to a similar but blunter conclusion:

> The next time that the crackers start a riot in this town, whether formented [*sic*] by the white newspapers and a bunch of white soldiers and sailors or by themselves, they will think a long deep think, as the colored men in Washington . . . have resolved to front the white mob by the colored mob and exact life for life. If they can't have protection of the Federal Government, and it has been shown that they had not had it, they have determined to defend themselves. And that is as it should be.[43]

Despite calls for a public inquiry into the "Washington riots" by the NAACP, by Black clergymen, and by sympathetic members of Congress, no inquiry took place. No reliable figures for the Washington casualties exist. What is known, however, is that when the dust settled, the Black/white casualty ratio was not the usual one. All indications are that more white than Black people were killed and injured.[44]

The underlying causes of these events were many and varied. At the level of immediate causality, it is clear that these incidents were instigated by white racist mobs. Not one of these conflagrations was initiated by African Americans, who were provoked and attacked. They responded in self-defense. This counterviolence on the part of African Americans was necessary in the absence of effective local, state, or federal response. The specific catalyst for each of these events varied from city to city. In Washington, it was the circumstances surrounding the arrest of a Black man on the night of July 20 and the "random" attacks on innocent Black people—encouraged by racist and alarmist reports in the *Washington Post*—by mobs of racist sailors, marines, and soldiers. In Chicago, it was the drowning of young Eugene Williams after being hit by missiles thrown at him by racists while swimming in Lake Michigan.

More broadly, increased economic competition between Black and white workers was at play in the immediate aftermath of the war. Before the war, for a variety of complex reasons, there was relatively little Black migration from the South to the North.[45] During the war, a number of circumstances facilitated this migration. First, there was a massive "labor shortage" in the industrial North as a consequence of war mobilization, which resulted in white men withdrawing from the labor force in large numbers. In fact, no fewer than 4,791,172 people served in the armed forces during the war. Second, the flow of European migrants to the United States declined drastically as a consequence of the war in Europe. Indeed, immigration to the United States—up to that point emanating mainly from Europe—dropped 91 percent between 1914 and 1918, from 1,218,480 to 110,618; net migration in 1918 was only 18,585. Exacerbating the labor shortage even further, European belligerents conscripted their eligible nationals residing in the United States.[46] Many others, fired by nationalism, voluntarily returned to Europe to fight. These developments, of course, increased employment opportunities for those left behind. Finally, the increased production demands imposed upon industry by wartime requirements created the need for extra labor. The vacancies in the industrial North were filled primarily by workers from the southern states. Though a largely overlooked fact, even more white than Black workers took the journey North.[47]

While these structural forces dramatically enhanced northern employment prospects for Black migrants from the South, increased opportunities in themselves do not explain the phenomenon of human migration. Mediating forces and agencies were necessary before actual movement occurred. The links between northern employment opportunities and prospective Black southern workers were established by a number of mechanisms: the activities of labor recruiting agents in the South; advertisements of northern employment opportunities in southern newspapers; the encouragement by Black people already residing in the North—including earlier migrants—of the northward migration of relatives, friends and loved ones left behind in the South; and the encouragement of similar action by Black northern newspapers, most notably the *Chicago Defender*. Added to these "pull" factors in Black northward migration were the "push," or repellent, factors in the South. Primary among these were the intensified racism during the war years, the deteriorating economic position of Black farmers, crop devastation by the boll weevil, and low wages in the South relative to those in the North—hence the African American jingle:

> Boll-weevil in de cotton
> Cut worm in de cotton,
> Debil in de white man,
> Wah's goin on.[48]

These developments, combined, constituted the key motors behind the Great Migration.[49]

Leaving aside the struggles and disappointments of the new migrants in the North during the war years, it was clear—given the culture of racism in the United States—that the perceived conflict of interests between Black and white workers would present severe problems after the war. The widespread new mood of Black militancy and self-confidence abroad—unparalleled since the long-gone days of Reconstruction—coupled with a deepening level of resentment and indignation against racism in its southern as well as northern disguises, challenged the racist status quo. Added to this was the fact that lynchings had increased during the war years.[50] That Black men—nearly two hundred thousand of them—were fighting and dying all the way across the Atlantic to preserve "freedom and democracy," to "make the world safe for democracy," made no difference to the lynchers.[51] African Americans who joined the army experienced some of the most humiliating indignities not at the hands of the "Kaiser's men," but at those of their own white officers and fellow American soldiers.[52] The Black soldiers read and heard about the lynchings back home. They enjoyed a relative freedom in France never experienced in the United States and vowed never to return to the status quo ante. Trained, as Haywood reminded us, in the use of weapons and in the conduct of war, they were distinguished soldiers, as their many honors testify. The Black community in America had changed, the black soldiers had changed—"We have a brand new Negro, if you please"—while American society, almost unimaginably, had actually regressed in its treatment of its black citizens. "You niggers are wondering how you are going to be treated after the war," a white man in New Orleans observed. "Well, I'll tell you, you going to be treated exactly like you were before the war."[53] Domestic peace, under such unfavorable circumstances, could not have been maintained. The Red Summer of 1919, at least in hindsight, was almost inevitable.

But the long Red Summer of 1919 was not solely a period of racist barbarism. It was also, as we have seen, a moment of organized, armed, and effective black resistance on a scale unprecedented in the postslavery period in the United States. And it is this which gave it—to paraphrase Yeats—its terribly beautiful quality.[54] This quality of the Red Summer is perhaps most eloquently expressed in a letter to the *Crisis* written by a black southern woman. The previous week, she had had a conversation with an old friend who had asked her what she thought of the events in Washington and Chicago. The friend was so moved by her response that she suggested it be shared with *Crisis* readers, "so that our men can know how we women have felt and how we feel now." The "Washington riots," she told her friend,

> gave me the thrill that comes once in a lifetime. I was alone when I read
> between the lines of the morning paper that at last our men had stood like
> men, struck back, were no longer dumb, driven cattle. When I could no
> longer read for my streaming tears, I stood up, alone in my room, held both
> hands high over my head and exclaimed, "Oh, I thank God, thank God!"
> When I remember anything after this, I was prone on my bed, beating the
> pillow with both fists, laughing and crying, whimpering like a whipped child,
> for sheer gladness and madness. The pent-up humiliation, grief and horror
> of a lifetime—half a century—was being stripped from me."[55]

The Black resistance of the Red Summer announced to the American public in the most spectacular fashion the existence of what became known as the "New Negro"—assertive and militant Black people, willing and prepared to resist to the death the racist mobs.[56] The New Negroes transformed potential pogroms into battles—an East St. Louis into a Washington, DC. And the Red Summer itself created even more New Negroes. Many African Americans, especially the youth, echoed the sentiments of the Black revolutionary socialist Cyril Briggs: "Right without might is moonshine!"[57] To paraphrase Stanley Norvell, Black people were bent on not simply being given their rights on paper but on receiving those rights in reality, even if they had to take them. W. E. B. Du Bois, who had fervently advocated African American unconditional support of the war effort, touched by the spirit of 1919, moved to the beat of a different drummer. In one of his most memorable pieces of writing since *The Souls of Black Folk*, his May 1919 editorial in the *Crisis*, "Returning Soldiers," Du Bois proclaimed:

> *We return.*
> *We return from fighting.*
> *We return fighting.*

> Make way for Democracy! We saved it in France, and by the Great Jehovah,
> we will save it in the United States of America, or know the reason why.[58]

Twenty years later, McKay identified that brief editorial, along with *The Souls of Black Folk*, as the reason why Du Bois "stands on a pedestal illuminated in my mind."[59]

A New and Strange Cry: To Sing in Dark Times

During the summer of 1919 McKay worked as a waiter on the Pennsylvania Railroad, traveling among New York, Philadelphia, Pittsburgh, Harrisburg, and Washington.[60] Years later, he vividly recalled the prevailing atmosphere. "Our Negro newspapers," he remembered, were "morbid, full of details of clashes between colored and white, murderous shootings and hangings." Traveling from city to city, unable to gauge the attitude and temper of each one, he and his fellow Black railroad men were "nervous." They were less lighthearted than usual, and they did not separate from one another "gaily to spend [themselves] in speakeasies and gambling joints," as they would otherwise have done. "We stuck together," he said. "I remember we waiters and cooks carried revolvers in secret and always kept together going from our quarters to the railroad yards, as a precaution against sudden attack." McKay, who had owned a revolver since 1914, when he ran a restaurant in a rough part of Brooklyn, now carried his gun with him. While stopping over in strange cities, he explained to a friend who questioned him about the revolver that he and his fellow trainmen were obliged to pass through "some of the toughest quarters" and had to be on guard against the "suddenly aroused hostility of the mob." They stayed in their quarters "all through the dreary ominous nights, for we never knew what was going to happen."[61]

Harry Haywood, who worked the Chicago–New York route as a waiter on the Michigan Central Railroad, reported exactly the same experience. It was only three months after his mustering out of the army that all hell broke loose in Chicago. Passing through Detroit on July 27, 1919, on their way to New York, Haywood and his fellow workers heard that rioting had broken out in Chicago. The next day, they became caught up in the mayhem themselves as they arrived at the Twelfth Street Station in Chicago and tried to make their way home to the South Side. Like McKay's group of trainmen, they too had armed themselves and prepared for the worst. Arriving in Chicago on the 28th, they—six waiters and four cooks—were warned by a friendly white trainman not to take Michigan Avenue, the street right in front of the station. "There's a big race riot going on out there," he told them, "and already this morning a couple of colored soldiers were killed coming in unsuspectingly. If I were you," he advised, "I'd keep off the street, and go right out those tracks by the lake." They thanked the trainman, followed his advice, and took the long but safer way home. "The battle at home was just as real as the battle in France had been," said Haywood. "Our small band, huddled like a bunch of raw recruits under machine gun fire." Having feared the worst, the whole family greeted him "emotionally" when Haywood finally arrived home. A recent disagreement with his father was now forgotten, and his mother and sister wept. As he explained, "Everyone was keyed up and had been worrying about my safety in getting from the station to the house." Neither Haywood nor any of his workmates returned to work until the disturbance was over, more than a week later.[62]

It was during those days—the high noon of the Red Summer—that a besieged Afro-America heard a sudden, loud, crisp, clear call to arms, sounding over the noise of battle like a clap of thunder. It was like reveille at midday—a "new and strange cry," Richard Wright called it. It "exploded out of me," McKay said, describing it as "an outgrowth of the intense emotional experience I was living through," along with thousands of African Americans.[63] McKay had previously explained to a friend that it was not easy being a poet working on the railroad. "Sometimes I carried lines in my thoughts for days," he said, "waiting until I found time to write them down." But at other times, he was driven to expression, come what may. He vividly related one such incident:

> For many days I was possessed with an unusually lyrical feeling, which grew and increased into form of expression until one day, while we were feeding a carload of people, there was a wild buzzing in my head. The buzzing was so great that it confused and crowded out all orders, so much so that my mechanical self could not function. Finally I explained to the steward that I had an unbearable pain in my belly. He excused me and volunteered to help the fourth waiter with my two tables. And hurrying to the lavatory I locked myself in and wrote the stuff out on a scrap of paper.[64]

McKay likened the experience to giving birth.[65] "If We Must Die" "exploded" out of him in similar fashion.[66] Fittingly, the first to hear "If We Must Die" was the same band of workmates, cooks and waiters, with whom he had tiptoed—Black, sad, afraid, angry, and armed—through the danger zones of the Red Summer. Probably huddled together in a corner of the dining car during a slack moment—just as the waiters and cooks did in his novel, *Home to Harlem*—McKay read his new poem to his Black brethren. Generally hating to recite his poems, he said it was the first and only time that he had read any of them to his workmates. He must have instinctively felt, as he came to understand later, that the poem stood out from the rest of his work—that it was unusual, special, and that it expressed the feelings of his colleagues on that summer's day in 1919, perhaps as much as it articulated his own. McKay read these words to his brothers and fellow workers:

> If we must die—let it not be like hogs
> Hunted and penned in an inglorious spot,
> While round us bark the mad and hungry dogs,
> Making their mock at our accursed lot.
> If we must die—oh, let us nobly die,
> So that our precious blood may not be shed
> In vain; then even the monsters we defy
> Shall be constrained to honor us though dead!
>
> Oh, kinsmen! we must meet the common foe;
> Though far outnumbered, let us still be brave,
> And for their thousand blows deal one death-blow!
> What though before us lies the open grave?
> Like men we'll face the murderous, cowardly pack,
> Pressed to the wall, dying, but—fighting back![67]

They were all "agitated" when he finished. "Even the fourth waiter—who was the giddiest and most irresponsible of the lot, with all his motives and gestures colored by a strangely acute form of satyriasis—even he actually cried. One who was a believer in the Marcus Garvey Back-to-Africa Movement, suggested that I should go to Liberty Hall, the headquarters of the organization, and read the poem."[68] Although McKay did not entertain the idea, never mind attempt to read the poem in front of the mass ranks at Liberty Hall, it was nonetheless widely disseminated, especially among Garveyites. And for this battle cry dressed as a sonnet, for "If We Must Die," Afro-America unanimously hailed McKay as a poet. "Indeed," McKay later observed, "that one grand outburst is their sole standard of appraising my poetry."[69]

First published in the July 1919 issue of one of the most exciting and radical journals in the United States at the time, Max Eastman's *Liberator*, "If We Must Die" was reprinted in innumerable Black journals and newspapers across the United States and abroad. It was published in the *Messenger* in its September issue, which made the poem's title its own for the editorial. The *Crusader* also carried it in their September issue.[70] Garvey's *Negro World* first carried it the following month, and as late as 1922, like the *Messenger*, it carried an editorial whose title was borrowed from that of the poem. After the publication of *Harlem Shadows*, which features "If We Must Die," the

Negro World carried not one but two laudatory reviews, within less than a month of each other. One of the paper's most popular contributors of poetry, Ethel Trew Dunlap, even wrote a long poem dedicated to McKay, which opens with the generous concession: "Your notes shall ring when mine are still, / Live on when mine the casket claim."[71]

Garvey may have had his differences with McKay, but his followers loved McKay. This is not surprising: no poet had captured more successfully and powerfully the spirit of the militant New Negro movement than McKay. And a key contingent of that movement comprised supporters of the UNIA. Even radical Black preachers, such as Rev. Francis J. Grimké, recited it from their pulpits to appreciative Black congregations. In his Thanksgiving address, delivered in Washington, DC, in 1919, Grimké—a veteran of Black America's long struggle for justice, and one of the most distinguished and highly respected churchmen in America at the time—told his congregation that the "new spirit" of resistance "that is taking hold of the Negro is very clearly and forcibly brought out by Claude McKay, one of the real poets of the race, in a little poem of his, entitled, 'If We Must Die.'" Grimké recited the poem. "There is no mistaking the spirit reflected in this poem that comes straight from the heart," he observed. "It has been a long time coming," he told his congregation, "but it has come at last, as is evident from all the recent race riots."[72]

Nine senior officials of the African Methodist Episcopal Church—including bishops from six states—signed and presented a memorial to the United States Senate in September 1919 urging a congressional investigation of the "race riots." "The Commission on After-War Problems of the African Methodist Episcopal Church," representing more than a million communicants, "prompted by a sense of stern duty, respectfully directs your attention to the solemn and ominous statements which characterize" the poem "If We Must Die." With harnessed passion and in an eloquent tone, the petitioners continued:

> Though the poem is the product of a West Indian negro, a native of Jamaica, it nevertheless reflects the conviction of a large group of American citizens of African descent—a group who feel that death is preferable to a state halfway between slavery and freedom. This group has sworn by the blood of their kinsmen who fell on the battle fields of France, in a death grip with the foe, to help make the world safe for democracy, that they will no longer tamely submit to a denial of the rights guaranteed by the National Constitution.[73]

Richard Wright observed that the poem emerged not only "when racial hate was at a hysterical pitch" but also "after the grinding processes of history had forged iron in the Negro's heart."[74] Black journalist and historian J. A. Rogers was not alone in regarding the poem as "the Marseillaise of the American Negro."[75] Wallace Thurman, who was only seventeen at the time of the Red Summer, welcomed "If We Must Die" and later rejoiced over McKay's militant poetry:

> There is no impotent whining here, no mercy-seeking prayer to the white man's God, no mournful jeremiad, no "ain't it hard to be a nigger," no lamenting of or apologizing for the fact that he is a member of a dark-skinned minority group. Rather he boasts:
>
> > Be not deceived, for every deed you do,
> > I could match—out match: Am I not Africa's son,
> > Black of that black land where black deeds are done?[76]

Had McKay not written another line or done anything else, "If We Must Die" alone, as he himself later acknowledged, would have winged his name into posterity. And it was "If We Must Die" more than anything else that promoted McKay to "the symbol of the New Negro and the Harlem Renaissance."[77]

Interestingly enough, published beside "If We Must Die" on the very same page of the *Liberator*, and on the same theme but in a different mood and tone, was another fine sonnet by McKay, "A Roman Holiday":

> 'Tis but a Roman Holiday;
> Each state invokes its soul of basest passion,
> Each vies with each to find the ugliest way
> To torture Negroes in fiercest fashion.
> Black Southern men, like hogs await your doom!
> White wretches hunt and haul you from your huts,
> They squeeze the babies out of your women's womb,
> They cut your members off, rip out your guts!
> It is a Roman Holiday, and worse:
> It is the mad beast risen from his lair,
> The dead accusing years' eternal curse.
> Reeking of vengeance, in fulfillment here.
> Bravo Democracy! Hail greatest Power
> That saved sick Europe in her darkest hour!

In sheer poetic form, "A Roman Holiday" surpasses in quality that of "If We Must Die." Yet "A Roman Holiday" has largely been forgotten, despite its emotional thrust and graphic imagery, including the lynching of Mary Turner—"They squeeze the babies out of your women's womb"—discussed in the previous chapter, and "If We Must Die" has not. This is mainly because in the latter poem, McKay gave poetic expression to the mood of his African American brothers and sisters (his masculine subject notwithstanding) in what Tolson describes as the "holocaustal year of 1919."[78] Almost twenty years after he wrote the poem, McKay was still somewhat perplexed at the reception Black people gave it. He recalled, in *A Long Way from Home*, that the poem was "reprinted in every Negro publication of any consequence."

> It forced its way into the Negro pulpit (a most interesting phenomenon for this black heretic). Ministers ended their sermons with it, and the congregations responded, Amen. It was repeated in Negro clubs and Negro schools and at Negro mass meetings. To thousands of Negroes who are not trained to appreciate poetry, "If We Must Die" makes me a poet. I myself was amazed at the general sentiment for the poem. For I am so intensely subjective as a poet, that I was not aware, at the moment of writing, that I was transformed into a medium to express a mass sentiment.[79]

The remarkable longevity of "If We Must Die" is also explained by its universality: the subject of the poem—the "We"—is never explicitly identified by race, color, nationality, gender, or any such attributes. It is quintessentially an advocacy of stern defiance in the face of formidable adversity, counseling what Huey P. Newton, leader of the Black Panthers in the late 1960s, would have called "revolutionary suicide": it imparts a strategy of siege warfare. This is why the poem has traveled well, as it were, and has appealed to as varied a group of people in time and space as Winston Churchill, allegedly, during the Battle of Britain; Jewish victims of Hitler's concentration camps; Garveyites in Harlem; frontline American soldiers in Europe during the Second World War; African American activists in the civil rights movement, including Stokely Carmichael; Black prisoners in revolt at Attica prison in 1971; George Jackson, who knew and quoted McKay's sonnet, even though, he confessed, "poetry is not my bag"; and an old Jamaican trade unionist in London who had it framed on his wall below a picture of McKay. The poem's enduring appeal is, as another Black poet put it, as "a pillar of fire by night in many lands."[80]

"If We Must Die" overshadowed everything else that McKay did in 1919. The poem was, in fact, one of a two-page spread of seven McKay poems published in the July *Liberator*. Additionally, "The Dominant White" (in April) and "The Tired Worker" (in August) were published that year in the *Liberator*; in September, "To the White Fiends," published a year earlier in *Pearson's*, was reprinted in the *Liberator*. Also in September, McKay published "Labor's Day," and in October "J'accuse," both in the *Messenger* magazine.

In these poems, McKay addresses issues of race and of class in an almost alternating sequence. "The Barrier," addressing the taboo of "inter-racial" love, closes:

> I must not see upon your face
>   Love's softly glowing spark;
> For there's the barrier of race,
>   You're fair and I am dark.[81]

"The Capitalist at Dinner" is classic socialist realist agitprop, rather like an early *Pravda* cartoon. Its subject is obese, round like the globe, greedy, exploitative, parasitic, repulsive. This poem may very well have drawn upon McKay's experience as a waiter, obliged to serve the rich and powerful:

> The entire service tries its best to please
> This overpampered piece of broken health,
> Who sits there thoughtless, querulous, obese,
> Wrapped in his sordid visions of vast wealth.

"If creatures like this money-fool," callous and uncaring must forever rule, driving the people like "helpless sheep," then "let proud mothers cease from giving birth; / Let human beings perish from the earth."[82]

The mood shifts in "The Little Peoples," where McKay bemoans the fact that the "big men of the world" in the postwar settlement at Versailles have decreed that "the little nations that are white and weak" shall gain their freedom. When it came to Black people, however, it is business as usual:

> But we, the blacks, less than the trampled dust,
> Who walk the new ways with the old dim eyes,—
> We to the ancient gods of greed and lust
> Must still be offered up as sacrifice!
> Oh, we who deign to live but will not dare
> The white man's burden must forever bear![83]

"The Tired Worker," like "The Capitalist at Dinner," draws upon McKay's life as a worker—a worker who is so exhausted that he prays for the night and curses the dawn.

> The wretched day was theirs, the night is mine;
> Come tender sleep, and fold me to thy breast.
> But what steals out the gray clouds red like wine?
> O dawn! O dreaded dawn! O let me rest
> Weary my veins, my brain, my life! Have pity![84]

"Labor's Day," was written in celebration of the historic holiday of the international working-class movement. In contrast to its European equivalent—May Day—in the United States, Labor Day, which became a federal holiday in 1894, is celebrated on the first Monday of September. May Day as a celebration of labor originated in the United States around workers' struggle for the eight-hour day in 1886. Later adopted by the European labor movement, it became truly international by the end of the nineteenth century. By the 1890s, Labor Day was seen by the government and bosses as an "antidote" to the more militant and "foreign" associations of May Day.[85] Although the poem was published in the month of September, it is perhaps significant that McKay's title is "Labor's Day," rather than Labor Day. He expressed the belief that the real poetry of "hope and vision" is being written by labor itself, for itself: the labor movement no longer needed the traditional poet; labor's struggle *is* poetry.

> For Labor, Lord, himself will limn his life
> And sing the modern songs of hope and vision,
> And write the inspired tale of long-drawn strife
> While mocked the poor blind world in grim derision,
> Until she opened wide her eyes in awe
> To see a new world under labor's law![86]

From one passion in September—the international proletariat and the promise of socialism—he turns to another in October, his "oppressed race." The mood, however, has changed; it is markedly different from that of "Labor's Day." McKay writes not with hope but sorrow. "J'accuse" is a monologue from the vortex of despair. The narrator witnesses the lynching of a "sinless" Black man, "my flesh and blood," in all its gory details. Having sought solace in the divine in some of his early American poems, the same force—the horrors of racist oppression—behind McKay's uncharacteristic religious turn now seems to have driven him away from religion and God. It is futile to maintain faith in a benevolent being when desperate hopes and prayers go unanswered: his tears ("burning gore") drop on the "earth's hard face" and rise up to heaven only to be met by "the idle guard that keeps / His useless watch before the august door." His conclusion: "There is no God, Earth sleeps, my heart is dead."[87]

Outside of this counterpointing field of race and class, of contending Black nationalist and socialist impulses, there sits a poem of yearning, of tenderness, of nostalgic charm, called "After the Winter":

> Some day, when trees have shed their leaves
>   And against the morning's white
> The shivering birds beneath the eaves
>   Have sheltered for the night,
> We'll turn our faces southward, love,
>   Toward the summer isle
> Where bamboos spire to shafted grove
>   And wide-mouthed orchids smile.
>
> And we will seek the quiet hill
>   Where towers the cotton tree,
> And leaps the laughing crystal rill,
>   And works the droning bee.
> And we will build a cottage there
>   Beside an open glade,
> With black-ribbed blue-bells blowing near,
>   And ferns that never fade.

It is intriguing that this poem was written by the same hand that wrote "If We Must Die." "After the Winter," moreover, appeared only one page away from the fire and brimstone of "If We Must Die" when it was first introduced to the public. To see these two poems—the one verso ("After the Winter"), the other recto ("If We Must Die"), facing each other across the page—is to get a tangible illustration of McKay's astonishing artistic range and diverse passions.[88] Yet these poems are not as unrelated as they may at first appear. The palpable yearning of "After the Winter," the warm, daydreaming, utopian embrace of that poem, cannot be explained without recognizing the lack, the absence, that it registers and draws our attention to. Like all utopian dreams it, perforce, indicts the status quo.[89] "After the Winter," like his Jamaican pastoral lyrics, reveals the extent to which existing conditions fell short of McKay's desire. The "winter" in the poem conjures up and signifies more than the literal; it is a metaphor for the bad times, of naked trees and shivering birds, the time before spring. Like his hero Shelley, another revolutionary poet, he yearns for the spring—for the radical transformation of society. "Drive my dead thoughts over the universe, / Like withered leaves to quicken a new birth!" sang Shelley. "If Winter comes can Spring be far behind?"[90]

But "If We Must Die" eclipsed and overwhelmed all the other poems—a not insubstantial body of work—from 1919. It is not surprising that this remarkable poem and what it stood for set alarm bells ringing among the American ruling class.

Being Black and Red

Combined with a high level of working-class combativeness in the United States and abroad, the African American militancy that McKay's poem symbolized and the Black popular response to it became objects of governmental investigation. The United States Congress ordered the attorney general, A. Mitchell Palmer, to investigate and report on radical and seditious activities in the United States. The New York State Assembly also commissioned its own elaborate investigation into radicalism; the report submitted ran to thousands of pages and several volumes. The year 1919 was the year of the Red Scare.[91]

The authorities nationally and at the New York state level attempted to gauge the radical "propaganda" of the Negro press with an eye to determining the extent to which these publications violated the law. Palmer discovered that "The Negro is 'seeing red.'" He talked patronizingly of the insolence, defiance, and insubordination of these publications, and reported ominously of "utterances" in the Black press "which in some cases have reached the limit of open defiance and a counsel of retaliation." There can, he said, "no longer be any question of a well-concerted movement among a certain class of Negro leaders of thought and action to constitute themselves a determined and persistent source of radical opposition to the Government, and to the established rule of law and order."[92] Palmer was alarmed by the fact that the number of "restrained and conservative" Black publications was "relatively negligible." Moreover, even some of these had "indulged in most intemperate utterance."[93]

The report concluded that there was widespread support in the Black press for the Industrial Workers of the World, the organization feared and hated the most by American industrialists. Even more alarming was the finding of widespread support for the Bolshevik Revolution. The *Messenger* magazine, like McKay and others, had expressed the hope that the Revolution would spread internationally, including to the United States. The report drew special attention to McKay's advocacy of Bolshevism. "Every Negro," McKay proclaimed in a letter to *The Negro World*,

> who lays claim to leadership should make a study of Bolshevism and explain its meaning to the colored masses. It is the greatest and most scientific idea afloat in the world today that can be easily put into practice by the proletariat to better its material and spiritual life. Bolshevism (as Mr. Domingo ably points out in the current *Messenger*)[94] has made Russia safe for the Jew. It has liberated the Slav peasant from priest and bureaucrat who can no longer egg him on to murder Jews to bolster up their rotten institutions. It might make these United States safe for the Negro. . . . Will their leaders educate them now to make good use of their advantages eventually?[95]

The Russian Revolution was indeed McKay's "golden hope."[96] Thus, by September 1919, in the words of the attorney general of the United States, McKay was advocating "Bolshevism as a means of freedom for the negro."[97] As Palmer made clear, McKay was by no means alone in proselytizing Black liberation through Bolshevism. Along with the *Messenger* and the *Crusader*, the *Challenge*—another Harlem publication, edited by William Bridges—also expressed strong support for the Bolsheviks.[98]

According to Palmer, Black people were being "insolently" counseled by the Black press to fight back. It was disturbing that "If We Must Die"— competently summarized as the famous poem "about the negro with his back against the wall and fighting to the death"—was "much-quoted," was "widely used in the negro press," and had "a constant place in many of the Negro publications."[99] The "Old Crowd Negroes"—as the *Messenger* dubbed its more conservative African American adversaries—were under unrelenting attack by the New Negroes for their alleged cowardice and misleadership. The report registered with alarm the Black radicals' denunciation of the "conservative element represented by Booker T. Washington and his successors."[100]

In short, things had changed. There was a new mood abroad in Afro-America. Palmer noted the existence of this phenomenon in alarmist terms. "If this report," he concludes, "serves to give a substantial appreciation of the dangerous spirit of defiance and vengeance at work among the Negro leaders, and, to an ever-increasing extent, among their followers, it shall have accomplished its purpose."[101]

The traditional establishment that Palmer protected and represented was not the only group alarmed by the new spirit of Black defiance and resistance. Even the white liberal and historic "friends of the Negro" were shocked and disturbed by the new African American militancy. McKay was angered and disappointed by those who deplored the fighting spirit of African Americans. The *Nation* magazine, for instance, editorialized on Black Washington's plucky response to the mobs, declaring that one of the "alarming features of this riot was the shooting-back of the Negroes." It was regrettable, the *Nation* thought, that the "doctrine of meeting force with force" was "making headway" among African Americans, partly due to the "mistaken teachings" of some of their leaders. The month before, it had condemned Du Bois by name for his *Crisis* editorial "Returning Soldiers" (quoted above), which urged African Americans, including Black veterans, to fight for their rights. "Dangerous and mistaken," declared the *Nation*.[102] Outraged, McKay drew upon the epistolary device that he had so often watched U. Theo deploy in his youth—the letter to the editor. "I am deeply interested," he inquired of the *Nation*, "in knowing what reasonable course it would advocate for the American Negro to adopt in helping to destroy the national pastime of lynching." Having dismissed Du Bois's "manly and courageous" editorial as "dangerous and mistaken" and the supposedly "mistaken teachings" of others advocating resistance, what better way does the *Nation* suggest? Using a metaphor repeatedly use by Malcom X two generations later, McKay continued:

> I have lived in the South, in the West, and in the East, not without remarking that Negroes are surrounded everywhere by mad dogs in human form. When a mad dog breaks loose, we call a policeman, and if one is not in sight, we kill the dog if we can. To me a lynching-mob bears a great resemblance to a pack of mad mongrels; but I may be wrong. Being black, I may see the hideous thing only through the eyes of prejudice, and not so clearly as you do from your pedestal of pure pity.
>
> But what would you advise Negroes to do when the Federal or State Government withholds from them its protection, as it invariably does? Should they stand by with folded arms and see a member of their race tortured and burned? Should a Negro let himself be taken and tormented without show of

resistance? Should Negroes remain supinely inactive while the womanhood of their race is outraged (and, incidentally, that of their tormentors cheapened)? In short, should not a Negro defend himself when attacked by the chivalrous Caucasian?[103]

"'Thou shalt not kill' remains the only sound precept for races, nations, and individuals," the editor (Oswald Garrison Villard) inserted parenthetically at the bottom of McKay's letter. "It is the meek alone who shall inherit the earth." He then grudgingly added: "The Negro, of course, has a right to defend his home." But what about his person, his life, and that of the Black community?

Like the Palmer report, the Report of New York State Assembly's Joint Legislative Committee Investigating Seditious Activities, five months later, found essentially the same manifestation of discontent among the Black population. But unlike Palmer, who saw nothing more than an unwarranted insolence on the part of African Americans, the New York report conceded that the expression of discontent among Black people was not groundless. "We believe," it concluded, "that much of this propaganda falls on fertile soil, by reason of lynchings, Jim Crow legislation and the abridgment of the rights of franchise to negroes in many states." But the report did not end there; it articulated the familiar, empty, and cruel liberal objection to the type of agitation that Black people were engaged in:

Instead of seeking to remedy these conditions in lawful manner, as we firmly believe they should be remedied, they are made the basis for the appeal to class consciousness. This propaganda seeks to make the negro believe that the only way in which his lot can be bettered is by the abolition of our form of government and the substitution therefor of a system of government similar to that of Soviet Russia and by the institution of the co-operative Socialist Commonwealth.[104]

What "lawful" remedy did Hayes Turner and Mary Turner have? After her brutal murder, the names of Mary Turner's torturers and murderers were handed over by Walter White and the NAACP to Governor Dorsey of Georgia. Nothing happened. No one was ever arrested, indicted, let alone convicted of the slaughter of Mary Turner and her husband, even though the governor had the names of the killers.

McKay's public embrace of the ideology of Bolshevism was far from unique. Even less so was his stance on Black self-defense as eloquently advocated in "If We Must Die." As he himself acknowledged, in writing the poem he was more a "medium" expressing the "mass sentiment" of African Americans than anything else.[105] The radical Black journals—most notably, Cyril Briggs's the *Crusader*, and the *Messenger* under the audacious editorship of A. Philip Randolph and Chandler Owen—had adopted an identical position to McKay's on Bolshevism. In a very real sense, Domingo, Briggs, Randolph, and Owen were McKay's comrades; they were all Black socialists, and they were all self-professed New Negroes. Indeed, the *Messenger*, in its "Riot Number" of September 1919, had declared in its editorial—aptly titled "If We Must Die"—that the "creed" of the New Negro "is admirably summed up in the poem of Claude McKay."[106] Both journals had published McKay's writings; indeed, as noted earlier, two of McKay's poems of 1919—excluding the republication of "If We Must Die"—were carried in the *Messenger*. From his self-imposed exile in London, McKay wrote a note of congratulation and support to Randolph and Owen in 1920: "I am all admiration of the unique style and high standard of your magazine. Every Negro who appreciates clean journalism should be proud of it."[107] On returning to the United States in the spring of 1921, McKay quickly joined forces with Cyril Briggs's African Blood Brotherhood. *The Crusader*, the organ of the Brotherhood, carried significant portions of his writings in 1921.[108]

What distinguished McKay from his Black radical contemporaries on the question of Bolshevism was the intellectual rigor with which he discussed the subject and the many occasions on which he returned to it in his writings. McKay also had the added ability and distinction to give his ideas on Bolshevism poetic expression. Addressing the "race question" and its relation to socialism was to preoccupy McKay for the rest of his life. The remedies he proffered changed somewhat over time, but the question remained essentially the same: the relationship between race and class, or the relevance of socialism to Black liberation. Uppermost in McKay's mind was not so much the project of socialism per se—though that was undoubtedly of deep and genuine interest to him—but the question of how best to secure the liberation of Black people, or at least to effect the amelioration of their lamentable condition, especially in the United States. Like his compatriot Wilfred Domingo, he was interested in finding out if Bolshevism could stop lynching. That the Bolsheviks had clamped down on anti-Semitism and had effectively brought pogroms against Jews in the territories they controlled to an end was the key bit of evidence that led many Black intellectuals to support the Bolshevik Revolution. The Bolsheviks' contiguous policy of supporting the rights of oppressed nations to self-determination was also important to winning Black support—to Cyril

Briggs this was the crucial element of Bolshevik policy that commanded his support for the Revolution as a whole—but the exemplary policy of the Bolsheviks toward stamping out anti-Semitism and other forms of racism was what caught the eye of oppressed Afro-America. The direct and burning question "Did Bolshevism Stop Race Riots in Russia?" was the title of Domingo's article in the *Messenger*. Having carefully weighed the evidence, Domingo came to the conclusion that it did.

> Will Bolshevism accomplish the full freedom of Africa, colonies in which Negroes are in the majority, and promote human tolerance and happiness in the United States by the eradication of the causes of such disgraceful occurrences as the Washington and Chicago race riots? The answer is deducible from the analogy of Soviet Russia, a country in which dozens of racial and lingual types have settled their many differences and found a common meeting ground, a country from which the lynch rope is banished and in which racial tolerance and peace now exist.[109]

McKay agreed with Domingo, and indeed invoked the article in his letter to the *Negro World* in support of Bolshevism. Within less than two years, McKay would once again be crossing swords with another African American editor over the significance of the Bolshevik Revolution. In his letter to the editor of the *Crisis*, W. E. B. Du Bois, McKay made an impassioned defense of the Revolution:

> I am surprised and sorry that in your editorial . . . you should leap out of your sphere to sneer at the Russian Revolution, the greatest event in the history of humanity; much greater than the French Revolution, which is held up as a wonderful achievement to Negro children and students in white and black schools. For American Negroes the indisputable and outstanding fact of the Russian revolution is that a mere handful of Jews, much less in ratio to the number of Negroes in the American population, have attained, through the Revolution, all the political and social rights that were denied to them under the regime of the Czar.[110]

Socialism was, in McKay's estimation, the most effective and promising vehicle to achieve the goal of Black liberation. "The greatest and most scientific idea afloat in the world today," is how he described Bolshevism. It is therefore significant, but not at all surprising, that the first essay McKay wrote in his post-Jamaican sojourn was entitled "Socialism and the Negro."

For McKay, the so-called race riots, as he intimated in his letter to the *Negro World*, brought into full relief—in the most spectacularly tragic manner—the urgent need to address the root cause of the oppression of Black people in America and to seek solutions to their gratuitous and excessive suffering.

Within a few months of the publication of "If We Must Die," McKay was off to Europe, thanks to a gift of money from an admirer of his work. Evidently, when he left the United States in 1919, he did so not only as a Black radical but also as a Black radical with decidedly revolutionary socialist sympathies and passions. There is no evidence that McKay was, in 1919, a member of either the Socialist Party or the newly formed Workers' Party, the American affiliate to the Third (Communist) International with its headquarters in Moscow. But by the time he sailed for Europe in the autumn of 1919, McKay was a member of the Industrial Workers of the World, the Wobblies. He was therefore more than a "fellow traveler" of the Bolshevik Revolution. The Fabian socialism that had accompanied him on his journey from Port Antonio to Charleston, Manhattan (Kansas), Brooklyn, and Harlem was now, like an old, worn-out coat, rendered obsolete, left behind, and abandoned. McKay had moved on, both figuratively and literally.

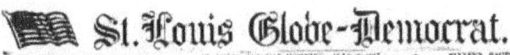

St. Louis Globe-Democrat.

EXTRA FINAL

100 NEGROES SHOT, BURNED, CLUBBED TO DEATH IN E. ST. LOUIS RACE WAR

Riot at Its Height Near Broadway and Fourth as Sketched by Artist Russell

WOMEN FAINT WHEN NEGROES ARE SHOT AS THEY FLEE FIRE

Captive Being Dragged to Lynching Post Is Beaten Down by Rain of Bricks — White Women Tear Clothes from Escaping Negresses

MAN-HUNTING MOBS BURN 60 HOMES AND SLAY FLEEING BLACKS BY BULLET AND ROPE

Women and Children Join in Blood Orgy as Flames Spread to Business Sections—Rioting Renewed in 'Reynolds Row' at 1 A. M., and 13 Homes Are Destroyed--Martial Law Virtually in Force.

17 Newspaper report on racist attacks in East St. Louis. July 3, 1917.

Source: Public domain

18 Mob dragging black man from street car, East St. Louis, July 1917

Source: Public domain.

19 Hubert Harrison (1882–1928), ca. 1919.

Source: Schomburg Center for Research in Black Culture, Photographs and Print Division, New York Public Library Digital Collections.

20 McKay in New York, ca. 1919.

Source: Schomburg Center for Research in Black Culture, Photographs and Print Division, New York Public Library Digital Collections.

21 Headline of the black-owned and run, *Chicago Defender* after racist mob violence broke out in the city.

Source: Public domain.

22 William Brown, the victim of mob violence in Omaha, Nebraska.

Source: Nebraska State Historical Society.)

23 William Brown, 1919

Source: Public domain; but see https://www.betweenthecovers.com/pages
/books/411374/c-b-mowrey/press-photograph-of-lynching-victim-will-brown
-the-lynchee-in-omaha-race-riot-1919?soldItem=true.

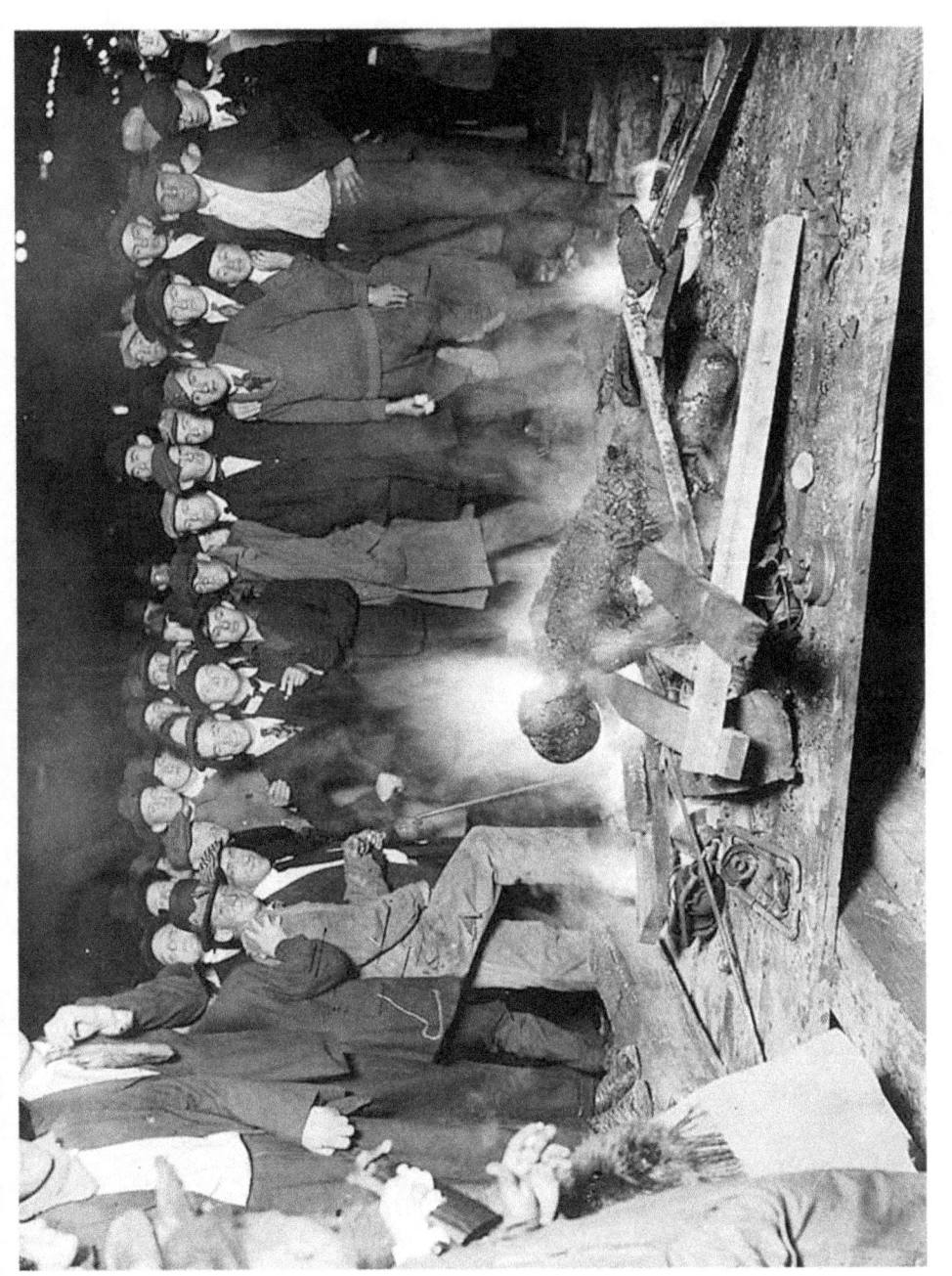

24 The burning of William Brown

Source: Nebraska State Historical Society.

25 The New Negro, as depicted by the *Messenger* magazine, 1919.

Source: Public domain.

26 Sylvia Pankhurst, 1919.

Source: Getty Images.

Workers' Dreadnought

FOR INTERNATIONAL SOCIALISM.

Vol. VI.—No. 45.   SATURDAY, JANUARY 31st, 1920.   PRICE TWOPENCE.

SOCIALISM AND THE NEGRO.

Chiefly through the efforts of Dr. Dubois, author of "The Souls of Black Folk," there came into being in the United States, some ten years ago, the National Association for the Advancement of Coloured People. In the main, the organisation strove to combat the wide and insidious influence of Booker Washington who, making light of the social and political status of his race, had put into practice, for its material benefit, the principle of work advocated by the latter-day Carlyle. A group of wealthy and socially and politically influential bourgeois of the North, helped to launch the movement and became its directing spirit.

In it were men and women representative of the old conservative and Quaker aristocracy of New England and Pennsylvania, and the liberal capitalists. It comprised intellectual and commercial Jews, and its finest spirit was Oswald Garrison Villard, editor of the American Nation and grandson of the great Abolitionist, who, vilified and denounced by the hide-bound capitalist press, stands out as the solitary and only consistent representative of the American bourgeoisie, counselling peace and moderation between aggressive Capitalism and its government, and Militant Labour and Socialism, and all the forces of passion struggling in America to-day. This group, palpably ignorant of the fact that the Negro question is primarily an economic problem, evidently thought it might be solved by admitting Negroes who have won to wealth and intellectual and other attainments into white society on equal terms, and by protesting and pleading to the political and aristocratic South to remove the notorious laws limiting the political and social status of coloured folk. So far as I am able to judge, it has done good work on the technically legal and educational side. It developed race-consciousness in the Negro and made him restive: but on the political side it has flirted with different parties and its work is quite ineffective.

Further, it has taken a firm stand against segregation, which is a moot and delicate question. While all Negroes are agreed that the social barriers must be removed, there is much difference in regard to educational and some institutions like hospitals and churches. The growing numbers of cultured Negro men and women find it extremely difficult to obtain employment that is in keeping with their education under the capitalist system of government. For one instance, had a scholar like Dr. Dubois been white he would certainly have secured a chair at Harvard, Yale or Columbia University, for which he is eminently fitted. Many Negroes have obtained a sound education at great sacrifice, only to be forced, upon completion of their studies, into menial or uncongenial toil. In the black belt of New York City, where there is an estimated population of 100,000 Negroes, the Police Force, hospital, library, and elementary schools—patronised chiefly by coloured people—are entirely manned by white staffs. It would be impossible for such conditions to exist under a soviet system of Government.

Just about the beginning of the late War the Socialists and I.W.W., realising that the Negro population offered a fertile field for propaganda, began working in earnest

among them. With the aid of the Messenger Magazine, edited by two ardent, young Negro university men, and The Liberator, they have done real constructive work that is now bearing fine fruit. The rank-and-file Negroes of America have been very responsive to the new truths. Some of them have been lured away by the siren call of the American Federation of Labour to color its ranks. For years this reactionary association held out against Negro membership, but recently the capitalist class, alarmed over the growth of revolutionary thought among the blacks, used its creature, Gompers, to put through a resolution admitting Negroes to membership at the last conference. It has, however, had no effect on the lily-white and inconsequential trade unions of the South.

A splendid result of the revolutionary propaganda work among the blacks was the Conference of the National Brotherhood of Workers of America (entirely Negro) which was held at Washington, D.C., in September of last year. Its platform is as revolutionary in principle as that of the I.W.W. Over 100 delegates were in attendance and the majority came from the South. As always, the coloured workers are ready and willing to meet the white workers half-way in order that they might unite in the fight against capitalism; but, owing to the seeds of hatred that have been sown for long years by the master class among both sections, the whites are still reluctant to take the step that would win the South over to Socialism. The black workers hold the key to the situation, but while they and the whites remain divided the reaction any South need not fear. The great task is to get both groups together. Coloured men from the North cannot be sent into the South for propaganda purposes, for they will be lynched. White men from the North will be beaten and, if they don't leave, they will also be lynched. A like fate awaits coloured women. But the South is boastful of its spirit of chivalry. It

believes that it is the divinely-appointed guardian of sacred white womanhood, and it professes to disfranchise, outrage and lynch Negro men and women solely for the protection of white women.

It seems then that the only solution to the problem is to get lowly and refined white women volunteers to carry the message of Socialism to both white and black workers. There are many of them in the movement who should be eager to go. During the period of Reconstruction a goodly number went from New England to educate the Negro; and, although they were socially ostracised by the Southerners, they stood to their guns. To-day they are needed more than ever. The call is louder and the cause is greater. Among the blacks they will be safe, respected and honoured. Will they rise to their duty?

Strangely, it is the professional class of Negroes that is chiefly opposed to Socialism, although it is the class that suffers and complains most bitterly. Dr. Dubois has flirted with the Socialist idea from a narrow, opportunist-racial standpoint; but he is in spirit opposed to it. If our Negro professionals are not blindly ignorant they should realise that there will never be any hope—no sound material place in the economic life of the world—for them until the Negro masses are industrially independent. Many coloured doctors, lawyers, journalists, teachers and preachers liberally starve and are driven to the wall because the black working class does not earn enough to give them adequate support. Naturally, the white workers will hardly turn from their kind to coloured aspirants to the professions, even though the latter should possess exceptional ability. And even when they are capable they are often up against the prejudice of their own people who have been subtly taught by the white ruling class to despise the talented of their race and sneer at their accomplishments.

During the War, Marcus Garvey, a West Indian Negro, went to New York and

THE ENTENTE AND RUSSIA

28 Douglas "Dave" Springhall, 1928.

Source: The National Archives, UK; public domain.

29 C. K. Ogden (c. 1930), as drawn by his friend and collaborator, James Wood.

Source: Public domain.

30 McKay in London as he appears in *Spring in New Hampshire*, 1920.

Source: Public domain

Part III

England, Their England: McKay's
British Sojourn, 1919–1921

7

English Innings and Left-Wing Communism

McKay's Bolshevization in Britain

In the East the clouds glow crimson with the new dawn that
   is breaking,
And its golden glow fills the western skies.
O my brothers and my sisters, wake! arise!
. . . . Lift your heavy-lidded eyes, Ethiopia! awake!
. . . . Wake from sleeping; to the East turn, turn your eyes!

—Claude McKay, 1920

McKay wanted to get away from the horror of 1919 and from his fame as
much as his notoriety. He had his chance through the aid of admirers
and booked a passage to Europe in the autumn of 1919. His American
friends provided him with contacts in London and a clutch of letters of
introduction to influential people. Frank Harris, editor of *Pearson's Magazine* and an ardent supporter of McKay's, wrote letters to George Bernard
Shaw and Grant Richards, the publisher. Harris asked Richards to introduce McKay to Siegfried Sassoon. "See that he gets a good welcome will
you," Harris wrote, in a tone at once beseeching and commanding.[1] Max
Eastman and his sister Crystal Eastman, editors of the *Liberator*, knew and
admired Sylvia Pankhurst and were apparently less formal in smoothing
the way for McKay, but no doubt encouraged him to drop in on Pankhurst.[2]
Crystal Eastman's English-born husband, Walter Fuller, was more formal.
The associate editor of the Progressive Era journal the *World Tomorrow*,

Fuller was also a close friend of Charles Ogden, editor of the *Cambridge Magazine*. "I am asking my friend, Mr. Claude McKay, the bearer of this letter, to call on you during his visit to London because I feel sure that you will be glad to know one another." Fuller also wrote to the publishers Allen and Unwin on McKay's behalf.[3] Through Harris's letter of introduction, McKay met Shaw soon after his arrival. Shaw, in turn, wrote a letter of reference to enable McKay to obtain a reading room ticket at the British Museum. As McKay explained, such a ticket "may seem easy enough for an ordinary person to acquire, but try, as a stranger in London, to find the responsible householder to sponsor you according to the regulations!"[4]

His good friends in America had placed McKay in good hands across the Atlantic. But what did the English make of McKay, and he of them? What impact did his "English inning," as he called the sojourn, have upon his political evolution? He had traveled to Britain with the primary intention of having a volume of his poetry published there. He could not have imagined, let alone anticipated, the profound effect that his British visit would have on his politics and general outlook on life.

England, Their England

McKay would soon learn the limits of what his new contacts in London, eminent though they were, could do for him. He did manage to find hotel accommodation on arrival in London, but, like so many nonwhites before and after him, McKay encountered serious difficulties when he tried to secure long-term lodgings. In an unpublished sketch of his time in London, McKay poignantly and vividly recalled five racist incidents he experienced in London, starting with the problem of getting a place to stay.[5]

After leaving his hotel, he found "the greatest difficulty" in obtaining lodgings in the area around the British Museum. There were many rooms to let, but when McKay presented himself, he was "invariably" told that they had been taken. Suspicious, he asked white friends to inquire for him, to test the validity of the claim. The result of the experiment was predictable, though no less disheartening: "*They* found rooms easily, but when they took me along as the lodger we were told at last that black guests were not accommodated." When he did find lodgings, it was not with the British, but with an Italian, a French couple, and finally a German family—all of which came about through the new friendships he developed at a radical club in East London, the International Socialist Club (ISC) and not through public advertisements. "And the Frenchwoman said that her English neighbours had taunted her about having a black person in her house."[6]

McKay relates the second incident in one sentence: "On Charing Cross Road [in central London] white friends invited me into a public house to drink and I was refused service."[7] McKay had always enjoyed exploring and strolling around big cities. In New York, his favorite, he often walked under the elevated train lines, expressing his liking for hearing the trains "clashing and clanging overhead."[8] In all big cities, he especially enjoyed strolling late at night in the central business district "under the great buildings when they are empty of life and traffic is stilled and the atmosphere[,] so different from the daytime[,] is almost eerie." It was a habit that probably developed out of his time as a Kingston cop, a "dog driver's friend," on night patrol. It was during one of his London strolls, on New Year's Eve 1919, that the third incident occurred. He was walking with a former militant suffragette in the City of London, the square-mile nucleus of the metropolis, which was then the financial and insurance center of the world. From the precision with which McKay relates it some fourteen years later, it is clear that the incident scarred him: "On Great William Street a ragged woman came out of the shadows and approached us, evidently to beg. But when she discerned to what group of humanity I belonged she stopped suddenly and cried at my companion: 'You dirty slut! On New Year's Eve too!' "[9]

McKay also related the fourth incident in *A Long Way from Home*, in a slightly more elaborate form.[10] Soon after his arrival in London, he learned of a colored men's club run by the YMCA that catered to the needs of non-white men who had served in the war. Located at the corner of Drury Lane and York Street, its membership comprised continental Africans, Afro-Caribbeans, African Americans, and a few Indians. McKay frequented the club and made friends with its somewhat besieged members.[11] Among the men were some boxers, one of whom came from the Caribbean. He gave McKay a ticket to a boxing match that he had in Holborn. The fight was with a white Englishman, and McKay's friend won. Some of the men from the club had gone to support their comrade. After the match, McKay and the rest grouped around their friend with congratulations. They proposed going to a Black restaurant off Shaftesbury Avenue for a celebration. At that moment, a white man pushed his way through the crowd to offer congratulations to the boxer: "Shake, Darkey, you did a clean job; it was a fine fight." The boxer shook hands and thanked his admirer. A "modest type of fellow," the boxer then turned to a little woman almost hidden in the group—a shy, typically nondescript and dowdy Englishwoman, with her hat set inelegantly back on her head—and introduced her to his white admirer: "That is my wife." The woman held out her hand, but the white man, ignoring it, exclaimed: "You damned nigger!" The boxer hauled back and hit him in the mouth and he dropped to the pavement.

They hurried off to the restaurant. "We sat around, the poor woman among us, endeavoring to woo the spirit of celebration. But we were all wet. The boxer said: 'I guess they don't want no colored in this damned white man's country.'" He moaned: "'I hate dis damn country. . . . Yet I doan' want to go back to de damn West Indies. Ah doan' know wha' fe do.'"[12] The boxer "dropped his head down on the table and sobbed like a child. And I thought that that," McKay added, speaking of his friend, "was *his* knockout."[13]

Finally, once when he was walking to the ISC in the East End of London with a female comrade, a white youth approached them and suddenly pulled his necktie. McKay hit him in the face and "immediately an angry crowd had gathered." Some of the local women raised their voices in McKay's defense. A policeman on the beat had witnessed everything. Luckily, "he strode up and ordered the white youth off."[14]

But there were other incidents that McKay never shared publicly. In April 1920, he wrote Ogden about how his color made him so conspicuous to racists. He would not mind if the encounters were "only amusing & tiresome, but at times they were positively dangerous." Were it not for some white friends, McKay told Ogden, "I should have been badly mauled in Limehouse a fortnight ago." And only

last Monday I was the chief actor in a near tragedy at the Old St. tube [underground] station. I was walking home from the [International] Socialist Club with a young Serbian & just as we said goodbye a drunken [white] South African soldier (discharged) came up to me and asked whether I came from Basutoland or some other place. I answered no & tried to pass but he held me up, got hold of my tie, & was rather threatening. Of course I know what the average S[outh] A[frican] white thinks of the blacks & what was evidently working in his sodden brain so I thought quickly & sent him sprawling to the street. Instantly a little mob gathered round me, but some friends of mine from the club came along & two policemen who perceived what was happening & drove them off. Had there been no help they wouldn't have reached me though as I would have dived into the tube immediately after hitting out. One must always be on one's guard.[15]

McKay at the time had lodgings with a German family at Provence Street in Islington. Despite its alluring name, Provence Street was a "hideous little gutter street near the Angel."[16] In February 1920, he claimed that he did not mind living there; a few months later, he became cautious of the area, making sure that he got home before it was too late at night.[17] He wanted to move farther to the west of London, where it was "a little safer" and "the grown-ups are more sensible & the children are not so disgustingly provocative & bad-mannered."[18]

One gets the distinct impression, especially from his correspondence with Ogden, that McKay's time in London was that of a man bewildered and besieged. In many ways, he could not have chosen a worse time to be in the imperial capital. Unemployment, especially among the demobilized servicemen, was rife. A few months before McKay arrived, there were racist attacks by mobs in Britain similar to those he had escaped in the United States. Liverpool, London, Cardiff, and Glasgow were the primary sites of outbreak. Black men were stabbed to death, and many more were badly beaten, burnt out of their homes, and chased by mobs. In 1920, another full-scale mob attack occurred in Hull and a smaller one in Limehouse, a part of the East End that McKay frequented.[19]

McKay's Radical Milieu and Network

Sylvia Pankhurst, the Workers' Socialist Federation, and the *Workers' Dreadnought*

Despite the many letters of introduction to representatives of London's literary world, the first person that McKay contacted in London was Sylvia Pankhurst. The contact must have been successful because he began work on her newspaper, the *Workers' Dreadnought*, within weeks of his arrival, thus becoming "Britain's first black journalist."[20] McKay's New York friends, Crystal Eastman and Max Eastman, almost certainly facilitated the contact. And Pankhurst was familiar with McKay's work, having devoted a generous spread to his poems in the *Workers' Dreadnought* in September 1919. Under the title "A Negro Poet," the *Dreadnought* acknowledged the *Liberator* as the source of the poems, explaining to its readers that they were by "Claude McKay, a negro of Jamaica, who, when he wrote them, was a waiter in an American dining car." The *Dreadnought* devoted a third of a page to five sonnets, "The Barrier," "After the Winter," "The Little Peoples," "A Roman Holiday," and ending with "If We Must Die."[21] Pankhurst therefore knew of McKay's background and radical politics by the time they actually met.

McKay's published recollection of his first meeting with Pankhurst is unreliable. Writing almost twenty years after the event, he reported that he met her after a letter he had written to the *Daily Herald* in April 1920 had been rejected. In fact, Pankhurst had employed him before she left for a tour of Italy and Germany in the fall of 1919, as he confided to Ogden. The *Dreadnought* published his revolutionary poem "Samson" as early as the January 10, 1920, issue, more than three months before the date when he claimed to have made contact with Pankhurst and her paper. His article "Socialism and the Negro" adorned the front page of the *Dreadnought* the same month.[22] Thus, when he wrote of his job on the *Dreadnought* as an "opportunity to practice a little practical journalism [which] was not to be missed,"[23] he obfuscated the fact that not only was he a member of the Central Branch of Pankhurst's Workers' Socialist Federation (WSF), but he had quickly become one of the organization's leading comrades.[24] In the summer of 1920, he probably attended the historic Communist Unity Convention in London, which laid the foundations for the formation of the Communist Party of Great Britain.

McKay's job at the *Dreadnought* formally entailed covering the volatile labor situation on the London docks, which had been the scene of racist mob attacks in the summer of 1919, getting news from non-European as well as white seamen and writing from a point of view that would be fresh and different. He was also assigned the task of reading the foreign newspapers from the United States, India, Australia, Africa, and other parts of the British Empire, with an eye to items that might interest *Dreadnought* readers. In this task, he worked closely with a "Comrade Vie," who read the foreign-language newspapers, mainly French and German. The mysterious Comrade Vie, who events later proved to have been a young Comintern agent, would compare his articles with McKay's, criticizing the latter's point of view while McKay corrected Vie's English.[25] In reality, McKay did much more than that at the *Dreadnought* office. He effectively became the paper's labor-relations correspondent, covering events from the annual conference of the Trades Union Congress to a strike at an East End sawmill. He wrote on the plight and struggles of the unemployed, racism among the British working class, the color bar in South Africa, socialism and the Negro, the Irish struggle, and the international money crisis. He wrote book reviews on topics ranging from the shop-stewards movement to Gorki on Tolstoy, and he published a large number of poems, including some of his most revolutionary, in the *Dreadnought*. He used his own name as well as a large number of pen names; many of his articles, especially the ones on international affairs, though attributable, went unsigned.[26] All told, McKay published at least nine articles and fourteen poems, including some of his most militant, in the *Dreadnought*.

Pankhurst entrusted him with great responsibility. As he later noted, apart from reporting, he corrected proofs, wrote and rewrote articles, and sold papers.[27] He privately complained in October 1920 of being overworked at the *Dreadnought* office. "I should have written before," he told Ogden,

> but I have been kept so frightfully busy by Sylvia Pankhurst since she came back [from Russia]. She has been experiencing all sorts of domestic and business difficulties, due to her own erratic nature, & all the routine work of getting out the paper falls upon me in consequence.[28]

As a good revolutionary, McKay also attended WSF meetings and other party functions. As he later told Max Eastman, he did "propaganda work among the colored soldiers." As early as February 1920, he was telling a London friend: "Although weak, I must also do my part to keep my poor people awake and discontented." But his political agitation was unconfined. He was, for example, responsible for selling his quota of *Dreadnoughts* and other "red literature" on the streets of London. He vividly recalled selling the paper along with Pankhurst's pamphlet *Rebel Ireland* and Herman Gorter's *Ireland: The Achilles Heel of England* at a big Sinn Fein rally in Trafalgar Square in the summer of 1920. He fondly recounted donning a green tie and being amused when he was welcomed with friendly banter as "Black Murphy" or "Black Irish" by the Sinn Feiners. He could hardly keep up with the "hearty handshakes and brief chats with Sinn Fein Communists and regular Sinn Feiners." He even recruited and cultivated disaffected members of the British Armed Forces to the revolutionary cause, to the great alarm of the authorities, military and civilian, whose intelligence branches kept him under close surveillance. Indeed, McKay's activities with radical sailors led directly to police raids on the *Dreadnought* office in the fall of 1920, ending with Pankhurst's arrest and subsequent imprisonment for sedition.[29]

McKay's involvement with the *Dreadnought* group was neither trivial nor innocuous. British intelligence exaggerated when they later alleged that McKay had entertained ambitions of taking over the leadership of the WSF from Pankhurst. There is no evidence to support that claim, but the accusation itself is an index of McKay's deep involvement with the British far left. Indeed, two of McKay's articles formed the primary evidence for the prosecution of Pankhurst in 1920. The motives behind his later understatement of his revolutionary activities in Britain is open to speculation.

The WSF had emerged organically out of Pankhurst's work among working-class women in London, developing out of a split within the mainstream suffragette movement. Pankhurst left the "suffragette legion" for the working-class movement "when she discovered that the leading ladies of the legion were not interested in the condition of working women," McKay noted.[30] It is therefore not surprising that the WSF was a predominantly women's organization based on working-class support, primarily in the East End of London.[31] Recognizing that working-class women were not only oppressed as women but exploited as workers, Pankhurst, as one historian noted, "came to see that women's liberation required more than the vote; it needed the overthrow of capitalist society." They fought an "unrelenting struggle, often coming into conflict with the forces of law and order."[32] As Harry Pollitt would later testify, the members of the WSF distinguished themselves in both toughness and commitment: "the most self-sacrificing and hard-working comrades it has been my fortune to come in contact with."[33] Contemporary newspaper reports of their tireless demonstrations and picket lines attest to the strength of their commitment.

The Bolshevik Revolution had its most enthusiastic British supporters in Sylvia Pankhurst and the WSF.[34] Indeed, the WSF was one of only two British left-wing organizations to wholeheartedly welcome the outbreak of revolution in Russia, and it was the first British group to affiliate with the Communist International (Comintern), or Third International, founded in Moscow in March 1919.[35] Less than three months after the founding of the Comintern, the WSF renamed itself the "Communist Party (British Section of the Third International)," a decision that was too fast even for Lenin, who preferred that all the British far-left forces first combine into one party before affiliation.

Thus, the WSF was one of Britain's most radical left-wing formations. "Left-wing communists," Lenin called them, as he chided Pankhurst and her followers for boycotting parliamentary elections and rejecting the notion of affiliation with the Labour Party. Such behavior was the symptom of an "infantile disorder," declared Lenin.[36] But it is perhaps for that very reason—its uncompromising political stance, its contempt for the dirty business of Realpolitik—that many respected, if not followed, Pankhurst and her group. As Raymond Challinor noted, "In the supreme test—that of its attitude to revolution—the Workers' Socialist Federation acquitted itself well." Resolutely anti-imperialist, of all the British groups on the left, the WSF came out by far the most strongly in support of the Irish Easter Uprisings.[37] And when the group changed its name in 1918 from the Workers' Suffrage Federation to the Workers' Socialist Federation, it explicitly called for self-determination not only for Ireland but also for India.[38]

Under Sylvia Pankhurst's moral leadership, the *Dreadnought* was far and away the most principled and explicitly antiracist organ on the left. From reading Guy Aldred's anarchist organ, *The Spur*, one would never know that the blood of Black men flowed in the streets of Liverpool, London, Cardiff, and Glasgow in 1919. *The Spur*, which was radical on everything, did not report, let alone condemn, the racist rampage on the part of white workers. In marked contrast, at the height of the madness in June 1919, Pankhurst did so in bold and clear tones. "I was returning home one evening down the East India Dock Road, and I found the place thronged," she recalled. "I asked, 'What is the matter?' and I was told, 'They are stabbing coloured men.' Some were killed that night, and for three nights the thing went on in Poplar. Out of work soldiers and other unemployed were stabbing coloured men."[39]

In "Stabbing Negroes in the London Dock Area," her editorial in the *Dreadnought*, Pankhurst "submitted," as she put it, "a few questions for the consideration of those who have been negro hunting."

> Do you think that the British should rule the world or do you want to live on peaceable terms with all peoples?
> Do you wish to exclude all blacks from England?
> If so, do you not think that blacks might justly ask that the British should at the same time keep out of the black peoples' countries?
> Do you not know that capitalists, and especially British capitalists, have seized, by force of arms, the countries inhabited by black people and are ruling those countries and the black inhabitants for their own profit? . . .
> Are you afraid that a white woman would prefer a blackman to you if you met her on equal terms with him?
> Do you not think you would be better employed in getting conditions made right for yourself and your fellow workers than in stabbing a blackman?[40]

This was in keeping with Pankhurst's lifelong stand against racism and ethnic chauvinism. She defied the wishes of her southern hosts and the racist press during her 1912 American tour and addressed students at the historically Black Fisk University, a blow against Jim Crow duly noted by the NAACP. She recorded her revulsion against the plight of Native and African Americans, especially prisoners. During the war, she expanded the complement of toys created in the East End factory she started for working women to include "Negro and Japanese" dolls, making her in all likelihood the first in Britain to have manufactured Black dolls. She worked closely with Jewish groups and individuals in the East End of London, wrote movingly about their plight and resilience, and denounced anti-Semitism in similarly outspoken terms. When German immigrants, including friends and coworkers, became victims of mob attacks in the East End for simply being German during the Great War, she came to their defense and spoke out.[41] Uncommonly decent and courageous, Pankhurst sought to challenge and to lead, not follow—to break the bigotry among some of her own constituents in the East End, rather than pander to it or remain silent, as so many others did. Small wonder, then, that with her, McKay found the most congenial political home in London.

Although he bluntly registered a notable political climb-down on her part—according to McKay, she refused an article of his critical of George Lansbury—McKay liked, respected, and admired Pankhurst. He did not get on with her closest friend and ally, Nora Smyth, with whom he worked at the *Dreadnought* offices in the Old Ford Road, but he remembered Pankhurst with kindness and admiration. He recalled her as "a plain little Queen-Victoria sized woman with plenty of long unruly bronze-like hair. There was no distinction about her clothes," he wrote, "and on the whole she was very undistinguished. But her eyes were fiery, even a little fanatic, with a glint of shrewdness."[42]

He noted, as have others before and since, that Pankhurst was "a good agitator and fighter, but she wasn't a leader. She had the magnetism to attract people to her organization, but she did not have the power to hold them. . . . It was a one-woman show."[43] He accused Pankhurst and her group of "rather hysterical militancy" and judged that the WSF was perhaps, in hindsight, "more piquant than important." But he conceded that Pankhurst had a personality "as picturesque and passionate as any radical in London." She had committed herself to working women, the poor and exploited women of the East End of London. In the labor movement, she was always "jabbing her hat pin into the hides of the smug and slack labor leaders." Her weekly, McKay thought, might have been called "the Dread Wasp." He observed that she had to deal with the "male-controlled radical groups," which were "quite hostile" to her and her group. Despite it all, to Pankhurst's eternal honor, wherever imperialism "got drunk and went wild among native peoples, the Pankhurst paper would be on the job." McKay gave her credit for having been one of the first leaders in Britain to "stand up for Soviet Russia." He praised her for founding the People's Russian Information Bureau, begun as early as 1918, which, he said, "remained for a long time the only source of authentic news from Russia." He was very protective of Pankhurst and came to her defense when he met up again with her former comrade turned nemesis, Arthur McManus, in Moscow in 1922. McManus, who knew and had worked with McKay in London, repeatedly described Pankhurst, in one of his "vodka-heated" rants, as "intellectually dishonest," to which McKay took exception. The basis of McKay's defense of Pankhurst opens up an important window on his views of the limitations of the British left and Pankhurst herself. Countering the charge of intellectual dishonesty, he told McManus that he thought "Sylvia Pankhurst was as honest as any imperial Briton could be." Furthermore, he "really preferred Pankhurst to persons like Lansbury, and perhaps even McManus himself." At this point:

> McManus shot up like a rabbit (he was a tiny man) and demanded in his remarkably beautiful Glasgow brogue if I meant to "insinuate" (that was the word he used) that he was an imperialist. I said that I had not said "imperialist," but "imperial," and that all Britons were imperial by birth and circumstances because of the nature of the political set-up of Britain. McManus asked if I did not believe that there were really radical Britons. I said that no man can be more radical than his system can stand.[44]

But there is more than enough evidence that one can be more radical than the system can stand—Marx, John Brown (the radical abolitionist), Lenin, Trotsky, Malcolm X. The real problem is the extent to which such radicalism can succeed in changing the system, not the presence of radicalism itself. And although Pankhurst may have been "imperial" by birth, she was anti-imperial and anti-imperialist by choice, in intent, purpose, conscious desire, inclination, and action; she was among those rare creatures who managed to break out of the ideological and political straitjacket of the structures into which she was born. She failed in transforming British society in the way she desired—and she should not be condemned for trying—but her radicalism extended well beyond what the "system" could stand, hence the aggressive persecution of her by the guardians of that system.

Pankhurst was, understandably, not happy with McKay's depiction of her. After reading *A Long Way from Home*, McKay's 1937 memoir, Pankhurst quickly wrote to McKay's publishers in New York telling them that she took "very strong exception to many statements" in the book. She particularly objected to McKay's rendering of a story concerning striking workers at a sawmill owned by George Lansbury and her reaction to his report for the *Dreadnought*. According to McKay, not long after he joined the *Dreadnought*, sawmill workers in London went on strike. Most of the sawmills were located in the East End, and one of the largest was owned by Lansbury. Many of the striking workers were friendly to the *Dreadnought*, and one of them volunteered to take McKay, assigned to cover the strike, around the mill. McKay discovered from the workers that Lansbury—a Labour Member of Parliament, and "symbolic of all that was simon-pure, pious and self-righteous in the British Labor movement"—was employing "scabs" (strikebreakers) in his mill. The strikers thought that it would "make an excellent story for the militant *Dreadnought*," as did McKay. Lansbury, McKay noted, as the boss of the *Daily Herald*, "stood at the center like an old bearded angel of picturesque honesty, with his right arm around the neck of the big trade-union leaders and Parliamentarians and his left waving to the Independent Labor partyites and all the radical Left. Like a little cat up against a big dog, the *Workers' Dreadnought* was always spitting at the *Daily Herald*." McKay thought the story would give the *Dreadnought* "some more spit to fire."[45] He had an additional incentive to try and take down Lansbury, because of his role in the racist campaign, largely waged in the pages of the *Herald*, over Black French troops in Germany after the war (discussed later).

Even Norah Smyth—Pankhurst's "upper-middle-class" personal aide and closest ally, with whom McKay never got on—when McKay showing her the story, "gasped" and said, "but this is a scoop." McKay noticed that her "gentle-lady poker face was lit as she read." But Pankhurst would have none of it. On reading the article, she summoned McKay to her office. "Your article is excellent but I'm sorry we cannot print it," she told him. "Why?" he inquired. "Because . . . we owe Lansbury twenty pounds. Besides, I have borrowed paper from the *Daily Herald* to print the *Dreadnought*. I can't print that." Disappointed, McKay surmised that Pankhurst's action may have stemmed from personal loyalty. She had very different politics to Lansbury's, but her friendship with him (and his family) went back to the early days of the suffragette movement, to which Lansbury gave whole-hearted support, never to be forgotten. Furthermore, McKay concluded, "one might concede that there are items which the capitalist press does not consider fit to print for capitalist reasons, and items which the radical press does not consider fit to print for radical reasons."[46]

This is the only item in McKay's book that Pankhurst specifically pointed to (going so far as to give pages and lines), declaring that it was "absolutely untrue" and that McKay had libeled her. She requested that Furman, the book's publishers, "immediately withdraw the book from circulation and delete those passages." Clearly feeling betrayed, she concluded her letter: "It is a pity that Claude McKay should have chosen to libel one who has treated him with consideration and kindness."[47] Though it is impossible to be absolutely certain about the accuracy of the story, it is unlikely, given the specificity of the details and his high regard for Pankhurst, that McKay would have fabricated or misremembered such an unflattering tale. He was probably guilty of indiscretion rather than mendacity. In any case, McKay stuck to his guns, and the book was never withdrawn from circulation nor the offending passages removed in subsequent printings.

McKay's work with and membership of the Pankhurst group provided him with important insights into various dimensions of the British scene. First, his association with the *Dreadnought* group placed him, as he put it, in the "nest of extreme radicalism in London."[48] He got to know intimately the politics and personalities of Britain's far-left groups, not just Pankhurst's. Second, he became acquainted with different sections of the trade union movement and especially the shop-stewards movement, which appealed to his syndicalist predilections. He also met and knew many of the key figures in the wider working-class movement. Third, McKay became deeply familiar with London proletarian life. Pankhurst and the WSF had their base in one of the most deprived working-class areas of the East End. He worked for much of his time in London at the production office of the *Dreadnought* at 400 Old Ford Road in Bow. For a time, he also lived in the neighborhood. His reporter's brief included coverage of struggles in the area, especially the docklands. He had friends in the area, and he was apparently rather fond of visiting Chinatown in Limehouse, about which he wrote with characteristic insight and compassion.[49] The International Socialist Club (ISC), at 23 East Road in Hoxton, of which he became a member and habitué soon after arriving in London, was also an East End locale.

Finally, because of his remit on the *Dreadnought*, McKay accelerated and deepened his knowledge of international affairs, especially as they pertained to the British Empire. Over the years, he augmented this store-house of knowledge, which served him well in analyzing the workings of imperialism and the international system. During his time with Pankhurst, he also became highly informed about the anticolonial struggle, especially in South Africa, India, and Ireland. It was, after all, part of his remit on the paper to know such things. But McKay not only wrote for the *Dreadnought*, he also read the *Dreadnought*, and Pankhurst's paper was a school in revolutionary socialism. Apart from her own remarkable contributions, others from Lenin, Trotsky, Kamenev, Rosa Luxemburg, Clara Zetkin, Alexandra Kollantai, and—especially during and after 1920, when Pankhurst started to explicitly express disquiet over Bolshevik domestic and foreign policy—left communists such as Anton Panakoek and Herman Gorter found a welcoming home in the *Dreadnought*.[50] Theoretical, strategic, and tactical questions were all discussed to the highest level of sophistication and openness, not only among the comrades at the ISC but also in the pages of the *Dreadnought*, and McKay was one of the beneficiaries of Pankhurst's Marxist cornucopia.

During his time with the *Dreadnought*, McKay acquired a greater appreciation of the dangers of revolutionary work, narrowly escaping arrest by the British Secret Service, MI-5. On October 18 and 19, 1920, the *Dreadnought* offices were raided by Scotland Yard.[51] McKay escaped arrest, but Pankhurst did not. She was charged and later convicted of sedition for four articles published in the issue of October 16: "Discontent on the Lower Deck," "How to Get a Labour Government," "The Datum Line," and "The Yellow Peril and the Dockers." In at least two of these, McKay had a direct hand.

"Discontent on the Lower Deck" emerged as an article from material furnished to McKay by Douglas (known mainly as "Dave") Springhall, a nineteen-year-old sailor in the Royal Navy. Springhall, who met McKay in early September 1920, had entered the navy at fifteen and had grown into a fine young man, physically and intellectually. He was an avid reader of the *Dreadnought* and other revolutionary propaganda, and he informed McKay that other men on his ship were also "eager for more stuff about the international workers' movement." Disillusioned by the horrors of the war, disgruntled over wages and conditions in the navy, and inspired by Bolshevik Russia, some sailors, among them Springhall, opted for revolution. Impressed with his ardor, McKay, on Springhall's visit to the Bow offices of the *Dreadnought*, provided him with many copies of the paper to share with his comrades. Before leaving, Springhall promised to send some navy news for the paper. He made good on his word and sent McKay various items, including an article, "a splendid piece of precious information," that was so incendiary that McKay waited for the material to be approved by

Pankhurst on her return from her trip to Russia. She was "enthusiastic" and personally edited what became "Discontent on the Lower Deck."[52]

Under the pseudonym "S.ooo (Gunner), H. M. S. Hunter," the article, covering the entire front page of the *Dreadnought*, adorned in the middle with a portrait of Marx (recently discovered in the Czar's archives), concluded:

> To the rank and file of the Navy I say: You are the Sons of the Working Class, therefore it is your duty to stand by that class and not the class and Government which is responsible for the starving of your ex-service brothers. Therefore, hail the formation of the Red Navy, which protects the interests of the working class, and repudiate the dirty financial interests which you are protecting now.[53]

The second article, "The Yellow Peril and the Dockers," was written by McKay himself under the pen name Leon Lopez. It addressed the racist objection of white seamen and dockers to the employment of Chinese seamen on British ships and in British ports. The authorities took especial exception to the final paragraph:

> The dockers, instead of being unduly concerned about the presence of their coloured fellow men, who like themselves, are victims of Capitalism and Civilisation, should turn their attention to the huge stores of wealth along the water front. The country's riches are not in the West End, in the palatial houses of the suburbs; they are stored in the East End, and the jobless should lead the attack on the bastilles, the bonded warehouses along the docks to solve the question of unemployment.[54]

McKay and Pankhurst were the only ones at the *Dreadnought* who knew the identity of the source for "Discontent on the Lower Deck." Interrogated by Scotland Yard, Pankhurst refused to name Springhall as the source for the article or to name McKay as the author of "The Yellow Peril and the Dockers." In her appeal hearing, she vigorously defended the latter article and the right of this "coloured man," the author, to speak out against racist propaganda and violence.[55] Her appeal rejected, she served five terrible months at Holloway until she was released a month early, in May 1921, on the grounds of ill health.

Thinking that he had outwitted the authorities, McKay was rather pleased with himself. When the detectives raided the Fleet Street offices of the *Dreadnought*, Pankhurst's private secretary tipped off McKay as he was leaving the top floor of the building. He quickly returned upstairs to his office and gathered the material that Springhall had sent him, tucking the papers into his socks. Pankhurst's office on the ground floor had been turned "upside down." "And what are you?" the detective asked him. "Nothing, Sir," McKay replied, with a "big black grin." The detective chuckled and let him pass. McKay left the building, entered another, went to the toilet, tore up the papers and flushed them away. Another detective was waiting for him at his lodgings in Bow Road when he got home: "He was very polite and I was more so. With alacrity I showed him all my papers, but he found nothing but lyrics."[56]

What McKay did not know is that the authorities knew far more about his activities than he could have imagined. They had intercepted his correspondence with Springhall and another radical sailor, George Crook, and they had even cracked the different pseudonyms used. McKay, to put it mildly, was not half as clever in such matters as he boasted. The detectives must have had another chuckle when they observed that the "letters of a suspicious nature" to Springhall "were sent by a man from Bow, London, who signed himself U. B. WARE in one letter and 'Claude McKay (my real name)' in another." They discovered this by the beginning of November 1920.[57] In short order, they noted in Springhall's file that he had been "receiving Communist literature and letters from Claude McKAY @ [sic; also known as] C. E. EDWARDS @ U. B. WARE . . . a negro Communist from Jamaica."[58]

It is a mystery why McKay was not picked up and arrested. The authorities might have decided that they had already got Pankhurst, the big fish, and they knew that McKay was about to leave the country. In one of his last intercepted letters, he told Springhall that "he is going to the Continent as it is getting too hot for him in London." In another, he wrote that he would be leaving for America in the next few weeks.[59] Apparently, they were happy to simply be rid of the Black troublemaker, letting him leave the country under his own steam.

Stoker Douglas Springhall and Able Seaman George Crook were discharged from the navy by mid-November 1920. But that did not stop Springhall.[60] Comrade Vie was apprehended with incriminating documents a week after Pankhurst's arrest, sentenced to six months, and then deported to Russia. He turned out to have been a Finnish-born agent (real name Erkki Veltheim) of the Comintern. Upon his release, Pankhurst's secretary followed him to Russia, where they were married. McKay met them again in Moscow during his "magic pilgrimage" in 1922.[61]

The International Socialist Club

The ISC served as McKay's primary redoubt in London. Crystal Eastman almost certainly told him about the place before he left the United States. Eastman was in Britain in the summer of 1919, only months before McKay sailed, and she knew the radical scene there well.[62] McKay joined the club soon after arriving in London and quickly became a familiar presence. At one point, he went there every day and even used it as an address for his mail. "No," he told Ogden, "I am not living at the Club but I go by every day." It was at the ISC that he established some of his most enduring friendships across the Atlantic, and it was there, he said, that he made his most interesting contacts in Britain.[63] It was at the ISC that he heard Britain's most distinguished left-wing orators of the day, including J. T. Walton Newbold, the first person elected to Parliament on the CP ticket; Indian-born Shapurji Saklatvala, who in 1922 was first elected an MP for Battersea as an independent, switching afterward to the CP; A. J. Cook of the Miners' Federation, of which he later became leader; Jack Tanner, a leader of the shop-stewards movement; Guy Aldred, the editor of the anarchist organ, the *Spur*; Arthur McManus and William Gallacher, labor agitators from the Clyde; George Lansbury, editor of the *Daily Herald*; and Sylvia Pankhurst herself. A strong supporter of women's liberation since childhood, McKay probably also attended the 1920 ISC conference on "Birth Control for the Workers," featuring birth-control pioneers Rose Witkop and Margaret Sanger as the main speakers.[64]

McKay paints a vivid portrait of life at the ISC. It was, he said, "full of excitement with its dogmatists and doctrinaires of radical left ideas: Socialists, Communists, anarchists, syndicalists, one-big-unionists and trade unionists, soap-boxers, poetasters, scribblers, editors of little radical sheets which flourish in London." He noted that foreigners formed the majority of the membership, among which predominated Jewish immigrants. "The Polish Jews and the Russian Jews were always intellectually at odds," he observed, while the German Jews tended to be aloof. Czechs, Italians, Irish nationalists, French, Serbs, wartime prisoners, deportees from America, and British Wobblies were among its members. There were also, McKay recalled, "rumors of spies"—and British intelligence reports show that they were not mere rumors; they were very real and apparently plentiful.[65]

But when McKay joined the ISC, cosmopolitan though it was, he was the only "African" among its members.[66] McKay took it upon himself to introduce other Black people to the club. Among them was a "Reverend Negro" whose great hope was to establish a church for the Black population of London. He liked the place and returned again and again and was soon busy sending "*billets-doux*, old style," to the female comrades who welcomed him with a cordial smile. McKay also introduced a Trinidadian student from Oxford. He, too, enjoyed the place.[67] It was different with the young medical student from Dulwich: one visit and sitting through a lecture was enough for him. "He disapproved of the club and the reckless and impertinent discussions of economic problems and established authority." He lectured McKay about "taking the wrong turn." He invited McKay one Sunday to his home in Dulwich and took him to his church; "the first and only time I ever attended religious service during my stay in London," noted McKay. "That pious long-faced congregation singing so solemnly those salvation hymns remains among my memories unforgettable."[68]

McKay also introduced some of his Black friends from the Drury Lane club to the ISC. He mentioned three soldiers and a couple of boxers. But undoubtedly the most important Black figure McKay introduced to the club was a man whom he simply describes in his 1937 memoir as "a mulatto sailor from Limehouse," probably to protect his identity.[69] His name was Reuben Gilmore. He figured prominently in East End and North London radical politics in the aftermath of the Great War but, with the notable exception of Ken Weller, has been overlooked by historians.[70] A twenty-one-year-old ship's steward, Gilmore was a member of the Pankhurst group and by 1920 was the secretary of the Poplar Unemployed Workers' Committee (PUWC).[71] He was the first of twenty taken into custody on January 3, 1921, for being among the assault party that tried to seize Islington Town Hall during a massive unemployed workers' demonstration, which attracted national attention. Gilmore was arrested with a rush basket containing three bottles of petrol and copies of the *Workers' Dreadnought* hidden under his coat. He was rescued by the crowd but was recaptured by the police, who charged with truncheons. Among the fourteen men who attempted to rescue Gilmore was his close friend and comrade, John O'Sullivan (also known as Jack Sullivan), chair of the PUWC. For his effort, O'Sullivan was also arrested, and the police found five rounds of ammunition on his person. Gilmore and O'Sullivan were each bound over with two sureties of £10 with six weeks imprisonment in default. The attempted assault on the town hall occurred in the aftermath of the occupation of the Essex Road library in Islington by unemployed workers demanding an increase in their allowance.[72]

Gilmore was a close associate of Lillian Thring, editor of *Out of Work*, newspaper of the unemployed movement. A militant suffragette and socialist, Thring worked closely with Pankhurst and was herself a leading member of the WSF.[73] She was a member of the ISC and, according to Scotland Yard, "took an active part in the Islington riot in January, 1921, when she suggested burning down the Town Hall and claimed that the incendiary mixture, found on the half-caste Gilmour [*sic*], was made in her rooms."[74] Gilmore attended the first national conference of the unemployed held at the ISC on April 15, 1921. As a merchant seaman, but with deep roots in the East End, Gilmore traveled widely and would have taught McKay much, including easing his way around some of the rougher parts of London, including Limehouse, his birthplace.

The men corresponded with each other up to at least the end of 1936, when their surviving correspondence breaks off. More than a decade had passed, but Gilmore remained as militant and indignant as ever. Unemployed in January 1934, he wrote to McKay from his home in Poplar, complaining during the Depression of having to "sell" himself to "Capitalist Shipowners whenever possible[,] that possibility only occurring at very long intermittent intervals and as I have not lived at home for a period upwards of thirteen years[,] life has shown me more uncongenial spots than otherwise."[75] Almost three years later, he wrote from a ship off Bermuda, telling McKay that he was working in the "menial capacity of 'Second Cook & Baker,' all work and very little play, but what can one do, one must live."[76]

On a lighter note, Gilmore shared news of their mutual friends—Christmas with Frank and Francine Budgen and another friend, Nancy, in 1933—"the best I have spent for years"; he wrote to Springhall but without reply; Jack Sullivan, he of the PUWC, "whom you knew as a somewhat callow boy is now a very much married man with two children." Bringing out the audacious, proletarian, autodidactic strain that had been on display at the ISC during McKay's time, Gilmore related that Sullivan had "for some years been working on a scientific idea which is more or less a refutation of Einstein's theory of Relativity based on a newer kind of mathematics." He had been to Russia twice in an effort to develop the idea in a "practical manner." But Gilmore confessed that although he had "always held a great faith in his [Sullivan's] method I still cannot help thinking now at this stage that his time would have been better occupied had he concentrated on his undoubted literary ability."[77] No one knew where Edgar Whitehead had gone, but rumor had it that he had "dropped out of the movement altogether." And Francine and Frank Budgen had had a son. Gilmore told McKay of his ship's visit to Jamaica and Haiti and other parts, including

Vancouver, where he wandered around its streets and, naturally, checked out its "Chinese quarter where I glean great interest."[78] He had read McKay's 1933 novel, *Banana Bottom*, "and to an extent, enjoyed your somewhat realistic style. When your new book is published I intend to give you my patronage, if I can find three dollars." Because of his travels at sea in 1936, he thought that McKay's inquiries about the British political scene would be better answered by Sullivan, whose Poplar address Gilmore provided. "In any case I think he would appreciate a letter. What kind of line are you hearing in New York just now and have you finished your book[?] I eagerly await your reply."[79] The men almost certainly remained in touch beyond this (McKay would have replied), their last surviving letter, which is dated December 1, 1936.

The ISC had a twofold impact on McKay, one political and the other intellectual, but both interconnected. He recalled later that it was the "first time" he had found himself in an atmosphere in which people "devoted themselves entirely to the discussion and analysis of social events from a radical and Marxian point of view." There were "always group discussions of social problems." At the ISC, he noticed "an uncompromising earnestness and seriousness about those radicals that reminded me of an orthodox group of persons engaged in the discussion of a theological creed." His contact with the ISC, he wrote, "stimulated and broadened my social outlook and plunged me into the reading of Karl Marx." McKay in fact sought his reading ticket from the British Museum primarily to keep up with the comrades at the club. "I felt intellectually inadequate," he confessed, "and decided to educate myself." He put his reading ticket to good use, earnestly plowing through volumes one and two of *Capital* and much else. He said that it "wasn't entertaining reading," that he felt like one "studying subjects you dislike, which are necessary to pass an examination." He felt pride, however, in "mouthing" that he was a "Marxian student." He certainly learned enough to appreciate the greatness of Marx: "I marveled that any modern system of social education could ignore the man who stood like a great fixed monument in the way of the world."[80]

It was during his stay in London that McKay, for the first time since his student days in Kansas, had the opportunity to engage in sustained intellectual activity. In the United States, he was obliged to work long shifts in physically demanding jobs, including as a Pullman waiter, with little time and energy to fully engage in a life of the mind. In his poetry, he repeatedly returned to the toll on the body of the work he did, most notably in "The Tired Worker" and "On the Road."[81] Now, thanks to a stipend from his

Dutch friend and benefactor, Johannes Ezerman, and the small income he earned at the *Dreadnought*, he had the time to read, to attend exhibitions, museums, the theater, and concerts, and to engage in the political life and lively discussions at the ISC.[82]

It was not all Marx and no play at the ISC. The comrades liked their concerts and dances, and so did McKay. Many of the events were fund-raising ones, but no less fun. On November 6, 1920, for instance, the Pankhurst-led Communist Party (British Section of the Third International) held a "Social and Dance" in aid of the *Workers' Dreadnought* at the ISC.[83] The manager of the ISC asked McKay's boxer friends from the Drury Lane club to put on a boxing exhibition. The men, one coffee brown, the other bronze, their bodies gleaming as if painted in oil, did not disappoint, "showing marvelous foot and muscle work, dancing and feinting all over the stage."[84] When Jack Tanner returned from his visit to Russia in 1920, he brought back with him a remarkable collection of posters and photographs of Bolshevik Russia. The ISC mounted an exhibition of them in the autumn of 1920.[85] McKay was especially impressed with the photographs and invited the art-loving C. K. Ogden to take a look.[86]

On a more practical level, the ISC provided a vital service for McKay. It was from the comrades there that he was able to secure lodgings in London, including one of the last places he stayed, which was the home of a Frenchwoman who used to serve at the ISC.[87] McKay established friendships at the ISC that endured well beyond his London days. As we have seen, he kept in touch with Reuben Gilmore. Henry Bernard, artist, writer, and cartoonist for the anarchist publication, the *Spur*, was a particularly close friend. It was Bernard's relatives who provided McKay with his first lodgings, at the Angel in Islington. The painter Frank Budgen (friend and biographer of James Joyce) and his wife Francine, both of anarchist persuasion, were also very close to McKay and kept in touch with him for many years after he left Britain. They interceded on McKay's behalf when he was being harassed by French and British authorities in Morocco in the 1930s.

The ISC delivered succor to many more than McKay and in very tangible ways. It provided loans to the unemployed and, according to McKay, almost went bankrupt on account of its inability to recoup the money because of the postwar recession. In November 1920, in an apparent cost-cutting measure, it drastically reduced its opening hours by half, closing at 6 p. m. instead of midnight.[88]

But it was not all sweetness and light at the ISC. The Trinidadian student McKay introduced to the club had "atrocious" manners and caused a spot of bother, requiring McKay's intercession to smooth things over. There was apparently at least one racist incident, of a "cockney lout" trying "to stir up race prejudice in the club," and McKay brought charges against him to the management committee of the ISC.[89] During the latter part of August 1920, he kept his distance from the club for a while: the Criminal Investigation Department (CID), comprising plainclothes detectives, had been "haunting" the place because "certain clever young criminals" had been using the ISC as a rendezvous to disguise their activities.[90] But on the whole, the experience of the ISC was a positive one for McKay. When he heard that his friend Joseph Freeman, the young poet, journalist, and contributor to the *Liberator*, was going over to London from Paris, he recommended the ISC: "If you ever want to meet some real proletarians in London who have no regular passport to intellectualism, I know of a club in City Road where you could drop in. It's a real den for revolutionary working folk, quite rough but once in a while one meets 'artists' and 'intellectuals' there."[91]

Having witnessed the operation of and benefits provided by the ISC, it is not surprising that McKay sought to create a similar club in New York. Thus, after he was appointed coeditor of the *Liberator* soon after his return in 1921, McKay made strenuous attempts to establish a Liberator Club in New York. He also attempted to organize social events along the lines of those he had observed and participated in at the ISC to raise funds for the financially strapped *Liberator* magazine.

Because of the prominence of the ISC in his London life, McKay operated within a largely foreign milieu, the most cosmopolitan one in which he had ever lived and operated, and as he later recorded, it broadened his outlook. He later reflected that he did not think he could have survived the "ordeal" of his yearlong sojourn in London had it not been for his enjoying the freedom of two clubs, the ISC and the Drury Lane club.[92]

The Drury Lane Club

The large amount of time McKay spent at the ISC was partly due to his being banned from the Drury Lane club. The club was founded by the YMCA during the troubles of 1919.[93] According to McKay, it came into being because of "the friction and mutual hatred" that existed between white American and colored soldiers and, "in a lesser, but nevertheless, ugly form, English and native colonials." McKay detested the patronizing and "overwhelmingly churchy" ambience of the club. Mrs. Newcombe, the woman who ran the place, insisted on referring to the men as her "colored boys" and told McKay in an interview of their virtues, "if white people knew how to manage them."[94] She "is one of those too-utterly-nice type of the English bourgeois," McKay wrote in the *Negro World*. "I didn't like her—the oleaginous way she talked about the Negro boys as if they were all a lot of silly children," McKay told Cunard.[95] "She has traveled in the East and she knows a little of life and books. Apparently she takes some interest in dark people and is not averse to working among her swarthy brethren." She has known "great sorrow," McKay acknowledged: she lost her husband and two brothers in France during the war. But she is "still narrow-minded enough to hate the German people and blame them for the terrible suffering that the imperial exploiters have brought upon a blindly submissive world."[96]

The club consisted of "three small and rather mean rooms," and McKay noticed, among the many cards on the wall, one in particular. It read: "Remember Booker T. Washington. Follow his leadership." The little library had only a few books. He remembered seeing a copy of Huxley's *Man's Place in Nature*, a few back numbers of *The Crisis*, and "some old newspapers from America and the West Indies that had no guts." He donated copies of both the American and English *Nation* magazines, *Workers' Dreadnought*, *One Big Union Monthly*, the *Negro World*, and "also some I. W. W. and other revolutionary literature." He reported the unhappiness of some of the men with the place and, in particular, with the obsequious behavior of an African American churchman who conducted a Christmas service in 1919 ending with the presentation of a gift to Mrs. Newcombe wrapped in cloying words. McKay was so "overcome with oppression" that he "had to leave."[97]

In time, a copy of the *Negro World* containing McKay's article arrived at the club. Mrs. Newcombe was not pleased and declared McKay persona non grata at Drury Lane.[98] But before he was banished, McKay had an opportunity—lasting about six months—to listen to the soldiers' stories of the war. He learned, as he told Leon Trotsky a couple of years later, that the men had all been "disillusioned" by the war. They kept on having "frightful clashes" with British and American soldiers. On top of this, the authorities treated them "completely differently from the white soldiers." Radicalized, they were "deeply aroused" by the Garvey movement.[99] "I am glad," he wrote in the *Negro World*, "that in the hearts of black men the 'grievance against things British' is rapidly growing greater instead of disappearing." He went on: "We should rejoice that Germany blundered, so that Negroes from all parts of the world were drawn to England to see the Lion, afraid and trembling, hiding in cellars, and the British ruling class revealed to them in all its rottenness and hypocrisy."[100]

McKay invited the most "forward-thinking" Drury Lane men to the ISC.[101] He was thus able to maintain close contact with at least some members of the club, including the boxers, as we have seen. He became deeply attached to them. Even their Caribbean creole speech provoked a nostalgic and visceral response in McKay. He explained to Ogden, who asked for some creole language poems for McKay's forthcoming anthology, that he had forgotten the "melody of the dialect." In the States, he mainly associated with African Americans, so "when I met some West Indian soldiers here speaking the dialect, it gave me a strange, pleasant sensation as of regaining some precious thing long lost."[102] His contact with West African soldiers at the club apparently triggered a desire to go to Africa. "I am thinking seriously of working my way to Africa before I return to America!" he wrote Ogden. He wanted to do his part to "keep my poor people awake and discontented."[103]

Grievances Against Things British: McKay and the "Black Horror on the Rhine"

The pervasiveness of such pernicious racism appalled McKay. He had, as we have seen, given moving testimony of his many personal encounters with it in London, but it hurt him even more to see it meted out to others, especially those weaker than himself—"for misery / I have the strength to bear but not to see."[104] It was for that reason that he felt impelled to publicly respond to E. D. Morel's "Black Horror on the Rhine" campaign, primarily disseminated by the *Daily Herald*, the newspaper of the British labor movement. Morel and, to a lesser extent, George Lansbury, the *Herald's* editor, used the most inflammatorily racist and sexualized language against Black French troops on the Rhine. Worse still, it was clear from the start that Morel had little regard for evidence and proof when it came to his incendiary charges. It was apparent then, and more so subsequently, that it was a campaign based on lies and misinformation to inflame and galvanize British and international opinion against the French occupation of the Ruhr. And what better way to effect this end than mobilizing the scoundrel language of antiblack racism?

On April 6, 1920, French troops extended their control of the Rhineland by occupying Frankfurt, Darmstadt, Duisburg, Hanau, and Homburg.

They moved into these cities east of the Rhine in response to German troops' violating the Treaty of Versailles by entering the demilitarized zone in the Ruhr valley. In the Rhineland as a whole, the French, who made up the majority of the occupying victorious Allied forces, had approximately 250,000 soldiers at the time of the crisis in the Ruhr. Of these, only about 10 percent, or 25,000, were non-Europeans. The majority of these were North Africans (Moroccans, Tunisians, and Algerians); only about 4,000, or less than 2 percent of the French total, were actually Black West Africans, primarily Senegalese soldiers.[105] All the French troops, including the non-European units, were under the command of white French officers.

Despite their relatively small numbers, Black troops became the target of racists, including those within the British labor movement, opposed to French and Allied policies in occupied Germany. E. D. Morel led the campaign in the English-speaking world. Morel, who had done creditable work exposing the atrocities committed against Africans in King Leopold's Congo, was highly respected in British Labour circles. A member of the Independent Labour Party, he had been a founder of the Union of Democratic Control (UDC) and spent six months in jail for his antiwar activity. His new campaign was an extension of his opposition to the Versailles Treaty, which he, as well as many others, regarded as excessive punishment of Germany for its role in the Great War.[106]

The campaign, which began in January 1920, was relatively low-key at the start. But when Moroccan units led the occupation of Frankfurt on April 6, as Morel himself put it, the gloves were taken off. Moreover, the Moroccans, who were renowned for their high level of discipline, had the audacity to open fire on a mob after severe provocation, including some having their rifles taken from them by the mob during an arrest of two German men. Five Germans were killed in the incident.[107] The *Daily Herald* reported the incident in racial and racist terms. "Frankfurt Runs with Blood / French Black Troops Use Machine Guns on Civilians," it screamed on the front page.[108] George Lansbury, the *Herald*'s editor, was a close friend of Morel's, and it is probable that the headline was inspired by Morel himself, who fed material on the subject to Lansbury. It is often overlooked in the literature on the subject that Morel actually began his racist outpourings before the Frankfurt incident of April 6. More than a week before, he had rehearsed his argument in a letter to the *Nation*, titled "The Employment of Black Troops in Europe." The French, he wrote, had "thrust barbarians—barbarians belonging to a race inspired by Nature . . . with tremendous sexual instincts—into the heart of Europe." It was in that letter that Morel first unveiled an argument that he repeated and that formed the crux of his objection to the use of Black troops: The garrisoning of European towns and countryside "with black barbarians *must* entail certain consequences. It does not matter whether available reports are few or numerous. Given the presence of this factor in the life of the Palatinate, the natural effects *must* follow."[109] But that was not enough for Morel. The *Nation's* liberal intelligentsia readership would not suffice. He sought to reach the more potent labor movement, and Lansbury provided him ample space to do so by means of the *Herald*. The following day, after Lansbury's intervention, Morel spoke directly and in his own voice—and he did so on the front page of the *Herald*. Morel was not interested in the rights and wrongs of shootings in Frankfurt; he was concerned with sex, the relations between Black soldiers and white women in occupied Germany. "Black Scourge in Europe / Sexual Horror Let Loose by France on the Rhine / Disappearance of Young German Girls," shouted the headline.[110]

Morel gave the game away in the opening passages of his article. "My information is not yet as complete as I should wish," he confessed, but he could not wait. "The news in to-day's papers, to the effect that France is thrusting her black savages still further into the heart of Germany, is such that I do not propose to hold my hand any longer." He also echoed the argument presented in his *Nation* letter that the absence of actual reports, let alone substantiated charges, of rapes by African troops was of little concern to him: "The abundance or otherwise of specific reports is immaterial." Specific evidence is immaterial because: "The African race is the most developed sexually of any. These levies are recruited from tribes in a primitive state of development. . . . Sexually they are unrestrained and unrestrainable. *That is perfectly well known*."[111] Thus the very presence of the Black troops, "unrestrained and unrestrainable" sexually, was tantamount to their committing crimes of rape. Significantly, Morel was not at all interested in what the 250,000 French troops were up to in the Rhineland, just what the small number of Black ones were alleged to have done. He condemned the "French militarists," but only for mobilizing Black troops in Europe, thus "perpetrating an abominable outrage upon womanhood, upon the white race, and upon civilisation." The Black troops, "primitive African barbarians," "have become a terror and a horror unimaginable to the countryside, raping women and girls." He then paused to enlighten his readers about the African body: "for well-known physiological reasons, the raping of a white woman by a negro is nearly always accompanied by serious injury and not infrequently has fatal results."

Morel ended his article by imploring the British working class to intervene. For the use of these "negro mercenaries . . . from the heart of Africa, to fight the battles and execute the lusts of capitalist Governments in the heart of Europe is . . . a terrific portent." The workers of Britain, France, and Italy would be "ill-advised if they allow it to pass in silence because to-day the victims happen to be German." He also appealed to white women, whose "decent instincts" might have remained more intact than the men's after the horrors of the war.

Lansbury, in an editorial note above Morel's article, declared that the *Daily Herald* was not in the business of encouraging color prejudice. On the editorial page itself, he returned to the subject. Under the heading "A New Horror," he stated:

> We are not amongst those who consider that because a man's skin is black he should be considered as an inferior human being to a white man; but nature has given us all qualities of temperament suitable to the conditions and climate in which we are born.
>
> It is an odious outrage to bring thousands of children of the forests from Africa to Europe without their womenfolk, and settle them down as enemies amongst the women and children of Germany. . . .
>
> For organised Labour there is another question, too. If the manhood of these races, not so advanced in the forms of civilisation as ourselves, are to be used against Germans, why not against the workers here or elsewhere?[112]

Thus, by his ostensibly antiracist words, Lansbury revealed his racist self.

You will look in vain to find a response to Morel's racist diatribe from the established labor movement. There was utter silence—silent acquiescence and, worse, not even mild protest by way of a letter to the editor. It is of course possible that Lansbury suppressed letters of criticism such as McKay's. But contrary to that hypothesis, he did publish a letter of criticism written by a fellow Christian Socialist and critic of empire, Norman Leys. A Scottish doctor, Leys had joined the colonial service in 1904 and worked in East Africa. Stating that he had lived in Africa for the previous seventeen years, the last three in company with African troops, Leys, who declared himself a Socialist, voiced his strong objection. "I write to bear evidence that the so-called physiological facts hinted at but not stated in Mr. Morel's article and in your leader to-day are simply untrue. That is to say, it is untrue that sexual passion in Africans is stronger than in Europeans." Such a belief, he continued, "is one of the great sources of race hatred. It should never be repeated by any honest man or honest newspaper. There is literally no evidence whatever in its favour." Leys concluded: "I regard the quartering of African troops on German towns with the same abhorrence as those who prefer to support their feelings and convictions by misstatements of fact."[113] What Leys left unsaid is whether he found foreign troops or French troops, not just African ones, quartered on German towns abhorrent. He certainly failed to disclose why he regarded African troops in particular as abhorrent. Leys's defense of African troops is therefore at best an ambiguous and somewhat equivocal one.

Morel objected to Leys's letter. Deliberately referring to Leys as "Dr. Leyds" (not once but on the two occasions he pretended to refer to Leys by name), he claimed that Leys misrepresented him when Leys noted that Morel argued that "sexual connection" between an African man and European woman is injurious to the European woman. No, said Morel: "I said the 'raping of a white woman' was." As to whether the African has stronger sexual passion than the European, Morel thought it a "general proposition upon which it is possible to hold different views without flinging about charges of dishonesty"—then immediately affirmed the proposition without evidence. What is particularly noteworthy in Morel's response is that he regarded even consensual relations between Black men and white women as "a monstrous outrage upon both races against which the women of Europe should protest on behalf of European womanhood."[114] Morel was remarkably dismissive of the charge of racism. Addressing a large meeting organized by the Women's International League at Central Hall, Westminster, he told his audience that he was "not in the least disposed" to respond to the accusation that he was "stirring up racial prejudice." Though fully aware of Leys's and McKay's critiques, both published just three days before his speech, Morel insisted that the charge of racism against him exceeded the bounds of "sweet reasonableness," evidently believing that his work on the Congo inoculated him from such a charge, making it obviously preposterous, as if he could not be both anti-imperialist and racist at the same time.[115]

Lansbury also received a curious letter from a Black man based in Cardiff. Its content reveals that he was a member of the West Indies Regiment and had served in the war. He was clearly excited by the Garvey movement—especially the launching of the Black Star Line, the movement's steamship company—and was probably a member of the UNIA. Very much attuned to developments within the movement across the Atlantic, he celebrated the emergence of the New Negro and signed his letter as "One of the

Oppressed." But his letter was very much out of tune with the radicalism of the New Negro movement. Either too easily mollified or misreading the horrible deluge of antiblack racism being spewed out by the *Herald* and Morel, the "New Negro" correspondent wrote to the editor: "Being a negro, although not from Africa, I was attracted by your comments on the scandal of the Black soldiers of the French Government in Germany. I must say that at first I thought I read in it an aggravation of colour prejudice, but I am pleased to say that your editorial in a subsequent issue dispelled any such fears." Remarkably, he concluded with praise and promotion of the *Herald*. "In my humble capacity," he told Lansbury, "I try my best to circulate the *Daily Herald*"; he had even won some senior officers over to the paper, which they had previously disparaged as "Bolshevik."[116] It apparently never crossed the correspondent's mind as to why his white officers' attitude to the *Herald* had been so radically altered—that the *Herald* that had so boldly condemned the Amritsar Massacre[117] had now become the *Herald* of E. D. Morel and the "Black Scourge on the Rhine."

Sylvia Pankhurst once again distinguished herself, standing well apart from the racist pack. "Much horror is being worked up because the French Army of Occupation is mainly manned by African troops," she editorialized in the very first issue of the *Workers' Dreadnought* published after Morel's bile in the *Herald*. But, she wrote, "the French have been using black troops all along in the occupied territories of Germany—we saw them ourselves last winter—yet the stories of rape and outrage are only now being told. Why is this?" She counseled her readers to "guard against the tendency to let our imaginations run riot under the influence of race prejudice on this question." Pankhurst conceded that "the women of the districts concerned are victimized to a certain extent," but quickly pointed out that "this is also the case where European troops are in occupation."[118] In other words, Pankhurst, unlike Morel and Lansbury, framed the matter as being about the alleged behavior of occupying troops, not the behavior of *Black* occupying troops. But she did more than that: she provided a platform for McKay to express his disgust and outrage at the dangerous racism propagated by Morel and the *Herald*.

McKay had picked up the *Herald* and was appalled by what he read. On the following day, he dispatched a letter to the editor. Lansbury refused to publish it and never replied to McKay.[119] The *Workers' Dreadnought* published it. Apart from Dr. Leys's brief letter and Pankhurst's concise editorial, no one had challenged Morel and the *Herald*. So McKay, once again, took upon himself the duty of speaking out against the racists. Not only was he virtually alone in responding, but his was by far the most sub-stantial rebuttal.

Under the heading "A Black Man Replies," McKay prefaced his letter by pointing out to *Dreadnought* readers that his letter had been sent to the editor of the *Herald* on April 11—the day after Morel's "Black Scourge" headline—"but apparently the *Herald* refuses a hearing to the other side, which is quite inarticulate." McKay told Lansbury that the "odiousness" of Morel's article was not mitigated by his explanatory editorial and note stating that he was not encouraging race prejudice and that he championed native rights in Africa. "If you are really consistent in thinking that you can do something to help the white and black peoples to a better under-standing of each other," he told Lansbury, "there is much that you might learn from Liberal and Conservative organs like the [British] *Nation*, the *New Statesman* and the *Edinburgh Review*, which have treated the problem . . . in a decent and dignified manner." McKay confessed ignorance of the "well-known physiological reasons that make the raping of a white woman by a negro resultful of serious and fatal injury." Any violent rape, he said, "whether by white, yellow or black, civilised or savage man, must entail injury, serious or fatal, especially if the victim be a virgin." In short, "Why all this obscene, maniacal outburst about the sex vitality of black men in a proletarian paper?" He concluded:

> I do not protest because I happen to be a negro (I am disgusted when I read in your columns that white dockers would prohibit their employers using Chinese and Indian labour), I write because I feel that the ultimate result of your propaganda will be further strife and blood-spilling between the whites and the many members of my race, boycotted economically and socially, who have been dumped down on the English docks since the ending of the European War. I have been told in Limehouse by white men, who ought to know, that this summer will see a recrudescence of the outbreaks that occurred last year. The negro-baiting Bourbons of the United States will thank you, and the proletarian underworld of London will certainly gloat over the scoop of the Christian-Socialist-pacifist *Daily Herald*.[120]

Rioting did recur in Limehouse in the summer of 1920, and American racists gobbled up and used Morel's expanded racist tract, *The Horror on the Rhine*, in their tens of thousands.[121] But the appeal of Morel's pamphlet extended well beyond the United States. It was translated not only into German but also into French, Dutch, Italian, and probably other languages. Following

Morel's lead, similar tracts were published as far afield as Buenos Aires and Lima. Others put out pamphlets in virtually all the languages of Europe, and at least one appeared in Esperanto. German merchants "routinely" enclosed Black Horror tracts in their catalogues, shipments, and bills. Leaflets were issued to passengers embarking ships at Hamburg. The British authorities discovered that delegates at an education conference in Edinburgh were "deluged with propaganda from Munich." Some of the publications even turned up on a British light cruiser squadron on duty at Riga. It appears that some pornography cranks tried to make some cash through lurid publications. A German racist published a novel on the subject and had it made into a film in Bavaria in 1921. A German film magazine thought it counterproductive, declaring that neutral opinion would not be won over by "such tendentious eyewash." But not only did the film do the rounds in Germany to packed houses, it also found an audience in Holland. Some theaters in Germany put it on as a stage play. The campaign was as vicious as it was effective. The French tried to rebut charges with their own counterpropaganda, but they could not match their adversaries' reach and output.[122] The campaign largely petered out in the late 1920s through its own excesses, imploding under the weight of its own exaggerations and lies.

What disheartened McKay most was that such blatantly racist propaganda could penetrate the British workers' movement so easily, pervasively, and deeply. At the annual conference of the Trades Union Congress at Portsmouth in September 1920, which McKay covered for the *Dreadnought*, the Standing Orders Committee gave permission to the UDC, publishers of Morel's pamphlet, to present each delegate with a copy of *The Horror on the Rhine*. According to one of Morel's friends, the pamphlet "produced a profound impression. . . . I was astonished at the number who came and expressed their views about it." It left the trade unionists with "a feeling of physical and spiritual revulsion."[123] Even a man such as Robert Smillie, whom McKay interviewed, admired and praised on the front page of the *Dreadnought*—ascetic, incorruptible, a cross between Gandhi and Big Bill Haywood, president of the Miners' Federation—even he was caught up in the sordid business, lending his name to Morel's campaign.[124]

McKay told Trotsky two years later that the propaganda was still under way, pointing to the fact that even the British Communist Party had become one of its purveyors. He specifically cited the British CP's daily paper, *The Communist*, as evidence of this.[125] On April 8, 1922, the *Communist* carried an anonymous Morelesque appeal, emanating from Germany.

"Outcry Against the Black Horror: Urgent Appeal to Englishmen" was unadorned racism:

> You members of the white race, help us to free our women, girls and children from the hell in the occupied districts into which they have been cast by the black and coloured hordes of Africa. . . .
>
> Englishmen! . . . You have taken our weapons from us, give them back to us, or help us by weight of your voices to put a stop to the darkest crime ever committed in the world's history: the Black Horror. Help us if you have any feeling for the awful disgrace which is being done to our white women on the Rhine by the eager lust of African savages.[126]

The fact that the four thousand mainly Senegalese Black troops had been withdrawn and had not been in Germany for almost two years was of little moment.[127] Not only did the CP print but it also endorsed the diatribe. The *Communist*'s editorial declared: "We have received the following appeal and reprint it verbatim believing it to be true in substance and in fact."[128] It was perhaps over this that McKay had a "serious dispute" with a leading member of the British CP, Nan Watkins, in Moscow. McKay complained to the Executive Committee of the Comintern that Watkins had failed to carry out its instructions.[129]

Morel suffered no ill effects from his racist campaign. He was elected to a seat in Dundee in 1922, defeating Winston Churchill, the sitting MP, and was reelected in 1924 with an increased majority on the Labour ticket. Not only was Morel popular among Labour voters, but he also received nothing but praise from leading members of the Communist Party. William Gallacher—a man who knew McKay from his London days and had worked with Pankhurst, a leading member of the CP, and a delegate to the Second Congress of the Comintern in 1920, who also ran for the two-seat Dundee constituency that Morel contested—recalled Morel's work in exposing the "appalling treatment of colonial peoples" but made no mention of his Horror on the Rhine campaign. He described Morel as a man of "superior ability who directed his life and work according to recognised moral principles." To Gallacher, "there was no doubt whatever about the honesty and integrity of E. D. Morel."[130]

The British liberal intelligentsia remained mute or, more often than not, fell in line with Morel. Even Bertrand Russell, titan of liberal politics and philosophy, lost his way. In his 1924 review of a book hostile to French foreign policy after Versailles, Russell averred, in speaking of the French "coloured troops," that the author "proves conclusively, what is obvious *à priori*, that these troops are constantly guilty of the worst moral offences, often of an unnatural kind," albeit encouraged by the French authorities.[131] At the height of Morel's campaign in 1920, Russell served by his side on the General Council of the UDC, which published *The Horror on the Rhine* that same year. A few years later, he occupied an even more elevated spot on its Executive Council, as did critics of empire J. A. Hobson and Leonard Woolf, Virginia Woolf's husband.[132] Russell loved and admired Morel, describing him as a man whom "on account of his purity of heart, I shall never forget."[133]

We have considered the propaganda of the Horror on the Rhine. But what were the facts of the Black presence in Germany? Both the evidence available then and subsequent historical scholarship have shown that the charges were demonstrably and overwhelmingly false, the poisonous fruit of German propagandists and their allies. The most judicious investigation of the subject has come to the clear conclusion that Morel and company were "long on outrage and short on solid facts."[134] One alleged complainant had left the district in which a crime is supposed to have been committed in 1916—four years before French troops, Black or white, had entered the area. In another complaint of several alleged rapes, after long investigation the French declared that the complainants must be fictional because no persons of those names lived in the town in which the incident was supposed to have taken place. Sally Marks reports that "formal complaints were made of black outrages in areas with no indigenous [non-European] troops or no troops at all. In some cases, complaints were provoked by local officials and in others, the women had clearly encouraged advances. Many cases collapsed for complete want of evidence."[135] In fact, Black troops in the Rhineland were generally well liked, and the Germans preferred them to white Frenchmen. The evidence is there and *was* there at the time Morel wrote.[136] Morel, Marks generously concluded, was either "imaginative or gullible or both."

> He claimed that 20,000 Senegalese occupied Frankfurt. His allegations about conditions in the Saar, including forced brothels, abductions of young girls, rape, and finding female corpses under manure heaps, led the French to investigate exhaustively, obtaining written refutations from the mayor of Saarbrucken, the barracks commander, the owner of the manure pile, his caretaker, and his employee. That stopped neither Morel's thunder nor its echoes in the German Reichstag and press.[137]

But the real problem was never Morel being "imaginative or gullible or both." It was far worse than that. Morel was happy to knowingly peddle false-hoods—lies—in order to undermine and destroy the hated Treaty of Versailles, and he sought to drive a wedge between Britain and France to achieve that goal. Even his German allies in the campaign counseled caution with his claims. "As to the black scourge," Count Max Montgelas wrote Arthur Ponsonby, Morel's closest colleague in the UDC, "you know yourself the difficulties of getting unmistakable evidence." Prince Max of Baden cynically conceded that the African soldiers "in some instances" were better behaved than the French, but "even then the atrocity of introducing black troops into the heart of Europe would be as great as ever." Ponsonby and Charles Trevelyan, cofounders of the UDC and Morel's friends and confidantes, visited Germany, investigated the allegations, and while there urged Morel to be more cautious. Ponsonby informed Morel that "the depositions of alleged victims might have been fabricated and advised avoiding references to individual cases." Even more tellingly, Trevelyan admonished Morel "not to exaggerate." "My only piece of first-hand evidence," he informed Morel, "is that the black troops are behaving exceedingly well, and that the native [white] French are feared far more." That was in a letter dated as early as 29 February 1920, more than a month before Morel went on his racist tirade in the *Herald*.[138] In short, Morel knew better, but strenuously resisted letting the facts get in his way.

Yet Bertrand Russell—that self-appointed guardian of truth, of enlightened and liberal values—applauded Morel's unforgettable "purity of heart." In his *Autobiography*, published more than a decade later, he declared that Morel had a "single-minded devotion to the truthful presentation of facts."[139] Of course, it was possible to tell the truth about atrocities in the Congo and the villainy of the Great War and at the same time lie about "coloured troops" in Germany, especially if that lie helped to undermine what one perceived as an unjust peace. It is unlikely that Russell did not know about the big lie of the Horror on the Rhine, since the falsehoods were exposed by, among others, Ponsonby and Trevelyan, eminent members and emissaries of the UDC, on whose Committee and Executive Council Russell served at the time. But maybe lying about "Negroes" and "coloured troops" committing atrocities did not count as lies—especially if those lies helped to undo the Versailles treaty. After all, it was Russell who declared that the "coloured troops," were "*obvious, a priori . . . constantly guilty of the worst moral offences.*" Facts and truth were thus unnecessary, redundant—the fact of their blackness in and of itself made them guilty of sexual crimes. Thus, the quarters from which McKay might have expected support in stemming the deluge of Morelian racism—the "revolutionary" left (including Gallacher) and the "liberal" intelligentsia (including Russell)—were firmly positioned on the other side. One can only imagine McKay's feeling of isolation, disappointment, and loneliness in taking on Morel.

Morel's biographer, who is by no means hostile to him, conceded that "it is difficult to avoid the conclusion that Morel . . . was prepared to use *any weapon* to discredit 'French militarism' and the Treaty of Versailles."[140] As McKay observed, in 1920 the "horror of German air raids and submarine warfare was still fresh in the minds of the British public. And it was not easy to work up and arouse the notorious moral righteousness of the English in favor of the Germans and against the French." In their search for a propaganda issue to mobilize British opinion against the treaty, Morel and his cabal found Black troops in the Rhineland. "Poor black billy goat," sighed McKay.[141]

What was also disturbing about the *Communist* giving vent to such racist propaganda was that by the time they published the appeal, many who had previously believed the allegations had discovered, through a wide variety of investigations, that they had been duped and had distanced themselves from Morel's diatribes.[142]

Looking back at the whole furor over the "Black Horror on the Rhine," McKay admitted that maybe he was not "civilized enough to understand why the sex of the black race should be put on exhibition to persuade the English people to decide which white gang should control the coal and iron of the Ruhr."[143] He noted that his "experience of the English" had convinced him that "prejudice against Negroes had become almost congenital among them." He was bewildered: "I think the Anglo-Saxon mind becomes morbid when it turns on the sex life of colored people. Perhaps a psychologist might be able to explain why."[144] Still, the damage was done, and what concerned McKay most was the impact it would have on a London and Britain that had seen widespread racist violence the previous summer.

Race, Class, Nation

On top of the hurt of racist propaganda in the press, the disillusionment of the Black men of the Drury Lane club, their sense of isolation, their anguish, their painful experience of racism in the theater of war and on the streets of London moved McKay deeply. The hurt and anger became his own, and he transmuted this anger into verse as well as prose. "Enslaved,"

one of his most powerful sonnets, was written at that time, probably soon
after the Holborn incident:

> Oh when I think of my long-suffering race
> For weary centuries despised, oppressed,
> Enslaved and lynched, denied a human place
> In the great life line of the Christian West;
> And in the Black Land disinherited,
> Robbed in the ancient country of its birth,—
> My heart grows sick with hate, becomes as lead,
> For my race, my race, outcast upon the earth.
> Then from the dark depths of my soul I cry
> To the avenging angel to consume
> The white man's world of wonders utterly:
> Let it be swallowed up in earth's vast womb,
> Or upward roll as sacrificial smoke
> To liberate my people from its yoke![145]

McKay wanted the anger and energy of the men to be joined with the
world revolutionary movement. As he explained to Garvey soon after his
arrival in London,

> radical Negroes should be more interested in the white radical movements.
> They are supporting our cause, at least in principle. . . . [T]hey are the great
> destructive forces *within*, while the subject races are fighting without. . . .
> [T]hey are fighting their own battle & so are we; but at present we meet on
> common ground against the common enemy. We have a great wall to batter
> down and while we are working on one side we should hail those who are
> working on the other.[146]

Tellingly, contemporaneous with his letter to Garvey, McKay sought to
enlighten his English comrades on the Black nationalist and the anticolonial
movements. In "Socialism and the Negro," carried on the front page of the
Dreadnought, he explained that although he was an "international Socialist,"
he supported the Garvey movement. He chided the English comrades who
disparaged the Irish and Indian movements because they were nationalistic. The British Empire, he argued, was the greatest obstacle to international
socialism, and the breaking away of any of its subjugated parts would be
helping the socialist cause. The breakup of the empire "must either begin

at home or abroad; the sooner the strong blow is struck the better it will be for all Communists." McKay believed that the nationalist, anticolonial revolution would not stop at the bourgeois phase; it would not "tamely submit" to a new capitalist order in place of the old one.[147] Thus, unless, "like some British intellectuals, they are enamoured of the idea of a Socialist (?) British Empire!" the Irish, Indian, Garvey, and other nationalist currents ought to be supported by English socialists.[148]

There are two especially noteworthy features of this argument. The first is McKay's formulation of what he perceives as the likely course of the anticolonial revolution. Students of the Russian Revolution will immediately perceive the identity of McKay's formulation with that of Leon Trotsky's theory of "permanent revolution." The theory can be traced back to Marx and Engels's analysis of the 1848 revolutions, as Trotsky himself acknowledged, but it was most fully developed by him.[149] Trotsky argued that in economically backward countries, such as prerevolutionary Russia, the bourgeois democratic revolution was organically tied to the socialist revolution and would become indistinct. The revolution would not come in two distinct stages, one bourgeois and the other socialist. The bourgeois revolution—carried out by the working class and peasantry because of the weakness of the domestic capitalist class—according to Trotsky, would grow into the socialist revolution. This, he argued, is precisely what took place in Russia in 1917, where between February and October the revolution had grown into a socialist one. Trotsky extended this analysis to the colonial world and anticipated a similar scenario, in which the nationalist phase of the revolution would develop into a socialist revolution.[150]

McKay might very well have come to this conclusion without knowledge of Trotsky's theory. Trotsky's *Results and Prospects*, in which the idea was first formulated, was published in Russian in St. Petersburg in 1906 in the aftermath of the 1905 revolution. It was first translated into English and published in Moscow in 1921.[151] An abridged edition did appear, however, in an English translation of Trotsky's writings three years earlier.[152] It is thus possible that McKay might have read this or other published excerpts in translation, either in the United States or in London, but his article makes no reference to Trotsky. At the Baku Congress of the Peoples of the East, held in Tashkent, the theory was hotly debated in discussions of the nature of the revolution in the non-European and colonial world, but that congress took place in September 1920, fully nine months after McKay's article.[153] It is therefore highly probable that McKay's argument was developed without recourse to Trotsky's theory.

The most remarkable quality of his argument, and indeed of the article as a whole, is the way it encapsulated McKay's political credo: I'm a socialist, but I'm also a Black nationalist; I'm a Black nationalist, but I'm also a socialist. In fact, I'm a socialist *because* I'm a Black nationalist, and I'm a Black nationalist *because* I'm a socialist.[154] For McKay, there was no intrinsic contradiction between the two; the potential contradiction was obviated by his deep and abiding commitment to the Black working class.[155] Moreover, he pointed out, there was no reason why the anticolonial revolution would not lead to socialist ends. History has shown him—and indeed Trotsky—to have been overly optimistic on this score, but not entirely unrealistic: China, Vietnam, Algeria, Angola, Guinea-Bissau, and Mozambique all provide qualified vindication of some of the basic tenets of the theory.[156]

In these two texts, his letter to Garvey and "Socialism and the Negro"—in effect, a diptych—McKay thus tried to bring together Black nationalist and anticolonial militants, on the one hand, and English socialists, on the other, to a common understanding and solidarity, if not collaboration. That was why he invested such great hopes in the Bolshevik Revolution and in bringing others to its cause. "Although weak," he wrote Ogden, "I must also do my part to keep my poor people awake and discontented." He sought to tap the race's "undeveloped energy."[157] Accordingly, in one of his London poems, he cried, "Ethiopia! Awake! / In the East the clouds glow crimson with the new dawn that is breaking. . . . / O my brothers and my sisters, Wake! Arise! / . . . Wake from sleeping; to the East turn, turn/ your eyes!"[158] He was working on his side of the "wall."

McKay's Black friends and associates in London were overwhelmingly working class, not members of the Black middle class, and his revolutionary politics and anticolonialism distinguished him from prominent Black figures as well as more moderate groups in Britain at the time. When he arrived in London in 1919, McKay stayed at a hotel located at 39 Woburn Place, a stone's throw away from Student Movement House, the newly established meeting place for "coloured" students at 32 Russell Square. Yet he never mentions setting foot in the place. He probably knew students who frequented the center but apparently kept away from it. This is not entirely surprising, given McKay's utter contempt for Christianity and its perceived role in the oppression of Black people. The center in Russell Square was run by the Student Christian Movement, a white philanthropic organization that noted the isolation of nonwhite students in London and sought a place for them to meet with dignity, among themselves as well as with members of the enlightened British public.[159]

He certainly would have heard of the Coterie of Friends, an organization begun in the spring of 1919 by Edmund Jenkins, a brilliant African American student-teacher at the Royal Academy of Music, and several other students from the Caribbean and West Africa and supported by London's Black notables. Jenkins's achievements were often featured in the press, and McKay probably even heard him perform at one of Jenkins's many outings on the London concert scene.[160] McKay, as his rich correspondence with Ogden shows, frequently went to the theater and music halls. He certainly went to see the Southern Syncopated Orchestra (SSO), which toured Britain and "took London by storm" during 1919 and 1920.[161] Ogden even reviewed one of their concerts in the *Cambridge Magazine* and would later draw a parallel between the SSO's achievements in music and McKay's in poetry.[162] Given his wide reading and contacts, McKay would also have known of the African Progress Union and the Society of Peoples of African Origin (SPAO) and the journal they produced, the *African Telegraph*, yet there is no mention of them either. Similarly, there is no mention of Dusé Mohamed Ali, who lived in London—albeit West London, far from McKay's East End redoubt—up to 1921, and his journal, the *African Times and Orient Review*, which McKay would have encountered. He certainly would have heard of Dr. Harold Moody and perhaps even met this fellow Jamaican and distinguished Black resident in London; virtually every Black person in London at the time knew Dr. Moody. And as we have seen, McKay visited Dulwich, where Moody lived and even dropped in at a church there.[163] Why, then, this lack of meaningful contact with Black organizations and the individuals who ran them?

The likelihood is that McKay regarded them as too conservative, too mixed up with Christianity, or both. As far as he was concerned, they were all too involved in the "amusing, but very pathetic" business of petitioning the British government, which he thought was utterly futile.[164] He was also in his most enthusiastically Bolshevik phase. Even the man with whom he had most in common, Felix Hercules of the SPAO, would have been too conservative for him. The platform enunciated by the *African Telegraph*, edited by Hercules, was not one that McKay could have endorsed:

> We stand, first and foremost, for the maintenance of our connection with Great Britain, and, for this reason, we shall resist any and every effort that may be made from whatever quarter to imperil this connection, because we regard Great Britain as the best and truest friend of the native races within the Empire.

It went on: "We are not going to be led astray by vague notions of self-determination. . . . Self-determination for us means the ultimate goal of political autonomy within the British Empire, which we hope to attain under the tutelage of Great Britain." The document concluded by distancing the journal from those whom it describes as "irresponsible agitators" whose one object is to "embarrass and to retard our development."[165]

McKay was a constellation away to the left of such men. He probably would have tolerated them during his long-gone Fabian days, before he "became Bolshevik."[166] McKay now wanted the destruction of the British Empire—not "autonomy" under its tutelage. He yearned for its "disintegration and the birth of a proletarian order."[167] Hercules would thus have counted McKay among the "irresponsible agitators." In any case, by the time McKay arrived in London, Hercules was in the Caribbean, estranged from his London colleagues, who regarded him as too radical. By 1920, the *African Telegraph* was dead. Its death was partly attributable to the colonial authorities' successful lawsuit against it for allegedly libeling a brutal colonial official in Nigeria, who had, the paper claimed, supervised the public flogging of Nigerian women after his men had stripped them of clothing.[168]

Amid the pain and bitterness that doubtless came out of his English experience, McKay's sojourn in London accelerated his political and intellectual development in a variety of ways.

First, his time in London destroyed any residual notion he might have had about his Britishness: to white Britons he was at best a "darkey"—not British at all. This discovery contributed mightily to McKay's Pan-Africanist and anti-imperialist identification and outlook on life, including the newly expressed desire to go to Africa and do revolutionary work there. It was in London, not Marseilles as is commonly believed, that McKay first developed a powerful identification with his ancestral home. It was there that he first expressed a desire to visit Africa. His befriending West African ex-soldiers at the Drury Lane club combined with the lacerations of British racism contributed to the yearning. Almost a decade before the publication of *Banjo*, McKay confided to Ogden his intention of going to Africa before returning to the United States and his wanting to "keep my poor people awake and discontented."[169] His more profound identification with Africa in London stimulated even further his interest in African history and culture, particularly African art, about which he systematically educated himself, especially among the rich collection he found at the British Museum's ethnological division. The art from the Kingdom of Benin, which McKay saw there, especially impressed and moved him deeply, leading him to conclude that "the treasure house of Benin are more complex in conception and more amazing than the strangest works of Picasso."[170]

His time in London also contributed to McKay's revolutionary socialist politics and worldview. To him, imperialism, colonialism, and racism required the strong medicine of revolutionary socialism of the Bolshevik variety to be thoroughly uprooted. And he was not at all sentimental about the process. He did not mind working with the "poor white devils," even when they called him darkey, as long as they got on with the demolition of their side of the capitalist and imperialist wall.

McKay brings this hard absence of sentimentality to the fore in fictional form in a striking but overlooked passage in *Banjo*, his 1929 novel. Ray, a leading character based on McKay, berates a French waiter for calling him "Joseph" (equivalent to American white racists calling every Black man "George") and later compounding the discourtesy by addressing him with the French familiar *tu*. Crosby, Ray's white British friend, is shocked at the ferocity of Ray's rebuke of the waiter. In the course of their discussion, Crosby says to Ray, "I thought you were a proletarian," to which Ray replies, "Sure. That's my politics. But you never asked me why I prefer Proletarian to Liberal, Democrat or Conservative." Crosby wants to know, so Ray tells him in a rather Socratic exchange:

"Because I hate the proletarian spawn of civilization. They are ugly, stupid, unthinking, degraded, full of vicious prejudices, which any demagogue can play upon to turn them into a hell-raising mob at any time. As a black man I have always been up against them, and I became a revolutionist because I have not only suffered with them, but have been victimized by them—just like my race."

"But you have no real faith in the proletariat," said Crosby. "Then what can you expect from proletarian politics?"

"I have never confused faith with politics. I should like to see the indecent horde get its chance at the privileged things of life, so that decency might find some place among them. I am not fond of any kind of hogs, but I prefer to see the well-fed ones feeding out of a well-filled trough than the razor-backs rooting all over the place. That's why I am against all those who are fighting to keep the razor-backs from getting fat and are no better doing it than fat swine themselves."

Crosby is taken aback by Ray's response. "Your being politically proletarian from hatred's got me stumped," he says. "I thought you loved the proletariat." Ray replies, "I love life—when it shows lovable aspects."[171]

Though McKay found the Irish proletariat more lovable than Ray made out,[172] he followed the same ruthless but compelling political logic when it came to the Irish and Indian nationalist struggles. At the Sinn Fein rally in Trafalgar Square, McKay heard the bourgeois Irish nationalist refrain—a racist one—that Ireland was the only "white" nation left under the yoke of foreign imperialism. "There are other nations in bondage, but they are not of the breed; they are colored, some are even Negro." McKay not only let it pass, he even expressed a little sympathy for their position.[173] What was significant about the Irish nationalists, even the bourgeois ones, was that they were contributing to the breakup of the British Empire. They were working on the wall, and that was all that mattered. His British experience—including being chased by a working-class mob in East London, his boxer friend being called a "damned nigger," being scorned by a Cockney beggar in the City of London, and his observation of Irish nationalism at close quarters—pushed him to such an unsentimental view of the socialist and anti-imperialist struggle. And it strengthened his commitment to the socialist cause: the razorbacks ought to be fed, and socialism was the most generous feeder.

It was also in London that McKay became properly acquainted with the socialist classics, including reading and studying the first two volumes of *Das Kapital* at the British Museum. In addition, as we have seen, both the *Workers' Dreadnought* and the ISC expanded his knowledge of revolutionary currents and anti-imperialist struggles around the world.

McKay submitted himself to the membership and discipline of a revolutionary party (Pankhurst's WSF) for the first time while living in London. On his return to the United States, he continued this activism, almost immediately joining the Workers' Party of America (the U.S. affiliate of the Communist International, later becoming the Communist Party) and its de facto Black section, the African Blood Brotherhood (ABB), headquartered in Harlem. He would serve on the executive committee of the ABB.

McKay was so well equipped by his journalistic work on Pankhurst's *Workers' Dreadnought* that, on his return to New York in January 1921, Max and Crystal Eastman, the coeditors of the *Liberator*, America's leading socialist magazine, not only appointed McKay associate editor but made him de facto managing editor.

McKay's positive experience at the ISC led him to attempt to establish an American equivalent in New York, which he called the Liberator Club, affiliated to the *Liberator* magazine. (It never really took off, but not for lack of effort on McKay's part.)

Finally, London was the place where McKay wrote not only his most nostalgic but also his most revolutionary poems, especially in the pages of the *Cambridge Magazine* and *Workers' Dreadnought*. "The Spanish Needle" and "Samson" are merely a couple from either category.[174]

In short, though lasting just over a year, McKay's sojourn in Britain had a huge and transformative impact upon his political and artistic development that can hardly be overstated. The experience was in many ways searing, but it accelerated McKay's maturation as a revolutionary and as an engaged artist, and overdetermined his political trajectory in the subsequent decades. London, in short, played a critical role in the deep, profound, and wide-ranging radicalization of Claude McKay.

8

Making *Spring in New Hampshire*, the 1917 Club, Standing Up, and Thinking of England

I am . . . a social leper, a race outcast from an outcast class.

—Claude McKay, 1921

Meeting C. K. Ogden

Outside of the radical circles around Pankhurst, the Workers' Socialist Federation, and the International Socialist Club, C. K. Ogden was the only member of the British intelligentsia with whom McKay had sustained relations. Born in June 1889, the son of a schoolmaster, Ogden was only four months older than McKay. He claimed that he was "good at everything" as a boy and earned a Classics scholarship to Magdalene College, Cambridge, in 1908. There, in the following year, he became the moving spirit behind and cofounder of the Heretics Society, which aspired to lift the smothering hand of religious orthodoxy from British intellectual and political life. Before graduation, he was recognized as an outstanding intellect and offered the opportunity to edit a journal of his own, *The Cambridge Magazine*, in 1912. A gifted linguist, antiracist, and cosmopolitan in outlook, Ogden carried news from all over the world through the translation and republication of articles from the foreign media. During the Great War, he had the courage to include antiwar writings from German publications. Ogden was vehemently against the war and earned ferocious opposition from British jingoists, who wrecked his offices on Armistice Day. By the time McKay met him in 1920, the *Cambridge Magazine* had been transformed from a weekly to a quarterly journal.

Still underappreciated, Ogden is best remembered as a polymath who made contributions in linguistics, aesthetics, and psychology. He was the first to bring the work of the then-obscure Austrian engineer and mathematician Ludwig Wittgenstein to the English-reading world, translating Wittgenstein's pioneering *Tractatus Logico-Philosophicus* in 1922. With his close friend and collaborator I. A. Richards, he published *Foundations of Aesthetics* (1921) and *The Meaning of Meaning* (1922). He spent most of the remainder of his life developing and advocating the use of "Basic English," an English-language-based alternative to Esperanto; he died in London in 1957.[1]

Though the two men were from very different backgrounds, Ogden's worldview converged with McKay's. Ogden was an agnostic, a supporter of birth control, and an outspoken advocate of women's suffrage, and like McKay, he deplored the futility and dreadful human and material devastation of the war. McKay was lucky to know Ogden, who, as his admirers and protégés all testify, was a talent scout and gifted editor with influential connections.

McKay first made contact with Ogden in February 1920. Their initial meeting was delayed and reticent. Although he arrived in London more than three months earlier with Walter Fuller's letter of introduction to Ogden (dated November 11, 1919), McKay did not write to Ogden until February 18. He informed Ogden that the primary reason behind his going to London was to get a collection of his poetry published there. Frank Harris had suggested, and McKay had accepted, the rather quaint idea that because the young man from Jamaica was "British," he would have a better chance of having his work published in London than in New York.[2] Before writing to Ogden, McKay, on his own initiative, had "tried a couple" of publishers in London but without success, "being unknown."[3] He thus turned to Ogden, sending along Fuller's letter of introduction and, under separate cover, some of his poems. McKay explained that he hesitated in writing to Ogden because he didn't "think it right to bother with business matters persons to whom one is practically a stranger." He informed Ogden that he had a friend in Holland committed to contributing fifty pounds to subsidizing the cost of publication.[4]

McKay need not have worried. Ogden welcomed the contact and quickly and positively responded to his letter and sample of poems. He wanted to know more about McKay and to meet him. Eagerly, McKay told him that he would be happy to meet him "any day that is convenient for you, and any hour."[5] They met in London and liked each other straightaway and soon became very good friends. Ogden offered to get McKay's book of poetry published. "Thanks very much for devoting so much time and being so naturally nice to me," McKay told him. And he put Ogden at ease:

> You mustn't think I mind criticism. I welcome it for it will make me do better work. Of course, I've never had much of it, from being outside literary circles & a writer is so often unconscious of bad things in his work which a critic, by virtue of his expert training, will find in a first reading.[6]

By May 1920, arrangements were well under way for the publication of McKay's book. Moreover, in the summer issue of the *Cambridge Magazine*, Ogden allocated a generous spread of no less than twenty-three beautifully laid out McKay poems. McKay had earlier published some of his revolutionary poems in the *Workers' Dreadnought*, but often under his nom de guerre Hugh Hope and not on this scale. Ogden, then, provided a splendid introduction of McKay to the British reading public, in one of Britain's most prestigious and adventurous journals.[7] By September 1920, Grant Richards had brought out *Spring in New Hampshire and Other Poems*, McKay's first book since *Constab Ballads*, published the year he left Jamaica.[8] Ogden not only helped to choose the poems but edited the volume as a whole, got his friend I. A. Richards to write a preface, and effectively supervised and closely liaised with Grant Richards over the design and production of the book.

McKay was grateful: "I must thank you for all the unselfish interest and trouble you have taken in making the selection and choosing the style of the volume." He now acknowledged apologetically that he was "often impatient and troublesome,"[9] which, based on the evidence of the correspondence, he was. McKay's reference to his own impatience and troublesomeness relates primarily to the delay in getting the book out. He had hoped to have copies from the printers in August to send to Alfred Knopf in New York, who expressed a keen interest in bringing out an American edition simultaneously.[10] In addition, McKay urgently wanted to get away from London. He had had enough of England and had intended to stay no more than six months: "I came [to London] with the definite purpose of having the poems published. Nothing else would have kept me in England so long."[11]

On Making *Spring in New Hampshire*

Despite their friendship, McKay had substantial disagreements with Ogden regarding *Spring in New Hampshire*. The first was over the selection, the

other about the title. Though intellectually adventurous and politically courageous, Ogden had particular difficulty accepting McKay's more revolutionary
poems. He regarded them as "propagandistic" and thought they should be
left out of the *Cambridge Magazine* selection as well as the anthology. Ogden
rejected "The White Fiends," "Pariahs," and McKay's most famous poem, "If
We Must Die," but he wanted to keep "The Black Fiends," a poem that McKay
describes as one that "goes for the black brute." "From purely racial motives,"
McKay informed Ogden, he could not agree to publish "The Black Fiends"
without the others as counterbalance. "You would understand why if you had
lived in America and tasted the poison of race hatred." He did not want his
poetry to be used as a weapon against African Americans, and he was "quite
sure" that the "Bourbon press of the South" would use "The Black Fiends"
in that way, "for the crackers will descend to the lowest depths to defeat the
cause of the blacks—but by including the other . . . poems the coloured press
will have a weapon for counter-attack."[12]

McKay was most disturbed by Ogden's exclusion of his most militant
and famous poem. "Coloured Americans will be disappointed if I should
leave ['If We Must Die'] out as it has been quoted & recited in nearly every
state. It is the best known of my rhymes in the coloured world." McKay
was perhaps too anxious to have his volume out and made a terrible compromise that he deeply regretted. He told Ogden that he would agree to
withdraw all four—"Pariahs," "The Black Fiend," "The White Fiend," and
"If We Must Die"—if *all* of them were not carried; he would not allow one
without the others. He insisted on the inclusion of "Exhortation to Ethiopia," which Ogden had initially rejected but included in the final version,
along with "The Harlem Dancer" and "Harlem Shadows," only at McKay's
insistence. Ogden, however, had his way in keeping out "A Prayer" and
"Soul and Body," though one was Max Eastman's favorite and the other
Frank Harris's, as McKay told Ogden. "When I Have Passed Away" was
also excluded. Ogden wanted to include some of McKay's Jamaican creole-
language poems, but McKay would have none of it. His main objection
was: "Some crabbed critic might begin by telling me to stick to it [Jamai-
can creole] for I can't write naturally in English in spite of my being able
to do so."[13]

"I don't like 'Spring in New Hampshire and Other Poems,'" he told
Ogden, objecting to the title. "The complementary title I never like on any
book. I much prefer a terse simple thing covering the collection or your first
suggestion, 'Poems' or 'Verses.' Or if it must be the title of one of the poems,
wouldn't 'Dawn in New York' do?"[14] The original manuscript of poems that

McKay had typed up in London bore the name "Songs of Struggle." But as Ezerman, McKay's Dutch friend who subsidized the publication, noticed when he saw the *Cambridge Magazine* selection, McKay's more revolutionary verses—what Ezerman called "the Labour and Russian" poems—were absent. Ezerman could also have mentioned the absence of the more militant race ones, too. "Did you yourself choose these or was it the Editor?" he inquired.[15] McKay allowed Ogden to have his way here again. The collection published was not called "Songs of Struggle," or "Poems," or "Verses," or "Dawn in New York." It was entitled *Spring in New Hampshire and Other Poems*. It is just as well that it was not called *Songs of Struggle* since only one of the thirty-one poems in the collection—the magnificent "Exhortation"—was written in this vein. And, as we saw, he had to fight with Ogden to get even that one included.

Though it does contain some fine McKay lyrics, including some of his best pastoral and nostalgic verses, *Spring in New Hampshire and Other Poems* is a tarnished book, unrepresentative of McKay's poetry at the time. In the end, it is far more Ogden's selection than McKay's. How and why did McKay allow this to happen? The answer seems quite straightforward, at least from the rich correspondence with Ogden: he was anxious to leave London, and he wanted to leave with a published book. But, in the end, he left with a book that was not truly his own. This was most uncharacteristic of McKay. It was the gravest political and artistic compromise he ever made, and he would make sure never to do it again.

When McKay dropped in on Frank Harris in New York, soon after his return from London in January 1921, he handed a copy of the book to Harris. Harris went down the contents list, McKay recalls, "his aggressive brow becom[ing] heavier and heavier and scowling."

Suddenly he roared: "Where is the poem?"

"Which one?" I asked with a bland countenance, as if I didn't know which he meant.

"You know which," he growled. "The fighting poem, 'If We Must Die.' Why isn't it printed here?"

I was ashamed. My face was scorched with fire. I stammered: "I was advised to keep it out."

"You are a bloody traitor to your race, sir!" Frank Harris shouted. "A damned traitor to your own integrity. That's what the English and civilization have done to your people. Emasculated them. Deprived them of their guts. Better you were a head-hunting, blood-drinking cannibal of the jungle than a civilized coward. You were bolder in America. The English make obscene sycophants of their subject peoples. I am Irish and I know. But we Irish have guts the English cannot rip out of us. I'm ashamed of you, sir. It's a good thing you got out of England. It's no place for a genius to live."[16]

Frank Harris's words, he said, "cut like a whip into my hide." McKay was glad to leave Harris's office, but felt relieved after the "castigation." Writing in 1937, he confessed, "The excision of the poem had been like a nerve cut out of me, leaving a wound which would not heal. And it hurt more every time I saw the damned book of verse." McKay resolved to get what was in effect a new collection, one more faithfully reflecting both his poetry and his wishes, published as soon as possible in the United States.[17]

In the spring of 1922, *Harlem Shadows: The Poems of Claude McKay* appeared to critical acclaim.[18] It was not an American edition of *Spring in New Hampshire*; it was a different book altogether. With seventy-four verses, *Harlem Shadows* had more than twice as many poems as the London book. McKay's militant socialist and Black lyrics, including what Hubert Harrison called his "manly, stirring poem," were given their rightful place, to the delight of Black and white socialists as well as the Garveyites—a unique achievement.[19] McKay's songs of struggle were finally sung, thanks to *Harlem Shadows*.

McKay seldom spoke of *Spring in New Hampshire* and remained for the rest of his life rather ashamed of the book. He was grateful to Ogden for getting it published, but over time he seems to have grown more resentful of what Ogden did and what he allowed Ogden to do with his first post-Jamaica collection. Ogden gets only two sentences in *A Long Way from Home*: "C. K. Ogden, the author of *Basic English* and *The Foundation of Esthetics*, besides steering me round the picture galleries and being otherwise kind, had published a set of my verses in his *Cambridge Magazine*. Later he got me a publisher."[20] Despite his insufferable arrogance, Ogden deserved much more than that from McKay. Though he perhaps enjoyed McKay's company as much as McKay did his, Ogden was, indeed, very kind to McKay. They frequently met in London, chatted, and indeed often visited the galleries together, especially the rich hoardings of the British Museum. He referred McKay, an extraordinarily curious man, to books on art, which McKay read and was never afraid to pass judgment on. McKay, in turn, put Ogden onto books about Africa. The two men wrote each other at least once a week for more than a year on subjects ranging from Benin bronze statues to the cost of printing.

In contrast to the rather perfunctory public acknowledgment of Ogden, privately McKay, from his very first meeting with him, praised and thanked Ogden effusively. In his first letter to Ogden on his return to New York, he thanked him again. "I feel that if I gained nothing by my first visit [to England] but meeting you, that was enough." He went on to especially thank Ogden for the close reading of his poetry: "When I think of the poor stuff that I should have piled into an American edition." In the United States, he told him,

> I had had critics but none that told me why, how, where this or that was wrong & showed me my real forte. Without dogmatism or any direct method you have shown me the key in which I should do by my best work. It has been a great experience for I now feel that I have a sound standard for artistic endeavour.[21]

He sought Ogden's advice on the design of the cover for his next book of poetry, *Harlem Shadows*, and promised to send the proofs to get his suggestions. As in London, the men discussed art and literature, and they sent books across the Atlantic to each other. Once McKay became an editor at the *Liberator* in April 1921, he repeatedly begged Ogden to contribute to the journal, but without success.[22]

The 1917 Club

After his offices in Cambridge were ransacked on Armistice Day, Ogden began spending more and more time in London. To the puzzlement of his friends, Ogden quickly acquired six houses in London, including two in Bloomsbury and one in Soho, but his primary redoubt in London, where he could often be seen at lunchtime, was the 1917 Club. It was there that he frequently met McKay. Despite his early syndicalist leanings, Ogden apparently never visited the International Socialist Club, with or without McKay.[23] He might have viewed the exhibition of Russian posters and photographs that McKay recommended to him, but there is no evidence that he did. McKay did not mind. When they first made contact by letter, McKay had extended an invitation to Ogden that was not an invitation at all, to meet at the ISC: "It . . . is quite a sordid place & there are no conveniences for private talk. But if you don't object, . . . [it] would do for me."[24] Thus, they ended up at the 1917 Club and never used the ISC as a meeting place.

Located in Gerrard Street in the heart of Soho, the 1917 Club was founded by Leonard Woolf and friends in December 1917. In contrast to the stuffy Athenaeum—the "nadir of respectability," Woolf called it—the 1917 Club was the "zenith of disreputability." Its Soho location set the tone. It was no Limehouse, but at the time Soho was still a relatively rough part of the city; Woolf recalled that Gerrard Street in those days was "the rather melancholy haunt of prostitutes daily from 2:30 p.m. onwards."[25] He described the membership of the club as a "curious mixture":

> It was mainly political and the politicals were mainly Labour Party, from Ramsay [MacDonald, who later became Labour's first Prime Minister] downwards. But there was also an element of unadulterated culture, particularly at tea time, so that if one dropped in about 4 o'clock and looked round its rooms, one would hardly have guessed that it was political. Virginia [Woolf] was often there and there was a strong contingent of Stracheys, including Lytton and a retinue of young women and young men often accompanied him.[26]

In short, the 1917 Club was the primary watering hole and haunt of the Fabians and the Bloomsbury Set.

Except in his correspondence with Ogden at the time they met there, McKay never mentioned the 1917 Club, not even in *A Long Way from Home*. He never felt particularly comfortable there. Woolf, a member of the enlightened bourgeoisie, might have regarded the place as the "zenith of disreputability," but to McKay the 1917 Club was hardly different from the Athenaeum: it was posh—"nice society," he called it—very different materially and socially from the ISC. With the help of Ogden, however, he did manage to get a little exhibition mounted there of the work of his anarchist-artist friend Henry Bernard.[27] He also ran into one of the daughters of former governor of Jamaica, Sir Sydney Olivier, at the 1917 Club. He liked her, and she tried to help with his getting a permit to the British Museum Reading Room. It was while he was having a conversation with her that McKay got involved in an unpleasant incident at the 1917. By his own account, the only one available, McKay was "merely telling Miss Olivier that [his] holding an I.W.W. card might prevent [his] getting back into the States" when a member butted into the conversation, jostled McKay, and "knocked [him] clean off [his] balance." McKay, not one to take such slights lightly, apparently retaliated either physically, verbally, or both. "I am really sorry if I caused you any embarrassment," he wrote Ogden.

"I could understand anyone intruding at the [International] Socialist Club—but at the 1917!—it quite beats me." The culprit, according to Ogden, was curiously an " 'extreme left' fellow." Ogden was relaxed about the whole matter, and McKay felt relieved because he thought the incident was "rather embarrassing for you [Ogden] & Miss Olivier." For himself, he did not care. "For I am always coming up against his type and worse—in America & also here, so I'm used to it. My colour alone makes me so conspicuous; I must reconcile myself to such things."[28]

Ogden was excessively secretive. He also tended to organize his friends in discrete units, either as groups or as individuals. Thus, one group of his friends may not have been aware of another equally friendly to him, and if they did know of the others' existence, they did not meet.[29] McKay, therefore, never entered Ogden's wider circle of friends. It comes as no surprise that I. A. Richards, probably Ogden's closest friend and certainly his closest collaborator, never met McKay, despite writing the preface to *Spring in New Hampshire*.[30] In July 1920, some six months after having met Ogden, McKay did meet the artist James Wood, another of Ogden's collaborators and close friends, who worked on the *Cambridge Magazine*. "I rather liked Mr. Wood," McKay wrote Ogden. "We went for a walk after you left and he said some very interesting things to me. He is really remarkable." Wood was based in Cambridge and seemed to have met McKay primarily because Ogden had involved him in the production of *Spring in New Hampshire*.[31] Apparently, McKay never met Wood again. Despite his limited contact, through Ogden and the 1917 Club McKay did get a glance at Britain's modernist intelligentsia after the First World War. And through his extraordinarily acute powers of observation, McKay made the most of this in trying to make sense of the British and his experience in London.

A Strangely Unsympathetic People

McKay described his time in London as "that most miserable of years."[32] An "ordeal," he called it. Even the "suffocating" fog of London—which "not only wrapped you around but entered your throat like a strangling nightmare"— seemed to McKay more welcoming than the Londoners themselves: "The feeling of London was so harshly unfriendly to me that sometimes I was happy in the embrace of the unfolding fog." "Oh blessed was the fog that veiled me blind!" he rejoiced in a poem on the city. To him, the English as a whole were "a strangely unsympathetic people, as coldly chilling as their English fog."[33]

McKay's disappointment with England stems not only from his experience but also from his expectations. Just as the stark reality of United States' racism shocked him despite having prior information about the situation there, so was he taken aback by British racism despite an abstract knowledge of its existence before going to London. In the end, he felt more misled and cheated—conned, even—than disappointed. Now he felt angry about his teacher in Jamaica (not U. Theo) marching him and his schoolmates around singing "Rule Britannia" in the breathless celebration of Queen Victoria's Diamond Jubilee in the Clarendon hills in 1897.[34] He felt angry because the colonial Jamaican notion that England was the "mother country" was so very far away from the facts on the ground as a Black Jamaican in London, where he had to dodge Cockney mobs as well as street urchins who saw him as nothing more than a nigger, at best a darkey, paradigmatically foreign, not British at all. "They called me 'Nigger,'" Una Marson wrote in 1933,

> Those little white urchins,
> They laughed and shouted
> As I passed along the street,
> They flung it at me:
> 'Nigger! Nigger! Nigger!'
>
> What made me keep my fingers
> From choking the words in their throats?[35]

McKay suffered the same torment and must have contemplated a similar response. Like Marson, a fellow Jamaican, he had trouble with them on the streets of London, as we have seen. But they were badly behaved even around their teachers in school. In December 1920, McKay visited a school in Islington at which a female friend from the International Socialist Club taught. "The children were horrible—terribly bad manners!" he told Ogden.[36] He almost certainly was called "nigger" by the little darlings.

McKay was also angered by the extraordinarily unequal knowledge between colonized and colonizers about each other. He was astonished, like so many others after him, at the crass ignorance of the British public about "their" empire. He, in marked contrast, had been drilled in British history from his childhood and, like any true Brit, took pride in the size and extent of the pink bits on the school map depicting the British Empire, on which the sun never set. In his 1933 novel, *Banana Bottom*, McKay depicted the ignorance even among reasonably "educated" persons in Britain. Bita, its Black Jamaican heroine, is at a posh English boarding school, sent there by English missionaries in Jamaica. Her schoolmates "asked her many curious questions about her native land."

> In what part of the Congo it [Jamaica] was situated. Were the cannibals very ferocious? And would they eat white flesh too or was their appetite restricted to dark? And when Bita said her home was in the West Indies, they said, Oh yes it was India and not Africa and was it North or South India and how did she feel the first time she changed from a fig leaf or straw apron and put on manufactured clothes to go abroad.[37]

At least until very recently, the British were asking which part of Jamaica was Trinidad, and they made no distinction between Guyana and Ghana. Yet the British working class were generally proud of "their" empire. "It came to me as a stupendous shock," wrote Barbadian novelist George Lamming, "that English workers could also see themselves as architects of Empire." "Do you belong to us or the French?" they asked him.[38]

Given the uncongenial, unsympathetic, and even hostile environment that London was for McKay, it is not surprising that it was there that he wrote his most powerful poetry of nostalgia about Jamaica. "The Spanish Needle," "Flame-Heart," "The Easter Flower," "December 1919," "My Mother," "Home Thoughts," "Reminiscences," "I Shall Return," an entirely new version of "Sukee River," and even "The Tropics in New York" were all written in London. These sorrow songs issued not only from the necessary distance, perspective, and loss that exile brings, but also from a new discovery of his un-Britishness and simultaneously a more thoroughly Jamaican, Caribbean, and Black identity; these poems were the fruits of a reverie of reminiscences triggered by a yearning for consolation and refuge from a harsh reality.

It is interesting to note that not only were these poems written in London, but they were *not* written in New York. It was not just the hostility of the British environment that stimulated them, for even McKay admitted that the United States was generally more uncongenial, if less hypocritical, than Britain. It was not just the loneliness of his life in London, because he was even lonelier in his early years in the United States. What distinguished his American from his British experience was the visceral and tangible shock of discovering that the "mother country" was not the mother country at all—that instead of being treated as a Black Briton coming home, he was scorned as a pariah, a nigger. McKay's shock and disillusionment stemmed from the conceptual contradiction and social clash of two logics of British imperialism, what I have elsewhere called the "logic of the empire" and the "logic of the metropole." The former declared colonial subjects as British while at home in the colonies, whereas the latter deprived them of such attributes once they arrived in Britain itself: McKay was British in Jamaica, but he was simply a nigger in Britain—quintessentially non-British and an outcast, "a social leper," as he puts it, in London. McKay, like other Black "subjects," belonged *to* the mother country but not *in* the mother country.[39]

It was this melancholic epiphany that sent him on such a long and intense journey down the road of nostalgia, contemplation, and self-discovery during his London interlude. Reflecting upon his time in London, McKay half-jokingly wrote, "London was not wholly Hell, for it was possible for me to compose poetry some of the time. No place can be altogether a God-forsaken Sahara or swamp in which a man is able to discipline and compose his emotions into self-expression."[40] That may be true as far as it goes. But why would he repeatedly take refuge in an idealized Jamaican past if London was not a "God-forsaken Sahara or swamp"? Why the emotional retreat? Why did he write not even one poem about London or Britain during his stay? McKay visited Westminster Abbey, but he no longer sang about it as he did (without seeing it) as a young man in "Old England."[41] Now, he told the readers of the *Negro World*, he felt that the place was the modern bastille of mankind's soul and that the workers of the world "would never know real freedom until they cease reverencing and worshipping" in it and put it to "practical, proletarian use instead."[42]

> Lovely dainty Spanish needle
> With your yellow flower and white,
> Dew bedecked and softly sleeping,
> Do you think of me to-night?
>
> Shadowed by the spreading mango,
> Nodding o'er the rippling stream,
> Tell me, dear plant of my childhood,
> Do you of the exile dream?[43]

Remarkably, "Spanish Needle" is the McKay poem—not "If We Must Die," "Enslaved," nor any of his Jamaican creole poems—that is best known in Jamaica. It has long been taught in its schools, and I have been always amazed at how many Jamaicans know this poem by heart and delight in reciting it. Yet no Jamaican on the island gives a thought to the Spanish needle; it is dainty, yes, but not that remarkable a plant or flower. (I freely confess not to have paid any attention to the flower during my Jamaican childhood. I only considered it after reading McKay.) It is the exile who sings of the Spanish needle, and McKay's is an exile's song that can never be fully appreciated by the untraveled Jamaican; it is taught to and recited by generations of Jamaicans who can never fully comprehend its ineffable pain of exile. Just as George Lamming's *In the Castle of My Skin* or V. S. Naipaul's *Miguel Street* or *A House for Mr Biswas*, despite Naipaul's ambivalence, could not have been written in the Caribbean, so too "The Spanish Needle" could not have been written in Jamaica. They are all, quintessentially, songs of exile, loss, longing, and remembrance.[44]

McKay felt a terrible sense of vulnerability—"helpless and wobbly," he said—when he could not find lodgings in London. London's "black boycott" was more effective and detrimental than that in America, for the United States had its Black Belts, "ghettoes," its "Negro pale," where one could "take refuge from prejudice."[45] As he repeatedly told Ogden in 1920, McKay dreaded the idea of being stranded in London. "I had to realize," he wrote in *A Long Way from Home*,

> that London is a cold white city where English culture is great and formidable like an iceberg. It is a city created for English needs, and admirable, no doubt, for the English people. It was not built to accommodate Negroes. I was very happy when I could get out of it to go back to the Negro pale of America.[46]

McKay was deeply disappointed by the British intelligentsia. Even his hero, George Bernard Shaw, suggested that it might be better for him to be a pugilist than a poet. The conversation between the two men has often been simplified by commentators, but McKay was taken aback and displeased by Shaw's suggestion. Only once, however, did McKay come close to explicitly saying so. And Shaw kept his place on the McKay pedestal. His conversation with Shaw, which he described as "the unforgettable joy of meeting with the most brilliant and energetic mind in the British Isles," remained the highlight of his London sojourn. In *A Long Way from Home*, he went so far as to declare: "Had I been a black Diogenes exploring the white world with my African lamp, I could have proclaimed: I saw Bernard Shaw!"[47]

Shaw might have got off relatively lightly, but the case of H. G. Wells was rather different. Despite the "beastly modern white savagery" of the Great War, Wells had the nerve, McKay observed, to wonder "whether the Negro is capable of becoming a civilized citizen of a world republic."[48] The depth to which racism saturated the British social fabric across all political persuasions (Wells saw himself and was seen as a "socialist") is perhaps best illustrated by the case of J. T. Walton Newbold, the country's first Communist MP. On winning his seat in the 1922 general election, he immediately dispatched a telegram to Zinoviev, president of the Communist International (Comintern): "Zinoviev Kremlin Moscow Russia have won Motherwell in Scotland for Communism Newbold." The sensational news came fortuitously during the Fourth Congress of the Comintern in Moscow. "We have a man in the British Parliament!" cried ecstatic delegates in the throne room of the Kremlin on hearing the news.[49] Soon thereafter, the conquering hero of Motherwell turned up at the congress. An elated Chinese delegate, pleased to meet and congratulate the British comrade on his historic victory, greeted him, "Comrade Newbold—." "Hello Chink," Comrade Newbold cut in. A member of the Chinese Young Communists, the young man was from a prominent family and had been educated in the United States. He fully understood Newbold's racist insult. "But Comrade Newbold, I am not a Chink." "Who said you weren't?" said Comrade Newbold as he strode away. McKay, who also attended the congress, heard the story, which "flashed like an arrow" around the halls of the Kremlin. To their eternal credit, the leading Bolsheviks gave Comrade Newbold a good going-over.[50] Less than two years later, Newbold wrote to the CPGB leadership: "I am, perhaps, too English in outlook and in thought too grounded in insularity and tradition to be a good Communist. Therefore, I am saying, farewell."[51]

British Reaction and *Spring in New Hampshire*

McKay's view of the British was not helped by the response, as well as the lack of response, to *Spring in New Hampshire* by London's literary establishment. The book was published at the beginning of October. He was disturbed at first by the silence, but the volume was soon met by a "rather starchy & grudging" review in the *Spectator*, about which McKay would have a lot to say.[52] In late November, he wrote: "I wish the *Times [Literary] Supplement* or *Athenaeum* would give me a review. It would help immensely in America." By early December, he discerned a pattern: "I notice that both [*sic*] the

Athenaeum, the *Times Supplement* & the [British] *Nation* give much space to all kinds of American poetry but ignore me altogether!" He reported that he did, however, see "a good notice" in the *Westminster Gazette*.[53] The following week, the *Athenaeum* did publish a review; in a letter written on Christmas Day, McKay informed Ogden that the review was very much like that in the *Spectator*, "a grudging little thing sandwiched between other notes on 'poetry overseas.'"[54] The *Yorkshire Post* and the *Daily Chronicle* took notice of the book, and the *Glasgow Herald* carried a short but laudatory review of it. Though he eventually got a review in the *Sunday Times*, the *Times Literary Supplement* (despite the fact that Grant Richards advertised the volume in its pages) and the *Nation* ignored the book.

The *Westminster Gazette*'s was much more than a good notice. It was by far the most extensive and laudatory review published in Britain—so much so that Ogden reproduced it in full in the *Cambridge Magazine* and gave it his explicit endorsement: "With every word of this we desire to associate ourselves." McKay, the *Gazette* noted, had "evidently" read widely in English poetry and had made use of good models for his form.

> But unlike the majority of our own versifiers he never borrows from the classics both form and content. He has far too much of his own to express. In him a whole race—unknown, mysterious—become at last articulate, and for this reason his work is at once a revelation and an indictment. The gentleness and generosity, the childlike delight in nature, the deep capacity for affection which are displayed throughout the volume lend an added poignancy to such poems as ["The Lynching" and "In Bondage," quoted in full], and, again, to this last verse of the last poem in the book ["Exhortation" quoted]. . . . [T]he whole volume reflects an original and charming personality, with which we are happy to have made acquaintance.[55]

McKay did not comment on it, but he would also have seen the short review in the *Glasgow Herald*, which shrewdly noted that what was new about his poetry was the thought, concluding:

> though this book gives but a hint, it holds before us the possibility of the coming of a negro poet who might make the grim pictures of the Divine Comedy seem pallid beside the realities of negro story. But for the hint he does give us we owe a spirit debt to Mr. McKay. His "Lynching" sonnet is to be remembered for its pitifully restrained indictment. . . . The sincerity of the book, alike in its racial songs of sorrow and its passionate love lyrics, gives it distinction.[56]

But these were not the reviews that drew McKay's attention; that in the *Athenaeum* and especially the one in the *Spectator* served as catalysts for one of his meditations on Britain.[57] McKay brought special notice to them, too, by assigning a chapter to the subject—aptly titled "Regarding Reactionary Criticism"—in *A Long Way from Home*. It is the shortest chapter in the book, but one of the most combative and angriest.

"If it is difficult to ascertain," McKay suggested, "the real attitude of the common people of any country regarding certain ideas and things, it should be easy enough to find out that of the élite by writing a book. The reviews will reveal more or less the mind of the better classes." He noticed a flippant note in most of the reviews of his book at the idea of "a Negro writing poetry." And after reading them, he said, he could understand better why Shaw had suggested pugilism over poetry. He then turned to the review in the *Spectator*, which he accurately described as "the organ of the Tory intellectuals." He has no doubt that the *Spectator* "represents the opinion of that English group, which, because of its wealth and power, its facilities for and standards of high education, and its domination of most of the universe, either directly or indirectly, is the most superior in the world."[58] The *Spectator* critic wrote:

> *Spring in New Hampshire* is extrinsically as well as intrinsically interesting. It is . . . written by a man who is a full-blooded negro. . . . Perhaps the ordinary reader's first impulse in realizing that the book is by an American negro is to inquire into its good taste. Not until we are satisfied that his work does not overstep the barriers which a not quite explicable but deep instinct in us is ever alive to maintain can we judge it with genuine fairness. Mr. Claude McKay never offends our sensibilities. His love poetry is clear of the hint which would put our racial instinct against him whether we would or no.[59]

Ogden was outraged. He waited four months after publication to see if the reviews would come in from the more established literary journals. But "only one [the *Westminster Gazette*] of the score or more of journals on which the modern public relies for literary information, has done more than briefly indicate that a 'nigger minstrel' or an 'overseas poet' has issued some verses." He recalled how McKay's set of verses first came to him after the poet had encountered difficulty getting a publisher because he did not have a "name." Yet, after receiving McKay's manuscript, it was "obvious" to him that "here was no ordinary set of verses." Given the prevailing cultural and political environment, McKay's color alone ought to have generated interest in his poetry. "From an academic point of view," Ogden noted,

> the emergence of a remarkable personality, the first of his race to express himself in such a medium, might alone have secured attention. Are we not ethnologists? Do we not send expeditions to strange parts to hunt for the dusky, bosky art-products of Hoo-doo and Voo-doo? . . . Yet here was the mountain come to Mahomet, a Daniel come to the lion's den for judgment.

He was quick to point out that these were not the considerations that had led to his accepting McKay's poems. "We took them," he explained, "because, with the exception of Siegfried Sassoon's 'Base Details' we had seen nothing of equal literary interest from a young man since Rupert Brooke sent us his essay on Tchekov." The deafening silence from the literary establishment therefore astonished as well as disappointed—and the silence was broken only by those who thought of McKay in terms of nigger minstrels and overseas poets. Ogden felt a need to apologize to McKay for the bad behavior of his English colleagues: "We hope that when Mr. McKay returns to this country the vanward cloud of evil days with which racial animosities threaten the world may have been dissipated by those rays of enlightenment and goodwill which are so hardly glimpsable to-day."[60]

To McKay, the *Spectator* only reconfirmed his contention that the British were obsessed with the sexuality of Black people, as revealed by the "Horror on the Rhine" campaign. "So there it bobbed up again," he wrote after quoting the passage. Just as it was there among the elite of the "class-conscious working class," so it was among the "aristocracy of the upper class": "the bugaboo of sex—the African's sex, whether he is a poet or pugilist." McKay could not understand why the love poetry of a Black man should be offensive to a "civilized" white man. "Now it seems to me that if the white man is really more civilized than the colored (be the color black, brown or yellow), then the white man should take Negro poetry and pugilism in his stride, just as he takes Negro labor in Africa and fattens on it." He pointed out that had the critic of the organ of the British aristocracy (the *Spectator*) used

> his facilities for education and knowledge and tolerance . . . to familiarize himself with the history and derivations of poetry he might have concluded that the love poetry of a Negro might be in better taste than the gory poetry of a civilized British barbarian like Rudyard Kipling.

McKay then informed his ignorant critic of the sixth-century warrior poet Antara ibn Shaddad, known in the West as Antar, "one of the greatest, if not the greatest, poets of love." McKay suggested, and modern scholarship has affirmed, that "European or white man's love poetry today probably owes much of its inspiration to Antar, who was the son of a Negro woman and an Arabian chieftain."[61]McKay probably did not know about Antar until he went to live in Morocco at the end of the 1920s. But he was astonished to discover that even the illiterate Moors were acquainted with the history and poetry of Antar. There, in the cafes of Tangiers, no one was taken aback when it was revealed that McKay was a poet. That knowledge provoked no *Spectator*-like instinct of revulsion in Morocco. On the contrary, he was applauded and flattered: "A poet! *Mezziane! Mezziane!* Our greatest poet, Antar, was a Negro."[62]

McKay could not help but contrast his Russian experience with that of Britain. One of the many things that delighted him when he visited Russia the year after leaving London was that no one in Moscow or Petrograd was taken aback on discovering that he was a Black man who wrote poetry. Reporting on his visit in the *Crisis*, McKay from his personal experience rated Soviet Russia well above Britain. When Shaw told him that it must be tragic for a sensitive Negro to be a poet, he was right, declared McKay. Some of the English reviewers of *Spring in New Hampshire*, he said, "touched the very bottom of journalistic muck." With the exception of those in the U.S. South, the English reviewer outdid his American cousin in "sprinkling criticism with racial prejudice." And in an implied rebuke of Shaw, who, though Irish, is obviously caught in the general condemnation, McKay wrote:

> The English people from the lowest to the highest, cannot think of a black man as being anything but an entertainer, boxer, a Baptist preacher or a menial. . . . Any healthy-looking black coon of an adventurous streak can have a wonderful time palming himself off as another Siki [a black boxing champion] or a buck dancer.

The Germans, he said, are only a little worse than the British. When an American writer introduced McKay as a poet to "a very cultured German, a lover of all the arts," the man simply could not believe it, "and I don't think he does yet," McKay added.[63]

But in Petrograd and Moscow, things could hardly have been more different. McKay could not detect "a trace" of such ignorant snobbishness among the educated classes, and in marked contrast to the Cockney thugs at Old Street tube station, "the attitude of the common workers, the soldiers and sailors was still more remarkable. It was so beautifully naive; for them I was just a black member of the world of humanity." McKay moved in various artistic circles in both Moscow and Petrograd. Some were Bolsheviks, some were anarchists, and others were sullenly anti-Bolshevik, bourgeois and aristocratic, licking the wounds of an historic defeat. But in none of these groups did he ever encounter any racism; no one rudely butted in on any of his conversations, let alone knock him clean off his balance as that nice chap did at the 1917 Club. They invited him to speak and read his poems. And despite their sophistication—many of them spoke two to four other European languages—among them McKay found

> no vulgar wonderment and bounderish superiority over a Negro's being a poet. I was a poet, that was all, and their keen questions showed that they were much more interested in the technique of my poetry, my views on and my position regarding the modern literary movements than in the difference of my color.[64]

Clearly, that English racist rejection hurt McKay deeply—to some, maybe McKay, the rejection of the mother country perhaps hurts as much as a mother's rejection. And rather than heal, it festered over time. Yet despite his professed hatred of the English, McKay engaged in working-class revolutionary activity in Britain. On the surface it appears to be a contradiction, but as the previous chapter made clear, it was not. It was this same logic that led McKay to support the international workers' movement and revolutionary socialism. He did not mind being pitied by white workers who were conscious of the fact that he was a "social leper, of a race outcast from an outcast class." He could see no other way "of upward struggle for colored peoples, but the way of the working-class movement, ugly and harsh though some of its phases may be."[65] He would later—in the 1930s, especially—have second thoughts, but by the early 1920s that was his conviction.

The Crisis of the British Left and McKay's Departure

In the latter part of 1920, the British Communist movement went into a deep crisis. Pankhurst's *Dreadnought* group was ostracized by the newly formed Communist Party of Great Britain (CPGB) which emerged out of the

Communist Unity Convention in August 1920. The CPGB received Lenin's blessings, while Pankhurst and the WSF were dismissed as ultra-leftists because of their continued refusal to participate in parliamentary politics and affiliate with the Labour Party. The *Dreadnought* group imploded with factionalism and mutual recrimination; many, including Edgar Whitehead, the general secretary of the Pankhurst-led Communist Party (British Section of the Third International, or BSTI), broke with Pankhurst, accepted the edict of the Comintern, and joined the CPGB. Whitehead, according to McKay, led a faction that wanted to put Pankhurst on trial![66] Despite his abiding admiration of Pankhurst, McKay also expressed grave misgivings about her leadership qualities, which he later made public in his 1937 memoir. In October 1920, in a letter marked "Private," McKay wrote to William Gallacher, chair of the Clyde Workers' Committee and an ally of the CP (BSTI), urging him to take up the leadership of the far-left forces instead of Pankhurst. "You seem so high above petty actions and deceit that you ought to be the man to weld the little warring forces together who are now wasting their energy fighting among themselves." Frustrated with Pankhurst, McKay expressed his criticism of her in even harsher terms than later expressed in *A Long Way from Home*:

> I am working quite close to Sylvia & the more I see of her & study her manner & gauge her intellect, the more I recognise how hopeless & what madness it is for her to aspire to be a leader. She is no doubt a sharp, clever woman, quick at grasping & sizing up current events. But I don't think she has any vision into the future nor has she the breadth & depth necessary in a great leader that gather followers round him & make them obey, trust & respect him. If Sylvia tries to be imperious she is funny, if she tries to be greatly sympathetic she is a failure. Her work is to be an editor and agitator & no more. The comprehensive mind necessary for high constructive work is lacking in her. But there is no doubt that she is splendid at "gingering" up people. I don't think she has an equal in that.[67]

Pankhurst was later boycotted and reviled by the CPGB when she refused to hand over the *Dreadnought* and its press to the new party—even though there is strong evidence that the paper was heavily subsidized by the Bolsheviks (sponsors of the CPGB), who also financed (partly if not wholly) the Agenda Press, publishers of the *Dreadnought*, from the end of January 1920.[68] It was, she insisted, her paper and her press, and she wanted them both to remain independent of the Party; she privately scoffed at "an absurd plot to seize the printing plant of my paper."[69] The party expelled Pankhurst in September 1921; the *Dreadnought* limped on and died less than three years later, in June 1924.[70]

By the end of 1920, the atmosphere in the Pankhurst group became toxic. Pankhurst had been arrested earlier, and Comrade Vie's arrest as a Bolshevik agent took many in the group by surprise, triggering "a lot of rubberneck gossip." Some even "asserted" that Vie had been "deliberately betrayed," a claim unsupported by evidence. Members accused other members of being "spies and traitors." Pankhurst's reluctance to join a united far left to form the CPGB had triggered Whitehead's desire to put her on trial. The group became so frenzied with paranoia that McKay himself had to give an accounting of his activities to his comrades. One evening, the secretary at the ISC showed McKay an anonymous letter accusing him, McKay, of being a spy. "I felt sick and was seized with a crazy craving to get quickly out of that atmosphere and far away from London," he recalled.[71] It was probably around this time that a mock hanging of McKay by some of the *Dreadnought* people apparently took place—an astonishing thing, if true.[72] For his part, McKay had also had enough of them. "I may be going away for a short while if I can," he wrote Ogden on October 28. "I am cutting myself loose from the *Dreadnought* people altogether. They are all so incompetent & under the circumstances there is nothing to be gained by keeping in with them but unsavoury notoriety."[73] McKay told Douglas Springhall, his young lionhearted friend and protégé, that it was "a pity the organization [WSF] was too small for him [Springhall]." But the wider context of these disquieting developments on the British left need to be acknowledged. McKay never mentioned the larger, unfolding processes that affected the latter part of his stay in Britain. But they are there explicitly and not so explicitly in some of his poetry. In "Re-Affirmation," published in July 1920, McKay was clearly cognizant of the revolutionary reversals in the West, especially Germany, and the challenges the new developments presented. He put a brave face on it, but morale was clearly affected. "I am downhearted not," he declared, "although it seems / The new birth is abortive in the West, / And men are turning from long-cherished dreams / Of world-wide freedom to ignoble rest." He tried to keep his own spirits up even though the foe "like boars disporting in the mud… Wallow obscenely in the workers' blood." After all, he tells himself and his fellow comrades:

The babe bursts from the mother's womb in pain
The night is darkest just before the dawn,

The heavens turn black to bless the earth with rain,
I am disheartened not, I will keep on.[74]

Finally, on January 5, 1921—the same day that Pankhurst lost her appeal against a six-months prison sentence—McKay sailed from Southampton on the SS *Adriatic* for New York. He was back in New York ten days later.[75]

McKay summarized his thoughts on Britain sixteen years after leaving London:

> I had looked upon the face of the British nation, fulfilling my boyish wish, complementing my education. And I was satisfied that England was a wonderful and perfect place for the English, but no place at all for colored persons, especially black. I left it feeling that I would never want to live there again, nor in any British territory, and I was happily excited to return again to the land of Segregation and Black Lynching. There the life of the spirit at least was more robust against the hot-brute hatred of America than the sepulchral-cold hostility of the English.[76]

Such harsh sentiments, however, were not entirely congruent with those McKay expressed soon after arriving back in New York. True, he was "happy to see New York again," after an "uncomfortable voyage." He wrote Ogden two weeks after his arrival: "the sun shines, the sky is invariably a brilliant blue & the air is splendid. Although it is much colder than London there is something exhilarating in the atmosphere."[77] And in what must be one of the finest passages ever written about the city—at once a praise song and a cautionary tale—he recalled in his 1937 memoir his feelings as he entered New York harbor on that winter morning in 1921:

> Like fixed massed sentinels guarding the approaches to the great metropolis, again the pyramids of New York in their Egyptian majesty dazzled my sight like a miracle of might and took my breath like the banging music of Wagner assaulting one's spirit and rushing it skyward with the pride and power of an eagle.
>
> The feeling of the dirty steerage passage across the Atlantic was swept away in the immense wonder of clean, vertical heaven-challenging lines, a glory to the grandeur of space.
>
> Oh, that I wished that it were possible to know New York in that way only—as a masterpiece wrought for the illumination of the sight, a splendor lifting aloft and shedding its radiance like a searchlight, making one big and

great with feeling. Oh, that I should never draw nearer to descend into its precipitous gorges, where visions are broken and shattered and one becomes one of a million, average, ordinary, insignificant.[78]

But McKay soon contemplated leaving again. Indeed, within weeks of returning, he hinted at going back to England—on "special business"—and asked Ogden for permission to use his name as reference for entering the country. "It isn't red matter, so you needn't be afraid," he assured him. There is no indication as to what this "purely business" matter was all about. But by October, far from expressing repulsion for Britain, he wrote Ogden: "I myself want to return as soon as I can induce some stupid sentimental bourgeois to give me some money."[79]

Nevertheless, McKay harbored "grievances against things British," as his contemporaneous writings reveal. They grew and intensified with time, and he grew even more bitterly anti-British toward the end of his life, becoming almost pathological.[80] He never ceased watching the British ruling class, noting its misdeeds at home and abroad. That the British in connivance with the French harried him, especially during his time in Morocco, did not raise them in his estimation. After he informed British consulate officials in Tangiers in 1928 of his wish to travel to Liberia and Sierra Leone, "to visit the land of his ancestors," the Foreign Office quickly banned him from all British colonies except his native Jamaica. The decision reached McKay in garbled form: he was informed in writing by an ostensibly friendly member of the British government that he had been banned from *all* British colonies. McKay was not pleased. Privately he referred to his British tormentors as "dogs," and "those dirty British bastards working respectably in the dark." The abusive language, though never exchanged between the parties, was not one-sided. Secretly, the British believed the charge of "sodomy" that the French had brought against McKay. Even though they admitted that the French had no proof, the word was spread from one British consulate to another, from the Foreign Office to the Colonial Office to the Home Office, that McKay was a "sodomite." And the British vice-consul at Fez, who went through McKay's luggage, read some of his poems, and noticed the radical literature, called him a "nasty dangerous fellow." When his French *carte d'identité* and his British passport were stolen from his little house on the outskirts of Tangiers in August 1932, he suspected the British authorities.[81]

The incident disturbed McKay and interrupted his work on his novel, *Banana Bottom*. One suspects that some of the strong anti-British feeling expressed in the novel, especially in the characterization of Priscilla Craig, the English missionary, was galvanized by his negative experiences at the time. Despite his "marvelous universal mind"—"a precursor of and king among the futurists, Shakespearean in comprehension"—even William Blake was chided by McKay via Bita, the chief protagonist. "The Little Black Boy," Bita thought, was a splendid poem but not one to be recommended to an impressionable Black child. "For it was murder of the spirit . . . to cultivate a black child to hanker after the physical characteristics of the white."[82]

Four years later, McKay recalled an ungenerous defense he gave of Sylvia Pankhurst. During his sojourn in Moscow, McKay spent a great deal of time in the company of Arthur McManus, the Scottish radical he had first met at the ISC, who was based in Moscow working for the Comintern. They were drinking buddies, and they were photographed together when, as honored guests, they toured the Soviet fleet at Kronstadt in 1923. Though he was only a "wee fellow," as Crystal Eastman described him—his comrades in Moscow called him Little Mac—McManus possessed a gigantic zest for life, courage, and revolutionary proletarian passion. When the American journalist Walter Duranty asked him why he became a Communist, McManus relished the opportunity to tell him—in his strong Glaswegian brogue:

> Because they put me to work at the age of six, stoppering bottles in a soda-water factory, and kept me at it ten hours a day, for all the laws against child labor. When the inspector came round all of us nippers used to rush to a hidey-hole and stay there quiet as mice till he went away; an' they still do it, as I know; don't tell me there's no child labor in Glasgow. That's why I'm a Communist, if you want to know.[83]

McKay was very fond of him. But, as we have seen, he did not like McManus's venomous sniping at the reputation of Sylvia Pankhurst. When McKay remarked that "all Britons were imperial by birth and circumstances," McManus accused McKay of being "a bloody bigoted black nationalist." McKay recalled that McManus's "*b*'s had such a wonderful ring (he stammered a little) that it made me laugh and laugh until both of us fell into a prolonged fit of black-and-white laughter."[84] But behind the humor and laughter stood—ominously and quietly like a ghost, unmoved, watching the laughing men—McKay's disturbing proposition that Britons were imperial by birth and circumstances. George Bernard Shaw, McKay insisted—despite the recommendation of pugilism—was the only person his Diogenesian lamp had spotted in all of Britain. And he was Irish. McManus was also of Irish descent, born in Belfast to a Catholic family and raised in Scotland.

McKay's claim that he had looked upon the face of the British nation is, however, questionable—itself deserving of being looked upon. The evidence and McKay himself explicitly contradict his own claim. He had never secured lodgings in a British, let alone an English, home; he spent time with Black ex-soldiers at and from the Drury Lane club; and he spent most of his spare time at the International Socialist Club. Because of his membership of these two clubs, which were "overwhelmingly foreign," McKay felt most of the time that he was "living on foreign instead of English soil."[85] His friends were mainly foreigners or outsiders in one way or another. Among his "little group that stuck together" at the ISC, Frank Budgen was the only white Englishman. Brought up in a strange and tiny religious sect called the Lampeter Brethren, which he renounced for socialism in his teens, he had spent many years in France, Switzerland, and Germany studying and practicing his craft of painting.[86] Budgen's wife, Francine, was Jewish and Belgian; Henry Bernard was half German and Jewish. In addition to these, McKay mentions a seamstress who was Jewish, as was a fur dealer. Reuben Gilmore was Black, as was the Trinidadian student. "Although I could say I lived in London," he told Nancy Cunard, "it was altogether in a foreign milieu—chiefly Russian-Jewish—except for the little time I worked with a Miss [Nora] Smyth on Sylvia Pankhurst's *Workers' Dreadnought*. And that was very uncongenial."[87]

In short, McKay can hardly be said to have known the British nation, for the British would not let him. This has been the general pattern with non-white immigrants, including Caribbean intellectuals in Britain, until very recently. It was the marginalization and isolation that set these Londoners apart, not so much their "loneliness."[88] McKay, in fact, never complained of loneliness in London, for he had his friends; he complained about the generally hostile environment. In any case, he had always loved his own company, which developed from when he was the only child in U. Theo's household.

One also needs to view McKay's complaints in context. He arrived in London at a time of racist upsurge, of mob attacks in 1919 and 1920. The East End, his primary site of work and recreation, was particularly hostile to Black people and non-Europeans in general, especially among the dock laborers who experienced a reversal of fortunes with the end of the war. The level of unemployment among them had increased dramatically at a time that the working class was hit by steep increases in the cost of living. Retail prices in 1920 were 176 percent higher than they had been in 1914. The cost of food had almost tripled, and that of clothing more than quadrupled, over the same period. Rents and rates (municipal taxes) went up by 42 percent, and would have been even higher had there not been local and central government price controls. Although economic historians disagree over the figures, it appears that wages in most sectors kept up with inflation during McKay's time in Britain; but for the unemployed, the wageless, including a large number of ex-servicemen, this was no consolation.[89] McKay was in Britain at a particularly bad time, and the East End of London, with the possible exception of Liverpool, was the worst place in the country for a Black man to be.[90]

This is not to diminish what McKay had to say about Britain: his experiences were his experiences, and he had every right to relate them in any way he saw fit. It is necessary to exercise caution, however, in relation to his more sweeping generalizations. We should also remember that he spent just over a year in Britain, and except for passing through for a week on his way to Russia in September 1922, he never returned. Almost all of his time in Britain was spent in London. Counterbalancing these qualifications, however, were McKay's exceptionally keen powers of observation and analysis, which come through in all his writings. Given the brevity of his stay, one is repeatedly struck by the fine and subtle nuisances of British society and culture that McKay picked up.[91]

There is certainly a great deal of bitterness in McKay's reflections on Britain. But who can blame him, given what he went through? As he said, in another context, "if the Negro is a little bitter, the white man should be the last person in the world to accuse him of bitterness." He also suggested that it matters not so much that one has had an experience of bitterness, but rather "how one has developed out of it."[92] Despite McKay's outbursts, he remained resolutely humane and resisted plunging into cynicism. Indeed, his bitterness stemmed from his deep humanitarian impulses and enjoyment of life. His friends recall his gift of laughter and mischievous sense of humor, which permeate his novels. It is precisely because of all this that he hated the denial of access to happiness and contentment not only to himself but also to others. His anger reached boiling point when this basic right to what the Spirituals call "the tree of life"—"Ain't we got a right to the tree of life?"—was denied people because of the color of their skin. He would later describe racism as the worst, the most dangerous, superstition in the world.

Despite his philippic against the British and the white world, in personal relations McKay always transcended the narrow boundaries of nationality, race, and color. Like Ray, the character in *Banjo*, he would have considered the white world an utterly contemptible thing from its attitude toward the black if it were not for his principle of stressing the exception above the average. The white mind in general approached the black world from exactly the opposite angle. He often pondered if an intellectual life could have been possible for him without that principle to support it.[93]

In a 1924 letter to a friend, he explicitly addressed this problem. "In ordinary propaganda language," he wrote,

> we say white vs. black but we know that it is more than that. The Irish and Indian peoples hate the English nation because they visualize it as the Power oppressing them. It is only from that point of view that their nationalist movement is at all tenable because when we look at facts we find many members of the English nation working for Irish and Indian Independence. And it is thus also with Negroes—the whites *en masse* represent a system that oppresses Negroes, but it is a system that a great body of thinking whites were accidentally born into and would like to change. . . . But it isn't an easy matter and in the common fight we use the ordinary phrases—black vs. white and working class vs. bourgeoisie—that are not at all correct. For life isn't narrow and definite like that.

He bemoaned the fact, however, that "the really fine people in this world are so few and *so powerless*" and admitted "that sometimes one is seized with a fit of despair in contemplating life."[94]

In that same year, McKay wrote a poem that remained unpublished at his death. It is called "England." When shall England be "hurled / From her pedestal proud, whence she sways power / Over the millions raped of strength and will," he wondered aloud. But he had reasons to be optimistic:

> The angry tempest will not lash in vain,
> Against thy granite, arch conspirator,
> Scheming to shackle men with the ancient chain.
> Afar the slaves revolt, the distant roar
> Tocsins thy plundered native multitude,
> That reach out hungry for thine ancient crown,
> Thine ancient titles, with strong hands and rude,
> From thy high eminence to dash thee down.[95]

He returned to New York a worldlier and a wiser man.

A Coda

Almost immediately after his return to New York, McKay not only became an editor of the left-wing *Liberator* magazine but also quickly linked up once again with his Black comrades and became one of the leading members of the African Blood Brotherhood (ABB), a semisecret, revolutionary, Black organization, whose leadership soon merged it with the Workers Party of America (later renamed the Communist Party of the USA), the American section of the Comintern. McKay, along with other leaders of the ABB, such as Cyril Briggs, Grace Campbell, and Richard B. Moore, became a bona fide member of the Workers Party.

But driven by the urge to "wander and wonder" and to see Lenin's Russia for himself, McKay was off again within less than two years of his return to New York. Arriving in Moscow in the fall of 1922, he attended and spoke at the Fourth Congress of the Comintern; met and corresponded with leading Bolsheviks, most notably Leon Trotsky; wrote *Negroes in America*; and published his first collection of short stories, *Trial by Lynching*. Feted by Bolshevik soldiers and sailors, McKay was also welcomed in the intellectual and literary circles of Petrograd and Moscow, by both those who supported and those who opposed the October Revolution and the Bolshevik regime. All told, he spent almost eight months in revolutionary Russia on what he would later call his "magic pilgrimage," the "most memorable experience" of his life.

Leaving from Petrograd, McKay arrived in Berlin in the summer of 1923 more convinced than ever of the revolutionary socialist cause. He espoused Bolshevism in his journalism—including articles published in

the *Crisis*—as well as in his private correspondence, with a zeal and eloquence surpassing his earlier, passionate pronouncements on the subject.
Although 1923 marked the high point of McKay's commitment to Bolshevism, it was also a peculiar and rather paradoxical moment. McKay
refrained from returning to the United States. Apart from a lack of desire to
return, he also correctly assumed that the authorities would not allow him
back into the United States, given his widely publicized activities in Russia,
especially his high-profile participation in and speech at the Fourth Congress of the Comintern in Moscow. (Indeed, the press reported influential
calls for his prosecution by the American authorities.) But he never joined
another socialist organization abroad. He was, for the first time since 1919,
outside the disciplinary framework of an organized revolutionary party.

Despite the urgings of his Black comrades in the United States and the
Comintern leadership in Moscow to return to New York and continue
his political work, McKay decided to stay in Western Europe, and later in
Morocco, without ever joining any of the Comintern's local affiliates, such
as the Communist Party in France, where he spent most of his time abroad.
Although he had serious misgivings about the antiracist commitment of
the Workers Party, which he publicly expressed in Moscow, and harbored
little hope of revolutionary transformation in the United States, McKay
decided to continue his support of the Bolsheviks. But rather than engage
in the type of direct political work that he had undertaken in New York
and London, McKay committed himself to a concentration on his writing,
shifting from poetry to the novel for the first time. As U.S. intelligence files
reveal, the Justice Department was fully apprised of his revolutionary activity abroad, but the likelihood of being barred from entry was a secondary
reason for his lack of effort to return. Thus, McKay's commitment to Bolshevism in 1923, though passionate, was more rhetorical and ideological
than active engagement. After arriving in Western Europe, he behaved, in
effect, more like a "fellow traveler" than an actual member operating under
party discipline—a freelance, wandering, Black, socialist vagabond.

During the rest of the 1920s, especially after Lenin's death, the rise
of Joseph Stalin, and the ousting of Trotsky—a man whom he greatly
admired—McKay denounced Stalin as an "unctuous tyrant" and watched
with alarm as his most cherished hopes in Soviet Russia were dashed. His
politics developed in a different direction as he increasingly became a Black
nationalist, albeit of a decidedly revolutionary kind, especially after his
return to the United States in 1934. Nonetheless, contrary to the prevailing
view, McKay's politics right up to his death exhibited remarkably strong

threads of continuity with the earlier, Bolshevik phase of his political evolution. Despite this continuity, however, the year 1921 marks a distinct and important moment in McKay's political development. It is a conspicuous inflection point, inviting our attention not so much because it marks a break with the pattern of the past, but because it brings into sharp relief the new departure of the later years. This we know in hindsight, but only in hindsight, by tracing McKay's political footsteps from his hilly and green Jamaican village to his journey's end in the city of Chicago in 1948.[1]

Notes

Prologue

1. *Negro World*, September 20, 1919, quoted in Exhibit No. 10: "Radicalism and Sedition Among the Negroes as Reflected in Their Publications," in A. Mitchell Palmer, *Letter from the Attorney General Transmitting in Response to a Senate Resolution October 17, 1919, a Report on the Activities of the Bureau of Investigation of the Department of Justice Against Persons Advising Anarchy, Sedition, and the Forcible Overthrow of the Government* (Washington, DC, 1919), 163–64; hereafter *Attorney General's Report*. Unfortunately, that issue of the *Negro World* has not survived, and our access to McKay's words is provided by the U.S. intelligence agency's quotation of them. However, their authenticity, in this case at least, is not in doubt. There is corroboration from McKay.

2. Quoted in W. E. B. Du Bois, "The Negro and Radical Thought," *Crisis*, July 1921, 102. Du Bois never printed McKay's letter as a freestanding contribution, but instead incorporated it into his editorial. He provided a long quotation, which probably comprises all of McKay's letter, but that is not certain.

3. Kenneth Ramchand, *The West Indian Novel and Its Background* (London: Heinemann, 1970); Lloyd Brown, *West Indian Poetry*, 2nd ed. (London: Heinemann, 1984); Laurence A. Breiner, *An Introduction to West Indian Poetry* (Cambridge: Cambridge University Press, 1998); Winston James, *A Fierce Hatred of Injustice: Claude McKay's Jamaica and His Poetry of Rebellion* (London: Verso, 2000).

4. The founders of the *négritude* movement in 1930s Paris, Leopold Sedar Senghor, Aimé Césaire, and Leon Gontran Damas, could recite by heart McKay's poetry and especially passages from his influential novel, *Banjo* (1929). When Senghor declared in a 1950 essay, "Claude McKay can be considered rightfully as the true inventor of *négritude* . . . not of the word . . . but of the values of *négritude*," he not only spoke for himself but expressed the shared view of the group. Leopold Sedar Senghor, *Liberté I: Négritude et humanisme* (Paris: Seuil, 1964), 116. See also Lilyan Kesteloot, *Black Writers in French: A Literary History of Negritude*, trans. Ellen Conroy Kennedy (1963; Philadelphia: Temple University Press, 1974); Jacques Louis Hymans, *Léopold Sédar Senghor: An Intellectual Biography* (Edinburgh: Edinburgh University

Press, 1971); Jacqueline Kaye, "Claude McKay's *Banjo*," *Présence Africaine* 73, no. 1 (1970): 165–69; Edward O. Ako, "*L'Etudiant Noir* and the Myth of the Genesis of the Négritude Movement," *Research in African Literatures* 15, no. 3 (1984): 341–53; Martin Steins, "Brown France vs. Black Africa: The Tide Turned in 1932," *Research in African Literatures* 14, no. 4 (1983): 474–97; Liliane Blary, "Claude McKay and Africa: *Banjo*," *Commonwealth: Essays and Studies* 5 (1981–1982): 25–35; Michel Fabre, "Beyond *Banjo*: Claude McKay's African Experience," *Commonwealth: Essays and Studies* 5 (1981–1982): 37–52; Bridget Jones, "With *Banjo* by My Bed: Black French Writers Reading Claude McKay," *Caribbean Quarterly* 38, no. 1 (March 1992): 32–39; Edris Makward, "Claude McKay: The African Experience," in *Claude McKay: Centennial Studies*, ed. A. L. McLeod (New Delhi: Sterling, 1992); Brent Hayes Edwards, "Three Ways to Translate the Harlem Renaissance," and Michel Fabre, "The Harlem Renaissance Abroad: French Critics and the New Negro Movement (1924–1964)," both in *Temples for Tomorrow: Looking Back at the Harlem Renaissance*, ed. Geneviève Fabre and Michel Feith (Bloomington: Indiana University Press, 2001); and Brent Hayes Edwards, *The Practice of Diaspora: Literature, Translation and the Rise of Black Internationalism* (Cambridge, MA: Harvard University Press, 2003), chap. 4.

5. McKay to Max Eastman, August 28, 1946; McKay MSS, Manuscripts Department, Lilly Library, Indiana University, Bloomington; hereafter CMI.

6. See *Attorney General's Report*, 161–87.

7. *Crisis*, June 28, 1928, 202; *Negro World*, September 28, 1928. Also see McKay to Arthur Schomburg [July 1925?], Arthur Schomburg Papers, Schomburg Center for Research in Black Culture, New York Public Library.

8. St. Clair Drake, introduction to Claude McKay, *A Long Way from Home* (New York: Harcourt, Brace & World, 1970), ix–xxi. Addison Gayle Jr., *Claude McKay: The Black Poet at War* (Detroit: Broadside, 1972), 18.

9. Langston Hughes, "American Negro Writers: IX. Claude McKay: The Best," unpublished manuscript, undated (but 1938), Langston Hughes Papers, James Weldon Johnson Collection, Beinecke Rare Book and Manuscript Library, Yale University, New Haven, CT; Wallace Thurman, "Negro Poets and Their Poetry," *Bookman*, July 1928, 559; James Weldon Johnson, ed., *The Book of American Negro Poetry*, rev. ed. (New York: Harcourt, Brace & World, 1931), 168.

10. "McKay Says Schuyler Is Writing Nonsense," *Amsterdam News* (New York), November 20, 1937; Arthur P. Davis, *From the Dark Tower: Afro-American Writers, 1900–1960* (Washington, DC: Howard University Press, 1981), 43.

11. Stokely Carmichael, "Black Power," in *The Dialectics of Liberation*, ed. David Cooper (Harmondsworth: Penguin, 1968), 168–69; Gayle, *Claude McKay*, 18.

12. Harold Cruse, *The Crisis of the Negro Intellectual* (New York: William Morrow, 1967), 115–17. I provide a corrective to Cruse's argument in Winston James, *Holding Aloft the Banner of Ethiopia: Caribbean Radicalism in Early Twentieth-Century America* (London: Verso, 1998), 262–91.

13. Hughes to Arna Bontemps, March 7, 1953, in *Arna Bontemps-Langston Hughes Letters, 1925–1967*, ed. Charles H. Nichols (New York: Dodd, Mead, 1980), 305.

14. Wayne Cooper, *Claude McKay: Rebel Sojourner in the Harlem Renaissance—a Biography* (Baton Rouge: Louisiana State University Press, 1987). Robert Giles, *Claude McKay* (Boston: Twayne, 1976) is a much slighter text, more literary criticism than biography. A more recent book, Tyrone Tillery, *Claude McKay: A Black Poet's Struggle for Identity* (Amherst: University of Massachusetts Press, 1992), is more polemic than scholarship. It not only repeats many of Cruse's arguments but also many of

Cruse's mistakes on top of the author's own. Gary Edward Holcomb, *Claude McKay, Code Name Sasha: Queer Black Marxism and the Harlem Renaissance* (Gainesville: University Press of Florida, 2007) is, unfortunately, similar to Tillery's book—a disappointment.

15. Robert A. Hill, ed., *The Marcus Garvey and Universal Negro Improvement Association Papers*, 13 vols. (Berkeley: University of California Press, and Durham: Duke University Press, 1983–); hereafter *MGP*.

16. McKay to C. K. Ogden, March 26, 1920, C. K. Ogden Fonds, William Ready Divisions of Archives and Research Collections, Mills Memorial Library, McMaster University; hereafter CKOF.

17. Claude McKay, *A Long Way from Home* (New York: Lee Furman, 1937), 76; hereafter *LW*.

18. Perry Anderson, *Arguments Within English Marxism* (London: New Left, 1980), 105; emphasis in original.

19. There are some very thoughtful and provocative recent reflections on biography as a genre. Those of Michael Holroyd (*Works on Paper: The Craft of Biography and Autobiography* [Washington: Counterpoint, 2002]); and Hermione Lee (*Body Parts: Essays on Life-Writing* [London: Chatto and Windus, 2005], and *Biography: A Very Short Introduction* [Oxford: Oxford University Press, 2009]) are especially noteworthy.

20. I am a great admirer of the majestic biographies written by Arnold Rampersad (especially of Langston Hughes) and David Levering Lewis (especially of W. E. B. Du Bois) and have learned a great deal from them. See Rampersad, *The Life of Langston Hughes*, vol. 1: *1902–1941—I, Too, Sing America* (New York: Oxford University Press, 1986) and *The Life of Langston Hughes*, vol. 2: *1941–1967—I Dream a World* (New York: Oxford University Press, 1988); Lewis, *W. E. B. Du Bois: A Biography of Race, 1868–1919* (New York: Henry Holt, 1993) and *W. E. B. Du Bois: The Fight for Equality and the American Century* (New York: Henry Holt, 2000). However, the work that comes closest conceptually and methodologically to what I have attempted is Michel Löwy's study of the political evolution of Georg Lukács, the Hungarian Marxist intellectual. I especially admire Löwy's attention to context and the erudition with which he evokes, lavishly and convincingly, the political and intellectual milieu out of which Lukács the Bolshevik emerged. Michael Löwy, *Georg Lukács: From Romanticism to Bolshevism* (London: New Left, 1979). Löwy's intellectual ambition is imparted more accurately by the title of the original French edition of his work than by its English rendering: *Pour une sociologie des intellectuels révolutionnaires—l'évolution politique de Lukács, 1908–1929* (Paris: Presses Universitaires de France, 1976).

21. George Lamming, *Conversations: Essays, Addresses and Interviews, 1953–1990*, ed. Richard Drayton and Andaiye (London: Karia, 1992), 24.

22. Mervyn Morris, introduction to Claude McKay, *My Green Hills of Jamaica* (Kingston: Heinemann, 1979), vii–viii; hereafter *MGH*.

23. Claude McKay, "A Negro Poet and His Poems," *Pearson's Magazine*, September 1918, 275.

24. Claude McKay, "To 'Holy' Russia," *Workers' Dreadnought*, February 28, 1920.

1. A Son of the Soil: Jamaica's Claude McKay

1. Prior to my discovery of McKay's birth certificate in 1995, McKay's year of birth was generally accepted as 1890. But following a hint from one of his autobiographical poems, I was convinced that he was actually born in 1889. The discovery of his birth

certificate provided definitive proof that the year was indeed 1889. The dispute and speculations over his year of birth are discussed in Winston James, *A Fierce Hatred of Injustice: Claude McKay's Jamaica and His Poetry of Rebellion* (London: Verso, 2000), 152–61.

2. *MGH*, 62; *Jamaica Times*, January 8, 1910.

3. *MGH*, 61. Rare though it was, some enslaved Africans were indeed brought from Madagascar and continental East Africa to Jamaica and elsewhere in the New World. The overwhelming majority came from West Africa, but not all. See W. J. Gardner, *A History of Jamaica: From Its Discovery by Christopher Columbus to the Year 1872* (London: Frank Cass, [1873] 1971), 97; Orlando Patterson, *The Sociology of Slavery: An Analysis of the Origins, Development and Structure of Negro Slave Society in Jamaica* (London: MacGibbon and Kee, 1967), 136; and Mavis C. Campbell, *The Maroons of Jamaica, 1655–1796* (Trenton, NJ: Africa World Press, 1990), 34–35.

4. Max Eastman, introduction to Claude McKay, *Harlem Shadows* (New York: Harcourt, Brace, 1922), xi–xii; hereafter *HS*. Eastman repeated the story thirty years later and added the coda: "With the blood of such rebels in his veins, and their memory to stir it, Claude McKay grew up proud of his race and with no disposition to apologize for his color." Max Eastman, biographical note in Claude McKay, *Selected Poems of Claude McKay* (New York: Bookman, 1953), 110; hereafter *SP*. Eastman was the first to publish this story, but he was not the only one. McKay also told his Russian translators (A. M. and P. Okhrimenko), who reported it in the introduction to his collection of short stories, *Sudom Lyncha*, published in Moscow in 1925 (retranslated into English by Robert Winter as *Trial by Lynching: Stories About Negro Life in America* [Mysore: Centre for Commonwealth Literature and Research, University of Mysore, 1977], 3–4). According to Jean Wagner, McKay's friend and last agent Carl Cowl "states that he too heard this anecdote related by the poet himself." Jean Wagner, *Black Poets of the United States: From Paul Laurence Dunbar to Langston Hughes* (Urbana: University of Illinois Press, 1973), 199n7. Cowl confirmed that McKay had told him this story directly (Cowl interview, September 25, 1991). It is, of course, impossible from this distance and sparse documentation to determine whether the story is or is not true; it is certainly plausible. What is clear is that McKay repeatedly told the story and believed it was true, and that belief is more important to our understanding of the man than whether it was actually true.

5. *MGH*, 59–60. McKay never disclosed that his father was illiterate, but the evidence from McKay's birth certificate suggests that Thomas was indeed unable to read and write. Even if he could read, he apparently could not write: instead of a signature, he left his mark (an X) on the birth certificate. It is possible that in subsequent years Thomas became literate. In 1928, a letter writer to the *Gleaner* claimed that Thomas McKay, still alive and vibrant, "reads without glasses" and was "a regular reader of the *Gleaner*." James, *A Fierce Hatred of Injustice*, 153, 159; *Daily Gleaner*, July 12, 1928. Thomas Edwards, a man of some standing in his community, was also for many years deacon of the local Baptist chapel, Mount Zion. Stephen A. Hill, ed., *Who's Who in Jamaica, 1916* (Kingston: Gleaner, 1916), 94.

6. *MGH*, 24, 60.

7. See Ken Post, *Arise Ye Starvelings: The Jamaican Labour Rebellion of 1938 and Its Aftermath* (The Hague: Matinus Nijhoff, 1978), 37, for a discussion of the emerging class differentiation in the countryside. Also see chapter 2 in this volume for more on the situation in Clarendon and Thomas McKay's position in the changing fortunes of the peasantry.

8. Lord Olivier, "The Dual Ethic in Empire," quoted in Post, *Arise Ye Starvelings*, 116.

9. Post, *Arise Ye Starvelings*, 116.

10. The color-class complex on the island is discussed further in chapter 2.

11. Jimmy Carnegie, "Claude McKay's Big Brother, U. Theo McKay (1872–1949)," *Caribbean Quarterly* 38, no. 1 (March 1992): 8.

12. Lloyd G. Barnett, *The Constitutional Law of Jamaica* (Oxford: Oxford University Press, 1977), 12.

13. Hume Wrong, *Government of the West Indies* (Oxford: Clarendon, 1923), 130–31; H. de R. Walker, *The West Indies and the Empire: Study and Travel in the Winter of 1900–1901* (London: T. Fisher Unwin, 1901), 183–84. Hume Wrong clearly exaggerated when he wrote that the vote had been "placed in reach of a very large section of the population"; when he noted that "of those in possession of the qualifications only a moderate percentage registered, and of those registered only a small portion trouble to go to the polls," his remarks applied almost exclusively to the white population. It is significant that in the three elections that took place between 1906 and 1920, almost half the winners were unopposed. Indeed, in the elections of 1920, nine of the fourteen seats had uncontested candidates. In all three elections (1906, 1911, and 1920), less than a third of those who were eligible voted. Calculations from Wrong, *Government of the West Indies*, 130. The supposed political apathy of the Negro proclaimed by writers such as Walker and Wrong has been effectively dismantled by Joyce Lumsden, "Robert Love and Jamaican Politics" (PhD diss., University of the West Indies, 1987), esp. chap. 5.

14. Calculated from H. A. Will, *Constitutional Change in the British West Indies, 1880–1903* (Oxford: Clarendon, 1970), 60. The "racial composition" of the population for 1886 was calculated as half the numerical change in population for each group between the censuses of 1881 and 1891; these census figures are given in George W. Roberts, *The Population of Jamaica* (Cambridge: Cambridge University Press, 1957), 65, table 14.

15. Will, *Constitutional Change*, 60–66; Wrong, *Government of the West Indies*, 130; Patrick Bryan, *The Jamaican People, 1880–1902: Race, Class and Social Control* (London: Macmillan, 1991), 14–20; *Handbook of Jamaica* (Kingston: Government Printing Office, annual), *1919*, 92; hereafter *HBJ*.

16. See the detailed report of the Legislative Council deliberations in *Gleaner*, May 15, 1919. The *Gleaner* provided extensive coverage of the campaign. For the large meeting—"epoch making event," the *Gleaner* called it—presided over by Lady Probyn, see *Gleaner*, September 26, 1918. For an overview of the campaign, see Linnette Vassell, "The Movement for the Vote for Women, 1918–1919," *Jamaican Historical Review* 18 (1993): 40–54.

17. *HBJ, 1921*, 91–92; Barnett, *Constitutional Law*, 12–13. Jamaican women were the first women in the British Caribbean to win the franchise. Wrong, *Government of the West Indies*, 130.

18. Vassell, "The Movement for the Vote." Also see the women's petition, *Gleaner*, September 16, 1918.

19. *MGH*, 60. In 1901, the entire parish of Clarendon had only 850 voters; Clarendon had a population of nearly 70,000 at the time. By the time McKay left the island in 1912, the proportion of voters was still only 2.6 percent of the parish's population: 1,940 registered voters out of a population of 73,914. Walker, *West Indies and Empire*, 184; Roberts, *The Population of Jamaica*, 51; *HBJ, 1919*, 92.

20. *MGH*, 60. For a vivid contemporary account of Jamaican electoral politics, see H. G. De Lisser, *Twentieth Century Jamaica* (Kingston: Jamaica Times, 1913), 149–68.

21. For the best analysis of this transition, see Ken Post's fine trilogy: *Arise Ye Starvelings*; *Strike the Iron: A Colony at War: Jamaica 1939–1945*, 2 vols. (Atlantic Highlands, NJ: Humanities, 1981). More recently, Colin A. Palmer made an outstanding contribution to the understanding of this moment: *Freedom's Children: The 1938 Labor Rebellion and the Birth of Modern Jamaica* (Chapel Hill: University of North Carolina Press, 2014), and Stuart Hall in his memoirs captured the visceral impact of the moment: *Familiar Stranger: Life Between Two Islands* (Durham, NC: Duke University Press, 2017).

22. From the correspondence of McKay's brother Thomas Edison and sister Rachel, and indeed from biographical information on another brother, Nathaniel, it is clear that oppositional political attitudes were not confined to U. Theo and Claude. See letters from T. E. McKay and Rachel McKay-Cooper in Claude McKay Papers, James Weldon Johnson Collection of Negro Literature and Art, American Literature Collection, Beinecke Rare Book and Manuscript Library, Yale University, New Haven, CT; hereafter CMPY. Also on Thomas McKay, see entry in L. A. Thoywell-Henry, ed., *Who's Who: Jamaica, British West Indies, 1941–1946* (Kingston: Who's Who [Jamaica], 1945), 444; for Nathaniel McKay, see Clifton Neita, ed., *Who's Who: Jamaica 1951* (Kingston: Who's Who [Jamaica], 1951), 403–4.

23. Rachel McKay-Cooper to McKay, June 13, 1929, CMPY.

24. T. E. McKay to McKay, September 26, 1929; undated [June 1936]; October 23, 1936; CMPY. Astonishingly, Tyrone Tillery confuses U. Theo—whom he repeatedly calls Theophilious although his middle name is Theodore—with his brother Thomas and attributes these letters to U. Theo. The effect of the confusion on his analysis is profound. Tyrone Tillery, *Claude McKay: A Black Poet's Search for Identity* (Amherst: University of Massachusetts Press, 1992), 18–19.

25. McKay to James Weldon Johnson, September 5, 1929, CMPY.

26. McKay to Nancy Cunard, March 29, 1932, Nancy Cunard Collection, Harry Ransom Humanities Research Center, University of Texas at Austin; hereafter NCC.

27. Langston Hughes, *The Big Sea: An Autobiography* (New York: Knopf, 1940), 165.

28. The regulations for admission into the civil service are outlined in the *Jamaica Handbook*; see, for instance, *HBJ, 1897*, 99–105, and *HBJ, 1919*, 229–32; see also Post, *Arise Ye Starvelings*, 213–14; *MGP*, 1:33n15.

29. Claude McKay, *Banana Bottom* (New York: Harper, 1933), 234–35; hereafter *BB*.

30. Marcus Garvey, "The British West Indies in the Mirror of Civilization: History Making by Colonial Negroes," *African Times and Orient Review* 2, no. 16 (Mid-October 1913): 159; J. A. Rogers, "The West Indies: Their Political, Social and Economic Condition," *Messenger*, October 1922, 506; Post, *Arise Ye Starvelings*, 213–14; Ethelred Brown, *Injustices in the Civil Service of Jamaica* (New York: Jamaica Progressive League, 1937); Mark D. Morrison-Reed, *A Dream Aborted: Egbert Ethelred Brown in Jamaica and Harlem* (Boston: Beacon, 1984); Winston James, *Holding Aloft the Banner of Ethiopia: Caribbean Radicalism in Early Twentieth-Century America* (London: Verso, 1998), 39–41; Joyce Moore-Turner, "The Rev. E. Ethelred Brown and the Harlem Renaissance, 1920–2020," *Journal of Caribbean History* 54, no. 1 (2020): 30–54.

31. C. A. Wilson, *Men with Backbone and Other Pleas for Progress*, 2nd ed. (Kingston: Educational Supply, 1913), 81.

32. The agitation began early. In his testimony to the West India Royal Commission of 1897, Rev. S. C. Morris of Port Antonio, although he was told that the inquiry had no remit to look into the subject, insisted on complaining. The blockage to the civil service, he said, was a "very great grievance. . . . [L]et us all have fair play and let us compete and get what we compete for." *Report of the West India Royal Commission,*

Appendix C, vol. 3, containing parts vi–xiii: Proceedings, Evidence, and Documents Relating to the Windward Islands, the Leeward Islands, and Jamaica [C. 8669] (London: Her Majesty's Stationery Office, 1897), 333.

33. Richard Hart, "Jamaica and Self-Determination, 1660–1970," *Race* 13, no. 3 (January 1972): 282–83; James, *Holding Aloft the Banner of Ethiopia*, 38–41; Francis Lee, *Fabianism and Colonialism: The Life and Political Thought of Lord Sydney Olivier* (London: Defiant Books, 1988), 120–24. In the nineteenth century, Jamaican-born (creole) whites also had their complaints, about "imported officials" being given preference over locals in recruitment to the civil service. Will, *Constitutional Change*, esp. 37–40, 77–80. The hierarchy was: British-born whites; creole (Jamaican-born) whites; "colored" / "mulatto" / "brown" Jamaicans; and at the bottom "black" / "Negro" / dark-skinned Jamaicans.

34. See Bryan, *The Jamaican People*, 216–21, for discussion of this category.

35. *MGH*, 60–61.

36. *Jamaica Times*, January 8, 1910; *MGH*, 59–60; Wayne Cooper, *Claude McKay: Rebel Sojourner in the Harlem Renaissance—A Biography* (Baton Rouge: Louisiana State University Press, 1987), 4, 6. Thomas's Staceyville origin comes from interviews Cooper conducted with McKay's relatives in the 1970s. The *Jamaica Times* obituary states that Hannah Ann was twenty-two when she married Thomas. This means that Hannah Ann was born around 1848, not 1856, as Cooper claimed. Cooper based this date on McKay's statement that his mother was fifty-three when she died, but she was in fact sixty-one, as the obituary states. See Cooper, *Claude McKay*, 6, 377n16.

37. *MGH*, 48–51.

38. U. Theo's daughter, Eloise McKay Edwards, told me that her father was "spoilt" as a boy by his mother. He never wanted to go to school, which perhaps explains why he was taught at home by his mother for so many years. Interview with Eloise McKay Edwards, London, August 23, 1995. See also letter to the editor by "Jamaican," *Daily Gleaner*, July 12, 1928, which claimed that Hannah Ann taught all her children to read and write before they went to elementary school.

39. According to the letter to the editor by "Jamaican," who claimed to have known the McKays "very well indeed," U. Theo entered elementary school in the "6th standard in reading, and 5th standard in arithmetic." *Daily Gleaner*, July 12, 1928.

40. *MGH*, 48–51; *Jamaica Times*, January 8, 1910.

41. *MGH*, 22.

42. *MGH*, 58.

43. *MGH*, 58; and see, for instance, the last stanza of "Strokes of the Tamarind Switch," in Claude McKay, *Songs of Jamaica* (Kingston: Gardner, 1912), 112; hereafter *SJ*.

44. *MGH*, 58. Hannah Ann would have been about forty-one years old when she gave birth to McKay.

45. *BB*, 7.

46. Telephone interview with Carl Cowl, March 18, 1993.

47. *Liberator*, March 1920, 24. According to the obituary in the *Jamaica Times* (January 8, 1910), Mrs. McKay died at "3:30 p.m." on Tuesday, December 21, 1909.

48. *LW*, 26.

49. *MGH*, 59.

50. *MGH*, 61.

51. T. E. McKay to McKay, undated [August 1929], CMPY.

52. *Jamaica Times*, January 8, 1910. See also letter by "Jamaican," *Daily Gleaner*, July 12, 1928.

53. *MGH*, 12. In his biography of McKay, Wayne Cooper insists that McKay's father was never a Presbyterian but had always been a Baptist (Cooper, *Claude McKay*, 5). I have my doubts, however, for it is unusual for McKay to make an error of this kind. McKay's description of his father is not figurative, as he repeated the statement in a clearly literal way elsewhere: "My father was converted and educated by a Presbyterian minister" (*MGH*, 25). It seems more likely than not that Thomas McKay was converted to Christianity by the Scottish Presbyterians and later became a Baptist, probably during his courting of Hannah Ann, whose influential father was a Baptist deacon. One might be puzzled by the Scottish influence and place names in Clarendon, not to mention McKay's family name, but in the 1770s it was estimated that a third of the white population on the island was from Scotland. They dominated the managerial positions on plantations, serving as attorneys, bookkeepers, and overseers. Some of the wealthiest planters and merchants were Scottish, as were the majority of doctors. Edward Long, *The History of Jamaica* (London: Frank Cass, [1774] 1970), 2:286–87; Richard B. Sheridan, "The Role of Scots in the Economy and Society of the West Indies," in *Comparative Perspectives on Slavery in New World Plantation Societies*, ed. Vera Rubin and Arthur Tuden (New York: New York Academy of Sciences, 1977), 94–106; Trevor Burnard, "European Migration to Jamaica, 1655–1780," *William and Mary Quarterly* 53, no. 4 (1996): 769–96; B. W. Higman, *Plantation Jamaica, 1750–1850: Capital and Control in a Colonial Economy* (Kingston: University of the West Indies Press, 2005), 77–81, 137–46; Douglas J. Hamilton, *Scotland, the Caribbean and the Atlantic World, 1750–1820* (Manchester: Manchester University Press, 2005); Eric J. Graham, "The Scots Penetration of the Jamaican Plantation Business," in *Recovering Scotland's Slave Past: The Caribbean Connection*, ed. T. M. Devine (Edinburgh: Edinburgh University Press, 2015), 82–98.

54. *MGH*, 22, 59.

55. *MGH*, 22–23.

56. McKay may have eventually gotten a photograph of his father sent to him, as there is one deposited among his papers at the Beinecke Library at Yale University, but it is possible that the picture may have been deposited after McKay's death by his daughter, Hope McKay-Virtue, who gave a number of items to the collection. See U. Theo McKay to Claude McKay, March 1, 1929, April 26, 1929, August 2, 1929, May 23, 1933, and Rachel McKay-Cooper to McKay, August 25, 1927, June 13, 1929, December 26, 1929, all in CMPY; and McKay to Nancy Cunard, August 20, 1932, NCC.

57. Claude McKay, "A Negro Poet and His Poems," *Pearson's Magazine*, September 1918, 275; hereafter "ANPP."

58. *MGH*, 25.

59. *MGH*, 11–12.

60. *MGH*, 33.

61. *LW*, 37.

62. *MGH*, 33; *LW*, 37.

63. *LW*, 37.

64. *LW*, 34. McKay said that the minister was trained at Calabar College, but he must have meant Calabar Institution; Calabar College was not opened until 1912, and then as a secondary school attached to the Institution. See *HBJ, 1913*, 359; and "Caribbean Man: The Life and Times of Philip Sherlock," an interview conducted by Edward Baugh, *Jamaica Journal* 16, no. 3 (August 1983): 23.

65. In *A Long Way from Home* (1937) and again in *My Green Hills of Jamaica* (1946–1947).

66. "Passive Resistance" is discussed in chapter 3.

67. See, for instance, McKay's "Sufi Abdul Hamid and Organized Labor," in his *Harlem: Negro Metropolis* (New York: Dutton, 1940), 181–262; hereafter *H*. McKay returned to the subject of the boycott in his posthumously published novel, *Harlem Glory: A Fragment of Aframerican Life* (Chicago: Kerr, 1990); hereafter *HG*. The novel was written in the early 1940s but was only published some fifty years later. I will discuss McKay's politics in the 1930s at length in a future volume, *Claude McKay: From Bolshevism to Black Nationalism.*

68. *MGH*, 55.

69. *MGH*, 61.

70. Original translator's note in Claude McKay, *Negroes in America* (1923; Port Washington, NY: Kennikat, [1923] 1979), xvi; hereafter *NA*.

71. *MGH*, 61.

72. "Personal Notes on the History of Jamaica," 10, in Claude McKay Papers, Schomburg Center for Research in Black Culture, New York Public Library, hereafter CMPS; McKay to Nancy Cunard, August 20, 1932, NCC. McKay wanted "Personal Notes on the History of Jamaica" to be published as a chapter of *My Green Hills of Jamaica*. See McKay to Charlie Smith, October 15, [1947], CMPS. It is omitted in the published edition.

73. "Personal Notes," 10. According to McKay, "the obeahman . . . devoured a lot of the peasants' money. He always demanded a pretty large payment for his work. So the British government was always pursuing him." In reality, matters were not as simple as McKay made them out to be. In his novel *Banana Bottom*, McKay would enjoy himself at the expense of his fictive obeahman. For more on the phenomenon of obeah in Jamaica, see Martha Beckwith, *Black Roadways: A Study of Jamaican Folk Life* (Chapel Hill: University of North Carolina Press, 1929); Joseph Williams, *Psychic Phenomena of Jamaica* (New York: Dial, 1934); Zora Neale Hurston, *Tell My Horse* (Philadelphia: Lippincott, 1938); Leonard Barrett, *The Sun and the Drum: African Roots in Jamaican Folk Tradition* (London: Heinemann, 1976); and Mervyn Alleyne, *Roots of Jamaican Culture* (London: Pluto, 1988); Brian L. Moore and Michele A. Johnson, *Neither Led nor Driven: Contesting British Cultural Imperialism in Jamaica, 1865–1920* (Kingston: University of the West Indies Press, 2004), chaps. 2 and 3.

74. McKay to Nancy Cunard, August 20, 1932, NCC; "Personal Notes," 14–15. The phrase "without any regrets" toward the end of the passage is written in by hand—presumably an afterthought. Thomas McKay was ninety-four (not ninety-eight as McKay wrote), when he died on January 24, 1933. And according to her obituarist, Hannah Ann was sixty-one when she died in 1909. (Inscriptions on Thomas McKay's gravestone and memorial plaque, presented by U. Theo, at Mount Zion Baptist Church, Nairne Castle, Clarendon [photographed by author]; and *Jamaica Times*, January 8, 1910.)

75. *Who's Who, 1916*, 94; *Who's Who, 1941–1946*, 444; *MGH*, 13; Cooper, *Claude McKay*, 12. Jamaica did not have a university in U. Theo's time. The University College of the West Indies (accredited by the University of London), forerunner of what was to become the University of the West Indies, was not established until 1948.

76. *Who's Who, 1941–1946*, 444.

77. *Gleaner*, August 8, 1922; *Christian Commonwealth*, March 27, 1912, 420.

78. *Who's Who, 1916*, 94. Although McKay writes in *My Green Hills of Jamaica* as though Sunny Ville was the name of a village, it was not—it was the name of the family home. As McKay had explained some years earlier, "I was born in a very little village high up in the hills of the parish of Clarendon. . . .The village was so small it hadn't a name like the larger surrounding villages. But our place was called Sunny Ville."

Countee Cullen, ed., *Caroling Dusk* (New York: Harper, 1927), 81–82. McKay therefore makes a clear distinction between the village and the home, "Sunny Ville," the original family seat, as his descendants pointed out to me on my visits. McKay's village was in fact called Nairne Castle, near James Hill in Clarendon. This is what his birth certificate states, and the village still exists. See Winston James, *A Fierce Hatred of Injustice: Claude McKay's Jamaica and His Poetry of Rebellion* (London: Verso, 2000), 152–61.

79. See Erna Brodber, "The Second Generation of Freemen in Jamaica, 1907–1944" (PhD diss., University of the West Indies, 1984), 57–70; and *The Second Generation of Freemen in Jamaica, 1907–1944* (Gainesville: University Press of Florida, 2004), chap. 2. For a wider context, see Raymond T. Smith, *Kinship and Class in the West Indies: A Genealogical Study of Jamaica and Guyana* (Cambridge: Cambridge University Press, 1988).

80. *MGH*, 15–16.

81. U. Theo McKay to Claude McKay, April 26, 1929, CMPY.

82. McKay to Nancy Cunard, August 20, 1932, NCC.

83. *MGH*, 19.

84. McKay, "On Becoming a Roman Catholic," *Epistle* 11, no. 2 (Spring 1945): 48.

85. "ANPP," 275.

86. *MGH*, 44. Strange and incredible though it may first appear, McKay's claim was not far-fetched. The records of the London-based Rationalist Press Association, the world's leading freethought organization, indicate a significant number of members on the island and that McKay was a signed-up member from 1911 to 1914. He appeared first in the 1911 records as F. C. McKay (carrying the initials of his birth name) and subsequently as Claude McKay, giving his location as Manhattan (Kansas). See the Rationalist Press Association, *Thirteenth Annual Report* (1911), 41; *Fourteenth Annual Report* (1912), 44; *Fifteenth Annual Report* (1913), 50; and *Sixteenth Annual Report* (1914), 48. Jekyll, who enlisted McKay, consistently appeared on the RPA's membership roster, listed every year between 1904 and 1928, the year before he died. There were twenty-two others in Jamaica listed as members between 1911 and 1928, which should not be confused with the reach and readership of the RPA. That reach and readership was noticeable enough for C. A. Wilson to remark in 1913: "The publications of the Rationalist Press Association find a ready sale, and eager readers among the more intelligent young men and women." Wilson, *Men with Backbone*, 90. U. Theo was among Jamaica's avid readers of RPA publications who never bothered to join. Also see *Jamaica Times*, February 8, 1908. Bill Cooke, *The Gathering of Infidels: A Hundred Years of the Rationalist Press Association* (Amherst, NY: Prometheus, 2004), provides the most detailed, recent, and authoritative account of the RPA.

87. *MGH*, 35–40.

88. *MGH*, 43.

89. *MGH*, 44.

90. See chapter 2 for discussion of Jamaica's emergent Black intelligentsia.

91. Rupert Lewis, *Marcus Garvey: Anti-Colonial Champion* (London: Karia, 1987), 26. There is disagreement over Love's date of birth. Lewis believes it was 1835, but others believe it was 1839; cf. W. Adolphe Roberts, *Six Great Jamaican: Biographical Sketches*, 2nd. ed. (Kingston: Pioneer, 1957), 66; and Joy Lumsden, "Joseph Robert Love, 1839–1914: West Indian Extraordinary," *Afro-Americans in New York Life and History* 7, no. 1 (January 1983): 26, 37n5.

92. One of the most notorious of these racist ideologues was James Froude, who in his 1888 travelogue fired his most poisonous arrows at the Black Republic, dismissing its citizens as mere cannibals. James Anthony Froude, *The English in the West Indies or the Bow of Ulysses* (London: Longmans, Green, 1888), esp. chap. 12. But Froude was far from alone in the maligning of Haiti.

93. Roberts, *The Population of Jamaica*, 73.

94. See *Voice of the Negro*, September 1905.

95. "The Condition *Sine Qua Non* of the Complete Elevation of the Negro Race," *Jamaica Advocate*, April 6, 1895.

96. "Truths to Be Remembered," *Jamaica Advocate*, September 14, 1895.

97. Lewis, *Marcus Garvey*, 27. These and related matters are discussed further in chapter 2.

98. See, for instance, *Jamaica Advocate*, April 8 and July 29, 1899. "Henry George," Love declared, "is right after all: and his doctrine (it is not a theory, but a principle) is the solution of our difficulties. Let it spread until it is known by heart, by every member of the community." *Jamaica Advocate*, November 26, 1898.

99. *Jamaica Advocate*, May 20 and September 23, 1899.

100. Harry Goulbourne, *Teachers, Education and Politics in Jamaica, 1892–1972* (London: Macmillan, 1988), 70–71.

101. *MGP*, 1:533.

102. See *Jamaica Advocate*, December 10, 1898, for report of the "sad news" of the termination of the *Jamaica Teacher*.

103. *Jamaica Advocate*, July 30, 1898; see also Bryan, *The Jamaican People*, 261; and Joy Lumsden, "The People's Convention: Celebrating the Diamond Jubilee of Full Freedom in Jamaica," in *August 1st: A Celebration of Emancipation*, ed. Patrick Bryan (Kingston: Department of History, University of the West Indies, 1995).

104. U. Theo McKay, "August 1 in Its True Setting," *Jamaica Times*, August Special, Saturday, August 21, 1909. For analyses of the rise and decline of Emancipation Day celebrations in the Americas, see, for example, W. H. Wiggins, Jr., *O Freedom! Afro-American Emancipation Celebrations* (Knoxville: University of Tennessee Press, 1987); Mitch Kachun, *Festivals of Freedom: Memory and Meaning in African American Emancipation Celebrations, 1808–1915* (Amherst: University of Massachusetts Press, 2003); J. R. Kerr-Ritchie, *Rites of August First: Emancipation Day in the Black Atlantic* (Baton Rouge: Louisiana State University Press, 2007); B. W. Higman, "Slavery Remembered: The Celebration of Emancipation in Jamaica," *Journal of Caribbean History* 12 (1979): 55–74; B. W. Higman, "Remembering Slavery: The Rise, Decline and Revival of Emancipation Day in the English-Speaking Caribbean," *Slavery and Abolition* 19, no. 1 (April 1998): 90–105; Bridget Brereton, "The Birthday of Our Race: A Social History of Emancipation Day in Trinidad, 1838–1888," in *Trade Government and Society in Caribbean History 1700–1920*, ed. B. W. Higman (Kingston: Heinemann, 1983); and Bridget Brereton, "A Social History of Emancipation Day in the British Caribbean: The First Fifty Years," in Bryan, *August 1st*.

105. Imanuel Geiss, *The Pan-African Movement*, trans. Ann Keep (London: Methuen, 1974), 110.

106. Scholes wrote at least three other books beside *Glimpses: Sugar and the West Indies* (London, 1897); *The British Empire and Alliances: or, Britain's Duty to her Colonies and Subject Races* (London, 1899); and, under the pseudonym Bartholomew Smith, *Chamberlain and Chamberlainism: His Fiscal Proposals and Colonial Policy* (London, 1903). The similar arguments developed later by Diop and Bernal may be found most

readily in Cheikh Anta Diop, *The African Origin of Civilization: Myth or Reality?* (Westport, CT: Greenwood, 1974), and Martin Bernal, *Black Athena: The Afroasiatic Roots of Classical Civilization* (London: Free Association, 1987).

107. See Bryan, *The Jamaican People*, chaps. 11 and 12.

108. Karl Mannheim, *Ideology and Utopia: An Introduction to the Sociology of Knowledge* (London: Routledge & Kegan Paul, 1936); *Essays on Sociology and Social Psychology* (New York: Oxford University Press, 1953), esp. his essay "Conservative Thought," 74–164; *Structures of Thinking* (London: Routledge & Kegan Paul, 1982).

109. U. Theo McKay, "August 1 in Its True Setting." Almost two generations later, Eric Williams, his fellow Caribbean intellectual, would famously (and more plausibly) ground the abolition process not in moral awakening but in the unfolding economic processes of the era. See Eric Williams, *Capitalism and Slavery* (Chapel Hill: University of North Carolina Press, 1944).

110. M. K. Bacchus, *Utilization, Misuse, and Development of Human Resources in the Early West Indian Colonies* (Waterloo, Ont.: Wilfrid Laurier University Press, 1990), 215; Peter Roberts, *From Oral to Literate Culture: Colonial Experience in the English West Indies* (Kingston: The Press University of the West Indies, 1997), 265–66.

111. "It is not in our blood," he chided his more radical brother, "to be revolutionists." U. Theo McKay to McKay, March 1, 1929, CMPY.

112. U. Theo McKay, "Some Questions Which Merit Consideration of Public," *Gleaner*, January 20, 1919. This is a long letter to the editor that provides a valuable overview of U. Theo's ideas on a wide variety of subjects. Income taxes were imposed for the first time in 1920, but contrary to U. Theo's wishes, they were extremely regressive. Gisela Eisner, *Jamaica, 1830–1930: A Study in Economic Growth* (Manchester: Manchester University Press, 1961), 23, 370–71.

113. U. Theo McKay, "Some Questions." (It is safe to assume that Robert Love would have supported the measure, but he died in 1914.) Like virtually all Black middle-class Jamaicans at the time, U. Theo did not call for universal adult suffrage. Indeed, while supporting the enfranchisement of women on the same basis as men, he suggested that "the occasion should be seized upon to raise the qualification for the franchise in general." The bill granting women the vote was passed in May 1919. For a useful discussion of the debate over the 1918 enfranchisement bill, see Vassell, "The Movement for the Vote." Unfortunately, she confines her discussion solely to the debate in the *Gleaner*, ignoring the other, more progressive island newspaper, *Jamaica Times*. Remarkably, she missed U. Theo's important intervention, even though it appeared in the *Gleaner*, and his name is unmentioned in her article.

114. Vassell, "The Movement for the Vote," 45. This episode in Smith's political career goes unmentioned by his biographer: Anthony Johnson, *J. A. G. Smith* (Kingston: Kingston, 1991). The bill was tabled in the Legislative Council by Hubert Simpson, a light-skinned colored man, who had a long and distinguished record in Jamaica's reform movement.

115. U. Theo McKay to Claude McKay, January 24, 1930, CMPY.

116. U. T. McKay, "To Conquer Material Success," *Jamaica Times*, December 16, 1911.

117. U. Theo McKay, "The Sons of Toil," *Jamaica Times*, July 20, 1912. The following year he called for "Medical Aid" for the poor: *Jamaica Times*, February 1, 1913.

118. U. Theo's last sentence is referring to the massive departure of Jamaican labor to work on the Panama Canal and elsewhere in the Americas and the debate it had generated in the island.

119. *MGH*, 21.

120. *MGH*, 21.
121. *MGH*, 27–28.
122. Without erasing the last phrase, McKay wrote above it "planter agent of an absentee landlord." That is to say, U. Theo had become a planter agent of an absentee landlord.
123. The notebook, with unnumbered pages, is located in Box 1, CMPS.
124. See especially Alain Locke, "Spiritual Truancy," *New Challenge* 2, no. 2 (Fall 1937): 81–85. Perhaps it was the frequent charge of ingratitude made against him that turned McKay against expressions of gratitude by others toward himself. The African American writer Ellen Tarry recalled in her memoir that she was "grateful" for the help McKay gave her, including teaching her "the meaning of craftsmanship," but he "forbade her to say so." She reported that when she attempted to express her gratitude to him, McKay always said, "Gratitude! I *hate* the word." Ellen Tarry, *The Third Door: The Autobiography of an American Negro Woman* (New York: David McKay, 1955), 129, emphasis in original. See also McKay to Joel Spingarn, March 12, 1937, Joel E. Spingarn Papers, Rare Books and Manuscript Collection, New York Public Library; hereafter JESP.
125. Teachers were not provided with pensions at the time U. Theo left the profession. Despite the recommendation of Education Commissions in 1886 and 1898 that teachers should receive a noncontributory pension, it was only in 1914 that the first cohort of retired teachers received a pension. Furthermore, though highly respected by the communities they served, teachers were poorly paid, generally earning less than artisans. Everybody knew this, and in rural areas the peasants often supplemented the teachers' income by giving them yams, bananas, chickens, eggs, and other farm produce. In the absence of savings or pensions, retirement often "dictated a return to the soil." Others who had left the profession before retirement became shopkeepers as well as farmers. These occupational shifts were directly related to low pay and the absence of provision for old age in the career structure of the teaching profession, not the product of free choice, or even preference. Goulbourne, *Teachers, Education and Politics*, 104–5, 112–14; Erna Brodber, *The Second Generation of Freemen in Jamaica, 1907–1944* (Gainesville: University Press of Florida, 2004), 61–62; Bryan, *The Jamaican People*, 221–25.
126. McKay's notebook, CMPS.
127. In a letter dated April 26, 1929, U. Theo informed McKay about his working for the United Fruit Company. Exactly when he began working as an agent for the company is unstated. In May 1933, he told McKay that his earnings as a fruit agent had fallen by 90 percent due to the combined effect of economic depression and a storm followed by drought. But employment as an agent, as one writer put it, "could be extremely lucrative." U. Theo McKay to McKay, April 26, 1929, and May 23, 1933, CMPY; Post, *Arise Ye Starvelings*, 117.
128. See Post, *Arise Ye Starvelings*, esp. 116–17.
129. James Carnegie, *Some Aspects of Jamaica's Politics, 1918–1938* (Kingston: Institute of Jamaica, 1973), 116.
130. U. Theo McKay, letter to the editor, "Branch Agricultural Societies," *Gleaner*, December 9, 1918.
131. U. Theo McKay, "Branch Agricultural Societies"; see also Carnegie, *Some Aspects of Jamaican Politics*, 109; and Carnegie, "Claude McKay's Big Brother," 8.
132. "What though before us lies the open grave? / Like men we'll face the murderous, cowardly pack, / Pressed to the wall, dying but—fighting back!" McKay, "If We Must Die," *Liberator*, July 1919, 21.
133. *Gleaner*, August 8, 1922; see also U. Theo McKay, letter to the *Gleaner*, February 24, 1923.
134. Carnegie, *Some Aspects of Jamaican Politics*, 73, 100, 116.

135. "Report on Marcus Garvey by Detective Charles A. Patterson," Kingston, January 2, 1928, reprinted in *MGP*, 7:84–86.
136. U. Theo McKay to Claude McKay, August 2, 1929, CMPY; the word *somebody* is underlined twice in the original.
137. *Gleaner*, July 14, 1923, August 6, 1932, and his obituary, June 17, 1949.
138. In *My Green Hills*, McKay said that he passed the examination "indifferently" (51) but in his notebook he wrote: "I did pass & very highly, my first years' pupil teachers' examination. I had the highest marks of all the pupils from the various neighbouring schools who wrote the examinations." The contradiction is only apparent. The pupil teacher examinations were spread over several years, and it is possible that McKay did extraordinary well in the first years' examination but indifferently in the subsequent ones.
139. *MGH*, 57.
140. Throughout *My Green Hills of Jamaica*, McKay's master is identified only as Brenga, or Old Brenga. However, in his 1911 interview with the *Gleaner*, McKay disclosed the name of his master as a Mr. Campbell of Brown's Town. *Gleaner*, October 7, 1911. McKay probably simply forgot Brenga's real name when he was writing his memoirs in the 1940s.
141. *MGH*, 58.
142. *SP*, 22.
143. "December 1919," *SP*, 23.
144. "My Mountain Home," *SJ*, 125.
145. *MGH*, 66.
146. His brother reported that when Jekyll lived in Bournemouth, he made friends with Robert Louis Stevenson. See Herbert Jekyll to Frank Cundall, March 16, 1929 (Walter Jekyll File, National Library of Jamaica), and detailed appreciation of Jekyll by Cundall, director of the Institute of Jamaica, and others, in the *Gleaner*, August 19, 1929; and Cooper, *Claude McKay*, 23.
147. Walter Jekyll, ed., *Jamaica Song and Story: Annancy Stories, Digging Sings, Ring Tunes, and Dancing Tunes* (London: Folklore Society, 1907). Jekyll's book, a real labor of love, is a major document in Jamaican cultural history.
148. *MGH*, 70.
149. Cooper, *Claude McKay*, 23–24, 29–31. See also Rhonda Cobham, "Jekyll and Claude: The Erotics of Patronage in Claude McKay's *Banana Bottom*," *Caribbean Quarterly* 38, no. 1 (March 1992): 55–78.
150. Jekyll's ascetic qualities are brought out strongly in the appreciation in the *Gleaner*, August 19, 1929. Also see letters of Herbert Jekyll to Frank Cundall, especially that of March 16, 1929 (Walter Jekyll File, National Library of Jamaica). The Oliviers developed a close friendship with Jekyll and testified to the simplicity of his life in Jamaica. Margaret Olivier, ed., *Sydney Olivier: Letters and Selected Writings* (London: Allen and Unwin, 1948), 110, 113. Jekyll's strong attraction to Buddhism is evident in *The Bible Untrustworthy: A Critical Comparison of Contradictory Passages in the Scriptures, With a View of Testing Their Historical Accuracy* (London: Watts, 1908), 265–84. There was hardly a charity or a good cause during his time in Jamaica that Jekyll did not contribute to, as reports in the *Gleaner* document. He also donated the books he reviewed and those he had read to the library of the Institute of Jamaica. Cundall mentions this in his obituary of Jekyll, but it is also there in reports on the Institute in the *Gleaner*.

151. Claude McKay, "My Green Hills of Jamaica," MS, Schomburg Center for Research in Black Culture, New York Public Library, 68–69; hereafter "MGH." See MGH, 70, where the important reference to Tolstoy is omitted.

152. Herbert Jekyll to Frank Cundall, March 16, 1929 (Walter Jekyll File, National Library of Jamaica). Jekyll definitely spent the winter in Jamaica in 1894. An advertisement for the Queen's Hotel in Kingston carried a letter by Jekyll, dated December 1, 1894, extolling the hotel's comforts. The advertisement ran in several issues of the Jamaica Advocate, including that of February 9, 1895.

153. MGH, 70–71.

154. Olivier, Sydney Olivier, 110. He, his wife, Margaret, and the rest of the Olivier family later became very fond of Jekyll and maintained contact right up to his death in 1929.

155. When Jekyll's father died in 1876, he left an estate worth £140,000. Jekyll was left "£300 per annum during the life or widowhood of [his] mother." At his mother's death or remarriage, he was to receive a further £20,000 from his father's estate. Jekyll settled in Jamaica soon after his mother's death. Cooper, Claude McKay, 23, 380n77; Gleaner, August 19, 1929.

156. BB, 71.

157. MGH, 70. David Levering Lewis, in When Harlem Was in Vogue (New York: Oxford University Press, 1989), 58, perceived the incident to be "as revealing as improbable." Revealing, it certainly is. For what other reason would McKay recall it? Improbable? It certainly is not. Lewis gave no explanation as to why he believed it improbable. The clear implication is that McKay was lying. Lewis is not an expert on McKay nor on early-twentieth-century Jamaican history. One can only surmise that he is stretching the canvas of the African American experience in the United States over the Jamaican landscape. What Lewis and others have failed to sufficiently appreciate is that the African American experience is the anomaly of the Americas, the aberration, not the norm. I have come across no parallel in the Americas to the uproar caused in the United States in 1901 when a distinguished Black man, Booker T. Washington, was invited to dinner by the president of the United States, Theodore Roosevelt. No other society in the New World had turned the brutal murdering of Black men and women into a regional if not a national pastime for more than a century; none other than the United States had formally institutionalized racial segregation, given it the imprimatur of law; none other than the United States had on their statute books so-called anti-miscegenation laws stretching into the second half of the twentieth century.

158. MGH, 66.

159. LW, 61.

160. LW, 13.

161. MGH, 66–67. "Cotch Donkey," is almost certainly the poem in question. See Claude McKay, Constab Ballads (London: Watts, 1912), 46; hereafter CB.

162. MGH, 67.

163. Indeed, the very first chapter of Black Skin, White Masks is titled "Le Noir et le langage." The chapter opens: "We attach a fundamental importance to the phenomenon of language." Frantz Fanon, Black Skin, White Masks (New York: Grove, [1952] 2008), 1.

164. Aimé Césaire, quoted in James Baldwin, Nobody Knows My Name (London: Michael Joseph, 1964), 39.

165. Mervyn Alleyne, Roots of Jamaican Culture (London: Pluto, 1988), 15.

166. Quoted in Richard Hart, "Jamaica and Self-Determination, 1660–1970," Race 13, no. 3 (January 1972): 283. Ronald Hyam has a striking discussion of some of the

key techniques through which this sense of inferiority is nurtured: Ronald Hyam, *Britain's Imperial Century, 1815–1914: A Study of Empire and Expansion* (London: Batsford, 1976), esp. 156–162.

167. Richard Hart, a veteran of the Jamaican nationalist struggles of the 1930s, told me the story of the response of a well-educated Jamaican woman to the nationalist ferment in Jamaica in the late 1930s. Knowing that Hart was a part of this political agitation, she turned to him and asked him one day, in all sincerity: "But, Richard, do you really think that the French or the Germans or the Americans could do a better job of ruling Jamaica than the British?" The thought simply never occurred to her, because to her and many Jamaicans at the time it was unthinkable, that the Jamaican people might have wanted to, and might have been able to, rule themselves.

168. Cited in Mervyn Morris, introduction to Louise Bennett, *Selected Poems*, ed. Mervyn Morris (Kingston: Sangster's Book Stores, 1983), xii–xiii. [Translation: "Is that what your mother sent you to school for?" i.e., to speak like that, to speak Jamaican creole.]

169. A. James Arnold, *Modernism and Negritude: The Poetry and Poetics of Aimé Césaire* (Cambridge, MA: Harvard University Press, 1981), 5. See also the introduction by Clayton Eshleman and Annette Smith to Aimé Césaire, *The Collected Poetry* (Berkeley: University of California Press, 1983), 1.

170. The most detailed documentation and analysis of Revert's influence on Césaire is provided by Vincent Clément, "Latitude and Longitude of the Past: Place, Negritude and French Caribbean Identity in Aimé Césaire's Poetry," *Caribbean Studies* 39, nos. 1–2 (2011): 171–93. See also Renée Larrier, "A Tradition of Literacy: Césaire in and out of the Classroom," *Research in African Literatures* 41, no. 1 (2010): 33–45.

171. *MGH*, 76.

172. "Cotch Donkey," *CB*, 46.

173. Morris, introduction to Bennett, *Selected Poems*, iv–v.

174. In a 1911 interview, McKay said: "I began writing dialect verses in 1909, my first attempt being a little thing entitled 'Hard Times.'" *Gleaner*, October 7, 1911. "Hard Times" was published in *Songs of Jamaica*, 53–54.

175. When Bennett was about seven years old a teacher gave her a copy of McKay's *Constab Ballads*, knowing the child's penchant for telling her classmates Annancy stories. "Here are some verses a man wrote in the Jamaican talk. You must read some of them. They're very funny!" Bennett took the book home and shared it with her Grandma Mimi who liked the poems. It was "thrilling" to see the language in print, Bennett said later. She memorized some of the poems and recited them to her friends and relatives. McKay "reinforced Bennett's love of her primary language." Mary Jane Hewitt, "A Comparative Study of the Careers of Zora Neale Hurston and Louise Bennett as Cultural Conservators" (PhD diss., University of the West Indies, 1986), 26–27; James, *A Fierce Hatred of Injustice*, 140.

176. *MGH*, 69.

177. McKay to Nancy Cunard, August 20, 1932, NCC. I discuss at greater length the politics of language in Jamaica as it relates to McKay's early poetry in James, *A Fierce Hatred of Injustice*, 139–51.

178. See James, *A Fierce Hatred of Injustice*, 36–41.

179. Jimmy Carnegie provides a useful portrait of U. Theo (Carnegie, "Claude McKay's Big Brother"), but it is very brief (five pages) and not entirely reliable. Wayne Cooper, in his pioneering biography of McKay, makes U. Theo secondary to Walter Jekyll in McKay's intellectual formation. One cannot help but be struck by the contrast between the Herculean effort Cooper made to reconstruct the life of Jekyll and the

relatively puny attempt to establish U. Theo's biography (Cooper, *Claude McKay*, chap. 1). In *Claude McKay: A Black Poet's Struggle for Identity*, Tyrone Tillery barely mentions U. Theo, gets his name wrong—inexplicably referring to him repeatedly as Theophilious—and confuses U. Theo with Thomas E. McKay, Tommy, another of McKay's brothers. He goes even further than Cooper in exalting the importance of Jekyll. Jekyll's recognition of McKay's "natural attributes" as a poet, Tillery claims, "proved crucial to Claude's development as a writer and intellectual." He writes that "the influence Jekyll exerted on McKay's intellectual development and person-ality was immense, the result being a peculiar combination of social inclinations" (Tillery, *Claude McKay*, 10, 11–12, 13, 19). Edward Brathwaite, in an unforgettably scornful, mocking, and self-righteous discussion of McKay's poetry refers to U. Theo as McKay's "*Dan-is-the-man-in-the-van* school-teacher brother" (Edward Kamau Brathwaite, *History of the Voice: The Development of Nation Language in Anglo-phone Caribbean Poetry* [London: New Beacon, 1984], 20n21). The reference is to the famous calypso song by The Mighty Sparrow satirizing the idiocies of colonial education. (The Mighty Sparrow [Francisco Slinger], "Dan is the Man." The lyrics are transcribed in Stewart Brown, Mervyn Morris and Gordon Rohlehr, eds., *Voice Print: An Anthology of Oral and Related Poetry from the Caribbean* [Harlow, UK: Longman, 1989], 129–30.) He does not condescend to tell us where he got this pearl of wis-dom; he simply throws it out without any recourse to evidence. He describes Jekyll as McKay's Svengali. But how can we take Professor Brathwaite's lofty pronounce-ments seriously when there is no evidence that he has researched his subject and when he does not even know basic facts about the subject on which he speaks with such authority and confidence? For instance, he has Claude six feet under fully eight years before the man was dead (Brathwaite, *History of the Voice*, 19, 20, 22, 28). The irony is that U. Theo was the sort of man Brathwaite would have admired—had he bothered to learn about him. More recently, Gary Edward Holcomb, *Claude McKay, Code Name Sasha: Queer Black Marxism and the Harlem Renaissance* (Gainesville: University Press of Florida, 2007), instead of engaging with the evidence of U. Theo's influence presented in my *A Fierce Hatred of Injustice*, suggested that I elevated the "heterosexual U. Theo" because he is "the acceptable fountainhead" for McKay, whereas because of Jekyll's supposed sexuality, his "role is abrogated" (234–236n9, quotation at 235). I leave it to the reader to judge, but I find it difficult to take Hol-comb seriously given the many errors of fact, let alone interpretation, that disfigure his book. McKay never called Jekyll "my special friend" (235); it was the other way round. McKay never spent "over a year" in the Soviet Union (14, 25); he was there for about eight months. The Easter uprising in Dublin occurred in 1916, not the year before. "Sasha" was never McKay's code name (that belonged to Rose Pastor Stokes); he used his own name. Anarchism, Marxism, Bolshevism, and Trotskyism are not synonyms. I could go on. Suffice to say that Holcomb's little book is astonishingly lazy, tendentious, and self-serving.

180. See especially U. Theo McKay to McKay, March 1, 1929, CMPY.
181. U. Theo to McKay, March 1, 1929.
182. U. Theo acknowledged receipt of the book in his last surviving letter to McKay, that of May 23, 1933.
183. U. Theo to McKay, May 23, 1933.
184. See U. Theo to McKay: March 1, April 26, August 2, 1929.
185. U. Theo to McKay, March 1, 1929. U. Theo was essentially a Fabian socialist, and this ideology was at least one of the strains in the McKay family "blood." As McKay

himself put it toward the end of his life: "I had imbibed Fabian Socialism with my mother's milk, so to speak." McKay, "On Becoming a Roman Catholic," 44.

186. U. Theo to McKay, August 2, 1929.

187. McKay, "On Becoming a Roman Catholic," 43.

188. *MGH*, 20–22.

189. *Gleaner*, October 7, 1911. The interview is introduced and reprinted in James, *A Fierce Hatred of Injustice*, 165–67.

190. "ANPP," 275–76; *NA*, xv–xvi.

191. Countee Cullen, ed., *Caroling Dusk* (New York: Harper, 1927), 82. *Songs of Jamaica* was in fact published in 1912.

192. McKay, "On Becoming a Roman Catholic."

193. "MGH," 36. In the original manuscript, McKay always referred to his brother as U. Theo, never once as Theo. Yet U. Theo is repeatedly referred to as Theo in the published version of *My Green Hills of Jamaica*.

194. Carl Cowl told me that McKay had always impressed upon him the profound role that his big brother played in his development, so he was rather surprised at the role attributed to Jekyll, relative to U. Theo, by commentators on McKay. "Judging from what Claude told me time and time again about his brother's library and about his discussions with U. Theo, it is clear to me that U. Theo was the single most important influence on his life. He spoke of Jekyll with respect and gratitude, but he talked about U. Theo with a great deal of warmth and enthusiasm." Conversation with Carl Cowl, March 28, 1993.

195. *MGH*, 15.

196. *MGH*, 67–68.

197. *Gleaner*, October 7, 1911.

198. *MGH*, 68. His official documents in the United States (immigration and naturalization applications) indicate that McKay was just over 5 feet 7 inches tall and so below the minimum height (5 feet 8 inches) required to join the police force.

199. In 1910, the force had a target of 748 but only had 730 at year's end. In 1911, it had 751 but wanted 785. See Government of Jamaica, *Departmental Reports*, 1911 and 1912 (Kingston: Government Printing Office). The *Gleaner* blamed the difficulties of recruitment and what it saw as the diminishing quality of the island's police force on the Panama Canal authorities. The latter had "drained" Jamaica of the "brain and sinew of the rural population" and had "encourage[d] resignations from the constabulary force by offering superior inducements to trained and capable policemen." See *Gleaner*, March 11, 1913, and discussion in chapter 4 below.

200. Herbert Thomas, *Story of a West Indian Policeman or 47 Years in the Jamaican Constabulary* (Kingston: Daily Gleaner, 1927), 353–54.

201. Author's taped interview with Mrs. Icelyn McKay Binger, May Pen, Clarendon, August 6, 1995.

202. C. A. Crosbie-Smith, "The Jamaica Constabulary Force, 1867 to 1938" (unpublished manuscript, Rhodes House Library, Oxford University, n.d. [c. 1960]), 4.

203. Crosbie-Smith, "The Jamaica Constabulary Force," 5; Richard Hart, "Blacks Under Whites: Racial, Religious, Social, Judicial, Constitutional and Armed Means of Control in a British Colony—Jamaica, 1660–1962" (unpublished manuscript; London, undated; in author's possession), 70.

204. Crosbie-Smith, "The Jamaica Constabulary Force," 6, 9, 14.

205. Thomas, *Story of a West Indian Policeman*, 35.

206. Crosbie-Smith, "The Jamaica Constabulary Force," 11–13.

207. Thomas, *Story of a West Indian Policeman*, 359.

208. Thomas, *Story of a West Indian Policeman*, 354–59.
209. Thomas, *Story of a West Indian Policeman*, 359–60.
210. U. Theo McKay, "Our Police: A Word for the Jamaican," *Jamaica Times*, September 10, 1910. "Let the way be open," U. Theo wrote, "that a young man joining the force may feel that his ability and character will take him to the rank of Sub-Inspector." Why not Inspector of Constabulary, the highest rank possible? Even U. Theo, it appears, despite his broad and progressive outlook, had limited horizons.
211. Hart, "Blacks Under Whites," 71–74. Orlando Patterson, the distinguished Jamaican-born sociologist, provides interesting vignettes of his father's time and struggles in the constabulary as a Black man. Detective Charles Patterson, one of the first Black Jamaicans to gain that rank, was given the job of following and reporting on Garvey after the latter's return to Jamaica. But his encounter with Garvey radicalized him, and he became a "covert Garveyite." In the aftermath of the labor uprisings of 1938, Charles Patterson claimed that he helped to form the police union, the Jamaica Police Federation, recognized by the authorities in 1944. For his agitation for union-ization, he was dismissed from the force without a pension and had to sue to have it reinstated. The young Patterson believes that his father was in the constabulary when McKay served. But McKay had left about a decade before Charles Patterson joined. David Scott, "The Paradox of Freedom: An Interview with Orlando Patterson," *Small Axe* 40 (March 2013): 100–102, 112.

2. Holding the Negro in Subjection: Claude McKay's Jamaica

1. Claude McKay, *A Long Way from Home* (New York: Lee Furman, 1937), 4; hereafter *LW*.
2. Edward Said, *Reflections on Exile and Other Essays* (Cambridge, MA: Harvard University Press, 2000), 173. See Claude McKay, "Flame-Heart," in *SP*, 13. Also see "Home Thoughts," in *HS*, 11.
3. McKay, "Flame-Heart," 13, first stanza. This version was first published in *HS*, 11. An earlier and slightly different version appeared in Claude McKay, *Spring in New Hampshire and Other Poems* (London: Grant Richards, 1920), 30; hereafter *SNH*.
4. Mervyn Morris, introduction to *MGH*, vii–viii.
5. Alistair Hennessy, series preface to Patrick Bryan, *The Jamaican People, 1880–1902: Race, Class and Social Control* (London: Macmillan, 1991), iii.
6. The most praiseworthy of the extant works are Ken Post, *Arise Ye Starvelings: The Jamaican Labour Rebellion of 1938 and Its Aftermath* (The Hague: Matinus Nijhoff, 1978), although its primary focus is the 1930s; Veront M. Satchell, *From Plots to Plantations: Land Transactions in Jamaica, 1866–1900* (Kinston: Institute of Social and Economic Research, 1990), whose remarkable story ends in 1900; Bryan, *Jamaican People*, a pathbreaking work that ends in 1902; and Thomas Holt, *The Problem of Freedom: Race, Labor, and Politics in Jamaica and Britain, 1832–1938* (Baltimore: Johns Hopkins University Press, 1992), which, despite its subtitle, is focused on the period up to Morant Bay (only two of its ten chapters deal with the period after 1865). Major contributions to filling this lacuna are Joyce Lumsden, "Robert Love and Jamaican Politics" (PhD diss., University of the West Indies, 1987); "Joseph Robert Love, 1839–1914: West Indian Extraordinary," *Afro-Americans in New York Life and History* 7, no. 1 (January 1983); "The People's Convention: Celebrating the Diamond Jubilee of Full Freedom in Jamaica," in *August 1st: A Celebration of Emancipation*, ed. Patrick Bryan (Kingston: Department of History, University of the West Indies, 1995);

"A Forgotten Generation: Black Politicians in Jamaica, 1884–1914," in *Before and After 1865: Education, Politics and Regionalism in the Caribbean*, ed. Brian Moore and Swithin Wilmot (Kingston: Ian Randle, 1998); Erna Brodber, *The Second Generation of Freemen in Jamaica, 1907–1944* (Gainesville: University Press of Florida, 2004), based on her PhD diss., University of the West Indies, 1984; and, more recently, Brian L. Moore and Michele A. Johnson, who focus on African Jamaican cultural history in two remarkable volumes, *Neither Led nor Driven: Contesting British Cultural Imperialism in Jamaica, 1865–1920* (Kingston: University of the West Indies Press, 2004) and *"They Do as They Please": The Jamaican Struggle for Cultural Freedom After Morant Bay* (Kingston: University of the West Indies Press, 2011).

7. John Stuart Mill, *Principles of Political Economy* (London: Routledge, 1900), 454. Developed by Latin American social scientists and historians, the metropolis-satellite economic model was popularized in the late 1960s and 1970s in the English-speaking world primarily by the work of André Gunder Frank; see especially his *Capitalism and Underdevelopment in Latin America: Historical Studies of Chile and Brazil* (New York: Monthly Review, 1967).

8. This was a contradiction McKay was to properly appreciate only after he had visited and spent some time in the "mother country" in 1919. There he discovered in no uncertain terms that he was not regarded as British at all. His experience in Britain is discussed in chapter 6.

9. The best overviews of the region's history are Gordon Lewis, *Main Currents in Caribbean Thought: The Historical Evolution of Caribbean Society in Its Ideological Aspects, 1492–1900* (Baltimore: Johns Hopkins University Press, 1983); Franklin Knight, *The Caribbean: The Genesis of a Fragmented Nationalism*, 2nd ed. (New York: Oxford University Press, 1990); and Eric Williams, *From Columbus to Castro: The History of the Caribbean, 1492–1969* (London: André Deutsch, 1970).

10. These global changes have attracted a vast and growing body of literature. Eric Hobsbawm, *The Age of Empire: 1875–1914* (London: Weidenfeld and Nicolson, 1987), is a masterful overview and interpretation of the period.

11. Calculated from J. R. Ward, *Poverty and Progress in the Caribbean, 1800–1960* (London: Macmillan, 1985), 27, table 2. For more on the transformations in the region during the late nineteenth century, see especially R. W. Beachey, *The British West Indies Sugar Industry in the Late Nineteenth Century* (Oxford: Basil Blackwell, 1957); Manuel Moreno Fraginals, *The Sugarmill* (New York: Monthly Review, 1974); Manuel Moreno Fraginals, Frank Moya Pons, and Stanley Engerman, eds., *Between Slavery and Free Labor: The Spanish-Speaking Caribbean in the Nineteenth Century* (Baltimore: Johns Hopkins University Press, 1985); Williams, *From Columbus*; Walter Rodney, *A History of the Guyanese Working People, 1881–1905* (Baltimore: Johns Hopkins University Press, 1981).

12. Gisela Eisner, *Jamaica, 1830–1930: A Study in Economic Growth* (Manchester: Manchester University Press, 1961), 244–45. The classic study of the subject is Noel Deerr, *The History of Sugar*, 2 vols. (London: Chapman and Hall, 1949–1950), which has been added to by Sidney W. Mintz, *Sweetness and Power: The Place of Sugar in Modern History* (New York: Viking, 1985).

13. Eisner, *Jamaica*, 203.

14. Veront Satchell, *From Plots to Plantation: Land Transactions in Jamaica, 1866–1900* (Kingston: Institute of Social and Economic Research, University of the West Indies, 1990), 38.

15. Satchell, *From Plots*, 42–44.

16. Eisner, *Jamaica*, 203.

17. Eisner, *Jamaica*, 294, 302.

18. Richard A. Lobdell, *Economic Structure and Demographic Performance in Jamaica, 1891–1935* (New York: Garland, 1987), 11; Eisner, *Jamaica*, 171.

19. See *Report of the West India Royal Commission*, Appendix C, vol. 3, containing parts 6–13: Proceedings, Evidence, and Documents Relating to the Windward Islands, the Leeward Islands, and Jamaica [C. 8669] (London: Her Majesty's Stationery Office, 1897), 249–430. The evidence and testimony are hereafter abbreviated as *Royal Commission*; the commissioners' own report, *Report of the West India Royal Commission, with Subsidiary Report by D. Morris, Esq . . .* [C. 8655] (London: Her Majesty's Stationery Office, 1897), is referred to as *Commission Report.*

20. Satchell, *From Plots*, 48–49; Lord Olivier, *Jamaica: The Blessed Island* (London: Faber and Faber, 1936), 377–78.

21. Olivier, *Jamaica*, 379.

22. Satchell, *From Plots*, 48.

23. Olivier, *Jamaica*, 379.

24. Holt, *Problem of Freedom*, 353.

25. *Royal Commission*, 339.

26. B. Pullen-Burry, *Jamaica as It Is, 1903* (London: T. Fisher Unwin, 1903), 187.

27. See Olivier, *Jamaica*, 377–98; Ansell Hart, "Banana in Jamaica: Export Trade," *Social and Economic Studies* 3, no. 2 (September 1954): 212–29; Post, *Arise Ye Starvelings*, 37–38, 63–67; Satchell, *From Plots*; Holt, *Problem of Freedom*, 347–56, where a photograph of Baker may be found on 351; Wilson Randolph Bartlett, "Lorenzo Dow Baker and the Development of the Banana Trade between Jamaica and the United States, 1881–1890" (PhD diss., American University, 1977), 56.

28. Bartlett, "Lorenzo Dow Baker," 56. Bartlett's dissertation reads disturbingly like an official biography and verges on the hagiographic; see especially 217–46. Despite his efforts, the thesis inadvertently exposes some of the unsavory sides to the author's hero.

29. The Aliens Law Amendment of 1871 gave aliens the right to acquire and dispose of real and personal property in the island. According to Satchell, this law "had the greatest impact on land ownership, as it enabled thousands of acres of prime lands to be transferred to multinational companies and foreign individuals." The Boston Fruit Company and Lorenzo Dow Baker himself were among the main beneficiaries. Satchell, *From Plots*, 79. See also H. A. Will, "Colonial Policy and Economic Development in the West Indies, 1895–1903," *Economic History Review* (Second Series) 23, no. 1 (April 1970): 129–47; and especially Bartholomew Smith [Theophilus Scholes], *Chamberlain and Chamberlainism: His Fiscal Proposals and Colonial Policy* (London: John Long, 1903)—a powerful, wide-ranging and uncompromising polemic, which perhaps explains the nom de guerre.

30. Quoted in Pullen-Burry, *Jamaica*, 238–40.

31. Satchell, *From Plots*, 38, 41.

32. Post, *Arise Ye Starvelings*, 37.

33. Satchell, *From Plots*, 41, table 3.3. Satchell's table mistakenly gives 25.6 percent instead of 35.6 percent as the 1900 figure for banana earnings. See text on 49.

34. Satchell, *From Plots*, 49; Eisner, *Jamaica*, 238. Jamaica's banana-export earnings were driven by the seemingly insatiable appetite for the fruit in the United States. Within the course of a generation, U.S. banana imports jumped more than thirteenfold in value, from just under $488,000 in 1875 to over $6,550,000 in 1901, even though banana consumption was confined largely to cities on America's east coast and

New Orleans. See Jesse T. Palmer, "The Banana in Caribbean Trade," *Economic Geography* 8, no. 3 (1932): 263.

35. Calculated from Eisner, *Jamaica*, 171, table 27.

36. Holt, *Problem of Freedom*, 353–56; Olivier, *Jamaica*, 379–98; Post, *Arise Ye Starvelings*, 37, 64, 117–18.

37. Bartlett, "Lorenzo D. Baker," 58–62, quotations from 61, 62.

38. *Royal Commission*, 417.

39. *Royal Commission*, 331.

40. *Royal Commission*, 325.

41. *Commission Report*, 20, 70.

42. Olivier, *Jamaica*, 382–83.

43. *HBJ, 1912*, 313.

44. Olivier, *Jamaica*, 379, 381, 386.

45. Bartlett, "Lorenzo Dow Baker," 190–91.

46. Holt, *Problem of Freedom*, 353; see also Satchell, *From Plots*, 103, 106.

47. Walton Look Lai, *Indentured Labor, Caribbean Sugar: Chinese and Indian Migrants to the British West Indies, 1838–1918* (Baltimore: Johns Hopkins University Press, 1993), 185; Holt, *Problem of Freedom*, 353. An American visitor to the island encountered none but Indian laborers on the large banana plantations in Portland: Allan Eric, *"Buckra" Land: Two Weeks in Jamaica*, 2nd ed. (Boston, 1897), 81–83.

48. Eisner, *Jamaica*, 342.

49. Many "squatters" had legitimate claims to the land from which they were evicted; see especially Satchell, *From Plots*, 71.

50. Satchell, *From Plots*, 106, 110.

51. Satchell, *From Plots*, 105–6.

52. Satchell, *From Plots*, 100, table 5.7, and 101–2.

53. Eisner, *Jamaica*, 221–22.

54. Satchell, *From Plots*, 109.

55. Satchell, *From Plots*, 111–50.

56. Satchell, *From Plots*, 75–78.

57. Woodville Marshall, "Notes on Peasant Development in the West Indies Since 1838," *Social and Economic Studies* 17, no. 3 (September 1968): 252–63.

58. Satchell, *From Plots*, 133.

59. Satchell, *From Plots*, 108–9.

60. *Royal Commission*, 427.

61. *MGH*, 60.

62. Calculated from Satchell, *From Plots*, Tables 3.7 and 4.3, 56, 75.

63. *MGH*, 25–26, 60.

64. In Jamaican parlance during McKay's time, *peasantry* was often used as a catchall term, equivalent to rural folk. Peter Fraser has forcefully argued that vagueness in the use of the term also afflicted scholarship on Caribbean rural society and rural groups, rightly pointing out that the term was often misapplied and lacked meaning. There were real peasants—meaning those with access to the soil (often owning it), reliant on their own or their family's labor, who did not need to sell their labor to survive. But such individuals and groups were far fewer in number and proportion than generally thought. See Peter Fraser, "The Fictive Peasantry: Caribbean Rural Groups in the Nineteenth Century," in *Contemporary Caribbean: A Sociological Reader*, ed. Susan Craig, vol. 1 (Maracas, Trinidad and Tobago: College Press, 1981), 319–47. Mindful of the common slippage between them, I have tried to maintain throughout

this text a distinction between *peasants* and *agro-proletarians* or *rural workers*, who lived primarily by selling their labor to the large plantation owners and others in the countryside.

65. Eisner, *Jamaica*, 379.

66. *Royal Commission*, 326.

67. *Royal Commission*, 418.

68. Eisner, *Jamaica*, 337–39, 341; see also Nadine Wilkins, "The Medical Profession in Jamaica in the Post-Emancipation Period," *Jamaica Journal* 21, no. 4 (November 1988–January 1989): 31, where it is claimed that doctors' fees during slavery could be as high as forty shillings a head per annum.

69. Cited in Wilkins, "The Medical Profession," 32.

70. Wilkins, "The Medical Profession," 31–32.

71. Eisner, *Jamaica*, 137, 340, 342.

72. Calculated from Satchell, *From Plots*, 56, table 3.7.

73. *Royal Commission*, 313–14.

74. Eisner, *Jamaica*, 163.

75. Karl Marx, *Capital*, vol. 1 (London: Lawrence and Wishart, 1974), 603. The desperate condition of the urban poor is captured in contemporary accounts carried by the local press; see the remarkable collection, *"Squalid Kingston,"1890–1920: How the Poor Lived, Moved and Had Their Being*, ed. Brian L. Moore and Michele A. Johnson (Kingston: Social History Project, University of the West Indies, 2000), esp. 90–107, depicting conditions in 1911.

76. Richard Lobdell, "Women in the Jamaican Labour Force, 1881–1921," *Social and Economic Studies* 37, nos. 1–2 (March–June 1988): 213–14, and 229–233, tables 9, 11, and 13.

77. Eisner, *Jamaica*, 351.

78. H. G. De Lisser, *Twentieth Century Jamaica* (Kingston: Jamaica Times, 1913), 97. The move from country to town and the world of the domestic servant in Kingston are powerfully evoked by De Lisser in his 1914 novel, *Jane's Career* (New York: Africana, [1914] 1971). For a general overview of domestic service in the island, see B. Higman, "Domestic Service in Jamaica Since 1750," in *Trade, Government and Society in Caribbean History, 1700–1920*, ed. B. Higman (Kingston: Heinemann, 1983); see also Michele A. Johnson, "'Problematic Bodies': Negotiations and Terminations in Domestic Service in Jamaica, 1920–1970," *Left History* 12, no. 2 (Fall/Winter 2007): 84–112.

79. Eisner, *Jamaica*, 350.

80. The Morant Bay Rebellion is discussed in chapter 3.

81. See H. de R. Walker, *The West Indies and the Empire: Study and Travel in the Winter of 1900–1901* (London: T. Fisher Unwin, 1901), chap. 4, esp. 204–5; and H. A. Will, *Constitutional Change in the British West Indies, 1880–1903* (Oxford: Clarendon, 1970), 156n16.

82. *Jamaica Times*, January 25, 1908. Scholes similarly noted that "every mouthful of food" was being taxed. Theo. E. S. Scholes, *The British Empire and Alliances, or Britain's Duty to Her Colonies and Subject Races* (London: Elliot Stock, 1899), 370. Also see the powerful testimony of Rev. Henry Clarke, *Royal Commission*, 286.

83. The taxation regime is listed in great detail in the *Handbook of Jamaica* over the years.

84. Eisner, *Jamaica*, 368–369.

85. *Royal Commission*, 288.

86. Eisner, *Jamaica*, 367.

87. The details of the Tax on Holdings are presented in *HBJ, 1898*, 138.

88. Theo. E. S. Scholes, *Sugar and the West Indies* (London: Elliot Stock, 1897), 5.
89. Scholes, *The British Empire and Alliances*, 369.
90. *Royal Commission*, 416.
91. In 1896 there were 251 estates of more than 1,500 acres; Clarendon led the parishes with thirty-six, followed by St. Ann, St. Catherine, and Westmoreland with thirty-one each. *HBJ, 1898*, 405.
92. The details of the property tax are presented in *HBJ, 1898*, 138.
93. *HBJ, 1898*, 402.
94. Olivier, *Jamaica*, 287.
95. This was a pattern that Theophilus Scholes drew attention to as early as 1897: Scholes, *Sugar and the West Indies*, 17–18.
96. For a good overview of the pattern, see *HBJ, 1898*, 406–10; *HBJ, 1903*, 370–74; *HBJ, 1912*, 416–20.
97. *HBJ, 1898*, 404; *HBJ, 1912*, 414; and Satchell, *From Plots*, 133.
98. The term "land-famine" is from Scholes, *Sugar and the West Indies*, 17.
99. On planter strategy to subordinate the former slaves to the wage labor system, see Williams, *From Columbus*, esp. chap. 18, and especially Holt, *Problem of Freedom*, chaps. 1–6.
100. *HBJ, 1898*, 406.
101. Letter to the editor from "A Cultivator," *Jamaica Advocate*, January 21, 1899.
102. "Exeter Hall," letter to the editor, *Jamaica Advocate*, September 16, 1899. The letter writer was using a pseudonym. The real Exeter Hall was one of the primary London venues for reformers of various kinds. Located on the Strand, it was opened in the early 1830s and closed its doors in 1907. The Caribbean planters and their allies, most notably Thomas Carlyle and James Froude, frequently railed against Exeter Hall, a symbol of philanthropic and liberal agitation.
103. *Commission Report*, 17–18.
104. For a good example, see John Henderson, *The West Indies* (London: Adam and Charles Black, 1905), 221–26.
105. See Winston James, *Holding Aloft the Banner of Ethiopia: Caribbean Radicalism in Early Twentieth-Century America* (London: Verso, 1998), 45–46, for the situation in Barbados.
106. See C. O. 137/742, despatch 711, Governor Probyn to Viscount Milner, Secretary of State for the Colonies, October 23, 1920; enclosure of report by Barclay and Cradwick, Oct. 9, 1920; also C. O. 137/746, Memorial from T. Gordon Somers and C. A. Wilson, on behalf of the Jamaica League, to Winston Churchill, Secretary of State for the Colonies, May 12, 1921; all in the National Archives, Kew, Richmond, Surrey, UK, hereafter TNA.
107. Harry A. Franck, *Roaming Through the West Indies* (New York: Blue Ribbon, 1920), 410.
108. Scholes, *Sugar and the West Indies*, 6, 18; Scholes, *The British Empire and Alliances*, 367–69; Franck, *Roaming Through the West Indies*, 410.
109. Rev. S. J. Washington, "Some Hindrances to the Greater Prosperity of Jamaica During the Last Fifty Years," in *Jamaica's Jubilee, or What We Are and What We Hope to Be* (London: S. W. Partridge, 1888), 80.
110. Washington, "Some Hindrances," 81.
111. See Walker, *West Indies and Empire*, 203; C. O. 137/746, Memorial from T. Gordon Somers and C. A. Wilson, on behalf of the Jamaica League, to Winston Churchill, Secretary of State for the Colonies, May 12, 1921. Also see C. O. 137/742, despatch 711,

Governor Probyn to Viscount Milner, Secretary of State for the Colonies, October 23, 1920; enclosure of report by Barclay and Cradwick, Oct. 9, 1920; TNA.

112. For evidence of the struggle and U. Theo's leading role, see *Jamaica Times*, July 9 and August 6, 1910; *Gleaner*, March 11 and 13, 1913; December 9, 1918; August 6, 1932.

113. *Gleaner*, March 11, 1913.

114. Some 36,412 Indian indentured laborers were brought to Jamaica from the 1840s to 1917, when indentureship ended. Far fewer Chinese indentures entered Jamaica: 510 were brought to the island in 1854 and another 696 in 1884 from Hong Kong. Although unindentured Chinese migrated to the island in the late nineteenth and early twentieth centuries, by 1911 there were only 2,111 in Jamaica. K. O. Laurence, *Immigration Into the West Indies in the Nineteenth Century* ([Barbados]: Caribbean Universities Press, 1971), 26; George W. Roberts, *The Population of Jamaica* (Cambridge: Cambridge University Press, 1957), 132; Orlando Patterson, "Context and Choice in Ethnic Allegiance: A Theoretical Framework and Caribbean Case Study," in *Ethnicity: Theory and Experience*, ed. Nathan Glazer and Daniel P. Moynihan (Cambridge, MA: Harvard University Press, 1975), 323–24; Look Lai, *Indentured Labor*, 276.

115. Ethelred Brown, "Labor Conditions in Jamaica Prior to 1917," *Journal of Negro History* 4, no. 4 (October 1919): 353–54; Douglas Hall, *Free Jamaica, 1838–1865: An Economic History* (New Haven, CT: Yale University Press, 1959), 54, 108; Williams, *From Columbus*, 357–58; Look Lai, *Indentured Labor*, 82–86.

116. Franck, *Roaming Through the West Indies*, 410. The significance of his remark is amplified by the fact that Franck, as is evident from his book, was a racist.

117. Post, *Arise Ye Starvelings*, 63–65; Sidney Mintz, *Caribbean Transformations* (Chicago: Aldine, 1974); Don Robotham, "The Development of a Black Ethnicity in Jamaica," in *Garvey: His Work and Impact*, ed. Rupert Lewis and Patrick Bryan (Kingston: Institute of Social and Economic Research, University of the West Indies, 1988); Swithin Wilmott, "The Growth of Black Political Activity in Post-Emancipation Jamaica," in *Garvey*, ed. Lewis and Bryan; Lorna Simmonds, "Civil Disturbances in Western Jamaica, 1838–1865," *Jamaican Historical Review* 14 (1984); Bryan, *Jamaican People*, 266–82.

118. See C.O. 137/627, encl. "Report of the Montego Bay Riot Commission (May 27th 1902)," TNA; hereafter "Riot Report."

119. "Riot Report," 106–7.

120. "Riot Report," 105.

121. "Riot Report," Annex No. 4. For examples of threatening letters of this kind during the Morant Bay crisis, see Gad Heuman, *"The Killing Time": The Morant Bay Rebellion in Jamaica* (London: Macmillan, 1994), 100–110.

122. Eisner, *Jamaica*, 332–33.

123. Eisner, *Jamaica*, 335.

124. Will, *Constitutional Change*, 66.

125. Quoted in Bryan, *Jamaican People*, 268–69.

126. Adapted from Roberts, *Population of Jamaica*, 330–31, and table I.1.

127. Figures calculated from Roberts, *Population of Jamaica*, 65.

128. For a pioneering discussion of this group, see Bryan, *Jamaican People*, 239–65.

129. Brown, "Labor Conditions," 351–52.

130. Velma Newton, *The Silver Men: West Indian Labour Migration to Panama, 1850–1914* (Kingston: ISER, University of the West Indies, 1984), 22, and 96, table 11. For a good analysis of the building of the Panama Railroad and its context, see Aims

McGuinness, *Path of Empire: Panama and the California Gold Rush* (Ithaca, NY: Cornell University Press, 2008).

131. Newton, *Silver Men*, 96, table 11; Roberts, *Population of Jamaica*, 43, table 7.
132. Newton, *Silver Men*, 118.
133. Williams, *From Columbus*, 359.
134. See Newton, *Silver Men*, 131–59.
135. Eisner, *Jamaica*, 136, table 6; Newton, *Silver Men*, 154, table 19.
136. Newton, *Silver Men*, 95.
137. For the conditions of these workers in Panama, see Lancelot Lewis, *The West Indian in Panama: Black Labor in Panama, 1850–1914* (Washington, DC: University Press of America, 1980); Elizabeth McLean Petras, *Jamaican Labor Migration: White Capital and Black Labor, 1850–1930* (Boulder, CO: Westview, 1988), 71–75, 187–203; Newton, *Silver Men*, 119–30, 139–59; Michael Conniff, *Black Labor on a White Canal: Panama, 1904–1981* (Pittsburgh, PA: University of Pittsburgh Press, 1985), chap. 3; Julie Greene, *The Canal Builders: Making America's Empire at the Panama Canal* (New York: Penguin, 2009), esp. chap. 3; Olive Senior, *Dying to Better Themselves: West Indians and the Building of the Panama Canal* (Kingston: University of the West Indies Press, 2014). See also David McCullough, *The Path Between the Seas: The Creation of the Panama Canal, 1870–1914* (New York: Simon and Schuster, 1977); and Matthew Parker, *Panama Fever: The Epic Story of the Building of the Panama Canal* (New York: Anchor, 2009), esp. chap. 21.
138. Quoted in Patrick Bryan, "The Question of Labor in the Sugar Industry of the Dominican Republic in the Late Nineteenth and Early Twentieth Centuries," in *Between Slavery and Free Labor: The Spanish-Speaking Caribbean in the Nineteenth Centtury*, ed. Manuel Moreno Fraginals, Frank Moya Pons, and Stanley L. Engerman (Baltimore: Johns Hopkins University Press, 1985), 241.
139. Cited in Newton, *Silver Men*, 59.
140. Newton, *Silver Men*, 62–63.
141. Cited in Newton, *Silver Men*, 63; Dr. Love and the milieu of which he was a part are discussed in chapter 1.
142. Newton, *Silver Men*, 63–64; Senior, *Dying to Better Themselves*, 118–24; Petras, *Jamaican Labor Migration*, 143–46.
143. See Franklin Knight, "Jamaican Migrants and the Cuban Sugar Industry, 1900–1934," in *Between Slavery and Free Labor*, ed. Fraginals et al., 97, 100, and 101, table 5.2. For a recent and detailed analysis of the migration to Cuba and the Black British migrant experience there, see Jorge L. Giovannetti-Torres, *Black British Migrants in Cuba: Race, Labor, and Empire in the Twentieth-Century Caribbean, 1898–1948* (Cambridge: Cambridge University Press, 2018).
144. Frank Snowden has shown that in previous epochs of European history the image of Africa had been quite different. See Frank Snowden, *Blacks in Antiquity: Ethiopians in the GrecoRoman Experience* (Cambridge, MA: Harvard University Press, 1970). See also Cheikh Anta Diop, *The African Origin of Civilization: Myth or Reality?* (New York: Lawrence Hill, 1974); and Martin Bernal, *Black Athena: The Afroasiatic Roots of Classical Civilization*, vol. 1 (London: Free Association, 1987).
145. Gordon Lewis, "Race Relations in Britain: A View from the Caribbean," *Race Today* 1, no. 3 (July 1969): 80; Lewis, *Main Currents in Caribbean Thought*, 9.
146. For some rare and qualified exceptions in the British colonies, see Edward Brathwaite, "Caribbean Women During the Period of Slavery," *Caribbean Contact* 11, no. 12 (May 1984): 13; see also Edward Brathwaite, *The Development of Creole Society in Jamaica,*

1770–1820 (Oxford: Clarendon, 1971), 188–91. The historical records of Barbados have so far yielded one exception during the entire period of slavery: a marriage between a colored man and a white woman that took place in 1685. See Jerome Handler, *The Unappropriated People: Freedmen in the Slave Society of Barbados* (Baltimore: Johns Hopkins University Press, 1974), 201.

147. Gad Heuman, *Between Black and White: Race, Politics and the Free Coloreds in Jamaica, 1792–1865* (Oxford: Clio, 1981). For a good overview of the position within the Americas as a whole, see D. Cohen and J. Greene, eds., *Neither Slave nor Free: The Freedmen of African Descent in the Slave Societies of the New World* (Baltimore: Johns Hopkins University Press, 1972); and on Jamaica, Mavis Campbell, *The Dynamics of Change in a Slave Society: A Socio-Political History of the Free Coloureds of Jamaica, 1800–1865* (London: Associated Universities Press, 1976), and for Barbados, Handler, *Unappropriated People.*

148. An estimated 80 percent of "freedmen"—manumitted slaves, women as well as men—in eighteenthcentury Jamaica were colored; the remaining 20 percent were Black (Heuman, *Between Black and White*, 4). At the time, well over 90 percent of the island's population was Black. The skewed pattern continued in the nineteenth century (B. W. Higman, *Slave Population and Economy in Jamaica, 1807–1834* [Cambridge: Cambridge University Press, 1976], 176–78).

149. Heuman, *Between Black and White*, 6.

150. Quoted in Higman, *Slave Population and Economy in Jamaica*, 189. Higman (208–10) argues that the pattern is partly explained by the planters' belief that colored slaves were weak and unsuited to labor in the field. This is not to say that domestic slaves did not experience atrocious physical abuse. See Brathwaite, *Development of Creole Society*, 156–57, for some examples of particularly gratuitous as well as gruesome acts of violence against domestic slaves. Despite the frequent and capricious cruelty their masters and mistresses dispensed in the house, domestic slaves were "regarded by most slaves and the master as being in a more 'honourable' position than the field slaves." Brathwaite, *Development of Creole Society*, 155; see also Patterson, *Sociology of Slavery*, 57–59.

151. Gardner, *History of Jamaica*, 97; Fernando Henriques, *Family and Colour in Jamaica* (London: MacGibbon & Kee, 1968), 33.

152. Brathwaite, *Development of Creole Society*, 167; Douglas Hall, "Jamaica," in *Neither Slave nor Free*, ed. Cohen and Greene, 196; and Higman, *Slave Population and Economy*, 139. According to Handler (*Unappropriated*, 6), this hierarchy did not exist in the same way in Barbados. There, one was "colored," "black," or "white". The permutations did not take the form of the ramified social categories that existed in Jamaica. The Spanish, Portuguese, and Dutch colonies had even more categories. Indeed, in Spanish America, no less than 128 gradations were possible, and in Brazil, one scholar counted 492 different categories. Magnus Mörner, *Race Mixture in the History of Latin America* (Boston: Little, Brown, 1967); Leslie Rout, *The African Experience in Spanish America, 1502 to the Present Day* (Cambridge: Cambridge University Press, 1976); Franklin Knight, *Slave Society in Cuba During the Nineteenth Century* (Madison: University of Wisconsin Press, 1970); Marvin Harris, "Referential Ambiguity in the Calculus of Brazilian Racial Identity," in *Afro-American Anthropology*, ed. Norman Whitten and J. F. Szwed (New York: Free Press, 1970); Roger Bastide, "The Present Status of Afro-American Research in Latin America," in *Slavery, Colonialism and Racism*, ed. Sidney Mintz (New York: Norton, 1974).

153. Higman, *Slave Population and Economy*, 176. "In Barbados . . . no one of *known* negroid ancestry, no matter how remote, could be considered *white* with respect to social or legal status." (Handler, *Unappropriated*, 6, emphasis in original).

154. Heuman, *Between Black and White*, 76.

155. Heuman, *Between Black and White*, 12.

156. Edward Long, *The History of Jamaica*, vol. 2 (London: Frank Cass, [1774] 1970), 332. The presence of such tensions did not mean that political alliances did not occur between freed Africans and coloreds; they did. Such alliances, however, were in general fragile, uneasy, and on the whole, ephemeral. Heuman, *Between Black and White*, documents this very well in the case of Jamaica. With the qualified exception of Cuba, Brazil, and Puerto Rico, this state of affairs was typical of the Americas as a whole. See James, *Holding Aloft the Banner of Ethiopia*, chap. 4.

157. Fanon's observation of the behavior of Caribbeans serving in the French army in Africa before 1939 provides an appropriate parallel here: "The West Indian, not satisfied to be superior to the African, despised him and while the white man could allow himself certain liberties with the native, the West Indian absolutely could not. This was because, between whites and Africans, there was no need of a reminder; the difference stared one in the face. But what a catastrophe if the West Indian should suddenly be taken for an African!" (Frantz Fanon, "West Indians and Africans," in *Toward the African Revolution* [Harmondsworth: Penguin, 1970], 30). It should be noted that a substantial number of Africans were owned as slaves by mulattoes: 16 percent of Jamaica's slaves (50,000 of the 310,368) were owned by mulattoes (Campbell, *The Dynamics of Change*, 62). They were not, however, the largest group of non-European slaveholders in the Caribbean. In Saint Domingue in 1789, on the eve of the Haitian revolution, their counterparts, the *affranchis*, owned no less than a quarter of the overall slave population estimated at 500,000 (Carolyn Fick, *The Making of Haiti: The Saint Domingue Revolution from Below* [Knoxville: University of Tennessee Press, 1990], 19).

158. Cited in Heuman, *Between Black and White*, 14. My translation: "If I must have a master or mistress, give me a white one—don't give me a mulatto, they don't treat black people well." Long, incidentally, had also suggested that "the middle class [the coloreds] are not much liked by the Negroes, because the latter abhor the idea of being slaves to the descendants of slaves" (Long, *The History of Jamaica*, 332).

159. Cited in Campbell, *Dynamics of Change*, 57. Long's and Carmichael's remarks were probably self-serving, but that does not make their observations ipso facto untrue, especially given the presence of corroborating evidence.

160. C. L. R. James, *The Black Jacobins* (New York: Vintage, [1938] 1963), 43.

161. Patterson, *Sociology of Slavery*, 146–47, 152; quotation at 152.

162. See Barbara Bush, *Slave Women in Caribbean Slave Society, 1650–1838* (London: James Currey, 1990), 105; she gives evidence of the positive and warm reception that newly arrived Africans sometimes received from creole slaves.

163. Karl Marx, "The Eighteenth Brumaire of Louis Bonaparte," in *Surveys from Exile* (Harmondsworth: Penguin, 1973), 146.

164. C. A. Wilson, *Men with Backbone and Other Pleas for Progress*, 2nd ed. (Kingston: Educational Supply, 1913), 80–81.

165. Marcus Garvey to Robert Moton, February 29, 1916, reprinted in *The Marcus Garvey and the Universal Negro Improvement Association Papers*, ed. Robert Hill, vol. 1 (Berkeley: University of California Press, 1983), 182; hereafter *Garvey Papers*.

166. Zora Neale Hurston, *Tell My Horse* [1938], in Hurston, *Folklore, Memoirs, and Other Writings* (New York: Library of America, 1995), 280.
167. Hurston, *Tell My Horse*, 282; emphasis in the original.
168. Hurston, *Tell My Horse*, 279, 282.
169. J. H. Reid, "The People of Jamaica Described," in *Jamaica's Jubilee*, 88.
170. Eric Williams, *The Negro in the Caribbean* (Westport, CT: Greenwood, [1942]1969), 66.
171. Wilson, *Men with Backbone*, 81.
172. Marcus Garvey, "The British West Indies in the Mirror of Civilization: History Making by Colonial Negroes," *African Times and Orient Review* 2, no. 16 (Mid-October 1913): 159.
173. Long, *The History of Jamaica*, 332. See, for instance, Frantz Fanon, *Black Skin, White Masks* (New York: Grove, [1952] 2008); and Walter Rodney, *The Groundings with My Brothers* (London: Bogle L'Ouverture, 1975), 32–33.
174. Franck, *Roaming Through the West Indies*, 412. The man, described by Franck only as an octoroon schoolteacher, also said that he "would no sooner marry a white woman, because it would be hell in a few years." What he meant by this is not clear.
175. Hurston, *Tell My Horse*, 280.
176. Henriques, *Family and Colour*, 171; Nancy Foner, *Status and Power in Rural Jamaica* (New York: Teachers' College, Columbia University Press, 1973), 27; Fanon, *Black Skin, White Masks*; Williams, *The Negro*, 66–67; Mervin Alleyne, *Roots of Jamaican Culture* (London: Pluto, 1988); and G. Kruijer, *A Sociological Study of the Christiana Area* (Kingston: Ministry of Agriculture, 1969), 22–23.

3. You Caan' Mek We Shet Up: McKay's Jamaican Poetry of Rebellion

1. *CB*, 7.
2. Claude McKay, *Home to Harlem* (New York: Harper, 1928), hereafter *HH*; *Banjo: A Story Without a Plot* (New York: Harper, 1929), hereafter *B*; *Romance in Marseille* (New York: Penguin, 2020); *Gingertown* (New York: Harper & Brothers, 1932), hereafter *G*.
3. See McKay to Max Eastman, August 28 and September 16, 1946, CMI.
4. See, for example, *Gleaner*, October 7, 1911; *Jamaica Times*, January 13, 1912; *Christian Commonwealth*, March 27, 1912, 420.
5. James Weldon Johnson, ed., *The Book of American Negro Poetry* (New York: Harcourt, Brace & World, 1931), 167. McKay was indeed the "poet of passion," but I shall argue and demonstrate, he was also the poet of thought, a philosopher-poet.
6. Jean Wagner, *Black Poets of the United States: From Paul Laurence Dunbar to Langston Hughes*, trans. Kenneth Douglas (Urbana: University of Illinois Press, [1962] 1973), 204.
7. McKay, incidentally, rated *Songs of Jamaica* above *Constab Ballads*; see McKay to Nancy Cunard, August 20 and 31, 1932, NCC.
8. In his memorable polemic against Sartre and Brecht, Theodor Adorno emphasized the negative as opposed to the prescriptive role of art. "It is not the office of art," he declared, "to spotlight alternatives, but to resist by its form alone the course of the world, which permanently puts a pistol to men's heads." Theodor Adorno, "Commitment," in *Aesthetics and Politics*, by Theodor Adorno, Walter Benjamin, Ernst Bloch, Bertolt Brecht, and Georg Lukács (London: New Left, 1977), 180.

9. *Buckra, backra,* or *bockra* is derived from the Efik *mbakara,* meaning "he who surrounds or governs." In the Caribbean, it soon became synonymous with white people. *Quashee* or *quashie* also has West African roots; in the days of slavery, it was used by enslaved Akan-speaking people to describe a male born on a Sunday. It was soon extended beyond this usage, and by the late eighteenth century, *Quashee* was taken as "a typical name for a negro," often with derogatory connotations. In the early twentieth century, *quashie* was generally used to mean a peasant. See Frederic Cassidy and Robert Le Page, eds., *Dictionary of Jamaican English,* 2nd ed. (Cambridge: Cambridge University Press, 1980); and Frederic Cassidy, *Jamaica Talk: Three Hundred Years of the English Language in Jamaica,* 2nd ed. (Kingston: Institute of Jamaica, 1971), 155–57. To avoid confusion, I spell *buccra* in this chapter the way McKay does; in more modern usage, it is generally spelled *buckra.*
10. "Quashie to Buccra," *SJ,* 13.
11. "Quashie to Buccra," 14.
12. "Hard Times," *SJ,* 53.
13. "Hard Times," 54.
14. "Fetchin' Water," *SJ,* 42.
15. "Fetchin' Water," 42.
16. "Retribution," *SJ,* 49.
17. "Two-An'-Six," *SJ,* 86.
18. "Two-An'-Six," 87–88.
19. "Two-An'-Six," 88.
20. "Two-An'-Six," 90.
21. "Two-An'-Six," 90.
22. "Two-An'-Six," 91.
23. Martha Beckwith, *Black Roadways: A Study of Jamaican Folk Life* (Chapel Hill: University of North Carolina Press, 1929), 50.
24. "Whe' Fe Do?" *SJ,* 28–29. Schopenhauer is also explicitly echoed in another of McKay's Jamaican poems: "De helpless playt'ing of a Will, / We'll spend our short days here; an' still, / Though prisoners, feel somehow free / To live our lives o' misery." McKay, "To W. G. G.," *CB,* 77.
25. The suicide-contemplating "Is It Worth While?" "ANPP," 276.
26. *MGH,* 19; *LW,* 13–14; *The Wisdom of Schopenhauer as Revealed in Some of His Writings,* selected and translated by Walter Jekyll (London: Watts, 1911). Since McKay did not leave Jamaica until July 1912, it is probable that he read even more of Jekyll's Schopenhauer book after its release in 1911.
27. Arthur Schopenhauer, "Additional Remarks on the Doctrine of the Suffering of the World," in *Parerga and Paralipomena: Short Philosophical Essays,* vol. 2, trans. E. F. J. Payne (Oxford: Clarendon, 1974), 300. This essay was among those selected and translated by Jekyll and, therefore, one that McKay might very well have read. See Jekyll, *The Wisdom of Schopenhauer,* 327–46.
28. Schopenhauer, "Additional Remarks," 293.
29. Schopenhauer, "Additional Remarks," 300.
30. Schopenhauer, "Additional Remarks," 299; the italicized words were written in English by Schopenhauer.
31. Schopenhauer, "Additional Remarks," 300; emphasis in the original.
32. Winston James, *Holding Aloft the Banner of Ethiopia: Caribbean Radicalism in Early Twentieth-Century America* (London: Verso, 1998), 32–36.

33. McKay to Josephine Herbst, August 18 [1924], emphasis in original; Josephine Herbst Papers, Beinecke Rare Book and Manuscript Library, Yale University.

34. Max Eastman, "Biographical Note," in *SP*, 110. It is expressive of the man and the times, that even after thirty years of friendship with McKay, Max Eastman felt comfortable using such language. And Eastman was McKay's best friend!

35. *HH*, 105.

36. See "Hard Times" and "Whe' Fe Do?" *SJ*, 54 and 28.

37. McKay never gives the name of U. Theo's wife. He reports that she was unhappy about moving from Mount Carey to rural Clarendon. It is unclear whether the couple divorced or the wife died. It is also possible that they were not formally married, but that was unlikely, given U. Theo's class and standing. U. Theo, however, did marry Hepzibah Elliott McKenzie of Clarendon; they had two daughters and a son who died in childhood. Interview with U. Theo's daughter, Eloise McKay Edwards, London, August 23, 1995.

38. *MGH*, 19–20.

39. Wagner, *Black Poets of the United States*, 215; see also Alan McLeod, "Memory and the Edenic Myth: Claude McKay's Green Hills of Jamaica," *World Literature Written in English* 18, no. 1 (April 1979).

40. Wagner, *Black Poets of the United States*, 215.

41. *LW*, 95.

42. Jean Wagner Papers, Houghton Library, Harvard University.

43. The manuscript of the anthology is among the McKay's papers at Yale, CMPY; reprinted in Claude McKay, *Complete Poems*, ed. William J. Maxwell (Urbana: University of Illinois Press, 2004), 223.

44. The original 1963 French edition of Wagner's book has an appendix (omitted from the English edition) of unpublished poems ("Poèmes Inédits") by some of the poets whose work formed the subject of Wagner's study. Wagner published in the appendix eight poems by McKay, which he claimed were previously unpublished. (In reality, at least two of them had been published.) McKay's poem on cities does not appear among Wagner's selection. See Jean Wagner, *Les Poètes Nègres des Etats-Unis: Le Sentiment Racial et Religieux dans la Poésie De P. L. Dunbar à L. Hughes (1890–1940)* (Paris: Librairie Istra, 1963), 580–84.

45. *MGH*, 52–53.

46. *MGH*, 56–57.

47. *MGH*, 53.

48. *CB*, 40–42; 57–58.

49. *CB*, 52–56; 13–14; 57–58; 71–72.

50. *CB*, 50–51; 66–68.

51. *CB*, 37–38.

52. See in *SJ*: "Reveille Soun'in," 61–62; "To Bennie," 127; "To a Comrade," 129; and in *CB*: "De Route March," 11–12; "Bennie's Departure," 15–22; "Fire Practice," 26–27; "Second-Class Constable Alston," 28–29; "Bound Fe Duty," 33. See also McKay's autobiographical story of his time in the police force, "When I Pounded the Pavement," in *G*, 203–20.

53. "The Bobby to the Sneering Lady," *CB*, 66.

54. "The Bobby to the Sneering Lady," 67n.

55. "The Bobby to the Sneering Lady," 67.

56. "The Heart of a Constab," *CB*, 62–63. It is likely that the disapproving Black people referred to in the poem included members of McKay's own extended, if not

immediate, family. The hypothesis is supported by his story "When I Pounded the Pavement," discussed below.

57. "ANPP," 276.
58. McKay, "When I Pounded the Pavement," *G*, 211.
59. McKay, "When I Pounded the Pavement," 211.
60. McKay, "When I Pounded the Pavement," 212.
61. McKay, "When I Pounded the Pavement," 212.
62. McKay, "When I Pounded the Pavement," 219–20.
63. *Gleaner*, March 4, 1913.
64. *Gleaner*, February 20, 1912. In marked contrast to the way they treated Black Jamaicans, the police were "extremely polite" and deferential toward tourists: Eric Allan, *"Buckra" Land: Two Weeks in Jamaica* (Boston: Boston Fruit Company, 1897), 40. The sordid tale of Jamaican tourism is very well told by Frank Taylor, *To Hell with Paradise: A History of the Jamaican Tourist Industry* (Pittsburgh: University of Pittsburgh Press, 1993).
65. *Gleaner*, December 10, 1912.
66. McKay to Nancy Cunard, April 30, 1932, NCC.
67. "ANPP," 275; "Original Translator's Note," *NA*, xv; Countee Cullen, ed., *Caroling Dusk* (New York: Harper, 1927), 82; Johnson, *Book of American Negro Poetry*, 165; *LW*, 199; *MGH*, 72, 78–79.
68. I have been able to deduce this even though my attempts at gaining a copy of McKay's police record files have been fruitless. According to the Jamaica Police Force, McKay's records are no longer extant. It is, nevertheless, possible to accurately determine how long he spent in the constabulary. In an interview published in the *Gleaner* in October 1911, McKay was asked "When did you join the Police Force?" To which he replied: "I enlisted last June—on the 7th of June." Wayne Cooper, in *Claude McKay: Rebel Sojourner in the Harlem Renaissance—A Biography* (Baton Rouge: Louisiana State University Press, 1987), understandably but wrongly deduced from this that McKay entered the force in June 1911 and also claimed that he spent less than a year as a policeman. Both claims are mistaken. We know that the first is incorrect because McKay's poem "To Inspector W. E. Clark," obviously written *after* he had spent time in the force, is dated "21st May, 1911." McKay's "last June" must, therefore, have meant June 1910. (Jamaicans frequently use English that way. The expression "last June" generally means "June last year," as opposed "this June" or "this past June," or in creole, "June jus' gaan") McKay's 1918 statement that he served between 1910 and 1911 is useful insofar as it corroborates the 1910 induction date. Furthermore, despite his obfuscations, we do know that at least as late as October 21, 1911, McKay was still a member of the force. The *Gleaner* of that date reported, "Some of his finest verses cannot be published owing to his position in the Constabulary Force, as they treat of present political questions." Within less than a fortnight, however, the *Gleaner* (November 1, 1911) informed its readers that McKay had resigned from the force, noting that he had been stationed at Half-Way Tree and, at the time of his resignation, "was attached to the clerical staff." Clearly, then, McKay left the force sometime between the twenty-first and thirty-first of October 1911, probably on the thirty-first. We can therefore conclude that McKay served just under seventeen months, from June 7, 1910 to October 31, 1911. *Gleaner*, October 7 and 21, and November 1, 1911; *Jamaica Times*, November 18, 1911; Cooper, *Claude McKay*, 28, 34; "To Inspector W. E. Clark," *SJ*, 105.
69. McKay to Nancy Cunard, April 30, 1932, NCC.

70. McKay to Nancy Cunard, August 31, 1932, NCC.

71. The description comes from Harry A. Franck, *Roaming Through the West Indies* (New York: Blue Ribbon, 1920), 410.

72. Cassidy, *Jamaica Talk*, 158–59; Cassidy and Le Page, *Dictionary of Jamaican English*, 80.

73. "Flat-Foot Drill," *CB*, 13–14. The *Gleaner*, the mouthpiece of the Jamaican ruling class, echoed the sentiments of McKay's drill instructor. In a long editorial on "The Number and Efficiency of the Colony's Police Force," it suggested that the authorities in Panama had "drain[ed] the island of the brain and sinew" of the rural population, "had . . . encourage[d] resignations from the constabulary force by offering superior inducements to trained and capable policemen." The problem was, accordingly, not just the number but the quality of recruits. The editorial was stimulated by a series of major burglaries in the business district of Kingston and the ensuing outcry of the merchants calling for law and order and greater protection from the authorities. The *Gleaner* was especially peeved at the audacity of one group of burglars and the incompetence of the police. The thieves struck in the vicinity of the *Gleaner* offices, and the paper could not "understand a gang of burglars getting into a store . . . and carting away a large haul, without being detected by the policemen on the beat." The paper did not suggest that the policemen may have been complicit in the theft, but that the incident showed a lack of "alertness, intelligence and efficiency of the men employed." Thus, the paper concluded, "If 'you cannot make a silk purse out of a sow's ear,' no more can police officers make competent constables out of uneducated rustics destitute of any real ability." *Gleaner*, March 11, 1913.

    The Isthmian Canal Commission (the American authority in charge of building the Panama Canal), did recruit men from the Jamaican constabulary, who in fact constituted the majority of the police force in the Canal Zone. As early as 1904, some were serving in the regular police force in Panama. See Velma Newton, *The Silver Men: West Indian Labour Migration to Panama, 1850–1914* (Kingston: Institute of Social and Economic Research, University of the West Indies, 1984), 137; Julie Greene, *The Canal Builders: Making America's Empire at the Panama Canal* (New York: Penguin, 2009), 128; Olive Senior, *Dying to Better Themselves: West Indians and the Building of the Panama Canal* (Kingston: University of the West Indies Press, 2014), 171–72.

74. "A Labourer's Life Give Me," *CB*, 71.

75. Ellen Tarry, *The Third Door: The Autobiography of An American Negro Woman* (New York: David McKay, 1955), 131.

76. "To Inspector W. E. Clark (On the Eve of His Departure for England)," *SJ*, 104; also see "To Inspector W. E. Clark (On His Return)," in which Clark is described as "An officer so dear an' true," *CB*, 89.

77. *CB*, 8.

78. "My Native Land, My Home," *SJ*, 84.

79. "My Native Land, My Home," 85.

80. "My Native Land, My Home," 85.

81. "My Native Land, My Home," 85.

82. Claude McKay, "Peasants' Ways o' Thinkin'," *Gleaner*, January 27, 1912.

83. It should be pointed out, however, that contrary to the arguments of British colonial apologists, the abolition of the slave trade and of slavery itself was not brought about by the disinterested goodness of the British ruling class, who had ostensibly recovered their moral posture at the end of the eighteenth and the beginning of the

nineteenth centuries. These progressive developments were brought about by the combination of a number of circumstances and forces: the frightening spectacle of emancipation from below exemplified by the Haitian Revolution (1791–1804); the emergence of new economic forces in Britain less dependent upon the slave trade and upon Caribbean slavery itself; the resistance of the enslaved Africans in the colonies; the declining economic significance of Caribbean slavery to the British economy; and the agitation of abolitionists in Britain. There is a substantial body of literature on the subject largely revolving around the seminal work of the Caribbean scholar-politician Eric Williams, *Capitalism and Slavery* (Chapel Hill: University of North Carolina Press, 1944). The decades-old debate over Williams's controversial text has not abated with time. For a good summary of the highlights up to the time of its publication, see Richard B. Sheridan, "Eric Williams and *Capitalism and Slavery*: A Biographical and Historiographical Essay," in *British Capitalism and Caribbean Slavery: The Legacy of Eric Williams*, ed. Barbara Solow and Stanley Engerman, (Cambridge: Cambridge University Press, 1987).

84. McKay, *Liberator*, September 1921, 32; the remark appears in an untitled review by McKay of Lytton Strachey's book, *Queen Victoria*.

85. Review of *Queen Victoria*, 32.

86. For further illumination of the subject, see Kathleen Montieth, "The Victoria Jubilee Celebrations of 1887 in Jamaica," *Jamaica Journal* 20, no. 4 (November 1987–January 1988).

87. Philip Curtin, *Two Jamaica's: The Role of Ideas in a Tropical Colony, 1830–1865* (Cambridge, MA: Harvard University Press, 1955), 197; Richard Hart, "Jamaica and Self-Determination, 1660–1970," *Race* 13, no. 3 (January 1972): 282–83; Gordon Lewis, *Main Currents in Caribbean Thought: The Historical Evolution of Caribbean Society in Its Ideological Aspects, 1492–1900* (Baltimore: Johns Hopkins University Press, 1983), 307–10.

88. Herbert Thomas, *Story of a West Indian Policeman or 47 Years in the Jamaican Constabulary* (Kingston: Daily Gleaner, 1927), 25–26.

89. Claude McKay, "Notes on Jamaican History," MGH, 7; CMPS.

90. McKay, "Notes on Jamaican History," 7. For a fine discussion of the "cult of monarchy and Empire" in Jamaica, see Brian L. Moore and Michele A. Johnson, *Neither Led nor Driven: Contesting British Cultural Imperialism in Jamaica, 1865–1920* (Kingston: University of the West Indies Press, 2004), chap. 9.

91. Hart, "Jamaica and Self-Determination," 286; George Eaton, *Alexander Bustamante and Modern Jamaica* (Kingston: Kingston Publishers, 1975), 95.

92. The hegemonic hold of the ideology of what we may call the "Crown as Protector" is completely ignored in Anthony Bogues's interesting discussion of Jamaican nationalism, which fatally undermines his argument: Anthony Bogues, "Nationalism and Jamaican Political Thought," in *Jamaica in Slavery and Freedom: History, Heritage and Culture*, ed. Kathleen E. A. Montieth and Glen Richards (Kingston: University of the West Indies Press, 2002). For a brief discussion of the rhythm of nationalism in Cuba and Puerto Rico compared to that of Anglophone Caribbean, see James, *Holding Aloft the Banner of Ethiopia*, chap. 4. For similar reasons to those in the British Caribbean (with "Republican France" the analogue of Queen Victoria), there has hardly been any significant nationalist aspiration in the French Caribbean. From time to time, one hears faint cries from Guadeloupe and even less from Martinique. This includes its remarkable line of Black intellectuals over the centuries. For a good overview of the case, see Richard Burton, "Between the Particular and the Universal:

Dilemmas of the Martinican Intellectual," in *Intellectuals in the Twentieth-Century Caribbean*, vol. 2, ed. Alistair Hennessy (London: Macmillan, 1992); also, Richard Burton and Fred Reno, eds., *French and West Indian: Martinique, Guadeloupe and French Guiana Today* (London: Macmillan, 1995).

93. "Old England," *SJ*, 63.

94. "Old England," 64.

95. See, for instance, Wayne Cooper, ed., *The Passion of Claude McKay: Selected Prose and Poetry, 1912-1948* (New York: Schocken, 1973), 4-5; Cooper, *Claude McKay*, 37; Wagner, *Black Poets*, 221; Lloyd Brown, *West Indian Poetry*, 2nd ed. (London: Heinemann, 1984), 43-44; and Tyrone Tillery, *Claude McKay: A Black Poet's Struggle for Identity* (Amherst: University of Massachusetts Press, 1992), 14.

96. "Old England," 65; emphasis added.

97. "To Inspector W. E. Clark," 104.

98. "Old England," 64; emphasis added.

99. "Notes on Jamaican History," 7.

100. McKay, to Max Eastman, June 18, 1932, CMI.

101. But see the very interesting discussion that John Henderson, a British visitor to the island, had with a Black Jamaican man at the turn of the century. Unnamed, he stands out on the Jamaican landscape, a strange creature, a cross between an apparition and a prophet. Well-groomed, dark-skinned, confident, traveled (he lived in England for ten years and traveled on the continent), prosperous (he describes himself as a planter), articulate, he calls for "Jamaica for the Jamaicans." Deeply resenting the Crown colony system in which the colonial governor has a built-in majority in the Legislative Council and de facto power of veto over the island's affairs, he nevertheless believes that the island should remain a part of the British Empire even though he envisages a free and independent Jamaica. The limits of his radicalism and nationalism are captured in the following remarks: "I would have Jamaica governed as England is governed. The people of this island have every moral right to govern themselves, to frame their own laws and to administer those laws. We are no longer barbarians; we are an educated people with ambitions, and the strength to attain our ambitions. We recognize that it is a fine thing to be part of the great Empire of Britain, but we recognize, even more clearly, that it is a finer thing to be a free, unfettered nation. England will always have our heartiest support and affection. When we have become a nation and ceased to be a crown colony, Jamaica will always feel that really she is the child of Britain." John Henderson, *The West Indies* (London: Adam and Charles Black, 1905), 145-51, quotation at 147.

102. On the relation between MacDermot and McKay, see McKay, "Personal Notes on the History of Jamaica," 7; W. Adolphe Roberts, *Six Great Jamaicans: Biographical Sketches*, 2nd. ed. (Kingston: Pioneer, 1957), 91; also see U. Theo McKay to Claude McKay, August 2, 1929, CMPY. For more on MacDermot's life and work, see the introduction by J. E. Clare McFarlane to Tom Redcam, *Orange Valley and Other Poems* (Kingston: Pioneer, 1951); J. E. Clare McFarlane, *A Literature in the Making* (Kingston: Pioneer, 1956), 1-11; Kenneth Ramchand, *The West Indian Novel and Its Background* (London: Faber and Faber, 1970), 51-55; and Mervyn Morris, "The All Jamaica Library," *Jamaica Journal*, March 1972, 47-49.

103. Redcam articulated this position in his newspaper, *Jamaica Times*. See, for instance, "An 'All Jamaica' Entertainment," *Jamaica Times*, June 15, 1912; "Our Writers," *Jamaica Times*, August 10, 1912; and "Sons and Daughters of Jamaica," front page, *Jamaica Times*, August 24, 1912. MacDermot deserves a biography, but has none. The most

detailed portrait of him is provided by Roberts, *Six Great Jamaicans*, 81–98; see also Leah Reade Rosenberg, *Nationalism and the Formation of Caribbean Literature* (New York: Palgrave Macmillan, 2007), chap. 2 for a useful assessment of MacDermot. Lloyd Brown loses sight completely of the nationalistic side of MacDermot; see Brown, *West Indian Poetry*, 28–32.

104. Before its demise, the National Club provided two of its officers, Marcus Garvey and W. A. Domingo, with valuable political experience before they also migrated to the United States. Hart, "Jamaica and Self-Determination," 282; Robert A. Hill, ed., *The Marcus Garvey and Universal Negro Improvement Association Papers*, vol. 1 (Berkeley: University of California Press, 1983), 20–21; Rupert Lewis, *Marcus Garvey: Anti-Colonial Champion* (London: Karia, 1987), 42–44; Francis Lee, *Fabianism and Colonialism: The Life and Political Thought of Lord Sydney Olivier* (London: Defiant, 1988), 120–24.

105. C. A. Wilson, *Men with Backbone and Other Pleas for Progress*, 2nd ed. (Kingston: Educational Supply, 1913), 81.

106. Wilson, *Men with Backbone*, 82.

107. Wilson, *Men with Backbone*, 83.

108. Wilson, *Men with Backbone*, 82.

109. *Gleaner*, October 7, 1911.

110. McKay's dedication reads in full: "TO / HIS EXCELLENCY / SIR SYDNEY OLIVIER, K.C.M.G., / GOVERNOR OF JAMAICA, / WHO / BY HIS SYMPATHY WITH THE BLACK RACE / HAS WON / THE LOVE AND ADMIRATION OF ALL JAMAICANS, / THIS VOLUME IS BY PERMISSION RESPECTFULLY DEDICATED."

111. *MGH*, 73.

112. In *My Green Hills*, McKay specifically recalled U. Theo telling him that Olivier's book *White Capital and Coloured Labor* [1906] was "very good"; *MGH*, 23. See also U. Theo's letters to the editor, *Gleaner*, March 13, 1913, and January 20, 1919, in which he credited Olivier with being the only person to have made a serious attempt to reform the Jamaican taxation system in a more equitable direction. U. Theo maintained contact with Olivier at least until 1938 and perhaps even later; see U. Theo's letter to Olivier in C.O. 950/28, September 14, 1938, TNA. For more on the objection of the oligarchy to better road and rail access by the peasantry, see C.O. 137/742, despatch 711, Governor Probyn to Viscount Milner, Secretary of State for the Colonies, October 23, 1920; enclosure of report by Barclay and Cradwick, October 9, 1920; also C.O. 137/746, Memorial from T. Gordon Somers and C. A. Wilson, on behalf of the Jamaica League, to Winston Churchill, Secretary of State for the Colonies, May 12, 1921; TNA. Also see discussion of the subject in previous chapter.

113. Lord Olivier, *Jamaica: The Blessed Island* (London: Faber and Faber, 1936).

114. Una Marson to Olivier, April 8, 1932; Dorothea Simmons to Olivier, January 31, 1939; Sydney Olivier Papers, Rhodes House Library, Oxford University. Also see Herbert de Lisser, "Notes on Lord Olivier's Official Career in Jamaica," in *Sydney Olivier: Letters and Selected Writings*, ed. Margaret Olivier (London: Allen and Unwin, 1948), 229–37.

115. See Newton, *The Silver Men*, 59–66; and James, *Holding Aloft the Banner of Ethiopia*, 28–29.

116. Olivier to Leonard Woolf, February 21, 1941; Sydney Olivier Papers, Rhodes House Library, Oxford University.

117. "De Gub'nor's Salary" does not appear in William J. Maxwell's McKay anthology, *Complete Poems* (Urbana: University of Illinois Press, 2004).

118. Olivier resigned from the governorship in January 1913, and on February 10, the *Gleaner* carried the poem.
119. "Claude McKay: One of the Early Poems of this Writer," *Gleaner*, February 10, 1913.
120. Claude McKay, "De Gub'nor's Salary," *Gleaner*, February 10, 1913.
121. Translated: "It is *us* who are minding [supporting, looking after] you [*unno*]."
122. Translated: "persecution cost a lot, eh!"; or "isn't persecution expensive!"
123. According to the *Gleaner* report, this is the line that Olivier found objectionable, calling it a "licentious metaphor." Olivier thus viewed the metaphor in sado-masochistic terms; to each his own, but McKay never meant it that way—he was talking about brutal oppression, nothing sexual. "Claude McKay: One of the Early Poems of this Writer," *Gleaner*, February 10, 1913.
124. But see Carolyn Cooper, " 'Only a Nigger Gal!': Race, Gender and the Politics of Education in Claude McKay's *Banana Bottom*," *Caribbean Quarterly* 38, no. 1 (1992); and A. L. McLeod, "An Ideal Woman: Claude McKay's Composite Image," in *Claude McKay: Centennial Studies*, ed. A. L. McLeod (New Delhi: Sterling, 1992).
125. "Ribber Come-Do'n," *SJ*, 118.
126. "Ribber Come-Do'n," 118.
127. "A Country Girl," *SJ*, 119.
128. "A Country Girl," 119–20.
129. *MGH*, 17–18.
130. *MGH*, 17.
131. *MGH*, 17–18.
132. *MGH*, 18.
133. Claude McKay, "Agnes o' de Village Lane," *Gleaner*, October 7, 1911.
134. *Gleaner*, October 21, 1911.
135. *MGH*, 18.
136. *Harlem Shadows* (New York: Harcourt, Brace, 1922); *HS*.
137. See especially "Harlem Shadows," "ANPP," 276; and "Africa," *Liberator*, August 1921, 10. These poems were subsequently included in a number of McKay's anthologies, including the posthumously published *Selected Poems*.
138. The colloquialism "bobby" is derived from the name of the founder of the modern British police force, Sir Robert Peel, Home Secretary when the force was created in 1828.
139. "A Midnight Woman to the Bobby," *SJ*, 74.
140. "A Midnight Woman to the Bobby," 75.
141. Strangely, "trace" and "tracing" do not appear in Cassidy's *Jamaica Talk* nor in his and LePage's *Dictionary of Jamaican English*, despite their local meaning and usage. It is interesting that Thomas, the white Jamaican police inspector, recognizes and speaks of it, correctly calling tracing "a favourite form of abuse." Thomas, *Story of a West Indian Policeman*, 357–58, quotation at 357.
142. "A Midnight Woman to the Bobby," 76.
143. "A Midnight Woman to the Bobby," 75.
144. "A Midnight Woman to the Bobby," 76.
145. *LW*, 315.
146. "The Apple-Woman's Complaint," *CB*, 57.
147. "The Apple-Woman's Complaint," 57–58.
148. "The Apple-Woman's Complaint," 58.
149. "The Apple-Woman's Complaint," 58.
150. "The Apple-Woman's Complaint," 58.

151. See Kimberlé Williams Crenshaw, "Mapping the Margins: Intersectionality, Identity Politics, and Violence Against Women of Color," in *Critical Race Theory: Key Writings That Formed the Movement*, ed. Kimberlé Crenshaw, Neil Gotanda, Gary Peller, and Kendall Thomas (New York: New Press, 1995), 357–83.

152. For examples of Bennett's work, see Louise Bennett, *Jamaica Labrish* (Kingston: Sangster's, 1966), and Louise Bennett, *Selected Poems* (Kingston: Sangster's, 1982).

153. In the 1920s, when McKay was getting a great deal of exposure in the Jamaican press, a local wag wrote anonymously to the *Gleaner* about rumors he or she had heard about McKay as a boy: "Strange thing about Claude McKay, I have been told, is that as a lad he was very fond of dolls, and he kept his dolls, making dresses for them, cutting out the dresses himself and was keenly interested in all the paraphernalia of doll-land." Letter to the editor, "The Life Story of a Jamaican Novelist," *Gleaner*, July 12, 1928.

154. See, for instance, Rachel K. McKay-Cooper to Claude McKay, August 25, 1927; CMPY and discussion in chapters 1 and 2 above.

155. Claude McKay, "The Park in Spring," "ANPP," 276. This poem was later revised and retitled "The Castaways." See *SP*, 73.

156. Gisela Eisner, *Jamaica, 1830–1930: A Study in Economic Growth* (Manchester: Manchester University Press, 1961), 155, tables 14 and 15.

157. George W. Roberts, *The Population of Jamaica* (Cambridge: Cambridge University Press, 1957), 72, table 17.

158. Roberts, *Population of Jamaica*, 145, table 33; 146, table 34; 149.

159. Richard Lobdell, "Women in the Jamaican Labour Force, 1881–1912," *Social and Economic Studies* 37, nos. 1 and 2 (March–June 1988), 213, table 11; 239, table 19.

160. Roberts, *Population of Jamaica*, 141, table 32.

161. *MGH*, 19. For discussions of women and Fabianism, see Eric Hobsbawm, "The Fabians Reconsidered," in *Labouring Men: Studies in the History of Labor* (London: Weidenfeld and Nicholson, 1964); Norman and Jeanne Mackenzie, *The First Fabians* (London: Weidenfeld and Nicholson, 1977); Barbara Caine, "Beatrice Webb and the Woman Question," *History Workshop Journal* 14 (Autumn 1982); Pat Thane, "Late Victorian Women," in *Later Victorian Britain, 1867–1900*, ed. T. R. Gourvish and Alan O'Day (New York: St. Martin's, 1988); Sally Alexander, "Equal or Different: The Emergence of the Victorian Women's Movement"; "The Fabian Women's Group, 1908–52"; "Fabian Socialism and the 'Sex-Relation'"; all in Alexander, *Becoming a Woman and Other Essays in Nineteenth and Twentieth Century Feminist History* (London: Virago, 1994).

162. *LW*, 12, 14.

163. "Strokes of the Tamarind Switch," *SJ*, 111

164. "Strokes of the Tamarind Switch," 111–12.

165. "Strokes of the Tamarind Switch," 112.

166. "Strokes of the Tamarind Switch," 113.

167. One cannot help wondering if this note was also aimed at placating the authorities at a time that McKay (guided and assisted by Jekyll) was seeking an early release from the police force. Nothing in the poem itself would suggest that the boy "deserved" such inhumane treatment, and nothing suggested that it was a "necessity," albeit a "miserable" one.

168. "The Bobby to the Sneering Lady," *CB*, 67; "The Heart of a Constab," *CB*, 63.

169. "Jim at Sixteen," *SJ*, 24.

170. "Jim at Sixteen," 26.

171. In his glossary to *Constab Ballads*, McKay explained "dog-driver" simply as "nickname for a policeman" (*CB*, 84), rather like "red-seam." But Thomas reports that the term was less neutral than McKay made it sound. "Those of the lower orders," he writes, "speak of the police as 'dog-drivers'—which used to be the *favourite term of opprobrium* in my young days." Thomas, *Story of a West Indian Policeman*, 351–52; emphasis added.

172. "De Dog-Driver's Frien," *CB*, 37.

173. "Killin' Nanny," *SJ*, 83.

174. McKay, "Snared!" *Jamaica Times*, July 27, 1912.

175. "Cotch Donkey," *CB*, 47.

176. The American anthropologist Martha Beckwith, however, noted in her 1929 study of Jamaican folk life that Bryan Edwards, an eighteenth-century Jamaican planter-historian, "complains of the cruelty the Negroes show towards animals, and I am afraid," she remarked, "they are not much improved in the ways of pity today." Beckwith, *Black Roadways*, 118.

177. I am not saying that McKay swallowed Schopenhauer's philosophical and ideological positions whole; he clearly did not. There is, most conspicuously, none of the militant misogyny of Arthur Schopenhauer in McKay's work or political outlook. For evidence of his misogyny, see, for instance, Schopenhauer's essay "On Women," in *Parerga and Paralipomena*, 2:614–26. Interestingly, Jekyll did not include this essay in his anthology of Schopenhauer's writings.

178. Schopenhauer, "On Religion," in *Parerga and Paralipomena*, 2:375. Much, but not all, of this essay is included in Jekyll's book. The passages quoted are included; see *Wisdom of Schopenhauer*, 356–72.

179. Schopenhauer, *Parerga and Paralipomena*, 2:297.

180. Schopenhauer, *Parerga and Paralipomena*, 2:375. It is not insignificant that even when Schopenhauer berated his poodle, he referred to him as "you, sir." Rudiger Safranski, *Schopenhauer and the Wild Years of Philosophy*, trans. Ewald Osers (Cambridge, MA: Harvard University Press, 1990), 284.

181. Schopenhauer, *Parerga Paralipomena*, 2:375; emphasis in original.

182. This is quoted from the McKay's original manuscript: "He [Jekyll] was a great follower of Leo Tolstoy, and a pessimist." It is somehow omitted from the published version. See MGH, 68; *MGH*, 70. Tolstoy, like Jekyll, was a great admirer of Schopenhauer. This is most explicit in Leo Tolstoy, "A Confession," in *A Confession and Other Religious Writings* (Harmondsworth, UK: Penguin, 1987).

183. MGH, 68.

184. See Margaret Olivier, ed., *Sydney Olivier: Letters and Selected Writings* (London: George Allen & Unwin, 1948), 110, 113. For further indication of the depth of the friendship between Jekyll and the Oliviers, see Jekyll to Sydney Olivier, 21 February 1928, Olivier Papers, Rhodes House. There is no evidence that McKay followed Jekyll's example in his eating habits; he remained a carnivore.

185. The following remarks on Salt and the League draw upon Norman and Jeanne MacKenzie, *The First Fabians* (London: Weidenfeld and Nicolson, 1977), and especially Dan Weinbren, "Against *All* Cruelty: The Humanitarian League, 1891–1919," *History Workshop* 38 (Autumn 1994).

186. Quoted in Weinbren, "Against *All* Cruelty," 90.

187. Quoted in Weinbren, "Against *All* Cruelty," 102n8.

188. McKay was baptized a Catholic on October 11, 1944, in Chicago; McKay, "On Becoming a Roman Catholic," 43.

189. *B*, 268. Earlier in the novel, McKay wrote that Banjo, the chief protagonist, despite his plight, "instinctively turned" his back against "the Helping-Hand brotherhood of Christian charity with all its sanctimonious cant" (242).
190. "Old England," *SJ*, 63.
191. "Old England," 64.
192. "Old England," 64.
193. "Cudjoe Fresh from de Lecture," *SJ*, 57.
194. "Strokes of the Tamarind Switch," *SJ*, 112.
195. "Hard Times," *SJ*, 53.
196. "The Apple-Woman's Complaint," *CB*, 58.
197. "Mother Dear," *SJ*, 78. McKay recalled that after reading Spinoza's *Ethics*, for a time he considered himself a pantheist. "Mother Dear" was perhaps written during this period. See *LW*, 14.
198. *Literary Guide*, January 1, 1912; review reprinted in the *Gleaner*, January 13, 1912, from which I have quoted. It is significant that McKay's second volume of poetry, *Constab Ballads*, was published by Watts & Co., the publishing arm of the Rationalist Press Association (RPA). Watts had published Jekyll's book, *The Wisdom of Schopenhauer*, in 1911, the year before *Constab Ballads* came out. Jekyll, of course, made the arrangements on McKay's behalf with Watts & Co. Charles Albert Watts (1858–1946) was the driving force behind the Rationalist Press Association in 1899 and the owner of Watts & Co. Bill Cooke, *The Gathering of Infidels: A Hundred Years of the Rationalist Press Association* (Amherst, NY: Prometheus, 2004), provides the most authoritative account of the RPA, its founders, and its publications.
199. Thomas MacDermot, editor of the *Jamaica Times*; see *Jamaica Times*, May 4, 1912.
200. *Christian Commonwealth*, March 27, 1912, 420.
201. In the end, however, Rev. Marwick had the last laugh: remarkably, both Claude and U. Theo converted to Catholicism shortly before they died. I was told of U. Theo's surprising conversion by both his niece and daughter. But unlike McKay, who converted more than three years before he died, U. Theo only rarely attended mass—his daughter remembered Easter and Christmas—in the last few years of his life; he converted on his deathbed in Kingston Public Hospital and took the last rites. It was also a surprise to learn that both U. Theo's daughters, who were born some years after McKay had emigrated, attended a Catholic school in Kingston. His daughter, however, could not recall whether the idea of sending the girls to a Catholic school was their mother's or their father's, and the decision might have been made on pragmatic rather than religious grounds. Apparently, U. Theo did not object. Author's taped interviews with Mrs. Icelyn McKay Binger, May Pen, Clarendon, August 6, 1995, and Mrs. Eloise McKay Edwards, London, August 23, 1995.
202. "Cudjoe Fresh from de Lecture," *SJ*, 57. This is an expression of a widely held doctrine, not just among African intellectuals of the diaspora but also on the continent, up to the early twentieth century. Wilson Jeremiah Moses calls it the "Fortunate Fall"— the belief that "slavery, although a terrible affliction on the African people, would become, through the workings of divine providence, a blessing in the fullness of time." Christianity and Civilization were the key benefits. Moses, *The Wings of Ethiopia: Studies in African-American Life and Letters* (Ames: Iowa State University Press, 1990), 141–58, quotation at 141.
203. "Cudjoe Fresh from de Lecture," 57.
204. "Cudjoe Fresh from de Lecture," 55.

205. "Cudjoe Fresh from de Lecture," 55.
206. "Cudjoe Fresh from de Lecture," 58.
207. McKay, "George William Gordon to the Oppressed Natives," *Gleaner*, May 3, 1912, and *Jamaica Times*, May 4, 1912.
208. Claude McKay, "Africa," *Liberator*, August 1921, 10.
209. The literature on the subject is large and growing. See, for instance, Lilyan Kesteloot, *Black Writers in French: A Literary History of Negritude*, trans. Ellen Conroy Kennedy (Philadelphia: Temple University Press, [1963] 1974); Jacques Louis Hymans, *Léopold Sédar Senghor: An Intellectual Biography* (Edinburgh: Edinburgh University Press, 1971); Jacqueline Kaye, "Claude McKay's *Banjo*," *Présence Africaine* 73 (First Quarter 1970); Edward O. Ako, "*L'Etudiant Noir* and the Myth of the Genesis of the Négritude Movement," *Research in African Literatures* 15, no. 3 (1984); Martin Steins, "Brown France vs. Black Africa: The Tide Turned in 1932," *Research in African Literatures* 14, no. 4 (1983); Liliane Blary, "Claude McKay and Africa: *Banjo*," *Commonwealth: Essays and Studies* 5 (1981–1982); Michel Fabre, "Beyond *Banjo*: Claude McKay's African Experience," *Commonwealth: Essays and Studies* 5 (1981–1982); Bridget Jones, "With *Banjo* by My Bed: Black French Writers Reading Claude McKay," *Caribbean Quarterly* 38, no. 1 (March 1992); Edris Makward, "Claude McKay: The African Experience," in *Claude McKay: Centennial Studies*, ed. A. L. McLeod (New Delhi: Sterling, 1992); Brent Hayes Edwards, "Three Ways to Translate the Harlem Renaissance," and Michel Fabre, "The Harlem Renaissance Abroad: French Critics and the New Negro Movement (1924-1964)," both in *Temples for Tomorrow: Looking Back at the Harlem Renaissance*, ed. Geneviève Fabre and Michel Feith (Bloomington: Indiana University Press, 2001); and Hayes Edwards, *The Practice of Diaspora: Literature, Translation and the Rise of Black Internationalism* (Cambridge, MA: Harvard University Press, 2003), chap. 4.
210. The classic statement of the problem is, of course, Frantz Fanon, *Black Skin, White Masks* (1952).
211. "My Pretty Dan," *SJ*, 114–115.
212. Cassidy, *Jamaica Talk*, 156–57; Cassidy and Le Page, *Dictionary of Jamaican English*; Izett Anderson and Frank Cundall, eds., *Jamaica Proverbs and Sayings*, rev. ed. (Kingston: Sangster's, [1927] 1972), 90.
213. "Fe Me Sal," *CB*, 64, 65.
214. *Gleaner*, October 28, 1911.
215. "Papine Corner," *CB*, 42.
216. *MGH*, 73.
217. "My Mountain Home," *SJ*, 124.
218. "My Mountain Home," 125.
219. "Sukee River," *CB*, 78, 79. McKay's river bathing did not end after he left the island. While he was living in North Africa in the early 1930s, one of the things he treasured about his little house near Tangiers was its closeness to a river suitable for bathing. "I am not much of a swimmer," he wrote a friend, "but very fond of floating in deep water and at high tide the sea drives up the river which is always calm and excellent for bathing when the sea is often rough because of the strait and Levant winds." McKay to Nancy Cunard, August 20, 1932, NCC.
220. All published in *SJ*: 59–60, 41, 79–80, and 69–71, respectively.
221. Theodor W. Adorno, *Notes to Literature*, vol. 1, trans. Shierry Weber Nicholsen (New York: Columbia University Press, 1991), 43.

4. The Man Who Left Jamaica: Claude McKay in 1912

1. *MGH*, 78.
2. *MGH*, 78.
3. "Free," *CB*, 73.
4. According to the *Jamaica Times* (November 18, 1911), McKay had returned by train to Clarendon on November 13.
5. *MGH*, 78–79.
6. *Gleaner*, January 20, 1912; *MGH*, 79.
7. *Jamaica Times*, January 13, 1912. Taking national pride in McKay's achievements, the *Gleaner* and the *Jamaica Times* reported on and carried reviews of the book published abroad.
8. *Gleaner*, February 20, 1912.
9. One farthing coin equaled a quarter of a penny.
10. In his report on the rioting, Kershaw, the Inspector General of Police, stated that McCrea regretted his arresting Judah and Heath "as it has engendered popular indignation against him and made matters worse, and admits that the whole population of Kingston appear to openly and bitterly resent his action." Report of Chief Inspector of Police to Colonial Secretary, March, 1, 1912, enclosed in Governor Olivier to Secretary of State for the Colonies, Rt. Honourable Lewis Harcourt, March, 2, 1912, C.O. 137/690, TNA (hereafter *Kershaw Report*).
11. *Gleaner*, February 22, 1912. The campaign of passive resistance, the riot, and the trials of protesters were extensively covered by the *Gleaner* and the *Jamaica Times* in February and March 1912. The account presented here draws heavily upon these reports, but I have noted only the issues of these newspapers from which I have quoted.
12. *Kershaw Report*.
13. "Lick" in such a context may be roughly translated as "hit," though it carries a connotation of great force, beyond simply hitting someone. Thus, it is more accurately captured by the phrase "Hit them *hard*," with emphasis on hard.
14. *Gleaner*, February 27, 1912.
15. *Gleaner*, February 27, 1912.
16. *Jamaica Times*, March 30, 1912.
17. *Jamaica Times*, March 16, 1912.
18. *Kershaw Report*.
19. Sir Sydney Olivier to Lewis Harcourt [Secretary of State for the Colonies], February 28, 1912; CO 137/690, PRO. The tramcar riots, including the stoning of the governor, were extensively covered in the British press. "The Governor of Jamaica Stoned," announced the heading of the report in the *Times* (February 28, 1912); also see *Times*, February 27 and 29, 1912; March 4 and 16, 1912.
20. Francis Lee, *Fabianism and Colonialism: The Life and Political Thought of Lord Sydney Olivier* (London: Defiant, 1988), 125.
21. Claude McKay, "Passive Resistance," reprinted in *The Passion of Claude McKay: Selected Prose and Poetry, 1912–1948*, ed. Wayne Cooper (New York: Schocken, 1973), 115–16. Cooper claims that the poem was published in the *Gleaner* of April 6, 1912. I think he is mistaken about the date. Despite my extensive search of holdings of the *Gleaner* in Jamaica, London, and the United States, none carried the poem on the date specified by Cooper. Nor was it found in either the *Gleaner* or the *Jamaica Times* for the period of the riots and their aftermath. It is possible that it was published in the magazine section of the *Gleaner* that was not microfilmed after Cooper

had carried out his research in the 1960s. Indeed, on Wednesday, March 13, 1912, the *Gleaner* announced prominently on its front page: "A BALLAD OF THE TRAM WAR / by Claude McKay / Will Appear on Saturday." On Saturday (March 16), again on the front page, with the same prominently boxed type, the paper informed its readers that the poem "APPEARS TO-DAY / SEE PAGE 17." But alas, page 17 has not been copied or digitized, and the Gleaner informs me that no hard copy for that issue exists. Only the first fifteen of the twenty-four pages were microfilmed or digitized. But there is another mystery here. Why was it announced as "A Ballad of the Tram War"? Was it simply an advertising tool to attract readers to the paper (McKay was always good copy in Jamaica), or was it the literal title of the poem, instead of "Passive Resistance"? In other words, could there have been a second poem by McKay on the subject called "A Ballad of the Tram War"? It is possible, but it seems highly improbable. Max Eastman and McKay himself (see below) have only mentioned *a* poem. My judgment is that "Passive Resistance" was actually the poem in question and that it was published on March 16 (not April 6), 1912. It is noteworthy that there is no banner notice of the poem on the front page of the *Gleaner* on April 6 as there was on March 16 (not to mention the advanced billing given the Wednesday before). There is no reason to doubt, however, the authenticity of the poem that appears under the title "Passive Resistance"; it has all the hallmarks of one by McKay. As further corroboration of McKay's authorship, "Passive Resistance" is obviously the poem that Max Eastman was referring to when he claimed that McKay's "first poem of political significance [was] a rally-call to the street-car men on strike in Kingston" (Eastman, introduction to *HS*, xii). The poem, of course, was not about striking tramcar men (though McKay may have supported their strike, which occurred in the aftermath of the "passive resistance" struggle in 1912), but about the resisters. Further corroboration of his authorship comes from McKay himself. During the labor uprisings of 1938, McKay, who was living in Harlem at the time, wrote to the *Gleaner* expressing his solidarity with the workers and peasants. He lamented that labor conditions in Jamaica were apparently "as bad as some 25 years ago, when the strike of the street-car workers precipitated the Kingston riots. On that occasion I wrote a poem on the situation which was published in THE GLEANER." He expressed the "fervent wish that The Gleaner, as the leading organ of opinion in Jamaica, will stand up with the forces standing for progress and justice for the people of Jamaica, so that instead of being harried by poverty and strife that beautiful and fertile island may become a really happy place for the majority of its inhabitants" (*Gleaner*, December 24, 1938).

22. For more on the Morant Bay Rebellion, see Lord Olivier, *The Myth of Governor Eyre* (London: Hogarth, 1933); Bernard Semmel, *The Governor Eyre Controversy* (London: McKibbon and Kee, 1962); Ansel Hart, *The Life of George William Gordon* (Kingston: Institute of Jamaica, 1972); Don Robotham, *"The Notorious Riot": The Socio-Economic and Political Bases of Paul Bogle's Revolt* (Kingston: Institute of Social and Economic Research, University of the West Indies, 1981); Catherine Hall, "The Economy of Intellectual Prestige: Thomas Carlyle, John Stuart Mill, and the Case of Governor Eyre," *Cultural Critique* 12 (Spring 1989): 167–96; Thomas Holt, *The Problem of Freedom: Race, Labor, and Politics in Jamaica and Britain, 1838–1938* (Baltimore: Johns Hopkins University Press, 1992), chap. 8; Gad Heuman, *"The Killing Time": The Morant Bay Rebellion in Jamaica* (London: Macmillan, 1994); Clinton Hutton, "The Defeat of the Morant Bay Rebellion," *Jamaican Historical Review* 19 (1996): 30–38; and Clinton Hutton, *Colour for Colour, Skin for Skin: Marching with the Ancestral Spirits Into War Oh at Morant Bay* (Kingston: Ian Randle, 2015).

23. Hutton, *Colour for Colour*, 172–83.
24. Claude McKay, "George William Gordon to the Oppressed Natives," *Gleaner*, May 3, 1912; and *Jamaica Times*, May 4, 1912.
25. Claude McKay, "Personal Notes on the History of Jamaica," MGH.
26. *Gleaner*, October 21, 1911. I could not find this essay in the extant issues of the *Jamaica Tribune*, nor, for that matter, any other publication.
27. The poem was first published in London in *T. P.'s Weekly*, April 12, 1912. See reports in *Gleaner*, May 3, 1912, and *Jamaica Times*, May 4, 1912.
28. If Jekyll had in fact written a letter, it was never published in either the *Gleaner* or the *Jamaica Times*.
29. "Peasants' Ways o' Thinkin'," *Gleaner*, January 27, 1912.
30. *MGH*, 79.
31. McKay sailed to America in July 1912 and spoke of making plans to leave eight months earlier. *MGH*, 83.
32. *MGH*, 84–85. The forces behind the migration to the United States and the characteristics of the Caribbean emigrants are analyzed in Winston James, *Holding Aloft the Banner of Ethiopia: Caribbean Radicalism in Early Twentieth-Century America* (London: Verso, 1998), chaps. 1 and 2; see also Winston James, "Explaining Afro-Caribbean Social Mobility in the United States: Beyond the Sowell Thesis," *Comparative Studies in Society and History* 44, no. 2 (April 2002): 218–62.
33. See especially *Jamaica Times*, March 9 and April 13, 1912; *Gleaner*, May 1 and June 1, 1912.
34. *MGH*, 82.
35. William Seraile, "Henrietta Vinton Davis and the Garvey Movement," *Afro-Americans in New York Life and History* 7, no. 2 (July 1983): 7–24; Robert A. Hill, ed., *The Marcus Garvey and Universal Negro Improvement Association Papers*, vol. 1 (Berkeley: University of California Press, 1983), 419–20.
36. *MGH*, 80–81.
37. *MGH*, 82.
38. Gisela Eisner, *Jamaica, 1830–1930: A Study in Economic Growth* (Manchester: Manchester University Press, 1961), 225–28; Patrick Bryan, *The Jamaican People, 1880–1902: Race, Class and Social Control* (London: Macmillan, 1991), 219–21; and *MGH*, 82.
39. *MGH*, 69, 78–79.
40. *MGH*, 79.
41. Claude McKay, "Clarendon Hills, Farewell!" *Gleaner*, August 5, 1912.
42. Claude McKay, "Christmas in de Air," *Jamaica Times*, December 16, 1912.
43. "Peasants' Ways o' Thinkin'." This poem and "Christmas in de Air" are reprinted in Winston James, *A Fierce Hatred of Injustice: Claude McKay's Jamaica and His Poetry of Rebellion* (London: Verso, 2000), 211–15, 210–11.
44. *MGH*, 80.
45. *MGH*, 85. C. A. Wilson provides the most detailed portrait of Plant; see C. A. Wilson, *Men of Vision*, 59–86. Bita Plant, the chief protagonist of *Banana Bottom*—despite its play on words (bitter plant)—almost certainly was given that last name out of respect for "Mr. Plant," as McKay invariably called the headmaster.
46. *Jamaica Times*, June 15, 1912; Anthony Johnson, *J. A. G. Smith* (Kingston: Kingston Publishers, 1991), 48.
47. The edition of the *Jamaica Times* for Saturday, July 27, 1912, reported that McKay "left the island on Wednesday," which would have been July 24, but U.S. passenger lists

indicate that he sailed from Port Antonio on the SS *Alfred Dumais* the following day, July 25, 1912. *Jamaica Times*, June 22 and July 27, 1912; *Passenger and Crew Lists of Vessels Arriving at Charleston, South Carolina*, NAI Number: 2723253; Record Group Title: *Records of the Immigration and Naturalization Service, 1787-2004*, Record Group Number: 85; National Archives, Washington, DC.

48. *MGH*, 84-85.

49. *Jamaica Times*, August 10, 1912.

50. *Jamaica Times*, August 17, 1912. A few months later, he reiterated that confidence in his American future by quoting Oliver Wendell Holmes's "The Chambered Nautilus" to readers of the *Jamaica Times* (December 14, 1912): "Build thee more stately mansions, O my soul, / As the swift seasons roll! / Leave thy low-vaulted past! /Let each new temple, nobler than the last, / Shut thee from heaven with a dome more vast, / Till thou at length art free, / Leaving thine outgrown shell by life's unresting sea!"

51. Translation: "If you cannot hear, you will have to feel."

52. *Liberator*, December 1921, 9.

53. Claude McKay, "On Becoming a Roman Catholic," *Epistle*, Spring 1945, 44; *MGH*, 23.

54. Quoted in Bryan, *Jamaican People*, 220.

55. *MGH*, 28-29.

56. Claude McKay, "Personal Notes on the History of Jamaica," 13.

57. *MGH*, 44.

58. McKay to Nancy Cunard, August 20, 1932, NCC; emphasis in original.

59. Nancy Cunard, "Jamaica—The Negro Island," in *Negro: An Anthology*, ed. Nancy Cunard (London: Nancy Cunard at Wishart, 1934), 449. See also Cunard to McKay, July 17, [1932], August 8, [1932], CMPY. W. E. B. Du Bois painted a similarly romantic image of the Jamaican peasantry after his visit to the island in 1915. He also overstated the level of racial harmony. Marcus Garvey and J. A. Rogers, among others, objected strongly to this superficial depiction of Caribbean societies. See W. E. B. Du Bois, "An Amazing Island," *Crisis*, June 1915, 80-81; Marcus Garvey to Moton, February 29, 1916, reprinted in the *Garvey Papers*, 1:179-83; J. A. Rogers, "The West Indies: Their Political, Social and Economic Condition," *Messenger*, September 1922, 484. Langston Hughes and Paul Robeson responded to Jamaica in a way similar as Du Bois: "MY NEW LOVE IS JAMAICA!" Hughes chirpily announced in the *Chicago Defender* on his return from visiting the island in 1947. "She is dressed in green, and her face is as dark and as beautiful as any in the world." Robeson, who toured Jamaica and Trinidad the year after Hughes's visit, said of Jamaica: "I felt that for the first time I could see what it will be like when Negroes are free in their own land. I felt something like what a Jew must feel when first he goes to Israel." Like Du Bois before them, they acknowledged the poverty. "Certainly my people in the islands are poor. They are desperately poor," said Robeson. And on more sober occasions Hughes spoke with insight about "color lines" in the Caribbean. Langston Hughes, *Chicago Defender*, November 29, 1947; Arnold Rampersad, *The Life of Langston Hughes*, vol. 2, *1941-1967: I Dream A World* (New York: Oxford University Press, 1988), 138-39; Langston Hughes, *I Wonder As I Wander: An Autobiographical Journey* (New York: Rinehart, 1956), 6-37; Charles Nichols, ed., *Arna Bontemps—Langston Hughes Letters, 1925-1967* (New York: Dodd, Mead, 1980), 235; Paul Robeson, *National Guardian*, December 20, 1948, reprinted in *Paul Robeson Speaks: Writings, Speeches, Interviews 1918-1974*, ed. Philip Foner (New York: Citadel, 1978), 190-91; Martin Duberman, *Paul Robeson* (New York: Knopf, 1988), 336.

60. The phrase is from Mervyn Morris, introduction to *MGH*, viii.

61. *MGH*, 61–63; for analysis of the substantial migration of Caribbean professionals to the United States, see James, *Holding Aloft the Banner of Ethiopia*, esp. 78–83, and James, "Explaining Afro-Caribbean Social Mobility in the United States."

62. "MGH," 59–60; CMPS. This is the original manuscript upon which the published version of *My Green Hills* is based. In this particular case, I felt it necessary to quote from the original version to restore elements that had been edited out for apparently no good reason. See *MGH*, 63–64. The man referred to was in fact Rev. A. Alexander Barclay (1876–1926), an important figure in Jamaican politics during the first three decades of the twentieth century. He had first worked as a teacher, became an activist pastor in the Presbyterian Church, serving in Clarendon when McKay's mother died in 1909, and later became a member of the Legislative Council. In 1920, he became the first Black person nominated to the Council, but was soon after elected by the Black voters of western St. Mary, whom he faithfully and tirelessly served until his untimely death in 1926. See Wilson, *Men of Vision*, 21–40. That Barclay officiated at Mrs. McKay's funeral is confirmed by her obituary in the *Jamaica Times*, January 8, 1910.

63. U. Theo's public objection to the ill-treatment of the laborers building the roads and the railway in Clarendon in 1912 was, according to members of the family, partly induced by the memory of his father having worked as a humble road mender. Wayne Cooper, *Claude McKay: Rebel Sojourner in the Harlem Renaissance—A Biography* (Baton Rouge: Louisiana State University Press, 1987), 49.

64. McKay to James Weldon Johnson, September 5, 1929, CMPY.

65. *MGH*, 69.

5. "Six Silent Years": McKay and America, 1912–1918

1. McKay landed at Charleston on July 29, 1912. The immigration officer noted that McKay entered the country with $60, he was "Going to Booker Washington School," and filled in the "marks of identification" column with the word "noon" (*sic*). *Passenger and Crew Lists of Vessels Arriving at Charleston, South Carolina*, NAI Number 2723253; Record Group Title: *Records of the Immigration and Naturalization Service, 1787–2004*, Record Group Number 85; National Archives, Washington, DC.

2. McKay reminded Eastman of the incident a few years later: McKay to Eastman, April 3, 1923, CMI.

3. Claude McKay, "Claude MacKay [*sic*] Describes His Own Life: A Negro Poet," *Pearson's Magazine* 39, no. 5 (September 1918): 275. The magazine's table of contents listed the item as "A Negro Poet and His Poems," hereafter "ANPP."

4. McKay alluded to Turner's case in "A Roman Holiday," *Liberator*, July 1919, 21.

5. Walter F. White, "The Work of a Mob," *Crisis*, September 1918, 222; White, *Rope and Faggot: A Biography of Judge Lynch* (New York: Arno, [1929] 1969), 28–29. See also Julie Buckner Armstrong, *Mary Turner and the Memory of Lynching* (Athens: University of Georgia Press, 2011). Mary Turner was only one of the estimated seventy-four women among the African Americans lynched in ten southern states between 1882 and 1930. Tolnay and Beck calculated that a total of 2,462 Black people were lynched in those states during the period. However, they could not identify the gender of twenty-four victims. Stewart E. Tolnay and E. M. Beck, *A Festival of Violence: An Analysis of Southern Lynchings, 1882–1930* (Urbana: University of Illinois Press, 1995), 51n1, 269 (table C-1).

6. "ANPP," 275.
7. Max Eastman, "Biographical Note," *SP*, 7.
8. "ANNP," 275.
9. This is discussed at length in Winston James, *Holding Aloft the Banner of Ethiopia: Caribbean Radicalism in Early Twentieth-Century America* (New York: Verso, 1998).
10. "ANPP," 275.
11. *LW, 63*. Actually, conscription was not introduced in Jamaica, but there was substantial mobilization for the war throughout the British Caribbean. C. L. Joseph, "The British West Indies Regiment, 1914–1918," *Journal of Caribbean History* 2 (May 1971). Two fine studies—Glenford Howe, *Race War and Nationalism: A Social History of West Indians in the First World War* (Kingston: Ian Randle, 2002), and Richard Smith, Jamaican Volunteers in the *First World War: Race, Masculinity and the Development of National Consciousness* (Manchester: Manchester University Press, 2005)—stand out in the growing literature on British Caribbean involvement in the Great War. The black Caribbean involvement and its radicalizing repercussions are also discussed in James, *Holding Aloft the Banner of Ethiopia*, esp. 52–69.
12. *LW*, 55.
13. *LW*, 123.
14. McKay to Max Eastman, October 16, 1944, CMI.
15. Jekyll warned McKay against Frank Harris, editor of *Pearson's*, simply because Harris expressed his opposition to the war. Jekyll's best friend (and alleged lover), Ernest Boyle, a colonel in the Royal Artillery, died on the front in 1917, which perhaps explains, but does not justify, his anti-German outburst. *LW*, 16; *Gleaner*, August 19, 1929; Wayne Cooper, *Claude McKay: Rebel Sojourner in the Harlem Renaissance—A Biography* (Baton Rouge: Louisiana State University Press, 1987), 30–31. Stuart Wallace has written a superb analysis of how a considerable number of British intellectuals of Jekyll's generation and background became raving jingoists: *War and the Image of Germany: British Academics, 1914–1918* (Edinburgh: John Donald, 1988).
16. Claude McKay, "To 'Holy' Russia," *Workers' Dreadnought*, February 28, 1920; hereafter *WD*.
17. See the discussion in chapter 6 below. See also Winston James, "To the East Turn: The Russian Revolution and the Black Radical Imagination in the United States, 1917–1924," *American Historical Review* 126, no. 3 (September 2021): 1001-1045.
18. See chapter 6 below.
19. "ANPP," 276.
20. The first university established in the state, Kansas State Agricultural College was founded as a land-grant institution in 1863. The early history of the college is authoritatively told by its official historian, Julius Terrass Willard, *History of the Kansas State College of Agriculture and Applied Science* (Manhattan: Kansas State College Press, 1940).
21. Max Eastman, introduction to *HS*, xvi.
22. McKay to William Aspenwall Bradley, May 17, 1927, William Aspenwall Bradley Archive, Harry Ransom Humanities Research Center, University of Texas at Austin, emphasis in original; hereafter WAB.
23. Transcript of Festus Claudius McKay, 1912–1914, Registrar's Office, Kansas State University, Manhattan.
24. *Cambridge Magazine* 10, no. 1 (Summer 1920), 55; I. A. Richards, preface to *SNH*; McKay Kansas Transcript. McKay may have burnished his college record for those at home. A July 12, 1913, report in the *Gleaner* assured readers that McKay was "doing

well" in his studies in America. "He has never failed in any subject so far, and has got E's (excellent) on several: Rhetoric, English, Literature, Zoology and Botany." But his transcript indicates that he earned "E" only in advanced grammar and agricultural education, he earned "G" (good) or "P" (pass) in his other subjects. However, the letter grade system, introduced in 1910 at KSC, meant that the difference between grades "E" and "G" could be very marginal. See Willard, *History of Kansas State College*, 193–94. There is every indication, in any case, that McKay did well academically at KSC, albeit less stellar than the *Gleaner* suggested.

25. *LW*, 110.

26. P. Okhrimenko, "Original Translator's Note," in *NA*, xvi.

27. Bryan D. Palmer, *James P. Cannon and the Origins of the American Revolutionary Left, 1890–1928* (Urbana: University of Illinois Press, 2007), 43.

28. See Ira Berlin et al., eds., *Free At Last: A Documentary History of Slavery and the Civil War* (New York: New Press, 1992); Theodore Draper, *American Communism and Soviet Russia: The Formative Period* (New York: Random House, 1960); James P. Cannon *The History of American Trotskyism* (New York: Pathfinder, 1972); James P. Cannon, *James P. Cannon and the Early Years of American Communism: Selected Writings and Speeches, 1920–1928* (New York: Spartacist, 1992); Paul Buhle, *Marxism in the United States: Remapping the History of the American Left*, rev. ed. (London: Verso, 1991); Palmer, *James P. Cannon*.

29. Claude McKay, "A Negro to His Critics," *New York Herald Tribune Books*, March 6, 1932, 6.

30. Claude McKay, "Review of *Home to Harlem*," in "Significant Books Reviewed by Their Own Authors," *McClure's* 60, no. 6 (June 1928), 81; hereafter "HH."

31. Susan Miller and Antonia Quintana Pigno, "Claude McKay: The Kansas State College Interlude, 1912–1914," *Minorities Resource and Research Center Newsletter* (Kansas State University), November 1982, 3. Official records indicate that in 1912 KSU had a student body numbering 2,928, which rose to 3,089 by the time McKay left in 1914. University Archives, Richard L. D. & Morse Department of Special Collections, Kansas State Libraries; also Willard, *History of Kansas State College*, 547.

32. The 1910 census records 303 African American residents out of a total Manhattan population of 5,722. Bureau of the Census, *Negro Population of the United States, 1790–1915* (Washington, DC: Government Printing Office, 1918), 97. Miller and Quintana Pigno, "Claude McKay," 3.

33. As late as 1921, Langston Hughes caused a real panic when, as a freshman, he showed up at the dormitory he had booked at Columbia University. "Oh, there must be some mistake!" the "startled" office lady told him. "All the rooms were gone long ago." To which Hughes responded: "But I reserved mine *long ago*, and paid the required deposit by mail." "You did? Then let me see," as she scurried around in a panic. The dormitories were not meant for anyone with a face the color of Hughes. Langston Hughes, *The Big Sea: An Autobiography* (New York: Knopf, 1940), 81–82; emphasis in original. *Students' Herald* quoted in Miller and Quintana Pigno, "Claude McKay," 2.

34. "HH," 81.

35. *LW*, 19–20.

36. See *Jamaica Times*, April 12, 1913, December 20, 1913, March 28, 1914; *Gleaner*, July 12, 1913.

37. Rhonda Hope [Claude McKay] to William Stanley Braithwaite, February 15, 1916, in the William Stanley Braithwaite Papers, Houghton Library, Harvard University, Cambridge, MA, hereafter WSBP.

38. Hope [McKay] to Braithwaite, January 11, 1916, WSBP.
39. "ANPP," 275. Among the five poems is "Harlem Shadows," which suggest that the apostrophe may have been misplaced: first *years'* residence rather than first *year's* residence. McKay had not been to Harlem before his move to New York City in 1914: he spent his first couple of months at Tuskegee, Alabama, and the rest of his first year in Kansas. There is nothing to suggest that he even made a trip to New York before 1914. It is plausible that the other four poems were written during his first year (1912–1913) in the United States, but not "Harlem Shadows," which clearly came from the poet's direct experience of Harlem.
40. "Is It Worth While?," "ANPP," 276.
41. *Jamaica Times*, December 20, 1913.
42. Hope [McKay] to Braithwaite, January 11, 1916; "To the White Fiends" was enclosed in this letter and later published in *Pearson's Magazine*, September 1918, 276; "After the Storm," *Jamaica Times*, March 28, 1914; "Is It Worth While?," "ANPP," 276.
43. The *Jamaica Times* had signaled as early as March 14, 1914, that McKay was not returning to Jamaica and intended working in the United States. The issue of August 1 announced that he had settled in Brooklyn. MacDermot, the editor of the *Jamaica Times*, repeated the hope that McKay would change his mind: "Jamaica wants him," he noted. See *Jamaica Times*, March 14 and 28, and August 1, 1914.
44. "HH," 81.
45. "HH," 81.
46. Bureau of the Census, *Negroes in the United States, 1920–1932* (Washington, DC: Government Printing Office, 1935), 5.
47. Bureau of the Census, *Negro Population, 1790–1915* (Washington, DC: Government Printing Office, 1918), 93; Bureau of the Census, *Negroes in the United States, 1920–1932*, 55. For more a general overview of this transformation, see Florette Henri, *Black Migration: Movement North, 1900–1920* (Garden City, NY: Anchor, 1975); and Isabel Wilkerson, *The Warmth of Other Suns: The Epic Story of America's Great Migration* (New York: Random House, 2010). For New York City and Harlem specifically, see James Weldon Johnson, *Black Manhattan* (New York: Knopf, 1930); Seth Scheiner, *Negro Mecca: A History of the Negro New York City, 1865–1920* (New York: New York University Press, 1965); Gilbert Osofsky, *Harlem: The Making of a Ghetto, 1890–1930*, 2nd ed. (New York: Harper and Row, 1971); and Marcy S. Sacks, *Before Harlem: The Black Experience in New York City Before World War I* (Philadelphia: University of Pennsylvania Press, 2006). For an analysis of Harlem as a unique Black urban formation, see Winston James, "Harlem's Difference," in *Race Capital? Harlem as Setting and Symbol*, ed. Andrew Fearnley and Daniel Matlin (New York: Columbia University Press, 2018), 111–42.
48. W. E. B. Du Bois, "Close Ranks," *Crisis*, July 1918, 111; also see Mark Ellis's valuable discussion of the background and reactions to Du Bois' editorial, " 'Closing Ranks' and 'Seeking Honors': W. E. B. Du Bois in World War I," *Journal of American History* 79, no. 1 (June 1992): 96–124. By the end of the war, almost 370,000 Black people had served in the armed forces, of which 200,000 saw service in Europe, mainly in France. Jack Foner, *Blacks and the Military in American History: A New Perspective* (New York: Praeger, 1974), 111, 121; see also Bernard Nalty, *Strength for the Fight: A History of Black Americans in the Military* (New York: Free Press, 1986), 107–24. The best analysis of the experience of African American soldiers during the First World War is Chad Williams, *Torchbearers of Democracy: African American Soldiers in the World War I Era* (Chapel Hill: University of North Carolina Press, 2010), but also see

the pioneering study of Arthur Barbeau and Florette Henri, *The Unknown Soldiers: Black American Troops in World War I* (Philadelphia: Temple University Press, 1974).

49. Ida B. Wells-Barnett, *The East St. Louis Massacre: The Greatest Outrage of the Century* (Chicago: Negro Fellowship Herald Press, 1917); Elliott Rudwick, *Race Riot at East St. Louis, July 2, 1917* (Carbondale: Southern Illinois University Press, 1964); Charles L. Lumpkins, *American Pogrom: The East St. Louis Race Riot and Black Politics* (Athens: Ohio University Press, 2008); Harper Barnes, *Never Been a Time: The 1917 Race Riot That Sparked the Civil Rights Movement* (New York: Walker, 2008). Garvey's speech is reprinted in *MGP*, 1:212–18; James, *Holding Aloft the Banner of Ethiopia*, chap. 5; Jeffrey B. Perry, *Hubert Harrison: The Voice of Harlem Radicalism, 1883–1918* (New York: Columbia University Press, 2009); Robert V. Haynes, *A Night of Violence: The Houston Riot of 1917* (Baton Rouge: Louisiana State University Press, 1976).

50. James, *Holding Aloft the Banner of Ethiopia*, and "Harlem's Difference"; Jervis Anderson, *A. Philip Randolph: A Biographical Portrait* (Berkeley: University of California Press, 1986).

51. James, *Holding Aloft the Banner of Ethiopia*, and "Harlem's Difference"; Perry, *Hubert Harrison*.

52. Kelly Miller, "After Marcus Garvey—What of the Negro?," *Contemporary Review* 131 (April 1927): 494.

53. James, *Holding Aloft the Banner of Ethiopia*, chap. 5. For a good analysis of intelligence gathering on Black organizations, see Theodore Kornweibel, Jr., *"Seeing Red": Federal Campaigns Against Black Militancy, 1919–1925* (Bloomington: Indiana University Press, 1998); and Mark Ellis, *Race, War and Surveillance: African Americans and the United States Government During World War I* (Bloomington: Indiana University Press, 2001), esp. chap. 4.

54. See Perry, *Hubert Harrison*; Jeffrey B. Perry, ed., *The Hubert Harrison Reader* (Middletown, CT: Wesleyan University Press, 2000); J. A. Rogers, "Hubert Henry Harrison," *World's Great Men of Color*, vol. 2 (New York: Macmillan, 1972), 433; James, *Holding Aloft the Banner of Ethiopia*, esp. 122–34.

55. Perry, *Hubert Harrison*, 148.

56. Rogers, "Hubert Henry Harrison," 439.

57. McKay to Alain Locke, October 7, 1924; Alain Locke Papers, Moorland-Spingarn Research Center, Howard University, Washington, DC.

58. McKay to J. E. Spingarn, March 7, 1937, JESP.

59. *LW*, 113.

60. Harrison, *When Africa Awakes: The "Inside Story" of the Stirrings and Strivings of the New Negro in the Western World* (New York: Porro Press, 1920), 34–35. For an excellent overview of the civilizationist strand in early Black nationalist and Pan-Africanist thought, see Wilson Jeremiah Moses, *The Golden Age of Black Nationalism, 1850–1925* (New York: Oxford University Press, 1988).

61. Harrison, *When Africa Awakes*, 34–35.

62. Harrison, *When Africa Awakes*, 130–31.

63. *LW*, 41.

64. *LW*, 113.

65. *LW*, 113–14.

66. *LW*, 41–42. McKay claimed that the offer of the trip to Europe came from an eccentric British brother and sister, whom he called "the Grays." There are good reasons to doubt this account (discussed in chapter 7), but every reason to believe that he called upon Harrison's counsel.

67. *LW*, 41.

68. *LW*, 55–56. An entire chapter of *A Long Way from Home* is devoted to an incident at a party held by Charlie Chaplin in Greenwich Village in which Hubert Harrison— who was specifically invited by Chaplin—figures prominently; see *LW*, 116–20.

69. *LW*, 108–9.

70. *LW*, 114; Hubert Harrison, "Another Negro Poet," *Negro World*, March 12, 1921; Harrison, "Poetry of Claude McKay" [review of McKay's *Spring in New Hampshire and Other Poems*], *Negro World*, May 21, 1921; Harrison, review of McKay's *Harlem Shadows*, *New York World*, May 21, 1922.

71. *LW*, 154.

72. *NA*, 11.

73. *LW*, 4–5.

74. *LW*, 4; "ANPP," 276; Eastman, "Biographical Note," 8. See also Harrison, "Poetry of Claude McKay."

75. *LW*, 4; McKay, "On Becoming a Roman Catholic," *Epistle* 11, no. 2 (Spring 1945): 44.

76. McKay, "A Negro to His Critics," 6.

77. *LW*, 139; McKay to Max Eastman, March 23, 1939, CMI.

78. McKay, "A Negro to His Critics," 6.

79. "The Negro's Friend," *SP*, 51.

80. *NA*, xvii; McKay to C. K. Ogden, March 26 and April 2, 1920, CKOF.

81. *LW*, 139.

82. McKay to Harold Jackman, March 10, 1928, CMPY.

83. Perry, *Hubert Harrison*, 17–18, 58. In the hard times of the 1930s, McKay spent even more time in these libraries as he did not have money to buy books. In 1935, for instance, he went to the "big library" and read *Negro Americans, What Now?* in one sitting. He immediately wrote and dispatched his response to the book's author, his friend James Weldon Johnson. McKay to James Weldon Johnson, May 16, 1935, CMPY.

84. *LW*, 21; McKay wrote in a footnote: "This poem was published years later in *Harlem Shadows*." This is true, but two years before it was published in *Harlem Shadows*, "The Lynching" appeared in the summer of 1920 in *Cambridge Magazine* and again, in the same year, in his first post-Jamaica collection, *Spring in New Hampshire and Other Poems* (London: Grant Richards, 1920), 11.

85. See, for instance, McKay to Joel E. Spingarn, January 9, 1917, and June 18, 1917. In the latter, McKay referred to "a long narrative poem and six sonnets which I enclosed," but these are not in Spingarn's papers. Also see McKay to Braithwaite, January 11, 1916, and September 29, 1918. Letters to Spingarn and Braithwaite are in JESP and WSBP, respectively. McKay had also submitted poems to the *Masses*, his favorite magazine at the time, as he mentioned in his memoir having received a couple of "So sorry" rejection slips from its editors. The *Masses*—bold, radical, iconoclastic, antiwar, and bohemian—persecuted by the government during the First World War, was finally suppressed out of existence in December 1917, but was resurrected a few months later as the *Liberator*. Evidently, McKay's poems must have been sent before that date (December 1917). See *LW*, 29; William L. O'Neill, *The Last Romantic: A Life of Max Eastman* (New York: Oxford University Press, 1978), 31–32, 65; Christoph Irmscher, *Max Eastman: A Life* (New Haven, CT: Yale University Press, 2017), chap. 5. It is probable that some, but by no means all, of these poems were submitted to more than one publication and that some are among the nineteen that have survived and been identified here; but there is no doubt that a number of poems that were written during this period are not among the ones found. For instance, none of the extant poems fits the description of the "long narrative poem" that McKay sent to Spingarn.

86. "ANPP," 275.

87. Much of the debate took place between one J. I. Dixon of Gordon Town and Walter Jekyll. Dixon regarded "dialect poetry" in general as "rubbish." He disagreed with Jekyll who encouraged budding writers to begin their writing in their Jamaican "mother tongue." "The English language," is the Jamaicans' mother tongue insisted Dixon. "The African language died with the imported Africans." McKay, he insisted, should have written in English. All "these dialect things" reflect "anything but credit on a people, every day advancing in intelligence." For key elements of the debate, see *Gleaner* April 17, April 21, April 26, April 30, 1913. Claude McKay, "The Liquid Negro Language of the South," *Gleaner*, July 12, 1913. In an address to the newly formed Universal Negro Improvement Association, the Mayor of Kingston used the occasion to disparage the use of Jamaican creole. See *Gleaner*, January 29, 1915; also February 12, 1915. The wider cultural and political contexts are discussed further in Winston James, *A Fierce Hatred of Injustice: Claude McKay's Jamaica and His Poetry of Rebellion* (London: Verso, 2000), 139-51.

88. "Claude McKay Defends Our Dialect Poetry," *Gleaner*, June 7, 1913. See Hughes's vigorous defense of the representation of ordinary Black folk and Black vernacular in art, "The Negro Artist and the Racial Mountain," *Nation*, June 23, 1926; also Langston Hughes, "Our Wonderful Society: Washington," *Opportunity*, August 1927, and McKay, "A Negro Writer to His Critics."

89. Claude McKay, "Longing for Thee," *Jamaica Times*, April 12, 1913; Claude McKay, "Home," *Jamaica Times*, December 20, 1913.

90. Claude McKay, "Bestman's Toast at Rustic Wedding Feast," *Jamaica Times*, December 14, 1920; reprinted in James, *A Fierce Hatred of Injustice*, 215-16.

91. McKay married his Jamaican sweetheart, Eulalie Imelda Lewars, in the summer of 1914, soon after he left Kansas State for New York. The marriage lasted less than six months, and the pregnant Eulalie returned to Jamaica, giving birth to a daughter that McKay never met. Eulalie tried to revive the marriage and turned up at McKay's apartment seven years later, but McKay was not interested and soon thereafter went on his trip to Russia, escaping what he called "domestic death." "ANPP," 276; *LW*, 149-50.

92. "My Ethiopian Maid," enclosure with McKay to Braithwaite, January 11, 1916, WSBP.

93. "To The White Fiends," in McKay to Braithwaite, January 11, 1916, WSBP.

94. Claude McKay, "Invocation," *Seven Arts*, October 1917, 741.

95. Claude McKay, "The Harlem Dancer," *Seven Arts*, October 1917, 741.

96. Claude McKay, "Harlem Shadows," "ANPP," 276.

97. Claude McKay, "Is It Worth While?," "ANPP," 276.

98. McKay, "Is It Worth While?"

99. W. E. B. Du Bois, *The Souls of Black Folk: Essays and Sketches* (Chicago: A. C. McClurg, 1903), 250-64.

100. McKay, "The Lynching," *Cambridge Magazine*, Summer 1920, 55.

101. *LW*, 21.

102. McKay to Braithwaite, February 15, 1916, WSBP; *LW*, 26-28.

103. See James, *Holding Aloft the Banner of Ethiopia*, esp. chaps 2 and 5.

6. Fighting Back: Claude McKay and the Crisis of 1919

1. Official reports suggest twenty-six, but through her diligent and enterprising research, Karen Sieber has discovered, so far, "nearly four dozen (known) riots and lynchings." This is all documented on her database, *Visualizing the Red Summer*,

http://visualizingtheredsummer.com/. For the official figure, see U.S. House of Representatives, 66th Cong., 2nd Sess., *Anti-Lynching Bill*, Report No. 1027 (Washington, DC: Government Printing Office, 1920), 2; hereafter *Anti-Lynching Bill*.

2. James Weldon Johnson, *Black Manhattan* (New York: Knopf, 1930), 246; and Johnson, *Along This Way* (New York: Viking, 1933), 341. The term *race riots*, generally used to describe the events of 1919, is misleading. By one common definition, the term *riot* means "disorder, tumult, disturbance of the peace, outbreak of lawlessness on the part of a crowd" (*Oxford Illustrated Dictionary*, 2nd. ed., 1975). But as E. P. Thompson noted, it is a "clumsy term which may conceal more than it reveals." It becomes even more problematic when the adjective *race* is added, concealing even more. These so-called race riots need a term that reflects what they really were: antiblack, racist mob violence, akin to pogroms and attempted pogroms. David Frugler noted the limitations of the term *riot* but elected to use it all the same, expressing reluctance to use the word *pogrom*—for unconvincing reasons—to describe these events. I, in contrast, aim to avoid the term *riot* and find *pogrom*—defined here as organized racial persecution, with tacit or explicit sanction by the state (governmental authorities, local, state, or federal) through mob violence, including murder—a more appropriate description of much of what racist mobs did, intended to do, or attempted to do during the Red Summer. Thus, I agree with Charles L. Lumpkins's depiction of the 1917 East St. Louis antiblack mob attacks as a pogrom. The only difference with the Red Summer was the far more sustained Black resistance, for a variety of reasons, in 1919 than in East St. Louis in 1917. E. P. Thompson, *Customs in Common: Studies in Traditional Popular Culture* (New York: New Press, 1991), 266; David F. Krugler, *1919, the Year of Racial Violence: How African Americans Fought Back* (New York: Cambridge University Press, 2015), 10–11; Charles L. Lumpkins, *American Pogrom: The East St. Louis Race Riot and Black Politics* (Athens: Ohio University Press, 2008), xi–xii.

3. John Hope Franklin and Alfred Moss, *From Slavery to Freedom: A History of Negro Americans* (New York: McGraw-Hill., 1988), 313.

4. C. Vann Woodward, *The Strange Career of Jim Crow*, 3rd rev. ed. (New York: Oxford University Press, 1974), 114.

5. *Anti-Lynching Bill*, 1: "77 Negroes" were lynched; but also see 14 and 15, where the numbers given are "74 Negroes" and "78 colored," respectively.

6. Vincent Mikkelsen, "Coming from Battle to Face a War: The Lynching of Black Soldiers in the World War I Era (PhD diss., Florida State University, 2007), 213.

7. Robert L. Zangrando, *The NAACP Crusade Against Lynching, 1909–1950* (Philadelphia: Temple University Press, 1980), 6; Walter White, *Rope and Faggot: A Biography of Judge Lynch* (New York: Knopf, 1929), 231; Herbert Shapiro, *White Violence and Black Response: From Reconstruction to Montgomery* (Amherst: University of Massachusetts Press, 1988), 147.

8. Walter White, "The Race Conflict in Arkansas," *Survey*, December 13, 1919, 233–34; White, "'Massacring Whites' in Arkansas," *Nation*, December 6, 1919, 715–16; Robert Kerlin, ed., *The Voice of the Negro, 1919* (New York: Dutton, 1920), 87–93; Arthur I. Waskow, *From Race Riot to Sit-In* (New York: Anchor, 1967), 121–42; Shapiro, *White Violence*, 148–49; Richard Cortner, *A Mob Intent on Death: The NAACP and the Arkansas Riot Cases* (Middletown, CT: Wesleyan University Press 1988), 30–31; Nan Elizabeth Woodruff, *American Congo: The African American Freedom Struggle in the Delta* (Cambridge, MA: Harvard University Press, 2003), chap. 3; Cameron McWhirter, *Red Summer: The Summer of 1919 and the Awakening of Black America* (New York: Henry Holt, 2011), chap. 19; Krugler, *1919*, 166–80.

9. Orville D. Menard, "Lest We Forget: The Lynching of Will Brown, Omaha's 1919 Race Riot," *Nebraska History* 91 (2010): 155, 157–58.

10. Lee E. Williams II, *Post-War Riots in America, 1919 and 1946* (Lewiston, NY: Edwin Mellen, 1991), 71–72, quoting the *Chicago Defender*, October 4, 1919; Kerlin, *Voice of the Negro*, 85.

11. Waskow, *From Race Riot*, 117.

12. *Wichita Protest* report reprinted in Kerlin, *Voice of the Negro*, 85; Clark quoted in Krugler, *1919*, 155.

13. Kerlin, *Voice of the Negro*, 86; Henry Fonda, *Fonda: My Life as Told to Howard Teichmann* (New York: New American Library, 1981), 24–25. It was more than fifty years before Henry Fonda spoke publicly about what he saw. Fonda's children, Peter and Jane, reference the experience as "a key to their father's concern for social justice." His biographer argued that that night in Omaha left a lifelong mark, supplying "the seeds of so much sorrow, anger and solitude in Fonda." Devin McKinney, *The Man Who Saw a Ghost: The Life and Work of Henry Fonda* (Detroit: Thorndike, 2012), 553–68.

14. Williams, *Post-War Riots*, 87.

15. For more on Omaha, see *Anti-Lynching Bill*, 2; Kerlin, *Voice of the Negro*, 85–87; Williams, *Post-War Riots*, 61–101; Waskow, *From Race Riot*, 110–20. Michael Lawson, "Omaha, A City in Ferment: Summer of 1919," *Nebraska History* 58, no. 3 (1977): 395–417, and Orville Menard, "Tom Dennison, the Omaha *Bee*, and the 1919 Omaha Race Riot," *Nebraska History* 68, no. 4 (1987): 152–65, provide a good overview of the toxic political environment in Omaha, which contributed to the racist outburst.

16. The Chicago Commission on Race Relations, *The Negro in Chicago: A Study of Race Relations and a Race Riot* (Chicago: University of Chicago Press, 1922), 48, 655–67.

17. National Association for the Advancement of Colored People (NAACP), "Supplementary Memorandum on Why Congress Should Investigate Race Riots and Lynchings," in *Anti-Lynching Bill*, 16.

18. *Anti-Lynching Bill*, 8.

19. NAACP, "Supplementary Memorandum," 16.

20. NAACP, "Supplementary Memorandum," 17.

21. Shapiro, *White Violence*, 147.

22. The Chicago rampage was the most serious of those that took place in 1919. At about 4:00 p.m. on Sunday, July 27, 1919, a Black boy, Eugene Williams, drowned after having being hit by a stone while swimming in Lake Michigan at the Twenty-Ninth Street beach. Eugene had apparently drifted across the de facto line of segregation on the beach into the "white" section. Black witnesses accused a white man of having stoned the youth and complained to a police officer patrolling the beach. The police refused to arrest the culprit and instead sought to arrest one of the Black men present. Coming on top of the notorious racism that African Americans had to endure in that city, Eugene's murder in broad daylight and the callous response of the police were the last straw. The white attacks and Black resistance lasted for almost a week. See Carl Sandburg, *The Chicago Race Riots, July 1919* (New York: Harcourt, Brace and Howe, 1919); Chicago Commission on Race Relations, *The Negro in Chicago*; William M. Tuttle, Jr., *Race Riot: Chicago in the Red Summer of 1919* (New York: Atheneum, 1970); and Allan H. Spear, *Black Chicago: The Making of a Ghetto, 1890–1920* (Chicago: University of Chicago Press 1967), chap. 11.

23. Spear, *Black Chicago*, 216.

24. "A Report on the Chicago Riot by an Eye-Witness," *Messenger*, September 1919 (Riot Number), 11–13.

25. Twenty-two percent—17 out of 77—of the Black people lynched in 1919 were ex-soldiers. *Anti-Lynching Bill*, 1; Mikkelsen, "Coming from Battle," 213. "Black soldiers may have returned home believing that their work and sacrifice entitled them to the rights of citizenship, but for the supporters of Jim Crow the black man in uniform was rather to be feared and hated than respected. . . . [In Georgia] blacks were lynched for a variety of alleged misdemeanors, and quite clearly returning soldiers were a high-priority target. During April [1919] one soldier was beaten to death at Blakely for wearing his uniform for too long. . . . Early in August a soldier was shot for refusing to yield the road, another was hanged for discussing the racial violence in Chicago. Another soldier was lynched at Pope City for firing a gun." Shapiro, *White Violence*, 146–47.

26. Harry Haywood, *Black Bolshevik: The Autobiography of An Afro-American Communist* (Chicago: Liberator, 1978), 82–83.

27. William M. Tuttle, Jr., "Views of a Negro During 'The Red Summer' of 1919: A Document," *Journal of Negro History* 51, no. 3 (July 1966): 213–14.

28. Tuttle, "Views of a Negro," 216.

29. William H. Harris, *The Harder We Run: Black Workers Since the Civil War* (New York: Oxford University Press, 1982), 55.

30. Mob violence took place in Washington from the 19th to the 22nd of July; that in Chicago began on the 27th of July.

31. James Weldon Johnson, "Views and Reviews," *New York Age*, August 2, 1919. The *Washington Post* not only encouraged the racists; it did much worse than that. The *Post*, in essence, appointed itself as the recruiting sergeant and strategist of the mobs. In its report on the first night of serious disturbance (Sunday, July 20), the *Post* included the following paragraph on its front page: "It was learned that a mobilization of every available service man stationed in or near Washington or on leave here has been ordered for tomorrow evening near the Knights of Columbus hut on Pennsylvania Avenue between Seventh and Eighth Streets. The hour of assembly is 9 o'clock and the purpose is a 'clean up' that will cause the events of the last two evenings to pale into insignificance" (*Washington Post*, July 21, 1919). The NAACP was furious with the *Post*, but there was very little that they could do. See Johnson, "Views and Reviews"; Johnson, "The Riots: An N.A.A.C.P. Investigation," *Crisis*, September 1919, 241–43.

32. Shapiro, *White Violence*, 154.

33. Carter G. Woodson, "Affidavit Concerning the Events of July 20, 1919," quoted in David Levering Lewis, *When Harlem Was in Vogue* (New York: Oxford University Press, 1989), 19; and Jacqueline Goggin, *Carter G. Woodson: A Life in Black History* (Baton Rouge: Louisiana State University Press, 1993), 147.

34. Quoted in Delia Cunningham Mellis, "'The Monsters We Defy': Washington, D.C. in the Red Summer of 1919" (PhD diss., City University of New York, 2008), 170.

35. *New York Times*, July 21, 1919; *Washington Herald*, July 21, 1919.

36. Mellis, "'The Monsters We Defy,'" 171; Krugler, *1919*, 77.

37. *New York Age*, August 2, 1919.

38. *New York Age*, August 2, 1919.

39. *New York Age*, August 2, 1919.

40. Johnson, "The Riots," 242.

41. Johnson, "The Riots," 242.

42. Johnson, "The Riots," 243.

43. *New York Age*, August 2, 1919.

44. Shapiro, *White Violence*, 154; see also Waskow, *From Race Riot*, 21–37; William G. Jordan, *Black Newspapers and America's War for Democracy, 1914–1920* (Chapel Hill: University of North Carolina Press, 2001), 149–50.

45. For a particularly cogent analysis of these inhibiting factors, see William Cohen, *At Freedom's Edge: Black Mobility and the Southern White Quest for Racial Control, 1861–1915* (Baton Rouge: Louisiana State University Press, 1991).

46. U.S. Department of Labor, Bureau of Immigration, *Annual Report of the Commissioner General of Immigration, 1925* (Washington, DC: Government Printing Office, 1925), 137–38; Tuttle, *Race Riot*, 84.

47. Between 1910 and 1920, net migration of white people from the South was almost 600,000; the corresponding figure for Black southerners was 482,300. Nevertheless, this meant that a higher proportion of Black people than whites left the South. See Jack Temple Kirby, *Rural Worlds Lost: The American South, 1920–1960* (Baton Rouge: Louisiana State University Press, 1987), 309–33; figures cited from 320, table 3. Many Black people in Chicago believed that some of the white southern migrants in that city constituted a "prime ingredient" in the outbreak of violence. Walter White (then national field officer of the NAACP), for one, insisted that in Chicago they "had spread the virus of race hatred." Tuttle, on the basis of his study of the riot, quite reasonably commented: "Even if they did, they were not indispensable to the forces that culminated in the rioting." The role that white Southerners played in the events in Chicago, Washington, or elsewhere in the North during the Red Summer is still unstudied and remains anecdotal and obscure. It is worth noting, though, that during rioting in Omaha in 1919, the wife of John Nassinger is reported to have said to her Alabaman husband: "Go on, dear, show them how they do it down in Alabama." Walter White, "Chicago and Its Eight Reasons," *Crisis*, October 1919, 294; Tuttle, *Race Riot*, 84n17; Williams, *Post-War Riots*, 91.

48. George E. Haynes, "Negroes Move North: Their Departure from the South," *Survey*, May 4, 1918, 120.

49. The literature on this subject is a vast and growing one. See, in particular, Joe W. Trotter, ed., *The Great Migration In Historical Perspective: New Dimensions of Race, Class, and Gender* (Bloomington: Indiana University Press, 1991); Carole Marks, *Farewell—We're Good and Gone: The Great Black Migration* (Bloomington: Indiana University Press, 1989); James Grossman, *Land of Hope: Chicago, Black Southerners and the Great Migration* (Chicago: University of Chicago Press, 1989); and Isabel Wilkerson, *The Warmth of Other Suns: The Epic Story of America's Great Migration* (New York: Random House, 2011).

50. In 1917, the year the United States entered the First World War, there were some thirty-six lynchings of Black people; in 1918, there were sixty, and in 1919 seventy-six. Robert L. Zangrando, *The NAACP Crusade Against Lynching, 1909–1950* (Philadelphia: Temple University Press, 1980), 6, table 2; Walter White, *Rope and Faggot: A Biography of Judge Lynch* (New York: Knopf, 1929), 231; Franklin and Moss, *From Slavery*, 307.

51. There was no irony meant by President Wilson when he asked Congress, on April 2, 1917, for a declaration of war against Germany with the following reasoning: "The world must be made safe for democracy. Its peace must be planted upon the tested foundations of political liberty. . . . We are but one of the champions of the rights of mankind." *Messages and Papers of the Presidents*, vol. 17 (New York: Bureau of National Literature, n.d.), 8231.

52. See Barbeau and Henri, *Unknown Soldier*; Jack Foner, *Blacks in the Military*, chap. 6; Robert Mullen, *Blacks in America's Wars* (New York: Pathfinder, 1973); Bernard Nalty, *Strength for the Fight: A History of Black Americans in the Military* (New York: Free Press, 1986), 101–124; Chad Williams, *Torchbearers of Democracy: African American Soldiers in the World War I Era* (Chapel Hill: University of North Carolina Press, 2010); and the testimony by Harry Haywood of his own experience in the army in France during the war, *Black Bolshevik*, chap. 2. The radical Black press at the time carried a number of important reports, testimonies, and analyses of the experience of African American soldiers. The *Messenger* magazine was especially copious in its reportage (January 1918, March 1919, May–June 1919, July 1919, August 1919, and October 1919); see also the *Crusader* (December 1919, January 1920, May 1920, and June 1920). The *Crisis* (May 1919) carried a powerful exposé of the treatment of Black troops in France, which was widely publicized and discussed within the African American community: W. E. B. Du Bois, "Documents of the War," *Crisis*, May 1919, 16–22.

53. Quoted in Charles H. Williams, *Negro Soldiers in World War I: The Human Side* (New York: AMS Press, 1979; [1923]), 220–21.

54. W. B. Yeats, "Easter 1916," in *Collected Poems* (London: Picador, 1990), 202–5.

55. *Crisis*, November 1919, 339.

56. No one is certain who coined the term "the New Negro." Although it is commonplace to associate the term with Alain Locke's anthology of Harlem Renaissance writing (*The New Negro: An Interpretation*, ed. Alain Locke [New York: Albert and Charles Boni, 1925]), there is abundant evidence of the term's currency from the turn of the century. Booker T. Washington and some of his associates published a book in 1900 entitled *A New Negro for a New Century*, but, as was to be expected from Washington, its ideological content was worlds apart from the meaning invested in it by militant Black America during and after the First World War. William Pickens in 1916 also published a book using the term (*The New Negro: His Political, Civil and Mental Status, and Related Essays* [reprinted, New York: Negro Universities Press, 1969]) in a way that approximated more to its later usage. Hubert Harrison spoke and wrote about the "New Negro" as early as his launch of the *Voice* on July 4, 1917, giving the term a new meaning—militant, fearless, outspoken. He also founded and edited a short-lived journal called *The New Negro*. His was the meaning adopted in the postwar period, as expressed in Cyril Briggs's *Cruasder*, A. Philip Randolph and Chandler Owen's *Messenger*, Garvey's *Negro World*, and a host of radical publications at the time. For an index of the mood of the time, see Kerlin, *Voice of the Negro*; Robert Kerlin, "The Negro Press," paper presented to the Southern Sociological Congress, Washington DC, May 13, 1920 (published in the *Crusader*, June 1920, 15–16); Frederick Detweiler, *The Negro Press in the United States* (Chicago: University of Chicago Press, 1922); Theodore Vincent, ed., *Voices of a Black Nation: Political Journalism in the Harlem Renaissance* (San Francisco: Ramparts, 1973); Tony Martin, ed., *African Fundamentalism: A Literary and Cultural Anthology of Garvey's Harlem Renaissance* (Dover, MA: Majority Press, 1986). For some background to the term, see Henry Louis Gates, "The Trope of a New Negro and the Reconstruction of the Image of the Black," *Representations* 24 (Fall 1988): 129–55.

57. Editorial, *Crusader*, January, 1921, 8.

58. W. E. B. Du Bois, "Returning Soldiers," *Crisis*, May 1919, 14; emphasis in original. In an editorial in the July 1918 issue of *Crisis*, Du Bois had counseled his fellow African

Americans: "Let us, while this war lasts, forget our special grievances and close our ranks shoulder to shoulder with our own white fellow citizens and the allied nations that are fighting for democracy." Du Bois was never allowed to forget this statement for the rest of his long life. The verdict of history has rather supported the editors of the *Messenger*, when they predicted that Du Bois's remarks "will rank in shame and reeking disgrace with the 'Atlanta Compromise' speech of Booker Washington." *Messenger*, May–June 1919, 9.

59. *LW*, 110.

60. Claude McKay, "A Negro Writer to His Critics," *New York Herald-Tribune Books*, March 6, 1932, 1.

61. *LW*, 31, 54; McKay, "A Negro Writer to His Critics," 1.

62. Haywood, *Black Bolshevik*, 1–3, 81.

63. Richard Wright, introduction to St. Clair Drake and Horace R. Cayton, *Black Metropolis: A Study of Negro Life in a Northern City* (New York: Harcourt, Brace, 1945), xxxiii; McKay, "A Negro Writer to His Critics," 1; *LW*, 31.

64. *LW*, 30.

65. *LW*, 30.

66. *LW*, 31.

67. Claude McKay, "If We Must Die," *Liberator*, July 1919, 21; the words "let us still be brave" in line 10 were changed when the poem was later reprinted to "let us show us brave." This revision, along with some smaller ones, was implemented in 1922 with the publication of *Harlem Shadows* and would be continued in subsequent publications of "If We Must Die"; see *HS*, 53; and *SP*, 36. The ambiance of a train's dining car when the rush is off is powerfully evoked in *Home to Harlem*, esp. 123–39.

68. *LW*, 31–32.

69. *LW*, 31.

70. *Messenger*, September 1919 (Riot Number), 4; *Crusader*, September 1919, 7.

71. "If We Must Die" was first published in the *Negro World* on October 4, 1919. This issue of the *Negro World* has not survived. The information comes from J. R. Ralph Casimir's unpublished anthology, "Book of Negro Poems and Songs, 1919," 3; J. R. Ralph Casimir Papers, Schomburg Center for Research in Black Culture, New York Public Library, hereafter JRRCP. For the editorial and reviews, see *Negro World*, June 17, May 6, and June 3, 1922. Ethel Trew Dunlap, "Lines Dedicated to Claude McKay," *Negro World*, May 27, 1922.

72. Carter G. Woodson, ed., *The Works of Francis J. Grimké*, vol. 1, *Addresses Mainly Personal and Racial* (Washington, DC: Associated Publishers, 1942), 607–8.

73. *Congressional Record and Proceedings and Debates*, 66th Cong., 1st Sess., vol. 58, pt. 6, Sept. 13, to Oct. 4, 1919 (Washington, DC: Government Printing Office, 1919), 5759.

74. Wright, introduction to Drake and Cayton, *Black Metropolis*, xxxiii.

75. *Pittsburgh Courier*, June 18, 1927.

76. Thurman, "Negro Poets and Their Poetry," *Bookman*, July 1928, 59. The poem quoted by Thurman is McKay's "To the White Fiends," first published in *Pearson's Magazine*, September 1918, 276.

77. Melvin Tolson, "Claude McKay's Art," *Poetry* 83 (1954): 290.

78. Tolson, "Claude McKay's Art," 290.

79. *LW*, 227–28.

80. Jessica Mitford, "A Talk with George Jackson," *New York Times*, June 13, 1971; Tolson, "Claude McKay's Art," 290. Despite the oft-repeated claim that Churchill recited the poem in one of his speeches during the Second World War, there is no definitive

evidence that he did so. I have searched for this evidence but have not found it, even though I heard an old Garveyite in London plausibly claim that he heard the speech in which the poem was quoted. If there is hard evidence, it has not been uncovered so far. Lee Jenkins also searched, and he too could not find it: Lee M. Jenkins, "'If We Must Die': Winston Churchill and Claude McKay," *Notes and Queries* 50, no. 3 (September 2003): 333–37.

81. "The Barrier," *Liberator*, July 1919, 20.

82. "The Capitalist at Dinner," *Liberator*, July 1919, 20; note the continuing echo of Schopenhauer.

83. "The Little Peoples," *Liberator*, July 1919, 21.

84. "The Tired Worker," *Liberator*, August 1919, 46.

85. Alexander Trachtenberg, *A History of May Day* (New York: International Pamphlets, 1935), 25–26; Philip S. Foner, *May Day: A Short History of the International Workers' Holiday, 1886–1986* (New York: International Publishers, 1986), 75–77.

86. Claude McKay, "Labor's Day," *Messenger*, September 1919, 31.

87. Claude McKay, "J'accuse," *Messenger*, October 1919, 33. The distinct echoes of motifs from his Jamaican poetry are clear, and of course Émile Zola's powerful denunciation of antisemitism expressed during the prolonged persecution of the French military officer, Alfred Dreyfus.

88. *Liberator*, July 1919, 20 and 21.

89. See Frank E. Manuel and Fritzie P. Manuel, *Utopian Thought in the Western World* (Oxford: Basil Blackwell, 1979); and Zygmunt Bauman, *Socialism: The Active Utopia* (London: Allen and Unwin, 1976).

90. Percy Bysshe Shelley, "Ode to the West Wind," in *Poetical Works*, ed. Thomas Hutchinson, corrected by G. M. Matthews (Oxford: Oxford University Press, 1970), 579.

91. See Robert K. Murray, *Red Scare: A Study in National Hysteria, 1919–1920* (New York: McGraw-Hill, 1955); and William Preston, Jr., *Aliens and Dissenters: Federal Suppression of Radicals, 1903–1933* (Cambridge, MA: Harvard University Press, 1963); Julian F. Jaffe, *Crusade Against Radicalism: New York During the Red Scare, 1914–1924* (Port Washington, NY: Kennikat, 1972); Todd J. Pfannestiel, *Rethinking the Red Scare: The Lusk Committee and New York's Campaign Against Radicalism, 1919–1923* (New York: Routledge, 2003).

92. A. Mitchell Palmer, *Letter from the Attorney General Transmitting in Response to a Senate Resolution October 17, 1919, A Report on the Activities of the Bureau of Investigation of the Department of Justice Against Persons Advising Anarchy, Sedition, and the Forcible Overthrow of the Government* (Washington, DC: Government Printing Office 1919), 162. This document, by Attorney General A. Mitchell Palmer, was generally referred to by contemporaries as the *Palmer Report* and will be so abbreviated hereafter. Theodore Kornweibel, Jr., *"Seeing Red": Federal Campaigns Against Black Militancy, 1917–1925* (Bloomington: Indiana University Press, 1998); Mark Ellis, *Race, War, and Surveillance: African Americans and the United States Government During World War I* (Bloomington: Indiana University Press, 2001).

93. *Palmer Report*, 162–63. The mood and temper of the Black press is captured well by two contemporary studies: Kerlin, *Voice of the Negro*; and Detweiler, *Negro Press*, chaps. iv–ix. See also William G. Jordan, *Black Newspapers and America's War for Democracy, 1914–1920* (Chapel Hill: University of North Carolina, 2001), chaps. 4 and 5.

94. McKay is here referring to W. A. Domingo, "Did Bolshevism Stop Race Riots in Russia?," *Messenger*, September 1919, 26–27.

95. *Negro World*, September 20, 1919; cited in *Palmer Report*, 163-64.
96. Claude McKay, "To 'Holy' Russia," *Workers' Dreadnought*, February 28, 1920.
97. *Palmer Report*, 163.
98. The Black radical responses to the Bolshevik Revolution are discussed at length in Winston James, "To the East Turn: The Russian Revolution and the Black Radical Imagination in the United States, 1917–1924," *American Historical Review* 126, no. 3 (September 2021): 1001-1045.
99. *Palmer Report*, 163, 166, 169.
100. *Palmer Report*, 166.
101. *Palmer Report*, 187.
102. *Nation*, July 26, 1919, 931, and June 14, 1919, 97.
103. *Nation*, August 16, 1919, 223.
104. *Revolutionary Radicalism: Its History, Purpose and Tactics with an Exposition and Discussion of the Steps Being Taken and Required to Curb It, Being the Report of the Joint Legislative Committee Investigating Seditious Activities, Filed April 24, 1920, in the Senate of the State of New York. Part I: Revolutionary and Subversive Movements Abroad and at Home*, II (Albany, NY: J. B. Lyon, 1920), 1520.
105. *LW*, 227–28.
106. "If We Must Die," *Messenger*, September 1919, 4.
107. Claude McKay, letter to the editor, *Messenger*, October 1920, 113. In 1928, McKay, who was by then in exile in France, inquired after the *Messenger* and recounted that "it was a splendid magazine during and right after the War. It had the *Crisis* licked miles and miles, it was so well-edited and strong in its opinion." McKay to James Ivy, May 20, 1928; reprinted in Wayne Cooper, ed., *The Passion of Claude McKay: Selected Poetry and Prose, 1912–1948* (New York: Schocken, 1973), 146.
108. See *Crusader*: "Tropical Night" [poem], March 1921, 5; "Afternoon in Herald Square" [poem], June 1921, 10; "English Journalists Investigate Bolshevism" [book review], June 1921, 18–19. In addition to these, there are references to and news of McKay, whom the editor, Briggs, hailed as "our brilliant poet" (January 1921, 5). See for example, May 1920, 6; April 1921, 21; May 1921, 13.
109. Domingo, "Did Bolshevism Stop Race Riots in Russia?," 27.
110. Quoted in W. E. B. Du Bois, "The Negro and Radical Thought," *Crisis*, July 1921, 102.

7. English Innings and Left-Wing Communism: McKay's Bolshevization in Britain, 1919-1921

1. Frank Harris to Grant Richards, November 8, 1919, Frank Harris Papers, Albert H. Small Collections Library, University of Virginia; McKay to Grant Richards, August 31, 1920, C. K. Ogden Fonds, William Ready Divisions of Archives and Research Collections, Mills Memorial Library, McMaster University. All McKay's correspondence with Ogden cited here are from this collection.
2. Pankhurst had known both Crystal Eastman, a socialist and ardent feminist, and her younger brother Max, who at the time of Pankhurst's 1911 U.S. tour was secretary and treasurer of New York State's Men's League for Woman Suffrage. During Pankhurst's 1912 tour, Crystal, who was then working with the suffrage movement in Wisconsin, hosted Pankhurst in Milwaukee. Sylvia Pankhurst, *The Suffragette Movement: An Intimate Account of Persons and Ideals* (London: Virago, [1931] 1977), 349;

Max Eastman to Sylvia Pankhurst, May 11, [1911?], Estelle Sylvia Pankhurst Papers, International Institute of Social History, Amsterdam; E. Sylvia Pankhurst, *A Suffragette in America: Reflections on Prisoners, Pickets and Political Change*, ed. Katherine Connelly (London: Pluto, 2019), 107, 122.

3. Walter Fuller to C. K. Ogden, November 11, 1919; McKay to C. K. Ogden, August 17, 1920.

4. *LW*, 64. The British Museum archives confirm that McKay applied for a ticket with a reference from Shaw and that he did receive one. See McKay to Director, British Museum, April 2, 1920, and Shaw's letter, dated March 29, 1920; in a note dated April 5, 1920, the director's office informed McKay that he had been granted a ticket lasting three months. It is almost certain that McKay sought extension of his permit, but there is no direct evidence of that in the museum's archives. The documents may be found in the British Museum Archives, London, Series CE83 1890–1973.

5. Claude McKay, "Up to Date" [1934], NCC. The manuscript is a fragment of an unpublished autobiographical sketch written for Cunard's anthology, *Negro* (1934). McKay, in the end, withdraw his contribution after a dispute with Cunard. Some of the material was reworked in McKay's 1937 travelogue, *A Long Way from Home*.

6. McKay, "Up to Date," 2.

7. McKay, "Up to Date," 2.

8. *LW*, 133–34.

9. McKay, "Up to Date," 2.

10. *LW*, 70–71.

11. McKay wrote a long article on the club for the *Negro World*, which was highly critical of the way it was run. See McKay, "Our London Letter," *Negro World* (Magazine Section), March 13, 1920. McKay's article is reprinted in Winston James, "Letters from London in Black and Red: Claude McKay, Marcus Garvey and the *Negro World*," *History Workshop Journal* 85 (Spring 2018): 281–93. Also see *West Africa*, June 14, 1919, 444.

12. *LW*, 70–71; McKay, "Up to Date," 3.

13. *LW*, 71.

14. McKay, "Up to Date," 3.

15. McKay to Ogden, April 2, 1920.

16. McKay to Ogden, February 25, 1920.

17. Provence Street was near a notoriously rough and racist area of London, known as Campbell Bunk. For a vivid depiction of the community, see Jerry White, *Campbell Bunk: The Worst Street in North London Between the Wars* (London: Pimlico, 2003).

18. McKay to Ogden, April 2, 1920.

19. Roy May and Robin Cohen, "The Interaction Between Race and Colonialism: A Case Study of the Liverpool Riots of 1919," *Race and Class* 16, no. 2 (1974); Neil Evans, "The South Wales Race Riots of 1919," *Llafur: Journal of Welsh Labour History* 3, no. 1 (1980); Neil Evans, "Across the Universe: Racial Violence and the Post-War Crisis in Imperial Britain, 1919–25," in *Ethnic Labour and British Imperial Trade: A History of Ethnic Seafarers in the U.K.*, ed. Diane Frost (London: Frank Cass, 1995); Jacqueline Jenkinson, "The 1919 Race Riots in Britain: A Survey," in *Under the Imperial Carpet: Essays in Black History, 1780–1950*, ed. Rainer Lotz and Ian Pegg (Crawley, UK: Rabbit, 1986); "Black Sailors on Red Clydeside: Rioting, Reactionary Trade Unionism and Conflicting Notions of 'Britishness' Following the First World War," *Twentieth Century British History* 19, no. 1 (2008): 29–60. The most comprehensive analysis is Jacqueline Jenkinson's fine study, "The 1919 Race Riots in Britain: Their Backgrounds

and Consequences" (PhD diss., University of Edinburgh, 1987), revised as *Black 1919: Riots, Racism and Resistance in Imperial Britain* (Liverpool: Liverpool University Press, 2009). For a rare firsthand account of the mob attacks from a Black eyewitness and victim, see Ernest Marke, *Old Man Trouble: The Memoirs of a Stowaway, Mutineer, Bootlegger, Crocuser and Soho Club Owner* (London: Weidenfeld and Nicolson, 1975), 25–32.

20. Peter Fryer, *Staying Power: The History of Black People in Britain* (London: Pluto, 1984), 318.
21. "A Negro Poet," *WD*, September 19, 1919.
22. *LW*, 76; McKay to Ogden, February 25, 1920; "Samson," *WD*, January 10, 1920; "Socialism and the Negro," *WD*, January 31, 1920.
23. *LW*, 76.
24. On October 23, 1920, for instance, the *Dreadnought* reported on a "very lively meeting," which finished at 11 p.m. at its Soho branch, and explicitly mentioned "Comrades McKay, Bishop, and others from the Central branch" as visitors.
25. *LW*, 76–77.
26. E. Edwards, Hugh Hope, C. E. E., C. E., C. E. Edwards, C. M., and Leon Lopez were among the pseudonyms used. Contrary to Wayne Cooper's assertion, Ness Edwards was not one of McKay's pen names. Ness Edwards (born Onesimus Edwards, 1897–1968) was at the time a Welsh revolutionary miner, a leading member of both the South Wales Miners' Federation and the South Wales Socialist Society, and a close associate of Pankhurst and the *Dreadnought* group. Wayne Cooper, *Claude McKay: Rebel Sojourner in the Harlem Renaissance* (Baton Rouge: Louisiana State University Press, 1987), 117, 394–95n57; and *The Labour Who's Who, 1927* (London: Labour, 1927), 62.
27. McKay, "Up to Date," 1.
28. McKay to Ogden, October 9, 1920.
29. Claude McKay, "How Black Sees Green and Red," *Liberator*, June 1921, 17, 20–21; McKay to Eastman, May 18, 1923, CMI; McKay to Ogden, February 25, 1920.
30. *LW*, 77. Pankhurst herself tells of the break in *The Suffragette Movement: An Intimate Account of Persons and Ideals* (London: Virago, [1931] 1977), esp. book 9, chap. 4.
31. Raymond Challinor, *The Origins of British Bolshevism* (London: Croom Helm, 1977), 168.
32. Challinor, *Origins*, 129, 168.
33. Harry Pollitt, *Serving My Time: An Apprenticeship to Politics* (London: Lawrence & Wishart, [1940] 1950), 110.
34. Walter Kendall, *The Revolutionary Movement in Britain, 1900–1920: The Origins of British Communism* (London: Weidenfeld and Nicolson, 1969), 198.
35. Challinor, *Origins*, 176; Kendall, *Revolutionary Movement*, 196–97.
36. See V. I. Lenin, *"Left-Wing" Communism, An Infantile Disorder* (Moscow: Progress, 1970), esp. 60–73. The pamphlet was first published in June 1920, in time for the Second Congress of the Communist International. For the most detailed discussion of Pankhurst's and other antiparliamentary communists' disagreement with Lenin, see Mark Shipway, *Anti-Parliamentary Communism: The Movement for Workers' Councils in Britain, 1917–45* (Basingstoke: Macmillan, 1988), chaps. 1–4; also see Ian Bullock, "Sylvia Pankhurst and the Russian Revolution: The Making of a 'Left-Wing' Communist," in *Sylvia Pankhurst: From Artist to Anti-Fascist*, ed. Ian Bullock and Richard Pankhurst (Basingstoke, UK: Macmillan, 1992).

37. Challinor, *Origins*, 168.
38. *WD*, June 1, 1918.
39. "The Appeal of Miss Sylvia Pankhurst Against the Sentence of Six Months Imprisonment," Guildhall, City of London, January 5, 1921, 16–17; folder 254, Estelle Sylvia Pankhurst Papers, International Institute of Social History, Amsterdam.
40. *WD*, June 7, 1919.
41. E. Sylvia Pankhurst, *A Suffragette in America: Reflections on Prisoners, Pickets and Political Change*, ed. Katherine Connelly (London: Pluto, 2019), chaps. 6 and 8; *Crisis*, April 1912, 228; Pankhurst, *Suffragette Movement*, 348–50; Pankhurst, *Home Front*, 73, 167–12, quotation at 73. When a young Jewish boy from the East End was executed for desertion, it made the front page of the *Women's Dreadnought* (predecessor of the *Workers' Dreadnought*). The boy had run away from home and joined the army. Evidently suffering from shell shock, he left his post, and for that his young life was taken away by the British authorities. When police and soldiers went on the rampage against Jewish men and boys in Whitechapel, accusing them of being "shirkers" (draft dodgers), Pankhurst was outraged and documented what had happened in a long and powerful editorial, "A Pogrom in London" (*Women's Dreadnought*, May 26, 1917). See also "Executed: East End Boy's Fate," *Women's Dreadnought*, April 22, 1916 (later published as a pamphlet, *Execution of an East End Boy* [London, 1916]), and Pankhurst, *Home Front*, 195.
42. *LW*, 76.
43. *LW*, 87. British intelligence was fully aware of Pankhurst's strengths as well as her weaknesses. One of their agents, reporting on the secret Communist conference in Manchester in September 1920 aimed at unifying the far-left forces, wrote: "This need not disturb us over much for no one has yet succeeded in working amicably with Sylvia Pankhurst." Harry Pollitt, who worked closely with Pankhurst in the WSF and the "Hands Off Russia" campaign, disagreed. "Though I often heard that Sylvia was very difficult to get on with, I never found it so," he wrote in his memoir. It is a striking remark, because Pankhurst was generally denounced by the male leadership of the orthodox left, especially the CP, after she broke with them in 1921. More remarkable still is that Pollitt was general secretary of the CPGB when he made that statement. TNA, CAB 24/112; Pollitt, *Serving My Time*, 110.
44. *LW*, 76–77, 198 (quotation).
45. *LW*, 78.
46. *LW*, 78–79.
47. E. Sylvia Pankhurst to Lee Furman, May 22, 1937, Box 6, Folder 177, CMPY.
48. *LW*, 76.
49. Leon Lopez [Claude McKay], "The Yellow Peril and the Dockers," *WD*, October 16, 1920. There is also an article published in the anarchist journal, *The Spur*, on Limehouse that was almost certainly written by McKay, though the author's name is given as "W. Winter": "More Limehouse," *Spur*, October 1920, 105.
50. See Bullock, "Sylvia Pankhurst and the Russian Revolution"; *Pannekoek and Gorter's Marxism*, ed. D. Smart (London: Pluto, 1978), and especially [Phillipe Bourrinet] and International Communist Current, *The Dutch and German Communist Left: A Contribution to the History of the Revolutionary Movement, 1900–1950* (London: Porcupine, [2001]).
51. "Sylvia Pankhurst Arrested," *WD*, October 23, 1920.
52. See "D. F. Springhull [*sic*] @ Silverhill," in Douglas Springhall file, KV 2/1594, TNA; *LW*, 81–82.

53. "Discontent on the Lower Deck," *WD*, October 16, 1920.

54. "The Yellow Peril and the Dockers," *WD*, October 16, 1920.

55. "The Appeal of Miss Sylvia Pankhurst," esp. 16–17.

56. *LW*, 81–83.

57. L. C. Lampen, Commander-in-Chief's Office, Devonport, to "My dear Peel," November 3, 1920, KV 2/1594, TNA.

58. "D. F. Springhull [*sic*] @ Silverhill."

59. Unsigned intelligence report, November 25, 1920; intercepted and transcribed letter from McKay to Springhall [no date, but envelope stamped in Bow, "4-pm 25 Nov. 20"], KV 2/1594, TNA.

60. Springhall rose up through the Communist youth ranks, becoming the national organizer of the CPGB by 1940. He was sentenced to seven years in prison for spying for the Russians in 1943. He died in Moscow in 1953 and is buried in China. (See the Douglas Springhall files, KV 2/1594.)

61. *LW*, 85–86; Kendall, *Revolutionary Movement*, 246–48.

62. See Blanche Wiesen Cook, ed., *Crystal Eastman on Women and Revolution* (New York: Oxford University Press, 1978) for a good sample of Eastman's writings, including some excellent analyses of the British political scene.

63. McKay to Ogden, November 25 [1920]; McKay, "Up to Date," 4.

64. *LW*, 69–70; Ken Weller, *"Don't Be a Soldier!" The Radical Anti-War Movement in North London, 1914–1918* (London: Journeyman, 1985), 79–80; William J. Fishman, *East End Jewish Radicals, 1875–1914* (London: Duckworth, 1975), 269.

65. *LW*, 68; McKay, "Up to Date," 4. During McKay's time in London, the British cabinet received via the Directorate of Intelligence at the Home Office, at least once a month, a detailed document titled "Report on Revolutionary Organisations in the United Kingdom." Hundreds of these reports, pertaining to the revolutionary ferment during and after the First World War, have been preserved. See National Archives series, CAB 24. Many of these relate the goings-on at the ISC, which the government regarded as the headquarters of the Communist Party in the early 1920s. One report in September 1921 claimed that the ISC was "entirely controlled by the Communist Party, which has paid 1,000 [pounds] towards its up-keep." CAB 24/128, Report No. 123, TNA.

66. *LW*, 70; McKay, "Up to Date," 4.

67. McKay, "Up to Date," 4; McKay to Ogden, April 30, 1920.

68. *LW*, 70; McKay to Ogden, April 30, 1920; McKay, "Up to Date," 4. Professor David Killingray, who is writing a biography of Dr. Harold Moody, informs me that the medical student in question was probably a Jamaican named I. O. B. Shirley. As Dr. Shirley, in 1929 he entered into a partnership with Moody, which dissolved in 1933. (Killingray to James, June 1, and July 17, 2002.)

69. Gilmore was still active, including working as a merchant seaman, at the time McKay wrote his memoir, *A Long Way from Home*. See below.

70. Barbara Winslow, *Sylvia Pankhurst: Sexual Politics and Political Activism* (London: UCL Press, 1996), 128 and 211n., gets Gilmore's name wrong (she calls him Reuben Samuels) and incorrectly states that he was a correspondent for the *Dreadnought*. Rachel Holmes, *Sylvia Pankhurst: Natural Born Rebel* (London: Bloomsbury, 2020), 571, presumably following Winslow (she gives no source), repeats the error. Others— notably Patricia Romero, *E. Sylvia Pankhurst: Portrait of a Radical* (New Haven, CT: Yale University Press, 1990); Mary Davis, *Sylvia Pankhurst: A Life in Radical Politics* (London: Pluto, 1999); and Katherine Connelly, *Sylvia Pankhurst: Suffragette, Socialist and Scourge of Empire* (London: Pluto, 2013)—do not even mention him.

71. "Islington Riots: More Stories," *Globe*, January 5, 1921; *Daily Gazette* (Islington), January 5 and 6, 1921; Ken Weller, "Direct Action and the Unemployed, 1920–21," *Solidarity*, July 1964, 24–30. McKay's biographical profile of a Comrade Gilmore, "The Leader of the Bristol Revolutionaries," *WD*, August 7, 1920, is of a different man. (See also *WD*, July 31, 1920, for a report on the march from Bristol and rally in Trafalgar Square.) The Gilmore who led a tramcar strike and the ex-servicemen's march to London is cited variously in the *Bristol Observer* and *Bristol Evening Post* as "G. Gilmore" or "J. Gilmore" and never referred to as "coloured" or "a man of colour," indicating that he was Black, as was the custom in the press at the time for nonwhites. The McKay profile made no reference this Comrade Gilmore's color.

72. *Holloway & Hornsey & Harringay & Muswell Hill Press*, January 8, 1921; *Daily Gazette* (Islington), January 5 and 6, 1921. Gilmore's defense claimed that the petrol was for the purpose of "making tea" when the Essex Road library, previously occupied by the unemployed (from which the authorities had forcibly expelled them), was "recovered." *Daily Gazette* (Islington), January 6, 1921.

73. "Islington Riot: Startling Document," *Globe*, January 4, 1921; Weller, "Direct Action"; and Weller, *"Don't Be a Soldier!"* 43–44, 76–80.

74. Directorate of Intelligence, "Report on Revolutionary Organisations in the United Kingdom," September 15, 1921, 5; CAB 24/128, TNA.

75. Three letters from Gilmore to McKay have survived, but none from McKay to Gilmore. See Reuben Gilmore to McKay, January 5, 1934 (quoted); November 1, 1936; December 1, 1936; CMPY.

76. Gilmore to McKay, November 1, 1936.

77. Gilmore to McKay, January 5, 1934.

78. Gilmore to McKay, January 5, 1934; November 1, 1936.

79. Gilmore to McKay, November 1, 1936; December 12, 1936.

80. McKay, "Up to Date," 1, 4; *LW*, 68–69; McKay to Eastman, September 16, 1946, CMI.

81. *Liberator*, August 1919, 46; March 1922, 22.

82. McKay, "Up to Date," 3–4. McKay met J. L. J. F. Ezerman (1869–1949), a radical and maverick Orientalist and Dutch civil servant, in New York in August 1919. Ezerman employed McKay to do research for him at the New York Public Library. Ezerman was called to Holland on family business and invited McKay to accompany him, paying his passage. From Holland they went to London in December 1919, where the relationship broke down. Ezerman, however, gave McKay his return passage to New York and £50 towards the publication of his book of poems. The wages from the *Dreadnought* only covered McKay's board in London. McKay to Ogden, February 25, June 23, and August 4, 1920; J. L. J. F. Ezerman to McKay, June 18, 1920, in CKOF; *LW*, 87. McKay's recounting of a mysterious couple, "the Grays," providing him with the passage to Europe (*LW*, 38–44), should not be taken literally. Nowhere—privately or publicly—does McKay explain the ruse of the Grays being his benefactors. One can only speculate. Maybe he felt the need or was asked not to disclose Ezerman's role in supporting him. The opening and title poem of *Spring in New Hampshire* (London: Grant Richards, 1920) is dedicated to "J. L. J. F. E.," who is clearly Ezerman. The same dedication accompanies the reprinted poem in the revised and expanded version of the London anthology, *Harlem Shadows* (New York: Harcourt, Brace, 1922), 40.

83. Advertisement in *WD*, October 23, 1920.

84. *LW*, 70. The *Dreadnought* over the years carried many advertisements for social events at the ISC.

85. Opened on October 21, the exhibition was advertised in the *Dreadnought*, October 23, 1920.

86. McKay to Ogden, October 30, 1920.

87. McKay to Cunard, April 30, 1932.

88. McKay to Ogden, November 25, 1920.

89. McKay to Ogden, April 30, 1920; McKay to Francine Budgen [August? 1920], quoted in Cooper, *Claude McKay*, 130–31.

90. McKay to Ogden, [undated but mid-August] 1920.

91. McKay to Joseph Freeman, March 19, 1921, Joseph Freeman Papers, box 29, file 35, Hoover Institution Archives, Stanford University.

92. *LW*, 67.

93. Writing in January 1920, McKay claimed that the club was "about three months old," but the June 14, 1919, issue of the magazine *West Africa*, 444, carried a report on the club's operations. See McKay, "Our London Letter." Although McKay's "letter"—in fact, a long article on the club—was published in the *Negro World* of March 13, 1920, it is datelined "London, Jan. 14, 1920."

94. McKay, "Our London Letter"; *LW*, 67.

95. McKay to Cunard, April 30, 1932.

96. McKay, "Our London Letter."

97. He appended Rev. Matthias's words to his article sent to the freethinking Hubert Harrison, who was then an editor on the *Negro World*. McKay, "Our London Letter." The report in *West Africa* (June 14, 1919) corroborated McKay's description of the place as "overwhelmingly churchy." The magazine reported that the club had a reputation as a "no drinking club." And one of its officials advised the men to "keep smiling": "The average Englishman does not understand coloured men, never having seen crowds of them, so is apt to stare and perhaps pass remarks. Don't let it get your goat" (444).

98. *LW*, 67–68.

99. "Pismo Mek-Kaia Tovarishu Trotskomu" ["Letter of McKay to Comrade Trotsky"], *Pravda*, April 1, 1923. Though *Pravda* carried it in April, McKay's letter was dated February 20, 1923.

100. McKay, "Our London Letter."

101. Letter to Trotsky.

102. McKay to Ogden, March 12, 1920.

103. McKay to Ogden, February 25, 1920.

104. McKay, "The Castaways," *Cambridge Magazine*, Summer 1920, 58.

105. Sally Marks, "Black Watch on the Rhine: A Study in Propaganda, Prejudice and Prurience," *European Studies Review* 13, no. 3 (1983): 299. Starting with Robert C. Reinders's pioneering effort, a burgeoning body of scholarship has developed on different aspects of the subject. Robert C. Reinders, "Racialism on the Left: E. D. Morel and the 'Black Horror on the Rhine,'" *International Review of Social History* 13 (First Quarter 1968): 1–28; Keith L. Nelson, "The 'Black Horror on the Rhine': Race as a Factor in Post–World War I Diplomacy," *Journal of Modern History* 42, no. 4 (December 1970): 606–27; Christian Koller, *'Von Wilden aller Rassen niedergemetzelt': Die Diskussion um die Verwendung von Kolonialtruppen in Europa zwischen Rassismus, Kolonial—und Militärpolitik (1914–1930)* (Stuttgart: Steiner, 2001); various works by Iris Wigger, "'Against the Laws of Civilisation': Race, Gender and Nation in the International Campaign Against the 'Black Shame,'" *Berkeley Journal of Sociology* 46 (2002): 113–31; "'Black Shame'—The Campaign Against 'Racial Degeneration' and Female Degradation in Interwar Europe," *Race & Class* 51, no. 3 (2010): 33–46; *The "Black Horror on the Rhine": Intersections of Race, Nation, Gender and Class in 1920s Germany* (London: Palgrave Macmillan, 2017); Peter Collar, *The Propaganda War in*

the Rhineland: Weimar Germany, Race and Occupation After World War I (London: I. B. Taurus, 2013); Julia Roos, "'Huns' and Other 'Barbarians': A Movie Ban and the Dilemmas of 1920s German Propaganda Against French Colonial Troops," *Historical Reflections* 40, no. 1 (Spring 2014): 67–91; Peter Campbell, "'Black Horror on the Rhine': Idealism, Pacifism, and Racism in Feminism and the Left in the Aftermath of the First World War," *Histoire sociale / Social History* 47, no. 94 (June 2014): 471–93.

106. The most thorough biography of Morel is Catherine Ann Cline, *E. D. Morel: The Strategies of Protest* (Belfast: Black Staff, 1980); see also Adam Hochschild, *King Leopold's Ghost: A Story of Greed, Terror, and Heroism in Colonial Africa* (Boston: Houghton Mifflin, 1998); A. J. P. Taylor, *The Trouble Makers: Dissent Over Foreign Policy, 1792–1939* (Harmondsworth: Penguin, 1985), esp. chap. 5; Reinders, "Racialism on the Left."

107. *Daily Herald* [hereafter *DH*], April 9, 1920; Marks, "Black Watch on the Rhine," 310.

108. *DH*, April 9, 1920.

109. E. D. Morel, "The Employment of Black Troops in Europe," *Nation*, March 27, 1920, 893; original emphasis.

110. *DH*, April 10, 1920.

111. *DH*, April 10, 1920; emphasis in original.

112. *DH*, April 10, 1920.

113. Norman Leys, "A Contradiction," *DH*, April 17, 1920.

114. E. D. Morel, "Black Troops," *DH*, April 21, 1920.

115. E. D. Morel, "Black Troops in Germany," Special Supplement to *Foreign Affairs*, June 1920, viii. The text, Morel tells us, is the "verbatim report" of his speech at Central Hall, delivered on April 27, 1920. The letters of both McKay and Leys were published on April 24, 1920. *Foreign Affairs* was the official organ of the Union of Democratic Control, founded and edited by Morel himself.

116. One of the Oppressed, "The 'New Negro,'" *DH*, April 24, 1920.

117. "Imperial Atrocities," *DH*, December 15, 1919.

118. Sylvia Pankhurst, "The German Situation," *WD*, April 17, 1920. As we will see, the Black troops were more highly regarded by residents of the occupied regions than the white French troops.

119. Privately, Lansbury claimed that the letter was too long—"of enormous length"—and that he had asked McKay's permission to shorten it, but he had refused. There is no evidence that McKay actually received a reply from the *Herald*. I believe that Lansbury's claim that he had replied to McKay and that the letter was too long is at best a red herring: the *Herald* did publish long letters, at least sometimes. (See, for instance, that of Clifford Allen, *DH*, April 13, 1920.) The fact is that McKay's letter was not welcomed and stood against the paper's editorial stance on the issue. Cutting of letter by A. W. Simpson to unidentified newspaper. Cuttings Album (F15/3/4), E. D. Morel Papers, British Library of Political and Economic Science, London School of Economics and Political Science, University of London.

120. McKay, "A Black Man Replies," *WD*, April 24, 1920. One of the reasons for McKay's eagerness to publish his exposé on the strikebreakers at Lansbury's sawmill was, he acknowledged, his chance for "getting even with the *Daily Herald* for its black-scourge-in-Europe campaign." *LW*, 78. McKay, as we have seen, claimed that Pankhurst refused to publish his article.

121. Morel's pamphlet came out in various editions in the early part of 1920 but was published in its most comprehensive form after his visit to Germany in the summer: *The Horror on the Rhine* (London: Union of Democratic Control, August 1920).

122. Reinders, "Racialism on the Left," 5–6; Nelson, "The 'Black Horror on the Rhine,'" 618–19; Marks, "Black Watch on the Rhine," 312–16; Collar, *Propaganda War*, esp. chaps. 4–7; Roos, "'Huns' and Other 'Barbarians'"; Wigger, *"Black Horror on the Rhine,"* esp. 7–10.

123. Quoted in Reinders, "Racialism on the Left," 6.

124. C. E. Edwards [Claude McKay], "Robert Smillie," *WD*, August 14, 1920; McKay, *LW*, 80–81; Woolf, *Beginning Again*, 219–21; Reinders, "Racialism on the Left," 8. Reinders's is an excellent documentation and analysis of the British labor movement's involvement in the campaign. At a time when Morel was at full tilt in his "Black Horror on the Rhine" campaign, Smillie wrote a glowing introduction to Morel's book, *Thoughts on the War: The Peace—and Prison* (London: Author, 1920).

125. McKay, "Letter to Comrade Trotsky."

126. *Communist*, April 8, 1922.

127. Black troops had been withdrawn in June 1920, "amid regret from the local German population," who preferred them to the white French soldiers. Collar, *Propaganda War*, 221.

128. *Communist*, April 8, 1922.

129. British intelligence had picked up the report of the dispute in a counterrevolutionary White Russian newspaper (*Svoboda*, March 8, 1923) published in Warsaw. In a report by a Captain H. W. Miller, Watkins's presence in Moscow is acknowledged, but Miller discounted the newspaper report. McKay (which he spelled Mackay), he claimed, "has been in the United States for a number of months." He was wrong. McKay was in Moscow until April 1923, when he went to Berlin; he never returned to the United States until 1934. See F.O. 371/9333/2567 and F.O. 371/9334/3085; TNA.

130. William Gallacher, *The Rolling of the Thunder* (London: Lawrence and Wishart, 1947), 65. Gallacher thought that Morel should have been made foreign secretary in the first Labour government led by Ramsay MacDonald.

131. Bertrand Russell, "French Policy Since Versailles," Supplement to *Foreign Affairs*, March 1924, viii. The book under review is C. J. C. Street, *The Treachery of France* (London: Philip Allan, 1924).

132. See "The Union of Democratic Control: Its Objects, Constitution, Personnel and Publications," *Foreign Affairs*, July 1919, 4; "Six Years," *Foreign Affairs*, December 1920, 94; and "Tenth Annual General Meeting of the U.D.C.," *Foreign Affairs*, April 1924, 204.

133. Bertrand Russell, "Eminent Men I Have Known," in *Unpopular Essays* (London: Allen and Unwin, 1950), 220.

134. Marks, "Black Watch on the Rhine," 319.

135. Marks, "Black Watch on the Rhine," 306–7.

136. Marks, "Black Watch on the Rhine," 300–301.

137. Marks, "Black Watch on the Rhine," 320.

138. Quotations from Cline, *E. D. Morel*, 127.

139. Russell, "Eminent Men I Have Known," 220.

140. Cline, *E. D. Morel*, 128; emphasis added.

141. *LW*, 75.

142. Marks, "Black Watch on the Rhine," 320–21.

143. *LW*, 75.

144. *LW*, 76.

145. McKay, "Enslaved," *Liberator*, July 1921, 6; "Africa Enslaved," is the title of one of the poems McKay sent to Ogden in a letter dated August 17, 1920. (The enclosure was not retained.) It is probably the one later published as "Enslaved."

146. McKay to Marcus Garvey, December 17, 1919; Hubert H. Harrison Papers, Box 2, Folder 66, Rare Book and Manuscript Library, Columbia University Library. The full text of the letter is reprinted in James, "Letters from London," 287.

147. McKay, "Socialism and the Negro," *WD*, January 31, 1920.

148. McKay, "Socialism and the Negro." The inserted question mark is McKay's. The notion of a Socialist British Empire was developed largely by Sidney and Beatrice Webb. To the Webbs, all of the nonwhite world (with the sole exception of Japan) comprised "Non-Adult Races" in need of tutelage and protection. Such races and communities—"American Indians, the Pacific Islanders, the Malays, the Arabs, the Kaffirs, the Negroes, and all the indigenous inhabitants of the Asiatic mainland"— would therefore still be under British imperial control even after the achievement of "Socialism." "The policy of Socialism with regard to the Non-Adult races is one of Collective Guardianship in their own interest," they declared. They further asserted that in "many parts of the British Empire, it would be idle to pretend that anything like effective self-government, even as regards strictly local affairs, can be introduced for many generations to come—in some cases, conceivably never." Sidney and Beatrice Webb, "What Is Socialism? XVII—The Guardianship of the Non-Adult Races," *New Statesman*, August 2, 1913, 525-26. They reiterated the point seven years later in *A Constitution for the Socialist Commonwealth of Great Britain* (London: Longmans, Green, 1920), 112, 323-324n. The prescriptions of the Webbs led Jay Winter to describe their politics as "socialist racialism," fully cognizant of the incongruity of the term. Such beliefs, far from uncommon on the left, were widely shared by many self-described socialists, including Morel. Similar arguments were supported by the Webbs' fellow Fabians, including George Bernard Shaw, the chief author of *Fabianism and the Empire*, the 1900 manifesto of the group, which J. A. Hobson described as "socialistic imperialism." See J. M. Winter, "The Webbs and the Non-White World: A Case of Socialist Racialism," *Journal of Contemporary History* 9 (January 1974): 181–92; Bernard Shaw, ed., *Fabianism and the Empire: A Manifesto of the Fabian Society* (London: Grant Richards, 1900); John A. Hobson, "Socialistic Imperialism," *International Journal of Ethics* 12 (October 1901): 44–59; and A. M. McBriar, *Fabianism and English Politics, 1884–1918* (Cambridge: Cambridge University Press, 1966), 119–30.

149. For the genealogy of the theory, see Michael Löwy, *The Politics of Combined and Uneven Development* (London: Verso, 1981), 1–69.

150. See Leon Trotsky, *The Permanent Revolution* and *Results and Prospects* (New York: Pathfinder, 1969).

151. See Trotsky, *Permanent Revolution*, Translator's Note, 25.

152. See "Prospects of a Labor Dictatorship," in Leon Trotzky (*sic*), *Our Revolution: Essays on Working-Class and International Revolution, 1904-1917*, ed. and trans. Moissaye J. Olgin (New York: Henry Holt, 1918), 65–149.

153. See *Congress of the Peoples of the East, Baku, September 1920: Stenographic Report*, trans. and annotated by Brian Pearce (London: New Park, 1977). A definitive edition was published in 1993, with a fine introduction by John Riddell: Riddell, ed., *To See the Dawn: Baku, 1920—First Congress of the Peoples of the East* (New York: Pathfinder, 1993).

154. The combination of these two ideological currents in early-twentieth-century Black radicalism in the United States is discussed in Winston James, *Holding Aloft*

the Banner of Ethiopia: Caribbean Radicalism in Early Twentieth-Century America (London: Verso, 1998), 128, 164–168.

155. This stance is markedly at odds with the false choice posed by Cedric Robinson, between what he calls "Western Marxism" and the "Black radical tradition." Cedric J. Robinson, *Black Marxism: The Making of the Black Radical Tradition* (London: Zed, 1983). There is no reason the two cannot be combined. Indeed, I would argue that the most potent elements of Black radicalism effect such a coupling. George Padmore, for instance, who was arguably the most effective and consequential Black radical of the twentieth century, even after breaking with the Comintern, never renounced his Marxism—he combined it with the anticolonial and Pan-Africanist struggles. Padmore denounced Stalinist and Soviet compromising of the anticolonial struggle, but he never disavowed his socialist beliefs—and there was much that he still admired about the Soviet Union after the break. Right up to his death, he remained a "race man" and a "class man," yearning for an independent *and* socialist Africa. Leslie James's recent biography, *George Padmore and Decolonization from Below: Pan-Africanism, the Cold War, and the End of Empire* (London: Palgrave Macmillan, 2015) does much to put to rest many false ideas about Padmore after his break from the CP. See also Theo Williams, "George Padmore and the Soviet Model of the British Commonwealth," *Modern Intellectual History* 16, no. 2 (August 2019): 531–59; James, "To the East Turn," 1043-1045.

156. For a judicious appraisal of the fate of Trotsky's theory, see Löwy, *The Politics of Combined and Uneven Development*.

157. McKay to Ogden, February 25, 1920.

158. McKay, "To Ethiopia," *Liberator*, February 1920, 7.

159. Jeffrey Green with Randall Lockhart, "'A Brown Alien in a White City': Black Students in London, 1917-1920," in Lotz and Pegg, *Under the Imperial Carpet*; and Paul Rich, "The Black Diaspora in Britain: Afro-Caribbean Students and the Struggle for a Political Identity, 1900-1950," *Immigrants and Minorities* 6, no. 2 (July 1987): 151–73.

160. Jeffrey Green, *Edmund Thornton Jenkins: The Life and Times of an American Black Composer, 1894–1926* (Westport, CT: Greenwood, 1982), esp. chap. 9.

161. McKay saw the SSO in December 1919 at the Coliseum. He was not as taken with Buddy Gilmore as most of the critics were. "His drum was more than noisy & practically drowned the whole band. There was no balance." McKay to Ogden, n.d. but marked "Saturday" [June/July?, 1920 (between June 23 and July 7, 1920)]; Green, *Edmund Thornton Jenkins*, 72; Howard Rye, "The Southern Syncopated Orchestra," in Lotz and Pegg, *Under the Imperial Carpet*.

162. *Cambridge Magazine*, August 16, 1919, 913, and Summer 1920, 55.

163. W. F. Elkins, "Hercules and the Society of Peoples of African Origin," *Caribbean Studies* 11, no. 4 (January 1972); Ian Duffield, "Duse Mohamed Ali and the Development of Pan-Africanism, 1866-1945" (PhD diss., University of Edinburgh, 1971); David Vaughan, *Negro Victory: The Life Story of Dr. Harold Moody* (London: Independent, 1950); Roderick J. Macdonald, "Dr. Harold Arundel Moody and the League of Coloured Peoples, 1931–1947: A Retrospective View," *Race* 14, no. 3 (1974); David Killingray, " 'To Do Something for the Race': Harold Moody and the League of Coloured Peoples," in *West Indian Intellectuals in Britain*, ed. Bill Schwarz (Manchester: Manchester University Press, 2003); Peter Fryer, *Staying Power: The History of Black People in Britain* (London: Pluto, 1984); Winston James, "The Black Experience in Twentieth-Century Britain," in *Black Experience and the Empire*, ed. Philip D. Morgan and Sean Hawkins (Oxford: Oxford University Press, 2004), esp. 351–62.

164. McKay to Garvey, December 17, 1919.

165. "What We Stand For," *African Telegraph*, July–August 1919, 271.

166. McKay to Ogden, March 26, 1920.

167. McKay, "English Journalists Investigate Bolshevism," *Crusader*, June 1921, 19.

168. See Elkins, "Hercules and the Society of Peoples of African Origin."

169. McKay to Ogden, February 25, 1920.

170. Claude McKay, *The Negroes in America* (Port Washington, NY: Kennikat, [1923] 1979), 56–59, quotation at 58. Evidently, McKay had extensive discussions of African art with C. K. Ogden, some of which were conducted in their correspondence.

171. Claude McKay, *Banjo: A Story Without a Plot* (New York: Harper, 1929), 269–71.

172. "I react more," McKay declared, "to the emotions of the Irish people than to those of any other whites; they are so passionately primitive in their loves and hates. They are quite free of the disease which is known in bourgeois phraseology as Anglo-Saxon hypocrisy. I suffer with the Irish. I understand the Irish. My belonging to a subject race entitles me to some understanding of them. And then I was born and reared a peasant; the peasant's passion for the soil possesses me, and it is one of the strongest passions in the Irish revolution." McKay, "How Black Sees Green and Red," 21. See also C. E. E. [McKay], "Under the Iron Heel," *WD*, August 14, 1920, and "The Martyrdom of Ireland," *WD*, October 9, 1920, where he passionately denounced the "Imperial rape of the Irish people" and pleaded with British Labour leaders to "take action" to assist struggling Ireland.

173. McKay, "How Black Sees Green and Red," 17. See also C. E. E. [McKay], "Under the Iron Heel," *WD*, August 14, 1920, where he more forthrightly denounced the idea as "vulgar and pernicious."

174. "The Spanish Needle," *Cambridge Magazine*, Summer 1920, 55; "Samson," *WD*, January 10, 1920.

8. Making *Spring in New Hampshire*, the 1917 Club, Standing Up, and Thinking of England

1. Ogden still has not been given full biographical treatment. His admirers have been delayed, they say, mainly by the formidable multidisciplinary and interdisciplinary range and depth of his interests and work. See P. Sargant Florence and J. R. L. Anderson, eds., *C. K. Ogden: Collective Memoir* (London: Elek Pemberton, 1977); and W. Terrence Gordon, *C. K. Ogden: A Bio-Bibliographical Study* (Metuchen, NJ: Scarecrow, 1990). James McElvenny recently took up the challenge of seriously engaging with Ogden's philosophy of language and linguistics in his remarkable study: *Language and Meaning in the Age of Modernism: C. K. Ogden and his Contemporaries* (Edinburgh: Edinburgh University Press, 2018).

2. Before he left for London, however, McKay had a promise of publication in New York. In a letter dated September 10, 1919, McKay informed William Stanley Braithwaite that the newly established firm of Alfred Knopf had "accepted my verse for publication this winter." But McKay wanted to travel and took the opportunity to do so. (It turned out that at the last minute, Knopf reneged on the deal to publish, "saying that he cannot publish for [McKay] as it won't pay him.") Frank Harris to Grant Richards, November 8, 1919, Frank Harris Papers, Albert H. Small Collections Library, University of Virginia; McKay to W. S. Braithwaite, September 10, 1919,

WSBP; McKay to Ogden, October 9, 1920, CKOF. All of McKay's correspondence with Ogden are from this collection.

3. McKay had sent Grant Richards Harris's letter of introduction but, he wrote Ogden, "as I never called with the poems I suppose he never troubled to answer." McKay to Ogden, June 19, 1920.

4. That friend, unnamed in McKay's letter to Ogden, was the Dutch colonial civil servant and Orientalist, J. L. J. F. Ezerman (discussed in the previous chapter).

5. See McKay to Ogden, especially February 18, February 25, and March 7, 1920. Unfortunately, Ogden's letters to McKay have apparently not survived. They are not to be found in any of the McKay holdings, nor are they among any of Ogden's papers. But the nature of Ogden's letters to McKay can be adduced from McKay's letters to him, which also sometimes quote or paraphrase Ogden's communications with him.

6. McKay to Ogden, March 7, 1920.

7. *Cambridge Magazine* 10, no. 1 (Summer 1920): 55–59.

8. Claude McKay, *Spring in New Hampshire and Other Poems* (London: Grant Richards, 1920).

9. McKay to Ogden, October 9, 1920.

10. Ogden and McKay had actually engaged a printer, who had started work on the volume, before Grant Richards formally agreed to publish. They were willing to bring out the volume independently, without the engagement of a publishing company, if necessary.

11. McKay to Ogden, August 4, 1920.

12. McKay to Ogden, March 12, 1920. "Pariahs" was probably the poem later published as "Outcast," but "The Black Fiends" was never published and has not survived even in manuscript form. "The White Fiends" and "If We Must Die" had been published in magazine form before McKay went to London.

13. McKay to Ogden, March 12, 1920.

14. McKay to Ogden, June 23, 1920.

15. J. L. J. F. Ezerman to McKay, June 18, 1920, copy included in McKay to Ogden, June 23, 1920.

16. *LW*, 98.

17. *LW*, 98–99.

18. Claude McKay, *Harlem Shadows: The Poems of Claude McKay* (New York: Harcourt, Brace, 1922).

19. Hubert Harrison, "Poetry of Claude McKay," *Negro World*, May 21, 1921. The *Negro World* (May 6 and June 3, 1922) ran two laudatory reviews of the book within less than a month of each other.

20. *LW*, 86.

21. McKay to Ogden, January 31, 1921.

22. McKay to Ogden, March 10, March 15, October 2, and December 24, 1921.

23. For Ogden's early syndicalist sympathies and his relation to the 1917 Club, see P. Sargant Florence, "Cambridge 1909–1919 and Its Aftermath," in Florence and Anderson, *C. K. Ogden*, 22–24, 41–43.

24. McKay to Ogden, February 25, 1920.

25. Leonard Woolf, *Beginning Again: An Autobiography of the Years 1911 to 1918* (New York: Harcourt Brace Jovanovich, 1975), 216.

26. Woolf, *Beginning Again*, 217. See also *The Diary of Virginia Woolf, Volume 1: 1915–1919*, ed. Anne Olivier Bell (New York: Harcourt Brace Jovanovich, 1977), which frequently refers to events at the club.

27. McKay to Ogden, March 26 and April 14, 1920. Bernard was the cartoonist for the *Spur*, the leading anarchist publication at the time.
28. McKay to Ogden, March 26 and April 2, 1920. The "Miss Olivier" referred to by McKay was most probably Noël Olivier (1892–1969), the youngest of Sydney Olivier's four daughters, who was unmarried at the time and a popular member of the Bloomsbury Set and the 1917 Club. See Sarah Watling, *The Olivier Sisters: A Biography* (New York: Oxford University Press, 2019). The man who jostled McKay was probably simply a racist (Ogden's "extreme left" attribution notwithstanding) who found it objectionable that McKay should be even speaking to a white woman, let alone one of the Olivier sisters and at the 1917 Club.
29. This is a theme that runs through the reminiscences of his friends. See Florence and Anderson, *C. K. Ogden*.
30. "I never met McKay and haven't read his poetry since." I. A. Richards to Robert C. Reinders, May 19, 1966, quoted in Wayne Cooper and Robert C. Reinders, "A Black Briton Comes 'Home': Claude McKay in England, 1920, " *Race* 9, no.1 (1967), 76.
31. McKay to Ogden, July 7, 1920.
32. *LW*, 303.
33. *LW*, 66–67; Claude McKay, "London," in his unpublished manuscript "Cities," CMPY.
34. See discussion in chaps. 1 and 2 above.
35. Una Marson, "Nigger," *Keys* 1, no. 1 (July 1933): 8.
36. McKay to Ogden, December 10, 1920.
37. *BB*, 46.
38. George Lamming, *Conversations: Essays, Addresses and Interviews, 1953–1990*, ed. Richard Drayton and Andaiye (London: Karia, 1992), 188.
39. Winston James, "The Black Experience in Twentieth-Century Britain," in *Black Experience and the Empire*, ed. Philip D. Morgan and Sean Hawkins (Oxford: Oxford University Press, 2004), 377–79.
40. *LW*, 73.
41. *SJ*, 63–65.
42. McKay, "Our London Letter."
43. McKay, "The Spanish Needle," *Cambridge Magazine* 10, no. 1 (Summer 1920): 55.
44. See George Lamming, *In the Castle of My Skin* (London: Michael Joseph, 1953); V. S. Naipaul, *Miguel Street* (London: André Deutsch, 1959) and *A House for Mr. Biswas* (London: André Deutsch, 1961).
45. *LW*, 304.
46. *LW*, 304.
47. McKay, "Up to Date," 3; *LW*, 66. But this was McKay's depiction of Shaw almost twenty years after meeting him. He was far more critical of Shaw during and in the immediate aftermath of his time in Britain. Writing in 1921, he was particularly critical of Shaw's non-revolutionary position on the Irish question, which was "similar to that of any English bourgeois reformist." See, Claude McKay, "How Black Sees Green and Red," *Liberator*, June 1921, 20.
48. *LW*, 123.
49. Robert Duncan, "'Motherwell for Moscow': Walton Newbold, Revolutionary Politics and the Labour Movement in a Lanarkshire Constituency 1918–1922," *Journal of the Scottish Labour History Society* 23 (1993): 47.
50. *LW*, 181–82.
51. J. T. Walton Newbold to Albert Inkpin, Secretary, Communist Party of Great Britain, 8 September 1924, 495/100/181, Russian State Archives for Social and Political History. See also James, "To the East Turn," 1014–16.

52. McKay to Ogden, October 28, 1920.

53. McKay to Ogden, November 25 and December 10, 1920.

54. McKay to Ogden, December 25, 1920.

55. *Westminster Gazette*, December 4, 1920; [C. K. Ogden], "Recent Verse," *Cambridge Magazine* 10, no. 2 (January–March 1921): 116–17.

56. *Glasgow Herald*, October 28, 1920. McKay would have seen this because he had employed Durrants' paper-clipping services to track notices of his book. McKay to Ogden, December 25, 1920.

57. E. B., "Poetry Overseas," *Athenaeum*, December 17, 1920, 833; [unsigned], "Poets and Poetry," *Spectator*, October 23, 1920, 539–40.

58. *LW*, 87–88.

59. "Poets and Poetry," 539. McKay quotes the passage in *LW*, 88, but not exactly; he has "pure-blooded" instead of "full-blooded"; he capitalizes Negro when the *Spectator* did not; and he does not indicate some of his contractions by ellipses. The *Yorkshire Post* (November 2, 1920), in its brief notice, "A Negro Poet," did speak of McKay being a "pure-blooded native of Jamaica," who had "just published some verses, and it is claimed that he is the first negro poet in English."

60. [Ogden], "Recent Verse," 116–17.

61. *LW*, 89. For two recent scholarly work in English on Antar, his poetry and reputation, see H. T. Norris, *The Adventures of Antar* (Warminster, UK: Aris & Phillips, 1980) and especially Peter Heath, *The Thirsty Sword: Sirat 'Anta and the Arabic Popular Epic* (Salt Lake City: University of Utah Press, 1996). See also Cedric Dover, "The Black Knight, Parts 1 and 2" *Phylon* 15, no. 1 and 2 (1st and 2nd Quarter, 1954): 41–57; 177–89.

62. *LW*, 89.

63. Claude McKay, "Soviet Russia and the Negro," *Crisis*, December 1923, 61–65, and January 1924, 114–18, quotations 114–15.

64. McKay, "Soviet Russia and the Negro," *Crisis*, January 1924, 116.

65. McKay, "How Black Sees Green and Red," 17.

66. *LW*, 86.

67. McKay to William Gallacher, October 10, 1920; Papers of William Gallacher, CP/IND/GALL/02/04, Labour History Archive and Study Centre, People's History Museum, Manchester.

68. Walter Kendall, *The Revolutionary Movement in Britain, 1900–1920: The Origins of British Communism* (London: Weidenfeld and Nicolson, 1969), 252, 413n116; see also Andrew Thorpe, *The British Communist Party and Moscow, 1920–43* (Manchester: Manchester University Press, 2000), 29–30.

69. Quoted in Kendall, *Revolutionary Movement*, 413n116.

70. Kendall, *Revolutionary Movement*, chap. 14; Ian Bullock, "Sylvia Pankhurst and the Russian Revolution: The Making of a 'Left-Wing' Communist," in *Sylvia Pankhurst: From Artist to Anti-Fascist*, ed. Ian Bullock and Richard Pankhurst (Basingstoke, UK: Macmillan, 1992), 141–42; Raymond Challinor, *The Origins of British Bolshevism* (London: Croom Helm, 1977), 273; Barbara Winslow, *Sylvia Pankhurst: Sexual Politics and Political Activism* (London: UCL Press, 1996), 162–71.

71. *LW*, 86–87.

72. Lucia Jones, "Interview with Nellie Rathbone," June 27, 1972, appended to Lucia Jones, "Sylvia Pankhurst and the Workers' Socialist Federation: The Red Twilight, 1918–1924" (MA thesis, Warwick University, 1972). The actual exchange between Rathbone and Jones went as follows. Rathbone: "and there was a West Indian—I

can't remember his name." Jones: "I know who you mean. . . . Claude MacKay [*sic*]." Rathbone: "Yes I don't know what happened to him but once they got so mad they pretended to hang him." Jones: "Really!" Rathbone: "They were just pretending of course."

73. McKay to Ogden, October 28, 1920. McKay did maintain contact with members of the group, including Edgar Whitehead, its general secretary, whom McKay had always liked if not agreed with. It was McKay whose name Edgar Whitehead gave to the suspicious U.S. authorities when he arrived at Ellis Island in January 1922. McKay was not pleased, for it threatened his own deportation, but he went and testified for Whitehead. Whitehead would reciprocate later that year when, as a Comintern official in Berlin, he smoothed the way for McKay's clandestine trip to Russia. As we saw in the previous chapter, McKay asked after Whitehead in his correspondence with Reuben Gilmore in the 1930s. Whitehead (who by then went under the name Edgar Bray) had joined the fascist movement and supported Hitler before and during the war. Tim Tate, *Hitler's British Traitors: The Secret History of Spies, Saboteurs and Fifth Columnist* (London: Icon, 2018), 362–65.

74. *LW*, 87. Hugh Hope [Claude McKay], "Re-Affirmation," *WD*, July 3, 1920; See also his "Song of the New Soldier," *WD*, April 3, 1920; "Reality," *WD*, April 24, 1920.

75. *Outward Passenger Lists*, BT27, Records of the Board of Trade, TNA. *Passenger and Crew Lists of Vessels Arriving at New York, New York, 1897–1957*, Records of the Immigration and Naturalization Service, U.S. National Archives.

76. McKay, "Up to Date," 4.

77. McKay to Ogden, January 31, 1921.

78. *LW*, 95.

79. McKay to Ogden, January 31 and October 2, 1921; see also McKay to Ogden, December 24, 1921.

80. One of his close friends, Mary Keating, noted: "At some point Claude began disliking the British, and this dislike became an almost psychotic fury before he died. . . . The past sins of the British became for Claude the very present." Mary Keating to Wayne Cooper, March 4, 1964; quoted in Cooper and Reinders, "A Black Briton Comes 'Home,'" 83n49.

81. McKay touches a little upon his Moroccan troubles with the Brits in *A Long Way from Home* (300–304). The South Africans authorities, on hearing rumors that McKay might slip into the country, had banned the "notorious negro and Communist" as early as March 1924. These matters are presented and analyzed in the companion volume to this book, *Claude McKay: From Bolshevism to Black Nationalism* (in progress).

82. *BB*, 268. "I am black, but O! my soul is white," Blake has the Black boy saying. "White as an angel is the English child: / But I am black as if bereav'd of light." But "round the tent of God," the Black boy and the "English child" will "lean in joy upon our fathers (sic) knee. / And then I'll stand and stroke his silver hair, / And be like him and he will then love me." See William Blake, "The Little Black Boy," in *Complete Poems* (London: Penguin, 1977), 106–7.

83. Crystal Eastman, "The Workers of the Clyde," *Liberator*, October 1919; reprinted in *Crystal Eastman on Women and Revolution*, ed. Blanche Wiesen Cook (New York: Oxford University Press, 1978), 336–49; McKay, *LW*, 197–98; Walter Duranty, *I Write As I Please* (New York: Halcyon House, 1935), 170–71.

84. McKay, *LW*, 198.

85. *LW*, 67.

86. Budgen tells his own remarkable story in *Myselves When Young* (London: Oxford University Press, 1970).
87. McKay to Cunard, April 30, 1932.
88. In fact, by the 1950s, the very moment that Sam Selvon wrote his famous novel, they were hardly lonely. Moses, after all, had his friends, and he was collecting more and more each day from the boat train. Sam Selvon, *The Lonely Londoners* (London: Longmans, 1956).
89. For a good overview of the immediate postwar conditions, see Charles Mowat, *Britain Between the Wars, 1918–1940* (Chicago: University of Chicago Press, 1958), esp. chaps. 1–3; and Gordon Phillips, "The Social Impact," in *The First World War in British History*, ed. Stephen Constantine, Maurice W. Kirby, and Mary B. Rose (London: Edward Arnold, 1995), 106–40, from which the figures are drawn.
90. For a good overview of Black working-class Britain at the time, see Laura Tabili, *"We Ask for British Justice": Workers and Racial Difference in Late Imperial Britain* (Ithaca, NY: Cornell University Press, 1994).
91. In *Banjo*, for instance, an Englishman is overcharged in a Marseilles bar and complains bitterly about it. He explains to Ray that he "didn't care about the few sous, but it was the principle of the thing." "You English certainly love to play with that word 'principle,'" said Ray. *B*, 142–43.
92. Claude McKay, "A Negro Writer to His Critics," *New York Herald Tribune Books*, March 6, 1932.
93. *B*, 275–76.
94. McKay to Josephine Herbst, August 18 [1924], Josephine Herbst Papers, Beinecke Rare Book and Manuscript Library, Yale University; emphasis in the original. Similar sentiments were expressed in McKay's poem, "Reality," *WD*, April 24, 1920 (published under the pen name Hugh Hope).
95. McKay, "England," in "Cities."

A Coda

1. The later period of McKay's life will be the subject of the second volume of this study, *Claude McKay: From Bolshevism to Black Nationalism*, but my interpretation of the broad arc of his life is presented in summary form in "Claude McKay," *Encyclopedia of the Harlem Renaissance*, vol. 2, ed. Cary D. Wintz and Paul Finkelman (New York: Routledge, 2004), 777–82.

Index

Association for the Study of Negro Life
and History, 238
atheism, 153, 192, 209

Baker, Lorenzo Dow, 102; banana market
and price control by, 72; banana
marketing initiated by, 71; BFC of,
71–73, 371n29; peasant producers
bargaining by, 72–73; UFC of, 71
Banana Bottom, 2, 20, 22, 294; anti-
British feelings in, 341–42; on British
ignorance, 328–29; on childhood and
youth, 66; on Christianity, 192; Jamaica
setting for, 55; Walter Jekyll dedication
in, 55, 57; Walter Jekyll depiction in, 48;
on obeah religious practice, 359n73
banana cultivation, in Jamaica, *165*; Baker
marketing initiation, 71; growth of,
72–73; indentured peasant laborers
for, 76; Alfred Jones Elders & Fyffes
shipping company for, 74–75;
landholders for, 78; of Thomas McKay
and U. Theo, 71; Norman and Smickle
on, 73–74; as peasant crop, 71; U.S.
imports of, 371n34; women and, *166.
167*
Banjo, 314–16, 344–45, 351n4; Great War
and, 204; influence on *négritude*
movement, 156–57; prostitute in, 106
Barclay, A. Alexander, 87–88, 396n62
Barnes, William, 221
"Barrier, The," 252, 279
"Base Details" (Sassoon), 335
Beckwith, Martha, 389n176
Bennett, Gwendolyn, 4
Bennett, Louise, 51; straight English poetry
of, 53, 366n175
Berlin, McKay in (1923-1934), 65
Berlin Conference (1884-1885), 68
Bernal, Martin, 37, 361n106
Bernard, Henry, 326
Besant, Annie, 38, 144–45
"Bestman's Toast at a Rustic Wedding
Feast," 222
BFC. *See* Boston Fruit Company
birth certificate, of Claude McKay, *161*,
353n1
Black Arts Movement, Gayle of, 4
Black Athena (Bernal), 37

"Black Fiends, The," 322, 422n12
Black Harlem: Black radicalism in, 211, 212;
Garvey in, 211; journals and magazines
in, 212; McKay support boycott by, 28;
McKay description of, 210; McKay in,
28, 209–13; population of, 210; UNIA
headquarters in, 211
"Black Horror on the Rhine" campaign,
335; antiblack racism of, 298; accused
Black troops of sexual misconduct,
300–301, 309; German propaganda
on, 307; labor union involvement in,
298–301, 418n124; McKay response
to, 303–4, 417n119; of Morel, 298–309;
French-Moroccan troops in Frankfurt,
299–300; Pankhurst on, 303, 417n118
Black Jamaicans: civil service selection
block for, 20; inferior colonial
education and, 51; Panama Canal
wealth of, 88; plantocracy land sale
refusal, 86–88, 374n99; voting and
literacy tests, 16
Black liberation: through Bolshevism,
205–6, 256, 348; nationalism and
socialism ideologies of, 4, 259
"Black Man Replies, A," 417n120
Black Marxism (Robinson), 420n155
Black Panthers, 251
Black people: "If We Must Die"
resistance rallying cry, 10, 44; Jamaica
Constabulary promotion blocks for,
60–63; Kingston population of, 143–44;
Love support of women, 34–35
Black Power movement, 4, 5
Black press: support of Bolshevik
Revolution, 256, 410n98; on Great
War racism, 407n52; IWW support
in, 256; Palmer on radicalism of, 255,
409nn92–93
Black radicalism: in Black Harlem, 211, 212;
of Padmore, 420n155; Robinson and,
420n155
Black Skin, White Masks (Fanon), 50
Black solidarity, 115–26
"Black Troops in Germany" (Morel),
417n115
Black working class: McKay member of
in U.S., 218–21; McKay loyalty to, 218;
women disenfranchisement, 16

CPSIA information can be obtained
at www.ICGtesting.com
Printed in the USA
JSHW020009060722
27815JS00002B/66